James D. Mackenzie

The Castles of England, their Story and Structure

Vol. II

James D. Mackenzie

The Castles of England, their Story and Structure
Vol. II

ISBN/EAN: 9783744735926

Printed in Europe, USA, Canada, Australia, Japan

Cover: Foto ©Andreas Hilbeck / pixelio.de

More available books at **www.hansebooks.com**

The Castles of England

Dunham Castle.

THE
Castles of England

THEIR STORY AND STRUCTURE

BY

Sir JAMES D. MACKENZIE,
BARONET OF SCATWELL AND TARBAT

WITH FORTY PLATES, ONE HUNDRED AND FIFTY-EIGHT TEXT
ILLUSTRATIONS AND SEVENTY PLANS

IN TWO VOLUMES
VOL. II.

NEW YORK
THE MACMILLAN CO.
1896

Contents

List of Plates

ST. MAWES

Cornwall

BOSCASTLE (*non-existent*)

ABOUT three miles along the coast N.E. of Tintagel is the scarped and partly terraced mound upon which once stood the Castle of Bottreaux. On the slope of the hill at the junction of two valleys, through each of which courses a stream, the Norman-French family of De Bottreaux built a castle in the time of Henry II., and from them the little town that afterwards grew round the stronghold took its name of Boscastle. Not a stone remains now of the building, whose site is marked only by a grassy mound called "Jordans."

William de Bottreaux and his younger brother Reginald espoused the side of the Barons in the Civil War with Henry III., 1264; and the last of the family, William, was killed at the second battle of St. Albans in 1461, leaving an only daughter, who married Robert, Lord Hungerford, with issue a daughter Mary, who was esteemed to be at the time the richest heiress in the country, being seised in her own right of over one hundred manors in different counties. Her husband, Lord Hastings, sold Boscastle in the reign of Elizabeth to John Hender, from whose daughters it has descended to its present owner, Miss Amy Hellier. The Marquis of Hastings still has the title of Baron Bottreaux, though he owns no estate here.

A

CARDINHAM, ANCIENTLY CALLED CARDINAN (*non-existent*)

CARDINHAM lies in the very centre of the county, N.E. of Bodmin. It seems to have been the seat of Robert de Cardinan (temp. Richard I.), who is said to have held no less than seventy-one knights' fees in these parts, which he acquired by his marriage with the heiress of Robert Fitz-William. Afterwards it was the abode of the Dynhams, or Dinhams, who derived from the former lord ; Oliver de Dinham being summoned to Parliament as a baron in 24 Edward I. After him came five direct generations of sons who were all knighted, and then John Dinham of Old Cardinham, Sheriff of Devon (39 Henry VI.), who was a zealous Yorkist, and was knighted for his active services by Edward IV., in whose sixth year he was created Baron Dynham and K.G. It appears curious that after this he should have acquired the favour of Henry VII., who made him Lord High Treasurer. This lord died in 17 Henry VII., aged 72, and, his son Charles dying *s.p.*, the estates were shared among his four sisters, who were all married to noblemen. Carew in his Survey says that "formerly at Cardinham lived Lord Dinham." One of the sisters, Margaret, was the wife of Sir Nicholas Carew, and her share of the Cardinham lands passed in 1573 to the Arundel family, from whom it was purchased in 1800 by Edward Glynn, whose descendant, Lord Vivian, now possesses the property.

This castle, the seat of the Dinhams, was situated on a considerable eminence, about half-a-mile from the church ; the site is still called The Castle, and traces of the old foundations, which were laid bare some years ago, are yet to be seen (compare *Wardour, Wilts.*).

CARN BREA (*minor*)

ON a rocky hill standing over Redruth, with an elevation of 738 feet, are the remains of a very ancient tower, about 20 feet square and 40 feet high, which once contained two timber floors, as may be seen from the beam-holes, windows, and chimneys, and a roof platform. There is but one entrance into it, through a small hole cut in the rock under the foundations. It stands at the E. end of the Carn Brea hill, on a ledge of vast rocks, which have been connected by arches turned across the cavities between the rocks. One part is ancient and is loopholed, but the other is of more modern construction, and seems to have been built in order to command the very extensive view. On the N.W. were some outworks, and on the W. side, near the summit, is a circular fortification called Old Castle (*Polwhele*).

FOWEY (*minor*)

THIS place was once one of the most important burghs in Cornwall; in 1347 it supplied forty-seven ships for the expedition of Edward III. to Calais. Leland writes: "The Frenchmen diverse tymes assailid this Town, at last most notably about Henry VI.'s tyme: when the wife of Thomas Treury, the 2 with her Man, repelled the French out of her House in her Housebande's Absence. Whereupon Thomas Treury buildid a right fair and stronge embatelid Tower in his House: and embateling al the waulles of the House in a Maner made it a Castelle: and onto this Day it is the glorie of the Town Building in Faweye." Place House is the seat of the Treffry family, and in its grounds is a statue of Elizabeth, the wife of Thomas Treffry, whose action is told by Leland.

Much of the house has been rebuilt, but its castellated appearance still remains. The principal entrance is from the churchyard through a ruined gate, with a strong wicket, flanked by a lodge pierced with loopholes.

Buck shows, in a drawing of 1734, a square tower on each side of the narrow entrance into Fowey Haven. From one of these to the other an iron chain was stretched, but this was removed, immediately after being placed there, by King Edward IV., who took umbrage at certain acts of piracy committed by the townspeople against the French. On a high rocky eminence outside on the W. are shown the remains of a large circular fort with embattled approaches. This fort of St. Catherine, built for the protection of the harbour in the reign of Henry VIII., is still in existence, and formerly mounted four guns.

HAYLE (*non-existent*)

AT the mouth of the estuary formed by the river once stood a castle for the protection of this port, but of what description cannot now be determined. Leland says: "Ryvier Castel almost at the est part of the mouth of the Hayle river, on the North se: now, as sum think, drownid with sand. This was Theodore's Castelle" (*Polwhele*).

HELSTON (*non-existent*)

THIS town, which stood on the great road from London to the Land's End, is a place of considerable antiquity, having been made by King John one of the four coinage towns. A castle was erected at Helston shortly after the Conquest, which fell into ruin about the time of Edward IV., and in the Itinerary of William of Worcester of 1478, given by Gilbert, it is called "dirutum." It stood on the site of the present bowling-green. Leland observed some vestiges of it, but at this date nothing whatever remains.

William of Worcester mentions thirty-four castles in Cornwall, eighteen of which were already destroyed, and he speaks of Helston Castle as sometime the residence of Edward, Earl of Cornwall, the grandson of King John, and as then being in ruins.

INCE (*minor*)

THIS was more a fortified house than a castle, being situated pleasantly almost on an island in the estuary of the Lynher or St. Germans River. It was a fortress built entirely of brick, with a flanking tower at each angle, and in 1646, during the Civil War, was garrisoned for the king, but soon surrendered to the Parliamentary forces. It was purchased by Mr. Alexander Baring, and is now a farm-house.

LAUNCESTON, once called DUNHEVED (*chief*)

BORLASE calls this "by far the strongest of our Cornish castles." It stands over the little stream Attery, nearly a mile distant from the banks of the Tamar, which here divides Cornwall from Devon, upon a high and rocky conical hill, commanding the principal ford of the river. Leland, writing in the middle of the sixteenth century, says : "The large and auncient Castelle of Lawnstun stondith on the Knappe of the Hille by S. a little from the Parsche chirch. Much of this Castel yet stondith ; & the Moles that the Kepe standeth on is large & of terrible highth, & the Arx of it, having 3 severale Wardes, is the strongest, but not the biggest, that ever I saw in any auncient Worke in Englande."

This castle is not named in the Domesday Survey nor in the list of the Earl of Mortain's castles and lands ; but though perhaps no masonry castle existed here before the Conquest, it is certain that this was one of the chief seats of the Earls or Princes of Cornwall from Roman times, if not before these (*Borlase*). It is said that Robert, Earl of Mortain, was established here by William I. in place of Othomarus de Knivet (of Danish extraction), who was hereditary Constable of Launceston Castle, that is, of the stronghold existing on the mound for centuries previous. This earl received from his half-brother the Conqueror, 280 manors in Cornwall, and 558 in other counties, together with the earldom of Cornwall. He was succeeded by his son William, who lost all by rebellion, his possessions being confiscated by the Crown, and retained until the creation of Richard, King of the Romans, as Earl of Cornwall by his brother Henry III. His son Edward inherited all after him, and at the death of this second earl *s.p.*, Edward I. laid hands on his lands and castles.

CORNWALL. 5

In 1329 the earldom was conferred on John of Eltham by Edward III., but at his death without issue this castle was settled, with the other possessions, upon the Black Prince, and thus passed into the Duchy of Cornwall, of which it still remains a part.

After its union with the duchy the fortress appears to have been little needed, and so fell into neglect and the ruin observed by Leland. But during the Civil War, in 1643, the fabric was partially repaired and strengthened for

LAUNCESTON

the reception of Parliamentary troops under the command of Sir Richard Buller, who, however, evacuated it on the approach of Sir Ralph Hopton with a force of 3000 men. In May of that year, Major-General Sir George Chudleigh, whilst endeavouring to prevent assistance reaching the castle, was attacked and beaten in the neighbourhood by the forces of Sir Richard and Sir Beville Grenville, who entered and garrisoned the place. In the next year Launceston was forced to surrender to the Earl of Essex, but it again fell into the king's hands at the capitulation of Essex at Fowey, and in 1645 Sir Richard Grenville, having refused to serve under Lord Hopton's command, was committed

prisoner to this castle by the Prince of Wales; he was removed hence to St.
Michael's Mount, from whence he escaped by sea to Flanders, dying three
years after in great destitution at Ghent. In March 1646 the fortress was
surrendered by Colonel Basset to the army under Sir Thomas Fairfax. After
the Restoration, Sir Hugh Piper for his services was granted a lease of this
castle and was made Constable of it, and it continued in his family till 1754,
when it passed to Hugh, 3rd Duke of Northumberland, remaining with his
descendants till 1867. During the occupation of this family, about £3000
was expended upon the castle and its grounds. It is now the property of
Mr. J. C. Williams. A large extent of forest originally surrounded the town
of Launceston, where in the time of Edward III. there was a deer park
a league in length.

In the drawing given in Buck (1734), as also in that by Borlase, of later
date, there is shown a large rectangular enclosure with a ruined wall. This
formed the outer ward of the castle, and is now covered by the town,—the
curtain wall being partly built on a rampart of earth, and defended by a large
encircling ditch on the S. and E. sides, while on the other quarters it was
protected by a deep valley. The chief entrance was on the S., where still
stands the large square gatehouse, with a broad Early English low-pointed gateway with portcullis grooves at the end of a walled passage, 120 feet in length;
access to this being by a drawbridge across the ditch. Some part of the archway remains, and also traces of the wall on the W. side. At the S. corner
of the rampart was a large circular bastion, called the Witches' Tower, which
fell down at the time a new road was constructed there; and there was also
a semi-circular tower with a gatehouse and guardroom, near the E. corner,
where rises abruptly the immense conical mound, crowned by the ancient
keep or *dungeon*.

This lofty hill, which occupies the N.E. angle, is partly natural and partly
artificial, and was orginally about 320 feet in diameter, rising to a height of
about 100 feet above the lower court. The ascent to the keep is from the
gatehouse up a flight of stairs between loopholed side-walls, the width being
7 feet. Around the summit of the mound at the edge ran a low stone wall
or breastwork, 3 feet high and 93 feet in diameter, behind which, at a distance
of 6 feet, is an annular wall 12 feet thick, with an entrance on the S. side
under a Norman arch, and containing a staircase which admits to the top of
the wall. In the centre and concentric with this outer wall, at a distance of
10 feet between, rises the inner tower of the keep, having an inside diameter
of 18 feet and a height of 32 feet, its walls being 10 feet through, with a
staircase contrived in the thickness running up to the top. This tower was
divided by a wooden floor into two rooms, the first being a store without
exterior lights, and the upper one having a large window on its E. and W.
sides. Below the ground-level is a cellar or prison. The space between

the tower and the encircling wall was covered with a wooden roof, at the
level of the first floor, resting on the top of this wall.

Following the line of the keep court wall to the N., and passing the deep
ravine which protected the castle here, one comes to the E. gate, the most
perfect part of the ruins, which contained the Constable's quarters. Beneath
the gatehouse, and entered by a small lancet doorway, is a chamber having
no chimney and only a loophole for air and light; this was the "noisome
den" in which George Fox, the Father of the Quakers, was confined for
eight months, in 1656, for contempt of Court in wearing his hat at his trial,
and for distributing tracts at St. Ives. Roman coins have been found here.
Launceston was sometimes called "Castle Terrible."

LISKEARD (*non-existent*)

THE very ancient place of this name was one of the four original stannary
and coinage towns, and as such was possessed by Robert de Mortain or
Moreton, Earl of Cornwall, in Domesday. Richard, Earl of Cornwall, the
brother of Henry III., made it a free borough, and is said to have built the
castle here, and to have lived in it. William of Worcester, who visited
Cornwall in the reign of Edward IV., speaks of Liskeard Castle as then standing,
and as one of the palaces of the duchy, but when Leland came there, about
1540, he says, it is "now al in ruine; fragments and pieces of waulle yet
stonde: the site of it is magnificent and looketh over all the towne." Carew
supposes it to have been of no great antiquity: "Of later times," he says, "the
castle served the Earl of Cornwall for one of his houses; but now that later
is worm-eaten, out of time and use." In the Survey of 1649, this castle was
found to be so much decayed that the materials were not worth taking down.
Some crumbling ruins only stand upon an eminence N. of the town, and
contiguous to these is a large field still called the Castle Park: the place was
disparked by Henry VIII., and once fed 200 deer.

PENDENNIS (*chief*)

THIS castle is built on a high and projecting peninsula on the W. side
of Falmouth Haven, nearly 300 feet above the sea, and a mile in compass.
In early times, the Danes visiting Cornwall seized this site and raised here a
rude triple entrenchment of earth and stones, but no regular fortification was
erected on the spot till the reign of Henry VIII. In 1537, in consequence
of Henry's relations with the Catholic powers, general insecurity was felt by
the country, and protection from threatened foreign invasion was demanded.
Accordingly, surveys and reports were ordered on those parts of the coast

where an invading army could most easily land; plans were submitted to engineers in London, and the works were at once taken in hand with most creditable promptitude, so that, in two years after, the greater part of all the exposed points suitable for a hostile landing were guarded either by a blockhouse or a fort, or by earthworks, from St. Michael's Mount to Portsmouth, and thence by Dover to the Thames. The king spared himself no exertion, and came personally to visit many spots chosen on the southern coasts, even to Cornwall.

In 1538 a small blockhouse was built, it is thought, under Pendennis Point, close to the water's edge and near the present rifle range, and in the next year the order was given for the erection of Pendennis Castle, which was completed in 1542-44, when Leland saw the work. At the same time, to support this fortress a corresponding castle was built on the opposite side of the water, called St. Mawes. The tradition is generally believed in Cornwall that Henry VIII. came to view the situation of these two castles, as proposed, and passed two nights at the Arundels' seat of Tolvern, whence he crossed the estuary to St. Feock at a passage that has ever since gone by his name. Elizabeth caused the castle to be greatly strengthened and enlarged, and a governor was appointed to it with a garrison of 100 men.

PENDENNIS

Pendennis consists of a large circular tower, 56 feet in outside diameter and 35 feet high, built of granite with walls 11 feet thick, which are pierced in three tiers with embrasures for guns, and carrying artillery likewise upon the roof, where a heavy sloping parapet protects the guns. Above this is a turret for observation. The arms of Henry VIII. are over the doorway.

On the N. side of the round tower projects a large embattled square building of two stories, in which are the lodgings, entered from a drawbridge across the wide moat, and through a highly ornamented gateway. A parapet wall pierced for guns surrounds the outside, and beyond are a ditch and glacis, and also an irregular fortification strengthened by four bastions, one of them mounting a large battery, and with a lunette on the E. side. The whole work covers an area of over three acres. There are still traces of a hornwork constructed during the Civil War.

The ancient family of Killigrew, whose residence of Arwenack stood directly below at the shore, furnished the three first governors of Pendennis Castle, which they held from the Crown, and on the death of Sir John, in 1597, Queen Elizabeth appointed Sir Nicholas Parker to the post. In 1626 Sir Robert Killigrew was governor and captain, his son Sir William being associated with him two years later; but in 1634 we find that from the governor's neglect the castle was reported to be in a ruinous state, and Sir William the next year gave place to Sir Nicholas Slanning, an energetic royalist, who was killed at the siege of Bristol in 1643. Then the king appointed Colonel John Arundel of Trerise to the governorship. During the next year Queen Henrietta Maria, who had just been delivered of her youngest daughter, was driven into Cornwall—always a loyal county—and rested at Pendennis for a night before embarking early the next day (June 29) in a Dutch vessel for France.

On February 12, 1646, the Prince of Wales, whose person the Parliament was anxious to seize, being in Cornwall, retired for safety to Pendennis, but after the flight of Sir Ralph Hopton, following the battle at Torrington, the place was deemed no longer safe for him, and on the night of March 2nd he went on board a ship which conveyed him to Scilly. The room in the castle where Charles lived is still called the king's room, and above it was contrived a closet with a fireplace, in which tradition relates that the prince was concealed. The place, however, with a recess opposite the fireplace, was removed in 1808 during some repairs in the castle.

Shortly after (March 16), in expectation of the immediate arrival of the Parliamentary army under Fairfax, Colonel Arundel sallied from the castle and caused fire to be set to the old house of the Killigrews, Arwenack, which lay directly below, surrounded by trees, in order to prevent its occupation by the enemy, purposing also to burn the adjoining town of Pennycomequick (the forerunner of Falmouth). But the sudden arrival of Roundhead troops prevented this, and saved also a part of Arwenack House, then esteemed to be "the finest and the costliest in the county." Fairfax arrived next day, establishing himself and his headquarters in the house, and with two regiments at once blocked up Pendennis.

Colonel Arundel had added to the defences, by forming a hornwork consisting of a pentagon redoubt, with flanks en tenaille, and had thrown up various other earthworks within the tracing of his lines. "The parapet and ditch of the redoubt still remain, though overgrown with bushes" (Oliver). He was a fine old cavalier, at that time, by his own account, seventy years of age, but probably older, as he is said to have been M.P. for Cornwall in the reign of Elizabeth, and to have been present at the review by her of her troops at Tilbury in 1588, on which account he went by the name of "Old Tilbury."

From his firm adherence to the cause of Charles, he was also known by the *sobriquet* of "John-for-the-King."

The castle contained a garrison of nearly 800 men, and was furnished with plenty of ammunition and provisions, as was supposed, for a nine months' siege; so when summoned on March 18th by Fairfax to surrender, old Arundel at once returned a decisive refusal. Thereon the place was closely invested by land across the isthmus, while Captain William Batten, the Parliamentary vice-admiral, blockaded it by sea. There appears to have been little actual bombardment, though shot-marks can still be seen on the N.W. side of the castle; but the besiegers trusted to reduce the fortress by famine, and in this they at last succeeded. Twice again a summons was delivered, but although provisions ran scarce, and the garrison was at last reduced to great extremities, the gallant old governor held out for five months, till August 17th, when only food for one day remained, and he then surrendered on excellent terms. The victors, on whom the investment had fallen very heavily, entering found in the castle only a cask of horse meat salted, "noe bread nor drink." Clarendon says that Pendennis "endured the longest siege and held out the last of any fort or castle in England," but Raglan appears to have been surrendered on August 19th. The list of the defenders includes 92 officers and 732 soldiers, of whom 200 were sick, and there were 200 women and children. The besiegers lost 17 men.

At the Restoration, Sir Peter Killigrew was appointed governor, and the town received a charter and its new name of Falmouth. Sir Peter died in 1662, and was succeeded by Colonel Richard Arundel, the son of Old Tilbury, who had assisted him in the siege. He was created Lord Arundel in 1665, and was followed at Pendennis by the Earl of Bath, who published here "with great contentment" the proclamations of the Prince of Orange on his landing in Torbay. In 1795 the Pendennis lands were purchased from the Crown in fee by the Killigrew family.

PENGERSIC (*minor*)

IN the S. of the parish of St. Breage, beautifully situated in a valley near the sea, is the site of an old fortress, which belonged since the Conquest mostly to the great family of Godolphin. The existing remains are those of a castellated blockhouse erected by Henry VIII., and consist of a square embattled tower of three storeys, and a small one annexed, with fragments of walls. In the lesser tower are winding stairs leading to the top; the walls of the ground floor are loopholed, and the door on the N. side is machicolated. Many of the apartments have fallen in. The wainscoted walls of the larger tower are enriched with carvings, paintings, and inscriptions. It was once occupied as a hiding-place by one Milliton, who in repentance for a secret murder, having purchased this barton and manor, secluded himself here for many years.

In Buck there is a drawing given of the place as it stood in 1734, showing a large oblong building of three storeys, battlemented at top, with a square tower attached to one corner rising above the roof, being the entrance tower, with a circular doorway. In front are the ruins of a still larger building. The place is the property of the Duke of Leeds.

RESTORMEL (minor)

THIS interesting ruin of an important stronghold stands on the crest of a rocky eminence, about a mile to the N. of Lostwithiel, with the rapid Fowey flowing below the precipitous face of the hill, which is covered with a thick wood. Leland wrote : "The Park of Restormel is hard by the N. side of the town of Lostwithiel. Ther is a castel on an hill in this park, wher somtymes the erles of Cornwall lay. The base court is sore defaced : the fair large dungeon (keep) yet stondith."

The Conqueror supplanted the last native Earl of Cornwall, giving his lands and title to his own half-brother, Roger le Mortain (or Moreton, as it came to be written), but on the subsequent attainder of Roger's son William the whole was confiscated, and the valuable property and the title of this earldom was ever after vested in the Royal family or the Crown itself. The Castle of Restormel may have been built by either of the Mortains, but is also said to have been reared by one of the Cardinham family, in the reign of Richard I., since they, as well as the Tracys, lived here in early times. Henry III. gave Restormel with other possessions to his brother Richard, King of the Romans, who was created Earl of Cornwall, and as one of the chief seats of this ancient earldom, it was used by him as a residence, and after him his son Edward kept his court here. At the death of this second earl without issue the whole again reverted to the Crown, and Edward III. annexed it to the Duchy of Cornwall ; since which time this castle and honour have never been alienated therefrom, though leased by the duchy from time to time. It must, however, have fallen early into neglect and ruin, and its great park was disparked by Henry VIII. at the instance of Sir Richard Pollard. In that reign the castle was unroofed and defaced.

During the Civil War of the seventeenth century Restormel, after these ages of ruin and desertion, was partially repaired by the Parliament and received a garrison ; and in the year 1644, when King Charles found himself in force in his loyal county of Cornwall, and was driving Essex before him, he came to Lostwithiel with his army, and on August 21st Restormel was stormed by Sir Richard Grenville.

The construction of the original fortress is that of a shell or annular keep, but in this case, being built upon the living rock and not on an artificial mound, its structure is much more massive than the ordinary masonry of a shell keep. An outer circular wall, 9 feet thick and about 34 feet high, having a diameter of 105 feet, fronts the open country, with its embattled parapet; within this and concentric with it is an inner wall of lighter masonry, and within the annular space between the two walls are contained the apartments of the castle, nineteen in number, on two storeys; there is the width of 19 feet between the outer and inner walls, the centre being an open circular court 64 feet in diameter. Three staircases lead up to the ramparts on the outer wall. Borlase gives a ground plan of the structure, the entrance to which is under the ruins of a square tower, and through a vaulted passage and second archway into a small open quadrangle adjoining the inner court.

On the opposite side to the entrance, that is on the E.N.E. quarter, is projected a tower called the Chapel, which afforded a flanking defence on that side as far as the centre of the deep ditch, 9 yards in width, encircling the whole castle. The outer wall contained some fine pointed-arch openings, perhaps for lighting the principal apartments, which were generally lighted from the inner court.

The lower or base court has perished, but in the reign of Elizabeth, when Carew wrote, some fragments remained of this portion of the fortress; and there was another large and deep moat, filled with water brought in pipes from the adjoining hill. Among these ruins was a huge ancient oven 14 feet in width.

ST. MAWES (minor)

THIS fort, a smaller work than Pendennis, on the opposite side of the haven, was commenced by Henry VIII. before the present Castle of Pendennis, and, like it, was completed about 1544, being stated to have cost £5000. Over the great door are Henry's arms, and on the doorways are these lines:

"Semper vivat anima regis Henrici octavi qui anno 34 sui regni hoc fecit fieri."

"May the soul of King Henry VIII. live for ever, who in the 34th year of his reign commanded this to be built."

It is a circular fort like Pendennis, with embrasures for guns on two storeys and the roof, having a small conning turret with a cupola roof. On the ground floor are three circular bastions with embattled parapets, embracing the central tower, which is 64 feet high, and stands 63 feet above sea-level. Of late years a formidable battery has been added below the old blockhouse, which can cross fire with the fortress opposite. It is quite commanded by higher ground in rear.

The first governors were all members of the Vivian family till 1630, when Sir Robert le Grys was appointed, in whose time much dispute arose with Pendennis regarding their relative rights over the shipping. Earl Arundel and Surrey became captain of the fort in 1635, with a garrison of sixteen men ; and at his death the lieutenant, Major Bonithon, was made keeper or captain. The latter, having been accused in 1644 of embezzlement, at once surrendered St. Mawes to General Fairfax in March 1646, with its armament of sixteen guns. After the Restoration, the Vivians again became the governors.

ST. MICHAEL'S MOUNT (*chief*)

THIS is a pyramidal isolated granite crag, in the parish of St. Hilary, 195 feet high and 5 furlongs in circumference, standing in Mounts Bay, E. of Penzance. It is said to have been cut off from the mainland by a mighty inundation which occurred in 1099, and is now joined to the shore only by a low causeway, 560 yards long, of land which is covered by the tide for sixteen hours out of the twenty-four.

The hill is crowned with an ancient building originally founded by Edward the Confessor as a priory for Benedictine monks, and which in after years was fortified. The first military occupation of this structure was effected by Henry de Pomeroy, who, having during the absence of King Richard I. at the Holy War assisted the usurping Prince John, was summoned by the vicegerent, Bishop Longchamp, from Berry Pomeroy (q.v., *Devon*). He, however, stabbed the messenger, and then fled to his castle of Tregony, the strength of which mistrusting, he thence proceeded with some followers to the Mount, where the party, disguised as pilgrims, introduced themselves into the monastic buildings, seized and fortified them, and remained there for several months. On the return of the king from his Austrian prison, Pomeroy, fearing the consequences, is said to have bled himself to death, and the Mount was surrendered to Walter, Archbishop of Canterbury, the Chancellor, who was sent to regain the place (1194). The king then restored the monks, placing a small garrison at the Mount to guard it in future. This Henry de Pomeroy being the grandson of the illegitimate daughter of Henry I., was thus a relation of Richard I. and his brother John.

The next we hear of the place is its capture in the fifteenth century by John, 13th Earl of Oxford, on fleeing from the battle of Barnet (1471). He came to Wales, and taking ship coasted round the S. coast to this place, where his grandfather had acquired possession. Here, after the example of Pomeroy, Oxford and his men, disguising themselves, obtained admission and seized the fortress, occupying it as they alleged for King Henry. Edward IV. at once sent a force under Sir John Arundel, the sheriff, to besiege and reduce the

Mount: Oxford, however, refusing to surrender, made a vigorous resistance, driving the besiegers back on the sands, where the sheriff and some of his men were killed. Thereon a new sheriff was despatched against Oxford, who again repulsed the force with loss, and on this being reported to the king he sent to learn on what terms Oxford would surrender. He demanded their lives, liberties, and lands, and Edward granted the terms asked, whereupon the fortress was delivered up. But the earl was sent prisoner to Ham in France,

ST. MICHAEL'S MOUNT

where he lived till the expedition of the Earl of Richmond against Richard III., which he joined, and, leading the van at Bosworth, was slain. In the reign of Henry VII. Perkin Warbeck landed here, and on proceeding on his raid in Cornwall left his wife, Lady Catherine Gordon, in security at the Mount. During the Cornish insurrection of 1549 (Edward VI.), many of the best families in the West fled for shelter to this stronghold, and were there besieged by the rebels under its governor, Humphrey Arundel. The place was stormed and taken, yielding rich plunder to the victors, who in their turn, however, were driven out.

In the great Civil War the Mount was made, as supposed, impregnable, and

St. Michael's Mount.

was held for King Charles by Sir Arthur Basset, but in April 1646 the Parliamentary troops, under Colonel Hammond, succeeded after a siege of fifteen days in reducing the place, when fifteen guns and 400 stand of arms fell into their hands (*Sprigg*).

A steep and difficult path leads up to the summit, defended midway by a battery, with another battery at the top. The church crowns the crest of the hill, surrounded by the old monastic buildings. On the centre tower is a turret once used as a beacon for sailors, and on the S.W. angle of this, overhanging the sea, is the famous seat called St. Michael's Chair. The whole structure has for long been the property of the St. Aubyn family (Lord St. Levan), and has been adapted to form a comfortable modern dwelling. It is a castellated house, retaining much of the monastic masonry, but great alterations were made in it during last century; the dining-room was the refectory of the convent, and the chapel has been fitted up in the Gothic style.

Queen Elizabeth granted the manor to Thomas Bellot, who conveyed it to Cecil, Earl of Salisbury; then, when forfeited by that family, King Charles gave it to the Bassets of Tehidy, but at the Restoration the St. Aubyn family purchased it from them and made it ever since their principal residence.

ST. RUAN, LANIHORNE (*minor*)

ABOUT three miles from Tregony, at the head of the creek of this name, and near the church, are some remains of a magnificent castle, which was the seat of the ancient family of Erchdeckne or Archdeckne. Leland writes: "At the Hed of Lanyhorne Creeke standith the Castelle of Lanyhorne, sumtyme a Castelle of an 8 Towres, now decaying for lack of Coverture. It longgid as principal House to the Archedecons. This landes descended by Heires general to the best Corbetes of Shropshir, and to Vaulx of Northamptonshir." Hals, writing early in the last century, states that six of the towers of this castle were standing a little time before he wrote, and that the largest of them, 50 feet in height, was then in existence; but in 1718 this was pulled down by one Grant, with the leave of the owner, and with its materials several houses were erected.

The family of Archdeckne was an ancient one in the country, Thomas le Arcedeckne being a knight of Parliament (33 Edward I.), and one of the same name was summoned to Parliament as a baron (14 Edward II.), as was likewise his son. His grandson left three daughters, coheiresses, by whom the estates came to the families of Vaux, Corbett, De Lacy, and the Tregrans.

TINTAGEL (*minor*)

THIS decayed fortress," says Carew in 1602, "more famous for his anti-
quitie than regardable for his present estate, abutteth on the sea; yet
the ruines argue it to have been once no unworthie dwelling for the Cornish
Princes;" and he continues: "Halfe the buildings were raised on the continent and the other half on an iland continued together (within men's
remembrance) by a draw-bridge, but now divorced by the downefaln steepe
cliffes on the farther side."

Here by tradition, about the year 450, the British King Arthur, the illegitimate son of Uther Pendragon, was born, and here it is said he kept his court
and held his diversions of the Round Table. At all events there existed here,
in early ages, a rude stronghold of the British earls of Cornwall, of which the
first mention is made by Geoffrey of Monmouth, about the year 1150; the
castle was probably built after the Conquest.

It consisted of an outer court on the mainland, enclosed by a curtain wall,
defended on the E. and N. outwardly by a ditch. Norden's sketch in 1626
shows on the land side a gate leading to a large square gatehouse, with a corner
watch-turret, from whence steps descended into a second ward, where a very
strong semi-circular wall, 7 feet thick, extended along a steep crag to the edge
of the cliff at the E. Toward the W. the wall rises to an eminence surrounded
by an embattled parapet, which is continued on that side to the cliff edge.
Beyond this comes the island or peninsula on which the keep and main part
of the fortress is said to have stood.

The great difficulty arises from the separation of this peninsula, which is
supposed to have been effected by the weathering, during the lapse of time, of
the soft schistose clay-slate which forms the rocks at this point of the coast.
In the *Journal of the Royal Institute of Cornwall* (vol. iv.), the Rev. R. B. Kinsman
states his opinion that originally this island was merely the point of the projecting headland of Tintagel Head, and that its isolation is due to the above
cause, which has formed a cove on both the E. and W. sides of it, and that
the original stronghold was one continuous fortress without any separation.
If so, the building must have been placed there in extremely remote ages,
since Geoffrey of Monmouth implies the situation as surrounded by the sea,
and with a narrow neck of land only joining it to the mainland, "which three
men shall be able to defend against the whole power of the kingdom." Since
that time this narrow neck, being broken through by the sea, gave place to a
drawbridge, which Hals in 1602 says was then remembered, and by degrees
the opening has been worn into the present chasm.

The ruins, as we see them, may have been of Plantagenet origin. In
1337 (temp. Edward III.) the buildings were in a ruinous state, a part of

Tintagel

them joining the work on the mainland to that on the island having fallen into the sea ; the drawbridge fell in the sixteenth century. The chasm which forms so picturesque a feature in the scenery is now about 200 feet across, and is gradually widening. For some time after the drawbridge went, the opening was crossed by a timber structure.

Leland wrote in 1538 regarding Tintagel : "This Castelle hath bene a marvelous strong and notable forteres, and almost situ loci inexpugnabile, especially for the dungeon that is on a great high terrible cragge, environed with the se, but having a drawbridge from the residew or the Castelle unto it. There is yet a chapel standing within this dungeon of St. Ulette alias Ulianne. Shepe now fede within the dungeon. The residew of buildings of the Castelle be sore wether-beten and yn ruine, but it hath bene a large thinge. The Castelle had belykhod 3 wardes, whereof 2 be woren away with gulfying in of the se : without the isle renneth alonly a gate house, a walle, and a fals braye dyged and walled. On the isle remayne old walles, and on the E. part of the same, the ground beyng lower, remayneth a walle embateled, and men alive saw ther, yn a postern, a dore of yren. There is in the isle a prety chapel, with a tumbe on the left syde."

The inner ward on the island contained the keep and the chief buildings, including the great hall, the timber of which was taken away by John of Eltham, then Earl of Cornwall, "when the hall was ruinous and its walls of no value." Adjoining the N. wall are still the ruins of six apartments where lived the Constable and the chaplain. The chapel, of the thirteenth century, measuring 54 feet by 12, has been unroofed and in ruins for several centuries ; part of its altar with a granite slab was unearthed in 1855. It had some mouldings of Transition Norman style.

Mr. Wilkinson (*Journal R. Inst. Corn.*) is of opinion that Richard, Earl of Cornwall (created 1225), built Tintagel, since he was active in repairing and enlarging other castles in the duchy, as Restormel, Liskeard, and other places, and it is likely that he added to any fortress he found there. In 1245 he entertained his nephew David, Prince of Wales, then in rebellion against Henry III. (*Matt. Paris*). His son Edmund, the last earl who resided in Cornwall, appointed in 1291 his "dearly beloved servant John, called le Barber, to be Constable of Tintagel for life, with a chaplain. After his death in 1300 all Cornish castles, except Launceston, ceased to be kept up, and so in 1337 there was no chaplain, and the castle was described as in a very dilapidated state ; it was then that the great hall was destroyed by John of Eltham. Some repairs, however, may have afterwards been made, as we find this castle in 1385 converted into a prison, where was then confined John of Northampton, Lord Mayor of London, condemned for his "unruly maioralty," and again in 1397 Thomas, Earl of Warwick, was imprisoned in the castle. Thenceforth a small sum was granted for repairs until the reign of Elizabeth, when the

Lord Treasurer Burleigh struck out the item as "a superfluous expense to the Crown." Since then the ravages of time, aided by Atlantic storms and landslips, have completed the wreck.

In the reign of Richard II., when much of the duchy lands were alienated for a time, Tintagel Castle and Manor were given to John Holland, Earl of Huntingdon, who had married the king's sister Elizabeth, and after he was beheaded his widow held the property till her death, when it reverted to the Crown. Mr. Wilkinson prints at length the Report and Survey on the fortress in December 1583, by Sir Richard Grenville, which speaks of the defensible landing-place on the E. side of the island called the Iron Gate. It was not a place of sufficient importance in the succeeding Civil War to cause any contention for its possession, and seems to have passed into oblivion.

TREGONY (*non-existent*)

AT the lower end of this town on the E. side of the Fal River, a little below the hospital, is an earthwork on a hill, still called the Castle Hill, where are some scanty remains of a castle built by Henry de Pomeroy (temp. Richard I.). Tradition says that this baron, being appointed lord of the manor in the reign of Henry II. on behalf of Prince John, Earl of Mortain and Cornwall, espoused the cause of John when in rebellion against his brother Richard, during his absence in the Holy Land.

The castle was standing and remained the seat of these Pomeroys till the reign of Edward VI. The last Pomeroy (temp. Elizabeth) left issue a daughter, married to Richard Penkivell of Resuna, whose descendant, having been ruined in the time of Charles I., sold the manor to Hugh Boscawen, Sheriff of Cornwall, in whose family it was settled on the Lady Anne Fitzgerald, who carried it to her second husband, Francis Robertes, youngest son of the Earl of Radnor (*Hals*).

Whitaker ascribes the site of this castle to the choice of the Romans, who placed a fort there to command the lowest ford of the Fal, having a high precipice on each side, and a brook which joined the river beneath it. The trenches of the later fortress built here are visible.

TREJAGO (*non-existent*)

AT the head of the large creek on the E. side of the Fal River is this place, which gave its name to a family who in Norman times built a castle here (*Hals*). This family of Trejago became extinct in the reign of Edward IV., at that time owning the manor of Fentongollan.

TREMATON (chief)

ON a high eminence over the river Lynher, which flows into the Hamoaze
near Saltash, stands the most entire of all the ancient castles of
Cornwall. Leland wrote : "The greaunt and auncient Castelle of Tremertoun
is upon a Rokky Hille : whereof great Peaces yet stond, and especially the
Dungeon. The Ruines now serve for a Prison. Great Libertees long to this
Castelle. The Valetortes, Men of great Possession, wer owners, &, as far as
I can gather, Builders of this Castel."

But its antiquity is probably superior to this, as the castle appears to have
been erected soon after the Conquest, on an ancient earthwork fortress belonging to the Saxon earls of Cornwall. Here, at the time of the Domesday
Survey, William, Earl of Mortain, or Moreton, and Cornwall half-nephew
of the Conqueror—had the head of his great barony ; but on the confiscation
of his possessions the Crown retained Trematon, which is said to have been
bestowed afterwards on a native British prince. From him it came by an
heiress to Reginald, the natural son of Henry I., and by their daughter to
Walter de Dunstanville, baron of Castlecombe, Cornwall, whose issue failing
it passed, in the reign of Richard I., by marriage to Reginald de Valletort,
whose grandson again passed Trematon, by his daughter Eglina, to Sir Henry
Pomeroy of Berry Pomeroy, Devon. His son made over the property to
King Edward III. in his eleventh year, and on the investment of the Black
Prince as Duke of Cornwall, this honour and castle, with the manor, were
granted to him and made part of the duchy, in which it still remains.

The fortress, as we see it, consists of a large oval enclosure of stone curtain
wall, 6 feet in thickness and 30 feet high, with an embattled parapet, encircling
an area of about three-quarters of an acre. In the direction of the longer
axis of this enceinte, in the N.W. corner, is a lofty and steep artificial mound,
on the top of which stands a fine Norman shell keep, oval in form and over
30 feet high, the walls of which are 10 feet thick, with crenellated parapet,
and measure 24 yards on the longest and 17 on the least diameter. The
entrance is through a circular-headed doorway at the top of the mound, which
is surrounded by a ditch of its own. The entrance to the castle is on the
S.W., under a square gatehouse, having a gateway with three arches and a
portcullis groove, with a guardroom over in a fair state of repair. Nothing
remains of the lodgings and buildings within the enclosure ; nor of those
within the keep which were built against the wall, as at Lincoln, without
any exterior lights. On the N. is a postern, and other buildings stood thereabout. A deep ditch surrounds the whole fortress.

During Kilter's insurrection of 1594, Sir Richard Grenville and his wife
took refuge in Trematon Castle, and were there besieged by the rebels at

three separate points, but unsuccessfully, until, by the treachery of some within the castle, Sir Richard was induced to leave its walls in order to parley with the enemy, when he was seized and made to yield up the fortress to the mob, who plundered the building and stripped their prisoners even of their clothing.

TRURO (*non-existent*)

THIS castle, of which no remains now exist, stood on an eminence on the W. of the town, where now is the head of St. Pancras or Pydar Street. Leland wrote : "Ther is a Castelle a quarter of a mile by West out of Truru longing to the Erle of Cornwale now clene down. The site thereof is now used for a shoting and playing place." It is supposed to have been the origin of the town, having served as a residence of the earls of Cornwall in very early times, as is evidenced by the artificial mound upon which it stood, but which is now constantly decreasing, as the site is included within the town, and its materials are being taken away.

Lysons says that the manor passed by coheiresses of the Lucy family, one moiety with the castle going to Thomas, son of Reginald de Prideaux, whose family conveyed the property in 1366 to the Bodrugans, and on the attainder of Sir Henry Bodrugans (temp. Henry VII.) it was given to Sir Richard Edgecombe, and still is included in the Mount-Edgecombe estates.

On the site of this building, when it was prepared in 1840 for the erection of a cattle market, the wall of the ancient castle was discovered, being possibly that of the keep. It had a diameter of 75 feet, and was built of slate. There is no sign at present left of any wall.

SALCOMBE

Devonshire

AFTON, or ASTON (minor)

THIS place is situated in the middle of N. Devon, in the parish of W. Worlington, at the stream of the Little Dart, a tributary of the river Taw; it was once the stronghold of the Devonshire Stucleys, and was restored by Sir George Stukeley. Lysons states that the manor belonged to a family who took the name of their residence (temp. Henry III.); a coheiress brought it in marriage to Crawthorne, and the heiress of this family to Marwood. In or about 1350 it was purchased of the Marwoods by Thomas Afleton of Afton, in the same parish. The heiress of Affeton brought it to Sir Hugh Stucley, or Stewkley, and it was long the seat of that family. The building is now a farm-house, but there are some remains of the more ancient castellated mansion which was the seat of the Affetons.

BAMPTON (non-existent)

POLWHELE claims this locality for a Roman station; at the Conquest it was a king's demesne, and was presented by the king to Walter de Douay. His son Robert, called De Bampton, held the lands, which by the marriage of his daughter Julian descended, in the reign of Richard II., to William Paganel, the brother of Fulk Paganel of Dudley, Stafford (*Risdon*). His son Fulk, Lord

of Braunton, married Ada, the heiress of Gilbert d'Albrincis, through whom
Bampton came by an heiress to Sir Milo Cogan (temp. Henry III.). "A very
stately family who kept great entertainment when they lived here, but residing
chiefly in Ireland" (*Risdon*). Sir James Cogan dying *s.p.* (12 Richard II.),
Bampton came to the Fitzwarrens, and then to the Bourchiers of Tavistock,
with whom it continued for six descents, and then fell by an heiress to the
Wrays of Cornwall, and afterwards to the family of Fellowes.

Richard Cogan had a licence from the Crown in 1336 to crenellate his
mansum at Bampton, and enclose his wood of Uffculme and 300 acres for
a park. The site of the keep of this castle is known near the town, but of
the building itself there are no vestiges.

BARNSTAPLE (*non-existent*)

THE original settlement of this ancient town stood in the angle between
the Taw and Yeo rivers, and a castle is said to have been built here
by King Athelstan, of which the mound still exists. The manor was bestowed
at the Conquest on Joel de Totnes (see *Totnes*), who founded here a priory
for Cluniac monks, and is supposed to have built a Norman keep on the
Saxon site, to which his son Alured retired. The manor followed the fortunes
generally of the Totnes estates, but the castle must have been destroyed at
an early date, as little mention exists of it. In Leland's time (cir. 1538) there
were "manifest ruins & a piece of the Dungeon" or keep, but at this date
nothing remains except the mound and a few fragments of walls.

BEER FERRERS (*non-existent*)

THIS is a small hamlet on the point of land lying between the Tamar
and the Tavy rivers, on the W. side of the latter, and almost at its
extremity. The lands here and northward were given by the Conqueror to
a Norman follower from Alençon, which word was corrupted into Alston, a
name taken by his family, and continued in the neighbouring village of
Beer Alston. In the reign of Henry II., Henry de Ferrariis, or Ferrers,
ancestor of the numerous branches of the ancient family of Ferrers in Devon
and Cornwall, held this honour and had his castle here. Many knights of that
family followed him (*Risdon*). In 1337 Sir William de Ferrers had a licence
for crenellating his manor-house at this place, and the last of the family was
Martin Ferrers, who was entrusted with the defence of the S. coasts against
an invasion of the French in the reign of Edward III. He left issue three
daughters, one of whom brought this estate to Alexander Champernown, from
whom it passed by his granddaughter to Robert Willoughby, Lord Brooke,

and thence through the Blounts (Earl of Newport, temp. Charles I.) by purchase to Sir John Maynard, whose granddaughter brought it in marriage to the Earl of Stamford. Afterwards Beer Ferrers came to the Duke of Northumberland.

The Lords Brooke resided in the old castellated mansion, which seems to have stood on the shore, and had a park here; but there are no remains of the castle (*Lysons*).

BERRY POMEROY (*chief*)

THESE magnificent ruins, the finest in the county, stand on a rocky ledge above a small stream flowing into the Dart, 2½ miles from Totnes, and in the midst of a thick wood. The manor of Beri was bestowed by the Conqueror on one of his followers, Ralph de Pomeroy or Pomerai (variously written), together with fifty-seven others in Devon, and the erection of the original castle is said to have been carried out by him. The family appear to have flourished, since Joel his son is said to have married one of the natural daughters of Henry I., and his successors were barons and nobles till 1257, after which date no Pomeroy was summoned to Parliament. Dugdale informs us that after this date (41 Henry III.) it became the custom for none to claim the peerage but such barons as were summoned to Parliament by the king's writ. The Pomeroys are said to have come from Cinglais, near Falaise in Normandy, where a fragment of their castle still remains.

But though not as nobles, the family maintained their lands here till the reign of Edward VI., the last of them being Sir Thomas Pomeroy, who served with distinction in France, and acquired the confidence of Henry VIII. In 1549 the new Act for reforming the Church Service was enforced for the first time on Whitsunday, and the riots which ensued in favour of the old ritual assumed in Devonshire the appearance of an insurrection, the whole county being speedily in a state of disorder. Sir Thomas, the last of his ancient family who resided at Berry, became the chief of the discontented gentry, and headed a force of 2000 men, who besieged Exeter, and kept up the blockade for a month, when a strong force under Lord Russell, partly of German horse and 300 Italian arquebusiers, came to the relief, and after some reverses succeeded in wholly defeating the insurgents, now 8000 strong, on Clist heath, and so ending the rebellion. Several of the leaders were beheaded, but Pomeroy managed to escape with the loss of his lands, which were confiscated, and were then acquired, probably by purchase, from the Crown by Lord Edward Seymour, son of the Protector Somerset.

The descendants of Sir Thomas Pomeroy afterwards resided in the parish of Harberton, till the beginning of the eighteenth century. A grandson of the Rev.

Arthur Pomeroy, the chaplain to Lord Essex in 1672, was raised to the peerage in 1783 as Baron Harberton.

The Seymour family at once inhabited Berry Castle, and Sir Edward Seymour, who succeeded in 1593, erected within the quadrangle of the castle the magnificent mansion whose outer walls still remain, and on which he is said to have spent £20,000. In the Civil War of the next century the castle was dismantled, but it was in a condition to be inhabited by Edward Seymour in the reign of James II. After his death, however, it went to decay, and being

BERRY POMEROY

set on fire in a thunderstorm in 1685 it became a ruin, and is now but an ivy-draped relic of its former state.

By the failure of the elder branch of the Seymour family, Berry became the property of the dukes of Somerset, to whom it still belongs, they being of the junior branch. It is said that William III. remarked to Sir Edward Seymour, on his presentation to him in 1686, that he believed Sir Edward was of the family of the Duke of Somerset. "Pardon me, sir," said he, "the Duke of Somerset is of *my* family." Macaulay says of Sir Edward Seymour, who was speaker temp. Charles II., that his fortune was large, and his influence in the west of England extensive, for he had long been at the head of a strong Parliamentary connection which was called the Western Alliance, and which included many gentlemen of Devon, Somerset, and Cornwall. Born in 1635, he played a prominent part in four reigns. He was one of the first who joined William of Orange on his landing at Torbay (November 5, 1688), and Berry Pomeroy Castle was made one of the first halting-places of the draggled army, toiling towards Exeter through the Devonshire lanes. Sir Edward died in 1708, and his son obtained the dukedom.

The S. front of the enceinte remains much as shown in Buck's drawing: at the W. end is the nearly perfect gatehouse, three storeys in height, with two hexagonal flanking towers supporting the great arched gateway, which is sculptured with the arms of Pomeroy. The passage is furnished with two portcullis grooves, and over it is a loopholed guardroom; stairs lead from this chamber down to small vaulted rooms in each side-tower, and a spiral stair ascends to the summit of the W. tower. The whole is embattled. A covered way leads from the guardroom to the E. end of this front, where is a large turret called Lady Margaret's Tower, in which it is said that Eleanor de Pomeroy, once mistress of the castle, was confined by her sister.

The walls of the castle formed a quadrangle within, and inside are the remains of the splendid mansion, four storeys high, built in the sixteenth century, but never finished on the W. side. The remains of the hall are there, and those of numberless apartments and offices, some of which must have been very fine.

Buck shows, on the W. side of the old castle, a square keep standing on the edge of the steep declivity of the valley.

CHULMLEIGH (non-existent)

AT this village, near the junction of the Little Dart with the Taw River, not far from Eggesford, it is said by Lysons that the Courtenay family possessed a castle, of which there are now no vestiges; they also had a park, which has been converted into tillage for more than two hundred years.

COLCOMBE (minor)

THE quondam seat of the Pole family is close to Colyton, and although it cannot ever have been a castle, it seems to have been a fortified house, the original building being alleged to have been erected by an earl of Devon (temp. Edward I.). It was rebuilt about the year 1600 by Sir William Pole, the county historian, who resided there till his death in 1635, when, the family leaving this house for the neighbouring one of Shute, Colcombe fell into decay. It is still owned by the Pole family, and is partly used as a farm-house.

COMPTON (minor)

AN ancient seat of the Pole family, in the parish of Marldon, about five miles from Newton Abbot, this is an excellent specimen of a fortified house of the fourteenth century. At the time of the Domesday Survey the manor was held by one Stephen, under Joel de Totais (see Totnes), and in the time of Henry II. was the property and seat of Sir Maurice de la Pole. In the succeeding reign Alice de la Pole bestowed the place on one Peter, who took the name of Compton, and after seven descents in his family a Compton heiress brought the estate in marriage to the Gilberts of Greenway, from whom it was purchased, about the beginning of the present century, by James Templer of Stover Lodge. In 1808, however, the estate was sold off in lots, when the ancient castellated seat of the Poles was bought by Mr. John Bishop and converted into a farm-house ; the hall was destroyed at that time, and several rooms at the back were pulled down. The Alice de la Pole who alienated the property originally must have been the widow of William de la Pole, the powerful statesman of the reign of Henry VI., who as Duke of Suffolk was murdered in the Channel in 1450 (see Donnington, Berks) : she was the grand-daughter of Geoffrey Chaucer the poet.

The structure is an interesting one, even in its ruins, as, having no moat, it shows the means adopted by its builders of protecting the foot of the walls from being undermined in an attack, by the provision of an overhead defence by means of projecting machicoulis and garde-robes at all vulnerable points, from which stones and burning matter could be discharged upon the heads of assailants.

Part of the N. front with its machicolated gatehouse and a part of the chapel still remain, but the ruin is partially filled up with modern farm-buildings, having been degraded from its high state to this purpose. The structure was originally in the form of a small quadrangle, with a square tower at each corner, the curtain wall, the greater part of which exists, being 20 feet high. Within this outer wall are seen the holes for the timbers of the roofing of the buildings or sheds which were ranged against it. The postern gate is at one end of the front, just within the wall of enceinte, and had a portcullis. The principal entrance was on the centre and also had a portcullis, being protected by very bold projecting machicoulis instead of side flanking towers. The outer ward in front was enclosed by a low wall only (Parker). The chapel is tolerably perfect, with a plain vault, and a priest's room over it. There is a good guardroom over the entrance.

COMPTON CASTLE

DARTMOUTH (minor)

THE estuary of the Dart, being a seaport of much importance from an early period, has received several fortifications at various times. At its mouth on the W. side, at the extreme point of the land, stands Dartmouth Castle, consisting of a square bastion and a round tower, embattled, in rear of which is the small church of St. Petrox. The round tower was built in the reign of Henry VII. by the Corporation of Dartmouth, who received £40 per annum for building "a strong and mighty tower, and arming the same with ordnance, and finding a chain of sufficient length and strength to close the entrance." The other end of this chain was made fast to the rocks, under a small turreted fort situated on the opposite side of the channel, where its groove can still be seen. Adjoining the before-mentioned tower is a gun platform, and the site of a far earlier fortress, for the erection of which a licence was obtained in the fourth year of Henry IV. (1405) by Johannes de Corp to crenellate "quoddam hospitium juxta introitum portus vill de Dertemuth, Devon." Polwhele says the chapel attached to this castle existed in the time of Edward III., and belonged to the neighbouring church of Stoke Fleming. On the eminence above the castle, at a height of 300 feet, are the remains of another strong work, which in the Civil War of the seventeenth century was called "The Gallant's Bower," and is spoken of in the despatches of Fairfax to the Parliament.

Across the harbour on the E. side, opposite to Dartmouth, is the still older town of KINGSWEAR, where on the hill above the church are the earthworks of a fort called Mount Ridley, but mentioned by Fairfax as Kingsworth Fort. Close to the shore, not very far below, stands the weather-beaten ruin of Kingswear Castle, an ancient defence of the harbour about which there is little or no information.

Altogether this group of fortifications formed an exceedingly strong position for the Royalists, heavily armed as it was with 106 pieces of ordnance, with ammunition and provisions, and a strong garrison of 800 troops.

Towards the end of 1645, after the fall of Basing House and Winchester, a final effort was determined on by the Parliamentary generals to clear out of Devon (never very loyal) the remaining strongholds of the king, which were chiefly on the S. of Exeter; Dartmouth and its port forming the headquarters of the district. General Fairfax reached Totnes on January 11, 1646, and at once made preparations for reducing Dartmouth, which had been fortified at considerable cost and with much skill. At the outbreak of the Civil War it had declared for the Parliament, and in 1643 was besieged and taken by Prince Maurice, since when its defences had been greatly strengthened, and earthwork forts and batteries erected.

Two men-of-war lay in the harbour, and at the mouth of this was Dartmouth Castle, commanding the entrance, having on the hill above the fort called the Gallant's Bower. Paradise Fort and Mount Flaggon guarded the line on the W., while Tunstall Church with outworks around it stood next, and Hardress with Mount Boon protected the N. These were supported on the other side of the water by Kingswear and Kingsworth Fort. The governor, Sir Hugh Pollard, was supported by some sixty officers.

DARTMOUTH

The harbour was blockaded by Captain Batten, the Parliamentary admiral, and three or four days were spent in preparations for storming. At last, on Sunday, January 18th, all was ready for the assault that night, and the troops were told off to their several stations. The dragoons with 200 sailors from the fleet were to threaten Kingswear, which, being a very strong place, the besiegers did not expect to take. Colonel Fortescue was appointed to attack the work at Tunstall Church, and Colonel Hammond the Westgate, Flaggon, and Paradise forts ; the attack on Mount Boon and Hardress falling to Colonel

Pride. The morning was spent in preaching and prayer, the password being "God with us," while the distinguishing badge of the attacking force was the wearing of their shirts outside the trousers.

At eleven o'clock at night the assault began, and was delivered with such vigour that the royal troops had but time to fire one round from their big guns and then, overpowered and disheartened, gave in after very slight resistance. The Roundheads were successful at each point, and after seven hours became possessed of the whole town, with the loss of only a single man; the governor retreating to Gallant's Bower, which fort, together with the castle, being summoned next morning, were surrendered by the governor, who lay wounded in the fort. Then the fort on the Kingswear side capitulated, and the whole position was won (*Sprigg*).

The defences of the castles being wholly seaward, their armament could have been of little avail against a land attack.

EXETER (*chief*)

THIS beautiful city, "Queen of the West," was originally a British settlement and an early fortified post under the name of *Caer Wise*; then it became the Isca of the Romans, and in Saxon times figures in the reign of Alfred as Exanceaster, or the castle on the Exe, having an English fortress, of great importance. It was the centre of the Cornish metal trade, and an object of capture and recapture more than once between the great king and the Danes. Athelstan surrounded the town with a defensive wall of stone with towers, preserving generally the plan of the Roman *castrum* which he found there; this was in 926. Then we read that the year after Duke William's victory at Senlac, or Hastings, he came as king into the West and advanced against this hill fort, in which Gytha, the Danish mother of King Harold, had taken shelter, with Harold's sons, and took the place by assault, whereupon he at once ordered the construction of a Norman castle upon the ancient British mound, to overawe the country round and the disaffected city; and thus reared upon the earthworks of earlier days, like so many other fortresses founded in those times, it effectually secured William's power in the West.

From its earliest days this Castle of Exeter was known by the name of *Rougemont*. It is referred to in Shakespeare's "Richard III.," where that usurper quails at the name, confounding it with Richmond.

In the Conqueror's days it withstood one or two sieges at the hands of the West Saxon insurgents, when its Constable and owner was one Baldwin of Okehampton, who had married William's niece Albreda, and in whose family it rested till 1230. In 1137 Exeter took the part of the Empress Maud, and King Stephen himself besieged and captured the fortress, destroying its outworks.

In Tudor times the castle was attacked, unsuccessfully, by the host that collected in the West in favour of Perkin Warbeck, in 1497 ; and again in 1549, when the religious insurrection, in defence of the old form of worship and the possessions of the Church, grew to an alarming height in this district,

Exeter was threatened, but was relieved by a force under the command of Lord Russel.

But neglect fell on the fortress, as it did upon most of the castles of the kingdom in the reign of Elizabeth, so that in the next century it is spoken of as entirely ruinous, and it is doubtful if in the Civil War the castle was of any actual value to the defences of the town. Exeter was taken in 1643 by Prince Maurice, but in 1646 was surrendered to Fairfax on the first summons and without sustaining a siege.

The ancient fortress is described by Clark as standing in the N. corner of the city, on the summit of a natural eminence of reddish stone, having the sides which grow out of the valley below artificially scarped ; the knoll is abrupt on the N.E. and N.W., sloping somewhat on the other sides. At the foot of the scarped front is a ditch, outside which the hill is again scarped down to the bottom of the valley :

EXETER

and a second ditch once existed on the S. At the top was a rampart of earth 30 feet high, but this has been reduced and the main ditch on the N.E. and N.W. filled up and converted into a boulevard ; the ditch on the S. and S.E. remaining still unaltered.

The Conqueror came before Exeter on the N.E., and summoned the city just below the castle at the E. gate, entering it through a breach in Athelstan's wall. The gatehouse is the oldest part left, and is probably his building ; it is

in two storeys, with a drawbridge over the ditch in front. At the W. angle, where the city wall sprang from the castle, stood a square bastion, the base of which remains, and a similar one stood at the N. angle, with the N.W. curtain between them, whereon there remain two half-round solid bastions, both of rough Norman work in rubble. A portion of the N.E. front is built of ashlar blocks of the time of Richard II. The bank and wall have been removed from the N.W. front to give place to an odious modern sessions house. The chapel was near the W. corner, but it cannot be told what buildings were contained in the enceinte, though it is evident that, as at Corfe and Taunton, no regular keep was ever erected here. The ancient entrance has been walled up, the existing one being on the W. of the main gatehouse.

The city walls were probably built at the same time as the castle, as there was a water-gate of Norman construction (removed in 1815); the walls crossed ditches and terminated on the castle. The E. wall has been rebuilt, but that on the N.W. is very perfect and strong (*Clark*).

In the Report of the Devon Association for 1895 is a paper by Sir J. B. Phear, giving an account of the repairs carried out in 1891, with photographs and sections of the old gatehouse, or Athelstan's Tower.

FORT CHARLES, or SALCOMBE CASTLE (*minor*)

THE ruins of this building are situated upon a rock in the Kingsbridge or Salcombe River, and are at high-water nearly surrounded by the tide. The position was an excellent one in early days for stopping the passage of ships up the river, and one authority speaks of the fortress as of Saxon origin. Hearne mentions this castle as "a round fort, built in the reign of Elizabeth a little before the Spanish invasion"; but it is more probable that it was one of Henry VIII.'s blockhouses, erected after his survey of the southern coasts, together with Pendennis and St. Mawes castles in Cornwall. Along with all other national defences, this one had been neglected from Elizabeth's to the Stuarts' time, and when it was taken in hand by Sir Edmund Fortescue, High Sheriff of Devon; during the Civil War it was known only by the name of "the olde Bullworke." A copy of the payments and disbursements made upon Fort Charles in January 1645 by Sir Edmund still exists "for the buildynge, victuallyne and fortifying it with great guns and musquets," and amounts to £1355, 18s. 9d. for building, and £1031, 19s. 9d. for the armament. The Parliamentary Admiral Batten had sailed up this creek previously, and on this account it was resolved to secure these waters, which formed a harbour of refuge for Royalist privateers. Hence, after the fall of Dartmouth, Colonel Ingoldsby was sent with a force to reduce Fort Charles, which was said to be "a verie stronge place," and impregnable to any but siege guns, which accordingly were sent for from Plymouth.

Colonel Fortescue, who held the place for King Charles, had a garrison of fifty-three men only and ten officers in the fort with him, but with these he held out valiantly as long as resistance was possible. We have no account of the incidents of the siege, but it is supposed that the Parliamentary artillery was placed on Rickham Common, where are still the remains of earthworks. One night Sir Edmund's sleep was disturbed by a shot carrying away the leg of his bedstead, "causing his sudden appearance among his men in his shirt"; but only two casualties occurred in the fort, and he held out till May 7th, when articles of capitulation were arranged, and the fort was surrendered. The key of Fort Charles, as it was named by its defenders, or Salcombe Castle, is now in the possession of Sir E. Fortescue's descendant, Mr. Fortescue of Octon, Torquay; it was the last place that held out for the king. Sir Edmund escaped to Delft in Holland, where he died soon after, and his son was made a baronet by Charles II.

GIDLEIGH (minor)

THIS fragment of an old Norman castle lies on the N.E. confines of Dartmoor, near Chagford. In the time of William I. the lands were possessed by a family named Prouse or Prowse, by ancient grants from the Crown; and here they had their castle. Adjoining is an extensive walled enclosure of moorland, three sides of it having a stone wall, while the remaining side is protected by a fine gorge of the river Teign, which rises up in this district. The Prouses became extinct in the reign of Edward II., and Gidleigh Castle and manor passed with its heiress to Mules, and from that family in the same way to Damerell. William Damerell of Gidleigh gave the estate to his daughter, wife to Walter Coade of Morval in Cornwall, with whose descendants it long continued. In later years the place belonged to an ancient family taking their name from the property; one Bartholomew Gidleigh being lord of the manor in 1772, and by marriage with this family the possessor at the time of Polwhele (1797) was one Ridley; after that time there was a Chancery suit respecting the property, followed by a sale.

HEMYOCK (minor)

THIS place lies in the valley of the river Culm or Columb, on the N.E. border of the county, south of Wellington, Somerset. An ancient family called Hidon had their settlement here from the time of the Conquest, and it was doubtless one of them who built the ancient castle at this place.

Polwhele says (temp. Edward I.) that the property was brought by Margaret, only daughter of Sir Richard Hidon, in marriage with Sir Joel Dinham or Dynham (see *Okehampton*), in whose possession Hemyock remained till the reign of Henry VII., when it was parted between the four sisters of John, Lord Dynham, High Treasurer of England, and then passed (temp. Elizabeth) by sale to Sir John Popham. After that time other divisions took place, and the estate and castle passed into the hands of various families. The descent, however, as given by Lysons, is that Roger de Hemiock possessed the lands at the Conquest; his son William had a daughter Beatrix, the wife of Sir Gerard de Clift, knight, and that from them it came by Isabel, daughter of William de Clift, to Richard Tremenet, and by an heir-general of that family to the Dynhams. Early in this century the castle and a quarter of the lands were purchased by General Simcoe.

Hemyock Castle stood out for Charles I., having been taken in 1642 by Lord Poulett, but it was held later and garrisoned as a prison by the Parliament. Soon after the Restoration it was dismantled.

The castle is situated at a little distance W. of the church, and was a regular, if not a very extensive, structure. The main entrance gateway and two flanking towers, built of flint, remain; the latter were tolerably entire till the end of the last century, when the tenant took down the upper part of them. The gateway has a portcullis groove. The enclosing curtain wall with its mural towers can still be made out, and there was a moat surrounding the fortress, filled by a rivulet running close by. A farm-house is on the site.

LYDFORD, or LIDFORD (*minor*)

THE town of this name which lies on the western edge of Dartmoor, nine miles from Okehampton, was one of the earliest in Britain, and one of the chief towns in Devon during the Heptarchy, possessing a mint for tin pennies in the time of Ethelred the Unready. At Domesday it was a walled town, and assizes were held there. The castle in this case dates many ages after the town, though a stronghold of some sort must have been placed on the mound, where, in the thirteenth century, Lydford Castle was built.

Little remains of the fortress except the walls of the square keep on this earthwork by the roadside; it is supposed to have been erected by Richard, "King of the Romans," the brother of Henry III., who created him Earl of Cornwall in 1225, with the gift of the Manor of Lydford, and also of Dartmoor Chase. Appointed to this important earldom, he worked strenuously to develop the mineral resources of his estates, and it was doubtless he who built the castle, on the site of a former stronghold, since a "Castrum de Lydford" is mentioned in the Close Rolls of 1216.

It was an important military point, commanding as it did the road on the W. of Dartmoor, but in the thirty-third year of Edward I. it had passed into the hands of the civil power, and is called "our prison of Lydeford," for the detention of offenders against the stannary laws.

In 1650, under the Commonwealth, a survey was held which reported that Lydford Castle was "very much in decay, & almost totally ruined. The walls are built of lime & stone, within the compass of which wall, their is 4 little roomes, whereof 2 are above stairs, the flore of which is all broken, divers of the chiefest beames being fallen to the ground, & all the rest is following; only the roof of the said castle being lately repaired by the Prince [Charles I.] and covered with lead, is more substantial than the other parts. The seite of the said castle with the ditches & courte, contain half an acre of land." A valuation of the ruin follows, and the dismantling seems to have been carried out in a very thorough manner. In 1703, the want of a prison being again felt, the castle was partially restored, and appropriated accordingly.

The Rev. E. A. Bray, early in the present century, describes the castle as a square building standing on an artificial mound, and entered at the N.W. side. Before it is a spacious area, having a gentle slope, and on the N.W. is the outer or "base" court, enclosed by two parallel earthworks, enclosing an oblong area of ninety paces in length, at the end of which is a precipitous declivity, or brae, which continues on the opposite side till it joins the river near the bridge. It was approachable only from the N.E. The stairs and floor were then in a ruinous state, but the Judge's Chair, with the royal arms over it, last occupied by the infamous Jeffries, still remained. A staircase in the wall led to the roof, while below is a cellar or dungeon, 16 feet by 10, attained by a ladder through a trap-door, and lighted by loops.

At the present time nothing remains but the bare walls, the decay having been caused by the removal, by George IV. when Duke of Cornwall, of the courts to the Duchy Hotel at Prince's Town, thus made the capital of Dartmoor. Lydford then fell into neglect.

The square keep stands on a moderately high mound on the N. side of the road, to the E. of Lydford Church. A low-pointed archway forms the doorway to the lower stage, which is not lighted, the upper storey having three square-headed loops, and slits for lighting the garderobes. On the S.W. face is a wide-arched window, with four openings, two on each storey; and on the right of the entrance is the staircase, at the head of which is the opening into the hall, or chief apartment. The whole building is divided by a transverse wall running E. and W., dividing it into two unequal portions, the lower stage having three rooms, and the upper stage two. There is but one fireplace in the castle.

OKEHAMPTON (chief)

ON the western confines of Dartmoor the ruins of this ancient castle stand boldly on a hill in the valley of the Okement or Oekment River, commanding the main road into Cornwall on the N. of Dartmoor from Exeter to Launceston. The rocky hill, still crowned by the castle keep, is about a mile S.W. of the town, being protected by a ravine on the N., and by a deep ditch on the W. side, and with the river defence on the S. It is a very strong position, approachable only on the E. slope, and from the extensive area covered by the ruins, the castle must have been a large and important fortress. The partly artificial mound on which the keep stands shows that long before Norman days this site was occupied by a stronghold and home of the former lords of the county.

OKEHAMPTON

In the Domesday Survey of 1089 it is written: "Baldwinus tenet de Rege Ochementon, et ibi sedet castellum"; the Conqueror having given the lands to Baldwin de Brionis, who made here the head of his barony. After him Richard Fitz-Baldwin held this honour, being Sheriff of Devon temp. Henry I., and on his death s.p. his property descended to another line, and from them was inherited by the great family of Courtenay, earls of Devon, by the marriage of Reginald Courtenay with Hawise, coheiress of Richard de Redvers, the eldest son of the last Brionis baron. Their son Robert succeeded in the reign of King John. The Courtenays were Lancastrians, and Earl Thomas was beheaded by Edward IV. after Towton at Pontefract in 1461, his head being set up at York in place of that of Edward's father, the Duke of York, which was taken down. His possessions were drafted to Sir Humphrey Stafford, knight, afterwards created Earl of Devon, who, however, in his turn came to the block (9 Edward IV.), when the castle and honour of

Okehampton were granted to Sir John Dynham, who yielded them to the Duke of Clarence. After the murder of this unhappy prince in the Tower, these estates were retained by the Crown till Henry VII. restored the Courtenays here as elsewhere.

Henry VIII. beheaded Henry Courtenay, Marquis of Exeter, alleging a secret and treasonable correspondence between him and Cardinal Pole, and with vindictive barbarism destroyed the ancient castle of Okehampton and devastated its noble park. The son of his victim, Edward Courtenay, was imprisoned in the Tower of London by Henry, but was released by Queen Mary and much favoured by Elizabeth. He died at Padua *s.p.*, and his large estates were divided between the descendants of the four sisters of his great-grandfather, Okehampton becoming the property of the famous rowdy Whig noble, Charles, 5th Lord Mohun, the duellist. In 1712 Mohun quarrelled with James Douglas, 4th Duke of Hamilton, concerning the reversion of the estate of the Earl of Macclesfield, and challenged the duke. A furious duel took place in Hyde Park in the early morning of November 15th, when, neither Mohun nor his adversary attempting to parry, both simply giving point, Mohun fell riddled with wounds, and is said to have given the duke a death-stab with a shortened sword as Hamilton was bending over him.

GATEWAY

The castle then came to Christopher Harris of Heynes, M.P. for the borough in the reign of Anne, by marriage with the heiress of that family. It was purchased about forty years ago by Sir R. R. Vyvyan, Bart., of Trelowarren, but is now the property of Mr. Reddaway.

Grose's drawing of 1768 shows the vast range of the outer walls supporting the interior lodgings, with some bastions and a large outside garderobe and buttresses; all which was possibly the building of Thomas de Courtenay, the first earl of that family (beheaded 1461), as stated by William de Worcester.

The remains now consist of the small quadrangular Norman keep on the crest of the hill, a portion only existing, which contains a small oratory, while below are parts of the hall and chapel, and ruins of the lodgings on the eastern slope, between walls narrowing to the main gateway. Beyond this are fragments of a barbican. The main buildings were probably erected by Hugh Courtenay, first earl, who succeeded 1292, and are in two ranges, divided by the yard; the least intact remains are those of the great hall with the solar and the cellar or undercroft. The hall was large, 45 feet long by 25 wide, lit by two large windows in the S. wall. On the S. range were a lodge, at the E. end, next two guardrooms, and then the chapel, all of Early English style; over the ground floor were the state apartments of the lord of the castle, with a central garderobe tower (see details in paper by Mr. Worth, *Devonshire Association Reports*, 1895).

PLYMOUTH CITADEL (*chief*)

THE town of Plymouth in 1411 was described as being without any defences, and it was not till after several attacks by the French that in 1439 the townsmen were granted a toll to enable them to fortify and protect themselves; at this time St. Nicholas or Drake's Island was fortified. Then in 1512 an Act of Parliament was passed for adding fortifications at Plymouth and other western seaports, and sometime after this Leland wrote regarding this place: "The mouth of the Gulph wherein the shippes of Plymmouth lyith is waullid on eche side, and chained over in tyme of Necessite. On the S.W. side of this mouthe is a Blok House: and on a Rokky Hille hard by it is a stronge Castel quadrate having at eche Corner a great Rounde Tower. It semith to be no very old Peace of Worke."

The existing citadel was built on the site of the old fort at the E. end of the Hoe, after the Restoration by Charles II., who went to see it in 1670. It consisted of three regular and two irregular bastions, with ravelins and hornworks.

Plymouth was the principal fortress and headquarters of the Parliamentary army in the West, from the commencement of the Civil War, and succeeded in 1643 and 1644 in beating off the attacks of the royal troops, who never were able to take the outworks of the town.

PLYMPTON EARL, or ST. MAURICE (*minor*)

PLYMPTON EARL is the ruin of a circular Norman keep on a very lofty mound. The town lay on the ancient Roman road from Exeter into Cornwall, and was a chartered stannary borough in 1241. The honour was granted by Henry I. to Richard de Redvers, afterwards Earl of Devon, who made it the head of his barony; from which cause its following name of " Earl" was derived, distinguishing it from the neighbouring Plympton St. Mary. The castle is said to be the work of Baldwin de Redvers, who took the side of the Empress Maud against Stephen, and was holding Exeter against him, when the knights whom he had entrusted with the defence of Plympton and its garrison revolted, treated with the king, and in 1136 surrendered the castle; Stephen then sent thither a force of 200 men and demolished it. The fortress appears to have been partially restored afterwards, since in John's reign some fighting took place there. It was then the dowry of Margaret, wife of Baldwin, 6th Earl of Devon, at whose death King John gave his widow, against her consent, in marriage to his worthless favourite Falk de Brent (see *Bedford*), after whose fall this castle and barony went to Isabella, sister of Baldwin, the wife of William de Fortibus, Earl of Albemarle, and who was called Countess of Devon and Albemarle (see *Eytham, Lincoln*). On her death in 1292 Sir Hugh Courtenay, baron of Okehampton, succeeded to the estates of De Redvers and to the earldom, till the death of the last earl in 1566, when this and his other large estates were divided between his four aunts or their representatives. The whole of this property became vested at last in the Earl of Morley, its present owner.

Leland wrote : " In the side of this town is a fair large Castelle & Dungeon in it, whereof the Waulles yet stonde, but the Logginges within be decayed." The earthworks on which this castle rested may have been British or even Roman originally, and within the last three centuries the upper waters of the Plym estuary were navigable up to the castle walls.

A fragment only of the keep remains crowning the mound, which is 70 feet high and 200 feet in circumference. The fortress enclosed two acres of ground, with a high rampart and a very deep ditch, but its walls have disappeared. It formed the headquarters of Prince Maurice's army during the siege of Plymouth in 1643, but was taken by Essex the following year. Scarcely any masonry remains, though the earthworks show it to have been a place of great strength.

POWDERHAM (*chief*)

THIS ancient inheritance of the Courtenays, possessed by them for over 500 years, stands on the W. side of the estuary of the Exe, three miles from the sea. "Powderham," says Leland, "late Sir William Courteneis Castelle, standith on the haven shore a little above Kenton. Some say that it was builded by Isabella de Fortibus, a widdowe of an Earl of Devonshires. It is stronge, & hath a barbican, or bulwark, to beate the haven." The site is near the confluence of the little stream Kenn with the Exe, about seven miles S.E. from Exeter. Polwhele supposes the original fortress to have been built to protect that district from the Danes, who landed at Teignmouth in 970. The Conqueror bestowed the lands on William, Count d'Eu, together with many other estates in different counties : he is styled in Domesday "Comes d'Ou." This lord conspired with Robert Mowbray, Earl of Northumberland, and others against Rufus, and being tried for treason by a council assembled at Salisbury in 1090, was afterwards vanquished in the duel which was granted to him, whereupon, according to the brutal course of law, he was by the still more savage king deprived of his eyes and barbarously mutilated (see Hutchins' "Dorset"). His lands being forfeited went to various new holders, and in the time of Edward I. this place, with its existing stronghold, together with Whitstone, Hereford, was held by John de Powderham, after whose death the property came to Humphrey de Bohun, Earl of Hereford and Essex, whose daughter Margaret, the granddaughter of Edward I., brought it in marriage to Hugh, Earl of Devon, in 1325. His fifth son, Sir Philip Courtenay (born cir. 1337), next obtained it, and the property has ever since been in the hands of that branch of the earls of Devon. It was this Philip who built the castle, which retained much of its mediaeval structure till 1752, when, Polwhele says, "the avenue to the castle was surrounded with stone walls, having battlements on the top; and in the middle, opposite the front of the castle, there was a square gatehouse." At that time there existed six square towers which, as well as the walls containing the quadrangle and the dwellings, were furnished with battlements. Over the gateway or entrance from the park was an antique tower also battlemented ; and in the N. wing was a neat chapel, which was rebuilt and beautified in 1717, having over it a library. But in 1752 Lord Courtenay remodelled and modernised the old fortress, and only two of the towers now exist, the chapel being converted into a new drawing-room, and another chapel which had long been used as a barn being restored to its proper character.

At Christmas 1645 Sir Thomas Fairfax, being then at Crediton with the headquarters of the Parliamentary army, detached a force of 200 men and some dragoons to take Powderham Castle, but the Royalists, having been reinforced by an addition of 150 men to their garrison, made a stout resistance ; and upon the enemy entrenching themselves in the church harassed them so warmly with hand-grenades and musketry that they forced them to withdraw. Then on January 24, 1646, Sprigg relates that Fairfax starting from Totnes "on the Lord's day, after forenoon's sermon, marched to Chudleigh, endeavouring first to take a view of Pouldram [Powderham] ; before which place Colonel Hammond was set down with some force. But night coming on (whilst he had yet two miles thither) he was forced to return to Chidley without viewing the castle, which ere the next day was happily put out of a capacity of being viewed by him ; for about twelve at night, the news came to him of the surrender thereof, and therein five barrels of powder, match and bullet pro-portionible, and four pieces of ordnance." Sir Hugh Meredith was the king's governor, and the garrison numbered 300.

TIVERTON (minor)

THE town of Tiverton stands on a point of land between the river Exe and the stream Lowman, flowing into the former, and above the town on the W. is a little hill which was chosen for the site of a castle, built early in the twelfth century by Richard Redvers, Earl of Devon, on whom Henry I. had conferred the town and the lands. The last of this family, Baldwin de Redvers, dying in 1262, left the manor in dower to Amicia his wife, upon whose death (12 Edward I.) it came to Isabella de Fortibus, Countess of Albemarle, the second wife of William de Fortibus, Earl of Albemarle and Holderness (see *Plympton Earl*), and her daughter. From her it passed to the great family of Courtenay, who enjoyed possession almost continuously, till the attainder of the Marquis of Exeter (20 Henry VIII.), when Tiverton came to the Crown, and was given by Edward VI. to his uncle the Protector Somerset, after whose fall the property was bestowed on Sir Henry Gate. From him it was taken by Queen Mary and given to Edward Courtenay, the prisoner of the Tower, son of the Marquis of Exeter, at whose demise at Padua, *s.p.*, his property was divided between his numerous coheirs. This castle and much of the property has long been vested in the old family of Carew.

The fortress appears to have been quadrangular in form, enclosing about an acre of ground, and to have been protected by a surrounding wall from 20 to 25 feet high. It had round towers at the S.E., N.E., and N.W. corners, 35 feet in height, battlemented, and a square one at the S.W. angle. A spacious gateway under a large square tower, projecting a few feet from the E. front, gave entrance to the quadrangle, and on the W. front was a some-what similar building. A steep declivity, 60 feet deep, below the W. wall protected the castle on that side, and on the N. and S. sides were two wide and deep moats filled by the town leat; these formed the defences as far as the causeway leading to the entrance at the E. side, and over one of these moats, near the round tower at the S.E. angle, was a drawbridge. The causeway and the outer gate were protected by battlements and machicoulis. Two other strong arched gateways, 18 feet apart, further defended the entrance passage, which was 36 feet long and 15 feet wide, all vaulted with stone. The vaultings were mostly removed at the end of the last century, as they threatened to fall. The chief apartments of the castle were towards the N., and are all now destroyed; the rooms of the gateway, however, are tolerably entire. On the top of the stone staircase is a small ruined turret called the Earl of Devon's Chair. A hundred years ago the remains of this fortress were extensive, but little is left now except the great gatehouse.

The second Earl Baldwin took the part of Maud against King Stephen, who came against him in force and deprived him of the castle. In later times, both Isabella de Fortibus, and the first Courtenay Earl of Devon lived here, and in the Wars of the Roses it was several times assaulted. It was afterwards chosen as a residence for the Princess Catherine, daughter of Edward IV., and widow of William, Earl of Devon. Her son, Henry, Marquis of Exeter, was beheaded by Henry VIII., and after his death the castle fell into decay and ruin, and the parks and much land were alienated from the estate and sold.

During the Civil War, Tiverton Castle was repaired and garrisoned for King Charles, its governor in 1645 being Sir Gilbert Talbert, but when in October of that year, after the fall of Winchester and Basing House, the army of Fairfax in the West detached General Massey with his cavalry and a brigade of foot under Colonel Welden to besiege this place, it was ill fitted to stand an attack. Talbert, however, having a force of 300 men and a few horse, did what he could to strengthen the defences, placing round the battlements a quantity of wool-packs, which had been stored for sale under the chapel, and including the church within the earthworks which he threw up. On Sunday the 19th, Fairfax, who was himself present, inspected the batteries and caused fire to be opened previous to storming the work, when Sprigg relates : "Our ordnance playing hard against the works and castle, the chain of the drawbridge with a round shot was broken in two, whereupon the bridge fell down, and our men immediately, without staying for orders, possessed themselves of the bridge, and entered the works and possessed the churchyard, which so terrified the enemy, that it made them quit their ordnance, and some of their posts and line, and fled into the church and castle; the governor shut himself up in a room of the castle and hung out a white flag for a parley, while the besiegers had forced their way by the windows into the church, and had made prisoners and stripped to their shirts all they found within. Fair quarter was however granted, and much plunder was found inside, besides provisions.

There was taken a Major Sadler, a former Parliamentary officer who had deserted and had made overtures of service again ; to him had been committed the defence of the bridge, and treachery on his part was believed. The victors now condemned him to death for his former desertion, after a formal court-martial. He managed, however, to escape, and got to Exeter ; there, however, he fared worse, for the Royalists tried him and hanged him, having detected him in treacherous correspondence with the enemy.

The capture of Tiverton opened the Western road between Taunton and Exeter to the Roundhead army.

TORRINGTON (*non-existent*)

ON the Torridge, S. of Bideford in North Devon, and S. of the town, are some scanty fragments of a Norman castle which once stood here. Leland wrote : "Ther was a great Castelle at Taringtun on Turidge Ripe, a litle above the S. Bridge, of 3 Arches of Stone. Ther standith only a Chapelle yn the Castelle Garth. I hard that one Syr William of Turrington & his Sunne after hym were Lordes of it." Early in the reign of Henry III., in 1228, we learn that the Sheriff of Devon was commanded to throw down the castle here of Henry de Tracy, and a little more than a century after, in 1340 (temp. Edward III.), Richard de Merton is said to have rebuilt it.

Lysons says that the place belonged to an ancient family who took their name from it, and made this their abode. After five descents the property fell to be divided between the coheiresses of Matthew, baron of Torrington, one of whom married Merton.

Little remains now but the site and traces of its protecting moat. It stood near the edge of a high and steep precipice overlooking the Torridge, upon what is now a bowling-green called Barley Grove.

TOTNES (*minor*)

THE ancient fortress of Totnes, which occupies the summit of an eminence near the town, is said to have been built by Judhael, or Joel, a Breton follower of Duke William and his grantee of the lands here. Leland says : "The Castelle waul and the stronge dungeon [keep] be maintained, but the logginges of it be cleane in ruine." The entrance is near the N. gate of the town, which is still standing, as are also the walls of the circular Norman keep, which this Joel raised on the lofty artificial mound of far earlier date that commanded the main road passing here from the important port of Dartmouth to Plymouth. The general area of the castle, which is irregular in form, contains several acres of land, and was wholly surrounded by a ditch. It closely resembles in its plan and defences the Castle of Plympton, placed, like it, on the ancient British road from Exeter into Cornwall.

Joel de Totnais, having espoused the cause of Robert Courthose, the Conqueror's elder son, was deprived of his lands by the Red King, who bestowed them upon Roger de Nonant ; Joel thereupon retired as a monk to the Benedictine priory which he had founded at Barnstaple.

The Nonants continued at Totnes till the 9th year of John, while Alured, the son of Joel, occupied a castle at Barnstaple or Barum in North Devon, and took the side of the Empress Maud with Baldwin de Redvers against

TOTNES

Stephen, being mentioned in the *Gesta Stephani*. He could have left no posterity, as we find that the descendant of his sister, who married into the great family of Braose (see *Bramber, Sussex*), William de Braose, the great-grandson of Joel de Totnais, claimed and obtained the honours of both Barnstaple and Totnes. His possessions were, however, afterwards seized, and conferred upon Henry, the natural son of Reginald, Earl of Cornwall. On the accession of Henry III., Reginald de Braose, the third son of William, had restitution of the estates, which passed in marriage by his sister Eva to William de Cantelupe, whose daughter Millicent married into the family of La Zouche ; her son William thus obtained the honour and castle of Totnes, and, after 18 Edward I., the manor and the possessions of the Braoses. The Nonants were succeeded in their portion of the lands by the family of Valletort, and after the failure of this line, the Nonant estate also fell to William la Zouche.

On the attainder of John de la Zouche in the reign of Henry VII., Totnes was granted (1485) to Richard Edgecombe, ancestor of the present Mount Edgecombe family, whose grandson (2 Elizabeth) conveyed the borough and manor to the Corporation of Totnes, and sold his interest in the honour and castle, with its fifty-six knights' fees, to Sir Edward Seymour, Lord of Berry; from that family it was conveyed in 1655 to William Bogan of Gatcombe, with whose descendants the property remained till 1726, when it was sold to John Taylor, whose son resold it to the Jeffery family. They, again, in 1764 parted with it to Edward, Duke of Somerset, and with this family it remains.

Although situated in an important position, there are no military events recorded in relation to Totnes Castle. It formed the temporary quarters of Lord Goring, in October 1645, and it was held by the king's forces in the following January, until the approach of Sir Thomas Fairfax towards Dartmouth.

NUNNEY

Somersetshire

BRIDGWATER (*non-existent*)

BRIDGWATER is one of the many splendid fortresses in the kingdom which, having survived from earliest times in a defensible condition until the Civil War of the seventeenth century, were then, by order of a commission which sat in London to attend to such matters, so thoroughly destroyed—either as a measure of precaution or from mere vindictiveness—that few traces of their very existence remain at the present day.

The lands were granted to Walter de Douai, perhaps a Netherlander who took kindly to the flat land and the waters, and who, having founded or improved a settlement at the furthest inland navigable point of the river Parret, called it "Walter's Bridge," or "Brugge-Walter," corrupted later into Bridgewater. He was followed by a son whose daughter-heiress married Paganel; her son Falk de Paganel conveyed the property to William de Briwere, who originated the prosperity of the borough. He was high in favour with four kings—Henry II., Richard I., John, and Henry III. and was for many years sheriff of this and eleven other counties, obtaining from King John a free charter for Brugge-Walter, with licence to erect a castle there. He also

45

founded here the hospital of St. John, and formed the haven, where he began the building of the original stone bridge of three arches across the river. The castle is said to have been built by him between 1202 and 1216, and although in 1540 Leland, passing there, describes "the Castelle, sumtyme a right fair & strong Peace of Worke," as then ruinous, it was in good preservation towards the middle of the seventeenth century, and owes its destruction to the Parliamentary War in 1645.

The second De Briwere dying *s.p.*, Bridgwater went to his eldest sister Graecia, the wife of the great noble, William de Braose, lord of Bergavenny, Bramber, Brecknock, &c., whose son William was killed by Llewellyn, when the borough of Bridgwater fell to Eve, the second daughter of De Braose, and wife of W. de Cantelupe; her sister Millicent succeeded, and brought these lands to her husband Eudo, Lord Zouch, but on the attainder of John, Lord Zouch and Seymour, the manor was given to Giles, Lord Aubeney, with reversion to Lord Zouch,—Lord Aubeney being appointed Constable of the castles of Bridgwater and Richmond. Henry VIII. created his son Earl of Bridgwater in 1539, and on failure of the title it was revived by James I. in the person of John Egerton, Baron Ellesmere. George I. advanced this family to the dignity of dukes of Bridgwater. The castle was sometimes held by queens of England, and Charles II. conferred the manor and castle on Sir William Whitmore, knight, but, soon after, the property was purchased by the Harvey family.

Little can be gathered regarding the structure of this castle, the only visible relic of it being a Norman archway, which perhaps formed the water-gate. There are also some bonded wine-cellars below the present custom-house and Castle Street, which formed part of a passage of communication between the castle and the river. In the *Proceedings of the Somerset Archaeological Society* for 1877, Mr. George Parker says he remembered the site of the castle in King's Square, now partly built over, as surrounded with wooden palings, with some of the walls still remaining. Vestiges also remained towards the W., leading to Dr. Morgan's school, which formed part of the defences, and at the E. side of the town, near Barclay Street, were some very high mounds of earth, in which, on their removal, were found bones, bullets, swords, and other weapons. At the end of 1645, when orders came for the demolition of the castle and the works around it, a dissension arose between the soldiers of the garrison and the country people, the latter insisting on the removal of the outside works, which the soldiers wished to retain; and the quarrel ended in the shooting down of numbers of the rustics.

Sir Thomas Fairfax and Cromwell, the general and the lieutenant-general of the "New Model" army, invested Bridgwater on July 11, 1645, the day after the rout of Goring at Langport, and just four weeks after the king's defeat at Naseby. As they were reconnoitring together, Cromwell was nearly killed by a shot from the castle, fired by Mrs. Wyndham, the wife of the governor, an officer to whom he was speaking being killed by his side. Several councils of war were held to decide on the operations to be commenced. Sprigg says the fortifications were very regular and strong, the ditch about 30 feet wide and very deep; the garrison was about 1000 strong, and on the ramparts and castle were mounted 44 guns. It was desired to storm the defences on the 14th, but delay was required in order to make bridges for crossing the ditches. Meantime, as the place was so strong, Fairfax was perplexed as to what course to pursue; he could not pass it by, nor could it be masked, because of the river. Again, regular approaches would be too tedious a process, and not easy in such low ground; so it was resolved to storm on the 21st. This was done at two o'clock on the morning of that day, when the Parliamentary troops, well led, crossed the moat, and, in spite of a very heavy fire, scaled the works and broke into a suburb of the town, called Eastover, capturing 500 Royalists, when the garrison retreated into the inner work and castle. From thence they fired the suburb, and next day great destruction was caused to the town. Colonel Edmund Wyndham, the governor, peremptorily refused the summons sent him, whereon Fairfax offered that all the women should leave the castle, and, as soon as they were out, the artillery, aided by guns taken at Naseby, played on the place with such dire effect that the garrison felt obliged to seek terms; these were at last arranged, and the town and castle surrendered on July 23rd. The Roundheads acquired great booty, in addition to the stores of provisions and 3000 stand of arms, since the country gentry, relying on the notion that the castle was impregnable, had sent in their jewels, and gold, and plate, for safe keeping, to the value of nearly £100,000. Resting only a day after this fighting, Fairfax at once passed on to attack Bath, and then to the siege of Sherbourne Castle.

BRISTOL. (*non-existent*)

IN Saxon times Bristol was a town of no mean importance; it had battle-mented walls with five gates, one at each extremity of its main streets. Centuries later the Normans reared, on rising ground upon a neck of land between the river Frome and the Avon, a mighty fortress covering an area nearly as large as the old city, at some distance to the E. of it. Leland says that this castle was built by Robert, the Red Earl of Gloucester, the natural son of Henry I., by Nesta, daughter of Rhys, Prince of S. Wales; but it is probable that the founder was Geoffrey, Bishop of Coutances, who in 1086 was in receipt of a large part (one-third) of the revenues of Bristol; he received large grants of land in this county from the Conqueror, and may have chosen the site of Bristol Castle for his chief fortress, as it held the only road by which

Bristol could then be approached from Gloucestershire, and as, besides, it commanded the harbour of this Western port.

Nor was this the first occupation of the important site, for a Saxon castle had been founded, as supposed, by King Edward the Elder, about 911, on the E. of the existing town; defended on the N. by the Frome, S. by Avon, and having a deep ditch on the E. where an arm of the Frome flows into the greater river; while on the W. was another deep moat meeting the Avon on the S. Probably there was also a wall inside the ditch, and stockades, and it seems certain that some stone buildings stood within the enclosure.

When the conspiracy of Bishop Odo was raised in the first year of the Red King, with the intent to dethrone him in favour of his elder brother Robert, the leaders of it used this fortress of Bristol as their headquarters. They were Odo and Robert de Mortain, the Conqueror's half-brothers; Eustace, Count of Boulogne; Robert de Belesme; Robert, Earl of Shrewsbury and Arundel; William, Bishop of Durham; Geoffrey, Bishop of Coutances, and Robert de Mowbray, his nephew; Roger Bigod, Hugh de Grantmesnil, and some others. Having crushed this rebellion, Rufus bestowed Bristol Castle and the earldom of Gloucester upon Robert Fitz-Hamon, one of the few Norman knights faithful to him, at whose death in 1107 his daughter Mabile brought both castle and title to Robert, King Henry's natural son, to whom Henry had married her, somewhat in despite of her dignity. This Earl Robert, however, proved himself the most valiant captain of his time, and was the stout supporter of his half-sister, the Empress Maud, throughout her war with Stephen. He was also the guardian of her son Henry, whom he kept for four years at Bristol, while his education and training were carried on. Lord Lyttleton bears testimony to the great benefits which the young prince derived thus from his uncle.

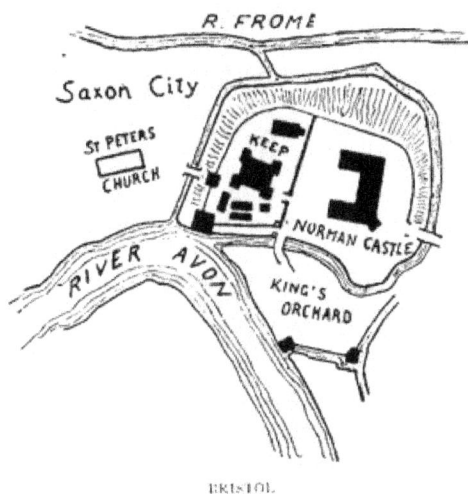

BRISTOL.

No doubt at this time Earl Robert added to the castle, and perhaps, as Leland says, built "the great square stone dungeon (keep); the stones whereof came out of Caen in Normandy." It was scarce finished when (1138) it was besieged by Stephen, who found it too strong and had to withdraw from before it.

When Stephen was taken prisoner at the battle of Lincoln in 1141 by Earl Robert, he was sent to his cousin the Empress for safe keeping in Bristol Castle; but Gloucester himself being captured soon afterwards whilst escorting Maud to Ludgershall, Wilts (q.v.), these two prisoners were exchanged, and the Civil War commenced again with more fury than ever. The earl died of fever 1147, - it is supposed at Bristol, since he was buried at the Priory of St. James. His son William had Bristol, but when his daughter Hawisia was married to King John, that monarch retained the place himself. He afterwards divorced his wife for a similar reason to that which separated Josephine from Napoleon —the want of issue—but Bristol remained with the Crown. Here the cruel king kept in confinement the unhappy Princess Eleanor, the *Damoiselle of Brittany*, after his murder of her brother Prince Arthur; she remained a close prisoner in this castle, and at Corfe, for forty years, till her death in 1241 (25 Henry III.), and this for no crime except her title to the crown. The boy king Henry was brought to Bristol Castle in 1216 to keep Christmas in it.

In 1263, Prince Edward was sent by Henry III. to secure Bristol at the opening of the Barons' War, when his troops behaved so badly to the burghers that they attacked him, and he had to take refuge in the castle, whence, fearing to stand a siege, he retreated in haste and left the west country.

Edward II. came here early in his reign to speed his favourite, Piers Gaveston, on his way to the government of Ireland; and four years later, Bartholomew, Lord Badlesmere, held the castle against the king, continuing there for three years, but it was finally taken in 1316. In 1326 the two Despencers, who had incurred popular dislike, fled hither with the king for safety, when Queen Isabella and Mortimer returned from France. Sir Hugh Despencer, who was ninety years old, was delivered up to the people of Bristol, and was "drawen, hanged, and beheaded," and his body in full armour having been hung up for four days, with two strong cords, was cut to pieces, "and dogges did ete it; and because he was Counte of Wynchester, his Ledde was sent thither" (*Leland*). This was done in sight of the king and his son in the castle. The king and the younger Despencer then attempted to escape by water, but being forced by ill winds to land in Wales, were captured and sent to the queen at Hereford, who caused Despencer, and also the Earl of Arundel and others, to be executed with much barbarity,—the She-Wolf of France being present, as is said. The king was sent to Kenilworth, and thence, after his enforced abdication, to Corfe; then to Bristol Castle again, where, a movement of the townspeople being made in his favour, he was sent off secretly with his keepers to Berkeley to his cruel end. It was in this castle that the Council sat, in Edward's absence, and proclaimed his son Edward guardian of the realm.

In 1399, Richard II. passed from here to Ireland, whence he only returned to find his throne usurped. In the same year, when William Scrope, Earl of Wilts, Sir John Bushy, Sir John Green, and Sir John Bagot were attainted, they fled from London to this castle, being followed by the Duke of Lancaster, who stormed the fortress, and took it in four days, when the three first named were seized and beheaded, Bagot escaping to Ireland.

Edward IV. came here in one of his progresses, and seems to have been present in the castle when Sir John Fulford and his companions were beheaded there. Next, in the 26th of Henry VIII. (1534), we get from Leland an insight into the castle and its condition. He says : " In the castell be two courtes ; in the utter courte, as in the N.W. part of it, is a great dungeon tower, a praty churche, a stone bridge, and 3 bullewarks. There be many towres yet standyng in both, the courtes, but alle tendeth to ruine." In Elizabeth's reign it was inhabited by beggars and thieves.

Again a lapse of a century, and in 1631 we hear of the sale by King Charles of the castle and all its lands to the municipality of Bristol, for the sum of £959 ; and this Corporation, at the commencement of the Civil War, thought it right that the walls and fortifications of the castle and town should be repaired, which was done in 1642, for, old as they were, the walls of the keep were strong. In addition, also, they built three regular forts to protect the town. Bristol was at first occupied by both sides in turns, but ultimately became the principal royal fortress in the West, and its loss, under Prince Rupert in 1645, was one of the final blows which the cause of the king received. Invited by the citizens, Rupert in 1643 came to Bristol with 20,000 troops, and at once attacked it, receiving the capitulation of its defenders after a siege of three days, when King Charles and his two sons visited the town.

Sprigg says that Bristol was at the time of its final siege the only considerable port which the king had in the whole kingdom for shipping and trade, and it was also his magazine for all sorts of ammunition ; so in August 1645 it was determined to attempt its capture, and orders were given to the Parliamentary army, under Sir Thomas Fairfax and Cromwell, to march against it. The town was accordingly invested about the 22nd of August.

As the siege and capture of Bristol concerned only the outlying forts and the defences of the city itself and did not apparently affect the castle, it will not be necessary to recount here the occurrences of the storming, which took place on the early morning of September 10th, when the defences were forced, and the chief fort of Priorshill was taken, its garrison being all put to the sword : Prince Rupert then made terms and surrendered, marching out on the 11th. Nothing seems to have taken place at the castle, which was victualled for six months.

Ten years after, the castle was slighted and demolished by order of Cromwell, and in 1656 a new road was opened through the site on which it had stood.

In Barrett's "History of Bristol" a drawing is given, copied from an ancient MS. of 1440, by the monk Rowlie, which shows a circular enclosure of embattled walling with the keep of Earl Robert in its centre, and a watch-tower on both the E. and W. sides of it. Its shape is a hollow square, with a cross in the middle. The elevations of the fronts of the keep shows embattled walls with turrets, having enriched Norman ornamentation. A chapel seems to have also existed in it.

CASTLE CARY (*non-existent*)

THE old stronghold of Castle Carey, belonging to the Percevals, stood on the brow of the hills above the sources of the Carey streamlet, upon an eminence called Lodgehill, in a fertile country, and in the midst of most picturesque scenery. The town was anciently called Carith and Kari. The existing remains of it would scarcely be worthy of notice, but for some historical associations connected with them. Two large mounds—grass-covered, lying in a field immediately above the lake, on its E. side, defended on the S. side by a deep ditch, and N.W. by a wall built against the hill-side are all that is to be seen of that ancient fortress, which for nearly 300 years was the seat of the Perceval Lovells, and which in early history resisted the attacks of even royal armies. In Barlow's Peerage, published 1773, it is stated, in a notice of Perceval, that the Norman Castle of Cary consisted of a mound with a great tower thereon, situated in an angle of a very extensive court, which was defended at other points by several lesser towers around the enceinte, and having a great gatehouse ; and Collinson says that upon this site implements of war and iron bolts have been dug up. Above the castle is a range of strong earthworks, supposed to have been thrown up by Henry de Tracy in 1153, but which are more likely to represent an original fortification of British tribes, as indeed is indicated by the prefix *Caer*.

The Conqueror took this place away from the Abbot of Glastonbury, and gave it first to Walter de Douai, with Brugge-Walter (now Bridgwater) and other lands. Soon after Domesday, however, it is found in the possession of Robert Perceval de Breberval or Bretevil, lord of Ivri and other places in Normandy, and in this family the lands continued till 25 Edward III. (1351), when they passed by an heiress to the St. Maur family, and afterwards by another heiress to Lord Zouche of Hemingworth ; but on the attainder of this noble by Henry VII. for his support of King Richard, Cary Castle and manor were granted to Lord Willoughby de Broke. They were then purchased by Edward, 1st Duke of Somerset, and in 1675 passed in marriage to Thomas, Lord Bruce, eldest son of the Earl of Aylesbury. In 1684 the estates were divided and sold to two persons, the manorial rights going to Henry Hoare, whose descendants still possess this part of the property.

The first Lord Cary, Robert Perceval, retired to Normandy after the battle of Hastings, and became a monk in the abbey of Bec, leaving his castle to his eldest son Ascelin, who, being a warrior of unusual fierceness and rapacity, acquired the name of *Lupus*. He married Isabel, daughter of the Earl of Bretteville, after storming her father's abode, and was succeeded at Cary by his second son, William Gouel de Perceval, who, according to the monks, was called *Lupellus*, or "The Little Wolf," a word softened later into *Lupell*, and then *Lovell*, which thenceforth became the name of two great families in the peerage.

This William Perceval, the first Lovell, is supposed to have built the castle, and it is certain that a Norman castle did exist in these times, for we are told by chroniclers of two sieges which it endured; one in 1138, and another in 1153. Henry of Huntingdon, an historian of the twelfth century, says that "in the third year of Stephen the rebellion of the English nobles burst out with great fury: Talbot, at their head, held Hereford Castle in Wales against the king, which place Stephen besieged and took. Robert, Earl of Gloucester,—the natural son of Henry I.,—with other lords, entrenched himself in the strongly fortified castle of Bristol (*q.v.*), and again in that of Leeds in Kent; William Lovell held Castle Cary; Payne held Ludlow; William de Mohun, Dunster Castle; Robert de Nichole, Wareham Castle; Eustace Fitzjohn held Melton, and William Fitzalan Shrewsbury Castle, which the king stormed."

The *Gesta Stephani* chronicle says the king lost no time in besieging Carith, and pressed on the siege with vigour, throwing by his machines showers of missiles and fire, without intermission, among the garrison, and reducing them to starvation, so that he at last forced them to surrender on terms of submission and alliance. Thereon he garrisoned and held it until 1153, when the Percevals recovered it by the aid of the Earl of Gloucester, son of the great Robert. At this time Henry de Tracy was keeping Castle Cary for Stephen, and had fortified it anew, but Earl William marched suddenly upon him with a large force, and demolished the works he had raised, compelling him to retreat. A brother of William, this Lord of Cary, was John, fourth son of Ascelin, who had Harptree, or Richmond, Castle, which Stephen took from him by stratagem.

There is no mention of Castle Cary after the twelfth century, and it is possible that before it passed to the Lords St. Maur, in 1351, it had fallen into decay. Some successor erected a grand manor-house near the site of the old fortress, and Collinson speaks of the "fine arches and other remains" of this second edifice as being visible in his time. Within comparatively recent times there was a large arched gateway, with stabling on one side, and a large groined room, which in the time of the war with France was used as a depôt for military stores.

It was in this house that Charles II. is said to have slept after his escape from Worcester. He came from Colonel Lane's, at Bentley, safely to Colonel

Norton's at Leigh Court, near Bristol, disguised as Mrs. Jane Lane's serving-man,
with that lady riding on a pillion behind him. Then from Leigh he came to
Castle Cary on September 16, 1651, and stayed there the night, passing on next
day to Trent, the house of Colonel Francis Wyndham. In the Boscobel Tracts,
Castle Cary is spoken of as the house of Mr. Edward Kirton, but no persons
there are mentioned; therefore it is likely that Kirton was the steward of
William Seymour, Marquess of Hertford, and afterwards Duke of Somerset,
who was then proprietor of the Cary manor-house, which he had purchased,
and in which his steward received the king.

During their long hold of this property, the Perceval or Lovell family threw
off several distinguished offshoots. The fourth son of William, Lord Lovell,
was ancestor of the Lords Lovell of Titchmarsh, Northants; one of whom, in
29 Edward I., was among the barons who supported this king in his pretensions
to the sovereignty of Scotland against Pope Boniface VIII., in a letter which
defied the Papal jurisdiction in this matter. Another was Lord High Chamberlain
to Richard III.; a personage of such great importance that the poet Colling-
bourne inveighed against him, with Catesby, Sir Thomas Ratcliffe and the king,
in his verses beginning—

> "The cat, the rat, and Lovell our dog,
> Doe rule all England under the hog:"

The last word meaning the device of Richard; and for it and the rest the poor
poet lost his head. It was this Francis, Lord Lovell, about whose uncertain fate
there is so curious a story. He was one of Richard's commanders at Bosworth,
having been created viscount by him, and, escaping to Flanders to the court of
Margaret, Duchess of Burgundy, joined the conspiracy of Lambert Simnel against
Henry VII., and with Martin Swartz invaded England in June 1487, with the Earl
of Lincoln; after their defeat at the battle of Stoke, Lovell was supposed to have
been drowned in crossing the Trent, and was never heard of more. Another
story, which is well authenticated, was to the effect that he lived long after in a
cave or vault; à propos of which report it is a fact that in 1708, on the occasion
of adding a chimney to the house of Minster Lovell near Burford, there was discovered a large room or vault underground, in which was the entire skeleton of a
man, sitting in a chair at a table, with a mass-book, paper, pen, &c., before him,
while near him lay a cup, "all much mouldered and decayed." This was judged
by the family to be the remains of Francis, Viscount Lovell, who might have
been shut up thus by friends, and by misadventure neglected and starved to
death. The clothing of the body had been rich, but on the admission of air
all soon fell to dust (see *Grey's Court, Oxon*).

The fifth son of the same Lord William of Cary was Sir Richard de
Perceval, ancestor of the present Lord Egmont, who is Lord Lovell and
Holland in England, as well as Earl of Egmont in Ireland. Another de-

scendant of this fifth son was Richard, born 1550, whose family retained the Perceval name ; having resided long in Spain, he was sought by Lord Burleigh, from his knowledge of the language, to decipher some letters supposed to refer to the Armada, which an English ship had taken out of a Spanish one in 1586. Perceval was able to read them, and thus to make known the designs of Spain against his country in time for preparations against the arrival of that dreaded armament.

DUNSTER (chief)

THE ancient stronghold of Dunster stands on the western edge of a deep valley, upon a tor, or hill, 200 feet in elevation, whence the valley passes in a short distance to the sea near Minehead, on the N. coast of the county. The old town of Dunster nestles at the foot of the castle hill—a quaint and interesting collection of old-fashioned and half-timbered houses. The old west-country name for the hill, of *Tor*, originally attached to the castle which in Saxon times stood on the summit of this natural mound or *burh*, probably a timber and stockaded fortress with a ditch, that in the time of the Confessor belonged to one Aluric. Soon after the Conquest, it passed into the hands of William de Mohun, and his family (whose name in modern days has been corrupted into *Moon*) held Dunster for nearly three and a half centuries.

This William was a landowner from the Côtentin in Normandy, who had followed Duke William and his fortunes, and having fought for him well at Senlac, was rewarded with some sixty-eight manors in the west of England, which were formed into an honour or barony, of which Dunster was the caput. On the site of the fortress of Aluric which doubtless was a strong one for protection against the sea-rovers, and also from the Welsh of the west— De Mohun built a stone Norman castle, which early in the next century was considered one of the most important in the west country, and was held by the second baron, also William by name, for the Empress Maud against King Stephen, who feared to attack it ; the character of this lord may be judged from the name which he acquired, in those terrible and lawless days, of " The Scourge of the West." In the time of King John, the owner, Reginald de Mohun, was a minor, and was kept in ward by the king, who appointed his trusty henchman, Hubert de Burgh, custodian of Dunster. This baron dying in 1213, the castle again fell to the Crown in ward till the heir, another Reginald, came of age. It is probably this baron or his son, who between 1246 and 1278 may have built the existing walls and towers of the lower court, the keep having been erected long before.

John de Mohun, 8th baron, died 1376, leaving daughters only, when his widow, Lady Joan, sold the estate and castle to Elizabeth, daughter of Hugh Courtenay, Earl of Devon, the widow of a second husband, Sir Andrew

Dunster Castle

Luttrell of Chilton. She was a dame of high birth and great wealth, and her son, Hugh Luttrell, eventually succeeded to the honour and castle of Dunster; but Lady Joan de Mohun retained possession for her life, and outlived Lady Elizabeth Luttrell, and when Sir Hugh succeeded, vexatious legal proceedings were instituted against him, by the daughters of the last De Mohun. He was poor, and had to borrow £50 from the Abbot of Cleeve to defend the suit, which terminated at last in 1404 in his favour (*Barrett*). Sir Hugh made many additions to the castle, and strengthened the gatehouse with two buttresses, which are still to be seen. He died in 1428, and his son John in 1430, whereupon his young son James, an infant, succeeded, who became a Lancastrian, and was killed on that side, at the second battle of St. Albans, in 1461, leaving two sons, minors. Edward IV. confiscated the Luttrell estates (1463), granting them to the Earl of Pembroke, and it was only after Bosworth that the family regained their possessions, and Hugh Luttrell the heir came to Dunster. Three generations of knighted Luttrells then continued here, the latter one, Sir John, serving in the war in Scotland and in France. He was knighted at Leith, after Flodden, and died in 1551, leaving three daughters, when the estate went to his brother's issue. Other three Luttrells succeeded him, of whom the last, Thomas, was owner during the Civil War, and seems to have begun as a Parliamentarian, like many of his neighbours, but to have faced both ways, since he was found even paying for the support of royalist troops when Colonel Wyndham managed to obtain possession of Dunster Castle for the king. It seems that in September 1642, when the Marquess of Hertford with a force of 400 men came to Minehead, Thomas Luttrell was ordered by the Roundhead general to defend Dunster, and being summoned by the Royalists, " Mistress Luttrell commanded the men within to give fire . . . which accordingly they did," from behind the castle rampart; whereon the king's troopers retreated, much to the vexation of Hertford, who charged them with cowardice. After this the castle was held for the Parliament till after the fall of Bridgwater, in 1643, when the king's star was so much in the ascendant, that Luttrell surrendered his castle to the royal troops, and it was garrisoned for the king under Colonel Francis Wyndham.

In 1645, after the reverses of Charles and the fall of Bridgwater and Bristol, Dunster remained the only fortress in the county held by king's troops, and Colonel Blake (afterwards the great admiral and vanquisher of Van Tromp), with Colonel Sydenham, was sent from Taunton to reduce it. They opened the siege early in November, and so completely blockaded the place that relief was impossible, and a speedy surrender was looked for; but the besieged, though straitened both as to water and provisions, gallantly held on, and returned a curt refusal to Blake's repeated summons. Meantime the approaches and batteries were pushed nearer, and mines were worked, which, however, the governor countermined, so that when on January 3, 1646, Blake sprang three mines, no great amount of damage was done, and the breach that was made was so inaccessible, that the intended storming could not be carried out. Incessant attempts were made for Wyndham's relief, and at last a force of 1500 horse and 300 foot managed to reach Dunster, and on February 5th threw in a welcome aid of four barrels of powder, thirty cows and fifty sheep; having done this, they spoilt the mines and destroyed the works of the enemy, and retreated to Devon. Then Exeter and other strong places in the West were lost to the king, and fresh troops were sent by Fairfax to the siege of Dunster; and at last, in April, on a fresh summons being made by Blake and Skippon, Colonel Wyndham, learning the king's losses and deprived of all hope of relief, demanded a parley, the result of which was that, after sustaining a close siege for a hundred and fifty days, with the loss of twenty men, he surrendered the castle on April 22nd, when six guns and two hundred stand of arms were all that fell to the captors. With this the fighting in Somerset ended. The war was then practically over, and the king's power destroyed.

Luttrell then felt the effects of his undecided policy. The Council sent down some one to supersede him, and gave orders for the castle to be pulled to pieces, which fortunately was not done as intended, nor was the building "slighted"; so the Luttrell family happily continue in the enjoyment of their old stronghold.

Nothing remains of the Norman keep which crowned the tor or mound, and its very shape is unknown. The mound is oval in shape and of natural formation, but has been scarped all round to render it less accessible. Below the tor on the N. side is a level platform of about half an acre, forming the lower ward, which conforms to the curve of the hill, and is continued on the N. by a curtain wall with flanking towers, below which the hill, somewhat scarped, falls thence to the valley. The ancient gateway from the lower ward is no longer used; it contains the old timber and iron gates of Henry VIII.'s time, or older, and stands at an angle with the old gatehouse to which the road from the town leads up. This fine building is still perfect, 45 feet in height, with two lofty octagonal towers, heavily battlemented, but without either portcullis or drawbridge. It is in three floors; the first with two good rooms and two closets; the second, which was formerly on the same plan, has been of late years converted into a fine hall, with an open roof: in it there are five Tudor windows and a fireplace. Upon exterior panels are carved various arms of the Luttrell family and their connections.

There seems to be no masonry here of earlier date than Henry III., who spoke of Dunster as "my castle." The curtain wall and low towers may be of that reign, while the gatehouse is Edwardian. The grand structure of the inhabited portion was rebuilt in the time of Elizabeth, on the old foundations.

ENMORE (*non-existent*)

THE site of the ancient castle of Enmore is four miles W. from Bridgwater. Before the Conquest the lands belonged to a Norman family named Courcelle, but soon afterwards we find them in the hands of the family of William Malet, the famous warrior of Duke William's army. His son Robert appears to have been the grantee, and after him the next brother Gilbert held the lands, and left them to his son and heir, William Malet. Of the same family were William and Robert Malet, who took part with the Duke of Normandy against Henry I., and were banished from England; and Baldwin, the eldest son of the former of these, on reconciliation with the king, settled at Enmore. which became the chief seat of the family. This Baldwin was a knight, and is designated "de Enmore." His son Sir William Malet followed, and then his son, likewise a knight; and so the succession went on in this family, generally from father to son, in curious and uneventful regularity, through all the changes of the country for more than 500 years, until John Malet in the seventeenth century dying, left an only daughter and heir, Elizabeth, married to John Wilmot, the Earl of Rochester, who thus acquired Enmore. Rochester, in 1684, left three daughters, coheiresses, the eldest of whom, Anne, was wife to Henry Bayntun of Spye Park, Wilts, and brought him this manor; from them it descended to Sir Edward Bayntun Rolt, Bart., who at the close of the last century sold Enmore to James Smyth, and from him it was conveyed to the Earl of Egmont. His son, Earl John, in 1833 sold the property to Mr. Nicholas Broadmead, whose son, Mr. Thomas P. Broadmead, is the present owner.

Nothing seems to be known about the earlier manor-house, which was undoubtedly protected by the existing ditch, and sufficiently fortified. It was pulled down on the purchase of the estate from Lord Egmont, and the present structure was reared in its place. It stands on gently rising ground in a very fine park.

FARLEIGH, OR FARLEIGH HUNGERFORD (*minor*)

FARLEIGH, being partly in Somerset, is sometimes claimed by that county; it lies about eight miles S.E. of Bath, and five W. of Trowbridge.

The castle stands on a rocky terrace, below which flows the Frome River, giving protection on the N.E., N., and N.W. sides, but there are commanding heights upon the S. side. Of the original Norman stronghold nothing can be said to remain; what now exists there is the work of the Hungerfords, some part being of the fourteenth century, but most of it belonging to the early fifteenth (*Parker*).

The lordship was given by the Conqueror to Roger de Courcelle, and on its reversion to the Crown, the Red King bestowed it on Hugh de Montfort, then lord of Nunney, a son of Thurstan de Bastenburgh, another Norman of distinction,—killed in a duel, who left a son having as his only issue a daughter, wife to Gilbert de Gant, whose son Hugh assumed the name of Montfort. This Hugh married Adeline, daughter of Robert, Earl of Mellent, and from his eldest son Robert was descended Sir Henry de Montfort, who, towards the close of the reign of Henry III., had his seat at Farleigh; whence this castle was also called Farleigh Montfort. After him followed later Sir Reginald de Montfort, who in 1337 alienated his property to Henry Burghersh, Bishop of Lincoln. He left it to his brother Bartholomew, Lord Burghersh, a baron of much power in the reigns of Edward II. and III., who did good service in the French and Scottish wars, and fought at Crecy. His grand-daughter, an heiress, married Edward, Lord Despencer, and dying *s.p.*, Farleigh was sold in 1369 to Sir Thomas Hungerford, knight, then of Hey-tesbury, who, with money acquired in the French wars (Leland says by the ransom of the Duke of Orleans), fortified the old manor-house with the four mighty towers and walls, and with two embattled gateways, in 7 Richard II.; but having done this without a licence, he had to pay a small fine and received the king's pardon. He died 1398, leaving Farleigh in dower for his wife Joan, who was succeeded by her son, Sir Walter Hungerford, in 1412.

The services of this knight must have been important in the French War, since he enjoyed a grant of a hundred marks a year (or about £1335 of our currency), secured on the town and castle of Marlborough, and the wool rates of Wells, in compensation for his outlays in that war. Henry VI. summoned him to Parliament as Lord Hungerford some years before his death, in 1449. On the death of his son Robert, ten years later, the widow founded the Hunger-ford chapel and chantry at Farleigh. Robert, the third lord, was a zealous Lancastrian, who married, in his father's lifetime, Alianore, daughter and heir of Lord William Molyns, and was in consequence occasionally called Lord Molyns. After the terrible defeat of Towton, on March 29, 1461, which established Edward IV. on the throne, King Henry, his queen and his son, fled northward in company with a few noblemen, of whom Lord Hungerford was one, and came to Scotland, where safety was purchased by the cession, to the King of Scots, of Berwick, a fortress captured fifty-six years before by Henry IV. Hungerford was attainted by the Act of Parliament 1 Edward IV., and when, two years later, Queen Margaret renewed the war, and got possession of some of the northern castles, he was the chief of those who defended Alnwick Castle with 500 or 600 French soldiers. Soon afterwards he was taken prisoner after the battle of Hexham, conveyed to Newcastle, and there beheaded, being afterwards buried in the N. aisle of Salisbury Cathedral. His eldest son, Thomas, joined Warwick upon his defection from Edward IV., and being taken and tried for high treason at Salisbury (8 Edward IV.), was condemned and beheaded. Edward IV. then gave Farleigh to his brother Richard, and George, Duke of Clarence, lived here. In the first year, however, of Henry VII. his attainder, and that of his father, were reversed by Parliament, and his heir had restitution of his lands and honours (*Brooke*).

This Lord Hungerford married Anne, daughter of Henry Percy, Earl of Northumberland, and left only a daughter, when, as the estates were entailed on heirs male, they descended to Walter, second son of the third lord. Sir Walter had naturally taken the side of Richmond, joining him on his march to Tamworth, and fighting at Bosworth with him. He was a Privy Councillor afterwards with Henry VIII. His grandson, Sir Walter, created Lord Hungerford of Heytesbury, was concerned in the troubles of 1540, at the time when Cromwell, Earl of Essex, was beheaded, and he also lost his life on Tower Green, at the same time and place, when his estates were confiscated. His son Sir Walter, however, recovered them, and eventually the property passed to the son of this man's daughter, Lucy, who had married a relative, Sir Anthony Hungerford of Black Bourton, Oxfordshire,—namely, to Sir Edward Hungerford of Corsham, K.C.B., who died in 1648, leaving everything to his half-brother Anthony, whose son, Sir Edward, succeeding, was knighted at the coronation of Charles II. He, in those spendthrift days, so involved his estates that they had to be sold by his trustees to Henry Baynton of Spye Park, Devizes, who with his wife, Lady Anne Wilmot, sister of the Earl of Rochester, resided at Farleigh; and they appear to have been the last occupants of the old fabric. The lands were afterwards resold, in 1702, to Joseph Houlton, the squire of a neighbouring property, and his descendant, Sir E. Victor Houlton, G.C.M.G., owned the property for many years. The castle, however, did not come to the Houltons till 1730, when it had fallen greatly to decay, and when a great part of its materials had been removed for other uses. It was advertised for sale in 1891, and was sold to the first Baron Donington, whose wife, Edith Maud, Countess Loudoun in her own right as daughter of the second Margaret of Hastings, was descended from Sir Thomas Hungerford (executed at Salisbury in 1469) by his only daughter Mary, married to Lord Hastings. Lord Donington, who died in 1895, settled the Farleigh Hungerford estate on the children of his third son, Gilbert, who are to bear the name of Hungerford-Hastings.

At Farleigh Castle was born the unfortunate lady, Mary Plantagenet, Countess of Salisbury, the daughter of George, "false, fleeting Clarence." After the murder of her brother, Edward, Earl of Warwick, by Henry VII., she petitioned and obtained from Parliament the restitution of his estates. She married Sir Richard Pole, a Welsh knight, cousin to Henry VII., and was made Countess of Salisbury by Henry VIII., having a fair claim to the title by her birth. One of her two sons was Reginald, Cardinal Pole, who excited the king's enmity by his opposition at the Papal court, and Henry accusing both his brother Henry and his mother of being implicated in a conspiracy against him, lodged them both in the Tower on a charge of high treason in 1538. First, the king caused her son, who was Henry, Lord Montague, to be beheaded, and after a rigorous imprisonment of two years, he brought the countess, who was nearly seventy years old, to the scaffold. Here a dreadful scene ensued, as the old countess refused to lie down at the block, and the executioner had to seize her grey hair and chop her head off the best way he could.

FARLEIGH

There is a story connected with Farleigh, also at the time of Henry VIII., which relates to Sir Walter or "Lord" Hungerford of Heytesbury. This man had three wives: how he dealt with the first two is not known, but a doleful tale exists about the third, Joan, daughter of Lord Hussey of Sleaford. In a "Humble Petition" addressed by her to one of the Secretaries of State, she complains that her lord had kept her locked up in one of the towers "for three or fower years, without comfort of any creature, & under the custodie of my lord's Chaplain, Sir John a Lee, who hath once or twice poyson'd me, as he will not deny upon examination. He hath promised my lord that he will soon rid him of me; & I am sure he intendeth to keep his promise, for I have none other meat nor drink, but such as cometh from the said priest, & brought me by my lord's foole; which meat & drink I have often feared, & yet do so every day more than another, to taste; so that I have been well-nigh starved, & sometimes of a truth I should die for lack of sustinence, & had, long ere this time, had not poor women of the country of their charity, knowing my Lord's demayne always to his wives, brought me to my great window in the night such meat & drink as they had; & gave me for the love of God; for money have I none, wherewith to pay them, nor yet have had of my Lord, these 4 years, four groats." This lord, who seems to have been crazy, was the man who was charged with other high crimes in connection with the Lincolnshire rebellion of 1536, and beheaded in 1540. His wife, whose father, Lord Hussey, had

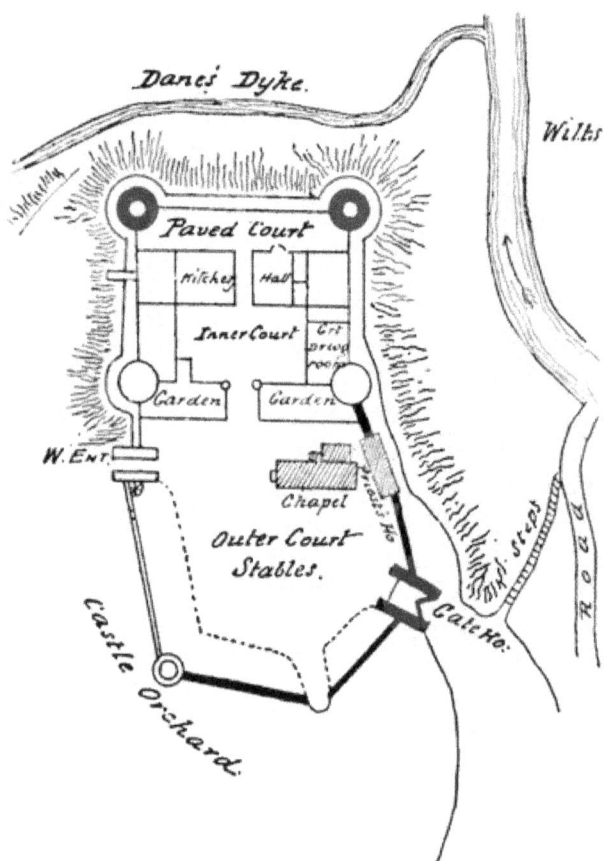

FARLEIGH

previously shared the same fate for the same offence, then married, as her second husband, Sir Robert Throckmorton ; she died in 1571.

Farleigh held a garrison for Charles I. under Colonel Hungerford, brother of the owner, Sir Edward Hungerford, who actually was at the time commander of the Parliament forces in Wiltshire ; but after the fall of Bristol and other fortresses in the West it surrendered, on the 15th September 1645, and thereby escaped demolition.

In the most perfect state of this stronghold, it consisted of two wards, surrounded by a high crenellated wall, outside of which, where not defended by the river and ditch, there was a moat. It had two entrances, the principal one being on the E., in the embattled gatehouse, the shell of which remains, having a drawbridge over the moat. There are some fragments of the other entrance, on the W. side. A spring of water in the adjacent hill supplied the moat, by means of pipes which were discovered in late years. This gate led into the outer ward, round which were placed the stables and offices, from whence another gateway opened to the N. or inner court, measuring 189 feet by 144. The wall of this court was flanked by four large circular towers, 60 feet high, containing three storeys; of these only the towers at the S.E. and S.W. corners remain. The N.W. and N.E. towers, with the intermediate buildings, are quite destroyed, except a small piece of parapet overlooking a deep dell, called Danes' Ditch. In the inner court were the great Hall and the State apartments, which are said to have once been magnificent in their appointments, "above any other baronial residence in England"; these were entire in 1701, but have now quite disappeared. They were decorated with tapestry, sculpture, and paintings, and the hall was hung with suits of armour, worn by possessors of Farleigh, and with spoils from the fields of Crecy, Poictiers, Agincourt, and Calais; but all has vanished except the lines of foundations. The chapel, on the right hand at entering, is the most entire of the buildings, and adjoining it, on the N., is the chantry or oratory dedicated to St. Anne, before mentioned. There are some interesting tombs of the Hungerfords, and below the chantry is a collection of bodies in lead cases, moulded to the shape of the figures and faces. E. of this building is a house built for the two chantry priests, and now converted into a dairy farm-house. The later owners have endeavoured to preserve the remains of these buildings, and have decorated the interior of the chapel with a fine collection of ancient armour. The park, which was 2¾ miles in circuit, lay on the N. and W. sides. The chief front of the castle in the inner ward, shown in Buck, faced the E., a grand flight of stairs leading up to its doorway.

MONTACUTE (*non-existent*)

THE village of this name, in the hills four miles to the W. of Yeovil, stands at the foot of a steep conical hill, somewhat detached from the ridge, which, as *Mons acutus*, is given by some as the derivation of the name.

In the time of Canute, that king's standard-bearer, Tofig, a Dane, owned the lands here, then called *Lutegarsbury*, and to the summit of this hill is

attached the legend of the Holy Rood of Waltham, which is briefly as follows:
The blacksmith of Montacute dreamed on three occasions of a vision enjoining
him to obtain the aid of the priest and to dig on this hill-top; at last he obeyed,
and under a stone were found two crucifixes, an ancient book, and a bell. Tofig
being informed of the treasure thus miraculously troven, brought a waggon
and oxen to cart it away to some minster. Glastonbury and Canterbury and
others were named, but the oxen refused to move. Tofig went through a list of
holy places in vain, and at last named Waltham in Essex, a place also belonging
to himself, whereon the cart at once started off and came to Waltham in time.
Here he built a small church wherein to house the Holy Rood and attract
pilgrims. In the course of years Tofig's lands became the property of Earl
Harold, afterwards the king, who built at Waltham a grand church for an abbey
of canons and a dean, and thus originated the Holy Rood or Cross of Waltham
which gave a war-cry to the English at Senlac.

After the Conquest, Tofig's lands were held by Drogo or Dru de Montacute,
—deriving his name from a township of that name in Normandy,— a follower
of Duke William, in the retinue of Robert de Mortain, or Morton, Earl of
Cornwall, under whom he held the manor, and who is said to have reared a
castle on the summit of the same hill soon after the Conquest. This castle was
attacked in 1069 by the men of Somerset and Dorset, in a last struggle for
freedom against their new and savage masters, but they were routed by the
warlike Geoffrey, Bishop of Coutances, when horrible sufferings were inflicted
upon the vanquished tribesmen. In 1091 William the son of Robert de Mortain
founded here a priory of Cluniac monks, and endowed it with this manor
and its castle. In the reign of Henry I., the castle being decayed, a chapel
was built on its site which existed in the time of Leland, but of which
no vestiges whatever remain at present. Round the hill are some traces of
earthworks which may be survivals of the old Norman castle, and a modern
look-out tower now occupies the hill-top.

Drogo's descendants held the rest of the lands here for many generations,
and in the persons of the earls of Salisbury became the greatest nobles in
England. Simon de Montacute was both a great soldier and an admiral
(temp. Edward I.), and his son was summoned to Parliament as baron in
2 Edward II. The next, William, Lord Montacute, after performing great
services for Edward III., was in 1336 made Earl of Salisbury, and was Earl
Marshal; and his son seems to have gone back to the old form of the name,
Montagu, which was adopted, and which followed the illustrious succession of
nobles and warriors and statesmen of the family who flourished after him.

The beautiful mansion known as Montacute House is in the possession
of a fine old Somersetshire family named Phelips, who have been settled at
Montacute since the middle of the fifteenth century.

NETHER STOWEY (*non-existent*)

O N the northern slopes of the Quantock Hills, some nine miles from
Bridgwater, upon the hill still called Castle Hill, above the E. end of the
village of the above name, are the remains of an extensive fortification, which,
in view of the artificial character of the mound, must be of remote origin.
To the eastward of this site the steep hill rises another 300 feet, and within
a mile in the same direction, on the highest point of the Quantocks,
is Dowsborough Castle, an early British or ante-Roman earthwork of oval
form. The mound of Stowey, which rises out of the steep slope of the
Castle Hill, is circular and about 100 yards in diameter at its base; a
steep ascent leads to the edge of a circular ditch, now 10 feet in depth,
which environs the upper and quite artificially formed mound above, on
the summit of which are the foundations of a large tower, measuring about
60 feet by 50, and 7 or 8 feet in thickness, said to be those of a somewhat
modern erection, pulled down about fifty years ago. The plan of these
foundations has, however, a close resemblance to that of a Norman keep,
with its forebuilding for the staircase, and it seems probable that below the
later erection may lie the walls of the Norman castle alleged to have stood
on the mound.

There do not appear to be any notices or records of this fortress in history,
nor do we know who were its owners or builders, except that it is said to have
been the residence of James (Touchet), Baron Audley, who was one of the
leaders of the Cornish insurgents who in 1497 were defeated by the forces of
Henry VII. at the battle of Blackheath (June 24). Lord Audley being taken
prisoner, is said by Lord Bacon to have been "led from Newgate to Tower
Hill, in a paper coat painted with his own arms; the arms reversed, the coat
torn, and he at Tower Hill beheaded."

Leland wrote: "Here is a goodly Maner place of the Lorde Audeley's,
stonding exceeding pleasauntly for good Pastures, & having by it a Parke of
redde Deare & another of falow & a faire Brooke serving al the offices of
the Maner Place. Lord Audeley that rebelled yn Henry the 7th Tyme
began great Foundations of Stone-work to the enlarging of his House, the
which can yet be scene onperfect."

Burke's Dormant and Extinct Peerages shows that Sir James de Audley,
4th Lord Audley (originally Alditheley), the great warrior of Poictiers
(*Froissart*), and one of the original knights of the Garter, was succeeded
by his son Nicholas, who died *s.p.* 1392, when the barony of Audley devolved
on the grandson of his sister Joane, the wife of Sir John Touchet. His
descendant, Sir George Touchet, 18th Baron Audley, was created Earl
Castlehaven in the Peerage of Ireland, in 1616. The second earl, his son

Mervyn, 19th Baron Audley, being convicted of high crimes, was sentenced to death, and executed on Tower Hill, August 14, 1631.

The site of the tower commands a wide prospect,- across the Bristol Channel to the Welsh mountains on one hand, and away to the Mendips and Glastonbury Tor on the other.

NUNNEY (minor)

ABOUT three miles from Frome, and the same from Witham Station, this castle stands in the lowland under the hills, among the trees which grow around the still perfect moat which almost washes the foot of the walls. It is described by Parker as a good example of a tower-built house or castle, that is, a house of tolerable refinement built in the form of a keep, in three or four storeys, with windows on all four sides of each floor, and having four towers or turrets, one at each angle, large enough to contain in one, bed-rooms, in another, closets, the third being devoted to offices, and the fourth to the staircase. In Nunney, the circular corner-turrets are so large as almost to meet at the two ends of the house, which is long and narrow, and with walls so thick as to curtail much the interior space. It is a strongly fortified dwelling-house of the fourteenth century, and an interesting one ; along the top of the walls outside are ranged the stone corbels, or brackets, which carried the wooden gallery for defence of the walls in place of machicolations.

The first notice of the place is in 1259 (temp. Henry III.), when its manor is granted to Henry de Montfort, the eldest son of the Earl of Leicester ; but in 1262 the owner is Elias de Noney, ancestor of the Delameres, and in 1315 (2 Edward II.), when a second Domesday Register was made of all owners of manors, "Noin" was owned by Nicholas de la Mare, and Alexander and Delicia de Montfort ; then followed a Thomas, whose son John Delamere is in 1372 scheduled as holding Nunney under Humphrey de Bohun, Earl of Hereford and Essex. This is the Sir John who, according to the Patent Rolls, obtained a licence in 1373 (47 Edward III.) as " John de la Mare, chivaler," to crenellate his house of "Nonny." He was a soldier of eminence, who served with Edward in the French wars, where no doubt, like others, he amassed sufficient wealth by ransoms and loot to build a suitable dwelling ; he served as sheriff in 1377, and dying about 1389, was succeeded by his son Philip, who had sufficient wealth to found a chantry there. After him John Delamere held the property, which is next found in the hands of an heiress Constantia, who had been the wife of one John Poulet, and at her death in 1443, her son John Poulet, aged fourteen, succeeded to the estate. He died in 1492, leaving a son and heir John, who is there in 1518. At the dissolution of monasteries, this estate and chantry seems to have

fallen to the Crown, for in 1560 the descendant of these Poulets, having
become Lord St. John, Marquess of Winchester and Treasurer of England,
obtained from Elizabeth a grant of the house and the chantry of Nunney.
Then the estate is sold to Richard Parker, who again alienates to Richard
Prater ; and it was this man's grandson, Colonel Richard Prater, who sustained
the siege in 1645, and surrendered the castle after a fight of two days. He
hoped to save his property, but it was sequestered and ordered to be sold.
Prater died before this could be carried out, but in 1652 the estate and castle
were divided and sold to various persons, and the widow and family left
to penury.

The walls of the castle are nearly perfect, and are 63 feet in height, the
oblong building measuring 61 feet by 25, but the roof and floors have gone ;
these have all been of timber, without any stone vaulting. The kitchen is on
the ground floor, where are two large fireplaces ; above on the first floor was
the hall, occupying the whole stage, and the two upper storeys contained the
family rooms and State apartments. The N.W. tower held the staircase,
which seems to have been of wood, and in the S.E. turret, second floor, is a
very perfect example of a private chapel or oratory, the entrance to which
is contrived curiously through the jamb of a deeply recessed window,
perhaps in order to secure orientation ; the other window opens eastward,
and its sill, bracketed out, forms the altar ; there is a piscina also. The
windows and architecture generally are of the transition from Decorated to
Perpendicular.

Leland visited Nunney twice ; for the first time in 1540, when he writes :
" A praty Castell, at the W. end of the Paroche church, having at eche end by
N. & S. 2 praty round Towres, gatheryd by Compace to joyne in to one.
The Waulls be very stronge & thykke, the Stayres narrow, the Lodginge within
some what darke. It standeth on the left ripe of the Ryver [which] dividithe
it from the Church Yarde. The Castell is servid by Water conveyed into it
owte of the Ryver. There is a stronge Waulle withe oute the Mote rownde
about, savinge at the E. Parte of the Castell, where it is defendyd by the
Brooke."

In the Additional MSS. in the British Museum Library (No. 17062) is a
diary kept by a Royalist officer at this time, giving a rough sketch of the castle,
which shows the turrets with conical tops and a high roof to the main building.
The outer wall of defence is not shown in Buck's drawing—it was only 12 feet
high nor are the gatehouse and drawbridge shown.

This, then, is the fortress which in 1645 Colonel Prater, its owner, garrisoned
for the king, and held against the Parliamentary force which Fairfax, on the
march to attack Bristol, detached under Colonel Rainsborough to besiege it,
and which consisted of the Colonel's own regiment and Colonel Hammond's
with two guns. Fairfax himself rode over to view Nunney, and found it to

be a very strong place (*Sprigg*). However, it was ill munitioned and provisioned, and after a day's battering, during which a breach was made in the
castle wall, Colonel Prater surrendered next day (September 20th), when his
garrison of eighty men were made prisoners. It is said that one of these, who
were chiefly Irish, deserted to the enemy and betrayed a weak spot in the
walls,—which is unlikely to have been known to him. The effects of the firing
are still visible on the wall, and were chiefly the work of a 36-pounder gun
brought over from Shepton Mallet. The besiegers lost five men, chiefly by the
fire of one marksman who seldom failed to hit his man. One of them had the
temerity to climb a tree in the garden, where now stands the manor-house, to
steal fruit, but he was brought down at the first shot. The castle flag, a red one
with "a crucifix-cross" in the centre of it, was sent to London as a Papist
trophy. Then the old castle was burnt, to prevent further use of it to the king,
and it was ordered to be "slighted," which happily could only partially have
been carried out.

RICHMONT, or HARPTREE (*non-existent*)

ON the northern slopes of the Mendips, near the village of East Harptree,
stood a castle which was a stronghold of the Gournay branch of the
Harptree family. After the Conquest this parish was granted to Geoffrey,
Bishop of Coutances, another of the warrior churchmen of the period, and
it was held of him by Azelin Gouel de Perceval, ancestor of the Perceval
family, and, by a younger son, of the barons Harptree and Gournay.

From Sir John de Harptree, in the reign of Henry I., descended Sir Robert
(temp. Henry III)., who assumed the name of Gournay, and was ancestor of
several barons of that name, long seated at this their castle of Richmont;
Joan, the daughter and heiress of the last of them, Sir Thomas, conveyed
the estate to her husband Walter de Cadicot, and thereafter it descended,
with the castle, by marriage to the family of Hampton, and then to that of
Newton, being held by Sir Richard Newton, who was Lord Chief-Justice
17 to 22 Henry VI. His family continued to possess the property till the
reign of Charles II., after which date it came to the Scropes of Louth in
Lincolnshire.

It is likely that Azelin built a strong Norman castle here in the time of the
Conqueror, or soon after, since in the time of Stephen, that king marched to
Richmont Castle, after the siege of Bristol, pretending to lay siege to it in
the ordinary way with his military engines. The garrison organised a sally
in force to some distance, when the king, galloping up to the walls with his
horsemen, before the garrison could get back again, set fire to the castle gate
and secured the walls, and so obtained possession of the fortress.

The old structure is said to have continued in preservation till the time of Henry VIII., when Sir John Newton destroyed it, even to the foundations, in order to build a new house near by, called Eastwood. It has now utterly vanished, but the site, overhanging on the N. and E. a narrow wooded ravine, is picturesque. It was an irregular fortress, approached from the S.W. only, and Collinson states that vestiges of a circular keep were visible in his time.

STOKECOURCY (pronounced Stogursey) (minor)

ON the border of the Lowlands, about two miles from the shore of Bridgwater Bay, lie the lands which were the head of the barony of Robert and William de Courcy, Sewers to the Empress Maud and to Henry II. William de Courcy died at the end of this king's reign, leaving a daughter and heiress Alice, who carried the estate, then of twenty-four knights' fees, to Warren Fitzgerald, Chamberlain to King John. They had two daughters, Margaret and Joan, who divided the property; Margaret married (1) Baldwin de Redvers, s.p., and (2), against her will, Falk de Brent or Brenté, a Norman of mean extraction, who, being disaffected to Henry III., fortified and garrisoned against him the manor-house of this barony; and it became under him such a

STOKECOURCY

grievance to the country round, that, on complaint made to the king, a writ was sent to the sheriff to dismantle it (see *Bedford*). Falk, who had been high in favour with King John, was banished 9 Henry III., and died not long after. Margaret, his wife, lived till 20 Edward I., but did not recover possession of the estate, which was granted to Hugh de Neville, and at his death to his son-in-law, Robert de Waleron. In the time of Edward II. it was the barony of Robert Fitzpayne, and from him, with the title of Lord Fitzpayne, it descended to Eleanor, wife of Henry Percy, Earl of Northumberland. During her lifetime, in 33 Henry VI., soon after the first battle of St. Albans, the castle was surprised and burned by William, Lord Bonville, the brother-in-law of the King-maker, and has lain in ruins ever since, continuing in the Percy family till 1682. The castle is on the S. of the village.

Buck's view of Stokecourcy (1733) shows a great deal of the fabric then remaining; there were half of the two round towers commanding the gateway, but the drawbridge is not given. In rear is a large rectangular enclosure with square towers at the extremities of the walls, remaining to about half their original height, and from thence is a long bank sloping to the moat surrounding the whole. The site only of the circular keep and a postern remain. A stream from the Quantock Hills supplied the moat, and worked the castle mill, which is still in use.

In the *Proceedings of the Somerset Archæological Society*, vol. viii., it is said that excavations have been made in and around the remains, but that very few characteristic portions of the original struc-

STOKECOURCY

ture are left, except the ancient bridge across the moat and parts of the main building, some walls, and the sally-postern.

It was a member of the De Courcy family who subdued the province of Ulster, of which he was created earl.

TAUNTON (*chief*)

INE, king of the West Saxons, in the beginning of the eighth century having extended his kingdom beyond the Parret River, built a strong fortress on his far west frontier, to protect his newly conquered lands from the Welsh of Devon. It was an earthwork, with a timber palace, surrounded by a moat and palisades, and some traces of it are said to be still visible; but it was captured and destroyed in 722 by Queen Ethelburga, and we hear of no stronghold at Taunton from that time till the reign of Henry I., when, a town having meantime arisen, the lordship belonged to the diocese of Winchester, and William Gifford, Bishop of Winchester, erected on the old site a stone Norman castle. Great additions were made by his successors in the Decorated or Edwardian period, of which there are still considerable remains.

The situation is on the right bank of the river Tone, upon a low elevation of gravel that rises above what was then a waste of fen land, which added strength to the position. The N. front, 180 yards in length, lies along the river, while the W. face is protected by a mill-stream, falling into the Tone here at right angles, and to obtain a water defence on the S. and E., a curved ditch, 340 yards in extent, was cut from the smaller stream round to the river, the whole enclosure thus forming somewhat the figure of a quadrant. An artificial ditch separates the inner court in the N.E. corner of this area, covering its S. and W. fronts; and this court was again divided by a wall into two parts, that on the W. containing the keep, which stood on the enceinte wall. The outer court is called the "Castle Green," and in it the dead were buried in war time, in the same way as the ground at the Tower of London, on the N. of the White Tower, was until of late years occupied by a graveyard.

Little is heard about the castle for a very long period after its building, except that it is known from deeds dated there that the bishops of Winchester occupied it, and from time to time enlarged and strengthened the fabric. In 1490 it had become ruinous, and Bishop Langton repaired the whole building, and on the strength of this placed his arms upon the inner gatehouse. In 1496 the Cornish miners and others rose against the taxation incurred by a subsidy given to King Henry by the Parliament, for prosecuting his war against the Scottish king, who espoused the cause of Perkin Warbeck. The rioters marched through Devon without committing any excesses, but on reaching Taunton, we learn from Lord Bacon that "they killed in fury an officious and eager commissioner for the subsidy, whom they called the Provost of Penrhyn," and who had sought shelter in the castle. The next year Perkin himself landed at Whitsand Bay, near Plymouth, under the title of Richard IV., and being repulsed at Exeter, came on to Taunton with between 6000 and 7000 men on September 20, 1497, and made show of attacking the castle; but being apprised of the near approach of the king with a formidable army, about midnight, he fled with sixty horsemen from Taunton to the New Forest in Hants, and took sanctuary at Beaulieu Priory there, leaving his supporters to their fate. On Henry's arrival at Taunton he was received with acclamations, and, the danger being past, he wisely pardoned the rebels. Again in 1577 we hear of this castle requiring repairs and alterations, which were then made by Bishop Horne, who built the Assize Hall.

When Sir Thomas Fairfax in May 1645 marched forth with his New Model army, the king held the whole of Somerset with the exception of Taunton,

TAUNTON CASTLE

which had been secured in 1642 by Waller, but was retaken soon after by Lord
Hertford, who drove out the Roundheads, and held the town and castle for the
king. This was only for a time, as in July 1644, soon after Marston Moor, Colonel
Blake (who was afterwards also the great admiral) and Sir Robert Pye again
captured the place, when they found in the castle one demi-culverin, and ten
other small pieces, two tons of match, eight barrels of powder, and also arms and

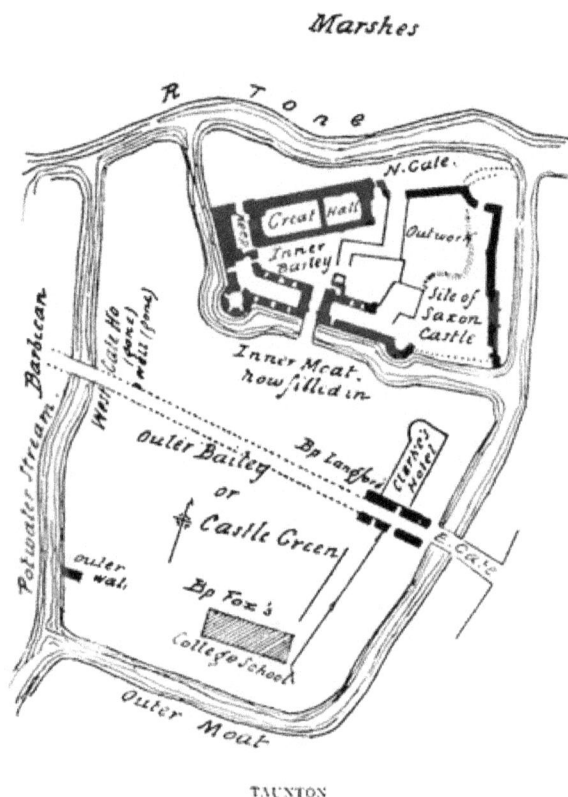

TAUNTON

ammunition, furniture, and plenty of provisions. Early the following spring,
Lord Goring was sent with 10,000 troops to attack the town, when he summoned
the castle, but was disdainfully refused by Blake. Meanwhile the army of
Fairfax had advanced to within ten miles of Taunton, and the Royalists, being
repulsed by Blake in a final assault of the trenches, after setting fire to two
whole streets of the town, drew off, and on May 11th the Parliamentary force

relieved their besieged comrades. The Royalists soon returned to the attack under Goring, and carried on a fresh investment of Taunton till July 3rd, when the advance of a strong Parliamentary force again obliged the raising of the siege.

In 1685 (June 18th) Monmouth entered Taunton and suffered himself to be proclaimed king here, but the castle of Taunton was not then concerned. After the collapse of this rebellion, the infamous Judge Jeffreys held his Bloody Assize in the great hall of the castle, causing it, according to his custom, to be draped in red hangings for the occasion; and here he sat, usually drunk, and subject to wild outbursts of passion, showing neither justice, pity, nor mercy. At this time the ancient castle must have become a heap of ruins, since at the Restoration, Charles II., taking a leaf from Cromwell's book, had caused the walls and defensive works of the fortress to be demolished, in return for the republican zeal of the town, whose charter also he annulled.

The entire enclosure, surrounded by river, stream, and moat, contains about seven acres, the inner bailey or citadel occupying its N.E. corner. Nothing remains of the outer walls of the lower bailey except a considerable part of the E. gatehouse, defending the entrance on that side to a road which passed through to the W. side, where the gatehouse has disappeared; there were drawbridges at each of these entrances over the moat and stream, and on the other side of these were wooden barbicans, some timbers of which have been dug up. None of the buildings exist now of the lower ward, Bishop Fox's school being, of course, early sixteenth-century work. A good deal of the Norman building of the inner ward remains; on the W. side is a portion of the rectangular keep, forming part of the wall along the inner moat, and measuring about 50 feet by 40, with walls 13 feet thick. The stone vaulting of its basement remains, and there was a staircase in the N.E. corner, from which extends the outer wall, forming, as at Leicester, the wall of the great hall. The W. wall of the keep ends in a large circular tower, of early Decorated or Edwardian architecture, and thence the S. inner ballium wall ran for 123 yards; but the E. end of it, with the base of a circular tower, has of late been removed. The inner moat was filled in by a municipal "benefactor," one Sir Benjamin Hammet, who likewise greatly injured the fabric. He also "restored" the great Hall, and placed therein a wall dividing the building into two courts.

In the centre of the S. front is a gatehouse with an Edwardian portal, portcullis groove, and gates, and in front are the holes for the drawbridge chains. On the E. side of this ward was thrown up the earth excavated from the ditches, forming a raised platform, whereon, in all probability, was erected the dwelling of King Ine. Thus we have here earthworks of the eighth century, walls and keep of the early twelfth, and towers and gatehouses of the thirteenth or early fourteenth century (*Clark*). The inner moat was 25 feet broad and

12 feet deep. Jeffrey's guards were taken from Kirke's regiment, who had lately formed the garrison of Tangiers (now 2nd Foot); these men were encamped during the assize on the W. of the Castle Green, which part, therefrom, is still called "Tangiers."

WALTON IN GORDANO (minor)

WALTON cannot be classed as a mediaeval castle, having been built probably in the reign of James I. as hunting quarters of the Paulett family. It lies W. of Bristol near the village of Clevedon, standing on the southern slopes of the hills there descending to the sea, and on the brink of the Bristol Channel.

It is an octagonal enclosure having a turret of like shape at its S.E. face. The place has a mediaeval look, but its embattled walls are slight, and the windows are large, and there is nothing venerable in the ruin, of which the roof and floors had fallen in at the beginning of the present century. The entrance is through a crenellated gateway.

The manor of Walton was given by the Conqueror to his kinsman, Robert de Mortain, Earl of Cornwall, one of the leaders in his army of invasion, and its possession followed the fortunes of the rest of his estates. In the third year of Edward IV., the manor was held by Sir Thomas de Cheddar, whose daughter brought it in marriage to Sir John Newton (see *Richmont*). In the reign of Mary it was owned by Sir Edward Seymour, who sold it to Sir John Thynne, and from him it passed to Christopher Ken of Ken, whose daughter and heiress conveyed the estate to the family of Paulett.

CHEPSTOW

Monmouthshire

ABERGAVENNY (minor)

AN observer in 1801 writes that "only a few scattered portions of the
walls and one poor gate are left" of this historic fortress, and guide-
books to-day say that what is left is "a shattered and shapeless ruin."
But Coxe's "Tour in Monmouthshire" gives a very intelligible plan
of these remains, which exist on a hill near the S. extremity of the town of
the same name, meagre though they be. The castle is said by Camden to have
been founded by Hameline de Baladun (or Barham) soon after the Conquest.
He left his nephew Brian of Wallingford, surnamed Fitz Count, his heir; but,
this man's two sons being lepers, he left the greatest part of his estate to Walter,
son of Milo, Earl of Hereford. To him succeeded his brother Henry, who was
slain by the Welsh during an invasion upon his lands, when the property was
brought by his sister and heir to the Braoses of Bramber, and from them, by
marriage, by the Cantelupes and Hastings family to Reginald Grey of Ruthin
(*Dugdale*, i. 710). William de Beauchamp, however, recovered it by conveyance

from Grey; and he again, in default of further issue, made it over to his brother Thomas, Earl of Warwick, and his heirs male. William de Beauchamp, lord of Abergavenny, had a son named Richard, who for his valour was created Earl of Worcester, and being slain in the French wars, his only daughter brought the estate in marriage to Edward Nevill. From that date the Nevills bore the style of Barons Bergavenny, although they did not then obtain the castle. Henry, the fourth lord, dying in 1586, left an only daughter Elizabeth, who married Sir Thomas Fane, knight, between whom and Sir Edward Nevill, knight, the castle and the greater part of the lands had fallen. The titles, then, of Berga-

venny and Le Despencer were contested by these two aspirants, when the House of Lords deter-mined the matter by Sir E. Nevill being summoned as Baron Abergavenny, while Elizabeth, Lady Fane, was made, or re-stored to the title of, Bar-oness le Despencer. The castle naturally remained with the heirs male.

The castle is now a picturesque ruin of the walls and towers of the fortifications, with no do-mestic portion left. In the centre of the outer court or bailey is a vast mound, where stood the keep until it was carted away as material for mending the

ABERGAVENNY

roads. There are vestiges only of various chambers, and some fragments of walls on the third storey remain, overhanging their supports. On the W. side, where the walls are now nearly gone, is a grand and uninterrupted view of the valley below the castle, with a chain of hills called the Blorenge rising beyond it, and the river winding along through the meadows, passing an ancient bridge of many pointed arches. The great gate of entrance remains, but the groining of its roof has fallen. In the court it is still possible to make out the great hall, the kitchens and other offices. Before the pacification of Wales and the Borderland, there was a constant struggle between the Welsh and their rulers and oppressors, the Lords Marchers, as the custodians of the marches were called, when this castle was more than once the scene of bloody deeds and murders. Giraldus Cambrensis declares it was dishonoured by treason oftener than any other castle in Wales. It was here that William de Braose—grandson of the lord of Bramber of same name, whose family was starved to death by King John (see *Bramber, Sussex*), one of the most powerful and unscrupulous of the Norman nobles, and famous, according to Matthew Paris, for his cruelty and treachery, even in those times—invited some Welsh chieftains to meet in friendship to arrange their differences, and whilst they were seated, unarmed, at table in his hall, caused them to be assassinated. It is satisfactory to read that this villain was afterwards hanged on a tree by Llewellyn, Prince of Wales.

The lordship passed through the above-named succession of families into the keeping of the Nevills, in which noble family it has remained since the reign of Henry VI., the Marquis of Abergavenny deriving his title from it.

CALDICOT

CALDICOT (*chief*)

CALDICOT, which is the most westerly place mentioned in Domesday, was originally held by Sheriff Durand, and afterwards by ten successive De Bohuns, earls of Hereford and hereditary Constables of England, who held it by this service. It passed from them by Eleanor, who was coheir of Earl Humphrey (see *Pleshy, Essex*), in marriage to Thomas of Woodstock, Duke of Gloucester, and was afterwards annexed as royal property, by Henry VIII., to the Duchy of Lancaster.

It must have been a fortress of considerable importance in early days, since, from its position near the Bristol Channel and the port of Portskewit, it protected the ingress and egress of Norman ships, and of the Angevin kings. Great care was evidently lavished upon the building of this castle, in the strength and finish of the masonry, which is all ashlar and of extraordinary fineness, most of the latter work appearing to be of the time of Edward II.,

CALDICOT

though the great gatehouse and north postern are the work of Thomas of Woodstock (Richard II.).

The plan is that of an irregular oblong, forming six or eight angles, two of which corners are occupied by towers, while on the lines of the curtain stand other towers. The W. front is the chief feature, having on it the principal vaulted entrance gateway. The portal is vaulted and groined, the corbels being portraits. The portcullis and bridge arrangements are by far the most finished in the kingdom, and the machicoulis are worked on corbels sculptured with portraits, of a richness rarely met with in this country. The flanking towers on each side of the entrance are machicolated, being in fact garderobe turrets, but the gatehouse has not this defence. On the other side of the court is a postern, defended by a portcullis and bold machicolations ; and on the E. of the gate tower is the great Hall, the windows of which still retain their tracery.

On the N.E. side is the circular keep, of thirteenth-century work, standing on a mound, and surrounded by its own ditch. The lowness of this keep tower is one of the peculiarities of Caldicot, a form which is shared also by Hawarden, but the excellence of its masonry is unsurpassed in England.

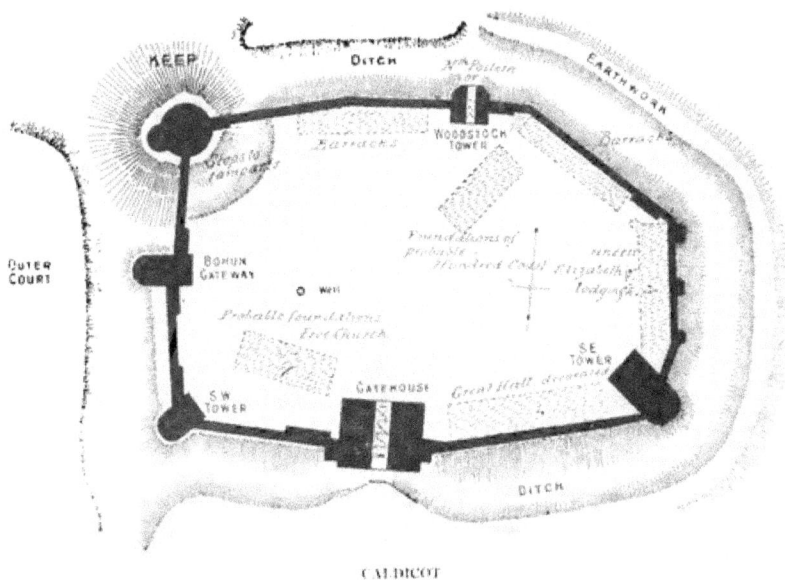

CALDICOT

The exterior walls, with their turrets, fortunately remain in very perfect condition, except on the E., and upon the inside of these curtains it is possible to observe how the offices and dwellings were contrived and built against them, probably in timber or half-timber work ; the fireplaces recessed in them, and the holes for the beams and rafters still remain. The most perfect of the towers is that at the N.E. angle, in which, in one of the window-sills, is an opening which may have led to a well. The towers attain a height of about 30 feet, and, with the walls, enclose an area of about 1½ acres. The great gatehouse, of Decorated style, is a noble structure ; it is still used as a residence, and has a high roof. The S. front was protected by a moat.

Caldicot gives a title to the dukes of Beaufort, who, however, were never more than lessees; it derives all its dignity from the grandeur of its design and from its architecture, since the position is not ennobling, being in low ground in the vale of the Trogoy, which falls into the Severn near this castle, and being only about a mile distant from the shore of the Channel, where troops and stores intended for South Wales were landed. The place is the property of Mr. Joseph R. Cobb, F.S.A.

CHEPSTOW (chief)

CHEPSTOW is a vast pile, to which or to its predecessor in Saxon or British times the name of Castle Gwent was given. It stands grandly on a rocky platform above the river Wye, on the summit of a perpendicular escarpment, being on the N. side in this manner quite inaccessible, and protected on the other three sides by deep ditches of great breadth. The general plan consists of four large courts having an entrance both on the E. and W. The narrow parallelogram enclosed by the fortress is about three acres in extent, and each of the courts is defensible. On the N. side, overhanging the river, are placed the principal apartments, the great hall with the kitchens, and all the chief chambers and "bowers"; here it was safe to indulge in decorations and fine windows and mouldings,

CHEPSTOW

while on the other fronts, susceptible of attack, the simplest and most defensible masonry was adopted, and the openings are loopholes and crenellations only. The main entrance is on the town side, on the E., by a gatehouse flanked by two circular towers, grooved for the portcullis. The whole is in a tolerable state of preservation. Near this entrance is the lesser hall, with windows of early Decorated style (about the time of Edward I.), and the chief offices, with the lord's oratory in the angle. Thence, passing through into the inner bailey, we arrive at the great Hall, of the same period, with rooms below it having some Norman work. Beyond this is another courtyard with entrance into the fourth, and leading to the western entrance.

The lords of this place were the Clares, earls of Pembroke, commonly called Earls of Strighull and Pembroke from the neighbouring castle of Strighall, where they resided ; though some wrongly assert that Chepstow and Strighull mean the same place. The last of the earls was Richard, a man of invincible spirit and of amazing strength of body, to whom, from the strength

CHEPSTOW

of the bow which he bent, the surname of "Strongbow" was given ; and he it was who by his valour first opened the conquest of Ireland to the English. By his daughter and heiress Isabel, Chepstow came to the Bigots, the Marshalls, and afterwards by marriage to the Herbert family, from whom the present noble family of Somerset, who now own it, acquired the property.

On entering the chief court, on the left is a large round tower in the angle of the wall, named Martin's Tower, because it served for twenty years as the prison of the regicide and wit, Henry Martin, till his death in 1680. His room was above and is still in fair condition ; in the basement of this tower there appears to have been a dungeon. Here also was imprisoned Bishop

MONMOUTHSHIRE   81

Jeremy Taylor, upon a charge of complicity with a Royalist insurrection. In
rear of the last and western court is another entrance, strongly defended, of later
date. Chepstow Castle endured many hard blows during the Civil War, being

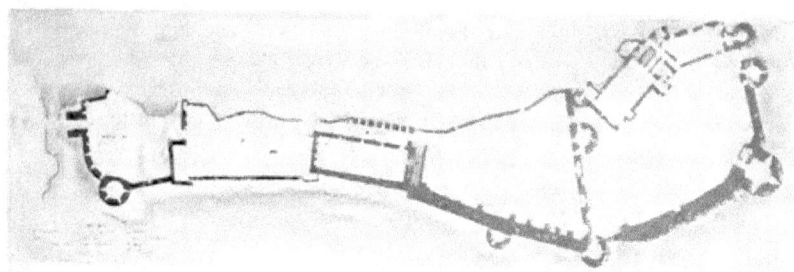

CHEPSTOW

taken and retaken several times; once it was besieged by Cromwell in person
in 1645, and was taken by assault; it was again attacked in 1648, when its
commander, Sir Nicholas Kemyss, and forty of his garrison were killed. The
Long Parliament granted the castle, together with several estates belonging
to the Marquis of Worcester and others, to Oliver Cromwell, but they were
restored at the accession of Charles II.

DINHAM (non-existent)

DINHAM is situated about one and a half mile N.W. of Caerwent, the
Roman station of Venta Silurum. Here was formerly a castle mentioned
as one of the six that compassed the forest of Wentwood. The ruins stand on a
gently rising ground near the road, and are so overgrown with trees as to be
scarcely discernible. They are on a bank above the combe through which an
old road led to Wentwood, and show foundations of some of the walls. Dinham
Castle is said to have been built upon the spot where the heroic British king
Caractacus was buried. It was built by the family of Le Walleys or Walsh,
who were here for many generations, and existed in 1128. In the reign of
Elizabeth, Dinham was purchased by William Blethyn, Bishop of Llandaff
(1575–1591), whose descendants lived in a mansion that stood on the site of
the present great Dinham farm, and from them the property came to the
Bayly family, with whom it still continues. It must have been demolished in
very distant times, since neither Leland nor Camden make any mention of
Dinham Castle.

VOL. II.   L

GREEN CASTLE (*minor*)

ABOUT one and a half mile S.W. of Newport are ruins, not mentioned by Leland or Camden, on the left bank of the Ebwy near its confluence with the Usk River. The castle formerly belonged to the dukes of Lancaster, and was esteemed a place of strength and security in the Civil Wars. The remains consist now of a building used as a farm stable or byre for cattle, a square tower with a spiral staircase, a building containing several apartments, one of which has a large fireplace, and a fine Gothic entrance and doorways. Close at hand is a circular mound surrounded by a foss overgrown with thicket, overhanging the old channel of the Ebwy, the probable site of the keep. The place now belongs to the family of Tredegar, and the farm is called Greenfield (*Coxe*).

GROSMONT, OR GRISMONT (*minor*)

IN the N.E. corner of the county is the celebrated "Trilateral" of Monmouthshire, being a group of three castles planted at a distance of from four to five and a half miles apart from each other, in the form of a triangle, the centre of which is occupied by the eminence known as the Graig Hill; the other two fortresses being the castles of Skenfrith and Whitecastle. Grosmont Castle, the most northern of the three as well as the latest built, stands on an eminence above the right bank of the river Monnow, on the confines of the county, and at the foot of the Graig Hill. It is in a very ruinous condition, and the remains are not extensive; they consist chiefly of a gateway and two circular towers, with a quadrangular enclosure of walls, attached to which is the shell of a great baronial hall, 80 feet by 27, lighted by four windows on each side. There are, too, on the N. side, the foundations of an apartment with a Gothic octagonal chimney, high and tapering, and surmounted by a sort of coronet or lanthorn. The castle is surrounded by a large and deep moat, and it was further strengthened by ancient earthworks. On the S.E. are more outworks, still partly visible, containing the barbican, and there are vestiges also on the S. of further works. Grosmont was granted, together with Skenfrith, by King John to William de Braose, the lord of Bramber; and Henry III. gave all three castles to Hubert de Burgh, who afterwards was forced to give them back to that monarch, who then annexed them to the Duchy of Lancaster (see *Skenfrith* and *Whitecastle*). The architecture is Early English of Henry III., with Decorated additions (*Clark*). Grosmont was once a favourite residence of the dukes of Lancaster, and Henry, grandson of Edmund Crouchback, was born there, and was from that fact surnamed "Grismont." In the

time of Henry III, this fortress was invested by Llewelyn, Prince of Wales
but the king relieved it by moving thither with a large army, when the Welsh
fled. Some time later this king, marching against Richard Marshall, Earl of
Pembroke, retreated to Grosmont in order to protect his supplies, and encamped
there; but he carelessly allowed his army to be surprised by Pembroke, who
beat up his quarters at night, and carried off 500 horses and much plunder.
The views here of the river flowing below the castle and of the country about
are very beautiful.

LLANGIBBY, FORMERLY CALLED TRAYGRUCK (minor)

LLANGIBBY is on the Caerleon road from Usk. It stood on a hill now
overgrown with brushwood, where little but the lines of the outer walls
can be traced. This castle was the possession of the earls of Gloucester, of
the family of Clare, and is given among the lands appointed as dowry to Maud,
the widow of Gilbert, the last male of that line, through whose daughter it
came to the earls of March of the Mortimer line. Roger Mortimer styles
himself Lord of Tragrucke in a charter granted to the town of Usk. In the
beginning of the seventeenth century it belonged to the Williams family, and
is mentioned by Oliver Cromwell as "a very strong house, well stored with
arms." Llangibby then belonged to Sir Trevor Williams (created baronet
1641), who, says Cromwell, is "a man full of craft and subtiltye, very bould &
resolute,—and very malignant."

The trace of the castle is a long parallelogram, now a cider orchard,
having the front above the ditch protected by a circular tower on the E.,
and an entrance between two circular towers on the left with a curtain
between. There are the vestiges of three or four other towers flanking the
long line of walls, a postern, some walls of apartments with columns, and
part of a roof supported by them; but all are greatly dilapidated. By the
several pointed arches, it must date subsequent to Norman times (Coxe).

LLANVAIR (minor)

ANOTHER fortress of twelfth-century origin is Llanvair, prettily situated on
the declivity of a hill, on the road to Usk across Wentwood Forest. It is
not of any great extent, but has been of considerable strength. There were three
round towers connected by walls, and one square one joined to a modern farm-
house; but the place has been too effectually destroyed to make out the buildings.

Llanvair was the ancient residence of the Kemyss family. Edward Kemyss,
who attended Hameline de Baladun in his conquests in Gwent, received these
and other lands for his services.

MONMOUTH (*minor*)

IN the middle of the town near the market-place are the ruins of this castle, which appears to have existed in the Conqueror's days. It belonged to John, Baron of Monmouth, from whom it came to the house of Lancaster, when Henry III. stripped him of his estates, because his heirs had taken the oath of allegiance to the earls of Brittany. The fact that it was thus in the possession of John of Gaunt and his son, in later years, accounts for Monmouth Castle being the birthplace of Henry V., hence called "Harry of Monmouth." An old writer in 1801, visiting the ruins, says: "Of the castle a poor diminished spot remains, a part of the walls of the chamber where the hero of Agincourt, the Conqueror of France, first drew his breath. The proportions of this chamber show an air of grandeur, and the decorations (from one perfect window yet in view) are of the first degree of refined taste." Only a small fragment exists of the great hall. Monmouth was certainly a Norman walled town, but only one gate is left—namely, the Bridge Gate, standing on the bridge leading to Abergavenny,— under which Henry V. may often have passed—and there are but few remnants of the walls. In 1646, Colonel Kyrle, who had originally sided with the king's party, made his peace with the Parliament by betraying his trust and handing over Monmouth to General Massy.

Here also was born, in 1152, Geoffrey of Monmouth, Bishop of St. Asaph, the compiler of the romancing chronicle which bears his name.

NEWCASTLE (*non-existent*)

A SHORT distance on the Monmouth road S. of Skenfrith are the vestiges of another castle to which this name was given, but they consist only of some tumuli surrounded by a moat 300 feet in circumference. Of the origin of this castle and of its demolition there are no records whatever in history.

NEWPORT (*minor*)

NEWPORT is not a large castle, but it deserves attention as a fine instance of the adaptation of the Perpendicular style to a strictly military structure. It stands on the right bank of the Usk, the walls and towers rising directly out of the water. Williams says that this part of the country was subdued by Martin, Lord of Cemais, who caused the castle to be built at the N.E. angle of the town, on the W. side of the river. Other authorities state that Robert Fitzhamon, the conqueror of Glamorgan, originally reared the edifice at the end of the eleventh century, to defend the passage of the river at this point ; the present fortress, however, was built by the Stafford family, who inherited the manor from the De Clares. Parker declares the river front, which alone remains perfect, to be "a beautiful composition," particularly in the way in which the towers, square and splayed at the base, become round or octagonal as they rise, and he remarks on the way in which round towers gave way to octagonal or square ones, as being better adapted to receive the newer square-headed or pointed windows. The castle is sadly degraded by being occupied as a brewery, which either destroys or conceals all except some few walls and two towers. There is a fine gateway tower with octagonal

NEWPORT

turrets, and a large pointed window over the entrance, but sadly blocked and mutilated. Along the river front three towers supported the curtain, but on the reverse side there is only the wall, without flank defence. The three front towers were in existence at the beginning of the present century in nearly a perfect state ; at each end of this face was an octagonal tower, with a large square tower in the centre having turrets at each angle. This latter formed the keep, which had a vaulted chamber called the State-room ; at the foot of it is the water-gate, beneath a high arched passage, defended by a portcullis ; between this and the lower tower was the hall, which can still be traced. The enceinte is a right-angled parallelogram, measuring about 46 yards N. and S., by 32 E. and W., and is built of rubble masonry, with ashlar quoins. The S. tower was once used as a nail factory.

PENCOED (*minor*)

TEN miles from Chepstow, this castle stands on a gentle ascent overlooking the Caldecot level, with a commanding view of the Bristol Channel. The original castle belonged to the twelfth century, but the ruins are chiefly those of an old mansion built in the reign of Henry VIII., partly with the materials of the former structure. The principal remains consist of a gateway with circular arches flanked by two narrow pentagon turrets, a round embattled tower, and portions of an ancient wall. It was the time-out-of-mind seat of the Morgan family, and afterwards of the Montagues, who divided possession of this county with the Herberts, Somersets, Seymours, and Morgans. Sir Walter Montague obtained the estate by marriage with the heiress of Sir Edmund Morgan, but it passed afterwards into several hands. When in the possession of a Mr. Jefferies it was lost at play, and then came into the possession of Admiral Mathews, whose grandson enjoyed it at the beginning of this century.

It is conjectured that Pencoed, with Troggy, Dinham, and many other petty castles existing in this district, were built for the protection of the fertile Wentwood district by the retainers of the Bohuns and Clares, or other great lords in the county.

PENHOW (*minor*)

THIS castle, which is of small size, is built on the top of a hill, on what was perhaps a Roman site, two miles from Pencoed Castle. It is now a farmhouse, and the chief remains of the old fortress are a square embattled tower of the twelfth century and some low irregular walls; the masonry generally is indifferent, being composed of rubble plastered and grouted. Penhow was for centuries the residence of the St. Maur, or Seymour, family, whose arms, cut in stone and painted on glass, appear in the neighbouring church dedicated to St. Maurus, whence is derived the name of St. Maur.

RAGLAN, OR RAGLAND (*chief*)

NOTICED by Parker ("Domestic Architecture," vol. iii. Part II.) as being a splendid ruin of the fifteenth century, more of a military than domestic character, the castle is still clearly inhabited as a nobleman's mansion of the period. It is believed to have been chiefly built by Sir William Herbert ap Thomas, who served with distinction in the French wars with Henry V. and was knighted by that king. His son William was created (8 Edward IV.) Earl of Pembroke, a title exchanged by his son and successor for the earldom of Huntingdon in 1479. Dying *s.p.* male, his only daughter and heiress Elizabeth brought Raglan in marriage to Sir Charles Somerset, who assumed the title of Lord Herbert, and for his services in France was in 1514 created Earl of Worcester by Henry VIII. The fifth earl, Henry, the gallant defender of Raglan for King Charles, was advanced to the dignity of Marquess of Worcester in 1642. The third marquess, Henry, was created Duke of Beaufort in 1682, and this family still includes Raglan Castle as one of the most cherished portions of their extensive domain.

The castle stands on rising ground, and is now almost hidden by trees.

RAGLAN

Its thoroughly defensible nature is shown at once in the noble gateway, which is contrived for this end as much as any castle of Norman or Edwardian times. Flanked by two hexagonal towers set cornerwise to the front, the entrance has grooves for two portcullises, being approached, after various external defences, by a bridge over a moat. Two massive towers stand on the extreme right and left of the fortress, that on the left of the entrance having the name of "The Yellow Tower of Gwent," and supposed to have been added temp. James I. This forms a genuine keep, standing detached on an island surrounded by a walled moat, with an outer circuit of low curtain walls, and only connected with the body of the castle by a drawbridge. The entrance gateway leads into the first court, at the far end of which is a pentagonal tower containing the kitchens and offices; on the right is the breach made by Fairfax at the siege, when he opened fire on the walls at a range of only sixty yards. On the left or W. side of the first court is the great hall, the walls of which remain, with its bay window; the roof, which was of Irish oak, is entirely destroyed. This hall is of stately proportions and preserves its importance, as in earlier times, while alongside it is the chapel, and on the other side of these chambers lies the fountain court, with the grand staircase and approach to the state apart-

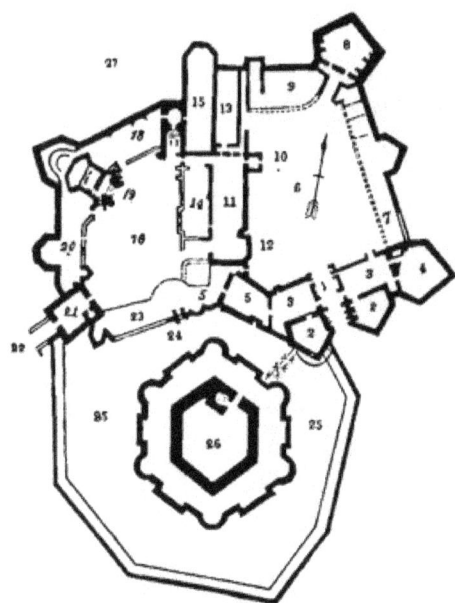

RAGLAN

ments. In the N.E. angle of these are the rooms occupied by Charles I. when he stayed at Raglan after the defeat of Naseby, one of the windows still bearing his name. A gate tower leads from this court out upon the terrace, which is called King Charles' Walk. The smaller gate, with its simple pointed arches, is one of the most pleasing portions of the castle. An old writer in the *Gentleman's Magazine* remarks how, on entering into the great court, the visitor sees the rich and uncommon front of the gallery-range, behind the entrance, the baronial hall with its porch and oriel, and the gallery door; while on the left is one of the gate towers,—the whole "presenting one of the most interesting castellated court scenes to be witnessed in the kingdom. The interior of the hall shows the grandeur of the style of what it once was, as does every other apartment

in this once splendid residence. Then there are the vestiges of the chapel, and the fountain court, and, passing on to the terrace with its still smooth enamelled surface, one beholds the mountains of Abergavenny with their cloud-capped summits."

The siege of 1646 was sustained by the old Marquess of Worcester, aged eighty-four, in company with his daughter-in-law, Lady Glamorgan, his sixth son, Lord Charles, his chaplain, Dr. Bailey, and a few friends, with a garrison

Raglan Castle.

of 800 men, horse and foot. The attack, which lasted for two months, was at first under the command of Colonel Morgan and a captain-engineer named Hooper, who had reduced Banbury a short while before, and a besieging force of 1500 men. The garrison made many desperate sallies, and in one of these captured a Parliamentary colour, while they lost several officers and men killed and wounded. Then 2000 troops reinforced the besiegers, and Sir Thomas Fairfax came himself from Bath to press the siege, and summoned the defenders. But the old marquess, with many excuses and objections, put off the demands

of Fairfax for many weeks, until, in the middle of August, the artillery of the besiegers being now advanced in the trenches close to the castle walls, he found it necessary to treat, and articles for surrendering the castle were eventually agreed on, and carried out on August 19th, the garrison marching out with all the honours of war (see Sprigg's "England's Recovery"). In the worst of bad faith, the Parliament refused to ratify Fairfax's articles of treaty, and sent the Marquess of Worcester to London, where he died in a few months. He had spent £60,000 in equipping and maintaining 1500 foot and 500 horse

RAGLAN

soldiers for the king, though they did small service, being routed at Gloucester without striking a blow. His estates with a revenue of £20,000 a year were confiscated, the woods of his three parks were destroyed, the deer killed, and the castle of Raglan was dismantled and "slighted," the lead and the timber being carted to Bristol. The great tower, after being battered at the top with pick-axes, was undermined, and the weight propped up with timbers, which being burnt, a great portion of the structure fell in a lump, and so remains to this day. The staircase fortunately was uninjured, so the summit of this keep is still attainable. The greatest injury to this splendid castle, however, was caused by the depredations of the country people, who for more than a century were allowed to use the place as a quarry, to obtain building stone.

Among the many historical personages who were immured in this castle was Henry, Earl of Richmond, afterwards King Henry VII. As a scion of Lancaster (on his mother's side), Edward IV. conceived a particular jealousy against this youth, and committed him for safe keeping in this fortress to the custody of Sir William Herbert, Lord of Raglan. Then, after the lapse of some time, Jasper, Earl of Pembroke, the lad's uncle, who had stayed in France since the battle of Tewkesbury, came over and paid a secret visit to the castle of Raglan in the absence of Sir W. Herbert; he managed to elude the vigilance or corrupted the fidelity of Lady Herbert, and carried off his nephew to Pembroke Castle, the place of Henry's birth, and soon after found means to send him over into Brittany, to the castle of Elven, where he remained hidden for a great many years, until the time came for him to strike for the crown of England.

SKENFRITH (minor)

THIS castle forms the S.E. point of the Trilateral group, about five miles S. of Grosmont, in the low land close to the same river, the Monnow (see *Grosmont*). It is built in trapezium form, with four outer walls and circular flanking towers at the angles, one of which is absent, and has in the midst a disconnected circular tower or keep, upon a low artificial mound. The walls are in good condition, but the upper parts are ruinous. It is probably the most ancient castle in the county, and during the prevalence of border warfare was of much importance, but after the settlement of Wales by Edward I., the necessity for these fortresses no longer existed, and from neglect they rapidly fell into decay. Skenfrith was conveyed with the other castles to Hubert de Burgh, but was afterwards seized again by Henry III. and granted to his son Edmund, Earl of Lancaster. It then, with the others, passed to John of Gaunt, and temp. Henry V. became parcel of the Duchy of Lancaster. In the reign of James I. it was reported as " ruinous and decayed, time out of the memory of man."

From the fact of the ground inside being from 6 to 10 feet higher than the level outside, there seems to have existed here an ancient earthen platform, having a mound on it, with probably a wooden fort and palisading defences, along the four sides of which the Norman curtain wall was built. Upon the mound was erected a circular stone tower 36 feet in diameter and from 45 to 50 feet high, having a battering base, like Coningsborough. There is a basement chamber for stores, a chief room above, 22½ feet in diameter and 14 feet high, with two windows, wherein was the only entrance. From this door a mural spiral stair led to the upper storey, in which is a recess for the kitchen fire, and the roof. The floors were all of timber.

The curtain wall of the work measures 74 and 71 yards N. and S., and 31 and 59 E. and W., has a thickness of 8 feet, and is from 30 to 40 feet in height, the battlements having been removed. The four circular corner towers are 11 feet diameter internally, closed in the gorge and entered by a door on the ground, and had three floors each; the S.W. tower has been removed. There is on the S. front a solid half-round buttress tower, and opposite this is a low-arched opening in the curtain, supposed by Mr. Clark to have admitted boats from the river, as was done at Tonbridge and Leeds. The moat cut from the Monnow River protected the three sides, while the river flowed beneath the N. front of the fortress. Leland mentions a stone bridge here, which crosses the river just below the castle.

STRIGUIL, or STRIGIL. (minor)

THE castle of Striguil is five miles W. of Chepstow, on the small stream of Ystriguil, which falls into the Usk. It stands in an extremely beautiful situation, on gently rising ground, commanding fine views of the valley. Williams says it was built by Gilbert, Earl of Ogie, the father of Richard Strongbow, and must be of later date than Chepstow, having Gothic windows and doorways. It was built, according to the Domesday Survey, by William Fitz-Osborn, Earl of Hereford, and it afterwards became the residence of the earls of Pembroke of the great house of Clare; it is remarkable in having given its name to a branch of this ancient family, who were called earls of Striguil from this their abode. Afterwards it was a seat of the Kemyss family, and in more modern times was acquired by the dukes of Beaufort. It has been a common error to give this name to the castle of Chepstow, which is sometimes called Chepstow or Striguil, the difficulty arising from both castles being possessed by the same family.

The remains are those of a square redoubt, having one face only existent, which contains a good circular tower attached to a piece of semicircular wall, and a straight curtain wall ending in part of a hexagonal tower, with some outworks and the remains of a moat in front.

TROGGY (minor)

CAMDEN says: "The little river Troggy falls into the Severn near Caldicot, where I saw the walls of a castle belonging anciently to the Constables of England," and held by the service of that office. It lies five or six miles from Chepstow, in a forest under a hillside, "very notable ruins." At the present day, an octagon tower with arched windows is all that is left.

U S K   (*minor*)

THE ruins of this castle stand over the little town of Usk, on the bank of the river of the same name. It is believed to have been commenced by William, Earl of Ewe and Matterel, who came to England with Duke William the Conqueror, and received from him certain manors in this west country, and "all he could conquer from the Welsh." With so promising a future, the noble Norman appears to have presumed too far, since he was banished for rebellion, and his lands were conferred on Walter Fitz Richard his nephew, who settled at Usk and built there; after which, carrying his inroads towards the west, he acquired Chepstow and Striguil. On his death without issue, his estates were granted to his nephew Gilbert de Clare, a still greater chieftain. In the time of Henry III., the castle belonged to Richard de Clare, Earl of Gloucester and Hereford. In the fifteenth century it was the property of Edward IV., and before that time had been a favourite resort of his father Richard, Duke of York; it was afterwards in favour with Henry VII., and with William, Earl of Pembroke, from whose female descendant's son by her last husband, Thomas, Viscount Windsor, it passed by purchase to the dukes of Beaufort.

Usk Castle has considerable remains, including the keep, the gatehouse, and the great hall. The outer walls are extant, enclosing a court and some outworks to the W., formed by two walls united by a round tower. At the end of the S. wall is a grand pointed gateway, grooved for the portcullis, and there remains a chamber of the castle, with an arched window and fireplace.

W H I T E C A S T L E   (*chief*)

WHITECASTLE, the third fortress of the Trilateral (see *Grosmont*), placed on its W. point, five and a half miles from Skenfrith, and five miles from Grosmont, upon very high ground, was one of the strongest castles of the Welsh marches. It consists of a central elliptical or hexagonal fortress, the longer axis of which lies N. and S., with a large outwork at each of these points, and the walls and towers are mostly standing. The centre ward is formed by a curtain wall 10 feet thick at base, and 30 feet high to the rampart walk, with circular towers at each angle, about 45 feet in height, all these towers having three storeys with wooden floors, and communicating with the wall. The two adjacent towers on the N. form between them the chief entrance or gatehouse, defended by gates and a portcullis, beyond which was a bridge over the moat, at this place 100 feet wide and nearly 40 feet deep. At the S. end of the ward was a smaller entrance, close to the S.W. angle tower. There was no keep, and the contained lodgings or barracks must have been of timber, as at Skenfrith; nor are there any traces of a hall or chapel.

In front of the main entrance is a large open barbican or outwork, somewhat rectangular in shape, and measuring 56 yards in depth, with a front of 74 yards, formed of a masonry wall 15 to 18 feet high, having flanking towers at intervals, three of which are circular, and a square tower containing the kitchen. A lesser outwork of half-moon shape similarly covers the S. entrance; it is composed entirely of earthwork, and connected with the main work by a bridge across the ditch, which encircles this outwork as well as the castle itself. The N. barbican is also defended throughout by a ditch, carried in a wide bend on the E. of the castle, and is defended on the outside by another huge earthwork, covering the flanks of the barbicans. The whole work is to afford protection to a large body of troops, as well as to the country people and their cattle, by earthworks and ditches of very great strength. It is believed to have been built by King John, and was conveyed by him, together with the other castles, to William de Braose (see *Skenfrith* and *Grosmont*).

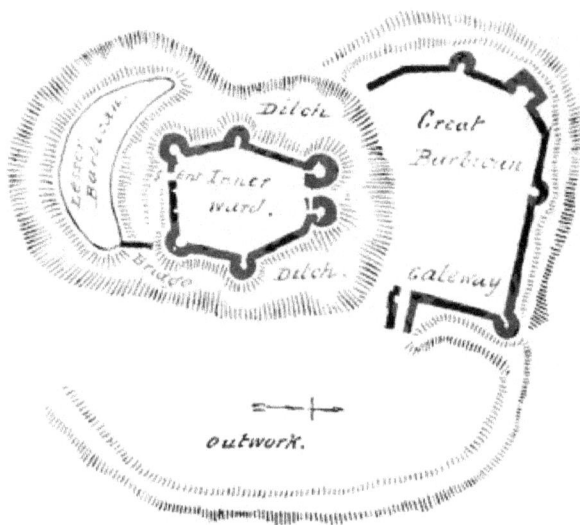

WHITLCASTLE

Henry III. first gave these castles to Hubert de Burgh, and afterwards demanding them from him, imprisoned and almost starved him to death, nor did De Burgh obtain his liberty until he had surrendered the castles to the king. From the Duchy of Lancaster they were held on lease by a family called Powell, of Llandilo, and afterwards by one John Lewis, who married the heiress of the Powells, and then by his son, after which they were demised to the dukes of Beaufort. The first Norman who overran the north of Monmouth was Brian Fitz Count, a companion of the Conqueror; he obtained these three castles, and also the castle of Abergavenny, in marriage, but they afterwards passed to the Braoses and the Cantelupes as lords of the manor of Abergavenny.

WILTON

Herefordshire

ALMELEY (*non-existent*)

IT is supposed that a Roman encampment first occupied the site of the lost castle of Almeley, which is on a turf-covered mound at the side of a small stream near the church of Almeley; at least it is thought that the keep was erected on this artificial mound, and there was a moat which was supplied by the rivulet. The name of the stronghold was Old Castle, and the site is now called Old Court, but nothing is to be found in history regarding its erection, except that the family of Oldcastle dwelt there in the fourteenth century, and the tradition goes that Sir John Oldcastle, better known as Lord Cobham, lived within its walls, his family being connected with this county at that period. Sir John was arrested for spreading the doctrines of Wicliffe, by command of that virtuous zealot Henry V., who caused him to be brought to London, and after interrogation, finding he denied the supremacy of the

Pope and other Catholic doctrines, handed him over to the priests; they caused him to be hung in chains over a bonfire on Christmas Day 1417, and so roasted him to death. He was both a most learned and accomplished man, and had been a great soldier in France. He was esteemed as the first English martyr after his cruel death (see *Couling, Kent*).

ASHPERTON (*non-existent*)

IN the parish of Stretton Gransham is a moat still holding water, which is all that remains of a castle of the Grandisons, who held lands in this county in the thirteenth century, and had a licence to crenellate a "mansum" or manor-house, in 20 Edward I., obtained by Willielmus de Grandison, the son of a Burgundian noble, the castle of whose territory is still on the Lake of Neuchatel (*Robinson*). It was this William's brother, or son, who was made Bishop of Exeter in 1327, and his elder brother, Sir Peter, was buried in Hereford Cathedral, on the N. side of the Lady Chapel, in a well-known tomb there. Sir Otho Grandison was a warrior and alderman temp. Edward II., and was sent by that king as ambassador to the Pope. Two hundred years ago there existed at this place a noble park belonging to the Lingen family; this is now a coppice wood, the property of Lady Emily Foley.

BRAMPTON BRIAN (*minor*)

THIS castle, which was built in the latter end of the reign of Henry I., seems to have been conferred on Barnard Unspee, Lord of Kinlet in Salop, as he made it his abode and took the name of De Brampton. His great-grandson married Matilda de Braose (see *Castles in Monmouth*), and their descendants for four generations held this castle, after which time it passed in marriage to Robert de Harley. In 1398, at the death of the last Bryan de Brampton, it is stated to have been held under the Mortimers, by the performance of a castle guard at Wigmore, for forty days in war time. Bryan, second son of Robert de Harley, succeeded to his mother's property, and serving with great distinction under the Black Prince, was made a Knight of the Garter by him. Either he or his son built the gateway at Brampton, the most ancient part of the ruins now existing, and of Edwardian date. The Harleys espoused the side of the White Rose; John Harley fought at the battle of Tewkesbury, and was knighted by Edward IV.; his grandson fought at Flodden.

Thomas Harley of Brampton Brian was sheriff 36 Elizabeth (1594), and was a distinguished councillor in the reign of James I., from whom he had a grant of the honour of Wigmore Castle. His son Robert was born in 1579, and was made a Knight of the Bath at James I.'s coronation; he was M.P.

for Radnor, and in 1623 married for his third wife Brilliana, second daughter of Lord Conway, who had been born and bred in Holland (whence her name), and who keenly joined in the extreme Puritanism of her husband, a strenuous supporter of Cromwell. Naturally, therefore, in the Civil War the Harleys were objects of offence in so loyal a county as Hereford, and Lady Harley, in the absence of her husband at Westminster, was harassed by the Royalists, and at last was shut up in Brampton with her family and some of her neighbours who sought shelter there with her. The eldest son, Edward, was serving with the Parliament army at Plymouth in 1643, when the long-expected attack was made upon the castle; but the Lady of Brampton was equal to the occasion, and placed her house in a fit state of defence, throwing up earthworks and getting in provisions and ammunition. She writes to her son in May (see her Letters, published by the Camden Society): "The water is brought quite into the greene court, & I think you will like the worke [fortifications] well. I like it soe well that I would not haue it undoun for a great deal." On July 25th the castle was besieged by Sir W. Vavasour and a force of 600 men, but so stout a defence was maintained by Lady Brilliana and her servants, that after six weeks no impression had been made, and, fearful of the enemy's operations in the Forest of Dean, the Royalists retired. But the strain was too much for the brave Lady Harley; delicate always, and with her health undermined by repeated illness and the anxieties involved by her troubles, she took "a verie bad colde" towards the end of the siege, and died a month only after its termination.

Early in 1644 Sir Michael Woodhouse, the Roundhead governor of Ludlow, came against Brampton again, after the taking of Hopton Castle, when the place was gallantly defended for a period of three weeks, but was then forced to surrender at the mercy of the victors, whose artillery had battered down some of the walls, the spoils being sixty-seven prisoners, a hundred stand of arms, two barrels of powder, and a whole year's provisions. The spelling of the name at that time was always "Brompton."

No traces exist of the original Border fortress, which the Rev. C. J. Robinson, in his "History of the Castles of Hereford," thinks may have stood on the N.W. side. The entrance gateway, with its pointed arches and vaulted passage with portcullis, has on each side a low circular flanking tower, with loopholes and crenellated parapets; the rest is what remains of the Tudor buildings, made in the middle of the sixteenth century. Sir Edward Harley, on his return from the governorship of Dunkirk, did what he could to repair the ruin of the Civil War, and built a new hall, partly on the site of the old structure. Some rooms over the inner gateway were inhabited till about the middle of the last century, when a violent storm did so much injury to the fabric that it was rendered unsafe and was dismantled. The existing front was added about 1748, on the marriage of Edward, 4th Earl of Oxford, of the Harley title. Here was born Robert, the first earl, grandson of Sir Robert Harley of the Civil War, the illustrious minister who in 1711 was created Baron Harley of Wigmore, Earl of Oxford and Earl Mortimer, Lord High Treasurer, and Knight of the Garter ; and here he died in 1724. Why they renewed in him the splendid dignity of the old De Veres is hard to say. Here too was formed the great Harleian Collection of MSS. and books, now in the British Museum. Brampton is now owned by Mr. Robert W. D. Harley.

BREDWARDINE (non-existent)

THE manor belonged at the Conquest to John de Bradwardyn, and afterwards was the property of the Baskerville family, and later of the Vaughans.

The site of this castle is now merely a huge green hillock, ornamented with trees, with a few fragments of masonry appearing. There remain some cellars and passages underground, whose entrance is choked with thicket.

BRONSIL (minor)

HERE in the parish of Eastnor was a castellated and defensible mansion of the Beauchamps. The ruins, overgrown with copse and ivy, lie in a deep glen below Midsummer Hill, a branch of the Malvern range.

Richard Beauchamp, son and heir of John, 1st Lord Beauchamp of Powyke, who was Lord High Treasurer to Henry VI., obtained a licence in 29 and 36 Henry VI. to enclose lands and to crenellate a mansion. In 1496, on the death of Richard, 2nd Lord Beauchamp, without male issue, his three daughters divided the estates ; one of them married William Rede of Lugwardine, and brought Bronsil to him. Mr. Robinson says that their occupation of the castle was much disturbed by ghosts, so that in 1600 Mr. Gabriel Rede went to consult the learned Mr. Allen of Gloster Hall, Oxford, on the subject. His advice was that some of the bones of old Lord Beauchamp should be taken from the distant place at which they were interred and brought to Bronsil. This was accordingly done, and the bones were taken in a box to Bronsil, "which ever after was quiet." These bones, which were portions of the vertebrae, were long regarded as heirlooms in the Rede family, and escaped destruction during the Civil War, when the castle was burnt. Bronsil was purchased from the Redes in the middle of the last century by Mr. Cocks of Castleditch, whose descendant now owns the property.

The enclosure of the walls was quadrangular, with an octagonal tower at each corner, one of which only was standing in 1770. A sketch made in 1731 of the ruins shows most of the outer walls and the towers then standing. It was defended by two moats, placed two yards apart, and these can easily be traced. The entrance gateway was on the W. side.

CLIFFORD (*minor*)

THIS historic fortress, the home of the Cliffords, stands on the summit of
a lofty escarpment of the bank of the Wye, guarding an important ford,
from whence the name is derived. It is one of the five castles of Herefordshire
mentioned in the Domesday Survey as belonging to Ralph de Todenei, and
was built by William Fitz Osborn, Earl of Hereford, -the same who built
Wigmore,—to whom the Conqueror gave lands here. On his son's revolt and
confiscation, it passed to the above-named Norman, his cousin, and went in
dower with his daughter Margaret to Richard des Ponts ; the second son of this
marriage succeeding to his mother's property of Clifford, assumed that surname.
His eldest daughter was the lady known as Fair Rosamond, the mistress of
Henry II., who may have been born at this castle, having spent her early life
there. Walter de Clifford, her brother, succeeded in 1221, and had many
contests with King Henry III., one of these being occasioned by his obliging a
king's messenger to eat up the royal letter that he had brought, seal and all,—a
joke which cost him a thousand marks. His only daughter Maud was married
to her cousin, William Longépée (the great-grandson of Fair Rosamond), who
was killed at a tournament in 1256, when his widow, in default of heirs male,
inherited the best estates of the De Cliffords. She was forcibly carried off and
married against her will by John, Lord Giffard of Brimpsfield (q.v., *Gloucestershire*), who fought on the king's side in the Barons' War, and died in 1290. He
was made to pay a fine of 300 marks for his escapade, which reminds one of
a similar feat perpetrated by Simon, Lord Lovat. Maud's daughter Margery
married Henry de Lacy, Earl of Lincoln, and in 4 Edward IV. is represented
as holding this manor and castle. Clifford next appears to have been given by
the Crown to the Mortimers, and after the House of York came to the throne,
it was retained as royal property. It is probable that at that period Clifford
Castle ceased to be inhabited, and therefore fell into neglect, disrepair, and ruin.
An account of the place, written early in the present century, says that from
the antiquity of some oak-trees growing about the ruins and mounds, 300 or
400 years old, it is likely that the castle has been disused as a fortress, if not
in ruins, at a very distant period. It speaks of the picturesqueness and beauty
of the scenery amid which Clifford stands, with the Wye flowing round it, and
winding about in glittering clearness among the rich meadows, encircled with
fine hills, which are fringed with forest and excellently cultivated fields.

The remains of this fortress, Fair Rosamond's cradle, are not very extensive ;
they consist of a fragment of the N. wall, very massive, standing on the edge
of the cliff. At the N.W. is a round tower, and there are scanty vestiges of the
square E. tower, which perhaps was the keep. There were an outer and an
inner bailey, or ward, and the existing remains belong solely to the latter,

which seems to have measured about 100 feet square. Only one of its many
towers survives, with some garderobes. On the N. front are to be traced the
foundations of the two circular towers flanking the gatehouse to the inner ward,
in front of which was a ditch dividing the two wards, and running from the
ravine on the E. to the river, along which ran the curtain wall. On the S. is
a curious triangular outwork without any traces now of masonry, perhaps
defended by a stockade. The outer ward had the river bank for its defence
on the W. and on the S. the ditch, the other sides being protected by the

CLIFFORD

ravine and a wall. In the centre is a mound, and the approach appears to
have been from the N. side. Whatever the antiquity of the earthworks, the
existing masonry does not appear to be older than Henry II. or Henry III.
The castle chapel, on the E. of the outer ward, was standing in 1657, near the
present cottage, which seems to have been built from its ruin.

There is an island higher up the river, below which was the ford; this was
a very shallow one, and there is another and a deeper one lower down the
stream. On the island stood the Castle Mill, and the Castle Park extended from
the river downwards, where is a tract still called "The Parks."

The manor of Clifford, together with the castle, was in 1547 granted to Lord

Clinton for his services against the Scots at the memorable battle of Pinkie. Clinton was admiral in command of the English fleet which co-operated with great effect with the land forces under the Protector Somerset, by lying in the bay of Musselburgh, near Edinburgh, and supporting them with fire from the ships. The late owner was Mr. Tomkyns Dew, whose grandfather obtained the ruins from the Wardour family.

CROFT (minor)

AT the time of the Domesday Survey, one Bernard held the manor of Croft, and from him the family of Croft deduce their origin, having been landowners in this county from the time of Edward the Confessor until the close of the eighteenth century. Richard Croft captured Prince Edward, son of Henry VI., at Tewkesbury, and for his valour during the insurrection under Lambert Simnel, was made a knight banneret on the field of Stoke by Henry VII. In the sixteenth century (1551) James Croft, only son of Richard Croft of Croft Castle by Catherine, daughter of Richard Herbert of Montgomery, was appointed, by Edward VI., Lord Deputy of Ireland, and was afterwards made Deputy Constable of the Tower of London; but when he headed the Protestant movement in Herefordshire in favour of Lady Jane Grey, he was himself brought to the Tower, and being examined on the charge of being also concerned in Wyatt's rebellion, was condemned, but allowed to escape. Queen Elizabeth made him governor of Berwick, and he was comptroller of her household. His grandson, Sir Herbert, succeeded him, whose son Sir William was killed in 1645 at Stokesay Castle, Shropshire, fighting for King Charles. His brother was Herbert, Dean and Bishop of Hereford, and chaplain to the king, whose son and heir, long time M.P. for the county, was made baronet. Sir Archer, the third baronet, straitened in means through the losses of the family in the Civil War, was in 1746 obliged to part with his ancestral estates, and the castle passed from the mortgagee to the families of Knight, and then Johnes, and then by sale to Mr. Somerset Davies of Wigmore, whose grandson, the Rev. W. K. Davies, is the present proprietor.

The approach to the ruins is through a fine avenue of beeches half a mile in length. Leland, early in the sixteenth century, speaks of Croft as a ditched and walled castle set on the brow of a hill. Perhaps a castle existed here in Norman times, but there are now no traces of any building earlier than the fourteenth century. Croft is a quadrangular structure having a circular tower at each of the four corners of the outer wall, enclosing a fine courtyard; but in 1746 there was no fourth side, and the building stood in the form of an **E**, after a custom not unusual in those days, in compliment to Queen Elizabeth.

In 1645 Croft was dismantled by the Royalists, to prevent the fortress proving of utility to the enemy, and much damage was wrought on it then. The N. side, where is a square centre turret between the two corner towers, suffered least. Since then the whole fabric has been modernised, and West Hall was built probably on the site of the old castle hall.

CUBLINGTON, or CUBBESTON (*non-existent*)

ALL traces of this castle, which was in the parish of Madley, have long disappeared.

CUSOP (*non-existent*)

THIS was a peel, the site of which is no longer visible. It belonged to a family named Clavenogh from the time of Henry III. to that of Edward IV.

DORSTON (*non-existent*)

MR. ROBINSON says this castle was situated on the river Dore, at the head of the Golden Valley, but it has disappeared. Henry IV. entrusted it to Sir Walter Fitzwalter, when the place was probably captured by Glendwr and destroyed. During the Civil War in 1645, it is mentioned that the forces of Charles met "neare Durston Castle." The lands belong to the Cornewall family.

EARDISLEY (*non-existent*)

THIS is included in a list of Hereford castles early in the reign of Henry III., and from its situation in the rich valley of the Wye, was exposed to the frequent inroads of Welsh invaders. The De Bohuns held it during the Barons' War, but Edward I. gave it to Roger de Clifford, who had afterwards to restore it to De Bohun (*Robinson*). On the extinction, however, of the earldom of Hereford, it vested in the Crown. Next it became the property and abode of the Baskervilles, a family of warriors who lived in the reigns of Henry V. to Henry VII. In the Civil War of the seventeenth century Sir Humphrey Baskerville took the king's side, and his castle was burnt to the ground, only one of the gatehouses remaining intact, in which the unfortunate family, then reduced to poverty, were living in 1670, but soon after the family was extinguished.

The castle stood on the W. side of the church, insulated by a threefold moat; but these and the mound of the keep are the only relics; not a fragment of the castle exists.

EATON TREGOZ (*non-existent*)

BUILT perhaps temp. John, in the parish of Foy, this castle was the property of the Tregoz family. Robert de Tregoz carried the Barons' standard at Evesham, and fell in that field of slaughter; then it came to the Grandisons, who had licence to crenellate in 1309, and who were extinct in 1375. There is no further notice of the place.

ECCLESWALL (*non-existent*)

THE castle now called Eccleswall Court lies 3½ miles from Ross, on the road between Broms Ash and Castle End, and is interesting as the cradle of the great family of Talbot in England, a castle being erected here between 1160 and 1170 by Richard de Talbot, who obtained the lordship from Henry II. He was succeeded by his eldest son and their direct descendants. In 1331 Sir George Talbot had summons to Parliament as Baron Talbot, and Richard, the second baron, died in 1356 possessed of immense estates, including Goodrich Castle, where he resided (*q.v.*), giving up Eccleswall, which accordingly declined, and finally, like Goodrich, on the death of the last Earl of Shrewsbury, in 1616, passed with his daughter Elizabeth in marriage to Henry Grey, Earl of Kent, and was sold.

About 100 yards E. from the farm-house is a circular green mound, about 40 yards in diameter, upon which, within the memory of living people, there stood a large square tower of masonry, and a building used as a barn. There existed also here at one time a chapel, and on the N. side is a large pond and a line of fish stews.

At the end of the last century, a silver seal of Philip de Henbury was found in the ruins.

ELLINGHAM (*non-existent*)

ELLINGHAM, in the parish of Much Marcle, was in the fourteenth century the property of the Audley family. It was the home of Sir James Audley, K.G., the hero of Poictiers, told of by Froissart. Nothing is recorded concerning the castle, the site of which is near the town, within a thick wood, but there is nothing to be seen (see *Stowey, Somerset*).

EWIAS HAROLD (*non-existent*)

THIS castle stood in the S.W. corner of the county, about six miles from the border, and being liable to attacks from the Welsh frontier, was well fortified against them. The position chosen for it was where two streams uniting formed an elevated triangle of ground, the larger one defending the

N. side, while on the S and E. were a brook and ravine; then a deep ditch was cut across the neck, and the excavation thrown up into a huge mound, in the usual manner, possibly in the tenth century. This circular burh, measuring 120 feet across, and from 60 to 70 feet high, occupied the W. end of the area, and upon it in Norman times was built a circular or polygonal shell keep. On the E. was a courtyard where were placed the castle buildings, and a curtain wall surrounded the whole, outside of which the slopes of the ground fell thirty or forty feet.

Not a particle of masonry exists, everything, even to the foundations, having been overthrown and removed for building purposes elsewhere.

In Domesday, this castle was held by Ahured de Merleberge, or Marleboro, a great tenant-in-chief in Wiltshire; and in 1100 it was owned by one Harold, son of Randulph, Earl of Hereford, "The Timid," of Sudeley, Gloucester, a grand-nephew of the Confessor. He had five sons (the castle of Sudeley going to John), the eldest of whom, Robert de Ewias, had this castle, and his grand-daughter Sybilla married (1) Robert de Tregoz, (2) William de Newmarch, s.p., (3) Roger de Clifford, from whom sprung the earls of Cumberland. Sybilla died 20 Henry III. Her son Robert de Tregoz was one of the barons killed at Evesham in 1265, and his son John de Tregoz, dying in 1300, left three daughters, the eldest of whom, Clarice, married Roger la Warre, whose descendants for three generations succeeded at this castle; but in 13 Richard II. it had been permanently alienated into the hands of the Montacute family, and in 1429 (7 Henry VI.) Thomas, Earl of Salisbury, possessed it. Thence it went, like other estates, to the Beauchamps, and finally Edward, Lord Abergavenny, died seised of the castle and manor, as well as of the manor of Trefiort Ewias, Wiltshire.

FROME, KINGSLAND, AND KINGTON (non-existent)

ALL these places are known to have existed in Herefordshire, but even their sites cannot now be traced.

GOODRICH (chief)

THIS splendid fortress occupies a commanding position on the top of a red sandstone hill, forming a small promontory in the S.E. corner of the county, on the border of Monmouthshire, and, environed with woods, has a fine appearance with the Wye sweeping along its base. It was founded in very early days, after an incursion of the Welsh hordes, in order to protect the ferry below it, which formed part of the chief thoroughfare between England and the marches of Wales. We find the possession of this castle by

William the Marshall, Earl of Pembroke, confirmed by King John in 1203, the
king being strenuously supported by him against the rebellious barons. He
became, however, at the death of John, the mainstay of the kingdom, and was
appointed governor of the young Henry III.; being chosen Protector of the
realm, he delivered it from the presence of a foreign army, defeating the French
with great loss at Lincoln, and thus putting an end to the Civil War. He died
in 1219, leaving five sons, who all succeeded to Goodrich, but all of whom died
without issue—the eldest son, William, having married one of the king's daughters.

GOODRICH

The tomb of this great noble is to be seen in the Temple Church, together
with those of two of his sons. His daughters therefore succeeded to his estates,
the eldest bringing Goodrich in marriage to Warren de Monchensi (Mont Cenis).
Her only son William fought on the popular side in the Barons' War at Lewes,
and accordingly, after his capture at Kenilworth, his estates being forfeited
were granted by Henry III. to William de Valence, the French half-brother to
the king, who was married to Monchensi's sister Joan; he obtained restitution
of them later, but was killed some years after, by the fall of a tower at the
siege of Drosselan Castle, when fighting under Edward I. He left an only
daughter, but the De Valences seem to have enjoyed Goodrich. William died
in 1296, and was buried in Westminster Abbey, and his son Aymer de Valence

was murdered in 1323, when attending Queen Isabella in France; then Goodrich, falling to his niece Elizabeth Comyn, went in marriage with her to her husband, Richard, 2nd Baron Talbot. This nobleman served in the French wars of Edward III., and gained much ransom-money there, which he expended on the fortress; he died in 1356, and was succeeded by his eldest son Gilbert, who also served in France under the Black Prince. His grandson was Sir John Talbot, 1st Earl of Shrewsbury, who, after taking his share of all the fighting in France during this reign and that of Henry V., was killed when eighty years of age at Châtillon in 1453 (see *Sheffield*). His son was one of the band of nobles who were killed fighting round the tent of their sovereign at the battle of Northampton in 1460, when his possessions were seized by the Yorkists and given to William Herbert, Earl of Pembroke; however, John, 3rd Earl of Shrewsbury, managed, probably after the reverse of the White Rose at Wakefield four months later, to recover his estates, and Goodrich remained with his descendants till the seventeenth century. Gilbert, the seventh earl, died in 1616 without male issue, and Goodrich was inherited by his daughter Elizabeth, wife of Henry Grey, Earl of Kent. The castle was held in the Civil War for the king, and bravely defended against the forces of the Parliament by Sir Henry Lingen in 1646 until, the fabric being much injured by the besiegers' heavy artillery

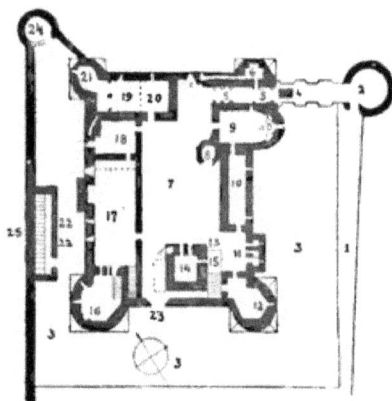

GOODRICH

1. APPROACH.	13. DUNGEON (below).
2. BARBICAN.	14. KEEP.
3. MOAT.	15. PRISON.
4. DRAWBRIDGE.	16. OFFICES' TOWER.
5. ENTRANCE.	17. GREAT HALL.
6. PORTER'S LODGE.	18. ANTEROOM.
7. INNER WARD.	19. DRAWING ROOM (kit hous
8. BEACON TOWER.	20. (under).
9. CHAPEL.	21. LADIES' TOWER.
10. STABLES.	22. GARRISON TABLES.
11. GARDEROBES.	23. PERCH'S WALL.
12. STATE PRISON.	24. PLEASANCE TOWER.

and the stores of the garrison being consumed, the fortress was surrendered, when it was slighted by order of Parliament, and left a wreck.

The general plan of the castle is a parallelogram with large towers at the four corners, protected by the river and a steep cliff on the N. and W. sides, and on the landward side by a deep ditch cut in the rock, with a circular barbican leading to a drawbridge at the N.E. angle, where the entrance lies through a narrow vaulted passage, 50 feet in length, defended by gates and two portcullises, and rows of machicoulis. Close to the entrance, on the left hand entering the courtyard, is the chapel, restored temp. Henry VI. and VII., and attached to it is the warder's or deacon tower, a tall octagonal turret;

next to which extended along the E. front a range of stabling for the lord
and his knights, with windows and seats looking down on the deep ditch.
Then comes a garderobe tower, and next to it at the S.E. angle the prison
tower in three storeys, on the recesses of which in the middle storey are
some curious carvings in relief, perhaps of the time of Henry IV., whose
cognizance, a swan, together with that of his victim Richard II., a white hart
couchant, are there sculptured, with other figures. The old Norman keep
of the twelfth century stands near the prison tower, close to the outer S.

GOODRICH (LADIES' TOWER)

wall. It is a small building, 14 feet square internally, in three storeys, the
floors having been of timber, and its inner front contains two windows; a
spiral stair in the N.W. corner leads from the first floor to the roof, the
entrance having been in the usual way by an exterior staircase, in a forebuilding, to the first floor on the E. side. Here is the breach made in the
outer wall by the Parliament cannon, at point-blank range, from the other
side of the S. ditch. The S.W. angle is occupied by the great circular W. or
officers' tower, which, together with the noble adjoining banqueting-hall, is
of the time of Edward I.; this hall is 65 feet long by 30 broad, a proportion
usual in Edwardian halls, and has a good fireplace and trefoil-headed lancet
windows, together with a fine oriel; at its N. end is the solar, with a window

looking into the hall, beyond which, along the N. face, is the great reception
or baronial hall, at the W. end of which is a very fine double-pointed arch,
supported by a single shaft, at the N.W. angle, leading to the Ladies' Tower,
which formed the lodging of the family. A large portion of this tower has
fallen—the work, it is said, of the siege in 1646; but it is difficult to see where
the battering-guns of that period could have been placed. Below this was
the pleasaunce or garden, with a small tower, and the garrison stabling.

In 1740, on the death of Henry, Duke of Kent, s.p., Goodrich was sold to
Admiral Thomas Griffin, from whom it passed to his brother George, whose
daughter Catherine, married to Major Marriott of Sellarsbrooke, inherited the
property. In 1876 Mrs. Marriott gave the castle to her adopted daughter on
her marriage with Mr. Edmund F. Bosanquet of Goodrich Court, and Mrs.
Bosanquet is the present lady of the manor and castle.

HEREFORD (*non-existent*)

THE absence of all vestiges of this great fortress exemplifies the lengths to
which a spirit of reckless destructiveness and careless vandalism, exerted
in favour of some supposed "benefit" to their precious townsfolk, frequently
lead municipalities. This we have seen of recent years in the lamentable
destruction worked in Rome, where, amongst other outrages on that ancient
mother of cities, the beautiful gardens of Sallust with their buildings have
been swept away, and the pleasant valley levelled up, to build a vulgar
boulevard. Leland says that Hereford Castle had been "one of the fayrest,
largest and strongest castells in all England." It was nearly as large as
Windsor, enclosing an area of about 5½ acres. A great portion of it remained into the last century, but in 1748 the site was levelled and converted
into "a public promenade." Stukeley speaks of it as "a noble work, built by
one of the Edwards before the Conquest." He says, "The city of Hereford
is encompassed with strong walls, towers, and lunets, all which with the
embattailments are pretty perfect, and enabled them to withstand a most
vigorous siege of the Scots army under General Lesly." The situation of the
castle was by nature very strong; on the S. side, the river Wye, flowing below
the steep bank 20 feet high, and the eminence whereon it was built, effectually
defended that front; while the little stream Eign in a deep ravine kept the E.
front; and the N. and W. lines were protected by a broad moat. Speed gives
a rough view of this castle, showing on the E. the great outer court, called
the Castle Green, or bailey, surrounded by strong walls with flanking towers,
the entrance gatehouse being on the N. side, approached by a drawbridge
with stone arches across the moat; on the W. end was a smaller enclosure
of pentagonal trace, walled, and with towers at the angles, which formed the

inner court, in the centre of which stood, on a high artificial mound, the great keep, consisting of a cluster of four or five lesser embattled towers with one lofty tower in the centre. Of this massive and extensive fortress not a vestige now remains; even the great mound of the keep was levelled, and all that is left are the names of the localities, Castle Green, Castle Street, and Castle Mill.

It is probable that in very early times a Saxon stronghold of earth was formed here, upon which Earl Harold began to erect a castle of stone, completed by others after his death. In the time of William the Conqueror, Fitz Osborn, the first Norman earl of Hereford, was governor of this castle, and these earls held it until Earl Milo, the son of Walter, the Constable of England, espousing the side of the Empress Maud, received the castle of Hereford from her, during her short period of success; he was displaced by Stephen, but his son and heir, Roger, was made governor by Henry II., who also restored to him his father's lost honours, together with "the mote and whole castel of Hereford." This earl, however, joined with Mortimer in resisting this king's order for the demolition of the numerous unnecessary castles that had been reared in England during the wars of Stephen and Maud, especially on the Borderlands, and Henry withdrew to himself the earldom of Hereford and the castle (cir. 1115). King John frequently came here, from 1200 to 1217, when endeavouring to obtain for himself the assistance of the Welsh, and in his time the castle was committed to the tutelage of Hubert de Burgh, his Grand Justiciary. Henry III. was here as often as his father, and it was at Hereford that the first hostile acts occurred at the opening of the Barons' War. Peter, son of Simon de Montfort, Earl of Leicester, was then governor, and hither was brought prisoner, after the battle of Lewes, Prince Edward. Here too it was that the prince cleverly escaped on the horse he was exercising on the plain of Widemarsh, N. of the town, by previously tiring out his companions' horses, and then riding away to the castle of Wigmore (q.v.). In Hereford Castle, 17 Henry III., "a fair and decent chapel" was added to the king's apartments. Here it was that Queen Isabella, the "She-Wolf of France," declared her son, afterwards Edward III., Protector of the Realm; here too the younger Despencer,—the great favourite of Edward II.,—who had been taken at Bristol, was hanged on a gallows 50 feet high. For a time this castle was under John of Gaunt, but after the disturbances had been quelled on the Welsh border, and no more troubles were expected, its repairs were neglected, and so fell rapidly into disrepair. "It hath been decayed," says Leland in 1520, "since the Bohuns' time"; the last De Bohun, Earl of Hereford, being Humphrey, who lived late temp. Edward III., and he adds that in his time the drawbridge was "cleane down, and the whole castel tended towards ruine."

After the battle of Mortimer's Cross, Owen Tudor, stepfather to King Henry VI., and some other officers of rank suffered death here, after confinement in the castle. In the Civil War of the Commonwealth, the keep, being

fortified and defended, received much damage; it was held by the Royalists
in April 1643, but on Sir William Waller appearing before it with a strong
force, it was surrendered to him after a very short resistance.

By a survey made in 1652, we learn that the outer court and governor's lodge
were then completely ruinous, for the fabric had evidently been deserted before
that date.   At last a Colonel Birch sold to the county members and sundry
other representatives, for £600, "all the circuit and precinct of the ruinous
castle of Hereford," when the ancient structure was left to the mercy of the
town authorities.

HUNTINGTON (*non-existent*)

MR. ROBINSON shows us that a few fragments of walls standing on
a circular hillock are all the remains existing of this castle, which was a
large one standing at the brink of a steep ravine which defended it on the
N. and W., while on the S. and E. it was protected by a moat, supplied by a
neighbouring rivulet.

North of the early mound, the outer walls formed an oval enclosure,
probably with towers, and on the mound there was a keep on the E. side, of
usual Norman construction.   The entrance was approached by a drawbridge,
but what the buildings were in the court cannot now be known, though by
the manor rolls they seem to have been complete.   The earthworks are very
perfect, and we see the outer and inner wards with the ditches and moat.

This castle seems to have been built temp. Henry III., and was then owned
by William de Braose, Lord of Bramber Castle and of Brecknock, and many
other places, which passed with Huntington to his widow Eva, sister of Richard
Marshall, Earl of Pembroke, and in 1248 to her daughter Elenor, married
to Humphrey de Bohun, eldest son of the Earl of Hereford.   He joined
the side of Simon de Montfort in the Barons' War, and after the fight and
slaughter of Evesham, was sent prisoner to Beeston Castle in Cheshire,
where he soon after died.   Still Huntington continued with the Bohuns
for four generations, and the story of this race of warriors is a part of the
history of our country.   The last of them dying 1372 without male issue, his
two daughters inherited, the eldest marrying Thomas of Woodstock, sixth
son of Edward III., and the other Henry, then Earl of Derby, afterwards King
Henry IV.   The latter, created Duke of Hereford by his cousin Richard II.,
possessed Huntington Castle among others through his wife, and lived here
occasionally until his accession to the throne; and it was here, at the ferry of
Huntington, that he heard of the birth at Monmouth Castle of his eldest son
Henry, who thereby acquired the name of Henry of Monmouth.   The earldom
of Hereford was then renewed in the person of Edmund de Stafford, Earl of
Buckingham, who married the only daughter of Thomas of Woodstock; he

was killed at the battle of Shrewsbury (July 31, 1403) fighting on the king's side, when the castle came to Humphrey de Stafford, 1st Duke of Buckingham, at whose death in 1460 it was found to be in a ruinous state. The unfortunate second duke Henry vainly sought refuge here from the wrath of Richard III. A survey of the castle was made when Edward, the last duke, fell a victim to Henry VIII. and Wolsey (see *Thornbury, Gloucester*), when there was evidently a tower in it used as a prison, and in 1670 the keep too was standing. After the attainder and execution of this last duke, the manor and the ruins became the property of the Crown, and then passed through many hands by sale. In 1818 Huntington was bought by Edward Watkins Cheese, whose representatives continue to hold it.

KILPECK (*non-existent*)

ABOUT seven miles from Hereford stood this once important Border fortress. It was by design of great strength, in order to restrain the incursions of the Welsh tribes. The Conqueror granted it to William Fitz Norman, who was succeeded by his son Hugh, and grandson Henry de Kilpeck. King John seems to have used the place as an abode when on his frequent journeys to the Welsh marches. Hugh de Kilpeck, about the middle of the thirteenth century, left a daughter who married William de Waleraund or Waleran, who thus obtained Kilpeck. His son Robert was a Royalist baron of much importance during the Civil War in Henry III.'s reign; he was one of the ambassadors to the French king in 1253 and 1260, and Sheriff of Kent and Gloster. The insurgent barons confiscated his lands, but the King, for whom he fought at Evesham, rewarded him with grants of Hugh de Neville's forfeited estates, and made him one of the four governors over London. He died without issue in 1272, leaving Kilpeck to his nephew and heir, Alan de Plukenet. In the Wars of the Roses, Kilpeck fell to the Crown, and was given by Edward IV. to William Herbert, 1st Earl of Pembroke; he however was taken prisoner at the battle at Edgecote (1469), and was beheaded at Northampton by order of the Earl of Warwick. After this, the castle came into the possession of James Butler, 1st Earl of Ormond, and early in the seventeenth century it passed to the family of Pye, at which time it was in a decayed condition, and though during the war in Charles' reign it held a garrison under Sir Walter Pye, it was of little use as a fortress, and was slighted and demolished. The Pyes followed James II. into exile, and had the title of Barons Kilpeck. Two large fragments of the keep, enclosing a space of from 70 to 80 yards in diameter, are all that remain now of this Border stronghold, built of massive masonry upon an elevation near the church. The site is partially surrounded by two wide moats or ditches, and as the hill they enclose is lofty, and the sides very steep, the situation was a commanding one in the valley of the river Worme. The keep was a polygonal shell one, set on an ancient Saxon artificial mound, and surrounded by earthworks of still greater antiquity.

KINNERSLEY (*non-existent*)

THERE was a mediæval castle here, belonging to the De la Bere family, who held it from the fourteenth till late in the sixteenth century, but the existing Elizabethan house, which was built on the site of the castle, has obliterated all traces of it.

LONGTOWN (*minor*)

THIS is one of a chain of fortresses built along the frontier to restrain the incursions of the Welsh, and was formerly called Ewias Lacy, or Clodock Castle. It stands on the site of a Roman station, and was reared by W. Fitz Osborne, the first Norman Earl of Hereford, who also built the castles of Wigmore and Clifford, and others; from him it went to Walter de Lacy, a warrior of Senlac, who died in 1085, when his family continued in possession. We find Walter de Lacy (see *Ludlow, Salop*) rebelling against John, and having a heavy fine to pay to retain his lands, a usual method with that king for obtaining money. He was son-in-law to William de Braose, Lord of Bramber and Brecknock, and Maud his wife, who with some of her family were starved to death by John at Windsor (see *Bramber, Sussex*). De Lacy was faithful to Henry III., and died worn out and blind in 1241, when his two grand-daughters inherited his estates; the younger of them married John de Verdon and brought him Longtown. De Verdon went to the Holy Land as a Crusader with the expedition which Prince Edward (afterwards Edward I.) led there in 1270; he died in 1274, and when his son died without male issue, his grand-daughter Elizabeth succeeded to the property; she was married to Bartholomew de Burghersh, who was one of the most distinguished warriors of Edward III. in the French wars, and was made a Knight of the Garter. Their son was the famous Thomas de Spencer, Earl of Gloucester, who adhered too closely to his king, Richard II., and thereby lost both his lands and his life.

His only daughter Isabel married Richard Beauchamp, Earl of Worcester, whose heiress Elizabeth Beauchamp became wife of Sir Edward Neville, K.G., 1st Lord Bergavenny, who thus obtained Longtown, and with whose descendants the lands still remain.

Longtown clearly occupied a position of much importance in times of border warfare, and was a place of great strength. Its trace resembled that of many similar fortresses. An outer wall, about 20 feet high, enclosed a bailey or court measuring nearly 100 yards on the square, in the N.W. angle of which, on an artificial mound, stood a circular tower or keep, of which the greater part still remains, having three round buttresses or turrets at equal distances, between which are circular openings for windows (*Murray*). The walls are very thick, and are composed of a hard laminated shale built in thin layers. Access to the inner court is through an arched gateway defended by a portcullis and strong circular flanking towers.

LYONSHALL (*minor*)

LYONSHALL is mentioned in the Survey of Domesday as Lenehalle, in the possession of Roger de Lacy, and was temp. Edward the Confessor the property of Earl Harold, son of Godwin, and under the De Lacys it was held by a branch of the family of d'Ebroicis or Devereux, who afterwards became its lords. One Stephen of that race adhered to the fortunes of King John, and his successor fell fighting on the side of the barons at the battle of Evesham, in 1265, when his lands were seized and granted by Henry III. to Roger Mortimer of Wigmore; the disinherited son, William Devereux, however, on payment of the fine of 100 marks, obtained restitution of Lyonshall Castle. Litigation appears to have supervened, and the castle afterwards passed to William Touchet (temp. Edward II.), on whose death it became part of the estate of Bartholomew, Lord Badlesmere, "a great baron and as great a rebel," as he is called. The story of the offence given to Queen Isabella in 1321 is told in the account of Leeds Castle, Kent (*q.v.*), and it is probable that the ignominious death inflicted on this baron, who being taken in arms with the Earl of Lancaster at Borough-bridge the next year was brought to Canterbury and hung there, was owing to the resentment of the queen at the insult offered to her by his wife at Leeds. At any rate Badlesmere's son Giles was permitted to succeed in the estates, and the attainder was reversed in 1328 in his favour; he died, however, *s.p.* in 1338, and his sister Maud inheriting Lyonshall, brought it to her husband, John de Vere, 7th Earl of Oxford, who fought at Crecy and Poictiers.

Towards the end of the fourteenth century, we find the estate transferred to Sir Simon Burley, who was a Knight of the Garter, and had been a favourite companion of the Black Prince; but he did not long enjoy it, for being concerned in the attempt of the Duke of Gloucester, uncle of Richard II., to usurp the royal authority, he was charged with high treason, and executed. Richard then conferred Lyonshall upon Sir John Devereux, the husband of Margaret, daughter of John, 7th Earl of Oxford, who also succeeded Burley in his stall at Windsor and other honours; but in default of male issue, his daughter brought the castle in marriage to Walter, 5th Baron

Fitz Walter, and again in the same way (temp. Henry V.) Lyonshall got back into the Devereux family, where it remained until the death of Robert, 3rd Earl of Essex, in 1641. His daughter, who was Duchess of Somerset, inherited it, and at her death bequeathed it to the Thynnes, whose descendant, the first Marquess of Bath, sold Lyonshall to John Cheese, and the representatives of that gentleman still possess the castle site.

The fortress was never made use of as a residence after the early part of the fifteenth century, and so fell into decay, as has been the fate of all such structures not suited to the improved requirements of the age. If the owner at that era was not wealthy enough to remodel or rebuild, he deserted the old fortress, whose accommodation was too scanty or too rude for the growing refinement of the family. Leland says, "It seems to have been a noble structure, but now [cir. 1538] nothing remains of it but the old walls." At the present day one can trace the form and extent of the castle by the two moats which still exist, and by the walls of the inner bailey, which are tolerably perfect. These walls enclosed an irregular space, about 60 yards across, with towers at the angles. On the N. side was a circular keep, about 12 yards in diameter, entered by a flight of steps on the S. As was generally the case in this country, the church was built close to the castle, and now the former alone survives.

MOCCAS (*non-existent*)

HUGH DE FRÊNE had a licence in 1291 (21 Edward I.) to build a stone and lime wall to fortify his house, such wall to be of the height of ten feet below the crenellation or battlement; and his family were here in 1375. The site can still be traced in a meadow on the E. side of the park, having a swampy circle round it, and a few grassy hillocks (*Robinson*).

MORTIMER'S CASTLE

VERY little is known about the castle that bore this name, except that it was one of the fortresses belonging to that powerful family. In the beginning of the last century its site could be traced near the church, but all marks are now effaced.

PEMBRIDGE (*minor*)

THIS castle, distant five miles from Monmouth, was a fee of the Honour of Wigmore, and was thus held in the beginning of the thirteenth century by Ralph de Pembridge, whose abode it was, though their chief seat was at Pembridge town. It was afterwards appended to the manor of

Newland, and was held temp. Edward III. by Richard Pembridge, whose son Richard was a great warrior, and a very important officer on King Edward's staff in the French wars, fighting at Crecy, and at the siege of Calais, and obtaining great renown at the battle of Poictiers. The king rewarded him with many honours, making him Custodian of Southampton Castle in 1361, and then of Bamborough Castle; he was also Lord Warden of the Cinque Ports. In 1368 he was made a Knight of the Garter, and appointed Chamberlain of the Royal Household; he died in 1375, and his tomb in Hereford Cathedral is well known. His castle of Pembridge was inherited by his sister, who was the wife of his comrade in arms, Sir Richard Burley, a nephew of Sir Simon Burley of Lyonshall (q.v.), and a soldier of almost equal renown. Sir Richard had one of the principal commands at the battle of Auray, Brittany, in 1364, and distinguished himself greatly in other engagements in France; he likewise obtained the Garter in 1382, and a splendid monument adorned his tomb in old St. Paul's. He too left no issue, and after his death we find Pembridge possessed by the Hopton family; they gave way in 1427 to Thomas, Duke of Exeter, the third son of John of Gaunt. It then fell into the hands of the Knights of St. John, and after the Reformation, in the sixteenth century, it belonged to a family named Baynham, and in the next century it was sold to Sir Walter Pye, knight.

During the Civil War it was held, in 1644, as an outpost of the royal forces, lying at the king's fortress of Monmouth. After the dastardly betrayal of the latter castle, Pembridge underwent some severe usage at the hands of the Parliamentary forces under General Murray, and was taken after a two days' siege; it was, however, recaptured by the Royalist troops, when, after an investment lasting two weeks, provisions failed the garrison. The castle was afterwards bought from the Pyes by one George Kemble, who repaired the ruins and rendered the place habitable in 1675. Afterwards we find it sold by the Townley family to Sir Joseph Bailey, baronet, and the structure is still owned by his descendants.

The trace of this fortress is quadrangular, enclosing an area of 45 yards by 35, the walls being protected by a moat 36 feet wide, with a defensible banquette of earth behind it. Part of it is in a tolerably perfect condition, although many of the buildings have disappeared, and what is left has been converted into a farm-house. The entrance is on the S. side, and is flanked by two unequal circular towers, the approach being through a long vaulted passage of pointed arches, 33 feet in length, well defended throughout by three gates and two portcullises. Of the keep in the S.W. angle only the basement remains; and the great hall has been converted into a parlour and kitchen for the farmer. In a square turret is a curious staircase formed of solid blocks of oak 5 feet long, which is undoubtedly original; there are also in the old fortress some remarkable towers which well deserve examination.

PENZARD

THIS was a castle belonging to the Talbot family in the thirteenth century, or perhaps only a fortified hunting lodge, like Knepp in Sussex (*q.v.*), in the wooded hillside above Weston, near Ross. There are still to be seen some fragments of massive walls and the remains of groinings (*Robinson*).

RICHARD'S CASTLE (*non-existent*)

THE place of this name is remarkable as having been possessed and built by a Norman lord, one Richard Fitz-Scrob, of the court of the Confessor, before the Conquest. It stood below the summit of the Vinnall Hill, which extends from Ludlow, on the borders of Shropshire, and commanded a grand and very extensive prospect over the rich lands of the Welsh frontier. Placed on the very high ground of the spur, it is amply defended on the W. and S. by a broad and deep ravine inclining to the S., and by a lesser valley on the N. which meets the gorge below the castle ; upon the E. side had been raised vast prehistoric defences of earthwork. Just above the meeting of the two glens had been thrown up a vast and steep mound, 60 feet in

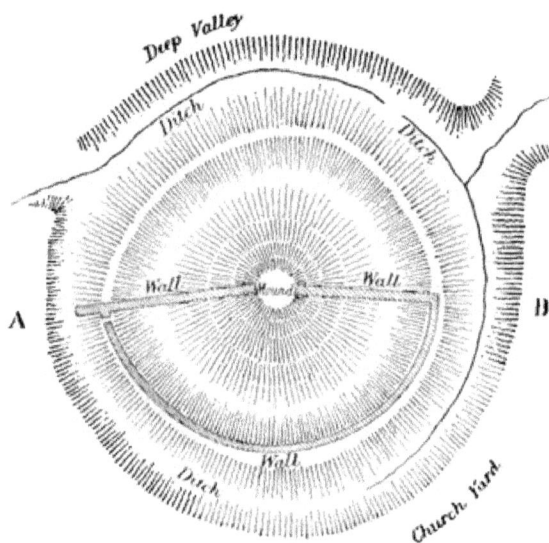

RICHARD'S CASTLE

height, with a summit 30 feet in diameter, 300 feet above the valley, and surrounded by a deep ditch, beyond which was a high rampart of earth, and, on the E. side, a second ditch.

The Norman parvenu coming here found himself opposed by Earl Godwin and the English in 1052, and again by Harold in 1056, but he appears to have held his ground, and after the coming of Duke William, Fitz-Scrob received from the Conqueror further grants of land in this county and elsewhere. He probably was at the outset obliged to further fortify his position, and this he did by erecting on the crown of the mound some sort of Norman keep, supporting it by two massive wing walls of masonry on either side, which ran down the sides of the mound, and thus divided it in half, N. and S.; he connected their two extremities by a semicircular wall, along and round the counterscarp of the ditch; then within this segmental enclosure were built the lodgings and other works of the castle. Outside this wall encircling the mound ran the outer moat, which was supplied with water from a brook above.

From this founder and his son Osbert, came Hugo Fitz-Osbert or Osborne, in the reign of Henry I., whose descendant dying cir. 1200, left a daughter Margaret at that time married to Robert de Mortimer, but who had, as her third husband, William de Stuteville, the possessor of the manor. He died in 1259, and devised the manor and castle to his stepson, Hugh de Mortimer, who actively espoused the king's side in the Barons' War, and received other lands from Henry in reward for his services. His descendants enjoyed the property until from want of male issue an heiress brought it in marriage to Sir Richard Talbot of the Eccleswall family; but after the lapse of many years this estate seems to have fallen to the Crown, since we find Edward VI. granting Richard's Castle to Nicholas, Bishop of Worcester. Then one Rowland Bradshaw obtained a long lease of it, and marrying into the Solway family, his son and grandson possessed the place, and the latter sold it to Richard Solway, the son of a member of the Long Parliament, whose descendants are still proprietors of the old ruin and of the parish of Richard's Castle.

Leland says : " It standeth on the toppe of a very rocky hill, well wooded. The Keep, the walls, and the Towers of it stand, but going to Ruyne." A serious engagement took place near this castle during the Civil War in 1645, between a body of Royalists 2000 strong, under Sir Thomas Lansford, who was surprised by the Parliamentary leader, Colonel Birch, and was routed with much slaughter. At the present day, all that survives to show us where this important old border stronghold stood are some fragments of very massive walls hidden in woods. The wall on the N.E. slope is " tolerably perfect " (*Clark*), as is that on the N.W. front. " Farther on the wall seems to have been lifted with gunpowder, and a vast fragment lies in the ditch." The entrance was in an arch on the S. side.

SNODHILL (*minor*)

THE ruin of this fortress, for 200 years the abode of the Chandos family, is on the top of a low hill in the Golden Valley, and near the vanished castle of Dorston. The manor was a barony of this family under the Plantagenet kings, and their manors were held subordinate to the superior court held within these walls. A follower of the Conqueror, with the queer surname of l'Asne, held Snodhill at the Domesday Survey. Then we find (temp. Henry I.) that Roger de Chandos owned it, and his descendants appear to have held the honour of Snodhill during the time of John and during the four succeeding reigns. A Roger de Chandos was knighted, and was governor of Hereford Castle, dying in 1355. His grandson Sir John held this castle against Glendower in 1403; he died *s.p.* in 1421, when the Chandos ownership ended. The castle during the reign of Henry VI. became the property of Richard Nevill, the mighty Earl of Warwick, in right of his wife Anne Beauchamp, who after her husband's death at Barnet, and the accession of the Lancastrian King Henry VII., settled this castle on the king. Queen Elizabeth conferred it on her worthless favourite Robert Dudley, Earl of Leicester; and in 1665 we find it purchased by one William Prosser of London, whose initials with the date 1665 appear on the house of Snodhill Court, which he erected out of the materials of the old castle. It still continues in the Prosser family.

The keep is Norman and octagonal in shape, and therefore it is likely that the castle was built before the end of the twelfth century. One of the gateways is tolerably perfect, being of Edwardian architecture, and with a portcullis groove, and there are still some fragments of the walls of the outer bailey. The place was ruinous even in Leland's time, and it suffered severely at the hands of the Parliamentary forces. Many cannon-balls have been found among the ruins.

STAPLETON

ON the extreme N.W. confines of the county was a mediæval castle, an appanage of Richard's Castle. In 1314 it became the property of Sir Geoffrey de Cornwall, a natural son of Richard, king of the Romans, brother of Henry III., and a family of the name of Cornewall held it till the beginning of the eighteenth century. The castle was demolished in 1645 by the Parliamentary troops, to prevent it falling into the king's hands, and a farmhouse occupies its site.

WEOBLEY

THIS castle stood on the S. side of the town of that name; it was held
by one William Talbot on behalf of Maud the Empress against Stephen,
but it was captured by that king, as were the neighbouring castles of Hereford
and Ludlow. A sketch of the plan of Weobley is to be found in the Harleian
MSS. (6726), Library of the British Museum, which shows its appearance in the
seventeenth century. The trace is a four-sided enclosure of considerable length,
having the S. wall much longer than that on the N. side, with circular towers
at the four corners, and a semicircular bastion midway on each E. and W.
curtain. The entrance was on the N. side between two square towers. At
the S. end of the area, almost touching the S. curtain, was the keep, a square
building with round towers at each angle, standing on a mound, and having
walls 12 feet thick. In front of the keep are shown two quadrangular buildings,
marked "dwellings."

At the entrance of the town exist some large grassy mounds, surrounded
by a wide ditch, the ground enclosed being planted with fine timber trees.

Walter de Lacy was lord of this castle temp. John, and was married to
Margery, daughter of William de Braose, the powerful lord of Bramber,
Sussex (q.v.), whose family were starved to death by John; De Braose took
refuge here in 1208-9. After De Lacy the castle was owned in succession by
the Verdons, the Blounts, and then by the family of Devereux, and so it came
to Walter Devereux, the unfortunate favourite of Elizabeth, by whose daughter
Frances, Duchess of Somerset, it passed in time into the hands of the Marquis
of Bath.

WIGMORE (chief)

WIGMORE is a most interesting ruin among the many castles of the
Welsh borderland, having been in its days of prosperity the splendid
abode of the warlike family of the Mortimers, who intermarried with the
Plantagenets, and themselves begat kings of England.

Ralph de Mortimer, one of the most valiant among the followers of Duke
William at Hastings, whose kinsman he was, being sent by him against
Edric, Earl of Shrewsbury, the then lord of Wigmore, gained possession of
his castle of Wigmore, after a siege, and led the earl himself in bonds to the
king, who consigned his prisoner to perpetual confinement, and granted his land
to Mortimer. Ralph's grandson Hugo or Hugh took part against Henry II.,
but being worsted was forced to surrender the castle to the king. In the fourth
generation later we find Roger de Mortimer, during the Baron's War, an eager
and active supporter of the side of Henry III.; he was married to Maud,

daughter of William de Braose, the lord of Bramber in Sussex (q.v.) and of large estates in Wales, whose bloodthirsty character seems to have been inherited by his daughter, as we shall see. This Roger Mortimer was a young, violent partisan, who, in 1263, by his desolating ravages on the neighbouring properties of barons opposed to the king, which naturally provoked retaliation, may be said to have begun the war. He was prominent at the storming of Northampton, and took part in the battle of Lewes in 1264, when, after being made prisoner, he must have found means to get back to Wigmore, since in the following year we find him assisting there at the escape of Prince Edward from the custody of the barons at Hereford. This escape was cleverly managed. The prince, who was treated as a prisoner on parole, was allowed the companionship of some of his friends, and took riding exercise with them beyond the town. A fine and spirited horse was presented to him, whose paces and speed he expressed a wish to try in order to approve its fitness for a tournament; so the party with the escort repaired to the plain N. of Hereford, called Widemarsh, where the prince, first trying and retrying the horses of his escort, galloped them till they were exhausted, and then mounting his own fresh horse rode straight away from the party, followed by two or three of his friends who were in the plot, and who, meeting the horsemen sent out by Mortimer to assist him, conducted the prince in safety the twenty-four miles to Wigmore Castle (see *Hereford* and *Kenilworth*). This escape raised at once the hopes of the Royalist party, and obliged a counter-movement on the part of Simon de Montfort and the barons, who on both sides collected their forces, and in August of the same year (1265) the fatal battle of Evesham was fought, where De Montfort lost his life, and where Mortimer commanded the third division of the Royal army. Not however content with his death, the old hero's body was mutilated in a horrible manner by the Royalists, and, with an excess of savagery, Roger de Mortimer caused de Montfort's head, fixed on a spear-point, together with his hands, cut from the body, to be sent as a worthy offering to his wife at Wigmore. When the messenger arrived there with this fearful trophy he found the Lady Maud away from the castle, attending mass at the neighbouring abbey founded by the Mortimers, and thither he followed her, still bearing the head, and having in his bosom the maimed hands, sewn up in a cloth. It is said that the lady refused to admit the hands into the castle, which implies that she received the head. Mortimer was rewarded for his services with the forfeited earldom of Oxford and the lands, but the De Veres managed to recover both shortly after.

The grandson of this man was the historical character of Edward the Second's reign. When in 1322 Queen Isabella took up her quarters at the Tower of London, she found in prison there two Mortimers, condemned for treason and attack on the property of the king's favourite, Despencer. The elder of them, Roger, the uncle, died of starvation; but Roger the nephew, the heir of Wigmore, being a handsome fellow of good address, managed to get into the good graces of the queen, and eventually became her paramour. With Isabella's help, he obtained commutation of his death-sentence into imprisonment in the Tower, and afterwards, when convicted of further treason, he made his escape by the queen's aid, and fled to Paris. Then began the hostility of Isabella to the Despencers, and later to the king, from whom she separated in 1325 for ever, to go to Paris to her brother Charles le Bel, King of France—the cruel torturer and murderer of the Knights Templar,—where she was joined by Mortimer. The scandalous attachment of the queen to Mortimer, leading to the murder of King Edward, attracted the odium of the nation against him. He was taken from the queen's side in Nottingham Castle in 1330 (see *Notting-ham*), conducted to London and hanged at Tyburn (being the first person executed there), and all his estates and honours, including the earldom of March, were forfeited to the Crown. His grandson, however, obtained their restoration, dying Earl of March and K.G. in 1360. His only son married the Lady Philippa Plantagenet, daughter and heiress of Lionel, Duke of Clarence, third son of Edward III., whose son, Roger Mortimer, was, in his mother's right, declared by Parliament heir presumptive to the Crown, failing issue of Richard II. He, however, was killed when Deputy in Ireland (1398), and his only son Edmund, 5th Earl of March, died *s.p.*, when the representation of the great house of Mortimer devolved on the son of his sister Ann, married to Richard, Duke of York, grandfather of Edward IV.

Thus Wigmore and the vast estates of the Mortimers fell to the throne, where they rested till Elizabeth granted them to one or two persons ; but in 1601 Wigmore, with a large estate, was conveyed to Thomas Harley of Brampton Brian (*q.v.*) for £2600. Here Sir Robert Harley was born, and, when Lord High Treasurer to Queen Anne, took his titles of Earl of March and Baron Wigmore from them, and his descendants continue in possession of the property.

The ruins of Wigmore extend over a large area, standing on rising ground above the stream that flows around. On the W. and N. it is defended by precipitous ground, but the dismantling which it received after the Civil War has destroyed most of its features. It has a square trace in the outer walls with four corner towers. The Norman keep, placed on a still more ancient high artificial mound, overlooks a wide range of country, and from this tower a strong battlemented wall is continued to the main buildings of the castle ; at the bottom of the hill is a second wall, each wall being defended by a ditch. A drawbridge led to the entrance gateway, on the S. side of the castle, and this is the most perfect part remaining ; the right tower has a staircase leading to the porter's room, from which the portcullis was worked. Lady Brilliana Harley wished to garrison it for the Parliament, like Brampton (*q.v.*), but Colonel Massy not being able to spare men and stores for its defence, it was decided to slight the fortress.

WILTON (*minor*)

THIS castle stands on the right bank of the Wye, which in former times flowed beneath its E. front, opposite the town of Ross, and is almost hidden by overshadowing trees. Leland says it was built by Stephen in 1141, to defend the ford over the river, but Henry I. had before granted the manor of Wilton to Hugo de Longchamp, to hold by service of two men-at-arms in the wars in Wales, and so it is possible that it was Longchamp who built the castle. His descendant, Henry de Longchamp, had a daughter Hawisia, who brought it and the lands in marriage to Reginald de Grey, Lord of Monmouth. Their descendant, Henry de Grey of Wilton, the fifth baron, was ancestor of that noble family, who held the title of Wilton till the beginning of the seventeenth century, and the lands belonged to Lord Grey de Wilton till 1555, when Edward, Lord Grey, being prisoner in France, had to sell Wilton to pay his ransom; then in the reign of Elizabeth the property was conveyed to the Hon. Charles Brydges, second son of Sir John Brydges, 1st Baron Chandos (see *Sudley Castle, Gloucester*), who was in Queen Mary's household. He was Deputy-Lieutenant of the Tower when the warrant was issued for the execution of the Princess Elizabeth, and his delay in obeying the mandate was the means of saving her life. It was in his day that the castle was rebuilt and added to. His eldest son, Giles, was created a baronet in 1627, whose successor, Sir John, incurred the enmity of his compeers and of the county by abstaining from taking any part in the war between king and Parliament, as he preferred to keep out of the way, and betook himself to Ireland. On his return after the war was over, the people of the county showed their aversion to him by burning down the greater part of Wilton Castle. At his death in 1651, his only son, Sir James, succeeded to the barony of Chandos; he died in 1714, and was succeeded by his son—the "Timon" of Pope—who was created Marquess of Carnarvon and Duke of Chandos. He parted with all his Hereford property about 1732, when Wilton Castle was purchased by the trustees of Guy's Hospital, and is still held by that institution. A small modern house has been incorporated with the S. end of the ruin.

The castle commanded the strong five-arched bridge (built 1599) which spans the rushing Wye opposite the town. It was a quadrilateral enclosure of 75 yards by 65 (about an acre), surrounded by a high curtain wall with towers at the four corners. That on the N.W. angle is a fine octagonal turret of three storeys, in tolerable preservation, the middle floor being furnished with good pointed windows. The N.E. tower has vanished, as likewise that which held the S.E. angle. The curtain wall, which was battlemented, remains upon three sides, and has a semicircular bastion on the E. face, *i.e.* fronting the river; the entrance was probably in the S.W. corner (where was a gateway that has disappeared), with a drawbridge across the broad and deep moat which still surrounds three of the faces. This was probably supported by a barbican. On the S.W. angle was the keep, of which a large portion exists, and upon the S. side are two large portions of the walls of the sixteenth-century mansion, which was burnt after the Civil War. The kitchens, at a great depth below the present level of the ground, can also be seen, and a fine bay-window in the apartments which are said to have received Queen Elizabeth. These later buildings are of the soft red sandstone of the district, and the whole of the area within the walls is now a fertile kitchen and fruit garden. All traces of buildings and of the lodgings, which must have been reared against the walls within the enceinte, have quite vanished, but in the cellars beneath the inhabited part of the castle are several lancet and pointed arches of the thirteenth century, with stairs in perfect preservation. The three lofty openings in the W. wall mark the position of the great hall.

Shropshire

ACTON BURNELL (*minor*)

LELAND wrote that Acton Burnell was "a goodly manor place and castle, 4 myles from Shrewsburie, where a Parliament was kepte in a great barne. It longed once to the Lord Lovel, then to the Duke of Norfolke, & now to Sir John Dudle. N.B. Burnelles daughter was married to the Lorde Lovel, thereby the Lovelle's landes increased."

Robert Burnell was a priest who in the reign of Henry III. was tutor to Prince Edward. The king wrote of him as his "beloved clerk," and sent him with the prince to the Crusade; but Burnell returned home before his master, and at the death of Henry III. in November 1272 was appointed, with the Archbishop of York and Roger de Mortimer, to the Regency during Edward's absence, who on his return in 1274 bestowed the Great Seal on Burnell. Having thus become Lord Chancellor as well as Lord Treasurer, Burnell was the following year consecrated Bishop of Bath and Wells. Acton was his native place, and he purchased the manor of it, and had here a house and a park. Edward I. stayed with him here in 1282, and two years later granted his old tutor a licence to strengthen with a wall of stone and lime, and to crenellate his mansion here, and also one to cut timber in the king's forests for the building. It is likely, therefore, that the old house was pulled down, and the new building erected some time between 1284 and 1292, the year of the bishop's death (*T. H. Turner*).

This eminent man died at Berwick while attending the king, when his nephew and heir, Philip Burnell, obtained his large property. He must have been a man of high standing, for he married Matilda, the daughter of Richard Fitz Alan, Earl of Arundel; but he enjoyed his fortune for two years only, dying 1294, and was succeeded by his son Edward, who, however, died *s.p.* in 1315, when his sister Maud inherited, and carried Acton to her husband, John Lovel, ancestor of the Lords Lovel, in which family the castle and lands continued till their forfeiture by Henry VII., after the battle of Stoke (see *Castle Cary, Somerset*).

Henry VIII. gave Acton Burnell to the Earl of Surrey, among other rewards, for his great services in the war which ended in Flodden Field.

Afterwards the property came into the possession of the family of Lee, and in the reign of Charles II. Sir Edward Smythe married the heiress of Sir Richard Lee of Acton Burnell, and in his family it still remains, the present owner being Sir C. F. Smythe, Bart., whose seat is the more modern mansion of at the same locality.

The ground plan of the building is a parallelogram measuring about 95 feet by 60, each corner being capped by a projecting turret, and the whole was battlemented throughout, and defended by a broad moat. The tower walls are very thick, and they contained dwelling apartments, the whole internal space of the building being occupied by large chambers, of which the hall, on the N. side, was 54 feet by 24 feet, and took up in height the whole of the three storeys of which the castle was composed. All this internal building has been destroyed, and stabling erected in its place; but the fine transomed pointed windows of the hall remain, and many interesting architectural details which are treated of in detail, and illustrated in the valuable work of Mr. Hudson Turner. Since Bishop Burnell also built the episcopal palace at Wells, the style of both buildings is similar, being Early English passing into Decorated.

Close to the castle are two curious gable walls, the remains of the earlier buildings, which formed the two ends of a huge barn, whose length was 157 feet, and width 40 feet. To these remains a high interest attaches, since this barn is supposed to have witnessed, in the autumn of 1283, the assembly, by adjournment from Shrewsbury, of the *first* Parliament in which the Commons had any share by legal authority. " In this assembly we find the earliest legitimate traces of that popular representation of the constitution, to which, under God, Englishmen have been indebted for all their subsequent prosperity."

The nobles were probably assembled in the manor-house hall, under the presidency of the king, and the Commons are said to have met in a tithe barn near by. The laws confirmed here are known as the Statute of Acton Burnell.

ALBERBURY (minor)

ALBERBURY was a small manor, on the W. of Shrewsbury, held at Domesday by Roger Corbet of Caus, and under the Corbets there was a castle which served as the fortress of the Fitzwarines before they obtained Whittington, as feoffees of the Corbets. Apparently, in 1145 Fulk Fitzwarine was here. All the family seem to have had the pre-name of Fulk, and were men of importance and power, esteemed by their sovereigns. The third Fitzwarine of King John's reign turned against that monarch and joined the side of the barons, and he was among the excommunicated ones in the Bull of Innocent III. in 1215. He made his peace, however, with the young King Henry in 1221, and was permitted to strengthen Whittington Castle. The fourth Fitzwarine was killed at the battle of Lewes in 1264, fighting on the king's side, being drowned in crossing the river. Towards the end of this reign Alberbury passed to a junior branch of the Whittington family, namely that of Fulk Glas, who were there in 1324.

The drawing given by Eyton shows the massive walls of a small keep of rectangular form, of which two corners exist, and the curtain wall is extended to the church, which, as usual, is close at hand.

This castle, as well as that of Wattlesborough, stood in the ancient park of Loton.

APLEY (non-existent)

APLEY is situated one mile to the N. of Wellington. It is said to be the third castle built here, the original one having been erected by John de Charlton, who owned the manor and married Hawise, the heiress of Powis Castle; he obtained in 1308 a licence to crenellate his house. The present owner of the site, Colonel Sir Thomas Meyrick, Bart., who is a descendant of this founder, still holds the original document.

There are no remains whatever of this first castle, and what is left of the fine Jacobean mansion that succeeded it is used as an outhouse for a third castle of Apley. The second house was built at a cost of £6000 by one Thomas Hanmer, who had married the widow of Francis Charlton, and was living when the Civil War broke out. Being so near to Shrewsbury, the fortress was coveted by both sides, and the owner, being obliged to declare himself one way or the other, or have his house blown up, fortified it for the king, arming his servants and tenants for a garrison. But the place was very soon taken from him, and at once dismantled, after being plundered to the extent of £1500, and the lead of the roof taken away for the repairs of Shrewsbury Castle.

BISHOP'S CASTLE, or LYDBURY (*non-existent*)

THIS castle, which was six miles N. from Clun, was reported by Leland to be "well mainteined" and "set on a stronge Rokke, but not very hy." There are now no traces of it,—the site being occupied by a bowling-green attached to the Castle Hotel,—with the exception of the old wall enclosing the green, on a level with the second floor of the inn. It was built about seventy years after Domesday by a bishop of Hereford,—that is, between 1085 and 1154, and it was then called Lydbury Castle, its intention being to guard the great episcopal manor of this name, whose lands had been given to the Church by a Saxon lord before the Conquest, in memory of his having been cured of palsy at St. Ethelbert's shrine. The bishops incurred the military service of Lords Marchers by virtue of their tenure here.

In the reign of Henry II. it was in the hands of Hugh de Mortimer, who, however, had to surrender it to the see. The bishops do not appear to have cared for it as a palace, for in the Barons' War we find the king insisting on the personal residence of a bishop, under threats of forfeiture, whereon the prelate returned to Lydbury, but only to fall into the hands of the rebellious barons, and to suffer imprisonment in the castle of Eardisland. In July (47 Henry III.) Sir John Fitz Alan of Arundel came to Bishop's Castle, and took it by storm, its Constable being treacherously slain, when its contents were plundered, much grain and some armour, including "an iron surcoat of the Bishop," being taken.

There is an account of a visit here of four days, in May 1290, by Bishop Swinfield with a large suite, and thirty or forty horses. The bishops of Hereford enjoyed full feudal rights of the seniory, with their forest lands, deer park, dovecotes, and gardens, and the garrison of the castle was efficiently provided for by the tenants of the great Lydbury estates, who all owed service here.

In 1610 James I. granted the manor and castle to Arthur Ingram and Thomas Williams, who in 1618 transferred the same to Henry, Earl of Arundel, together with the honour of Clun. From that time the castle appears to have been neglected, and allowed to go to ruin, since no allusion occurs to it during the Civil War of the seventeenth century.

An old sketch of the fortress shows an outer ward surrounded by a wall on one side and a rampart on the other, with an entrance gatehouse and a drum tower in front of the keep, which appears as a rectangular building with turrets at the four corners, and its entrance flanked by two circular turrets. It was built in two storeys and a basement, and was evidently a place of great strength.

BRIDGNORTH, ANCIENTLY CALLED BRUGGE AND BRUGES (minor)

ETHELFLEDA'S Mound, raised by that Lady of the Mercians in 912 at
the river-side as a fortification against her neighbours, is still there; it
was called in the time of Edward I. the Old Castle, and its modern appellation
is Pan-pudding Hill. It is but a short distance from the commanding site
above the bridge over Severn whereon afterwards the fearful third Earl of
Shrewsbury, Robert de Belème "The Devil Belème"—built his castle. On
the death of Hugh de Montgomery, Earl of Shrewsbury, in 1098, his elder
brother Robert, of Belème in Normandy, obtained the earldom from the Red
King, but retained it for four years only, being then outlawed for treason against
Henry I., in supporting the just claims of that king's elder brother Robert,
Duke of Normandy.

During his tenure he had transferred the settlement of a borough with
a castle and church, made by his father and mother, Earl Roger and the
Countess Adeliza, at Quatford, a short distance down the river, to this place,
where he reared a very strong Norman castle on a barren rock, which was
naturally fortified on three sides by ravines, and on the fourth overhung the
Severn at a still greater elevation. The original building was doubtless the
usual square keep, called for long after in the Rolls, the Tower of Brug, and
though it is said to have been erected within a year, was yet of sufficient strength
to stand a vehement siege.

The king having with great sagacity first come to terms with his brother,
Duke Robert, and induced him to return to Normandy, promptly proceeded
in force against the conspirators. He cited Belème to appear before him,
and then, proclaiming him an outlaw, went with a strong force against his
castle of Arundel in Sussex, which he took, and sending the Bishop of London
to besiege the earl's house of Tickhill, he passed northwards against him in
person at Bridgnorth, where he had been working day and night to complete
the defences of the new fortress. Belème had effected this before the king
could arrive, and had garrisoned the castle with stipendiary soldiers under the
command of Robert Corbet, while he himself retired to await the king at
Shrewsbury Castle. Henry came with all his army to Bridgnorth, and laid
siege to the castle; after three days he summoned the fortress a second time,
threatening to hang the whole garrison, whereon Corbet surrendered the place
to him. The king then advanced to Shrewsbury, and Robert de Belème, seeing
the game was up, hastened to make peace, and meeting the king on the road,
threw himself at his feet, and sued for mercy. His life was spared, but he
was sent prisoner into Normandy, and his estates and castles were forfeited
to the Crown. It is said that this Earl Robert died paralytic in St. Osyth's
Priory in Essex, a place founded by him as a set-off against his many crimes.

Thenceforth Bridgnorth was a royal castle, whose importance may be fairly estimated from the large amounts expended on its repairs and improvements during succeeding reigns, its custody being remitted to the sheriffs of the county.

In 1155 Hugh de Mortimer of Wigmore, a supporter of King Stephen, defying Henry II. here, was besieged by him, but was soon forced to yield the place, which was at once garrisoned for the Crown. The most interesting story connected with this siege is that of the devotion of Hubert St. Clair, Constable of Colchester, who, while reconnoitring with the king, saved Henry's life at the sacrifice of his own by interposing his body to receive a shaft aimed at him from the walls.

King John was here on five several occasions, on one of these being entertained with costly festivities. On another visit here it is related of this scrupulous monarch that, having on a Friday indulged in food twice, he atoned for this misdeed by feeding one hundred paupers with bread, fish, and beer. Henry III. also was frequently at Bridgnorth on account of the disputes between himself and Llewellyn, Prince of Wales, and its Constable, Hamo le Strange, held the castle bravely for him against De Montfort.

During the civil war, about 1321, which followed Edward II.'s pursuit of Badlesmere, the confederate barons besieged Bridgnorth, burned the town and took the castle, when the king came with a strong force and retook it. He came here again, a fugitive from Mortimer, who led him thence to his deposition at Kenilworth (q.v.). Shakespeare makes Henry IV. name Bridgnorth as the point for assembling his army before the battle of Shrewsbury.

Charles I. in the fourth year of his reign granted the castle to Gilbert North, one of his gentlemen, who at once sold it to Sir William Whitmore of Apley, in whose family it has ever since continued. The town was Royalist in the seventeenth century, when it and the castle were put into a state of defence in 1642, and Charles and his two sons were there and lodged in the castle eight days before the battle of Edgehill. He was here again in 1645. In March 1646 the Parliamentary Committee holding Shrewsbury sent a party of horse and foot against Bridgnorth and summoned the place, but received from Colonel Howard, commanding in the castle, a defiant reply. The Roundheads then attacked the town at three points, and penetrating through St. Leonard's churchyard opened the town gates and took possession, the Royalists retreating to the castle and firing the town. A furious siege against it was then commenced; a battery was established on Ethelfleda's Mound, and a bombardment kept up for three weeks, but with little effect. It was next determined to undermine the walls, and a large hole was made on the S. side of the hill, which can still be seen, called Lavingstone's Hole; the governor, accordingly, being short of ammunition, and foreseeing that the explosion of a mine here would ruin his defences, capitulated with all honours.

By order of the committee, the castle of Bridgnorth was entirely demolished, and in the lapse of time the whole of the ruins have been taken away with the exception of an immense corner fragment of the Norman keep, on the S.E. of the Castle Hill, which having been undermined and partially thrown over, is called the Leaning Tower.

King, in his *Munimenta Antiqua*, says that, from the fragment left of the keep, it was a building 41½ feet square, containing three storeys, and had walls 8 to 9 feet thick. The side of the tower next the town was covered with iron hooks, said by tradition to have been placed for hanging woolpacks during the siege ; but King thinks them far more ancient, and that they rather remind one of the savage custom which sometimes prevailed of fastening the bodies of enemies on the outside of the walls of fortresses.

Mr. Eyton in his paper on Bridgnorth shows that in 1281 this castle was in grievous disrepair ; the great tower was rotted, from the lead having been carried away from the roof ; the chambers in the barbican were uninhabitable and threatened to fall ; the king's and the other stables were thrown down and the woodwork was stolen ; the bridge, too, was in so bad a state that it could scarce be crossed on foot. Again, after the lapse of 250 years, Leland wrote thus of the fortress : "The walles of it be of a great height. There were 2 or 3 stronge wardes in the Castle, that nowe goe totally to ruine. I count the Castle to be more in compasse than the third part of the towne. There is one mighty Gate by North in it, now stopped up, and one little posterne made by force thereby through the wall to enter into the Castell. The Castell ground & especially the base court hath now many dwelling houses of tymbre in it newly erected."

There is a pleasant terrace walk about the ancient walls nearly 600 yards in compass, which was much admired by King Charles I.

BRONCROFT (*non-existent*)

LITTLE is known of the origin of this castle. Leland calls it "a very goodly place like a Castell longging to the Erle of Shrewsbire. It stondeth in the Cle Hilles." The present building has the appearance of a farm-house. It was made a royal garrison in King Charles' war, but, like other untenable quarters hereabout, was abandoned by the royal troops in January 1645. A strong force of 500 foot and 300 horse from Shrewsbury garrison then made a reconnaissance through that part of the country to block Ludlow, and viewed Broncroft and Holgate, both of which stations had been greatly demolished. The latter place was left untouched, but at Broncroft they made repairs, and

placed a garrison under Lord Calvin, who fortified it anew. It was then the
property of Mr. John Lulley, whose family inhabited the house for many
generations.

Of late years the castle, which is believed to have been built in the
fourteenth century, has been restored, and converted into a stately residence
by the present owner, Mr. James Whitaker. It lies about five miles S.E. from
Rushbury station.

CAUS (minor)

CAUS is believed to be the place called "Alretone" in Domesday, whose
lord, then Roger Fitz Corbet, built a castle and called it Caux, from his own
Norman home. The situation is most imposing, being on an isolated eminence
overlooking the valley of the Rea, about ten miles W. of Shrewsbury.

Caus is shown to have been by some means in the hands of Pagan or
Pain Fitz John, sheriff of this county in 1134, at which time Ordericus relates
that it was taken and burnt by the Welsh. The Corbets renewed their
tenure at the accession of Henry II., and Roger Corbet became baron of
Caus, and in 1155 attended the king at the siege of Bridgnorth (q.v.) against
Robert de Beléme. In 1165, probably on the death of this Roger and the
minority of his heir, it was garrisoned by the king.

In 1217 the castle was again in royal hands, owing to a recent rebellion of
Thomas Corbet, eldest son and heir of Robert, the holder of the barony, but
it was restored to the family at the end of the same year. The three grandsons
of this Thomas Corbet all dying s.p. before the middle of the fourteenth century,
the barony passed (temp. Edward III.) to the descendants of his daughter
Alice, the wife of Robert de Stafford, and thence to the earls of that name.
With them it remained, like their other properties, till the execution of the
last Duke of Buckingham, when it was forfeited to the Crown, but was at
length restored to his son, by whom the property was sold to Robert Howard
(temp. Elizabeth); from him it came to Lord Weymouth, whose family held
it during the Civil Wars.

The ruins of Caus Castle give no clue to the date of its erection; for
the masonry remaining is little more than rubble hearting, from which all
the ashlar facing and dressings have been removed. The massive keep, which
stood on the summit of a lofty conical mound, partly raised and scarped
from the natural hill, and proving the prior antiquity of a former fortress
here, can be traced.

An old drawing, copied into "The Garrisons of Shropshire in 1642 to 1648,"
shows this castle with its lofty and steep mound, its enceinte wall forming a
parallelogram round the crest of the hill, with a massive round tower at each
corner. This formed the outer ward or bailey, from the E. end of which—that

nearest to the mound—is formed a three-sided inner ward, having another round tower at its inner corner, with its walls running up to the mound, half of which is thus included in the work, as at Castle Acre, Clare, and other places. The commanding keep was probably one of the shell type, and the whole formed an enclosure of about six acres. At the foot of the hill was a ditch. In the time of King John there was a town which covered eight acres at the base of the hill. An enormous well existed in the castle, which can still be traced, and vestiges of other water-works can be found on the N. side, near the brook supplying the great ditch, intended for the necessities of the crowd of country-folk who, with their cattle, might take refuge in this stronghold during a sudden irruption of the Welsh.

In the Civil War a force of 300 men held Caus for King Charles, and in June 1645, as it still displayed the royal colours, a strong force under Colonel Hunt was sent against the place, and, as is related, "sat down before Cause Castle, a place of great strength and little inferior to Basing : it standing on a rock not mineable ; which was surrendered to them after seven days' siege. By this the country is cleared on that side Severne to Ludlow, and so quite up to Montgomery."

To exemplify the effect of the war on the proprietors of such castles, Lord Henry F. Thynne, the owner of Caus, having submitted to the committee at Shrewsbury, before December 1645, was imprisoned and fined £1750. He then went to the Fleet, and so late as 1652 was unable to raise sufficient money to clear the claim. His family appears to have been in great distress.

CLUN (minor)

THE village, church, and castle of Clun stand in an amphitheatre of hills in the ancient forest of Clun, on the left bank of a bend of the river of the same name. The castle is placed on a mound which has been originally formed by cutting and scarping a natural elevation of rock surface, surrounded by a deep ditch on its S. and E. sides, the river bank forming its defence N. and W. It was further defended on the S. and E. by three other raised and scarped platforms on the other side of the castle ditch, each of these again being separated and insulated by ditches or moats. It is not known when these four mounds, or burhs, were formed, but the strength of the position was early recognised by a Norman follower of the Conqueror, Picot de Say, and taken possession of and held by him, together with Hopton, as a fief of Roger de Montgomery, the great Earl of Shrewsbury.

Picot lived till 1098, and was succeeded by his son Henry (alive in 1130), and next by Helias de Say, whose daughter Isabel, the Lady of Clun, married, first, William FitzAlan ; secondly, Geoffrey de Vere ; and thirdly, William Boterell, in whose time the castle was stormed and burned by Llewellyn. FitzAlan left a son, William, who inherited Clun, and probably built this castle on the site of the original timber one which had been burnt. John, the third FitzAlan from him, acquired through his mother Arundel Castle in Sussex; he died 1267, leaving John Fitz-Alan, lord of Clun and Earl of Arundel; he died in 1272.

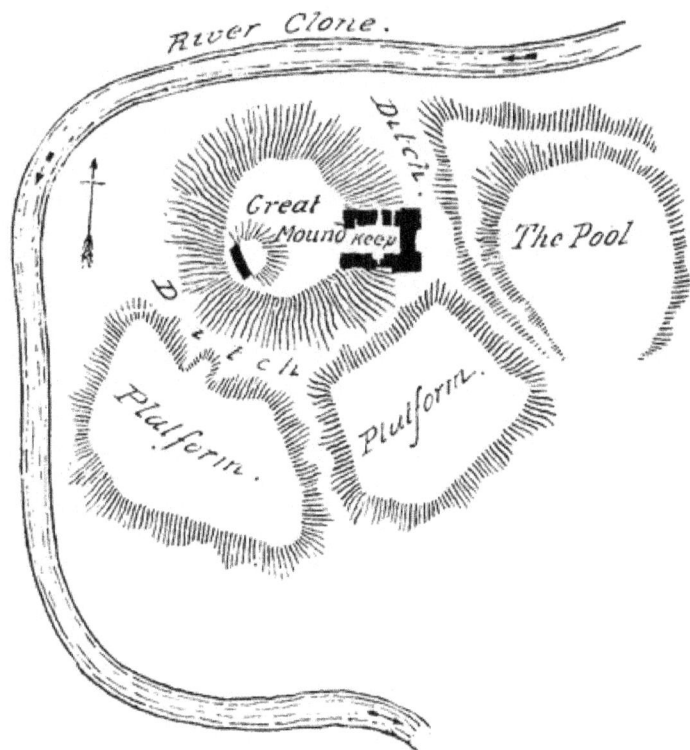

CLUN

About that time a report was made on this fortress, in which it appears that a bridge existed, and that outside the castle was a bailey enclosed by a ditch and gatehouse. Clun continued to be held by the FitzAlans, but they no longer resided here, and when Philip, Earl of Arundel, died under attainder in 1595, his son Thomas did not retain Clun, which King James granted to the brother of that earl's grandfather, Henry Howard, Earl of Southampton, and his descendants sold the property. It lately passed to the Duke of Norfolk, under whom careful restoration is proceeding.

The barony or honour and hundred of Clun formed a tract of vast extent, having on the N. and W. sides the ancient forest of the same name, extending to a radius of about five miles. From this forest four streams descending combine to form the river Clone or Clun, which, a short distance from their union, now a stream of considerable volume makes a sudden bend to the S. and then again another eastward, enclosing a space in which, on the left or inner bank, the fortress of Clun is situated, thus surrounded on three sides by the river. Within this space there is a cluster of rocky knolls that have been artificially scarped and formed into raised platforms and mounds, whereon the works of the castle were placed. The most northern forms a lofty mound, the top of which is 40 yards in diameter, and standing 60 feet above the enclosing ditch, which area formed the inner ward, on which are the remains of the keep. Southward are three other islands, forming the defences and approaches on this side, and divided from each other and the first mound by ditches. On the inner side of the platform on the W. appear the rudiments of the bridge which led to the central mound, the approach road from the village lying through this work. In the middle of the third platform on the E. is a hollow pool which perhaps formed a stew and was furnished with sluices.

When these earthworks were formed it is impossible to decide, but it was probably in the ninth or tenth century (*Clark*); they were taken by the Normans, and made into a stronghold, which in the twelfth century developed into buildings of which we have now some remains.

The keep is a rectangular tower built, like Guildford, on the edge of the mound, measuring 68 feet by 42 feet, with walls 11 feet thick, and with three storeys. Its height is about 80 feet, and the floors were of timber. The W. wall has disappeared. The quoins were strengthened with pilasters of the late Norman style, and ended perhaps in corner turrets. Each floor had five windows and a fireplace, the second containing the state rooms, and the upper one the bed-chambers. The entrance door is on the S. side, and a mural staircase led to the several floors. Round the summit of the mound ran a curtain wall attached to the keep on two sides, two large fragments of which remain, and within the enceinte is a small artificial mound, which seems to have carried a separate tower. There are no traces of walls on the outer platforms, the defences of which may have been of timber.

Further earthworks appear some way to the E., and beyond the fine old church of St. George, where is a natural ravine, whose sides have been scarped.

Clun is supposed to form the scene of Sir Walter Scott's "Betrothed."

ELLESMERE (*non-existent*)

ELLESMERE, which lies between Oswestry and Whitchurch, was the most important castle entrusted or granted by Henry I. to his half-brother William Peverell of Dover, and was fortified against Stephen in 1138 by his nephew, William Peverell the younger, for this lord naturally and gallantly supported the cause of his cousin, the Empress Maud, in the south, afterwards ending his life of devotion in Palestine. Henry II. on his accession resumed possession, but in 1177 gave Ellesmere to David ap Owen, who had married his illegitimate sister Emma.

King John held the castle himself, but gave it in 1205 to his son-in-law, Llewellyn ap Jorworth, the husband of his natural daughter Joan, who forfeited it by rebellion, recovering it afterwards from Henry III. In the Welsh wars it again became royal property, and was granted to Prince Edward, after being repaired at the king's expense. The "Mad Parliament" of 1258 made Peter de Montfort governor of Ellesmere, and in 1260 Hamo le Strange was rewarded for his loyal services by a grant of the place for seventeen years, which on the death of Simon de Montfort was extended into possession of the fee; he died at the Crusade of 1270, *s.p.*, when Ellesmere was seized, but was given up in 1276 by Edward I. to Roger le Strange, Hamo's brother, a great and successful man, who was Sheriff of Yorkshire, and Justice of the Forests E. of Trent. At his death, it again reverted to the Crown (1311), and was farmed to different people till 1330, when Edward III. gave it back to the Strange family, in the person of Eubolo le Strange, and then to his brother, who transmitted the property to his descendants. Thus it continued till the heir-general carried Ellesmere to the Stanleys. Eyton says that at present this barony is in abeyance between the representatives of the three daughters and coheirs of Ferdinando Stanley, 5th Earl of Derby of his line (see *Middle Castle*).

In 1644 Prince Maurice took up his residence at Ellesmere, defeating a cavalry attack by Colonel Mytton in the neighbourhood at Oateley Hall. The fortress was utterly destroyed, and its site is now occupied by a bowling-green.

HOLGATE (*minor*)

THIS castle lies about six miles to the N. of Ludlow, in the head of Corve Dale. It was owned by a soldier of the Conqueror named Helget, whose son or grandson, Herbert Fitz Helget, entertained Henry I. in 1109 at this place, which at that period must have been a timber stronghold taken from its Saxon lord, and strengthened by its new Norman master. In 1115 a court was held here to settle some disputes regarding the estates of the priory of Wenlock.

In the reign of Richard I. the manor and castle passed to the Mauduits

of Warminster, as collateral heirs of Helget, but the barony was forfeited by
them in the Barons' War, and, temp. Edward I., was sold to Richard, Earl of
Cornwall, the king's uncle, who conveyed it to Robert Burnell, Bishop of Bath and
Wells, the chancellor (see *Acton Burnell*). By an inquest held in 1295 it is thus
recorded : "The old castle is not to be retained because it is worth nothing."

In the next reign the heiress of Burnell brought Holgate by marriage to the
Lovels, with whom it rested till the forfeiture of the last lord, Francis Lovel,
in the reign of Henry VII. (see *Castle Cary, Somerset*), when that king gave
Holgate to Jasper, Duke of Bedford, at whose death it reverted to the Crown ;
Henry VIII. granted it to the Duke of Norfolk, beheaded by Elizabeth, but
before his death he had exchanged it for lands of the Dudley family.

Holgate became the property of the Cressetts before 1584, and it continues
with their descendants, being now in the possession of Mr. Thursby Pelham.

When the Civil War broke out between King Charles I. and the Parliament,
Holgate received a royal garrison, but, as it was deemed untenable, the Royalists
abandoned it, as they did Bromcroft, and they then dismantled and demolished this
fortress so completely, that in 1645 the Parliamentary Committee of Shrewsbury
reported it as too far dilapidated to be worth holding, and in this state it was left.

The ruins consist of a fine circular tower, built into the modern farm-house,
which tower is perhaps the surviving portion of the Norman castle, while an
ancient lofty mound, standing near it on the edge of what was the water
defence, shows that a far earlier settlement had been formed, where perhaps
the Norman lord built a keep. The tower, which has a conical roof of wood,
has a broad spreading base, and is lighted by loops on two floors. When this
castle was rebuilt is not recorded.

The neighbouring church is Norman.

HOPTON (minor)

THE castle of Hopton lies about five miles S.E. of Clun, and one mile from
Hopton Heath railway station. The remains consist of the strong square
keep of a fortress of the Decorated period, in good preservation, standing on
a knoll of gravel in a low situation, and surrounded by a circular moat fed by
a passing streamlet. The manor was granted by the Conqueror in his third
year, as we learn by a curious metrical deed, which runs thus :

"I, Will king, the third of my reign,
Give to the Northern Hunter,
To me that art both Laine and Deare,
The Hoppe and the Hoptoune,
And all the bounds up and downe,
Under the earth to Hell,
Above the earth to Heaven," &c.

The place was a fief of Clun, and was held by Picot as the successor of Edric. In 1165 it was held by Walter de Opton, as two knights' fees, under Geoffrey de Vere, one of the three husbands of Isabel de Say (see *Whittington*)—that is, Sai near Exmes, the Norman viscounty of Earl Roger)—and by Peter de Opton in 1201. Then two Walters de Hopton succeeded from 1223 to 1272, on the tenure of war service to Clun Castle, and the family continued here for many generations, enjoying much of the surrounding property.

In the reign of Henry VI. the heiress of Thomas Hopton married, first, Sir Roger Corbet of Moreton ; secondly, the Earl of Worcester ; and lastly, Sir William Stanley.   Hopton went to the Corbets, and by an heiress of that family to the Wallops of Hampshire, one of whom, Henry Wallop, a fierce republican, owned it during the Civil War of the seventeenth century, when the old castle was still strong enough to stand a violent siege.   It was held for the Parliament by one Samuel More with a small garrison of thirty-one men, and was attacked in February 1644 by a Royalist force which took the outer wall, and then retired for a week or so, returning 500 strong, under Sir Michael Woodhouse, when the place was summoned in the name of Prince Rupert. A fierce attack followed, in which a breach was made, but was repulsed, whereon the Royalist force again retired for a week, and came back with three pieces of ordnance. A fresh summons being rejected they bombarded the castle ; ninety-six shots were fired, and a breach was again made, and unsuccessfully stormed ; but the next day the governor, finding the castle was mined, asked for a parley, and surrendered unconditionally, other terms having been refused him.

The Parliamentary account makes out that the garrison were inhumanly mutilated and butchered by the king's troops, which is a very unlikely story, although 150 Royalists were killed in the siege.   The fortress was then dismantled.

Hopton was long the property of Mr. Salwey Beale, whose ancestor purchased it early in the last century, but Sir Edward Ripley, Bart., is the present owner.

From the tower mound with its earthworks and ditches, the work is evidently of Saxon origin. The keep measures 50 feet by 48, and the walls are 10 feet thick ; each angle is strengthened by a broad projecting pilaster on both faces, which quoins were probably carried up in turrets above the battlements. The entrance is in the N.W. angle by a circular stair, and a gateway without portcullis, but well guarded by a bold machicoulis chamber overhead. The basement forms a single large chamber with several mural recesses and a garderobe ; the floors above this were of timber, and a spiral stair led to them, the first having recesses like the lowest stage, and some windows of large size. The roof was formed with two gables, N. and S., and a ridge roof over, and altogether it was more like a Scottish than an English tower ; it is all of one date, being probably the work of Walter de Hopton, who died 1304 or 1305, and who seems to have been a man of wealth and power (*Clark*).

KNOCKYN (non-existent)

THE fortress of Knockyn, which lies six miles S.E. from Oswestry, was one
of the outer chain of castles on the borders of Wales. It was founded
by Guy le Strange of Weston and Alveley (temp. Henry II.), and passed at his
death in 1179 to his son Ralph, who dying s.p. 1195, left his three sisters his
coheirs. They and their husbands concurred in transferring Knockyn, manor
and castle, to their cousin John le Strange of Ness and Cheswardine, since " a
Border Castle and Estate was no fit matter for female coparcenary" (Eyton).

This castle followed the fortunes of Middle Castle (q.v.), and passed to the
Stanleys. It was first demolished in the troublous times of King John, and was
repaired by John le Strange in the following reign.

There is now scarcely a vestige of the castle remaining, its stones having
been appropriated for building the churchyard wall and the adjacent bridge,
and even for road mending. The site of the keep is to be seen.

LUDLOW (chief)

LUDLOW, the glory of the Border castles, chief of the thirty-two that guarded
the Welsh Marches, occupies the summit of a rock which stands over
the river Teme at the point of its confluence with the Corve, from whence
they flow together to meet the Severn. The green meadow-lands on the N., as
we now see them, were anciently a marsh protecting the fortress on that side
as effectively as did the river channels elsewhere. The broad point of this
promontory, having thus a natural defence upon two sides, was chosen, in very
early times probably, for the site of a fortress. One Osborne Fitz Richard
was the Norman lord of the place called Lude, after the Conquest, and from
him Roger de Lacy is believed to have obtained enough land to build a castle
shortly after Doomsday. In 1088, however, he rebelled against Rufus in favour
of Robert Curthose, Duke of Normandy, and again in 1095 he took part in the
Mowbray or second rebellion, when he was exiled, and his possessions, torn
from him, were bestowed on his more loyal brother Hugh, who died s.p.
between 1108 and 1121, when the estates were escheated to the Crown.
Henry I. then gave Ludlow to Pagan, or Pain, Fitzjohn, but on his being slain
by the Welsh in 1136, Stephen placed here a Flemish knight, Sir Joyce de
Dinant, who is said to have completed the building of the castle, and is called
"a strong and valiant knight." He it was who built at this time the beautiful
circular Norman chapel in the middle ward, and extended the structure generally over the ground as we now see it. Before, however, Sir Joyce could
obtain his grant King Stephen had to wrest the castle from Gervase de Paganel

who in 1139 held it on behalf of the Empress Maud, and who offered an
obstinate and successful resistance. It was at this siege of Ludlow that Stephen
is said to have by bodily strength and great courage rescued his hostage, Prince
Henry of Scotland, from being seized and dragged off his horse by a grappling-
iron (*unca ferrea*) thrown on him from the walls which he had incautiously
approached.

On the accession of Henry II. we find Joyce de Dinant at war with Hugh
de Mortimer, lord of Wigmore, whom he contrived to waylay and capture, and

LUDLOW

then immured in a high turret at Ludlow, called to this day Mortimer's Tower.
Sir Hugh only regained his liberty by payment of 3000 marks, together with
all his plate, horses, and hawks. Sir Joyce died *s.p.* about 1166, when Henry II.
gave Ludlow to Hugh de Lacy, a descendant of the original lord by a sister of
Roger and Hugh de Lacy. This Hugh was a powerful baron both here and
in Ireland; but on his suspected treachery the king seized on Ludlow in 1181,
and retained it till 1190, when, Hugh de Lacy being slain in Ireland, he allowed
the lands to go to his son Walter, who was made to pay a fine for Ludlow in
1206 by King John. That monarch, however, seized the castle the next year,
and gave it in charge temporarily to several barons, restoring it at last in 1214
to Walter de Lacy. He died in 1241, when Ludlow went to a granddaughter,

who was married, first to Peter de Geneva, one of the foreign favourites of Henry III., and, secondly, to Geoffry de Geneville or Joinville, who had custody of Ludlow and held half the manor, Matilda's other sister Marjory having the other half, and being married to John de Verdon. Matilda's son Peter de Geneville then succeeded.

Rishanger says that Simon de Montfort, in his raid into Wales after the victory of Lewes, actually reduced Ludlow Castle (1264), but it was certainly recovered by the Royalists after the escape of Prince Edward from Hereford Castle in May 1265, and it was here that the prince assembled his friends and their forces before the battle of Evesham, being joined by Gilbert de Clare, Earl of Gloucester.

Peter de Geneville had Ludlow from his father and mother in 1283, but he predeceased them in 1292, leaving three daughters, two of whom became nuns. The other, Joan, carried the whole Geneville property, and a moiety of the great estates of De Lacy, to her husband Roger de Mortimer, 1st Earl of March (born 1287), famous as the paramour of Queen Isabella, the "She-Wolf of France," and who, taken at Nottingham Castle (q.v.) by Edward III., was hung at Tyburn in 1330.

Ludlow soon eclipsed Wigmore as the *caput* of the Mortimer baronies; hence in a short time Wigmore was deserted for Ludlow, and fell into neglect and consequent ruin. Roger Mortimer's story is sufficiently told in the memoirs of Nottingham and other castles. His eldest son Edmund died the year after his father's execution, leaving a son Roger, in whose favour Edward III. repealed the judgments against his grandfather, and restored to him his title, with Ludlow and other large possessions. He died in 1360, and was followed by his son Edward (born 1351), whose marriage with the Lady Philippa, the daughter of Lionel, Duke of Clarence, third son of Edward III., gave to his son and heir, Roger, a title to the throne of England, as heir-presumptive, which was recognised by Richard II., and worked incredible woe to his country in the Wars of the Roses. Being appointed Viceroy of Ireland, he was slain there by a party of rebels when his son and heir was a child of six years. The fourth earl obtained by exchange with the Ferrars family the moiety of Ludlow which had gone to the Verdons by the marriage of the coheiress Marjory, and the fifth earl therefore, Edmund, now enjoyed the entire Ludlow estates.

This Earl Edmund held a command in the French wars under Henry V., having been as a boy, together with his brother, the jealously watched prisoner of Henry IV., whose right to the crown was undoubtedly second to his (see *Berkhamstead* and *Windsor*). He died *s.p.*, at the age of only twenty-three, when his nephew Richard Plantagenet, Duke of York, son of his sister Anne, Countess of Cambridge, was returned heir to his honours, including Ludlow; his son, afterwards Edward IV., enjoyed them as an appanage then of the Crown.

Ludlow Castle became famous in its later days as the place where the Lords Marchers (*Barones Marchiæ*) held the courts of their peculiar jurisdiction.

In 1472 King Edward gave the Castle to his two young sons as a residence, and here they remained till 1483, when they were taken by their mother to the sanctuary of Westminster, from which their uncle Richard III. removed them to their prison in the Tower of London, where they were subsequently murdered. Henry VII. also made Ludlow the abode of his eldest son, Prince Arthur, coming here frequently to visit him ; and here the prince died in 1502. Under

LUDLOW

Henry VIII. it was neglected and fell into disrepair, although still used by the Lords President as the Court of Council of the Marches under the Prince of Wales. In 1559, however, Sir Henry Sidney was appointed by Elizabeth Lord President of this Council, and he retained the post and lived here in much state for twenty-seven years, during which time large alterations were made on the castle. Sidney built the gatehouse into the middle ward (on which is an inscription dated 1581) and the bridge leading to the castle, and he repaired the chapel and the structure generally, particularly the keep, which was used as a prison for the principality, the inner ward forming the exercise ground for the prisoners. He died in 1586.

In 1642 the Earl of Essex with an army of 20,000 horse and foot advanced

Birch must have retired, as Charles came there after Naseby, and held a council in the castle, at which a levy was decreed of one foot soldier from every person worth £30 a year, to be maintained at his charge, and from those of an income of £200 was demanded a horse and rider. In May 1646 Ludlow, the only royal garrison in Shropshire, was surrendered to the Parliament. Then it was dismantled by order of the committee, and in 1651 the fittings and furniture were sold.

LUDLOW

The Court of the Council continued to be held here nominally after the Restoration, but this was abolished by William III., at which time the rooms of state were all in tolerable repair. George I., however, caused the destruction of the old fortress by selling the lead off the roofs. Buck's drawing of 1731 shows the outer walls almost uninjured, therefore much ruin must have accrued since that time. The Powis family held a lease of the place, which was in 1811 converted into a freehold.

At the site of the castle, before described, the point of the promontory was cut off by a great ditch like a quadrant excavated in the rock from cliff to cliff, 13 yards wide and 4 yards deep, inside which the main fortress was erected, with a line of walls following the cliff edge and carried round the curve of the ditch. By prolonging the N. and W. walls and returning them on the E. and S. a large outer court was formed, of rectangular figure, containing about four acres.

The entrance gatehouse is in the middle of the E. curtain, and N. of it is a square Norman tower projecting from the wall. On the W. curtain is an Early English bastion of semicircular form, closed at the gorge, called Mortimer's Tower, in three storeys; and in the S.W. corner, where was the junction with the town wall, are the ruins of some later buildings. Against the E. wall is a range of Tudor stabling.

The entrance in Castle Street is through a Decorated gatehouse with two flanking walls covering the drawbridge, and under a low-pointed gateway — the walls here being 35 feet high and 6 feet thick. Crossing the outer ward we enter through a second gateway, by a bridge over the ditch, under a low arch which is a Tudor insertion in the Norman wall. There is no portcullis, and the long passage has doors on the left into the keep and porter's lodge, and on the right into the lodgings.

The keep, which stands on the highest part of the ground, and consists of a basement and three floors, was probably built by Roger de Lacy, and forms on its S. face part of the wall of the ward; it is rectangular, and has had later constructions added to it on the E. and W. The basement is vaulted, and has an arcade of Norman work. A newel stair conducts to the several floors; the first being a room 30 feet by 17½ feet, having a mural chamber and a garderobe, and the stair communicates on both sides with the walls, an unusual feature in a keep. The floors were of timber, and Tudor windows have replaced the Norman lights.

The salient is formed by a group of towers with wondrous thick walls, having the buttery below, and giving exit to a large sewer. Set against this is a second tower, half octagonal, from which stretches S.E. a strong short wall forming the W. end of the great hall, of which the curtain continuing is its N. side, pierced with three tall Early English windows on the exterior. Below this wall on the outside is a broad platform, whence a second steep slope descends to the fields beneath. Beyond the Hall are the state apartments, and attached to these, projecting from the wall, is an immense garderobe tower of five stages. Then come the private lodgings, of Decorated style, with much Tudor alteration and insertion. The N.E. angle of the inner ward ends in a Norman tower at the junction of the inner and outer curtain walls. This outer wall, which continues along the N. face and curves round to the first-named square Norman tower, seems to have been partly rebuilt in Elizabeth's reign as far as a small postern. The outer ditch has been filled in for a great length of time. The Hall was a grand chamber, 60 feet long, 30 feet broad, and 35 feet high to the springing of its open roof; all this and the state rooms are of Decorated work of the fourteenth century.

Ludlow Castle.

The chapel of St. Mary Magdalene is "the most remarkable part of the castle," standing alone in the centre of the ward between the gatehouse and the hall. Only its circular part remains, being twelfth-century work, with a good Norman doorway. This is 28 feet in diameter inside, with walls 4 feet

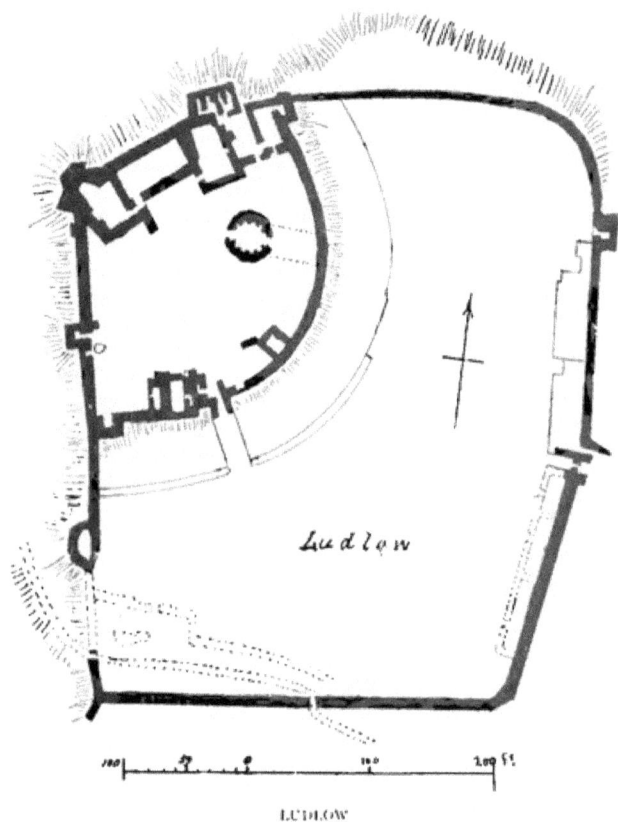

LUDLOW

thick, and there is a chancel arch on the E. side, but the chancel has vanished. It has three Early English windows.

It is of interest to know that Milton was from Ludlow, and wrote his *Comus* there, taking as his scene a lovely valley some two miles out on the Wigmore road. The masque was first acted in May 1633 in the banqueting-hall of this castle.

MIDDLE CASTLE (*minor*)

THE remains of this castle are situated between Shrewsbury and Chester, about 2½ miles from Baschurch. It was embattled and fortified in 1308, in the reign of Edward II., by John, Lord le Strange, who held the manor under the FitzAlans. The original founder is said to have received from the Conqueror, Myddle, Knockyn, and Nesse Strange, and this manor remained in the same family for over 400 years, during the reigns of eighteen kings. In the time of Henry VII., on the failure of male issue, Joan, daughter of the last Lord le Strange, brought it to her husband Sir George Stanley, the son of Lord Stanley, who being held by Richard III. as a hostage for his father's loyalty, was ordered to be executed by the king, just before the commencement of the battle of Bosworth, when Lord Stanley failed to join the royal army. He took the title of Lord Strange, and dying before his father, was succeeded by his son Thomas, 2nd Lord Derby.

The Stanleys held Middle for about 110 years, when William, Earl of Derby, sold it to the Lord Keeper Egerton, who was created Baron Ellesmere and became Lord Chancellor. After his death King James made his son Earl of Bridgwater, and in that family Middle continued.

The castle was a small one, of which Richard Gough (born 1634) gives a description as he remembered it sixty years before. It was built square, with a courtyard in the centre, and stood within a moat; beyond it on the E. side was a piece of land, nearly an acre in extent, also enclosed by a moat, evidently the site of an outer ward. There was a drawbridge and a gatehouse near the N.E. corner of the castle moat, the latter containing two chambers on each side of the entrance passage which led into the courtyard. On the S. side was a large room, supposed to be the kitchen, having a huge fireplace, and another pleasant apartment; on the W. were two rooms together, perhaps the hall and solar, that were used for holding "the court leet of the manor." The castle was only two storeys in height, and had a flat roof. In the N.E. corner of the inner court was a high tower with a staircase, giving access to the upper floors and the roof, a part of which tower was thrown down by an earthquake in 1688. Another stair was in the S.W. angle. The whole buildings stood in the N.E. corner of a pretty large park which had a lane round it, called Moor Lane.

This castle appears to have been committed to the charge of a constable or keeper, who at one time was Sir Roger Kynaston of Hordeley, being succeeded in the office and as tenant by his son Humphrey about 1564—a dissolute man who was called Wild Humphrey, and was outlawed for debt; he allowed the fabric to go to ruin for want of repairs, and after him it was never inhabited, and became a wreck.

MORETON CORBET (*minor*)

THE beautiful ruin of Moreton Corbet is situated about nine miles N. from Shrewsbury, having been erected in 1576 and 1578, adjacent to the foundations of a more ancient castle, which was probably demolished to make room for it. This early building may have been the work of one of the Turret family who were long settled here, and from them the place received its name of Moreton Turret, and continued to be so called until the year 1516. The heiress of that family married, in the reign of Henry III., Sir Richard Corbet of Wattlesbury, and the Corbets have possessed the place and lands ever since.

The above dates are those of Sir Andrew Corbet, knight, who died in 1578, and of his son Robert, who, having travelled in Italy, brought back a craze for renaissance art and a design for a house in that style. Camden says that he began to build "a most gorgeous and stately house, after the Italian model; but death prevented him, so that he left the new work unfinished, and the old castle defaced." He died of the plague in London *s.p.*, and his estates passed to his cousin Sir Richard, who died 1606, and was succeeded by his brother Sir Vincent, created a baronet in 1642. He served King Charles zealously, and had afterwards to compound for his estates so heavily that he was obliged to sell a part, including Moreton Corbet, but this property was redeemed in 1743 by Andrew Corbet of Shawbury Park.

The ruin consists of two houses of different characters, and, not being defensible, could not have been noticed here, but for the fact of its representing an ancient castle now vanished. It must have been sufficiently completed to contain, with closed doors, a small garrison of eighty foot and thirty horse, to keep the place for the king in 1644. In September of that year, however, a Parliamentary force was sent against Moreton Corbet under Colonel Rinking, who, coming from Wem in the night, surprised the garrison and captured the house with little difficulty, losing only one man. After that the building was ruined and the roof removed. It is now the property of Sir Walter O. Corbet, of Acton-Reynald, Bart.

OSWESTRY, OR OSWALDESTRE (*non-existent*)

OSWESTRY is so called in memory of a battle fought here A.D. 642, when Oswald, King of Northumbria, fell fighting against Penda, the pagan Prince of Mercia. Within a mile is the ancient earthwork called Old Oswestry, the British Caer Ogyrvan, the birthplace, it is said, of King Arthur's third wife, the fair and frail Guinevere.

Oswestry lies on the N.W. frontier of Salop, almost upon Welsh territory, having been supported by the castle of Whittington, two miles off. In Saxon times it was the head of the lordship, and here was one of the many earthwork mounds which are found in this region, where the Saxon chief had his timber house fortified with palisades and ditches.

In 1071, when Morcar and Edwin were deprived of their possessions, the Conqueror bestowed this district on Roger de Montgomery, Earl of Shrewsbury, who granted the fee to Warin the Bald, Sheriff of Shropshire under him—"a man little in body but great in soul"—married to the earl's niece. On the death of Warin in 1085, Oswestry, or as the place is called in Domesday, Meresberie, was enjoyed by Reginald de Bailleul, who married his widow, and built a castle here, called "Luure" or Luvre (*i.e.* l'Œuvre, or *The Work*), held after him by his stepson Hugh, the son of Warin. He died young, and was succeeded here by Alan Fitz Flaen.

In the metrical Norman history of Fulke Fitz Warine (translated by Mr. Thomas Wright) is given the first mention of this castle, such as it then was, in the year 1608, when all the N.W. and S.W. of England rose against the Normans, and York was stormed, 3000 of the usurpers being massacred (a manifest exaggeration). William I. travelling in the Forest of Dean, learning this, swore "by the splendour of God" to avenge himself, and the Norman garrison at Shrewsbury being besieged at the time, he marched thither and relieved the place. Then he is said to have come to a little castle "which is called 'The Tree Town of Oswald,' but now Oswaldestre. Here the king called a knight Aleyn or Alan Fitz Flaen and gave him the little castle and the honour appertaining to it ; and from this Alan came all the lords of England who had the surname of FitzAlan. Subsequently, this Alan caused the castle to be much enlarged."

Eyton, however, shows that Alan did not obtain Oswestry till after William's death, and tradition traces him to the court of Macbeth in Scotland. He was undoubtedly of the royal house of Stuart, and the ancestor of the FitzAlans of Oswestre. His eldest son William acquired also the lordship of Clun (*q.v.*), by his second wife Isabel de Say, and both places were long held by the Fitz-Alans, earls of Arundel, and afterwards by their representatives the Howards. His second son was Walter, Steward of Scotland, who supported the Empress Maud, and during her reverses took refuge in Scotland at the court of her relative David I. ; he died in 1177, and his great-great-grandson Walter, who died cir. 1320, married Marjory Bruce, whose son was Robert Bruce, King of Scotland. His successors were Lords Marchers, who, with other Norman nobles, had power and lands conferred on them on condition that they kept the Welsh quiet, and any territory they were able to annex was to be counted their own. It followed therefore that these Border fortresses of theirs should be strongly built and garrisoned, and in their dealings with the wretched natives these lords were domineering, rapacious, and unscrupulous, ill-treating the inhabitants, confiscating their property, and ignoring their rights. Many of the castles in this district were held by military service due at Oswestry Castle.

William FitzAlan dying in 1160, during the minority of his son William, the sheriff, Guy le Strange, had custody of Oswestry and Clun, with other castles, and in 1165 a determined onslaught was made on the Welsh by Henry II., who advanced to this castle and encamped his forces near it. In 1188 William FitzAlan entertained here Baldwin, Archbishop of Canterbury, and Giraldus Cambrensis; he died in 1210, when, his son being a minor, King John seized the place, and during his wars in Wales made Oswestry his headquarters, storing in the castle immense quantities of munitions of war. Upon his coming of age young FitzAlan was called on to pay a fine for his inheritance of 10,000 marks (equal to about £70,000 now), and as he was unable to do this his lands were given to Thomas de Eardington. William FitzAlan died, and his brother John at once attacked and took Oswestry Castle by force, and joined himself to the party of the barons in their revolt. When in 1216 the raging king proceeded to retaliate on his opponents, he came to avenge himself at Oswestry and burned that town to the ground. During the next reign Prince Llewellyn overran the district, burning Clun and Redcastle, but Oswestry was too strong for him.

Then came King Edward I., whom Green describes as "a born soldier, tall, deep-chested, long of limb, capable alike of endurance and action, and sharing to the full his people's love of venture and hard fighting." He, in 1277, built a wall round Oswestry, including the castle in its circuit; he visited the place in 1282, and again in 1295 after an insurrection of the Welsh. During the minority of Richard, the young Earl of Arundel (8 Edward I.), his mother Isabel had the custody of this castle; he died in 1302, and his son Earl Edmund became a warm supporter of Edward II., in whose defence he gathered a force together at Oswestry, but being taken prisoner at Shrewsbury, was executed at Hereford in 1326. His enemy the notorious Roger Mortimer then took possession of Oswestry Castle, on being made Lord of the Welsh Marches (from whence his descendants took their title of Earls of March), but after his execution the family estates were restored to Earl Edmund's son Richard. This earl was present at Crecy with 200 retainers from Oswestry and Clun.

In 1397, on the attainder and execution of Richard, Earl of Arundel, Richard II. gave his estates to William Scrope, the newly created Earl of Wiltshire; but when Henry IV. led that unfortunate king from Flint Castle to Chester, he delivered the captive prince to Thomas, the son of Earl Richard, saying: "Here is the murderer of your father, you must be answerable for him." It was shortly before this time that Richard II. had adjourned the great Parliament of Shrewsbury to Oswestry, when the remarkable scene took place, wrongly portrayed by Shakespeare as happening at the Tower of London,—when the king determined the dispute between Bolingbroke, Duke of Hereford, and Mowbray, Duke of Norfolk, these two nobles having there referred their quarrel to the king, who directed that they should fight out their feud at Coventry (see *Baginton* and *Caludon, Warwickshire*).

Little is heard of Oswestry during the Wars of the Roses, and the property went to heirs male, with the earldom of Arundel, till 1580, when, on the death of Earl Henry FitzAlan *s.p.* male, his daughter and heiress Mary married Thomas, Duke of Norfolk, and carried the titles and honours of FitzAlan to the Howards, with whom the title of Baron Oswaldestre still remains. Philip, Earl of Arundel, died in the Tower in 1595, when the Crown took possession of his lands, but James I. in 1603 granted, by letters patent, the lordship, manor, and castle of Oswestry, to Philip's half-brother, Thomas Howard, Earl of Suffolk, one of the captains of the fleet which defeated the Armada. He sold the property to Dame Elizabeth Craven, from whom it descended to William Herbert, Marquess of Powis, and by the female line to the present lord of the manor of Oswestry, the Earl of Powis.

In June 1644, Oswestry town having been captured by the Earl of Denbigh with a large Parliamentary force, the besieged took refuge in the castle, which was held for the king; but the gate was blown in with a petard, and the garrison surrendered, 400 of them marching out. Then in 1647, by order of the committee, the castle was demolished, and that so effectually that after the Restoration a proclamation was made at Oswestry that "the swine market will be kept on the hill or voyd place where the castle is."

The mound, which recent excavations have proved to be chiefly a natural elevation, has on it some fragments of the ancient keep which crowned it, and this is all that is left of the historic Border fortress. The hill is about 30 feet high and 200 feet in circumference; according to Mr. Clark the keep was one of the shell type, and polygonal. The moat, which extended to the Beatrice Gate of the town on the one side and to the Willow (Wallia, or Wales) Gate on the other, has disappeared with all the walls and buildings. A sketch of the last century given in the *Transactions of the Shropshire Archæological Society* (vol. vi. Part II.), shows that a considerable portion of the castle was then standing, a plain strong building with a gatehouse and drawbridge. Edward's "History of Oswestry" (1815) says: "It had a tower called Madoc's Tower, while the Bailey's Head, as we now term it, formed the ballium or courtyard. The barbican or outer gate, where the maimed and blind were relieved, would be situate on the mound in Castle Street,—cleared away about thirty years ago, and then called Cripple's Gate." It was probably approached by a bridge over the moat, which ran across the site of the new municipal buildings.

QUATFORD (*non-existent*)

THIS district is an important historic position on Severn-side, where the Danes in their last campaign with Alfred had left their name at a ford on the river, still called Danesford. Near to this, on the right bank, they appear to have raised a mound, or rather scarped and fortified a natural eminence, which at the Domesday Survey was called Oldbury, and still bears that name. Then, after sixteen years, came the Lady of Mercia, Ethelfleda, who on a high cliff on the same side, separated from Oldbury by a marshy tract of land, reared a Saxon timber fortress at the place called Brugge or Bridge, afterwards Bridgnorth (*q.v.*).

About two miles lower down the river, and on the E. side of it, is the ditched and scarped natural mound where was a Saxon stronghold called Quatford, and near it, on a little isolated hill, somewhat above on the river-side, Earl Roger de Montgomery, soon after the Conquest, with his pious countess, erected a Norman castle and a church, and lived here when not at Shrewsbury or at his southern home of Arundel. At his death his possessions went to his second son Hugh, who, being killed in 1094, was succeeded by his terrible elder brother Robert. He had hitherto been in the enjoyment of Belême (or Belesme) and all the other family possessions in Normandy, and now came over to espouse the cause of his patron, Duke Robert of Normandy, eldest son of the Conqueror, against the Red King. This "Devil of Belême," as he is called, seeing the inferiority of his father's castle at Quatford, demolished it, and transferred the stones to the very superior site, higher up the river, at Brugge, where, on a commanding position not far from Ethelfleda's Mound, he built, in the short period of twelve months, the strong Norman castle of Bridgnorth (*Freeman*).

REDCASTLE (*minor*)

THIS ancient ruin lies about four miles E. from Wem in Hawkstone Park, the seat of Viscount Hill. Camden wrote : "Upon a woody hill, or rather rock (which was anciently called Radcliffe), stood a castle, upon a very high ground, called from the reddish stone, Redcastle, and by the Normans Castle Rous, heretofore the seat of the Audleys by the bounty of Mawd the stranger, or Le Strange : but now there is nothing to be seen but decayed walls." And Leland, cir. 1539, declared it to be "now at ruinns. It hath been strong & hath decayid many a Day." Henry, the first of the Aldithley or Audley family noted by Dugdale, had a licence in 16 Hen. III. to build a castle upon his demesne, but it is believed that the hill was fortified in earlier days.

The most famous of the Audleys was James, Lord Audley, who, according to Walsingham, by his extraordinary valour at the battle of Poictiers in 30 Edward III., "brake through the French army, and caused much slaughter that day to the enemy." And Froissart recounts how, with his four esquires, "he fought always in the chief of the Battle. He was sore hurt in the body, and in the visage. As long as his breath served him he fought;" for which service the Black Prince gave him a yearly fee of 500 marks, and when Lord James handed this to his esquires, the prince added 600 marks a year more. He died in 1386.

In 1459, James Touchet, Lord Audley, issuing from Redcastle with the Lancastrian forces 10,000 strong, to oppose the march of the Yorkists before the battle of Bloreheath (a place distant ten miles only from Redcastle), was there defeated and killed. Lord James, the son of John, Lord Audley, was in 1497 beheaded for his share in the Cornish rising, after the battle of Blackheath (see *Nether Stowey, Somerset*), when his possessions were confiscated, but restored to his son John 25 Henry VIII., though he regained his title in 1513.

Then we hear no more of that family, and Redcastle passed through many hands, a partition of it being made in 1654.

The ruined castle and the demesne were purchased in the last century by Sir Rowland Hill, between 1737 and 1756, and his family have continued there. The ruin spoken of in the sixteenth century must have been repaired subsequently, since during the Civil War "Mr. Rowland Hill of Hawkstone, a zealous Royalist, hid himself in the Tower glen, and being discovered, was imprisoned in the adjacent castle, commonly called Redcastle, whilst his house was pillaged and ransacked by the rebels. The castle was soon after demolished."

A few remains exist. One ancient tower, perhaps the keep, is still standing, in great dilapidation, and there is a part of a tower containing the well, 200 feet deep. A ravine divides the Castle Hill into two parts, and this has been fortified by a cross ditch, while a wall carried round the top of the rock defended the buildings on it.

ROWTON (minor)

ROWTON is on the W. of Shrewsbury, near the Severn, and is said by Camden to be the most ancient of Shropshire castles. It was held in the twelfth century by Roger de Say, under the Honour of Montgomery, and from him passed to his two daughters, Lucia and Amice. Towards the end of the thirteenth century, Robert Burnell, Bishop of Bath and Wells, obtained a grant of the estate, holding it of the king *in capite* by the serjeantry of providing two archers at Montgomery Castle in war time. The value was small. Thence it came to the Le Strange family, and was held by John le Strange of Knockyn, when Llewellyn, Prince of Wales, levelled it to the ground in 1282. In 1482 William Lyster was in possession of Rowton, and his family retained it, as in the seventeenth century we find its owner was Thomas Lyster, an active Royalist, whose wife, on his being taken prisoner at Shrewsbury, continued to hold the castle against the Parliamentary general, Mytton, and with such effect as to obtain good terms for its surrender. Sir Thomas, who was knighted by Charles I., had to pay a heavy composition for its restitution.

It is now the property of Lord Rowton, who as Mr. Montague Corry was long the private secretary and close friend of Lord Beaconsfield.

SHRAWARDINE (*non-existent*)

THE name of Shrawardine is derived from the words *Shire-reeve-worthine* (the county of the shire reeve, or sheriff): the locality having been the residence of Saxon sheriffs before the Conquest and of Norman ones after it. It occupied a commanding position guarding an important ford over Severn, E. of Shrewsbury, and on the E. side of the river is the Saxon or Danish mound, which was left by the Normans who built their castle opposite to it.

Mr. Eyton says the fortress stood upon land of the FitzAlans, but was probably built by order of King Henry I. It was for about a hundred years repaired and garrisoned by the Crown, and at least twelve estates were held in this county and in Stafford by serjeantry, or the service of certain quotas of castle-guard at Shrawardine, of which records exist as being returned as early as 1165. At the close of John's reign this castle was razed by the Welsh, when its ruins were handed by the king to the first FitzAlan, who rebuilt it about 1240. Its name was commonly "Castle Isabel," perhaps from the coincidence that one of its possessors, William FitzAlan, married Isabel de Say; and his grandson the first John, who rebuilt it, married Isabel de Albine, a coheiress of the Earl of Arundel, while the wife of his son John was Isabel de Mortimer, whose dower house it became. Ceasing thus to be royal property, the fortress lost the feudal services rendered there, which were transferred to Montgomery.

On the death of Richard, Earl of Arundel, in 1302, this castle was deemed of no annual value, but in 1322, when Edward II. commenced the war against his barons, Earl Edmund joining him (as is shown also at Oswestry), came to his castle of Shrawardine, and for long held the Welsh Marches. In 1326, when Queen Isabella and her "gentle" Mortimer appeared in arms against the king, Earl Edmund was seized by the townsfolk near Shrewsbury, and being handed over to the queen's party was beheaded at Hereford, when his lands were seized by Mortimer.

Nothing is recorded after this of Shrawardine until August 1485, when

Henry, Duke of Richmond, on his way from Milford Haven to the field of Bosworth, came here desiring to pass at Shrewsbury. Leland says the place is two miles from Montford Bridge, and elsewhere mentions a child of FitzAlan's "which by the Neclygeance of his Norice, fell, as is sayd, out of his norice's armes, from the Batlements of the Castle of Shrawardig, and was killed."

Sir Thomas Bromley, afterwards Lord Chancellor, who presided over the mock trial of Mary Queen of Scots at Fotheringhay, purchased the Shrawardine Castle estates in 1583, and his son Sir Henry made the castle his chief residence. In the time of his grandson Henry Bromley, the fortress was garrisoned for King Charles under Colonel Sir William Vaughan, who from his successful sallies and his long resistance in 1644 was called "The Devil of Shrawardine"; but the castle was taken by treachery at last, burnt down and totally destroyed by the Parliament forces in 1645, its very stones being taken away for repairing Shrewsbury. Vaughan's descendant Henry was created Lord Montfort in 1741, a title which died with his grandson, the third baron. A story is related that during the investment (which could not have been very close) Colonel Mytton, the Parliamentary commander, coming on Sir W. Vaughan and twelve of his officers abroad, out of the castle, made prisoners of them and brought them before the walls, summoning the place, " which upon capitulation seemed willing to surrender, but Sir William, slipping in, drew up the bridge and returned a denial," when the other officers were carried off.

About 1760, after his return from India, Robert, the great Lord Clive— among his other purchases of land—acquired Shrawardine and Montford from the second Lord Montfort.

SHREWSBURY (chief)

BOTH Britons and Romans possessed themselves in turn of the vantage point of land where the river Severn, in its course southward, forms a large loop of flat ground, about 500 yards across, leaving a narrow neck on which was a natural eminence commanding the passage of the river between England and Wales. Here afterwards the Saxons erected a lofty mound, where now is Laura's Tower, and a line of earthworks, within which, after the fifth century, grew the town of Shrewsbury.

The Conqueror bestowed nearly the whole of Shropshire on his kinsman Roger de Montgomery, besides 158 manors in other parts; and here, as Earl of Shrewsbury, he installed the *caput* of his earldom, and about the year 1080 commenced to build a Norman castle, clearing away fifty-one houses of the town on the northern isthmus to procure a site for it. At first there was probably only a keep with its surrounding wall; and this his successor, Robert de

Belême (see *Bridgnorth*), extended on both sides to the river bank, where stood the Norman Gerewald's Tower. This (temp. Henry III.) formed the starting-point of the circuit of the city walls, which were carried thence on the W., and round the city back to the castle again, including on each side the approaches to the two bridges over Severn.

The same "Devil of Belême" fortified this castle against Henry I., at the beginning of his rebellion (1102), but when his other castle of Bridgnorth had fallen, and Henry advanced to Shrewsbury, Earl Robert, forsaken by his friends and seeing no means of resistance, left his castle here, by the gateway which we still see, and, meeting the king on his road to Shrewsbury, threw himself at Henry's feet, giving up the keys and suing for mercy. The cruel and crafty rebel received a safe-conduct to the coast, but all his lands and honours were taken from him. Afterwards, in 1113, King Henry put an end to the mischief which Belême was still working in Normandy, by seizing him and sending him over to Wareham Castle in Dorset, where he died in captivity.

The castle thenceforth became royal property, and was entrusted to a sewer or steward, one Richard de Belmeis, and next to Pagan Fitz John, and so it remained for twenty-four years, when Henry gave it to his second wife, who placed it in the hands of William de FitzAlan, the elder brother of Walter, Steward of Scotland, and ancestor of the Arundel family. FitzAlan adhered to the cause of the rightful heir to the crown, the Empress Maud, and Shrewsbury had to stand a siege in 1138 by King Stephen, who carried the fortress by assault after four weeks, and ruthlessly hanged the captain, Arnulf de Hesding, and ninety-three men of his garrison. William FitzAlan fortunately escaped. When the young Duke Henry, afterwards Henry II., came over, he obtained possession of Shrewsbury Castle, and it was once more attached to the Crown.

During the Barons' War, although this part of the country was greatly disturbed, no mention of this castle occurs; it continued to be held by the sheriffs of Salop. In 1283 the Parliament which sat at Shrewsbury under Edward I., after his final defeat of the Welsh, executed the barbarous sentence for treason on David, the sovereign of Wales, which was carried out here, with all its horrors, probably in the castle-yard, under the eye of the king. Afterwards the whole assembly adjourned to the castle of Bishop Burnell at Acton Burnell (*q.v.*), where was held the celebrated parliament in which for the first time the Commons of England participated.

To Shrewsbury Henry IV. brought his forces on the eve of the battle with Hotspur, in 1403, arriving there only a few hours before the insurgents, who also were advancing on this town. By this measure he secured the passage of the Severn and cut off the assistance which Percy was expecting from Owen Glendower from Oswestry. The fight, fatal to him, took place on the second day at the place since called Battlefield, three miles from Shrewsbury, but there was some skirmishing the day before under the N. walls of the town.

Many succeeding sovereigns came here ; but after the union with Wales the importance of this fortress, as the door of Wales, passed away, and when Leland visited it he wrote : "The Castle hath beene a stronge thynge. It is now much in ruine." In the reign of Elizabeth it was leased to one Richard Onslow, who conveyed his interest in it to the corporation.

In the Civil War of the seventeenth century the place was garrisoned for the king, the outer walls being repaired and the gates strengthened. Charles visited Shrewsbury on several occasions. In February 1645 a Parliamentary force of 1200 men under Colonels Bowyer and Mytton managed to surprise the castle at night, a bad watch being kept. A party coming round on the E. side by water obtained possession of the palisading and let in the rest of the force, which captured the stronghold almost without a blow, losing only two men ; the place was surrendered the same day, upon which the town also was taken.

Somehow the castle escaped destruction at the hands of the London Committee, and at the Restoration was given back to the municipality, who kept it in a fortified state till the reign of James II., when the guns and ammunition were removed, together with the outworks. It is probable that the fine Norman church of St. Nicholas was removed at that time.

What remained was leased (about 1730) to a Mr. Goswell, who made the old place into a gloomy habitation, in which state it remained till Sir William Pulteney improved the appearance of it, as now seen.

The castle, which is built of a reddish coloured stone, still retains a considerable portion of its old fabric. The keep is a square building with circular turrets at the angles, and a good deal of the walls of the inner ward remain, together with the old Norman gateway. Modern constructions have been erected on the mound.

STOKESAY (minor)

THIS fine structure stands at the foot of the hills at the N. entrance of the valley of the Onny River, seven miles from Ludlow, and is an almost unique specimen of a mansion of the thirteenth century, fortified subsequently to the erection of its domestic portion. Its principal defence consists in a moat, which points to its being intended rather for use as a family abode than for military purposes. Stokesay is of peculiar interest to the archæologist and historian, since of all early embattled houses in this county it retains most of its original character.

The De Lacys of Ludlow, who from Domesday till 1241 held this and other manors directly from the Crown, about the year 1115 enfeoffed at Stoke the De Says, whose ancestor, Picot de Sai (a place nine miles to the W.

of Exmes in Normandy), had followed Duke William, and fought for him
at Senlac. Five generations of De Says dwelt here, and in 1241, when the
last of the De Lacys, their superiors, died, a blind old man, his estates were
divided between his two sons-in-law, Peter of Geneva, married to his daughter
Matilda, and John de Verdun, the husband of the younger, Margaret, by whom
he obtained Stokesay with other manors. He died in 1274, and during the
life of his son this manor was conveyed to Lawrence de Ludlow, who in 1291
(19 Edward I.) obtained a licence to crenellate his house of Stokesay and
strengthen it with a wall of stone and lime. He seems at this time to have
built the great S. tower, the Hall having been previously * built in all probability
by John de Verdun,
who was an active
Royalist during the
Barons' War, and re-
sided here as one of
the Lords Marchers.

After this, ten gene-
rations of Ludlows
held Stokesay: they
seem to have been
prosperous merchants,
and to have made
their money in trade.
At last, in 1497, the
property fell with
Anne, daughter of
John Ludlow, to
Thomas Vernon, son
of Sir Richard Vernon

STOKESAY

of Haddon, and they were living here when Leland visited Stokesay Castle.
Their son held the place and died in 1570, when Stokesay was sold to Sir
George Mainwaring, and after being settled in 1616 on the families of
Baker and Francis, was in 1620 resold to a Shropshire lady, the widow
of the wealthy Sir William Craven, knight, Alderman of London. Her
eldest son, the heir of Stokesay, who is spoken of as one of the most
accomplished and honoured gentlemen in Europe, distinguished himself as
a soldier at the early age of seventeen, in the Low Countries under Henry,
Prince of Orange, and was knighted in 1626, being created Baron Craven
eight days after.

The story of this nobleman's life is romantic and interesting. His admiration

* As the style of this castle is earlier than that of Acton-Burnell, whose licence is dated 1284, it seems
likely that the licence granted to Ludlow was only for an addition to an already existing fortress.

of the beautiful but unhappy Elizabeth, daughter of James I., and wife of the Elector Palatine Frederick, called the Queen of Hearts, led him to adventure his life in the enterprise for placing the Elector on the throne of Bohemia ; he was taken prisoner, and was obliged to purchase his liberty with £20,000. Then when Elizabeth's kingdom was gone, and she and her family were destitute, Craven continued her friend and adviser ; he is said also to have bought Combe Abbey near Coventry, from the romantic wish to possess the place where Elizabeth had passed her childhood. In her early days she had

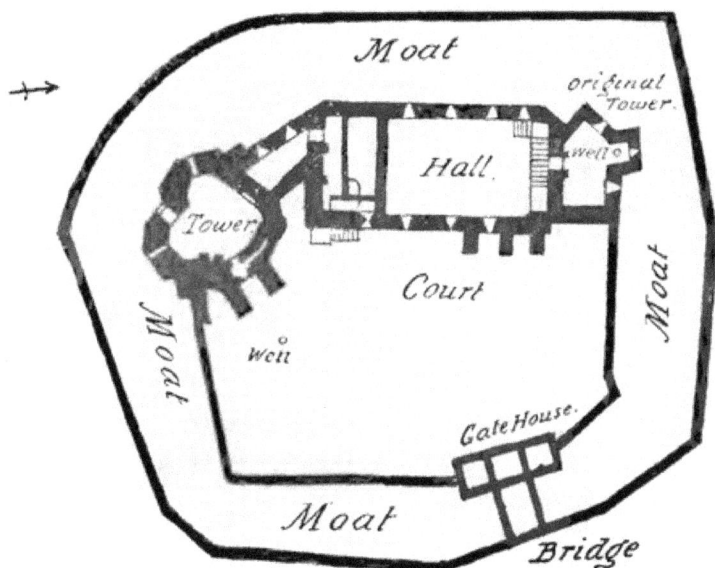

STOKESAY

been placed here under the guardianship of Lord Harrington, who was entrusted with her education, and it was while she was here that the gunpowder plotters formed a plan to surprise Lord Harrington, and seize the princess, whom they intended to proclaim a Catholic queen. She was removed then for safety to Coventry. To Craven's munificence it was due that Elizabeth in 1661 was enabled to return to her native country ; Combe Abbey was placed at her disposal, and it was there, 'tis said, that she gave her hand and was privately married to her devoted friend, Lord Craven (see the *Verney Papers*, vol. i.). But she died the next year, leaving him her papers, books, and pictures, which are still in the collection at Combe. Additional interest attaches to this princess, since she was the mother of Prince Rupert, the gallant general of the great Civil War, and of his brother Prince Maurice, and was the grandmother of our first Hanoverian king, George I.

Lord Craven lost £5000 in assisting the Royal Family of England during the war, and in their exile, and was by Charles II. in 1663 created Earl of Craven. He died in 1697, aged nearly eighty-nine, and was succeeded in his estates by his cousin, on whom the barony alone descended. During Lord Craven's absence, Stokesay was let on a very long lease, not many years expired, to a family called Baldwyn, and it was surrendered to the Parliament forces besieging Ludlow, thereby escaping demolition, only the battlements of the N. tower being re-

moved. The old mansion recently passed into the hands of the late Mr. Allcroft, who has preserved the fabric with much skill and judgment, and his son, Mr. H. J. Allcroft, is the present owner.

The buildings, which are set in a courtyard of oblong shape, are surrounded, close to the walls, by a moat 22 feet wide, and now 6 feet deep, fed from a small stream flowing into the river Onny. The present

STOKESAY

gatehouse is a fine half-timbered Tudor building, replacing the old drawbridge house which led into the courtyard, where traces of several buildings may be seen, in existence at the beginning of the century, including the kitchen and buttery.

The Hall is, with that of Winchester, the most perfect remaining of the thirteenth century. It is the main feature of the house, standing opposite the gateway, and measures 51 feet by 31 feet internally. It has a fine open roof, and is lighted by four Early English windows on the W. over the moat, and by three on the E. There is no fireplace, the fire being put into a central brazier, and the roof is blackened with smoke. At the N. end some steps lead into what is probably the oldest part of the fabric, a small defensible out-building, the ground floor of which is a cellar with a large chamber upstairs, and at the end of which is a small tower projected into the moat. At the S.

end are the lower apartments, and an external staircase to the solar above, from whence a covered passage leads into the great tower, which has the appearance of two octagon turrets joined together. It is in three storeys, with a conical roof, and is of an imposing appearance, being 66 feet high, with walls 2 yards thick. Hudson Turner declares Stokesay to be one of the most perfect and interesting buildings of the thirteenth century which we possess.

TONG (*non-existent*)

TONG lies on the E. of the county, near Boscobel. Leland says of it: "There was an olde Castell of stone caullid Tunge Castel. It standeth half a myle from the towne, on a Broke. Sir Henry Vernoun a late daies made the Castel al of bricke."

Its early history is not known; that ascribed to it regarding King Vortigern and Hengist belongs to a castle of the same name in Kent, with which this one has been confused.

Tong passed through the hands of various families. At one time it was owned by the Pembrugges, the last of whom, Sir Fulke, dying *s.p.*, his sister and heir, Benedicta, carried Tong to William Vernon of Haddon; from whom it came by an heiress to the Stanleys, and was purchased from them by a lawyer, Sir Thomas Harris. His daughter marrying William Pierre-point in 1638, brought the property to the dukes of Kingston. Evelyn, the last duke, sold Tong in 1764 to George Durant, whose family were here for a hundred years. The Earl of Bradford purchased Tong from Captain Durant.

George Durant, having as Paymaster of the Forces acquired a large fortune, built the present curious house in the place of Sir H. Vernon's. The view of the old house, as it was in 1731, is given by Buck.

In Symon's list of Shropshire garrisons in May 1645 it is added: "Tong Castle,—first the king had it, and then the rebels gott it; then Prince Rupert tooke it, and put in a Garrison, who afterwards burnt it, when he drew them out to the battails of York." . . . "A fayre old Castle neere the Church called Tong Castle belonging to Pierrepoint this 18 years."

The owner was then William Pierrepoint, second son of the Earl of Kingston, who was killed in Charles' service; his son being on the side of the Parliament.

The castle is partly surrounded by a deep artificial ditch; the entrance gateway is curiously carved with a representation of the ancient castle.

WATTLESBOROUGH (*minor*)

THE castle of this name lies to the W. of Shrewsbury, a little beyond Rowton Castle, in a district once traversed by a Roman road—a branch of the Watling Street. The manor was among those held by Roger Fitz Corbet of Caus, whose Corbet ancestor had received it from the Conqueror, and the house formed the Border residence of that family. A Richard Corbet is shown here in 1179 (26 Henry II.), belonging to a branch of the Caus family and holding under them; and after four more generations of these Corbets the lands came to the De la Poles, by the marriage of Elizabeth, only child of Sir Fulke Corbet, with John de la Pole, Lord of Mawddy, or Moethe, and other lands, through his mother, the daughter of Llewellyn. She died in 1403, her son, Fulke de Mawddy, being born 1390, and her grandson, Sir John de Burgh—the son of her daughter Elizabeth, the wife of Hugh de Burgh—succeeded.

The family of Leighton then obtained Wattlesborough by the marriage of Ankaret, a daughter of this last Sir John de Burgh, with John Leighton, whose family thenceforth made it their principal seat until the year 1711, when Sir Edward Leighton removed to Loton, about a mile distant. Since that time Wattlesborough has been used as a farmer's house.

There is not much recorded regarding the place, except that in 1584 the Earl of Essex, Elizabeth's favourite, stayed here with Sir Edward Leighton for nearly eight weeks, perhaps "with a view of raising forces for the expedition against Holland" (Canon Blake's paper in the *Archæological Journal*, 1868).

The engraving of this building, as it lately was, shows a tolerably perfect square Norman keep of small size, having double pilasters at the end of each face, not meeting but with an open arris, as is seen at Helmsley, Yorks. Some Norman windows remain, but most of them are enlarged loopholes with square heads, one being of later insertion. The roof is formed by a four-sided frame and is tiled. The tower now has but three stages, but by tradition there was formerly a fourth, and also a battlemented parapet; while the original roof was flat, and had a look-out turret above it.

The remains now consist of this tower only, with a small building or wing on the N. side; but it is said that there once were four such towers, the stones of which were used in the construction of the neighbouring church. Traces of foundations occur in various spots, and there are vestiges of the moat. Connected with the tower is a large earthwork, 56 yards square, of possibly prehistoric origin.

WHITECHURCH (*non-existent*)

WHITECHURCH was formerly called Weston, and was situated in the N.W. corner of the county, near Flint and Cheshire. Some ruins of the walls of this castle existed as late as 1760, on the Castle Hill on the side of the mill, but they have now vanished entirely. The manor belonged at the Conquest to Harold the king, and was given by William I. to his stepson-in-law William, Earl Warren, afterwards Earl of Surrey. Eyton says that the Warrens held this place until the death of Bertred in 1281, when Whitechurch passed to his sister Eleanore, the wife of Robert le Strange. Thenceforth the history of Whitechurch merges in that of the Barons le Strange of Blackmere.

WHITTINGTON (*minor*)

THE remains of the castle of Whittington stand on low marshy ground near the railway station. The manor, after the Conquest, was held by a Welsh owner named Tudor, under Earl Roger de Montgomery; his younger son Ramulph, styled "Pefr" (the "Fine," or the "Swell"), married Maud, daughter of Ingelric, a noble Saxon, once the mistress of the Conqueror, and who had by him a son called William. She had also by her husband three other sons, who, being all brought up together, bore the name of Pefr, anglicised into Peverell. The king's bastard son received grants of land in Notts, Northamptonshire, and Derby, and Maud's other sons also were provided for; one of them, on the attainder of Robert de Belême (see *Oswestry*), had Whittington, which afterwards went to his niece Miletta Peverell, who was the wife of Warine, the son of Fulke Fitz Warine, who thus became possessed of the property.

Henry II. annexed it to the Crown, placing there first Geoffrey de Vere, and then Roger de Powis, who was Lord of Whittington temp. Richard I.; but in the sixth year of King John, Fitz Warine succeeded in recovering his family property. He was a strenuous supporter of that reckless king, and was at one time lord of Ludlow. A story is told of his once playing a game of chess with King John, when the monarch, losing the game, in a rage broke Fitz Warine's head with the chess-board; "but Fulke, nothing daunted, returned the blow, and almost," says an old writer, "demolished the king" (see Harper's "Marches of Wales," 1894). In 1219 his son, the third Fulke, paid Henry III. £262 and two chargers (*destriers*), for the possession of this castle, with licence next year to fortify it. This we can take as the date of the castle. Fulke was slain at Lewes in 1264, fighting on the king's side, when Henry was forced by De Montfort, his captor, to grant Whittington to Llewellyn of Wales.

SHROPSHIRE

The fourth Fulke served with such gallantry in the Welsh campaigns under Edward I. that Whittington was restored to him, and his son, the fifth Fulke, was summoned to Parliament as a baron, in 1295, till 1314. After him the descent of the Fitz Warines of Whittington Castle and manor continued for a long period, until by the failure of heirs male the property passed by Elizabeth, a sister of the tenth Fulke, to her husband, Sir Richard Hankford, knight. Their daughter and heir, Thomasine, married William Bourchier, ancestor of the Bourchiers, earls of Bath, whose descendant Earl John exchanged Whittington with Henry VIII., and from the Crown it passed to the FitzAlan family, from whom, in 1570, it was purchased by William Albany, and the manor has since continued with the descendants of that gentleman.

Mr. Clark shows that this place is the site of a very early fortification, in which water formed the main defence, the proof of which is in an artificial mound, 30 feet high, with sides about 150 feet long by 100, that have been scarped and revetted. A wall surrounded this, defended by five or six circular towers, of which the two supporting the entrance remain entire, and there is the base of another. In front of this mound was another large earthen platform, separated from it by a moat, containing the main entrance and the outer ward. Westward of these islands are two others, likewise divided by water, and behind these ranges a sort of semicircular work, with three more islands forming long ramparts and ditches, protecting the inner fort from the S.W. to the S.E. A swiftly running stream from the E. supplied water, flooding the whole intermediate ground between the islands, and rendering them quite unapproachable.

Upon the mound, which must have been formed by Saxon or Danish hands, was the keep, or an enclosed fort within a strong revetment wall, 30 feet in height, with a second gatehouse and drawbridge. The outer ward was approached by a drawbridge and the gatehouse, of which part is still tolerably perfect; this enclosure was rectangular, with strong walls flanked by circular towers at the angles, and having the entrance on its E. side. The whole of the older part seems of the reign of Henry III., and is, no doubt, Fitz Warine work, but there is a chamber in the S. wall with a sharp-pointed window of late Decorated style. No masonry remains on the other islands (*Clark*).

In a drawing of this castle dated 1790, five towers are shown in the outer ward, with a large extent of curtain wall, each tower being battlemented, and a low-pointed entrance doorway with machicoulis over is given. In that year the E. tower fell, and the N. one was then undermined for the purpose of getting stone for road repairs. In 1809 the smaller tower was taken down to repair the gatehouse, which is now nearly all that remains of the castle of the Fitz Warines, who were lords here for nine generations. Their shield is still to be seen on the wall.

VOL. II.

BEESTON

Cheshire

ALDFORD (*non-existent*)

ON the right bank of the river Dee, three miles S. of Chester, and near Pulford, is the village of Aldford, and below it is the ford across Dee, from which it derives its title. On an eminence above are the earthworks of a castle, erected for the defence of this important point, the ancient junction of the North and South Watling Streets.

The fortification is of singular shape, somewhat resembling a harp in the outline of its earthworks and ditches, which alone remain. The outer ward forms a large triangle, whose sides measure respectively 130, 120, and 55 yards along the enclosing ditch, which is 20 yards wide, where unaltered. The N.W. angle of this figure is occupied by a large circular mound, 40 yards in diameter, surrounded by its own moat, 40 yards wide, and intersects the main ditches before mentioned. Upon this mound of still earlier origin was the Norman keep of the castle of a family who took their name from the locality, but the buildings of which have quite disappeared. The country people call the mound Blobb Hill, and the lower or outer court, the Hall Croft, it being the site of a mansion built by the Arderne family, which, like the castle, has vanished.

It is probable that the structure was built in the reign of Henry II., when the Aldford family lived here, having succeeded to certain manors of the Bigods.

Richard de Aldford was succeeded in his fee and castle of Aldford, between 10 John and 13 Henry III., by Sir John Arderne, who appears to have been either his son or his son-in-law, and who was confirmed here by Randle, Earl of Chester, as his *miles* (" pro homagio et servitio suo "). This family of Arderne continued here in a direct line till the reign of Henry IV., when, towards the end of that time, Matilda de Arderne brought Aldford to her husband, Thomas Stanley, the third son of Sir John Stanley, of Lathom and Knowsley, K.G. (see *Liverpool*). On the attainder and execution of Sir William Stanley, Aldford fell to the Crown, and temp. Henry VIII. was bought by Sir William Brereton, who was himself beheaded in 1546, when the property was again seized by the Crown, and granted by the king to Edward Peckham. It afterwards passed to various persons, among whom was the infamous Lord Mohun, whose second wife sold Aldford manor to the Grosvenor family, in whom it is now vested.

BEESTON (*chief*)

BEESTON stands on the summit of a bold hill of new red sandstone, which, rising out of the flat, plain country, attains an elevation of nearly 400 feet above it. Towards the S. the hill slopes evenly and swiftly downwards, but denudation on the N. and E. has left a precipitous cliff, on the brink of which Randle the Third, surnamed Blundeville or Blondeville, sixth Earl of Chester, in 1220 built a magnificent castle. There are no records of any earlier work, but we may well surmise that so commanding a position, overlooking an immense panorama of country, and so close to the main roads passing through this district, was occupied by the original possessors of this county long before Norman days. Little is known of the early history of this fortress. Randle, the founder, was certainly the greatest of the Norman earls of Chester, and to his support King John was mainly indebted for his security on the throne ; while the reign of the young king, Henry III., was established by the victory which Earl Randle gained over the French troops at Lincoln. He raised an army, and, taking Henry with him, marched to Lincoln, where the Comte de Perche and the Dauphin lay waiting for him. Walter de Wittlesey, the Peterborough monk, relates how the two earls met before Lincoln Cathedral, when De Perche, observing the small stature of Randle, exclaimed, "Have I waited here all this while for so small a dwarf !" To which Randle replied, "I vow to God and Our Lady, whose church this is, that before to-morrow evening I will seem to thee greater and taller than that steeple."

The following day he gave battle to the French, destroyed them, and slew the Comte de Perche. Then seizing on Louis the Dauphin in the cathedral, he made him swear on the relics on the high altar never to claim the crown of England, and to quit the country with all his followers. This being done, he sent for the young king, Henry, a child of ten, who had been waiting in the cow-house of Bardley Abbey near Lincoln, and placing him on the altar delivered him seisin of the kingdom by a white wand, and did homage to him, as did all the nobles present. This Earl Randle died without issue in 1232, having held his earldom fifty-one years, and his nephew, John Scott, Earl of Huntingdonshire, succeeded as seventh and last Earl of Chester. On his death in 1237, Henry seized the castles of Chester and Beeston, and caused homage to be done to Prince Edward by the Cheshire nobles and gentry as Earl of Chester.

Later, in 1264, Simon de Montfort after the battle of Lewes took possession of Beeston Castle, and governed it with his supporters; but he could not have held it in force, as the next year the king's men, James de Audley and Urian St. Pierre, took it on behalf of the king. After this, nothing is recorded about the place until the last year of Richard II., who, on his way to carry out his fatal expedition to Ireland, chose Beeston Castle for the repository of his treasure and jewels, leaving them here to the amount of 200,000 marks (£134,000), in charge of a garrison of a hundred men. But on the coming of Bolingbroke all was delivered over to him. The last mention of it as a regular fortress is in 1460, during the Wars of the Roses, when it is recorded among the castles and manors belonging to the earldom.

In Leland's time it was in ruins, and so continued till the Civil Wars of the seventeenth century. In 1640 it was taken and held by the Parliamentarians with a garrison of three hundred, when occurred the only warlike incident connected with the place of which we have any account. In December of that year Captain Landford with some Royalist soldiers came here, and, attended by only eight men, scaled the steep side of the rock and got into the upper ward, and then, as is believed, by the treachery of Captain Steel, the Parliamentarian governor, gained possession of the castle. The whole transaction seems to have been peaceably arranged, but, when Steel marched out after giving up the castle and all its contents, his soldiers mutinied against him, and he was put in prison, and finally shot for his act at Nantwich. Mention of his death is found in the diary of the siege of Nantwich, in which an entry for January 1643 records that "Steel, late governor of Beeston Castle, was shot to death in Tinker's-croft by two soldiers, according to the judgment against him . . . he confessed all his sins, among the rest, that of uncleanness; he prayed a great while, and to the judgment of charity died penitently."

By the capture of Beeston Castle ammunition and stores for one and a half years were secured for the king, and much treasure also was taken, which the country people had sent in for safe custody. Further vicissitudes were in store for Beeston Castle, however, for in 1644 the Parliamentarians advanced from their quarters at Nantwich and besieged it. The Royal garrison, ill provided with both fuel and stores, gallantly held out from October till the middle of the following March, when the princes Rupert and Maurice came in force and compelled the siege to be raised. It was at this time that Prince Rupert caused the manor hall to be burnt, in order to avoid its being used by the enemy; and it is said that, being at dinner in this building, "he did not communicate his intentions to the lady of the house until he rose from dinner, when he expressed his regrets at being compelled thus to requite her hospitality" (*Ayrton*).

BEESTON

The Roundheads returned to the attack again in the next month, and raised a strong mound and other works against the fortress, but the approach of the king again obliged them to retire. The Royalists continued their gallant resistance here till 1645, when, after the defeat of Sir Marmaduke Langdale on Rowton Heath, the king's power in that quarter was destroyed. Then on November 16th, after a further protracted defence of eighteen weeks, the garrison of fifty-six men had to surrender the place, marching out with all the honours of war. It is said there were no provisions found, with the exception of a turkey-pie, the garrison having been reduced even to eating all the cats in the place. The next year Beeston Castle was dismantled and left to ruin.

The manor of Beeston remained with the family of the name of Bunbury, descended from the Bunburys who held it in Henry II.'s time. Sir George Bunbury had it in 44 Queen Elizabeth, and at length, by the marriage of the daughter of Sir Hugh to William Whitmore, it went to the latter, but was soon after transferred by Bridget his heir to Thomas, Viscount Savage of Rock Savage, whose granddaughter Bridget brought it to Sir Thomas Mostyn, Bart., from whose heiress, Lady Champneys, Beeston was purchased by the Tollemache family, and they still own it.

The main fortress stands on the crown of an abrupt precipice, which renders it inaccessible on three sides, i.e. on the N., W., and S. sides, the N. and S. faces being connected by an immensely deep ditch at the base of the walls enclosing the inner ward, which is a rectangular space of an acre. The entrance to it is by a drawbridge and a gatehouse, having two semicircular flanking towers, and an Early English pointed archway with portcullis. This gateway and the castle wall, which descends to the level of the brook at the foot of the cliff, 90 feet below, are all that remains perfect in any degree. There are but few vestiges of the rooms in the castle.

From the drawbridge, externally, stretches the outer ward, a large area of 7 or 8 acres, sufficient to give shelter to flocks and herds, enclosed by an irregular circular wall, strengthened by eight mural towers, which extends across the neck of the hill from N. to S. The entrance to this ward was by a gatehouse similar to that of the inner ward, and it was defended by a strong square tower. Owing to the repairs and additions of the seventeenth century all the masonry of the thirteenth has now quite vanished.

BRUNSTATH, or BRIMSTAGE (minor)

ON a bleak tract of moorland lies this original settlement of the Domvilles, who were probably a younger branch of the barons of Montalt, under whom they held their lands. The elder line is represented by the Earl of Shrewsbury, and another branch continued in uninterrupted male descent at Lymme in this county until the beginning of the last century.

The first Hugh Domville appears in the reign of Henry III., and his descendants continued until the time of Richard II., when an heiress brought the lands to Sir Hugh de Holes or Hulse, by whose granddaughter they passed to the Troutbecks in 10 Henry VI., and from them the property came to the Earl of Shrewsbury, as it is now vested.

At the end of the village is the hall, a building of no great antiquity ; but attached to it is a lofty and ancient peel tower, the surviving member of the former fabric. It is a massive building of four storeys, connected by a newel staircase, and surmounted with a heavy crenellated parapet and machicoulis. The lowest stage has a stone ribbed vault, said to have formed the chapel.

Hugh Hulse and his wife Margery had a licence in 1398 to build an oratory at this place, and the tower is supposed to have been built temp. Henry V. The period of the castle's demolition is uncertain; it was habitable at the end of the sixteenth century, and was then tenanted by John Pool of Poole, as the superior bailiff of the Talbots.

CHESTER CASTLE (*chief*)

THE foundation of this castle is ascribed by Ordericus Vitalis to William the Conqueror three years after the Conquest. It was not only the chief stronghold, but often also the palace of the powerful earls of Chester, and this dual character it retained until alterations made at the beginning of the present century utterly destroyed its interesting details; a Grecian barrack or court-house was then erected, with a Doric temple by way of entrance. One portion only of the old building remains in the shape of a square tower, called Cæsar's or Julius Agricola's Tower, which was long used as a powder magazine. This tower dates from a period later than the Conquest, being Transitional Norman in style, and stands partly on the Roman walls of the ancient city. Within it is the Chapel of St. Mary, infra castrum, built between 1190 and 1200, measuring 19 feet 4 inches by 16½ feet in area, and 16½ feet in height, the roof being vaulted and groined. In this chapel King James II. received mass on his visit to Chester.

The castle is situated near the S.W. angle of the city walls, the upper ward standing on high ground which falls precipitously on the S. and W., and it is further defended on the N. by an artificial elevation. Pennant describes the castle of his time (1784) as "composed of two parts, an upper and a lower, each with a strong gate, defended by a round bastion on either side with a ditch, and formerly with drawbridges. Within the precincts of the upper ballium are to be seen some towers of Norman architecture, square, with square projections at each corner, slightly salient. The handsomest is that called after Julius Cæsar. The arsenal, some batteries, and certain habitable buildings occupy the remaining part. On the side of the lower court stands the noble room called Hugh Lupus' Hall, in which the courts of justice for the county are held; its length is very nearly 99 feet, and the breadth 45 feet; the height is tremendous, being 50 feet, and the chamber is fitting for the state apartments of a great baron. Adjoining the end of this great hall is the Court of Exchequer, or the Chancery of the County Palatine of Chester. This very building is said to have been the Parliament house of the little kings of the palatinate. It savours of antiquity in architecture, and within are a number of neatly carved seats enclosed by Gothic arches and pillars. At the upper end are two chairs of state, one for the earl, the other for the abbot. The eight others are allotted to his eight barons, and occupy one side of the room." Ormerod gives the rare plate by Hollar, of Earl Lupus holding his parliament here. This beautiful Hall was ruthlessly demolished in 1830 to make room for the Grecian designs of Mr. Thomas Harrison. The upper ward remained little altered, however, except that the gatehouse and its towers were removed. Lysons' *Magna Britannia* gives a bird's-eye view taken from the Harleian MSS. (2073.) William I. granted to his nephew Hugh, surnamed Lupus, son of Richard, Earl of Avranches, the County Palatine of Chester "to hold by the sword, as he held England by the crown" (as see under *Halton*). Hugh divided the county between four barons; 1. his cousin, Sir Nigel of Halton; 2. Sir Piers Malban of Nantwich; 3. Sir Eustace of Malpas; 4. Sir Warren Vernon of Shipbrook. Hugh's son Richard was drowned at Barfleur in the shipwreck which caused the death of Prince William, son of Henry I., in 1120; and as he left no issue, the earldom of Chester then descended to his cousin, Ranulph Bohun, as third earl. Ranulph married Maud, daughter of Aubrey de Vere, Earl of Oxford, and died in 1130, being succeeded by his son Ranulph, who took the side of the Empress Maud, and was the great warrior by whom Stephen was defeated (see *Lincoln*). He married Alice, daughter of Robert, Earl of Gloucester, and died in 1152. His son, Hugh, the fifth earl, took the part of the sons of Henry II. against their father, whom he fought in Normandy, but was defeated and made prisoner by the king. Hugh died in 1181, and his son Ranulph, surnamed Blondeville, became sixth Earl of Chester, being also Earl of Lincoln. This earl was not only a very learned man, but also a good soldier. He defeated the French army at Lincoln, thus ending the claim of the Dauphin to the English throne. His first wife was Constance, widow of Geoffrey, third son of Henry II., and father of Prince Arthur, killed by King John at Rouen, and of the hapless Princess Isabel, his sister. Earl Ranulph died at his castle of Wallingford in 1232, *s.p.*, when his lands were divided, his nephew John, surnamed "Scot," succeeding as seventh earl. John married Jane, daughter of Llewellyn, Prince of Wales, by whom he was poisoned (*Matthew Paris*) in 1237. Dying without issue, his four sisters became his heirs 1. Margaret, married to the Earl of Galloway; 2. Isabel, married to Robert Bruce, and grandmother to King Robert Bruce; 3. Maud, died *s.p.*; 4. Eva, wife of Henry, lord of Abergavenny, one of the competitors for the crown of Scotland, temp. Edward I. At Earl John's death Henry III. annexed Chester and its title to the Crown, and his descendants were earls until the time of Edward the Black Prince, since when the eldest sons of all sovereigns of England have from their birth borne the title of Earls of Chester.

It was in Chester Castle, in the year 1477, that Eleanor, Duchess of Gloucester, was confined. The most memorable event which occurred in its history was the great siege, begun in 1643, and lasting, on and off, for three years. The castle itself is not especially mentioned in the accounts of this siege, but we are told that the city had received a tolerably strong line of fortifications, and was able to sustain repeated attacks of the enemy—Lord Byron being in command, with twelve commissioners. The besieged refused nine summonses for capitulation from the Parliamentarian general, Sir William Brereton ; but at last, towards the end of January 1645, having consumed all their horses, dogs, and cats, they made an offer to treat. Articles of surrender were drawn up and at length agreed to, and Chester and its castle were on very honourable terms given up on February 3, 1645.

The old walls which surround the city and their towers are still kept in good order, and afford a pleasant promenade, two miles in length. At their N.W. angle is the Water Tower, which has been rebuilt on the site of the ancient one which stood on the N. bank of Dee for five hundred years. It is described by Fuller in 1662, and in an old record of events at Chester by Hemingway it is said : "1322. In this year the new Tower was built at the cost of the city by John Helpstone, a mason, who conditioned to build the same for the sum of £100." It is of circular shape, 10½ yards in diameter and 24 yards in height, having at convenient distances loopholes for the discharge of missile weapons. But by the desertion of the old river channel, and the sanding up of the haven, this ancient tower has been left high and dry ever since the days of Richard II.

DODDINGTON CASTLE (minor)

IN the fourth year of Henry IV.'s reign John de Delves had licence to crenellate a tower in Doddington Park, about four miles S.E. of Nantwich, where there is a sumptuous house, built about fifty years since. A short distance N. of this modern building are the ancient remains of a castle, or fortified mansion, erected by Sir John Delves in 1364, to which, perhaps, the above mentioned licence applied. Whether the tower was a detached building or an addition to the castle does not appear.

The Delves family was in Staffordshire in the time of Edward I., and its members were esquires of the lords Audley. In 38 Edward III. Sir John Delves had a licence to fortify Doddington, which he had purchased thirteen years previously from John de Bresey (25 Edward III.). It was his grandson who obtained permission from Henry IV. to build the tower ; his great-grandson, Sir John Delves, knight, being slain at Tewkesbury. This Sir John's son, also called John, was beheaded after that battle. In 1621 Sir Thomas Delves of Doddington was made a baronet, and his great-grandson, also Sir Thomas, left an only daughter and heiress, Elizabeth, who brought Doddington to her husband, Sir Brian Broughton—whence the family of Delves-Broughton, the present owners.

The drawing in Ormerod shows a square tower of two storeys, of fourteenth-century style, with a later outer stair of approach, having a battlemented turret capping each angle. "A mansion of middle date, built in the reign of Elizabeth near this castellet, and which was thrice occupied by the Parliamentary troops during the Civil Wars, has been wholly taken down; but five statues of Lord Audley and his esquires, which decorated the portico, and some other ornamental stone-work of the mansion, are preserved in the outer staircase attached to the remains of the castellet."

In January 1643 the Royalists besieged Doddington Hall, when held by Captain Harwar and 160 men, and took it, but it was retaken in February by the Parliament, who planted "great ordnance" against it.

DODLESTONE (*non-existent*)

ON the S.W. of Chester, opposite to Eaton, is the site of a castle, once the seat of a family named Boydel, descendants of Osbern Fitz Tezzon or Taisson, who held Dodlestone at the Domesday Survey. This Tezzon family was an illustrious one in Normandy, and once held in fee a fifth part of that province, being seigneurs of Cinqueleiz. Raval Taisson fought at Hastings, and seems to have been the first of this English branch (*Ormerod*). Osbern's son was Hugh, and his grandson, Helto, who assumed the name of De Boydel. He had two brothers, Alan and William, who both succeeded during the reign of King John, and were known as benefactors to the Church. The son of the latter brother, Sir William de Boydel, knight, made grants also in 1245 to the abbey of Dieulacres.

Here the Boydels continued for many generations, maintaining themselves "with a degree of consequence little inferior to that of the barons of the earldom." A partition of the estate took place temp. Edward III., when Dodlestone fell to Howel ap Owain Vaughan, whose son and heir, William, assumed the name of Boydel, and his descendants continued here till 3 Henry VI., when the castle and lands were brought in marriage by a daughter to Hugh de Radyche or Redishe. This family remained long in possession, until an heiress, Maud, in the eleventh year of Queen Elizabeth's reign, married William Merbury, when a part of the property was sold to the Grosvenors. They conveyed it afterwards to Thomas Egerton, the Lord Chancellor, who made his residence at Dodlestone Hall. The residue of the estate was sold in 1627 by Thomas Merbury to several holders, from whom it came to the Grosvenor family, its present owners.

The site of the old home of the Boydels can still be traced on the W. of the church, where is a rectangular enclosure, about a Cheshire acre in extent, formed by the moat, having in its N.E. corner a circular mound, the site of the ancient keep, surrounded by its own moat, which is connected with the principal ditch, outside of which again are the remains of a circular earthwork. The Manleys of Lache erected within this enclosure a house which formed the headquarters of Sir William Brereton during the siege of Chester, but it has now vanished.

D U N H A M - M A S S Y (*non-existent*)

THE castle of Dunham-Massy was formerly the seat of the ancient Barons Massy, and was situated near Altrincham. The first baron, Hamon Massy, held his lands under Hugh Lupus, Earl of Chester, temp. William the Conqueror. Sir Hamon, the sixth and last baron, left four daughters, the eldest of whom, Cicely, married John Fitton of Bollin, temp. Edward II. On the death of Sir Hamon, who had sold Dunham to Oliver de Ingham, a judge of Chester, a lawsuit subvened, after the settlement of which Ingham held Dunham till his death, when the Fittons entered into possession. Thereafter Henry, Duke of Lancaster, bought the manor and gave it to Roger le Strange, lord of Knocking, whose wife was heir to Ingham. Dunham seems, however, to have reverted to the Fittons, and from them to have come, through the Venables of Kinderton, to Sir Robert Booth of Barton, Lancaster, descending from the Fittons by an arrangement dated 11 Henry VI. In the first year of Richard III.'s reign George Bothe, *armiger*, son of William Bothe, *miles*, was seised of the moiety of Dunham-Massy among others. His descendant, Sir George Booth, having represented the county in the Long Parliament, and having been actively engaged in the service of the Commonwealth, "conceived a subsequent disgust" for that cause, and became a prime mover in the Restoration. For this tardy piece of loyalty, and for his losses, he subsequently received £10,000, and was created Baron Delamere of Dunham-Massy. His son Henry, who strongly espoused the cause of the Prince of Orange, was raised in 1690 to the earldom of Warrington, and his granddaughter and sole heiress married in 1736 Harry, 4th Earl of Stamford, whence came the union of these titles.

The Norman barons constituted Dunham the chief seat of their barony, and built a castle at this place, of which, however, nothing whatever remains. Nor, indeed, are there any local traditions of it having existed, although there are charters which mention both the castle and the dependent fort of Ullersford. A drawing exists of the mansion of Dunham as it appeared 200 years ago, standing within a garden surrounded by a moat, and having in one angle of the grounds a high circular mound, similar to all such round mounds, on which sometimes were built the Norman shell or hollow keeps. Doubtless this drawing represents the last relic of the fortress of Hamon de Masci.

FRODSHAM (non-existent)

THE town of this name lies at the foot of the lofty and precipitous Overton Hill, on the S. side of the Weaver River near its confluence with the Mersey estuary. The lands here were among the possessions of the Norman earls palatine of Chester, and there exists a charter to the burgesses of Frodsham, dated in the early part of the twelfth century, from Randle Blundeville, Earl of Chester, who appears to have lived in Frodsham Castle, built perhaps by his ancestors.

The position of this castle was important, commanding as it did a narrow pass on the road to Chester from Lancashire, between some marshes and the steep sides of Overton Hill; in ancient times it was protected by the waters of the Mersey, and in front by marshes. There are no longer any remains of the fortress, the site of which was at the W. end of the town, but in the collections of the Bucks is a drawing of it as it appeared in 1727, when a good deal of the Norman fabric still existed. Ormerod says that the building was of stone with semicircular arches of early Norman work, and walls of enormous thickness.

From the reign of Edward III. to that of Elizabeth the castle seems to have been used as a manor gaol, and the office of Constable to it was hereditary. After its acquisition by the Savages of Rock Savage (a place on the opposite side of the stream), that family resided there till 1654, when the castle was consumed by fire, on the day of the death in it of John, Earl Rivers.

The ruins were taken down to make room for the erection of the house called Castle Park, the residence of Mr. D. Ashley, who bought the site, under an Act of Parliament, from the Daniels of Daresbury. They had acquired it in 1721 by purchase from the trustees of Lord Barrymore. Then from Mr. Ashley the property came for a time to descendants of his, called Wright. Portions of the foundation walls of the old castle form the cellars of the modern house.

The manor is said to have been granted by the Earls of Chester at an early period to a family who assumed the name of Frodsham, the first of the name whom we meet with being Hugh de Frodsham (temp. Henry II.), but there is no proof that they possessed a castle for a long period after this. In John's reign they farmed the lands here, and there is a pedigree of their family up to 1396.

In 1279 Edward I. granted the place and lands to David, brother of Llewellyn, Prince of Wales, with whom he had been at variance, in order to give him an interest outside his own country; but David, being afterwards reconciled to his brother, broke his treaty with Edward I., and having surprised and captured the castle of Hawarden in Flint, put its garrison to the sword. For this, after Llewellyn's death, and the subjugation of Wales, David, though a sovereign prince, was seized by Edward and tried for high treason at Shrewsbury in 1283, and was put to death there with every circumstance of horrible cruelty borne in the sentence, which was now for the first time passed and practised, the savage king looking on while his royal victim was partially hanged, but cut down alive and disembowelled, his members being then severed and distributed through the kingdom (see *Shrewsbury*).

In 1357 Thomas de Frodesham performed important services for Edward III. and the Black Prince in Gascony and at Poictiers, for which he obtained rewards.

Henry VI. in his thirty-second year granted Frodsham and its appurtenances to Edmund Tudor, Earl of Richmond, the father of Henry VII., though the lordship was still attached to the royal earldom of Chester.

At the beginning of the seventeenth century the property was bestowed on the Savages of Clifton, whose representative, the Earl of Rivers, enjoyed it till deprived of it by litigation (temp. George I.). At a later date it passed to Lady Penelope Barry, the wife of Lord Barrymore, and daughter and heir of Earl Rivers. She afterwards brought the estate in marriage to the Earl of Cholmondeley, whose descendants still own the lands.

HALTON (chief)

AT the head of the Mersey estuary, to the N.E. of Chester, on the brow of a lofty hill, was built this fortress shortly after the Conquest. When William I. had concluded the pacification of the kingdom in 1070, he appointed all this part of the country to one of his Norman earls, Hugh Lupus, "to hold from him by the sword as he himself held the realm of England by the crown." Hugh at once divided his great palatinate between his eight followers, who were constituted barons, on condition of supporting him, in some manner, by the sword. One of these was Nigel, a Norman warrior, who became the first baron of Halton, and made it the head of his barony, it being his chief fortress. Nothing, however, remains now of the Norman castle, which in its general plan, before its dismantling, resembled Beeston.

Nigel's son and grandson succeeded, and at the death of the latter in Normandy temp. Stephen, *s.p.*, his sister's husband, Eustace FitzRoger, acquired the lands and castle as fourth Baron of Halton. This man had already inherited Knaresborough (Yorks) from his uncle, Serlo de Burgh, and had also obtained the valuable baronies of Halton and Alnwick through his first wife, the daughter and heiress of Ivo de Vesey, and to him Earl Randle Gernons gave the hereditary Constableship of Cheshire. He fell in the Welsh campaign of 1157, and was succeeded by his son Richard, whose son John after his mother's accession to the vast estates of Robert de Lacy, her half-brother, assumed the great name of Lacy. He died in the Crusade before Tyre in 1190.

His son Roger followed as seventh Baron of Halton (see *Clitheroe, Lancashire*), and was known as a valiant soldier who fought together with Cœur de Lion at Acre in 1191. He it was who defended the Château Gaillard so long against the French king, and was taken prisoner when, vanquished by famine, he and his men were trying to cut their way through the French host.

Roger Lacy married Maud de Clare, and dying in 1211, was succeeded by his son John, who was one of the Magna Charta barons appointed to see that the faithless king executed the requirements laid upon him. In 1218, after serving in the Crusade at Damietta, he obtained from Henry III. the earldom of Lincoln. This elevation of the Lacys, however, brought ruin to Halton, since, no longer needing that castle for their constant abode, it was deserted and neglected by them.

John de Lacy died in 1240, and his son Edmund dying before his mother, never became Earl of Lincoln, but lived as Baron of Halton only. He died in 1258, being followed by his son Henry, tenth baron, whose name is historic. After receiving knighthood from Henry III., in the fifty-seventh year of that king's reign, he became a companion-in-arms, and likewise a trusty councillor, of Edward I., whom in energy of character and in bravery he resembled. In 1272 he assisted Edmund, the king's brother, in the siege of Chartley Castle, which had been seized by Robert, Earl Ferrers. In 1290 Edward appointed him Chief Commissioner for reforming law abuses. In 1296 he commanded the English forces in the south of France, when he expelled the French from Toulouse. We next find Baron Henry in 1299 leading the van at the battle of Falkirk, where 40,000 Scots are said to have been slain.

At the Parliament of Carlisle of 1307 our Baron of Halton was placed above all peers except the king's son; and such was his high standing in the country, that when Edward II. advanced into Scotland, Henry de Lacy was appointed Protector of the Realm during the king's absence. He died in his great mansion of Lincoln's Inn in 1310, when, leaving no son, his honours fell to his young daughter Alice, who, as a child of nine, was married to Thomas, Earl of Lancaster, whose rebellion in 1321, and retreat from Tutbury, with the loss of his treasure-chest, are mentioned in the account of Tutbury (Stafford). Taken prisoner at Boroughbridge and then beheaded at Pontefract, his possessions were seized by the Crown, and we hear no more of his poor child-wife. Although probably a weak man, he was idolised by the monks, who, after their own fashion, canonised him after his death. Edward II. came soon after this to inspect Halton Castle, and stayed there several days.

When the lands were restored, it was Henry of Lincoln, surnamed

Grismond, who obtained them as twelfth Baron of Halton, and was succeeded at Halton in 1345 by his son Henry, Earl, and afterwards Duke, of Lancaster. He claimed the right to have his castle of Halton crenellated and embattled, together with a castle ward and a prison. Duke Henry's daughter Blanche brought Halton to John of Gaunt, as fourteenth baron, and he seems to have built here as he did in so many other places, so that his name still lingers in the neighbourhood. At the death of "time-honoured Lancaster," Halton fell to his son Bolingbroke as the fifteenth and last baron, and on his death passed to the Crown.

In 10 Henry VI. Sir John Savage was made Constable of Halton Castle, and mustered the Cheshire men under its walls. Afterwards, little is heard of the fortress during the Wars of the Roses, and in 1579, after a century of neglect, this proud castle, so long the head of a great barony, was turned into a prison.

James I. came here in August 1617 to hunt, and killed a buck in the park. The importance of Halton was recognised at the opening of the Civil War, when a garrison was placed there for the king by Earl Rivers in June 1643, but a year after the post was reduced and taken possession of for the Parliament by the force under Sir William Brereton. Shortly afterwards the castle was dismantled and turned into a ruin.

An ancient print reproduced by the Historic Society of Cheshire (*Journal*, vol. ii.) shows the old fortress standing on a cliff over the river, with the town below it; the enclosure of high embattled walls is of circular form, holding nine large square mural towers, at intervals, the lower gatehouse being flanked by two of them. On the opposite side of the enceinte is shown a similar gateway, leading probably to an inner ward not seen. Ormerod too gives a sketch of the ruins as they may have been at the beginning of the present century. This view shows half-octagonal flanking towers to the entrance gateway, with the lofty Edwardian windows of John of Gaunt's period.

KINDERTON CASTLE (*non-existent*)

SITUATED on the river Dane at Middlewich, this place belonged at the Domesday Survey to Gilbert de Venables, a Norman from the town of Venables, between Rouen and Paris, and near to Vernon. This Gilbert is supposed to have been a younger brother of Stephen, Earl of Blois, and his descendants continued here as Barons of Kinderton for many generations. Sir Richard de Venables was beheaded after the battle of Shrewsbury, in which he took part against Henry IV. Sir Hugh served on the side of Lancaster under Lord Audley, and was slain at Bloreheath. Peter, the Baron of Kinderton, died in 1679, and his sister's daughter, Anne, the sole heiress, having married

Henry Vernon of Sudbury, county Derby, her son George Venables Vernon was in 1762 created Baron Vernon of Kinderton.

The ancient hall of Kinderton stood near the banks of the Dane, two fields distant from the supposed Roman work of Condate. A part only of the moat remains, but formerly it enclosed a parallelogram of several acres, in the S.W. angle of which is still left a large circular mound. All remains of the ancient castle and of the later hall which succeeded it have been removed, and a brick mansion called Kinderton Lodge was erected by Lord Norreys in another part of the manor; this also has in its turn vanished. It was a large quadrangular fabric of timber and plaster, decorated on the exterior of the upper storey with imaginary portraits of the Barons of Kinderton.

MACCLESFIELD (non-existent)

MACCLESFIELD was a castle which belonged in demesne to the Earls of Chester, and seems to have been fortified at the Domesday period by a *haia* or palisade. At the extinction of the local earldom, the manor passed to the Crown, where it is still vested.

On the S. of the church, and in a steep and narrow pathway leading from the town to the river, called the Black Wall Gate, is a lofty stone wall, behind which were once the remains of a castellated palace built by Humphrey, Duke of Lancaster. In the lower part of the wall is a small doorway under a pointed arch of considerable antiquity.

Ormerod also says that near the Congleton road is a place called Castle Field, which is probably the site of the local palace of the Earls of Chester. In this a circular mound, or tumulus, is still remaining.

MALPAS (non-existent)

THIS position was chosen by the first Earl of Chester as the site of one of his many Border castles, and was given by him to one of the eight barons of his court, Robert FitzHugh, who was said to be his bastard son. He obtained the forfeited estates of the dispossessed Earl Edwin, and of other Saxon owners, and at his death *s.p.* male, his two daughters divided his lands between them. One of them, Letitia, was the wife of Richard Patric, whose heiress (temp. Henry II.) carried the Malpas manor, with others, to the family of De Sutton of Shropshire; the other, Mabel, married to William Belward, became the ancestress of the elder line of Egerton, afterwards represented by the Breretons.

The FitzHugh estates, thus divided, were reunited in the reigns of Henry VIII. and Elizabeth by purchases carried out by the Egertons; and in the eleventh year of Charles I. Sir Richard Egerton of Shotlack (*q.v.*) and his brothers parted with the property, which was afterwards conveyed to Robert, Viscount Cholmondeley, ancestor of the present marquess, whose second title is Baron Malpas, and in whose family the Malpas estates remain.

The Castle of Malpas, the original head of the barony, has long been destroyed. The only remains are those of the circular mound, measuring 40 yards in diameter, the relic of a still earlier fortress, on which it is likely that the new Norman lord erected his tower or keep, soon after the Conquest, to strengthen the earldom against the Welsh. The castle ditch has been traced out for a long distance.

Like most fortresses in Cheshire upon the Welsh marches, this castle was situated immediately adjacent to the church, which most probably was comprehended within the works.

The intricate pedigrees of the various families connected with the succession to these lands, are given at length by Ormerod.

NORTHWICH (*non-existent*)

THE site of the ancient fortress lies on the road to Chester from Northwich. After passing the bridge the road ascends a very steep hill, on the right of which are the remains of this stronghold, in a small field bounded on one side by a brook. It commanded the junction of the Dane with the Weaver at a point where the latter stream was crossed by the Watling Street.

However important this point may have been in Roman or Saxon times, it is doubtful whether any stone fortress was ever placed here, since no mention is made of any military service connected with the castle, nor was it ever in the hands of any but obscure families.

The remains consist of two high mounds of unequal height; the higher is nearly circular, and about 30 yards in diameter, while the lower one measures only 17 yards across. There are no remains of walls or of other earthworks; but for all that, a formidable stronghold may have been formed here in Saxon times in timber with palisades.

OLDCASTLE (*non-existent*)

OLDCASTLE was situated S.E. of Malpas, directly on the Welsh frontier, from which a little brook divides it. The surface of the land here rises in a number of small hills and inequalities, and on the summit of one of them are indications of the works of this ancient fortress, which was perhaps one of a line of forts erected along the Border after the Norman

Conquest, or may be of still earlier derivation, as might be inferred from the name.

On the subdivision of the Malpas estates, Oldcastle passed to the St. Pierre family, and from them to the Cokesays ; thence it went to the Dudleys, and in the reign of Henry VIII. to Sir Rowland Hill.

In 1644 Oldcastle Heath was the scene of a bloody encounter between 2500 Royalist cavalry, who had been driven out of Lancashire, and 900 Parliamentary troops from Nantwich, when the king's troopers were routed, leaving Colonel Vane and Colonel Conyers dead on the field, with sixty of their men.

PULFORD (*non-existent*)

THIS fortress stood on the road from Chester to Wrexham, in a flat country, on the bank of a small brook dividing Cheshire from Denbighshire. All that remains is a strong semicircular earthwork facing the N.E., containing within it a round mound, the rear of the work being protected by the brook. The whole encloses about an acre, and in front stands a church, the predecessor of which was there in the time of the Confessor.

Hugh Fitz Osborn ejected the Saxon owner of the place, and was succeeded in it by his son. Subsequently it was divided between the Ormesbies and the Pulfords, the latter family being the supposed descendants of the Norman grantee ; but their estates were united again (28 Henry III.) by Ralph de Ormesbie, who gave his moiety to Robert de Pulford, with the castle of Pulford. The father of Robert had granted some of his lands to the neighbouring Cistercian abbey of Pulton, which no longer is visible.

The Pulfords were a numerous and strong family, and retained the property till the reign of Richard II., when Joan, the sister and heiress of the last Pulford owner, married, first, Thomas de Belgrave (*s.p.*), and second, Sir Robert le Grosvenor of Holme, becoming the ancestress of the Grosvenor family, to whom these lands descended. In the time of Edward IV. they passed by an heiress to the Winningtons, who held them under Henry VII. as Earl of Chester ; and thence they came by marriage, at the end of Henry VIII.'s reign, to the Warburtons. In this family the estate descended regularly until early in the present century, when it was bought by the Earl of Grosvenor, to whose domain of Eaton it is contiguous.

There is little recorded about the castle ; the last occasion on which its defences were in requisition, was during the rebellion of Owen Glendower (4 Henry IV.), when Sir Thomas de Grosvenor received a mandate to hasten to his castle of Pulford for the defence of the marches of Wales.

SHIPBROOK (*non-existent*)

SHIPBROOK is situated on the S. of Northwich, on the right bank of the Weaver, and opposite to the town of Davenham. The position, being a strong one on high ground, was chosen by the Norman lords of Shipbrook for their residence, and the site of their castle is still indicated by the name of Castle Hill attached to an elevation between Shipbrook Bridge and Shipbrook Farm. The remains existed till the middle of the last century, when they are said to have been cleared away by one Tomkinson, a tenant.

Richard de Vernon, deriving from Vernon in Normandy, was grantee of the lands at the Domesday Survey, and his descendants continued here till the reign of Henry VI.,—one of them, called "Sir Ralphe the Olde," living as is alleged to the age of 150 years, and dying during the reign of Edward II.

SHOTLACK (*non-existent*)

SHOTLACK was a Welsh frontier fortress on the banks of the Dee. The manor was held at Domesday by Robert FitzHugh of Malpas, who had dispossessed Dot the Saxon proprietor, and at his death it passed to the Suttons and the St. Pierres. John de Sutton held it 17 Edward III., and at the end of the reign of Henry VII., it had come from that family to Lord Dudley, the judge; and, again (temp. Henry VIII.), from Dudley by the family of Hill to Sir Richard Corbett of Stoke, who sold it in the fourteenth year of Elizabeth to Sir Randolph Brereton, knight, from whom it went by marriage to the Egertons. At the wreck of the Egerton property, in the reign of Charles I., it passed by purchase to the Pulestons of Emral. The Breretons were high in the favour of Henry VIII., Sir William being Groom of the Chamber to that king, but he was one of the unfortunates whose head Henry brought to the block at the time of the trial of Queen Anne Boleyn (1536).

Shotlack formed an important link in the chain of Cheshire castles between Aldford and Malpas, the Chester road passing through the fortress. Lord Dudley claimed the right, in 15 Henry VII., to maintain this castle fortified, ditched, and crenellated; and as he does not mention the castle of Malpas, it is possible that that castle was not in such good repair as Shotlack. The earthworks of the place were very strong, occupying an important pass, near the church, where the present road to Chester crosses a deep ravine, watered by a small brook. On the W. side of the road is a lofty circular mound or burh, 20 feet high, of very early derivation, on the top of which the Normans placed their keep; it is half encircled by a deep ditch, close to the road, and on the left or W. side, where must have existed the castle buildings,

the ground falls rapidly towards the ravine. On the E. side of the road is
another raised platform, shaped like a kite, also of ancient formation, which
seems to have protected the communications between the Watling Street on
the N. and that on the S., commanding as it did the road passing through.
The area of the castle occupied about an acre, and its situation, protected as
it must have been by marshes and forests, would be impregnable.

There are now no vestiges of the masonry of this castle, and "the fair and
goodly seat" of Sir Richard Egerton, called Shotwick Hall, is also completely
destroyed.

SHOTWICK (non-existent)

THIS was one of the Norman forts erected by the Earls of Chester to
protect their frontier from the Welsh, Shotwick being intended to guard
the shallow channel of Dee in the Wirral Hundred. In later times, when the
river at Chester shrunk back, the embarkation of soldiers for Ireland became

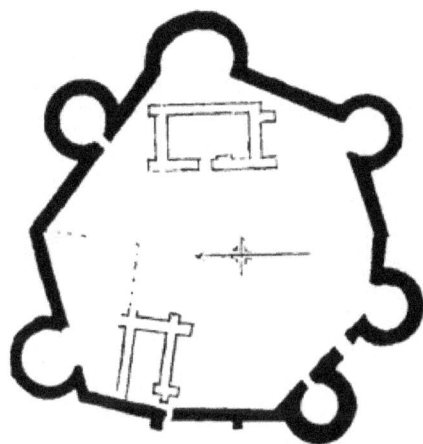

SHOTWICK
Cheshire

difficult there, and the Cheshire
archers and other troops were then
collected on the shores of Wirral
and embarked from this point.
The castle was more than once
honoured by the presence of the
sovereign when starting on these
expeditions. Leland speaks of it
as existing in his day. "A myle
lower is Shottewik Castle, on the
very shore, longing to the king,
and therby ys a parke."

In the Harleian MSS. (2073) is
a drawing and plan of this fortress
by Randle Holme, as it appeared
then, in a ruinous condition. Its
trace was a pentagon strengthened
by six towers, one of which, according to Camden, was five storeys

high. The wash of the tides, and the cultivation of the lands, have not
quite obliterated these remains, those seen at present consisting merely of a
large mound, supported by a huge earthwork of crescent form, and two deep
entrenchments on the land side.

In 1256 Fulco de Orreby, Justiciary of Cheshire, received charge of
Shotewyke Castle as one of the chief strongholds of the palatinate. Various
persons are spoken of as being wardens of it, or of the royal park, during

successive reigns, but after a time the castle is no longer mentioned, and in 17 Charles II. this and other manors were sold to Thomas Wilbraham.

In 1734 the property was bequeathed to the Brereton family, and afterwards passed from them to the Trelawneys of Shotwick Park at the beginning of the present century.

STOCKPORT *(non-existent)*

THE family of De Stockport, or Stokeport, derived the manors at this locality from Waltheof, in the reign of Richard I., and, intermingled in blood with another family named De Eton, were here at the end of the reign of Edward III. Stockport is finely situated on the Mersey, and appears to have been a place of importance from the time of the Romans to that of William I., although it is not noticed in the Domesday Survey.

On the N. of the church is the site of the ancient castle, and of some Roman works which originally held the position and guarded the fords and passes to Chester. The castle, which may have been founded by the Earls of Chester, was in 1173 held against Henry II. by Geoffry de Cotentin, a Norman supporter of Henry's son whose title is obscure. Afterwards the place became the property of the Despencers, and was held under them by the Stockports. Subsequently, after the forfeiture of Hugh Despencer, Earl of Winchelsea, for the part he took with Simon de Montfort, the headship reverted to the Earls of Chester. From the Stockports the property descended to the family of Warren of Poynton, and through them to the Lords Vernon.

ULLERSFORD CASTLE *(non-existent)*

ON a neighbouring part of the property of Hamon de Masci was a place called the Ullerswode, to the N. of Bollin, also called in one deed Ulresford, whence came the name given to another fortress held by the same Baron Hamon, together with his baronial castle of Dunham, against Henry II. About one mile W. of this point and at the back of Bollin is Castle Mill, where there are vestiges of earthworks, being the site of Ullersford Castle, which was perhaps an outwork of Dunham Castle.

HOGHTON TOWER

Lancashire

BURY (non-existent)

IN 1865 some labourers, while constructing a sewer in a piece of waste ground called Castle Croft, came upon the foundations of the ancient castle of Bury. Further examination showed the walls, 6 feet thick, of an entire parallelogram measuring 82 feet by 63; and more extended investigation opened up the outer walls, which proved to form a figure 120 feet by 113, in the centre of which stood the inner enclosure, or bailey, built with very thin walls. It was evident that a mound had also existed, on which this inner court abutted. There was little to show the date of the building, but some pieces of carved stone which lay about were of the Decorated period.

Aiken's map shows that the castle of Bury was protected on the N. and W. by a steep bank, below which ran the Irwell. The name and the mound both point to a Saxon settlement and stronghold at this spot, probably of the usual type.

The earliest known reference to the place occurs temp. Henry II., when Robert de Lacy made a grant of lands here; and the name of Adam de Bury is entered in 12 Henry III., in the Lansdowne MSS.

The chief part of the lands was afterwards held by Pilkington of Pilkington and Bury, which family came under forfeiture at the termination of the Wars of the Roses, and Henry VII. conferred the estate on his supporter, Lord Stanley, afterwards first Earl of Derby of the present family, with whose heirs it continues. Leland speaks of the ruins of a castle here, and there remained some portions above-ground at the end of the last century.

CLITHEROE (minor)

THIS name may come from *Cled-dwr* (Brit., "The rock by the water"). The castle stands on the summit of a bare isolated limestone hill, or rock, that rises boldly in the valley of the Ribble which flows at some distance below. Camden says that Roger de Poictou at the time of the Domesday Survey owned all the land between the Ribble and the Mersey; he was the son of Roger de Montgomeri, who commanded the centre division of the Norman host at Senlac, and upon whom the Conqueror conferred the two earldoms of Shrewsbury and Arundel. Roger de Poictou obtained the lordship and honour (or seigniory) of Lancaster, but taking part with the cause of the Empress Maud, his property was confiscated by Stephen.

Whitaker (History of Whalley) says "there can be little doubt that Roger of Poictou was

CLITHEROE

the real founder of the castle of Clitheroe," though Gregson believes it to have been built by Robert De Lacy (temp. Henry II.). It was certainly one of the residences of the De Lacy family in Norman times, the other being at Pontefract. Alice, daughter of Henry, Earl of Lincoln, the last of the De Lacys, in 1310 brought the honour of Clitheroe by marriage to Thomas Plantagenet,

Earl of Lancaster, the son of Edmund Crouchback, fourth son of Henry III.
by Blanche, Queen-Dowager of Navarre. He being beheaded 15 Edward II.
(1322), Clitheroe was forfeited and became Crown property, being absorbed
into the Duchy of Lancaster, where it remained until Charles II. gave it to
General Monk, from whom it passed to the Duke of Buccleuch.

The cap of the rock on which this castle is built is not sufficiently large
to admit of a very spacious structure, and nothing more appears to have
been intended by the founder than to provide a temporary residence when
called to this part of his domains. The castle was slighted by order of
Parliament after the Civil War, and therefore little now remains of it; but,
from a drawing made just before its destruction, it appears that there was a
fine entrance gate-tower of circular form, on the site of the present gates,
having a semicircular Norman archway, and a lofty embattled wall running
round the brink of the hill, turning first on the back of the present steward's
house, and secondly behind the present courthouse, towards the keep. It
is recorded that coeval with the foundation of the castle, and forming part
of it, was the chapel of St. Michael de Castro, erected and endowed by the
founder, but within the whole bailey there is no appearance of this chapel,
nor of any other building except the keep, which is of the usual Norman
form, square, with flat square towers at each of the four corners, or rather
turrets, one of which has a spiral staircase. This keep is well built and
is of small dimensions, and though much undermined, stands as firm as the
rock upon which it was erected. The other remains consist of portions of
the castle wall, several feet in height, and of great thickness.

DALTON (minor)

THIS castle is near Ulverston, in the Furness district. What is called the
Castle of Dalton stands in the town of that name, formerly the capital
of Furness, and occupies the site of a *castellum* of Agricola, of the fosse of
which there are yet traces to be seen in an advantageous position commanding
the valley below (*Gregson*). All that remains is a plain oblong structure of
two storeys, the upper part of which is of the Decorated period, perhaps temp.
Edward III. The Abbot of Furness held his secular court here, and for
many years the chief chamber has been used as a gaol for debtors. In
Baines' "History of Lancashire," we are told that the frequent irruptions of
the Scots, and the exposed situation of the northern parts of Lancashire to
their inroads, during the reigns of the early Edwards, rendered frontier fortresses necessary for the protection of the inhabitants, and the tower of
Dalton, which is supposed to have been erected by the monks of Furness, as
well as the peel of Fouldry, contributed to their security. In the district of

Furness a number of beacons were erected, and when the hills of Langdale and Coniston were illuminated with these ominous presages, the more opulent inhabitants flocked to their castles, and removed their effects out of the reach of their unwelcome visitors, to await more tranquil times.

For some time before the Dissolution this castle had been falling to ruin, and in 1544 a commission ordered its repair with stone, lead, and timber from the dismantled abbey of Furness; after which it "was used for a pryson and common gaole for the whole lordship and domynyon of Furness in the liberties of the same." Later on, the courts of the Duke of Buccleuch, lord of the liberties and manors of Furness, were convenable here, and in 1850 the old tower was put into a thorough state of repair. It is now also used as the armoury of the Rifle Volunteers.

FARLETON (non-existent)

AT this place, about a mile S. from Hornby, on low ground near the banks of the Lune, is the site of a castle which in the fifteenth century belonged to a younger branch of the Harrington family. How the lords of Hornby became possessed of it cannot now be ascertained, but in a survey of that honour in 1581, the park and castle of Farleton are enumerated. Even at that time it was probably much dilapidated.

Adam de Mont Begon gave to Geoffrey de Valons, to be held by knights' service, certain lands in Farleton and Cancefield, which in an inquisition of 12 Edward II. are described as the manor of Farleton, being then in the hands of the lady of the castle and honour of Hornby, Margaret, widow of Geoffrey Nevile (see *Hornby*). As it was then a dependence of Hornby, it followed the fortunes of that estate, and in the reign of Edward III. a younger branch of the Harringtons of Aldingham was seated here, and Sir William Harrington, who fell at Agincourt, became lord of the property with Hornby.

There was formerly a park with the castle, but two and a half centuries ago the castle had gone into ruin, and the park has quite disappeared. There are still some vestiges of the castle.

FOULDRY (minor)

THE strong castle called the Piel (or peel) of Fouldry stands on a small flat island of nineteen acres extent on the N. shore of Morecambe Bay, just where the coast-line turns towards the open sea, a fordable narrow channel separating the island from the shore. It is thought that the Danes had a fortification here of earlier date, but this stronghold was built originally in the reign of Stephen for the protection of the excellent harbour, as well as against Border inroads. It was rebuilt in the fourteenth century as an outpost, and in all probability greatly strengthened by the Abbot of Furness and his monks, who were alarmed by the terrible invasion of Scots which followed their victory of Bannockburn in 1322. Here, in 1487 (temp. Henry VII.), a landing took place of the Earl of Lincoln and Lord Lovel, with 2000 German soldiers, in support of Lambert Simnel, who was joined by Sir Thomas Broughton at this place, in their attempt to dethrone the king, an attempt which ended in the battle of Stoke. In the Survey of Elizabeth's reign the fortress is called " ane old decayed Castell."

The castle is an early instance of a concentric fortress—a keep or central tower surrounded by an inner girdle of fortified wall, and, beyond that, an outer wall of curtains and bastions, each wall being protected by a wide ditch. Buck gives a view of the work as it was in 1727, from which we see that a considerable change has taken place. There is no trace of the outer entrance, and the N.E. tower has lost its sea front and its wooden floors on both storeys, most of the outer towers being of similar construction. Adjoining this tower was the chapel, which was small, measuring 34 feet by 15 feet. There are steps up to the ramparts which communicated with each of the towers, and the wall, including battlements, was 8 feet thick; part of it has vanished, but most of the towers remain. Across this outer ward is the moat defending the inner wall, through which the entrance lies on the W. side, where is the barbican with drawbridge and portcullis groove; and the other towers with the curtains remain. The entrance to the central tower or keep is on the N. side, through a projected approach guarded by a portcullis at either end, and partly vaulted. The main staircase is here, and there is another on the S. side. The keep was a square of about 60 feet inside, but its E. face has gone. It has two lofty storeys, and its corners were supported by grand and bold buttresses, the total height being 45 feet, with two centre and four corner turrets of fine construction. The roof and floors were of wood; the pointed windows had mullions and quatrefoils.

Before the days of artillery the castle must have been impregnable. It is constructed of excellent concrete formed of the shingle of the beach, but the whole has been much injured by the action of the sea. The port of Fouldry is very large and commodious, and a battle-ship of the first class could float safely in it at low water. Some fifty years ago there were dredged up at Walney Island, off the coast at this spot, some specimens of early English guns, the origin of which has been referred to the time of Richard II., when John Bolton, Abbot of Furness, made an attempt to demolish the peel of Fouldry, rather than be at the cost of keeping it up against the enemies of the country, i.e. the Scots. This was a difficult measure for a churchman to adopt, when so little could be known about the power of artillery, and so little strength was in either guns or powder; the pickaxe would have been more certain. The guns in those days were only rough tubes of either brass or sheet-iron, welded at the overlap on a mandrel, and having iron hoops shrunk or driven on them (*Wylie*).

At the Restoration this castle and its manors were given to the Duke of Albemarle by Charles II., and through him came to the Dukes of Buccleuch. The whole edifice was repaired, and some restorations made, by the late duke.

GLEASTON (*minor*)

THIS castle lies at the foot of a hill in Dalton in Furness, two miles E. of Furness Abbey, and is pleasantly situated on a trout stream flowing through the fertile valley.

The castle is a quadrangular figure whose N. end is larger than that on the S., and consists of four corner towers connected by curtain walls, which enclose a ward about 265 feet in length, and measuring 170 feet at the N., and 120 feet at the S. end. The walls are three yards in thickness, and the towers were of great strength and lofty, but the masonry is bad, and the lime mortar used for the hearting earthy and poor, so that a great part has crumbled away into mere mounds.

The keep was at the N.W. corner, at the highest point of the ground, and was exterior to the enceinte. Two fragments of it remain, from 30 to 40 feet high, showing that it consisted of two floors and a dungeon or cellar. Close to it is a postern in the W. wall. In the centre of the wall was a semicircular bastion, which has fallen. At the end of this curtain is the S.W. tower, which is square and has a basement without lights, with three floors over, the whole being 43 feet high, with a newel stair leading to the battlements and several garderobes. At a distance of 120 feet from this, and connected by a straight curtain, stands the S.E. tower, of larger size than the last, having two floors only ; there is a newel staircase, and the upper room led on to the allure. The greater part of the N.E. tower and the whole of the N. curtain have perished.

Buck gives a drawing showing the ruin to have been in much the same condition in 1727 as we see it now. It is difficult to say where the principal entrance was situated, and there is no ditch.

The lands at the Conquest were possessed by one Ernulph, who gave way to a Fleming named Michael, and his domain was formed into a manor called Muchland, after him (Michael being corrupted into the old Northern word *mickle*, or *much*). After three or four generations of Flemings, the manor passed (about 1270) by an heiress to a family named Cancefield, from whom it went with an heiress in 1293 to Robert de Harrington, whose family remained here till 1457, when the property was again transferred by an heiress to Lord Bonville of Shaton. He took the name of Lord Harrington, and his grand-

daughter brought it in marriage to Thomas Grey, created Duke of Suffolk, the
father of Lady Jane Grey. In 1554, after Wyatt's rebellion, he with his two
brothers, his daughter—the nine-days' queen—and her husband, Lord Guildford
Dudley, were beheaded, when his estates, including Gleaston, were forfeited to
the Crown, being afterwards bestowed separately on various people, first to the
queens of Charles I. and II., and afterwards to the Duke of Montague on lease.
At a point on the coast 1½ miles S.E. of this castle is the ancient mound,
called Aldingham Moat Hill, where no doubt Ernulph and the Flemings had
their "burh" and wooden fort, before the building of Gleaston. The writer
of a paper in the *Transactions of the Cumberland Antiquarian Society* (H. S.
Cowper, F.S.A.) is of opinion that this castle is the work of the owners, Cance-
fields or Harringtons, late in the thirteenth century, or temp. Edward I. In 1340
John de Harrington had leave to enclose a part. The dwellings and domestic
buildings were probably built of wood or wattle against the inside of the
curtain wall.

GREENHALGH (manor)

THIS is about a mile N.E. of Garstang, and is called by Gough "a pretty
castle of the Lord of Derby; only one tower remains near the town;" this
tower is now in a very shattered state. There appear to have been seven or
eight towers of great height and strength. Greenhalgh Castle was erected by
Thomas Stanley, Earl of Derby, under a licence dated at Lancaster, August 2,
5 Henry VII. (1490), "to build and crenellate and embattle," also to make
there a park, with free warren and chase. He built the castle for his protection, being under apprehension of danger from certain of the nobility of this
county who had been outlawed, and whose estates, having been confiscated by
Henry, had been conferred upon him; several hostile attempts had already been
made against him. "The Wyr, a little river coming from Wierdale, runs with
a swift stream by Greenhaugh Castle" (*Camden*). The plan of the work was a
rectangle, approaching a square, with a tower at each corner standing diagonally
to each adjoining wall. Between the walls the distance was only 14 yards on
one side and 16 yards on the other, and the whole was surrounded by a circular
moat. The masonry of what is left is extremely plain and unfeatured.

The castle was garrisoned for the king in 1643 by James, Earl of Derby,
and it was besieged unsuccessfully in 1644. Rushworth, in his "Historical
Collection," says: "There remained, in 1645, of garrisons belonging to the
king unreduced, Lathom House and Green Castle in Lancashire, besieged
by the Lancashire forces." On the death of the governor, however, Greenhalgh surrendered, and was dismantled and destroyed in 1649 or 1650. In
1772 Pennant speaks of the single tower as "the poor remains of Greenhaugh
Castle." A few years since Lord Derby sold the castle to Lord Kenlis.

HOGHTON TOWER (SOMETIMES SPELT HOUGHTON) (chief)

IN the valley of the Ribble, five and a half miles to the W.S.W. of Black-
burn, is a lofty ridge of rock on the summit of which stands the old
mansion of the Hoghton family, between the two streams of the Derwent
and the Orr. It is an eminently fine situation for a stronghold ; on the
E. the cliff is steep and very rugged, and the hill slopes gently to the N.
and W. It is the only specimen in this neighbourhood of a true baronial
residence, and is well worthy of comparison even with Haddon Hall, for
its extent is such that from a distance Hoghton appears almost like a fortified
town.

The family of De Hoghton held property here in the time of Henry II.,
but their first residence was built down at the foot of the hill, by the riverside.
The existing castle was built by Thomas Hoghton in 1565, after the most
approved rules then observed in domestic architecture, with an upper and
a lower court, divided by a very strong tower or gatehouse, which in the
Civil War appears to have been used for storing powder, and was accidentally
blown up, together with the adjacent buildings, when Captain Starkey and
200 men were killed. The stables and offices of the farm constitute the
lower court, in exact conformity with Andrew Borde's directions for the construction of great houses (1542).

For ages the castle was a dilapidated ruin, and Britton wrote in 1818 :
"Within a few years the roof of the gallery and some of its walls have fallen
prostrate, though some parts of this ancient and extensive building are
inhabited by a few families of the lower class. The building is falling fast
to decay, and presents a view at once picturesque, grand, melancholy, and
venerable." It is satisfactory to find that the old fabric has since then been
put into partial repair.

Sir Richard Hoghton obtained permission to enclose a park, and the
place was once surrounded with a large park full of fine timber, though
too closely planted, which has now mostly disappeared. In those days it
was well stocked with game of all sorts ; there were wild cattle of the white
Roman breed, red deer, and wild boars, and we possess an account (given
by Whitaker) in the Journal of Nicholas Assheton, of a sporting entertainment offered here to King James I. in 1617. He came from Preston, on
one of his royal progresses, on August 15, with a great train of courtiers and
servants, and half Lancashire came to assist at the sports, and to pay respects
to their sovereign,—Sir Richard Hoghton, the proprietor, meeting the king
at the foot of the hill with a large company of the chief country gentry.
James remained at the Tower until August 18, and was amused each day
with sports of various kinds, feasts, dancing, masques, and stag hunts. The

diary contains the following entries, which give us some insight into court
life 300 years ago :—

"Soe away to Houghton : there a speche made.   Hunted and killed a
stagg. Wee attended at the Lord's table [that means as gentlemen waiters].
August 16.—The king hunting,—a great companie : Killed afore dinner a brace
of staggs. Verie hot : we went in to dinner. About 4 o'clock the king went
down to the Allome [alum] mines, and was there an hower and viewd them
precisely, and then went and shot at a stagg and missed. The king shot again
and brake the thigh bone. A dogge long in coming, and my Lord Compton
shott again and killed him. Late in to supper. August 17 (Sunday). We
served the Lords with briskett, wyne, and jellie. The Bishopp of Chester
preached before the king. To dinner. About 4 o'clock there was a rush-
bearing and pipering afore them, afore the king in the Middle Court :
then to supper. Then about 10 or 11 o'clock a maske of noblemen, knights,
and gentlemen, and courtiers afore the king [see Cattermole's painting of
this], in the middle room in the garden. Some speeches : of the rest,
dancing the Huckler, Tom Bedlo [" Tom of Bedlam," an interlude], and
the Cowp Justice of Peace. August 18. The king went away about 12 to
Lathom. Ther was a man almost slayne with fighting. Wee back with
Sir Richard ; as merrie as Robin Hood and all his fellowes." It was during
one of these banquets at Hoghton that King James is said to have knighted
the loin of beef, and ordered it ever after to be called Sir Loin, although,
according to some, the joint was already called *sur-loin*, and his Majesty only
made a pun.

The main building, which is entered from the quadrangle by a circular flight
of steps, contains some fine rooms, including the King's Room, where James I.
was lodged at his visit above described.

HORNBY (*minor*)

TURNER has placed this castle and the surpassingly beautiful scenery of
the Lune valley among his grand delineations of English hill and dale.
On a tongue of land between the rivers Lune and Wenning, about a mile
distant from their confluence, the Romans selected the site of a post for
guarding the fords here, and some remains of their buildings, coins, and
perhaps of a villa, have been found. The termination *by* would lead to the
inference that a Dane named Horne had his dwelling here (there is a town in
Denmark called Hornby), and not far off are the earthworks of a grand Saxon
fortress, of elliptical trace, covering 2 acres 9 perches, and proving the position
to have been one of importance.

The Norman builder chose for the site of his castle an abrupt cone-shaped

Court Yard. Houghton Tower.

rock, at the base of which flows the Wenning River, but the date of this construction is not known. Alric, a Saxon, is mentioned as living here at the Conquest, and his grandson Adam Fitz-Swain left two daughters, one of whom, Maud, married a Norman named Adam de Montbegon. In the fifth year of Stephen we find Roger de Montbegon here, and again in 1225 the castle is given into the custody of William, Earl Warren ; but only temporarily, for three years later (13 Henry III.), the king granted the manor, castle, and honour of Hornby to his great minister and justiciar Hubert de Burgh and his wife Margaret ; and after the death of Hubert in 1242, his widow, Countess of Kent, continued in possession during her lifetime.

On her death in 1250 claimants deriving from the Montbegons appeared in the family of Longuevillers, who succeeded in recovering the property, which passed with an heiress Margaret, daughter of Sir John Longuevillers, in marriage to Geoffrey Nevile, who obtained from Edward I. a grant of free-warren here and a market.

This Geoffrey died in 1285, and his widow held Hornby until 1318, when it went to her grandson John Nevile, and at his death to his cousin Sir Robert Nevile, who dying in 1413, left the estates to his daughter Margaret, the wife of Thomas Beaufort, Duke of Exeter. This nobleman left Hornby to two cousins of the Neviles, John Langton and Sir William Harrington, between whom the property was partitioned, Hornby Castle falling to Harrington, who was killed at Agincourt. After him, his son Sir Thomas and his grandson Sir John both fell at the battle of Wakefield, fighting on the over-matched Yorkist side. The great rampart and ditch forming a boundary between Hornby and the forest of Bowland are called the Harrington Dyke.

Sir Thomas left a son James, and Sir John two daughters, Anne and Elizabeth, who were harshly treated and imprisoned by their uncle James. He took possession of Hornby, and ruled there until Lord Stanley obtained from Edward IV. the custody of the castle, and a deed of wardship over the sisters and heiresses, together with the attainder of James Harrington ; then Lord Stanley married Anne, the elder girl, to his own son Edward Stanley, and Elizabeth to his nephew, John Stanley of Melling. Edward Stanley and his wife took up their abode in the castle in 1485, and, on Anne's death (4 Henry VII.), Stanley obtained a right to one moiety of the estates. At the death of John and Elizabeth Stanley, he obtained from his father, now Earl of Derby, a re-lease of the entire property in his own favour, and he is said to have even caused the death of his cousin John, a son left by the attainted James Harrington, by means of poison administered by a servant.

Murderer and perjurer as Sir Edward Stanley is said, on no certain foundation, to have been, he must have been a stout soldier. At Bosworth he commanded a wing of his father's troops, and at Flodden field, in 1513, where he led the third line or rear of the English forces, under the Earl of Surrey, he stopped and routed, with the archers of Lancashire and Cheshire, the fierce attack of the Highlanders under Lennox and Argyll, and, later in the day, by a flank movement over the hill, brought his men upon the rear of the Scottish troops that were fighting round their king, completing their overthrow. For these services, Sir Edward was created Lord Monteagle by the king at Eltham. He died in 1524, and sometime before had, by way of strengthening the credit side of his account, begun to build the chapel of St. Margaret near the castle, whereon is still read the inscription :

G Stanley: Miles: Dns: Montegle me fieri fecⁱ.

The octagonal tower and chancel were finished soon after his death, but the nave was completed by the parish in an inferior manner. It has all, however, been restored recently in excellent taste.

On the S. side of the tower Sir Edward's shield of arms, surrounded by the motto of the Garter, is still perfect. His will is dated in April 1523, and in it he gives explicit directions for his burial, and temporary interment in the priory ground pending the completion of the " new Chancell to be made at his cost and charges and with all convenient haste at the East ende of the Chapell of Saint Margaret at Horneby." Whitaker gives an engraving of the old chapel with its Stanley additions. During the ownership of Mr. Marsden the old nave was totally destroyed, the pillars and arches removed, and the walls taken down and reconstructed ; and thus this poor edifice stood until Colonel Forster and his brothers restored the church and rebuilt the nave in admirable manner. The work of Sir E. Stanley remains in excellent preservation.

Of his son Thomas, the second lord, there was a tradition, long preserved in the country, that it was his hand which gave the final *coup de grace* to King James at Flodden ; he died 1564, and his son William held Hornby until his death in 1581. This third lord left a daughter Elizabeth, married to Edward Parker, Lord Morley, whose son William became fourth Lord Morley and Monteagle ; he was one of the commissioners who sat at the trial, ending in the judicial murder, of Mary Queen of Scots at Fotheringay, but he was an enthusiast for the Catholic cause, and in 1601 was sent to the Tower, and heavily fined for participation in the rebellion of Essex. On the accession of James, Monteagle modified his ways, and was in full favour at court. He it was who on October 26, 1605, while at supper in his house at Hoxton, received the letter, now preserved in the Record Office, warning him of the "terrible blow" intended for those who would come to the meeting of Parliament on November 5th. Monteagle at once took the letter to Whitehall, whereupon the arrest of Guy Fawkes and the other conspirators followed, and he was rewarded with a grant of £200 a year in land, and a further annual pension of £500. The letter was written by Francis Tresham, the brother of Lady Monteagle. In 1617, King James stayed with Lord Monteagle at Hornby Castle for the night of August 11th.

This lord was succeeded in 1622 by his son Henry, who as a Catholic suffered severely under the Penal Acts, his castle being searched for arms in 1625, when all that were found, with the armour, were confiscated.

During the Civil War, Hornby received a royal garrison, and repulsed a strong assault made on it in May 1643 by three companies of foot under Colonel Ralph Assheton. Having, however, acquired the knowledge that the east window of the hall was a vulnerable point, the Roundheads renewed the attack on the gates, while a second party provided with ladders assailed the back of the castle. After a stout resistance of two hours the defenders, taken in rear, were driven back and the fortress was captured. Its demolition was at once decreed by Parliament, but could only have been carried out partially, since at the time of the second siege of Thurland Castle the Parliamentary forces made it their headquarters.

Lord Morley and Monteagle was deprived of his estates after the war, and died in 1655, and his son, though he recovered the castle, was reduced to part with it and its lands in 1663 to Robert, 2nd Earl of Cardigan, whose successor George, the third earl, sold Hornby in 1713 for £14,500 to Colonel Francis Charteris. This disreputable man, who had been turned out of Marlborough's army in the Low Countries, amassed a fortune by gambling and cheating at cards, and lived at the castle, which he altered and disfigured. His only daughter married the fourth Earl of Wemyss, and their son Earl Francis sold the property in 1789 to John Marsden of Wennington Hall. Mr. Marsden died in 1826, and his will, devising Hornby, was contested by his cousin Admiral Tatham, whereon ensued the memorable lawsuit of Tatham v. Wright, commenced in 1830, in which the ablest judges and barristers of the day were concerned, and which was only ended in 1838, when the family of Lister-Marsden were ejected finally by Admiral Tatham, who then entered into possession. He died seventeen months after, and was succeeded by a relative, Mr. Pudsey Dawson. His nephew sold the estates and castle to Mr. John Foster of Queensbury, Yorks, whose grandson, Colonel W. H. Foster, M.P., is the present owner.

Nothing now remains of the original castle of the Monthegons, but the foundations of two round towers and of the ancient keep, 36 feet across, were laid bare during various rebuildings: these were perhaps early Nevile work. The oldest existing portion is the great tower erected by the first Lord Monteagle, which bears his crest of an eagle's claw. In front of this tower was a large quadrangle, while an outer or lower court extended to the town. All this was perhaps destroyed after the Civil War. A new front seems to have been built by the Charteris family, as shown by Buck's drawing, with its octagonal eagle tower built by Lord Wemyss in 1743. Lord Elcho slept at Hornby during his march south in 1745 with the Pretender's army, and when Lord Wemyss returned here a year or two later, he was so ill received that he left Hornby in disgust, and allowed the castle to go to ruin. Later restorations and additions to the fabric by Pudsey Dawson and the Foster family "have built up a castle which adorns a landscape scarcely rivalled for beauty in the length and breadth of England."

LANCASTER (chief)

WHERE this castle stands, on a hill above the river Lune, or Loyne, was the Roman camp and settlement of Longovicum, and Stukeley declares that portions of Roman walls might be seen there in 1721 ; traces certainly of the Roman fosse are still to be found on the N. side of the Castle Hill. Then followed a Saxon wooden fort or blockhouse, which gave way to Norman erections at the hands of Roger de Poictou, to whom the Conqueror gifted 398 English manors, including the honour and nearly the whole county of Lancashire, and who built the Lungess Tower in 1094. He was the younger son of Roger de Montgomery, who also came over with Duke William, and both father and son seem to have deserved well at the Conqueror's hands by their services at Senlac. Roger de Poictou fell on evil days in the time of Stephen, who deprived him of his lands, and conferred them on his own son William. John kept court here in 1206, receiving within the walls an embassy from France, perhaps in the tower which had been erected about that time by his friend and supporter Hubert de Burgh. Later in the thirteenth century, Henry III. bestowed all the lands that had been held by Simon de Montfort, Earl Ferrers, and John of Monmouth, on his second son Edmund Crouchback, with the title of Earl of Lancaster ; these lands, being inherited temp. Edward III. by his descendant Blanche, Duchess of Lancaster, were brought in marriage by her to Edward's fourth son, John of Gaunt, who was then created Duke of Lancaster, and who fixed his residence at this castle and made several noble additions to the fabric. To him succeeded his son Henry of Bolingbroke in the title of Lancaster, which dignity, on his accession in 1399, was absorbed in the Crown. As Henry IV. he held his court for some time here (cir. 1409), and in one of the smaller rooms of the gate-tower received the King of Scotland, and also the French ambassadors.

During the Civil Wars of the seventeenth century Lancaster Castle was besieged and taken more than once, and the remains of earthworks and batteries raised for breaching the walls may still be traced on the S.W. side. In 1745

LANCASTER CASTLE

Prince Charles Edward entered Lancaster on his march to Derby, passing there again on his retreat. This was not the first Scottish invasion which Lancaster had seen, since the Scots under Bruce, in their Southern foray after the English defeat at Bannockburn, laid waste the town and inflicted much injury upon the castle.

The great feature of the building is the superb gatehouse, 66 feet high, erected by John of Gaunt, partly with Norman materials. It has two fine octagonal flanking towers, a four-centred arch to the gateway and portcullis, a fine machicoulis carrying an allure, or rampart terrace, and a battlement (*Parker*). The oldest portion is the massive keep of Roger de Poicton, 80 feet square, with walls 10 feet thick; this too was much altered by John of Gaunt, but the original Norman windows are intact. The upper portion was rebuilt, temp. Elizabeth, though the S.W. turret is still popularly known as John of Gaunt's Chair. There is a chapel in

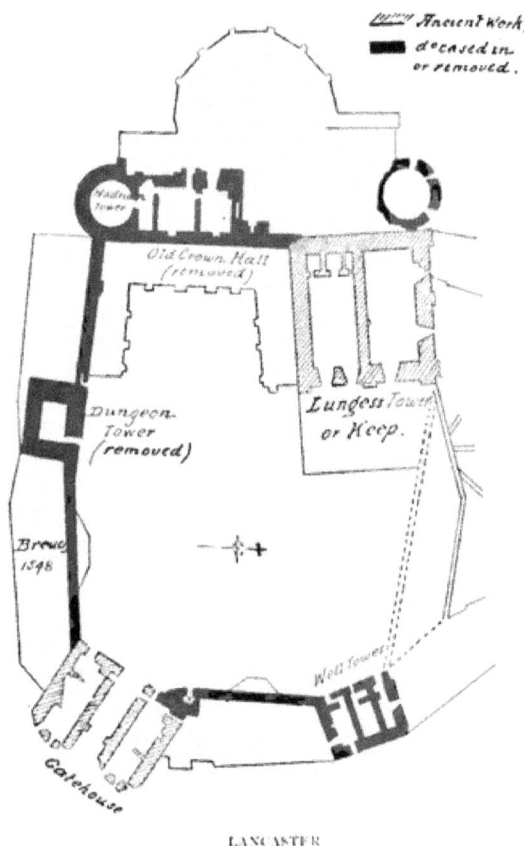

LANCASTER

the basement, and the dungeons are placed in two floors below the ground level (*Grindon's Lancashire*). There are now four grand towers in all, the ancient dungeon tower on the S. side, which had been used as a debtors' prison, having been demolished in 1812. The entire area of the castle measures 380 feet by 350 feet, but the old courtyard has now a sufficiently modernised appearance from the erection of modern courts and prisons necessary for the adaptation of the castle to its present purposes of county buildings, courts, and jail. Here too are held the assizes of the county of Lancashire.

Hadrian's Tower was cased over, at the time when the new buildings were formed, and made into a muniment store for the county records.

LATHOM HOUSE (*non-existent*)

LATHOM is a township, three miles N.E. of Ormskirk, where was the ancient baronial residence of the Lathams of Lathom, a family who had held these estates from Saxon times, and whose heiress brought them in marriage to Sir John Stanley in the reign of Edward III. (see *Liverpool Tower*). The estates continued in the Derby family for 300 years, and at the death of the ninth earl they were sold to the Bootle Wilbrahams, ancestors of Lord Skelmersdale, who was created Earl of Lathom in 1880, and whose seat the existing structure is.

The old house was a noble and strong fortress, and from its siege in the seventeenth century has a memory of unfading historic interest, second to few in the country. Of this structure nothing whatever remains, and as the fine mansion built in its place in 1724 has nothing in common with it, it will be well to record here what was the nature of the old place, called Lathom House, and also, briefly, the outlines of the siege which it stood so gallantly in 1643, under the command of an heroic woman, against very superior forces.

The house stood on a low site, on soft and boggy earth, and was surrounded by a high stone wall, 2 yards thick, furnished with a very fine gatehouse defended by two flanking towers, and having no less than nine strong towers in the length of the wall, on each of which were mounted six guns. Outside the wall was a moat, 8 yards wide and 2 yards deep, encircling the whole, and between the moat and the wall was a strong row of stout palisades. The mansion, in the centre, which is described in Bishop Ratter's MS. as being large enough to receive three kings and their trains, had in its midst a high and strong building called the Eagle Tower. On all sides the house was screened by high rising ground which effectually covered the place, so that an enemy could not open batteries for direct fire upon the walls; and thus we find the garrison annoyed by the fire of "grenades," or shells—that is, by vertical fire, from which they suffered latterly.

At the time of the outbreak of civil war in England, James, 7th Earl of Derby, the owner of Lathom, had been sent, as Lord of the Isle of Man, to preserve the peace in that island among the Manx population, who being disaffected, were also expecting there an invasion of a Scottish force; thus he was long detained there, and during his absence his Countess Charlotte, *née* De la Tremouille, a worthy descendant of the renowned Count William of Nassau, was in charge of Lathom House and her husband's property in the district. This was the state of affairs when, in May 1643, the Parliamentary general at the nearest station sent her a summons to yield up Lathom House. Her answer was a refusal: that she had been entrusted with the place, and that without contrary orders from the earl she would hold and defend it to the last extremity; and drawing all her garrison within the walls and closing the gates, she endured something like a state of siege there till February 1644. At this time Sir Thomas Fairfax sent her a fresh summons, and repeated it several times, offering the countess leave to transport her arms and goods, and liberty for all to move where they pleased, on yielding up the house; but she returned a final reply, that not a man should depart from her house

that she would keep it, whilst God enabled her, against all the king's enemies, and that she would await her lord's pleasure. Her garrison consisted of eleven officers and three hundred men. Little went on during the first few days, while the besiegers were drawing their lines and raising batteries against the place; but on March 12th a notable sally was made by a party of horse, who killed thirty of the enemy and took several prisoners. Then batteries were advanced, but the guns could make no impression on the big walls; while it does not appear that the "grenades," when they managed to throw them into the enceinte, did much harm, though they were an object of dread to the plucky garrison, including the countess and her children and chaplain (see "Memoirs of Colonel Hutchinson"). Thus the siege lingered on, the forces of the Parliament being variously put at from 1000 to 2000 men, until on May 29th Prince Rupert came to the relief of the sore-tried and gallant defenders, when their enemy raised the siege and decamped. Of the garrison only six men had been lost.

In July the siege was renewed by General Egerton, with a force of 4000 men; but just at that moment occurred the battle of Marston Moor, which cleared the North of the friends of Lathom, and gave Rupert other work to look after than its relief. The place also was badly provided with munitions of war, and necessaries and food for the garrison. The king therefore advised that both parties should treat, and commissioners were being named, when, through the treachery of an Irish soldier connected with Lathom House, this compromise was defeated and the defenders were led to surrender to the Parliamentary forces on the 2nd of December. It was one of the last places that held out for Charles. Then the order came for its demolition, which was carried out effectively, the materials being sold, and part given away to any who chose to help themselves.

At the Restoration, Lathom returned into the possession of the Earl of Derby, but as the house was almost destroyed, the family residence was now fixed at Knowsley. The ninth earl, intending to rebuild it, erected a sumptuous and grand front, part of the S. front of the present house, but did not live to complete his design, the execution of which should have devolved upon his eldest daughter Henrietta, the wife first of the Earl of Anglesey, and secondly of Lord Ashburnham. She, however, sold the place to Henry Furnese, from whom it was purchased in 1724 by Sir Thomas Bootle, Chancellor to Frederick, Prince of Wales, whose niece and heiress married Richard Wilbraham of Rode Hall, Cheshire ; the estate thus came to Lord Skelmersdale, the eldest son of that marriage, and is now possessed by the same family. To finish the personal history : the brave countess joined her husband in the Isle of Man, but she had to send her children to England, under a safe-conduct from Fairfax, in spite of which they were made prisoners by order of the Parliament.

In 1651 the Earl of Derby joined Charles II., and after the defeat of Worcester surrendered as prisoner of war, and was beheaded by the Parliamentary generals on October 15th, in his own town of Bolton-le-Moors, upon a scaffold made of timbers taken from Lathom House. His heroic countess, betrayed into her enemies' hands, remained a prisoner till the Restoration, and died at Knowsley in 1663.

> " Of Lathom-house by line came out,
> Whose blood will never turn their back."
> —*Ballad of Flodden Field.*

It is believed that no drawings or plans are in existence to show what Lathom House was, or the nature of its fortifications ; and we have therefore to content ourselves with the little that is known of this famous place, as repeated by Whitaker (" Richmondshire," vol. ii. p. 254).

"The whole must have been surrounded by a deep fosse, immediately within which, and beyond the drawbridge, would appear a strong gateway, more lofty and of larger dimensions than the other towers. The curtain walls ranging off to right and left from the great gateway would have eight angles, in each of which was placed a flanking tower. Within this outer enclosure would be another fosse, with its drawbridge, and an inner gateway opposite to the former ; but the eight towers of the second enclosure, instead of flanking a curtain wall like the former, must have been attached to the walls and angles of the body of the house, and from the time at which they were erected, may have been either square or octagonal. One of these was unquestionably the Eagle Tower, known from the account of the great siege to have contained 70 yards of flooring, in which were probably the principal apartments."

LIVERPOOL. (*non-existent*)

ACCORDING to Camden, Roger of Poictou, lord of the honour of Lancaster, who at the time of the Domesday Survey owned all the lands between the Mersey and the Ribble, built the castle of Liverpool on the south side of the town in 1076, and bestowed the custody of it on the noble family of Molyneux, whose seat was at Sefton, their descendants being the Earls of Sefton, who were constables of this castle.

The keep of Liverpool Castle was a square building, heavily battlemented, having four circular flanking towers at the angles, with an enclosed area of 50 square acres. It was surrounded by a deep moat 30 yards broad, with a drawbridge and a fosse partly cut out of the live rock; there was also an entrance gatehouse, the strongest part of the fortress, and other buildings were enclosed. The whole structure had been pulled down before 1663, and since then, the church of St. George has been built on the site of it. Early in the fifteenth century Sir Richard Molyneux was hereditary Constable of this, the king's castle, while Sir John Stanley lived in his own tower, higher up the river; between these two there were constant fighting and disturbances, highly prejudicial to the town and its prosperity.

LIVERPOOL TOWER (non-existent)

THERE was also a strongly fortified tower at the bottom of Water Street, called the Tower of Liverpool, the origin of which is quite forgotten. Sir John Stanley, a young knight, attended a tournament in London in the reign of Edward III., and being conspicuous by his courage and his good looks thereat, did gain the affections of the beautiful daughter of Sir Thomas Latham of Lathom, Isabella, whom her father unwillingly gave to this knight in marriage; being the heiress of Lathom, she brought that estate, and also this tower by the river, to the Stanleys. Sir John Stanley obtained a licence in 1405 to fortify his house, and he built or enlarged this tower in 1406, after which, through the reign of Henry VI., it served as an occasional residence for the Stanley family, lords of Man, and was their town abode. It was a square embattled building with corner towers, forming three sides of a quadrangle, and commanded both the town and the Mersey, where lay the ships of the Stanleys, in which they sailed to their new kingdom of the Isle of Man. In the lapse of time the destinies of the old tower changed, and it became an assembly-room, and latterly a prison. It was razed to the ground in 1820, and the site of it is now covered by Tower Buildings. The area it occupied was 3700 square yards.

TOWER (non-existent)

AT one time there was, commanding the Pool on the west side of Liverpool, a fortalice built by King John, who was windbound here when on an expedition to Ireland, and conceived the necessity of the fortress. This has of course vanished.

MANCHESTER (*non-existent*)

CAMDEN says: "Two flyte shottes without the town beneth on the same side of Irwell yet may be seen the dikes and foundations of old Man Castel yn a ground now enclosed: the stones of the ruins of this castel were translated towards making of bridges for the town."

PENWORTHAM (*non-existent*)

THE Castle Hill of Penwortham is on the N.E. spur of the heights below Preston; in front of it is a level area, and on the S. it is divided by a deep gully from the site of the church. In early times the river Ribble, when the channel of that stream was larger than it now is, washed two sides of the conical rocky cliff whereon the castle stood, and on the W. a sunk lane ran below it. Thus the position was an extremely strong one, and had been selected in very early times for a stronghold, since, in 1856, some excavations made in the hill exposed the remains of prehistoric wooden dwellings of probably British origin, and a Saxon kitchen-midden; a prick-spur and some ironwork of refined make were also found.

The Conqueror bestowed Penwortham manor on Roger de Busli, and his son, Warin de Busli, or Bussel, succeeded him, and ranks as the first baron of Penwortham; he it probably was—if not Roger de Poictou—who reared a fortalice at this spot. The property remained with his family until the time of John, who succeeded in wresting the estate from Hugh, the fourth baron, and then sold it to Roger de Lacy for 310 marks of silver. Next it is recorded that Ramulph, Earl of Chester, held his courts at Penwortham Castle, and after the Earls of Chester and Lincoln, the barony passed by marriage to Thomas, Earl of Lancaster, and became merged in that duchy.

The castle has totally disappeared, owing perhaps to the great land-ships which have taken place on the river banks, and no signs of a ditch or of the walls are to be seen; but the memory of the place is retained, as usually is the case, in the name of Castle Hill. It is believed to have been a strong square Norman keep, surrounded by a rampart and ditch.

RADCLIFFE TOWER (minor)

A BLUFF, or cliff of red stone immediately opposite and overhanging the river Irwell at this point, seems to have been the origin of the name of one of the noblest, most ancient, and most honourable families in this kingdom. Sir Bernard Burke, no mean authority, declares that the house of Radcliffe has produced fourteen earls, one viscount, five barons, seven knights of the Garter, several bannerets and knights of the Bath, together with many privy councillors, warriors, and statesmen. It is stated in Murray's guide-book that Edward the Confessor bestowed Radcliffe on Roger de Poictou; but there was an Edward Radeclive here at the time of the Domesday Survey, therefore Roger cannot have held it long, and the manor appears to have fallen to the Crown and so remained till the reign of Stephen, when it was given to Ranulph de Gernons, Earl of Chester. It is in the time of Henry II. that we first hear of a De Radeclive, and the pedigree of that family shows that in 6 Richard I. there was a William de Radeclive of Radcliffe Tower, Sheriff of Lancaster; and these lords bear this name down to the sixteenth century. In the time of Henry IV., James Radclyffe had a licence to enclose his manor of Radcliffe, and to crenellate and embattle his house and walls. One of the family, Sir John Radclyffe, was a great commander of the armies of Henry V., his father being Sir Richard Radclyffe, Seneschal of the Royal Forests; his grandson Sir John married the heiress of Walter, Lord Fitzwalter, and succeeded to that title, and it was he who, riding without his helmet, was killed at the skirmish at Ferrybridge, the night before the bloody battle of Towton. One of the Sir John Radcliffes lost five sons in different battles in the years 1598-99, and his daughter, who was maid of honour to Queen Elizabeth, died of grief for the loss of her brothers.

The grandson of the Lord Fitzwalter slain as above, named Robert, Lord Fitzwalter, succeeded in 1518 to Radcliffe Tower, and was created Earl of Sussex in 1529. Edward Radcliffe, the sixth and last Earl of Sussex, died without issue in 1641, aged eighty-seven.

What was called Radcliffe Tower was enlarged into a manor-house of the first rank. It has been a quadrangular structure, but two sides only remain. In 1801 it contained a noble old hall, 42 feet in length, with a splendid ancient roof of oak, and oaken windows and doors, and other fittings in good order; but now, alas, all this has disappeared, and the fine old mansion, a mixture of stone and timber, has been all but destroyed. In decay it shows traces of strong masonry, but the lower storey alone is now remaining; the old hall and the adjoining tower having been taken down of late to make room for a row of modern cottages.

To this ancient building and to the family that owned it are attached the ballad and tradition given in Dr. Percy's "Reliques" under the name of "The Lady Isabella's Tragedy; or, The Stepmother's Cruelty," which are sometimes given under the title of "Fair Ellen of Radelyffe." The story is that of the sacrifice and murder of a young and beautiful heiress by her stepmother, the Lady of Radelyffe, who causes the cook to kill the fair Isabella, "the white doe," and serve her up for the repast of her father. This Thyestian story is related in this wise :—

> "Fair Isabella was she called,
> A creature fair was she :
> She was her father's only joye,
> As you shall after see.
>
> Therefore her cruel step-mother
> Did envy her so much,
> That daye by daye she sought her life,
> Her malice it was such."

So the dame "bargains with the master-cook to take her life awaye," and then sends the fair Isabella to him with this message :—

> "And bid him dress to dinner straight
> That fair and milk-white doe,
> That in the park doth shine so bright,
> There's none so fair to showe."

But when she gives the cook the message he says, "Thou art the doe that I must dress," and prepares accordingly.

> "O then cried out the scullion boye,
> As loud as loud might bee,
> 'O save her life, good master-cook,
> And make your pyes of mee!'"

However, the tragedy is accomplished, and the pye is made; and when the lord of the tower comes home from the chase, and is set down to dinner with the pye before him, he calls for his daughter deare, and says he will neither eat nor drink, until he did her see.

> "O then outspake the scullion boye,
> With a loud voice so hye,
> 'If now you will your daughter see,
> My lord, cut up that pye,

' Wherein her flesh is mincèd small,
   And parchèd with the fire,
All causèd by her step-mothèr,
   Who did her death desire.'

Then all in black this lord did mourne,
   And for his daughter's sake,
He judged her cruel step-mothèr
   To be burnt at a stake.

Likewise he judged the master-cook
   In boiling lead to stand,
And made the simple scullion boye
   The heir of all his land."

THURLAND (minor)

THE castle stands on slightly elevated ground in the Vale of Lune, about twelve miles from the county town, near the high-road, but shrouded by trees. It is one of the few old moated mansions in Lancashire. In very early times a fortress was placed at this point to assist in repressing the border forays, which perhaps served as an abode to the Tunstalls who owned the lands.

There appear to have been lords of Tunstall in the county of Lancaster since the time of William the Conquerer, as Topsi, the then lord, gave one messuage and one toft in Bolton (le Sands) to the Abbot of Rivaulx; and they are frequently mentioned in Henry I. and following reigns. Sir Thomas Tunstall is spoken of by Camden as an *eques auratus* living here under Edward III., Richard II., and Henry IV. and V., serving with the last king in his French wars, and being present at Agincourt. In 1402 (4 Henry IV.) this knight obtained a licence "kernellare manerium suum de Thorslond," and also to enclose the manor. This date, therefore, may be taken for the foundation of the existing castle. The grandson of this man, Sir Richard Tunstall, was a man of high renown during the Wars of the Roses, and a staunch Lancastrian, holding Harlech for Henry VI. longer than any place in England; still in spite of this he was highly esteemed by the Yorkist kings, and Richard III. employed him and made him a Knight of the Garter. He died in 1492. His nephew was the great Bishop Tunstall of Durham, the friend of Erasmus, Sir Thomas More, and other great men little liked by Henry VIII., who placed him in confinement in Lambeth Palace, where he died in 1550, aged eighty-five. Sir Richard's son, Bryan Tunstall, must have been a warrior of note, having confided to him, with Sir Edward Howard, the command of the English right wing at Flodden.

The poet of this terrible fight makes a most important character of this "stainless Knight of Flodden," and in the ballad many stanzas are devoted to him, descriptive of his valour and of his slaying.

> " And never a nobleman of fame,
>   But Bryan Tunstal bold, alas!
> Whose corpse home to his burial came,
>   With worship great, as worthy was."
>
> —(*See also* " Marmion.")

There is no record of Bryan Tunstall having been knighted, and he is described elsewhere in the ballad as "that bold Esquire." Neither is there any authority for believing that his body was brought home. He is not buried in Tunstall Church. His son Sir Marmaduke succeeded him at Thurland, and his descendant of the third generation, Francis Thurland, owing to the encumbered condition of the estate, exchanged the manor of Tunstall, Thurland Castle, &c., for the manor of Hutton Longvillers.

Thurland Castle has changed hands several times. The Tunstalls were, with the exception of a period between 1466 and 1474, the owners until 1598. Sir Richard Tunstall, the son of Francis, having been attainted, forfeited his estates; but these, including the castle, were restored to him in 1474. In 1598 the castle and manor were sold to John Girlington, the head of a wealthy Catholic family, whose grandson, Sir John Girlington, fought and died for Charles I. In 1643 this Sir John garrisoned his house, and sustained a short siege in it by Colonel Assheton, but had to yield. It is said that a large quantity of money and plate, together with a number of disaffected ladies and gentlemen of the county who had shut themselves up in the castle, fell into the enemy's hands.

A month later, however, we find Sir John holding the castle against a fresh enemy, Colonel Rigby: he sustained a seven weeks' siege and again had to yield possession. The castle was then dismantled, and it remained in ruins till 1663. Sir John is said to have been killed in a fight at Melton Mowbray, and his family sank into poverty. In 1698 Thurland was sold to John Borrett of Shoreham, Kent, from whom it passed to his daughter, whose husband, Evelyn, sold it in 1771 to one Welch, of Leek, from whom it was purchased by Miles North, of Kirkby Lonsdale, in 1781. It was sold by North's grand-nephew in 1885 to the present owner, Colonel Edward B. Lees.

The castle was rebuilt early in the present century from the designs of Wyatt, and little remains of the original massive pile. A small stone vaulted building with one narrow window, called by Whitaker the gatehouse, is all

that is left of a large block of buildings that extended along the western side
of the court, removed, together with a fine gateway which spanned the
approach near the gatehouse, some seventy or eighty years ago.

The castle stands on a gravel mound about 40 feet high, and is surrounded
by a moat, 30 feet wide and 6 feet deep. It is a **L**-shaped building, the walls
in the old part being from 6 to 14 feet thick. During recent alterations, several
portions of human skeletons have been discovered.

TURTON TOWER (minor)

FOUR miles N.E. from Bolton, is one of the oldest halls in England,
and as it is said to have been built originally in the time of Henry II.,
it follows that in those times it must have been a defensible work, although,
rebuilt as it was, it can scarcely be called a castle now, being chiefly an
Elizabethan house, with a square stone tower, battlemented. It was surrounded by a moat, of which there are still some traces, and is a picturesque,
irregular old pile, partly of stone and partly half-timbered, or "black-and-
white," the latter portion being gabled, with each of the four storeys projecting. The walls of the tower, which is three storeys high, are 5 feet in
thickness.

The manor of Turton in the reign of John was held by Roger Fitz Robert
(De Holland) ; afterwards it belonged to the good Duke of Lancaster, from
whom it passed into the hands of an ancient and famous family called
Orrell, whose seat it was from 1408 to 1628, when they became impoverished
and sold Turton to the philanthropist Humphrey Chetham for £4000. He
resided here, and dying in 1653 the place next went to the Blauds by a
Chetham heiress, from whom it came by a similar way to the Greenes,
and from them by marriage to the father of Sir Henry Bartle Frere, and
thence by purchase to Mr. J. Kay, with whose family Turton remains. It
was almost entirely rebuilt in 1596 by William Orrell, who carefully retained
the old timber and plaster construction and the ancient square tower. Mr.
Kay in 1835 restored and renewed the fabric in the state in which we
now see it.

The chief curiosity here is a number of subterranean passages. One is
entered at the foot of the staircase and leads towards the neighbouring
village of Chapelton — originally, it is said, to Bolton ; and there are others.
In the breakfast-room is a secret niche behind the panelling, where, it is
said, a concealed spy overheard the orders of Cromwell when he rested
here on his way to meet the Royalist forces after he had gained the victory
at Dunbar. He ordered an attack on Wigan that somewhat failed, owing,
as said, to the plan being divulged. Near the dining-room, off the passage

to the billiard-room, is a priest's hole, giving access to the battlements, and another has been found lately. A steep circular stair leads to the cellars, and beyond, to a circular chamber supposed to be a dungeon, with loop-holed walls. The old house was well filled with curious oak furniture, which has of late years been in great measure sold and dispersed.

WRAYSHOLME (*minor*)

THIS tower is on the way to Gleaston, a little S. of the village of Allithwaite. All that remains of the place is a massive tower. There is a tradition that the last of the English wolves was killed near this building (*Grindon*), which is an ancient peel, erected on the marches, and once belonged to the Harrington family.

MIDDLEHAM

Yorkshire

BARDEN TOWER (*minor*)

IN the neighbourhood of Bolton Priory, where the Strid comes down from the high moors, in the old forest of the Cliffords, is this ancient building. Originally one of the six lodges with which the Barden forest was provided, it was chosen for a retreat by Henry Clifford, the Shepherd lord of Skipton, whose story is noticed under Skipton. It is probable that during his twenty-four years of exile from society, he came frequently into this district and got to love the place, so that when the accession of Henry VII. enabled him to return to his property, he rebuilt this house, to form for himself a quiet home for study and retirement. And here he generally dwelt, resorting to the company of the monks of Bolton for assistance in his favourite studies of astrology and alchemy. After his death the tower was neglected, and so in the time of Countess Anne had become ruinous, and was repaired and rebuilt by her in 1659. Whitaker saw it entire, he says, in 1774, but it is once more a ruin. It is a large square building, and has a chapel attached. The walls are strong, but it does not seem more capable of defence than an ordinary peel tower would be.

BEDALE (non-existent)

THERE was a castle here belonging to Sir Brian FitzAlan, the viceroy of Edward I. for Scotland, whose tomb, together with that of his wife, is in the church of Bedale. He was a very distinguished baron in the reigns both of Henry III. and of his son (see *Richmond, Yorks*). This was his residence, and was probably built by him; it was placed in a position, without any natural advantage, a little to the S.W. of the church, and its foundations have been traced to a considerable distance, extending from the gardens of the house of the owner of the site into a field N.W. of the church; no vestiges, however, remain above-ground.

BOLTON (chief)

THIS grand and grim old castle of the Scropes, which they built in the days of Richard II., and inhabited with baronial splendour till nearly the epoch of the Long Parliament, stands on the edge of high, bleak, and barren moors, on the N. side of Wensleydale, in the N. Riding, three miles from Wensley, and four miles from Middleham Castle, across the river Ure, on the opposite side of the valley. Above, at the back of the castle, the ground rises to Stanton Moor, from whence it falls again into the valley of the Swale. Dreary and desolate as was its situation, the wealthy Scropes continued to use it as their home while their race lasted, and much additional interest attaches to the grey ruin in the castle which was one of the prisons of Mary Queen of Scots. The Scrope family seem originally to have been of plebeian origin, perhaps deriving from Normandy, and Dugdale traces them back to one Robert le Scrope, who in 13 Henry III. obtained a footing in Yorkshire. The elevation of the family was effected by the two able sons of Sir William le Scrope (temp. Edward I.), Bailiff of Richmond, who both rose to be Chief Justice of the King's Bench, and each of whom purchased lands in this county and elsewhere. The elder brother, Sir Henry le Scrope, died in 1336, and was followed by his son Richard, who served in the wars of Edward III., and was twice Chancellor; he inherited vast property from his father in Herts, Middlesex, Yorkshire, and other places, and was the founder of Bolton Castle. Leland (*Itin.*, vol. viii. f. 53) says: "*Richard*, Lord *Scrope*, was Chancelor of *England* in Richard the 2 Dayes. This Richard made out of the Grownd the Castle of *Bolton* of 4 greate stronge Towres and of good lodgings. It was a making xviii yeres, and the Chargys of the Buyldinge came by yere [annually] to 1000 marks. . . . It was finished or King Richard the 2 dyed. . . . Most parte of the Tymber that was occupied in buylding of

BOLTON CASTLE

this Castell was fett out of the Forest of Engleby in Cumberland, and Richard Lord Scrope for conveyance of it, had layde by the way dyvers drawghts of oxen to carry it from place to place till it came to Bolton."

This first lord of Bolton was actively employed in the French wars of Edward I., and in the forty-fifth year of that monarch's reign was made Treasurer of the Exchequer; in 2 Richard II. he became Chancellor of England and Keeper of the Great Seal. He died in 1403, leaving three sons—William, created Earl of Wilts, who was beheaded at Bristol in the revolution of 1399 for fidelity to King Richard; Roger, who became second lord of Bolton, and died six months after his father; and Stephen, who was Deputy-Lieutenant of Ireland. The brother of Sir Henry the Chief Justice was Sir Geoffry Scrope, who also rose to be Chief Justice, temp. Richard II. Henry was also a brave soldier, and was knighted for his prowess at a royal tournament. He purchased Upsall and Clifton on the river Ure, a short distance to the S.E. of Masham, and his son Henry became first lord of Masham. Henry was a very warlike personage, and of great repute, who served actively in all the foreign and other wars of Edward III. (see *Wylie*, ii. 197), and his third son Richard, born 1346, was the pugnacious Archbishop of York, who, opposing the distasteful rule of Henry IV., was ruthlessly beheaded by him. This Archbishop Scrope had been one of Henry's strongest supporters at his outset, and had himself obtained from King Richard in the Tower his renunciation of the throne; he had read it to the Parliament at Westminster, and had assisted in placing the crown on Henry's head. Soon after, with the Percys, he became hostile to the king, and being taken in arms at the insurrection of 1405, was brought from Pontefract to his palace at Bishopthorpe. The Chief Justice Gascoigne refused to pass sentence on a prelate of his rank; he was, however, condemned by a mock tribunal at Henry's bidding, and executed at once in the fields near York. His tomb is in that Minster. The eighth Lord Scrope of Bolton was a stout Yorkist during the Wars of the Roses; and Henry, the ninth lord, is celebrated in the Ballad of Flodden Field as bringing thither all the men of that country-side with him to join the English host, and marshalling them below this castle.

When Queen Mary of Scotland sought an asylum in England, after the fatal battle of Langside, in May 1568, she was brought to Carlisle, being there attended by Henry, 10th Lord Scrope, as Warden of the Marches, and was by him, in compliance with orders from London, conducted to his castle of Bolton, where his wife, sister to the Duke of Norfolk, was detailed to wait on her. But when Mary realised the intentions of the English to make a prisoner of her, she warned her captors that they would have a difficult task, and so, for fear of her escaping, the queen's windows at Bolton were grated with iron, her male servants were sent out of the castle at sunset, and when she walked or rode out she was attended by a hundred men of the Berwick guard. She came to Bolton in July 1568 and remained until January 26, 1568-9, when, after the discovery that Lady Scrope had acted as a means of communication between the queen and the Duke of Norfolk, she was removed to Tutbury in Staffordshire and placed under the care of that dour and grim pair, the Earl of Shrewsbury and his wife. An episode in Mary's life at Bolton is given in Froude's History (vol. ix.), affording an interesting view of life in that fortress. Many plots were formed to effect the queen's escape during her detention here, but they all miscarried, including the one of local tradition, which tells how, having passed through one of the windows in the S.W. tower close to which her apartments are said to have been located, she had managed to escape as far as the "Queen's Gap" on Leybourne Shaw, when she was overtaken and brought back. Her signature, "Marie R.," long remained scratched on a window-pane of her room, but this being removed for better preservation to Bolton Hall, it was accidentally broken ; the fragments, however, are preserved. The Queen's Room has one window looking into the court, and another over the country to the W. In 1645, after the reduction of Tickhill, Knaresborough, Scarborough, and other Yorkshire castles, Bolton, which was held by a garrison for the king under Colonel Scrope and Colonel Henry Chaytor of Croft, was seriously attacked by a strong Parliamentary force, and after a lengthened resistance, in which the garrison were reduced to the eating of their horses, was surrendered, and its defenders were removed to Pontefract.

The structure consists of a huge square central block, having a quadrangular courtyard in its midst, round which the apartments stand, and at each of the angles were the great strong towers of Leland, one of which has disappeared, for the N.E. tower, having been injured by artillery fire in the siege, fell to the ground suddenly in 1649 ; the rest of the walls are nearly perfect. The great hall is on the N. side, and there is on the S. front also a banqueting-hall, with the kitchens and offices. The only entrance is at the E. end through a well-protected gateway, and each of the small doors into the buildings from the court is said to have had a portcullis—the fire from which would have rendered this courtyard untenable by an enemy. There is no ditch, nor are there any outworks to the castle, which is gaunt and devoid of ornament, while the rooms are small, and many of them dark and sombre. The chapel is outside the walls. The ground rooms were vaulted, and the upper floors were of timber, and the roofs nearly flat. The garderobes are placed in a turret in the centre of the S. front, and have passages leading to them in the walls. Bolton is altogether the most perfect house of its period remaining in England (*Parker*).

BOWES (minor)

ORIGINALLY written Boghes, near Barnard Castle, on the crest of the hill S. of the town, this castle was erected by the Earls of Richmond at the site of the Roman station of Lavatræ, the stones of which furnished a vast and ready quarry for the building of the castle and the church. The fortress was intended as a defence on that side against the incursions of the Scots, and they placed at this spot a large Norman rectangular tower, with the usual pilasters in the centre of the faces and double at the angles, with walls 4 yards in thickness. It is called Bowes Castle, but, as is observed by Mr. Clark, a keep or tower like this is only a part of a castle proper, "a single structure being usually termed a tower or peel." It is evident that no other buildings ever existed here. It stands near the high road, which replaces the Roman road from Greta Bridge by Brough, Appleby, and Brougham, and is actually within the camp of the Roman station. Roman remains have been discovered round it.

Little is known as to the history of this tower, which was always held by the Earls of Richmond, who had highway rights, and set up a gallows. King John was here in 1206, and again in 1212. What part of the country did that restless and active monarch not visit? Boghes or Bowes is mentioned in many grants, in conjunction with Richmond, from Henry III. to Henry VI.

The tower is very Late Norman, built probably in the twelfth century. It is 82 feet long by 60 feet, and about 50 feet high, and contained a basement and two upper storeys. It is built in the usual way, with broad double pilasters at the angles, and a single one in the centre of each face; the top storey is ruined, and there are no remains of battlements. One angle on the S.E. held the staircase, which probably terminated in a turret. Two cross walls divided the basement into three chambers, whose roofs were vaulted, and one of these cross walls, rising, divided the first floor into a large hall and a solar; the entrance was on this floor, on the E. side, 10 feet above the ground, under a round arch, and defended only by a door. Several small apartments and a garderobe were contrived in the thickness of the walls, lighted by loops, and three windows lighted the large rooms. The floor above was timber. A mill on the river Greta ground the corn for the garrison.

CASTLETON (non-existent)

ON the N. face of Cleveland, near the station of Danby, on the railway from Whitby to Stockton, is a village of this name, which has a mound called Castle Hill, and probably represents one of the earliest holdings of the Bruces in England. After the Conquest Robert de Brus was granted the manor of Danby (q.v.) at this place, which he must have fortified. The presence of a mound refers almost invariably to a settlement of Anglo-Saxons or Danes, and we have the Danish name Danby to prove the residence of some settler of the latter nation.   And we can still see the trace of the early fortress — the usual mound surrounded by a ditch formed by the deblai, and protected by a close double palisading, somewhat like that of a New Zealand Prah. This fortified point must have been adopted, as in other places, by the incoming Norman, who strengthened it with further defences, and perhaps with stonework, and whose representatives continued in it until the building of a fit and proper castle at Danby (*q.v.*).

CAWOOD PALACE (*minor*)

ORIGINALLY, it is said, King Athelstan had a stronghold here, which was held by the archbishops as a palace long before the Conquest, probably by royal grant.   In the reign of Richard II., his faithful friend Archbishop Nevill used this house in preference to his other palaces in the county, Bishopthorpe, Sherburn, Ripon, and Otley ; but at the deposition of that prince he had to flee the country, dying in extreme poverty at Louvain.

The palace was fortified and made into a castle temp. Henry IV., and was added to and strengthened by Archbishop Bowett, temp. Henry VI., and by his successor Archbishop and Chancellor John Kempe, who added the great gatehouse which is still remaining.   He was translated to Canterbury, and died in 1415.

The chief interest of the place is its association with Wolsey, at his fall. In 1529, when his relations with the king were broken off, Wolsey came to Cawood to brood over his disgrace, and passed the autumn at this palace. Then the Earl of Northumberland was sent hither to arrest him, and on November 6th he was removed by the earl, through Pontefract and Doncaster, to Sheffield Castle, where he was received by the Earl of Shrewsbury, and was treated with every mark of respect.   Wolsey remained here for sixteen days, and it appears that the profound melancholy in which he was plunged resulted in a mortal attack of dysentery.   Ill as he was, however, he was urged on, by orders from London, where he was to take his trial for high treason, and came the first night to Hardwick Hall (Shrewsbury's house also), and the next to Nottingham, and thence to Newark.   On arriving at Leicester Abbey next day he was unable to proceed, and there on the 28th he died, in his fifty-ninth year.

In 1642 Cawood received a garrison for King Charles, which did good service the next July in attacking the retreating forces of Sir Thomas Fairfax while crossing the ferry at Selby after the repulse at Adderton Moor.   But in 1644 the castle was surrendered to Sir John Meldrum, the Parliamentary chief, and two years after was dismantled and made untenable.

The principal building remaining is Kempe's Gatehouse, a large and lofty structure with buttresses at the angles, and between them are the broad entrance, under a low-pointed archway, through which the dejected cardinal must have ridden on his mule,—and a narrow one for foot-passers. On a broad panel running across are displayed eleven shields of arms, not decipherable. In the chamber above is still held the court of the manor, and above this there is another storey; both rooms have pointed lights. There is also a chapel of brick, now used as a barn, on the right of the tower, while a modern farmhouse is joined on the left.

Cawood stands in a flat country by the river Ouse, about five miles from Selby.

CLIFTON-UPON-URE (*non-existent*)

THIS ancient stronghold of the Scropes stands four miles to the N. of Masham, and its possession generally followed that of Upsall (*q.v.*). There are but scanty vestiges of it remaining; some tottering piles of masonry with small-pointed windows, standing on the banks of the Ure, are all. Leland says that Clifton was only a tower or castlet, and Camden speaks of it as in ruins, "formerly the seat of the Lords Scrope of Masham," part of it being then inhabited by a farmer. And it is evident that, being so small, the abode of the Scropes must have generally been at Upsall and not here.

In White's "Gazetteer of Yorkshire" we are told that the manor of Clifton passed (like Upsall) from the lords Scrope to Sir Ralph Fitz Randolph, and afterwards to the Wyvills, the Daltons, and the Prestons, a member of which last family sold Clifton to John Hutton in 1735.

From its nearness to Masham, Clifton seems to have stood in the place of a manor-house to that town.

CONINGSBOROUGH (*chief*)

THE town of this name is on the banks of the Don, five miles from Doncaster, and was a place of importance in earliest times. The manor was in Earl Godwin's family, and belonged at the Conquest to King Harold. At Domesday it was held by William de Warenne, the first Earl of Surrey, who was son-in-law to King William, and one of the most important of his Norman followers. He seems to have lived much here when in England, and would no doubt strengthen and fortify the old dwelling of his Saxon predecessors, until the time arrived for the building of a strong fortress. This place, which became the *caput* of his Yorkshire estates, was to Earl Warenne the same as Lewes was to his great possessions in Sussex, and he

cemented the connection between the two districts by giving the church of
Coningsborough to Lewes Priory.

His son William, 2nd Earl of Surrey, was a supporter at first of Robert,
Duke of Normandy, but made his peace later with Henry I., and retained and

CONINGSBOROUGH

transmitted the estates and honours of his earldom, which were enjoyed by his
son, who left but one daughter, Isabel de Warenne, who in 1163 married as her
second husband Hameline Plantagenet, the brother of Henry II. He became,
jure uxoris, Earl Warenne, being an active soldier, and serving with Richard
Cœur de Lion; their son William succeeded in 1201 as fifth Earl of Surrey,
and was one of the great barons concerned in Magna Charta. His son and
heir John was the fierce and blunt soldier who defied the "Quo Warranto"

edict of Edward I.; he was summoned to Parliament as Earl of Surrey and Sussex. His grandson, the last earl, John, died in 1347, his will being dated at Conesburgh Castle, when his title of Surrey, in default of legitimate heirs, went to Hugh, Earl of Arundel, his sister's son. This estate was left, by royal permission, to his natural sons. In 1 Edward III. homage had been done for this castle by Thomas, Earl of Lancaster, but soon after John, Earl Warenne, held it for his lifetime, and after his death it fell to the Crown, when King Edward granted Coningsborough to Edmund of Langley, his fifth son, who died 1402, when it went to his son Edward, Duke of York, who was stifled in his armour at Agincourt, 1415. He was succeeded by his brother Richard, called of Conisburgh, Earl of Cambridge (beheaded 1415), whose son and successor was Richard, Duke of York, the father of Edward IV. and Richard III. His second wife and widow, Maud Clifford, had this castle in dower, and died there in 1446, when Coningsborough again became Crown property, and

THE KEEP

appears thenceforth to have been neglected. Edward IV., its owner, was king, and did not want the castle, and his brother Richard of Glo'ster had Middleham and Barnard. Constables were appointed and stewards, &c., of "the lordships of Conysborowe" from time to time, and at last James II. bestowed the place on Carey, Earl of Dover; it in later times became Conyers' property.

Coningsborough is best known in its connection with "Ivanhoe," where the Wizard of the North has described its position thus: "There are few more

beautiful or striking scenes in England, than is presented by the vicinity of
this ancient Saxon fortress. The soft and gentle river Don sweeps through an
amphitheatre in which cultivation is richly blended with woodland, and on a
mount ascending from the river, well defended by walls and ditches, rises this
ancient edifice, which, as its Saxon name implies, was, previous to the Conquest, a royal residence of the Kings of England." The natural mound of
gravel and rock, steep on all sides, rises 175 feet above the river, its summit
having been levelled into a platform measuring ⅜ of an acre, 60 feet below
which the scarped sides end in an immense ditch. On the W. side is the
village, between which and the hill is the outer ward of the castle, from
whence a path rises to the entrance between lofty parallel walls. There is
no gatehouse into the inner ward, and none perhaps ever existed, though the
entrance may have been well protected in the passage through the dwellings,
which were built against the curtain wall; right and left extended a range
of these containing the hall, kitchen, and offices, and probably a chapel. The
wall of this ward follows the edge of the platform, and is from 20 to 35 feet
high, but the allures and battlements have disappeared. On the S. and E.
sides some flanking defence was obtained by five half-round turrets, and other
towers may have stood where the wall is broken.

But the chief object and glory of this castle is the Keep standing at the
N.E. corner, on the line of the curtain which abuts on it, and without any
special ditch of its own. It is a huge cylindrical building, almost solid below,
being 60 feet in diameter, and even now 90 feet in height; its base is broadly
splayed, and the sides are supported by six huge buttresses, each of which projects 9 feet, and is also splayed outwards for 20 feet above the foundations. The
masonry is magnificent. Entrance is had by an outer staircase to the level of
the first floor, through a flat-headed doorway which had no protection. There
are four stages, the uppermost being in the roof, which was conical, and all the
apartments are circular. The room on the first stage is 22 feet in diameter and
had no light or air except from the doorway; it was doubtless a store. A small
mural stair with a loop conducts to the next, or state floor, 25 feet in diameter,
lighted by a square-headed window, in two lights. Opposite is a huge fireplace,
and near the entrance is a wall passage conducting to a garderobe furnished
with a loophole. On the opposite side is the opening of the staircase which leads
to the third stage, or oratory floor, 27 feet in diameter, containing a window
and other arrangements as the floor below, both of these rooms having had
timber floors. The remarkable feature is the small oratory, contrived within the
S.E. buttress, the roof being groined and vaulted, and ornamented with Norman
mouldings. The piscina is there, but the altar is gone; it had a vestry and three
lights. Another wall staircase leads to the uppermost stage, the opening being
on the allure behind the parapet. Above this parapet the buttresses rise in
turrets, three of them containing a half-round cavity, one forming an oven,

and two being cisterns; the third was a dove-cote, in all probability. Below the first floor is a large domed cellar, and in the centre of it is the well opening. The thickness of the wall at the ground level is 5 yards between the buttresses.

The curtain wall and buildings attached are the work of an early Norman owner, perhaps of William, the third and last original Earl Warenne, while the

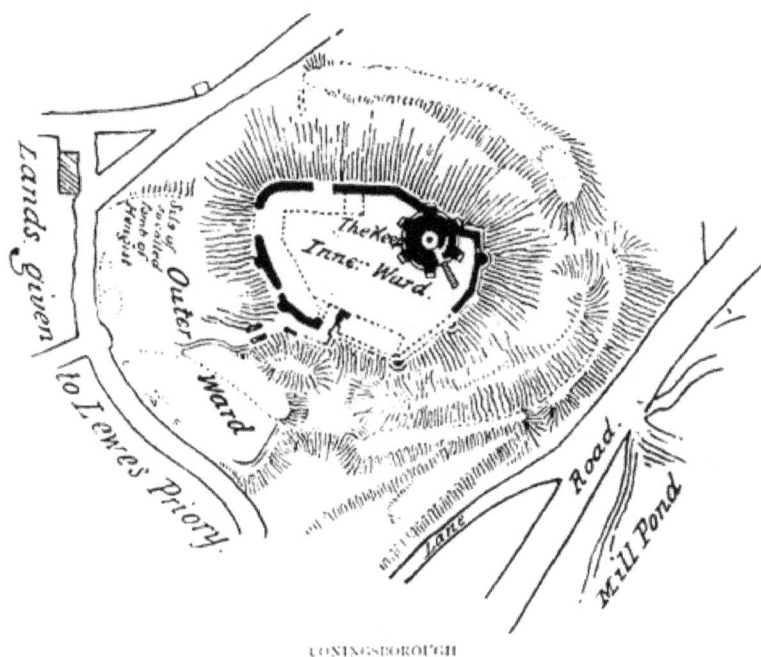

CONINGSBOROUGH

keep is certainly fifty years later, and may be the building of Hameline Plantagenet, who held the place from 1163 to 1201. The keep of Orford, Suffolk, somewhat resembles this one (*Clark*).

COTHERSTONE (*non-existent*)

THIS was another manor of the Fitzhughs, in which they occasionally resided from very early times. The date of the castle is uncertain, but in a charter given between the years 1182 and 1201 mention is made of the Porta de Cutherston, then the residence of the lord. The tradition runs that it was burnt and destroyed in one of the Scottish raids, the plunderers having been irritated at some expressions used by the lady of the castle. But the marauding

hordes who came for booty would not want a reason for their acts. At all
events, fragments of charred wood have been dug up on the site. Cotherstone
stands in a highly picturesque position near the confluence of the Balder Beck
with the Tees, on an eminence between the streams, but only some fragments of
the tower survive. In the chapel garth have been dug up some stones of pointed
windows, and an ancient font, proving that a domestic chapel must have existed.

The Fitzhughs, deriving from one Boden, lord of Ravenswath before the
Conquest, continued in Richmondshire until the fourth year of Henry VIII.,
when their ancient line ended in George, lord of Ravenswath, who died *s.p.*
One of them, Henry Fitz Henry, was summoned to Parliament as a baron in
15 Edward II.; his grandson adopted the name of Fitzhugh, and this man's
son attended Henry V. in France. They are described as a noble and chivalrous
race (see *Kirkby Ravenswath, Yorks*).

COTTINGHAM, or BAYNARD'S CASTLE (*non-existent*)

ABOUT three miles from Beverley stood this old twelfth-century fortress
of the Stutevilles and Wakes. Leland says: "Entering into the South
part of the great Uplandish Town of Cotingham, I saw wher Stutevilles Castelle,
dobill dikid and motid, stoode, of the which nothing now remaynith."

Robert de Stuteville was Sheriff of Yorkshire in 21 Henry II., and is said
to have built the castle. His descendant William, who was here in John's
reign, quarrelled with the churchmen at York, and was excommunicated by
the archbishop; and the king, with a fellow-feeling, paid him a visit to inquire
into the matter, which ended in a victory for the layman, and permission
granted to fortify his house. William's great-granddaughter Joan brought
the manor and castle of Cottingham to her husband, of the De Wake family,
and her son Baldwin de Wake inherited these, with many other lands.

In 1319 Thomas de Wake obtained a charter of confirmation, and a further
licence to convert his manor-house into a castle of defence, under the name
of Baynard's Castle, with authority to keep it armed and garrisoned, which
patent was renewed by Edward III. on his accession.

The vast property of the Wakes then came to royal hands, by the marriage of
Edmund of Woodstock, youngest son of Edward I., to Margaret, the sister of
Thomas de Wake; she bore him a daughter, Joan, the Fair Maid of Kent, who
had as her first husband the warrior Thomas, Earl of Holland, and after his early
death held the manor of Cottingham and its dependencies; afterwards, becoming
the wife of the Black Prince, she was the mother of King Richard II.

Nothing is known as to the description of the buildings which composed
this castle. It was burnt to the ground in the reign of Henry VIII., and
was never rebuilt. There is a story given by Allen, but scarcely worthy

of belief, that the Lord Wake during that period himself caused his house to be destroyed by fire, to prevent the coming thither of the king, whose power and fascinations he dreaded on behalf of his beautiful wife.

The last Wake dying *s.p.*, the manor was divided into three parts, in favour of his three daughters, who were married respectively to the Duke of Richmond, the Earl of Westmorland, and Lord Powis, and the names of these nobles are still attached to the properties.

The area covered by the castle was about two acres, but nothing now remains to mark its site except the traces of the outer and inner moats and some banks.

CRAYKE (minor)

THREE miles from Easingwold, on the summit of a hill, stand the remains of this old castle of the Bishops of Durham, the lands of it having been made Church property as far back as A.D. 685. There was an early castle here, built by one of the bishops in Norman days, but the existing later structures were added by Bishop Nevill (1438-1457).

Leland described the castle thus: "There remaineth at this tyme small shew of any Castel that hath beene there. There is a Haul, with other offices, and a great stable voltid with stone, of a meatly auncyent building. The great squar towre, that is thereby, as in the toppe of the hille, and supplement of loggings, is very fair, and was erected *wholly* by Nevill, bishop of Duresme." And there is a survey extant, made a hundred years after Bishop Nevill, in Elizabeth's time, from which it appears that the bishop only added to an earlier castle. It appears that the base of the "New Tower" belongs to a work built between 1280 and 1320, and that at the beginning of the fifteenth century the Great Chamber, *i.e.* the present castle, was built, after which the New Tower, containing a hall and solar, was erected on the N.E. Then were appended by Bishop Nevill the kitchen and larder to the Great Chamber. The parlour of the tower has a garderobe attached, with a sunk pond below for drainage. There are some traces of the gatehouse near the present entrance to the grounds, but the barn and the chapel have disappeared, together with the surrounding wall. The whole stood once in a large and well-wooded park, which was provided with a sunk fence called a saltery (*saltatorium*), or trap for deer, which leaping into, they could not leave again (Canon Raine in *Architectural Societies' Report*, 1869).

The committee that sat in London on the castles, doomed this one to destruction, and it was accordingly slighted, and remained in this ruined state until restored by Mr. Waite, who made the place into a modern residence.

As we see it, it is a square building of Tudor style, four storeys in height, with a battlemented parapet, from which a lovely view of the Vale of Mowbray is obtained, and away to the hills of Craven and Westmorland.

DANBY (minor)

AT Danby and in the neighbouring ancient fortress of CASTLETON, the
Norman follower of Duke William, Robert de Brus, obtained his first
shelter in this part of Cleveland. He held ninety-three manors in all in
Yorkshire, and dying cir. 1094, was followed by his direct descendants, lords
of Skelton, who continued here till 55 Henry III., when, by the marriage of
Lucia de Brus, a coheiress, Danby went to Marmaduke Thweng. There had
been a break, however, and a difficulty with the Crown, for Adam de Brus
took part with King Stephen, and when Henry II. ascended the throne, it
was natural that he should, in his raid against the Stephanic strongholds,
remember his grudge against De Brus. Accordingly, he seized Danby Castle
which proves that some edifice existed here at that time—and it was not
recovered until 2 John, when Peter de Brus had to yield lands and a large
sum of money to the king for its restoration.

From the Thwengs the manor and lordship passed, temp. Edward I., with
Lucia, heiress of Robert de Thweng, to the powerful Latimers, and from them
through their heiress Elizabeth, cir. 1374, to the Nevills of Raby (q.v.). John Nevill,
4th Lord Latimer (temp. Elizabeth), left four daughters, the youngest of whom,
Elizabeth, brought Danby in marriage to Sir John Danvers, whose grandson, Sir
Henry, sold the property to five freeholders; and from them, in 1656, Danby
was acquired by John Dawney, an ancestor of the present owner, Lord Downe.

The castle is a picturesque ruin, commanding from its elevated site, about two
miles from Castleton, a very fine prospect over the Esk valley. The present building is not earlier than the reign of Edward I., and was probably built by William
Latimer on acquiring the manor from the Thwengs (Ora). The Latimer arms,
with those of Bruce and Thweng, appear on the walls, as if anterior to the
Nevill marriage. The buildings covered a space about 120 feet square, with a
court in the centre, and corner turrets projecting diagonally at each exterior
angle, which latter seem to have been additions. A farm-house occupies part of
the later buildings. The kitchens, a room in the W. tower, and other parts are
tolerably perfect, and the S. wall exhibits the magnificence of the ancient fabric.

A tradition exists that the bridge near the castle was built by three sisters, that
is, by Lucy, Margaret, and Catherine de Thweng, daughters of Marmaduke de
Thweng. And it is asserted that a Queen of England once lived here,—a tradition which refers to Queen Catherine Parr, the sixth wife of Henry VIII., and
daughter of Sir Thomas Parr of Kendal Castle (q.v.). She married John Nevill,
3rd Lord Latimer, as her second husband, and subsequently the king, and immediately after his death—as her fourth husband—Admiral Seymour, the luckless
brother of the Protector Somerset. They were both beheaded (see Sudeley,
Gloucestershire). As Lady Latimer she must have resided at Danby.

GILLING (minor)

THIS castle of the Fairfaxes is near Byland Abbey, and the name must not be confounded with the parish in Richmondshire, the patrimony of Earl Edwin. It stands on an eminence on the W. side of the village of that name, and was originally a fee of the Mowbray family, lords of Thirsk and the Vale of Mowbray.

One of the most notable warriors who came over to the Conquest of England was Roger de Mowbray (spelt variously), whose name is in the roll of Battle Abbey, and his son Robert succeeded to the large tract of country with which his father had been endowed by William I. He took part with Duke Robert against the Red King, with whom he was afterwards reconciled, and was by him created Earl of Northumberland. He did good service in 1093 in repelling the invasion of Malcolm, King of Scotland, but soon after he again broke into rebellion. Rufus came against him at Bamburgh (q.v.), and in the end Mowbray was captured, and died a prisoner at Windsor after thirty years of confinement. All the Mowbray estates were confiscated, and were held by the Crown until granted by Henry I. to Nigel de Albini, brother to the Earl of Arundel, who assumed the name of Mowbray. His son Roger succeeded him, and was one of the leaders at the Battle of the Standard (1138). Besides Gilling, he owned in Yorkshire the castles of Thirsk, Slingsby, and Kirkby Malzeard, and he it was who founded the abbey at Byland, whither he retired to die in peace at the close of his long and troublous life (see *Bamburgh*).

This great house of Mowbray, and their successors, are intimately woven into the history of the country, but there is little regarding them connected with Gilling Castle, which in after-times became the property and the seat of the Etton family.

In the seventh year of Henry VII. Thomas Fairfax of Walton married the heiress, Elizabeth Etton, and Gilling has been in the possession of his descendants or representatives ever since, though on some occasions it has passed by marriage. Francis Cholmeley received it through his wife, Harriet Fairfax, and the present owner is Mr. Hugh C. Fairfax-Cholmeley.

The keep is a square one of Edwardian architecture, built temp. Edward II., and the basement of the eastern portion contains much Decorated work. The buildings on the other side are of Tudor date, the rooms being ornamented with fine sixteenth-century carvings and painted glass. The castle is well situated and surrounded by timber, and the views eastward are very fine.

GUISBOROUGH (*non-existent*)

GUISBOROUGH Priory, in Cleveland, where was buried Robert Bruce, who contested the crown of Scotland with Baliol, was built in 1120, and it is likely that a castle of some sort existed here even earlier than this date. The manor was among the many given to Robert le Brus by the Conqueror, and here, as at Castleton (*q.v.*), was an ancient stronghold, probably a British earthwork, but no appearance of masonry remains.

It stood in a field near the lane leading from Church Street to Redcar, called War's Field, and can still be traced by the moat in this and in the adjoining field, having well elevated ridges and uneven surfaces, the whole occupying several acres of ground (*Ord*).

HAREWOOD (*minor*)

CAMDEN, who passed here about the year 1582, says: "Afterwards the river [Wharfe] runs between the banks of limestone, by Harewood, where I saw a handsome and well-fortified castle, which has often changed its lords by the vicissitudes of time. It formerly belonged to the Curceys; but came by their heiress, Alice, to Warin Fitz-Gerald, who married her; whose daughter and coheiress, Margery, was given in marriage, with the fine estate belonging to her, to Baldwin Rivers, Earl of Devon, who died before his father; afterwards to Falcasius de Brent, by favour of King John, for his good services in pillaging. But upon the death of Isabella de Rivers, Countess of Devon, *s.p.*, this castle fell to Robert de Lisle, son of Warin, as kinsman and coheir. Lastly, by the family of Aldburgh, it came to Rithers."

The original ancient date of the castle is shown in the drawing given by King in *Archæologia*, where two windows of late Norman type appear—now not in existence; but the present remains belong to a much later date. The castle is supposed to have been built in the reign of Edward I. or Edward II., and to have been finished temp. Edward III. Over the entrance are the arms of Sir William de Aldburgh, who married Elizabeth, only daughter of Robert, Lord de Lisle, about 1327, and obtained this castle with her; he repaired and added to it, and made it his chief residence. He was called (Harleian MSS. vol. lxxxv. f. 5) "the messenger of Edward Baliol, King of Scotland," a post of high rank; and the Baliol arms appear with his above the doorway. After Baliol's deposition he lived at Wheatley, near Doncaster, where Sir William was his close and faithful attendant. Sir William died without male issue, leaving two daughters who divided his estates: Elizabeth, married to Sir Richard Redmayne or Rednam, and Sybil, the wife of Sir William Ryther of Ryther Castle, Yorks. But the two families continued to live together, alternately, at

Harewood, where the last inhabitant was James Ryther, an esquire of Queen Elizabeth, and his only son Robert, who left Harewood in 1620. The castle was dismantled during the Civil Wars, and was thus purchased in 1657 by Sir John Cutler, a London merchant, cruelly and unfairly satirised by Pope.

In 1582 the manor had come into the possession of Thomas Wentworth, married to Margaret, the heiress of Sir William Gascoigne, who inherited the Redmayne moiety, and had bought the Ryther half. The grandson of this Thomas Wentworth was the unfortunate Lord Strafford, whose son subsequently recovered the confiscated estates, but was forced to sell them, when the manor was bought by Cutler.

The castle is in the form of a rectangular parallelogram, with two lofty towers at the S.E. and N.E. angles, four storeys in height; there were also towers on the N. and S. sides. The main entrance is on the N., and was defended by a portcullis. The great hall is 55 feet long by 29 feet, and in it are still the stone seats used at times of courts; at one end is a curious arched recess in the wall which appears to have covered a buffet or sideboard. The portcullis room over the entrance communicates by stairs with the hall, and with the rooms over it, and the chapel, wherein are many shields bearing the arms of the different allied families. A dungeon exists under the entrance tower, and beneath the hall is a cellar or store. Access to all parts of the castle was gained by mural passages.

Sir William Aldburgh obtained in 40 Edward III. (1367) a license to crenellate his *mansum manerii*, and the building seems to have been embattled throughout.

Harewood Church contains the tombs of many of the above-named persons, including that of the celebrated Chief Justice, Sir William Gascoigne, who was born, lived, and died almost beneath the shadow of these walls, and whose daughter was the wife of Sir Richard Redman, before mentioned. Shakespeare in the play of *Henry IV.*, part ii., makes the young king, Henry V., to reappoint Gascoigne as Chief Justice in return for his committal, but this does not appear to have been done.

HARLSEY (non-existent)

THIS castle was in the neighbourhood of Sigston or Beresend Castle, and was held by the family of Strangewaies, who twice intermarried with the Pygot family, the owners of the Sigston and Winton estates. It was probably a building of similar form and date to the latter stronghold. Some portions still remain incorporated with the farm buildings belonging to a modern farm-house.

Leland mentions the place as "where Strangwaise the Judge builded a pretty Castle." His family had succeeded that of Hotham, who long held possession of Harlsey (see *Sigston, Yorks*).

HELMSLEY, near Rievaulx Abbey (chief)

THE lordship of Helmsley was granted by the Conqueror to the Earl of Moreton, but passed, temp. Henry I., to Walter d'Espec, or Spec, the great leader at the Battle of the Standard. He, losing his only son in 1122, devised Helmsley to his youngest sister Adelina, wife of Peter de Ros or Roos, after whom it went to her son Robert, called "Fursan," who was one of the twenty-five barons chosen to carry out the provisions of Magna Charta. He built here a castle about 1200, called "Castle Fursan," of which we see some remains in the lower part of the keep with its circular - headed apertures. He married Isabel, daughter of William the Lion, King of Scotland, and at her death joined the Templars, his effigy being still at the Temple Church, London. Robert de Ros died seised of the manor and castle, 13 Edward I., and left them to his son and heir, William, who for eminent services performed temp. Edward II. received from King Edward III. a tower in London to hold as an appurtenant to Helmsley. In 1339 this king, apprehending an invasion by the Scots, placed this William de Ros in command of the northern district, acting from his castle of Helmsley. He died in 1343, and his descendants continued to possess the property, till it was temporarily confiscated by Edward IV. It was afterwards restored to Edmund, the last De Ros, whose

HELMSLEY

sisters became his heirs, and one of them, Eleanor, marrying Sir Robert Manners of Etall, Northumberland, brought him Helmsley, and also BELVOIR (*q.v.*), which had previously been brought into the De Ros family by marriage. One of this family was created Earl of Rutland by Henry VIII. in 1525, and the sixth earl of this name, temp. James I., had an only daughter, Catherine, married to George Villiers, 1st Duke of Buckingham, who was stabbed by Felton, and thus Helmsley became a part of his large possessions. In the Civil War, in 1644, the castle was granted by the Parliament to Sir Thomas Fairfax, the general, but being held for the king by Colonel Jordan Crossland, an able and determined cavalier, it was besieged after Marston Moor, by Fairfax himself, who was shot in the shoulder by a musket-ball during the siege; he was removed to York in a dangerous condition, and it was feared that the wound would prove fatal. The castle being forced to surrender was dismantled by order of the House, and partly blown up.

The trustees of the last duke, who recovered Helmsley at the Restoration, sold the property in 1695 to Sir Charles Duncombe, a Secretary to the Treasury, for £95,000, when

> "Helmsley, once proud Buckingham's delight,
> Slid to a scrivener, and a City knight."

He left it to a nephew, one Thomas Brown, who took the name of Duncombe, and in 1718 built the house and formed the place called Duncombe Park, at the gates of which the castle stands. His great-grandson was made Lord Faversham in 1826.

The ruins, standing on a gentle eminence on the W. of the town, with the keep rising above the grove of trees which surrounds it, form a picturesque object. The whole is encircled by a double moat—the outer one—wide and deep, filled from the river Rye, and at the distance of 27 feet is the inner moat, 50 feet wide, and 20 feet deep; the extent of the area contained is about 10 acres.

The main entrance is on the S., through a square tower with a portcullis, embattled and machicolated above, and strengthened by two circular flanking towers. There is a gateway into the river court or bailey, of which not much remains; the portcullis groove of it can be seen. The great keep occupies the N.E. corner of the inner bailey, its E. side being quite destroyed, the fragments of it lying in the moat; injured as it is, the structure rises to a height of nearly 100 feet above the dungeons below it. The lower part dates from the reign of John, and the turrets and battlements were added in the reign of Edward II. The fine barbican between the moats and the gatehouse was perhaps of the time of John. The outer walls of the enceinte on the E. and N. sides have been destroyed, and the moat filled up. There was an entrance to the castle also on the N. side, and part of a bridge across the moat remains. On the W., against the moat, is the later mansion, added in Elizabeth's reign, with square-headed, heavy mullioned windows, this range being in good preservation, with many windows still

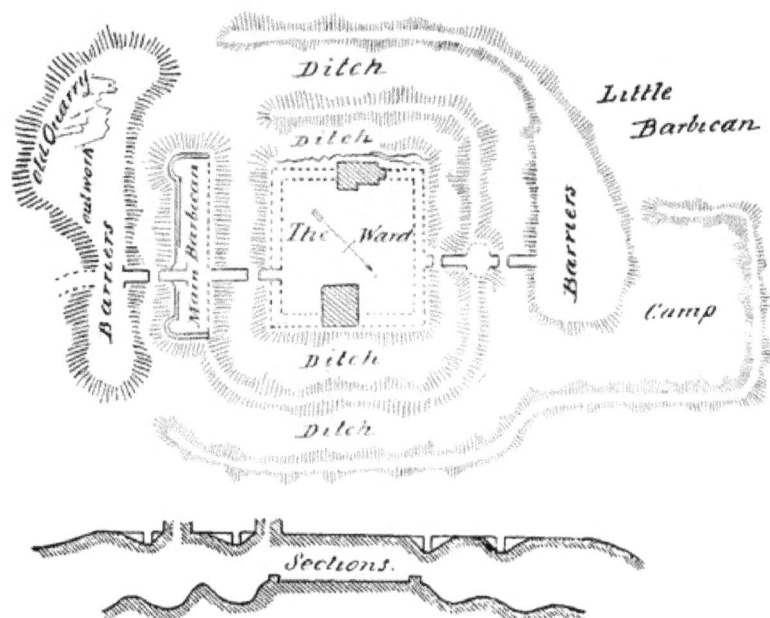

HELMSLEY

glazed, and a part remaining roofed. A large upper room, indeed, is still used for the rent audit of Lord Faversham; and here doubtless the last duke carried on his gay life. Beneath the high building, in the corner, is a sub-terranean passage said to extend to the neighbouring abbey, for not far off, in the sweet valley of the Rye, is old Walter d'Espec's own abbey of Rievaulx, certainly one of the most beautiful monastic ruins in the country.

HORNBY (chief)

THIS stately structure, like Belvoir, has little to show of antiquity in its walls, though replacing or overlaying a more ancient abode, as it is thought to do, of the St. Quintins, and having been built by the first Lord Conyers early in the sixteenth century. All the knowledge we have of its origin is from the Itinerary of Leland, who says that the Conyers rose to importance through the patronage of Richard, Lord Scrope of Bolton, temp. Richard II. "Richard, Lord Scrope that buildid Bolton Castle boute the heire generall of St. Quintine, that was owner of Hornby Castle in Richemount-shire. This Richard was content that one Coniers, a servant [vassal] of his, should have the preferment of this warde, and so he had Hornby Castle. Gul. Coniers, the first lord of that name, grandfather to him that is now (1540), dyd great coste on Hornaby Castle. It was before but a meane thing." Perhaps a border tower only.

John Conyers was a Chief Justice, and married Margaret, daughter and heir to Anthony St. Quintin. Their son Christopher is described as of Hornby, and his son, again, Sir John Conyers "of Hornby Castle," was grandfather to William, first Lord Conyers, the holder of the existing castle. His family ended in his grandson's children, the two sons dying s.p., and the property going to the eldest daughter, Elizabeth, married to Thomas Darcy (died 1605), whose grandson, Conyers Darcy, was summoned to Parliament in 1661 as Baron D'Arcy and Conyers, and was in 1689 created Earl of Holderness.

The fourth earl left an only daughter to inherit his lands, Amelia Darcy, and she, by her marriage in 1773 with Francis Osborne, afterwards fifth duke of Leeds, brought Hornby to that family, whose residence it is.

The castle, which is not very extensive, is built in the form of a quadrangle, and has been modernised to accord with the requirements of the day. One ivy-clad tower remains, to which is attached the name of St. Quintin, in memory of the early possessors.

HULL (non-existent)

IN 1541 King Henry VIII., accompanied by his queen, Katherine Howard, made a progress to the North, and came to Kingston-upon-Hull. He surveyed the town with a view to its security, and ordered that a castle and two blockhouses should be erected, with other fortifications for the defence of the town. The works were carried out at a cost of £23,755, which was found by the king. Hollar's plan of Hull shows a strong fortification on the left bank of the river Hull, extending from the North Bridge over that river to its mouth in the Humber. This fort consisted of two strong circular block-houses, one beside the bridge, and another at the junction of the two rivers, the centre of the line being occupied by a larger fortress, called the castle, a rec-tangular structure with semicircular bastions ; these three works are connected by a strong curtain wall about three-quarters of a mile in length. A citadel was erected here in the reign of Charles II. The blockhouses were of brick.

In the commencement of the Parliamentary War, King Charles attempted to make himself master of the important position of Hull, but the gates of the town were closed against him by the governor, Sir John Hotham, and a more serious attempt in the same year (1643) made by a strong force under the Marquess of Newcastle, failed after a six weeks' siege,—the new governor, Fairfax, placing the country all round under water by means of the sluices. We know not what part in the warfare was taken by Henry VIII.'s forts.

KILTON (minor)

LIES near the coast, on the way from Whitby to Saltburn. Here are the remains of an immensely strong fortress, built in Norman times, on the summit of a bold promontory, 300 feet long and 60 feet wide, with precipitous sides, and ending in a narrow ridge on the W. side, which was defended by strong walls still standing : an ancient road led up to this point. The outer earthworks have vanished, with the barbican and other defences, but the position of the gatehouse and main entrance can be traced, with its protecting ditches, one of which measures 26 feet across. Ord laments the destruction which has been permitted, the masonry having been used as a quarry for the neighbourhood. Still the buildings can be made out,—the hall with its two huge fireplaces, and the great tower on the E., which con-stitute the most interesting part of the ruins. The castle was semicircular in plan, of Early English style, built perhaps at the end of the twelfth century ; there are good loops and two lancet windows in it.

Kilton Manor, like Danby, came to the Thwengs by Lucia, the daughter of Peter de Brus, lord of Skelton, and her granddaughter, also Lucia, being a coheiress, brought Kilton to her husband, Sir Robert Lumley, temp. Edward III. With this family it remained till 29 Henry VIII., when George Lumley, the owner, was tried for his share in the insurrection called the "Pilgrimage of Grace," and was beheaded ; then Kilton Castle passed by attainder to the Crown.

Afterwards the place became the property of a family called Tullie, and from them came to the Rev. Dr. Waugh, Chancellor of Carlisle, whose daughters sold it to Mr. John Wharton, the predecessor of the present proprietor. There are some remains of the old manor-house.

KIRKBY-MALZEARD (*non-existent*)

THIS stronghold of the Percy family was situated a few miles to the E. of Ripon, upon an eminence commanding an extensive range of country to the N.E. and E., in the district once called Mashamshire. It was one of the many belonging to Roger de Mowbray (see *Thirsk* and *Gilling*), a great warrior who fought at the Battle of the Standard (1138), and who, on his return from the Crusade in 1173, took part with Prince Henry against his father; but after losing his castle of Epworth in the Isle of Axeholme (Lincoln), and being taken prisoner by Geoffrey, the Bishop Elect of Lincoln, a natural son of the king, he was made to surrender his castles of Malzeard and Thirsk to Henry II., who at once caused them to be demolished. The work was oval in shape, covering about half an acre. Not a stone, however, remains above ground to show what this building was, but much carved stone of Norman workmanship has been dug up on its site. It was probably within sight and signal of Thirsk Castle, and its traces are still apparent in the huge earthworks seen at the E. of the church-yard. The foundations can be traced of the hall, kitchen, and chapel, and some other buildings in the inner bailey. The position was a strong one sloping in front to the Kesbeck stream, and with a pool on the north side.

KIRKBY-RAVENSWATH (*minor*)

ABOUT five miles N.W. from Richmond, was the seat of the historic family of Fitzhugh. At the time of the Domesday Survey, Bodin, the progenitor of that line, obtained the manor here, and as the high ground was already occupied by the church, either he or his successor was forced to make their dwelling and fortress in the swampy ground below. Leland says (cir. 1538): " Ravenswarthe Castel, in a mares [marish] grownde, and a parke on a litle hangginge grownde by it. . . . Lord Parr is owner thereof. The castle, excepting 2 or 3 square towers, and a faire stable ,with a conduct [conduit] cumming to the haull-side, hath nothing memorable."

And Camden, sixty years later, wrote: " Ravensworth Castle rears its head with a large extent of ruinous walls, which had barons of its own, named Fitz Hugh, of old Saxon descent, . . . and famous to the time of Henry VII., for their great estates acquired by marriage with the heiresses of the illustrious families of Furneaux and Marmion, which at the last came by females to the Fienes, Lords Dacre of the South, and to the Parrs." The Fitzhughs were a notable family, many of them being renowned in the history of the country, and some being crusaders. They were usually buried at Jervaux Abbey, where, among others, is the tomb of Henry, Lord Fitzhugh, who attended Henry V. at Agincourt with 66 men-at-arms and 209 archers ; he fought also in the Holy Land, and died at Ravensworth.

The remains of this castle, which, like Richmond, covers a much larger space of ground than any other in this part of the country, consisted of three quadrangles formed by the buildings around them, and of eight chief towers, all of them square ; but their remains are so broken up and so little distinguished architecturally, that it is impossible to determine their antiquity, though there are certain Norman forms (*Whitaker*). The S. front seems to have been semi-circular. The whole area is covered with hillocks and low banks indicating the remains of masonry. In a turret, near the middle and between two of the courts, is the following inscription in the black-letter of Henry VIII.'s time :—

(*The Labarum.*) rp'c . dus . ih'c . bia . fons . & origo . alpha . & oo .
Christus dominus Jesus via fons et origo alpha et omega.

This seems to be the work of some disciple of the Reformation, and surrounds a small oratory of the castle. Ravenswath was transferred, at the death of Lord Fitzhugh (10 Henry VIII.), to the Parrs, one of whom, being a Protestant, may have caused the inscription to be set up.

KNARESBOROUGH (*minor*)

IN the beautiful valley of the Nidd, where a lofty cliff projects into the stream ; on the summit of this, some 250 feet above the river, was built this old fortress. Knaresburg was in Saxon times the head of an extensive lordship, including the large tract of the forest of the same name, and was royal property. William I. granted the lands to one of his followers, Serlo de Burg, who probably began the buildings which his grandson Eustace Fitz John, a Justiciary in the North with Walter Lespee of "the Standard," completed. Eustace was the lord of Alnwick Castle also by his marriage with Beatrice de Vesey, and their eldest son took his mother's name and continued at Alnwick. His other son Richard married Albreda de Lacy, heiress of Pontefract Castle and honour, to which her son John succeeded in 1193, together with Knaresborough, and then took his mother's name of De Lacy, for hitherto the family seem to have had no name. Eustace FitzJohn built Alnwick Castle, and added to Knaresborough, dying in 1157, when the Crown granted it to various castellans.

One of the first of these was Hugh de Morville, one of the murderers of Thomas à Becket in 1170, and one of the memories of this castle is that it afforded a refuge to the four assassins during a whole year. The Estotevilles or Stutevilles were governors there, and temp. King John it was held by Brian de Lisle, who added the ditch and some buildings to the castle. Henry III.

KNARESBOROUGH CASTLE.

granted Knaresborough to Hubert de Burgh, and afterwards conferred the manor and honour on his brother Richard, King of the Romans, who founded a priory on the river bank below the castle. Edward II. gave the place to Piers Gaveston, and in 1371 Edward III. granted all to his son John of Gaunt, since when it has ever remained in the Duchy of Lancaster. They shut up the captive King Richard II. here before taking him to Pontefract, and from this the keep has ever since been called the King's Tower.

The area enclosed, which was oval in shape, is 2½ acres; the lines of the external walls being discernible, with six circular mural towers. Besides the gorge of the Nidd there are two ravines which protected the castle on other sides, while there is a broad ditch on the land front. The outer wall was 7 to 8 feet thick, and from 30 to 40 feet high, but it has been quite destroyed and removed, except close to the keep; it edges the cliff and the ravines and ditch, outside which latter is the town, built under the castle's shelter, the entrance gateway being in front of the town between two flanking mural towers;

KNARESBOROUGH

the arch of the gateway is gone, but the portcullis and gate grooves remain, and the place of the drawbridge over the ditch. A cross wall divided the area into an E. and a W. or inner ward, the keep being placed on the line of this wall, whereby it was made to form the passage, or gatehouse in fact, from one ward to the other, and was provided with drawbridges.

There are considerable remains of the keep, which must have been of grand design and finish; it was rectangular, 64 feet long by 52 feet broad, but the N. angle is lost. The W. angle has a turret, some 60 feet above the court. The S.W. front, looking into the inner court, is the most perfect; it consists of a large apartment on the first floor with Decorated windows and a fireplace;

below in the basement is a large kitchen having a beautifully vaulted roof, and supported by two pillars, with three or four other rooms, underneath being a small dungeon with a staircase.   On the first floor are two fine pointed doorways, one with a portcullis groove, and with arrangements in the masonry for raising and lowering a bridge which gave access from the roadway on arches in the outer court, a part of which roadway remains.   There is nothing left of the upper room in the keep, which had a wooden floor.   The ornaments and details are late Decorated of Edward II. (*Clark*).

We owe the destruction of this fine castle and its beautiful details chiefly to the fire of Parliamentary guns in the Civil War, at which time, in 1644, it was besieged for about a month by Colonel Lilburn, who was sent, after the easy capture of Tickhill, to demand the surrender of Knaresborough, then held for the king by the townsmen, who determined to hold out, relying on a promise of assistance from the North.   Unprepared for such resistance, Lilburn sent to York for two guns with which he battered the walls from Gallow Hill, but to little effect, until he was traitorously informed of a weak point in the defences, and opened fire upon this from a new battery near Briggate, then a garden.   The garrison, who were meanwhile reduced to a state of famine, maintained an heroic defence, and made serious sallies on the besiegers' lines, but a breach being effected and the storming imminent, they offered a parley, and surrendered on honourable terms.   In the castle were found four pieces of fine ordnance, a large store of arms and powder, and silver plate and valuables worth £1500, with other booty.   In 1648, the castle was dismantled and made into the ruin we see.

LECONFIELD (*non-existent*)

AN old castle of the Percys, 2½ miles N. from Beverley.   Leland wrote : "Lekingfeld is a large House & stondith withyn a greate mote yn one very spatius Courte.   3 partes of the House, saving the meane gate that is made of Brike, is al of tymbre.   The 4 Parte is made of Stone & sum Brike."   The lands were given to the De Brus family, and in the reign of King John Henry Percy married Isabel de Brus, and received from her brother Peter de Brus certain lands in Leconfield, on the curious tenure that every Christmas day he should call upon the lady of Skelton Castle (*q.v.*), and should lead her to mass.   In 1308 Henry Percy obtained a licence to crenellate and fortify his house of Leconfield, and his successor Henry, 2nd Earl of Northumberland, made this castle his chief residence, some of his children being born in it.

After Towton Field the manor was granted to George, Duke of Clarence, but in 1469 the Northumberland estates were restored to the new earl, who lived here till he was slain by the mob at Cockledge. The fifth earl, Henry Algernon, lived in great state here and at Wressel, as is shown by the regulations for his household, drawn up in 1512 ; and in 1541 he entertained at this castle and at Wressel King Henry VIII., when on his northern journey, but was himself absent.

After the attainder of the Percys, John Dudley, the new Duke of Northumberland, obtained Leconfield and its castle, but when Queen Mary deprived him of his head (1553), the place was restored to Thomas Percy, seventh earl.

But further affliction befell the Percys. The ninth earl was fined £30,000 by the Star Chamber, and was imprisoned during fifteen years for neglecting to administer the oath of supremacy to a Percy relative, who had been concerned in the Gunpowder Plot. This fine so greatly impoverished him that he could no longer find money to keep up his castles, and so they fell to decay. The site of Leconfield is a little S.W. of the village, and it must have been a very large and strong place ; the moat spoken of by Leland is about half a mile in circumference, enclosing nearly 4 acres. In 1574 it was reported that the decay of this castle was much more serious than that of Wressel ; that new roofs were required and new timbers ; that the surveyors "cannot speke of the particular harmes of the said howse, the waste is so universal." And in all probability it never was repaired, but was afterwards demolished, and the materials used for the mending of Wressel ; a return of these is extant, showing what wood, glass, and carved or painted work was thus removed in the reign of James I. This seems an authentic instance of the causes which have effected the disappearance of so many of our mediaeval fortresses.

LEEDS (*non-existent*)

IT seems likely that the castle of Leeds was built shortly after the accession of William I., by one of the Paganel family, who were feudatories of the great Anglo-Norman house of De Lacy of Pontefract (*Wardell*). The site of it is the ground now surrounded by the streets called Millhill, Bishopsgate, and the W. part of Boar Lane. It is said to have been besieged and taken by Stephen on his march into Scotland in 1139, and the only other historical interest attached to it is that it was the scene of the imprisonment of King Richard II. after his deposition. Hardyng's Chronicle says :

> "The King then sent Kyng Richard to Ledis,
> There to be kepte surely ;
> Fro thens after to Pykeryng went he nedes,
> And to Knaresburgh after led was he,
> But to Pountfrete last where he did die."

After this the castle is not noticed, nor is anything known of its destruction; nothing whatever remains of it. There was an outpost work on the N. belonging to it, a tower near Lydgate, the foundation stones of which were chanced on many years ago, deep in the ground.

MALTON (*non-existent*)

THE lordship of Malton was given by the Conqueror to one Gilbert Tyson, who left it with other lands to his son William, whose daughter possessed it at her death. Her son Eustace Fitzjohn held the lordship and castle of Malton temp. Henry I., with whom he was in great favour, and who gave him the towns of Malton, and of Alnwick in Northumberland. He took the side of the Empress Maud, and opposed Stephen to the length of giving over Alnwick and Malton Castle to David, King of Scotland, who, occupying the latter, did much injury to the neighbourhood, till Thurstan, Archbishop of York, defeated and drove out the Scottish garrison. Then Eustace shelved his patriotism so far as to fight in the ranks of the Scots army at the Battle of the Standard; but making peace afterwards with Stephen, he rebuilt the burnt town of Malton, which was thereafter called "New Malton," and died fighting in Wales for Henry II. in 1156. His son William assumed the name of Vesey, and in the family under that name Malton continued till temp. Edward II., when, the owner being killed at Bannockburn without heirs, the estates fell to the Crown. The manor remained in the possession of a family who took the name of Vesey until the reign of Henry VIII., when it was broken up by marriages among the families of Clifford, Conyers, and Eure, which last obtained Old Malton. Ralph, Lord Eure, temp. James I., built a fine mansion on the site of the Norman castle; but in 1674 his two granddaughters, being heiresses of the estate, quarrelled over its division, and the whole edifice, with the exception of the lodge, was pulled down to satisfy their claims. Then this lodge and the manor were acquired by Sir Thomas Wentworth, who in 1728 was made Lord Malton, and afterwards Marquis of Rockingham, and his son's nephew, Earl Fitzwilliam, succeeded in 1782 to the manor of Malton.

In Leland's Itinerary, he says: "The Castel of Malton hath been larg, as it apperith from the ruine. There is at this time no habitation in it, but a mene house for a farmer." Of course nothing now exists.

MARKENFIELD (minor)

A GRAND castellated and moated house of defence, situated three miles S.W. from Ripon. It was the home of a family of that name of long standing in the county and of importance, one of whom, John de Merkyngfeld, in the reign of Edward II., obtained a licence to crenellate his house in 1311, and erected this castle. One of the family, Sir Thomas, with his wife Dionisia, is buried in a fine tomb in Ripon Minster. They died at the end of the fifteenth century.

In 1513, among the gentry who went with Lords Lumley and Latimer and Conyers to Flodden Field, with their tenants and servants, rode

> "Sir Ninian Markenville
> In armour coat of cunning work,"

having succeeded his father Sir Thomas (as above) in his honours and estates. He died 20 Henry VIII., and was followed by his son Sir Thomas, knight, who died 1550, and was succeeded by his son Thomas, aged seventeen, who had livery of his father's inheritance in the second of Elizabeth. But he had little good from it, for in 1569 he took an active part in the insurrection called "The Rising of the North," being prompted thereto by his uncle, Richard Norton, who was one of the more prominent leaders, and who was the bearer of the famous banner:

> "The Norton's ancyent had the crosse,
> And the five wounds our Lord did beare."

This rebellion is written of in the accounts of the castles of Barnard and Brancepeth, Durham, and was of terrible consequences to those who took part in it. Young Markenfield, after being hidden, like the Earl of Westmorland, in Scotland by Lord Hume, escaped to the Low Countries, and like the earl also dragged out a weary existence in exile, a pensioner on the pittances doled out by the King of Spain. His estates were forfeited to the Crown, and Markenfield became the property of the Egertons, Earls of Bridgwater, and was so held until its purchase by Sir Fletcher Norton, the first Lord Grantley, and Baron Markenfield—being now held by his descendants. The house is still inhabited, being built on the plan of a large courtyard made up of the main building, which is in the form of the letter L, in the N.E. angle, and the stables and outbuildings, surrounded by a wide moat. The hall occupies the whole N. side— a noble building, about 40 feet long, lighted by four Decorated pointed windows, two on either side—with its wooden screens and minstrels' gallery. At the S.E. is the chapel, which is reached also by a doorway from the dais of the hall. At the E. end of the hall is the solar, with a large garderobe attached to it. The rest of the house is Perpendicular, of the fifteenth century. The kitchen and cellars, &c., are in the vaulted basement. Access to the upper rooms is given by a newel stair enclosed in a turret, which leads to the battlements, and is capped with its original pointed roof. Nine shields of arms ornament the courtyard, bearing the coats of the various families related.

J. H. Parker observes that this manor-house bears a greater resemblance to Southern than to Northern buildings, since the use of large Decorated windows, facing the moat, is not characteristic of a house built for defence.

MIDDLEHAM (chief)

THIS famous stronghold of the Nevills, the most important after Raby of the many they possessed, and the favourite home of the great Earl of Warwick, the King-maker, stands on high ground over the river Ure at the entrance of Wensleydale in the moor country of the North Riding, N.W. of Ripon. The lands of Middleham were part of the territory granted to Alan, son of Eudo of Brittany, by the Conqueror. This Alan founded Richmond Castle, which is not far off, and he gave the manor of Middleham to his brother Ribald, whose grandson Robert Fitz Ralph was the builder of the keep of this castle in 1191. He married Helewise, daughter and heir of Ralph de Glanville of Coverdale, where that lady founded the abbey of that name. His grandson Ralph Fitz Ranulph left three daughters only, the eldest of whom, Mary, married Robert, eldest son of Robert de Nevill, lord of Raby and Brancepeth, and thus brought the honour and castle of Middleham to the Nevills, who enjoyed the possession for nearly 250 years. This Robert was caused by his wife to be barbarously mutilated on account of a *liaison* which he had formed with a lady in Craven, and died soon after, when his son Ralph succeeded, who, dying in 1331, was followed first by his eldest son Robert, called "The Peacock of the North," and then by his second son Ralph. This lord of Middleham died 41 Edward III. (1367), and was succeeded by his son John, Baron Nevill, whose eldest son by his first wife was Ralph, the great Earl of Westmorland, Earl Marshal of England, whose abode was at Brancepeth. This John Nevill must have been a personage of high worth and importance, since he married as his second wife Joan Beaufort, the daughter of John of Gaunt, Duke of Lancaster, by whom he had a daughter, Cecilia or Cicely, "The Rose of Raby," mother of King Edward IV. and of Richard III. (see *Berkhamstead, Herts*), by Richard, Duke of York; and an eldest son Richard, created Earl of Salisbury, who was Lord of Middleham, and was beheaded after the battle of Wakefield, and whose eldest son was Richard the King-maker, Earl of Warwick in his wife's right, killed at Barnet in 1471, when all his property, including Middleham, was confiscated by the Crown. This great man lived chiefly at Middleham, and seems to have sought the solitude and security of this fortress in the many troubled periods of his life. It was here that it is said he confined King Edward IV. after surprising and capturing him in his camp at Wolsey. Edward was placed there by Warwick under the custody of the Archbishop of York, Warwick's brother. Edward was allowed to hunt in the park, and one day was met by a strong force of his friends, who enabled him to make good his escape. Edward gave Middleham to his brother Richard, Duke of York, afterwards Richard III. He seems to have been attached to this place, and to have lived there frequently, and his only son by Anne, the daughter of Warwick, was born in this castle and died in it. There is scarcely any mention of Middleham in history after that epoch, and the fabric was probably neglected, though inhabited partially in the seventeenth century; the finishing stroke being put to its existence when the Roundhead Committee at York, during the Civil War, sent orders to make the place untenable, at which time the walls were rent and greatly injured by gunpowder, huge masses of them now lying about the ruins. The castle was sold long ago to Mr. Wood of Littleton, an ancestor of the present owner. It stands a little above the town, the N. side of the fortress, where is the entrance, being next the town; the whole is in ruins. The plan is an oblong rectangular enclosure, measuring 245 feet by 190 feet, having at three of the corners of the outer wall a square tower, and at the fourth a circular or drum tower, three storeys in height. The walls, which are about 30 feet high, and 3 to 4 yards thick, and exist partly on three sides, had attached to them inside numerous chambers and offices, the designation of which can now scarcely be made out. In the centre of the area stands the Norman keep of 1191, measuring 100 feet by 80 feet, and 55 feet in height, having at its E. face a grand ascent of many steps leading to the entrance, and a barbican which contained an oratory; besides the gate at the top of the stairs there was another half-way up, and a third at the vestibule. The keep is built of coursed rubble with ashlar dressings, and is divided unequally by the usual Norman wall in the middle, with a vaulted basement of two chambers on the ground level, and state rooms upon the first floor, where was the grand hall, very lofty, and lighted by round-headed windows, with an adjoining apartment on the W. side; there were two large fireplaces, the shafts of which rise clear of the roof. There are two small rooms, perhaps garderobes, in the centre buttresses. The buildings of the outer ward, which are of the Decorated period, and were rebuilt by the Nevills between 1331 and 1367, encroach so much round the keep as to leave little space between the buildings; some of the state chambers of these dwellings must have been very grand. On the outside of the enceinte, on the S. and E. fronts, are indications of a ditch. The home of a character so interesting in English history as the Earl of Warwick, Richard the Third, and Anne Nevill, is worthy of more than a passing glance, however ruined.

MULGRAVE (minor)

ABOUT a quarter of a mile from the modern seat of the Normanby family, near Whitby, lies the ruin of this ancient castle, on a ridge between two ravines, through which flow two rapid streams, rendering it difficult of access. It is supposed to have been formed in very early times upon the site of a Roman work, by a Northumbrian earl named Wada, who was concerned in the murder of "Ethelred of Northumberland" (*Hinderwell*), but the whole tradition savours of folk-lore and fiction. The place was long a stronghold of the De Mauleys, whose fortunes are said by Dugdale to have been formed by King John, who had used the services of one of them, named Peter, in the murder at Rouen of his nephew Prince Arthur. This man he caused to be married to Isabel, daughter of Robert de Turnham, and heiress of Mulgrave. Seven De Mauleys of the name of Peter successively enjoyed the estate and castle, but the seventh dying without issue, the inheritance passed by his sisters into various hands. At last, about 1625, it came to Edmund, Lord Sheffield, whom Elizabeth had made a Knight of the Garter, and who was created Earl of Mulgrave by Charles I. The family failing temp. George II., a lease of the Mulgrave estates was granted to Constantine Phipps, of the Anglesea family, who was made Lord Mulgrave in 1767, and who permanently acquired the estates by purchase, for the sum of £30,000, and an annual quit-rent to Government.

There have been considerable buildings on this rugged site, consisting of large state rooms and domestic offices, bakeries, &c., and the remains are mostly Edwardian, with additions of later days. There are some very large fireplaces and chimneys, but not much remains that is of interest or remarkable. It is said that many farm-houses have been built from these ruins. The entrance to the outer court is on the W. between two circular towers, one of which is of great height, and is covered with ivy; outside the walls there is a deep ditch crossed by a drawbridge. The keep is square, with a round turret at each angle; at the S.E. angle of the outer wall are the remains of a square tower, the inside measurement of which is 12 feet by 9 feet; it is two storeys high, and a fireplace exists in it. The whole is in a very ruinous state. The area is irregular in shape, and extends 110 yards E. to W., by 80 yards.

NORTHALLERTON (non-existent)

A CASTLE stood at this place, on the W. side of the town, said to have been built by Bishop Galfridus Rufus, who was Chancellor in the reign of Henry I. William Cumin, Chancellor of Scotland, on the death of the Bishop of Durham in 1140, usurped the see, and held this fortress for three years ; he is said by some to have been its builder : he yielded it to Bishop Hugh Pudsay in 1144, and this Prince Bishop added to and fortified it in the year 1173, and then gave it over to his nephew Hugh, Count of Barre. This must have drawn on him the wrath of that royal destroyer of castles, King Henry II., who obliged the bishop to demolish the building, though he offered a large sum to redeem it ; nor does it appear to have been ever rebuilt. All that Leland saw in 1538 was "the ditches and the dungeon hille wher it sumtyme stood."

The bishops had also a palace which stood near the church, said to have been "stronge of building & welle motid." It was quite a ruin in 1658, and is represented as being in 1694 "a weather-beaten castle, demolished with age and the ruins of time a receptacle for bats and buzzards, owls and jackdaws." A considerable portion of the gatehouse was standing about 140 years ago, of which not the smallest vestige now remains.

The castle mound is a relic of still earlier times ; it is 100 feet in diameter and 20 feet in height, and is surrounded by a dry ditch. At a slight distance are the remains of a rampart and a ditch, beyond which a third dry ditch and rampart formed an outer defence. The whole must have been a formidable work.

PICKERING (minor)

LELAND in his Itinerary says : "This Castelle hath longgid to the Lancaster bloode ; but who made the Castelle, or who was the owner of it before the Lancasters, I could not lerne there." Indeed there is no record of the place until 32 Henry III. (1250), when William, Lord Dacre, was constituted keeper of Pickering Castle. After this Henry gave it to his son, Edmund Crouchback, from whom it came to his son Thomas, Earl of Lancaster, who was beheaded after the defeat at Boroughbridge, at Pontefract, in 1322, when his estates were forfeited by Edward II., who made Henry Percy, Earl of Northumberland, governor of Pickering. The castle and manor have both been attached to the Duchy of Lancaster ever since John of Gaunt obtained them and the other estates through his wife Blanche, the granddaughter of Henry, brother of the beheaded earl, who obtained a reversal of the attainder. Henry of Bolingbroke, when he landed at Ravenspur in 1399, came first to this castle, where he was joined by his Northern allies, and to Pickering also was his victim, Richard II., taken before being made away with at Pontefract, as is recorded in Hardyng's Chronicle (see Leeds, Yorks).

In the Parliamentary War, Cromwell's troops opened a battery against this castle from the opposite side of the valley, and succeeded in driving a large breach into the W. wall. One may still see, on the crest of the opposite hill, two or three grassy hillocks which mark the site of this battery. William III.

sold a long lease of Pickering to one Hart at a yearly rent of £10, after which it passed into the possession of various persons.

The castle stands at the N. of the town, on the brow of the hill; the walls of it and the towers being continued round the hill side; in the words of Leland: "In the first Court of it be 4 toures, of the which one is called Rosamonde's Toure. In the ynner Court be also 4 toures, whereof the kepe is one. The Castelle waulles and the toures be neatly welle. The loggins that be yn the ynner Court that be of timber, be in ruine." The cross walls divide the area into three

PICKERING

courts, and where they meet is the keep, which is multangular, and stood on a circular mound surrounded by a deep ditch. The Mill Tower, on the left of the entrance, and the Devil's Tower, on the outer wall, close to the moat of the keep, and the Rosamond Tower (so called because Fair Rosamond is said to have been imprisoned there), in the outer court, three storeys high, are tolerably perfect, and are of Edwardian architecture, but there are some remains of earlier Norman work. There is a sallyport in the Devil's Tower giving to the outer ditch. The chapel is poor. Lovely views are seen from various parts of this castle over the well-wooded country around.

PONTEFRACT (chief)

WHERE the ruins of this fine castle stand on its commanding height, was an earlier fortress from which its English lord was expelled by the Conqueror, to make room for Ilbert de Lacy, to whom he granted 150 manors in Yorkshire. In most cases the Norman choice of sites followed the Saxon lead, which in very many cases throughout the land had depended

on the previous military experience of the Romans or of the Britons.
William ordered the erection of this castle, recognising the great importance
of its position, which commanded the main road from Doncaster to York,
with the passage of the river Aire, and also the intersection of the road from
Chester and the Riching Street at Castleford, where was the Roman station
of Lagentium (*Stukeley*). De Lacy founded the castle about 1080, together
with the chapel of St. Clement inside it. He was succeeded by his son
Robert (who, or perhaps his brother, built Clitheroe, Lancaster), and with his
son Ilbert, on the death of Rufus, espoused the cause of Robert Courthouse
against Henry I., who in return dispossessed them of their lands, and granted
these first to William Traverse, and afterwards to Guy De la Val, a baron who
was there temp. Stephen. Then Ilbert de Lacy regained his property, and
Henry his brother succeeding, built the later Norman work of the castle.
In 1193 Albreda, his sister and heiress, brought it in marriage to Richard
Fitz Eustace, Count of Chester, and their son assumed his mother's name of
De Lacy. John de Lacy succeeding in 1213, married Margaret, daughter of
Hawise, Countess of Lincoln, and coheir of Ranulph, Earl of Chester and
Lincoln, at whose death these titles were transferred to John de Lacy, before
his death in 1240. The grandson of this man, Henry de Lacy, Earl of Lincoln,
was perhaps the best of his race; he married the daughter of Longspee, and
in her right became Earl of Salisbury. Earl Henry lost his two sons early,
one of them being drowned at Denbigh Castle, and the other killed by falling
when he was attempting to run round the battlements of one of the towers
of Pomfret Castle. After the death of this poor boy, De Lacy, dying in 1310,
made King Edward I. heir to all his estates, and at his death the king
conferred them on his own brother Edmund "Crouchback," Earl of Lancaster.
Queen Margaret "of France," Edward's second wife, was staying at Pontefract
when, on a hunting expedition to Brotherton, she was unexpectedly confined
of her eldest son Thomas, who was surnamed of that place. Then, after the
failure of the De Lacys, Pontefract became indeed "a bloody prison."

Earl Henry left a daughter Alice, who was married to the king's nephew
Thomas, the son of Edmund Crouchback: this was Thomas Plantagenet, the
great Earl of Lancaster, the bitter enemy of his weak cousin's favourites,
Gaveston and the two Despencers, and therefore the beloved of England,
and, like Simon de Montfort, worshipped as a saint when dead. He was
a mighty builder, and, as owner of Dunstanburgh, at that fortress erected
extensive additions, while at Kenilworth he made the Lancaster Buildings.
Here at Pontefract he built the Swillington Tower, and some of the best
portions of the structure. After the defeat at Boroughbridge he was taken to
Pontefract, where his cousin, the weak and vindictive Edward, awaited him,
and imprisoned him in the Swillington Tower; then, brought into his own
hall, he was tried and condemned by his enemies, and was beheaded on the

hill above, which still bears the name of St. Thomas. The earldom and property were suffered to pass to his brother Henry, whose son was created in 1351 Duke of Lancaster. He died without male issue, and the castle and honour of Pontefract went with his daughter Blanche in marriage to John of Gaunt, fourth son of Edward III., who in her right became Duke of Lancaster. He lived partly here, and rebuilt and restored some portions of the castle, which at his death (1399) passed to his son Henry of Bolingbroke, Duke of Hereford, who at once deposed his cousin, Richard II., and usurped the crown. Then occurred at Pontefract the cruel murder of Richard either, as given by Shakespeare, at the hands of Sir Piers Exton, or more probably, according to Archbishop Scrope, by the slow torture of starvation. Richard had confiscated Bolingbroke's estates, and thus Henry took his revenge. Since the accession of Henry IV. Pontefract has always vested in the Crown.

This king was a frequent visitor at Pontefract, and in 1405 came thither to receive from his crafty supporter the Earl of Westmorland, Archbishop Scrope, and Mowbray, the young Earl Marshal, victims of Nevill's treachery at Shipton Moor. The warlike prelate, having acted as a prime mover in placing the crown on Henry's head, took in 1405 a leading part in a Northern revolt, set about ostensibly to lighten the burdens of the clergy and others, and to free the country from unjust exactions. A Yorkshire force, 8000 strong, led by Scrope and Mowbray, advanced from York against the royal troops under the earl and Prince John, encamped on Shipton Moor, six miles N.W. of York. Here Nevill, at a parley held between the two forces, pretending sympathy with Scrope's manifesto, and extreme friendship, joined hands with him over a friendly cup of wine in view of the rebel troops, who were thereby persuaded that all was conceded, and at once disbanded in large numbers. Then the earl's men took possession of the ground, made prisoners of the archbishop and the Earl Marshal, and hurried them off under guard to Pontefract to await the king's arrival. When Henry arrived, the archbishop, who had been watching for him from the castle battlements, came down to meet him, throwing himself at his feet; but the king, refusing to hear him, had him hustled away to Bishopthorpe, and following thither himself, caused trial and condemnation to be carried out at once in the hall of that palace. The Chief Justice, Gascoigne, refused to pronounce sentence of death upon an Archbishop of York, but by Henry's order both Scrope and the Earl Marshal were led away towards York and were beheaded in a field near the city.

Here were tried the abettors of the Earl of Northumberland and Lord Bardolph; and Pontefract became the prison of the unfortunate King James I. of Scotland, made prisoner, and so long held by Henry IV.; and in the next reign the accomplished Duke of Orleans, with other prisoners from Agincourt,

was confined in it. Henry V. writes in 1419: "Wherefore I wolle that the
Duc of Orliance be kept stille within the Castil of Pomfret with owte goyng
to Robertis place or to any othre disport, for it is bettre he lak his disport then
we were disceyued" (*Facsimile autographs, British Museum*).

Many stirring events occurred here during the Wars of the Roses. At the
close of the year 1460 the Royalist leader, the Duke of Somerset, repaired to
Pontefract before the battle of Wakefield, with his Lancastrian contingent, and
after that bloody fight, the Earl of Salisbury, Richard Nevill, father to the King-
maker, was carried wounded to the castle, with other Yorkist persons of
distinction, all of whom were, with short shrift, next morning beheaded.

Three months after this (March 1461), the newly proclaimed king, Edward
IV., and the Earl of Warwick were at Pontefract with their forces two days prior
to the great battle of Towton; but the story of Warwick killing his charger
under the castle walls, to animate his troops when on the march towards the
enemy, is not worthy of credit, although from the legend of the Red Horse in
Warwickshire (see *Fulbroke*) some foundation for it may have occurred during
a panic at Towton Field. Then Edward, returning to Pontefract, reverently
restored to the coffin of his father, Richard, buried there, the head which, since
his death at Wakefield, had surmounted one of the gates of York. Edward IV.
was here again in 1463, and again, in great state, in 1478, remaining a week.
Hither were sent by Richard III., in 1483, his unfortunate victims, Earl Rivers,
Sir Richard Gray, Sir Thomas Vaughan and Hawse, for execution without even
the formality of a trial, and they were beheaded at this bloodstained castle.
The leaders of the insurrection called "The Pilgrimage of Grace," which broke
out in defence of the old creed in 1536, came to Pontefract with their whole forces
and succeeded in obtaining temporary possession of the fortress from Lord
Darcy, and Lee, the Archbishop of York, who were secretly favourable to their
cause. Elizabeth, towards the end of her reign, repaired the castle and
restored the chapel; and in 1603 James I. came thither, the castle and honour
being part of his queen's dower.

In the Civil War, Pontefract became a military post of great importance,
keenly contended for on both sides. It was the rallying-place for the cavaliers
of Yorkshire, and was garrisoned by a very strong force of gentry and
volunteers, under the command of Sir William Lowther. At Christmas, after
the victory at Marston Moor (July 1644), Fairfax came before the castle and
opened the siege; his main attack was on the N.W. angle, where he threw
down one of the seven towers, called the Piper, which flanked the defences, and
which carried down with it a part of the wall. The breach was made good
with earth at once, and the enemy then ruined the S.E. angle, near the King's
Tower, an attack which the garrison met by countermining, no easy matter in
the solid rock. Great spirit was shown on both sides, especially in the heroic
sallies of the garrison, who were at length weakened by losses of men and by

dearth of stores. At this moment they were relieved by Sir M. Langdale and 2000 men from Oxford, at whose coming the enemy (March 1, 1645) broke up in haste, and raised the siege. Very shortly after, however, they again beset the place, and after a second siege, which lasted three months, succeeded in obtaining its surrender. In 1648 Pontefract was recovered for the king by a ruse ; Colonel Morrice, a young officer who had faced both ways, introduced some carts with provisions into the castle, accompanied by a few soldiers disguised as peasants, who surprised the guard and captured the fortress. It was an old trick, which succeeded at Scarborough Castle and on other occasions in ancient times, and irritated by it, the Parliamentary forces soon after appeared again before the castle, whose garrison had by that time been greatly reinforced. Cromwell himself, having viewed the works, wrote to the Council of War in London stating that as "the place is very well known to be one of the strongest inland garrisons in the kingdom, well watered, situated upon a rock in every part of it, and therefore difficult to mine," he desired additional troops and money, "500 barrels of powder, and 6 good battering guns, with 300 shot for each." Too much honour cannot be accorded to the brave garrison for the stand they made, for at that time the Parliament had triumphed all along the line. The king had been killed, and only Scarborough Castle held out ; but they proclaimed Charles II., and made such vigorous sallies on the enemy's works as to prolong the siege for six months, when their lessened numbers, reduced from 500 to 100 men, obliged them to capitulate. Six persons were excepted from mercy, including Morrice and another who cut their way through and escaped for a time ; the other four were walled up in an underground chamber, and so eluded capture till opportunity occurred to get away. The Parliament immediately ordered the wreck of this blood-stained old fortress to be demolished, and the materials to be sold ; the only marvel being that anything of it should have survived to our day.

The summit of the elevated rock, from which Pomfret Castle looked down on the surrounding country, occupied an area of 7 acres, with a high wall, having large, flanking, mural towers at intervals, and a deep ditch encompassing the whole. Two huge round towers remain, portions of the keep, the lower part of them probably the work of the great Earl of Lancaster. The entrance to the keep is by a long flight of stairs; it contains in its chapel some Norman work. Narrow staircases lead in it to a sallyport and to a dungeon, and below are vast subterranean passages and chambers in the rock of the time of Edward II. The walls are those built by Henry I., Duke of Lancaster.

In Drake's Journal of the two first sieges (published by the Surtees Society), a drawing is reproduced giving a bird's-eye view of the fortress as it appeared in 1648. By this the great keep, with its clustering round towers, is shown on the W., with the square mural towers in succession on the outer curtain

wall: first the Red, or Gascoyne's Tower; the Piper Tower (wrongly called
the Pix), with a doorway, which lay next the keep, having been destroyed in
1645; then the Treasurer's Tower; the Swillington, advanced from the wall;
the Queen's Tower; the King's Tower; the Constable's Tower, with its chapel
of St. Clement attached on the W., of which the basement remains; and the
great gatehouse into the inner ward occupying the whole summit—all, except
the keep, being perhaps Norman (*Clark*), as is the greater part of the masonry.
Only the keep and the ruin of the Piper Tower are now traceable, the rest, with
the hall, kitchens, and the lodgings, having been removed by the Parliament.

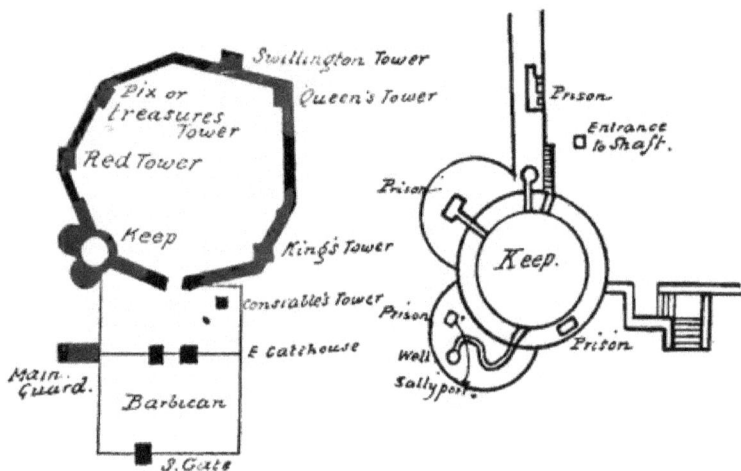

PONTEFRACT

In front of the gatehouse stood the barbican, whose wall on the E. ended in
the E. or lower gatehouse; and further S. was another enclosure of wall, com-
mencing at the keep and continued on three sides of a square to the lower
gatehouse, with a lower barbican and gateway in its midst. On the W. below
the keep was the west gate, with a bridge and guardhouse in front.

The keep was formed upon the ancient mound, faced with masonry, and
supporting a regular shell keep 60 feet in diameter. From the irregularity of
the rock base this building was supported by the circular bastions mentioned
by Leland, only two of which now remain; on the S.W. is the platform,
20 feet above the main ward, and at its S. angle rises the conical mound.
Among the ruins of early masonry is the end of an arched vault, which bears
the name of "King Richard's Prison," having near it the shaft of a garderobe.

Mr. Clark alleges the greater part of the remains to be early Norman work;

while the enceinte wall, the buildings on the W. platform, the old postern, the interior of the keep, and the deep magazine seem also to be Norman; very little being extant of Early English or Decorated.

The purpose to which this historical enclosure, so full of tragic memories, has been applied is the cultivation of liquorice.

RICHMOND (chief)

IT was probably during his marches through Yorkshire when engaged in his fiendish destruction of that North country, that William I. observed and chose as a point to be fortified the rocky peninsula here, around which the Swale—that "ryght noble ryuer" bends its dark course. The lands below this height were the home of his friend, or prisoner, the Saxon Earl Edwin, who had his earthwork and timber fortress of Gilling there; but a stronger position was needed for the Norman tower to which was to be confided the subjugation of this wild country, and the Breton count to whom the lands were given was directed to build his castle on these well-protected heights. This was Alan Fergeant, the second son of one of Duke William's followers, Eudo, Duke of Brittany, on whom, possibly at his Christmas festivities at York amid the ashes of that city (December 1069), the Conqueror conferred 199 manors, chiefly then "waste," and after Earl Edwin's defection and death the bulk of the estates of that noble. The "Registrum honoris de Richmond" tells how this Alan, who was a cousin of William, and is called Rufus, at once drew a protecting line of wall round the site, and in 1071 began his castle of the French name of Richmond; he took also the title of Richmond for his earldom. His brother Alan Niger succeeded him, and dying in 1093, was followed by another brother, Stephen, whose son Alan, marrying the heiress of Conan, Duke of Brittany, united in his son Conan this dukedom and the earldom of Richmond. To him is ascribed the existing keep of the castle. He seems to have been worked on by King Henry II. to resign the Breton Duchy, and also to betroth his daughter Constance to Henry's son Geoffrey. This is Shakespeare's Constance in *King John*, the mother of the murdered Prince Arthur, Duke of Brittany, after whose death the earldoms of Richmond devolved upon his half-sister Alice, the daughter of Constance by her third husband, Guy de Tours. But the richness of Earl Edwin's patrimony caused it to be coveted by English monarchs to such an extent that the succession to the honour of Richmond was greatly disjointed over a long period. First, the estates were arbitrarily seized and retained by Richard I., and John followed his example, Richmond Castle being placed under Geoffrey de Nevill as Constable. Alice, meanwhile, the sister of Prince Arthur, was titular Countess of Richmond and Duchess of Brittany, of which latter possession her husband,

Richmond Castle

Peter de Dreux, was deprived by Louis IX., on his becoming a vassal of Henry III. (1237), the unfortunate condition of an owner of rank and lands in two opposed countries. His son, however, at last obtained restitution of Brittany, and also in 1266 of the county, honour, and castle of Richmond. Dying in 1286, he was followed by his son John, Earl of Richmond, whose wife was Beatrix, the daughter of Henry III.; he was accidentally killed at Lyons in 1304, leaving two sons—Arthur, who became Duke of Brittany, and John, who succeeded to Richmond, and who was made by his brother-in-law, Edward I., Regent of Scotland (35 Edward I.), an honour continued by the next king. This earl was taken prisoner at Bannockburn, and was deemed of so much importance that the Queen of France and the Bishop of Glasgow were exchanged for him; poor compensation perhaps "for an active and warlike earl." He again fell into the hands of the Bruce at the disaster of Byland Abbey, and paid ransom, but soon after retired to France, giving up his earldom. On his death in 1330, John his nephew was admitted by Edward III. to the honour and dignity, and at his death s.p. in 1341, his honours were claimed by John de Montfort, son of Duke Arthur of Brittany, but his claims were put aside by Edward III., who, anxious to retain this great fief, conferred the earldom on his fourth son, an infant, afterwards John of Gaunt, and confirmed his title to Richmond in his twenty-seventh year, under the Great Seal. In the eighth year of Richard II., this earldom was conferred on Anne his queen. The Dukes of Brittany, however, long after continued ineffectually to seek restitution of the lands and dignity ravished from John de Montfort.

Henry IV. bestowed the county of Richmond, but not the title, upon his then faithful friend Ralph Nevill, Earl of Westmorland, for his lifetime; and he was followed in the possession by John, Duke of Bedford, and next by Prince John of Hadham, half-brother to Henry VI., whose title of Earl of Richmond expressly gave him precedence of dukes. His wife, Margaret, Countess of Richmond, was one of the most illustrious women in the world, for learning, wisdom, and piety; she was the mother of Henry VII. by her Tudor husband, and her son only resigned this title of hers for that of king on the field of Bosworth.

The ground plan of the castle is triangular, with its apex pointing N., and occupied by the keep, in front of which is a circular barbican, covering the main entrance. The base is the curtain, 150 yards long, below which runs the cliff, 30 feet high, and then a long slope down to the river, while the W. side, 130 yards in length, crowns a very steep depression to the town. The E. side has in front of it the outer ward on a gentle slope towards the river. A portion of the barbican wall remains, connected with what has probably formed part of an outer gatehouse; all its W. side has been built over.

The great Norman keep measures 52 feet by 45 feet, and is nearly 100 feet high. Its walls at the base are 10 feet thick, the usual broad pilasters forming the angles on each side, with two pilasters strengthening the wide fronts, and one on each of the others; each angle carries a turret at top, which had two stages. The lower part of the keep building being of better masonry than the upper part, would suggest an addition in the upper of the three floors.

The basement is a chamber 32 feet by 21 feet, having lights or recesses, and in Decorated times the wooden floor above it was removed and a vaulted roof substituted for this stage, with ribs supported by an octagonal pier of stone, at the foot of which is the castle well. A Decorated spiral stair ascends from this chamber to the first floor, the chief apartment, lighted by three windows on the N. side. The only entrance was, as now, by a door on the S. face, inside which a straight stair leads up in the wall to the floor above, which is provided with three sleeping apartments in the thickness of the W. and E. walls, that on the N. being quite solid. The upper floor has a stair to the roof and battlements. The entrance to the basement was by an enormous archway, that to the first floor by an outer stair. There were neither fireplaces nor garderobes in the building.

Near the keep was the chapel founded in 1278 by Earl John, which, with the various domestic offices, kitchens, hall, &c., was built against the wall. The most perfect of these is called Scotland's Hall, standing against the S. wall, through which its ground floor has loopholes. Its upper floor measures 70 feet by 26 feet, and is lighted at its E. end by a Decorated window, and at the W. by one of Early English construction, the side windows being Norman. Next to this fine building is a rectangular tower occupying the S.E. angle of the outer walls, having once an ancient postern in its basement.

Extending from the hall along the E. wall is the kitchen, which had over it a large apartment, and next to that is the chapel. Outside the E. wall and sloping down towards the river is the outer ward, now a garden; it is known by the name of "The Cockpit."

Although so near the great road to the North through Doncaster, Pontefract, and Boroughbridge, there is no recorded siege of this fortress, nor any account of warfare in or about it.

RIPLEY (minor)

ON a slope of ground on the side of the Nidd stands this fine residence of the Ingilby family, who have been here for more than five centuries. Originally there was here a tower of the Ripleys, the heiress of which family, marrying Sir Thomas Ingilby about the year 1378, brought him these lands, and his descendants continued here till 1642. At the breaking out of the Civil War, a baronetage was conferred on Sir William Ingilby. By the death of the fourth baronet, Sir John, in 1779, unmarried, the title became extinct, but was revived by patent in 1781, in favour of his successor in the property.

It appears from an inscription on the oaken wainscoting of an apartment in the tower, that the castle was built by Sir William Ingilby in 1555, and in later years many additions have been made to the structure.

Nothing of historic interest is recorded regarding the place, but a noteworthy incident happened here when Cromwell, after the victory of Marston Moor, came through Ripley, and desired to be received for the night in the castle. Sir William Ingilby being absent with the king, his wife, a daughter of Sir James Bellingham, at first refused to admit him, saying she had strength enough to defend herself and her house against all rebels; but at length,

RIPLEY

being persuaded not to resist, Lady Ingilby received the general in the great hall, with a pair of pistols stuck in her apron-strings, and told him she expected that both he and his men would behave properly. Then, to assure herself, she kept watch over him, and "there, sitting or reclining, each on a sofa in different parts of the room, these two extraordinary personages passed the night, equally jealous of each other's intentions. At his departure in the morning, this high-spirited dame caused it to be intimated to Cromwell that she was glad he had behaved in so peaceable a manner, for had it been otherwise, he would not have left that house alive" (*Baine*).

The lodge and the great tower are battlemented, and preserve their original traces of strength and security.

SANDAL (*non-existent*)

WAKEFIELD formed a part of the fee of the great family of De Warenne, of which Coningsborough was the head. John, the eighth and last Earl of Warenne, succeeded his grandfather in the barony in 1304, his father having been killed in a tournament in 1286. Edward I. honoured him by giving him his granddaughter, Joan de Barr, in marriage ; but it was not a happy union, and both parties would have had a divorce if they could, but the Pope would not grant one. The earl separated from her, consorted with a Norfolk lady of rank, Maud de Narford, formerly the wife of Thomas, Earl of Lancaster, and if he could, would have made her his countess, and the two sons he had by her owners at his death of Coningsborough, and all his other property N. of Trent. It was as a residence for her that he built this castle of Sandal about the year 1320 ; he, however, survived both her and her sons, and when he died in 1347, his estates fell to the Crown. In the time of Edward III., John Baliol resided at Sandal during the time that an army was being raised to place him on the throne of Scotland. But the strongest interest which attaches to this fortress centres in its connection with the war of York and Lancaster. In 1446 Richard, Duke of York, father of Edward IV., entered into possession of Sandal, deriving it from his uncle Edward, Earl of Rutland, and he was slain there fourteen years after, at the battle of Wakefield.

After the battle of Northampton, in which Warwick captured King Henry and drove Queen Margaret into Scotland, the Duke of York made formal claim to the throne, and it was settled in Parliament that after Henry's death he should succeed. But to this negation of her son's rights the queen was naturally opposed, and gaining over the king and nobility of Scotland to her cause, she collected, with their aid, a large army and invaded England ; her forces were stated to be 22,000 strong, and were under the chief command of the Dukes of Somerset and Exeter. The Duke of York, getting together what troops he could, left London in December to meet the queen's army, though his numbers did not amount to 5000 men. At Worksop his van came in collision with Somerset's rear and suffered a slight check ; but York pushed on, and on December 21 reached his castle of Sandal, where he intended to await the arrival of his son Edward, Earl of March, with reinforcements, before attacking the enemy. After a short armistice during Christmas, the Royalists, breaking up from Pontefract, advanced to Wakefield, from whence Sandal was about a mile distant, and coming near the castle, sought by taunts and menaces to draw Richard of York out of his moated stronghold. Unfortunately for his cause—perhaps straitened for provisions after nine days— he allowed himself to accept battle without waiting for the rest of his army, and on December 30 drew his small force out of the castle to meet his challengers. Sandal Castle stood on the summit of a conical mound, probably of Saxon or Danish origin, and its chief gate opening to the S., York was obliged, in order to meet the hostile army in the N., to wheel round the base of his castle hill, a movement which gave Somerset time to make his arrangements for entrapping the Yorkists, which was effected by advancing his two wings to a position on the right and left of the road by which York would have to attack his main body. Thus it came about that as soon as the head of the Yorkist column came to close quarters with the Royalist centre, posted across the roadway, these wings were brought round and fell upon the flanks and rear of Duke Richard's force, which had marched blindly into the snare, and was at once overwhelmed and cut to pieces by overpowering odds—some 2800 being said to have fallen. The duke himself was slain, with many of his best officers, and the whole affair was over in half-an-hour. The duke's body was beheaded, and the head set up over the Micklegate Bar of York :

> "So York may overlook the town of York."

But Shakespeare's account is poetical, and there is no doubt that at that time Queen Margaret was not in Yorkshire. Two months later, however, the young Edward was proclaimed king, and his first act was to take down his father's head, and give proper burial to the remains at Pontefract.

The ground slopes gently down from Sandal Castle to Wakefield Bridge, where the murder of Richard's young son, the Earl of Rutland, by Lord Clifford occurred, and where is still the beautiful chapel of Edward II.'s reign. The spot on which tradition places the death of Richard of York is about a mile from this bridge, near the Barnsley road, where in a marshy place stood till lately two very aged willow trees ; here it is likely the fugitives were rallied by the duke, but soon overpowered.

Meagre, indeed, are the vestiges of this castle, consisting of the rubble hearting of some pieces of wall, from the outside of which the ashlar has been torn, and many heaps of rubbish ; a circular moat, which has been wide and deep, surrounds the castle still, 40 or 50 feet below its site.

Richard, Duke of Gloucester, inhabited Sandal at times during his brother's reign. The place was always the manor-house of the barony of Wakefield, and the Saviles of Thornhill, who acted as hereditary stewards of these estates, sometimes resided here. It was held for Charles I. by Colonel Bonivert, and after a siege was surrendered to the Parliamentary forces in October 1645 ; the next year it was slighted and dismantled by orders from the Council.

SCARBOROUGH (chief)

THERE could be no finer ideal situation for a fortress of a maritime power than that held by the Castle of Scarborough, reared on the summit of its lofty headland or scar, 300 feet high, and peering thence over hundreds of square leagues of ocean. The promontory forms a bay and harbour on its S. side, while on the N. it advances boldly into the North Sea, so that the precipitous cliff is washed by the waves on all sides, except where its neck of rock joins the land side, and here the cliff is scarped, and deep ditches cut off all access to the castle.

The chief authorities for this part of Yorkshire are the chronicle of William of Newburgh, an East Riding man, who wrote at the end of the twelfth century, and the writings of the antiquary Thomas Hinderwell, published in 1798. From these it appears that the noble castle of Scarborough was built (temp. Stephen) about the year 1136 by William le Gros, Earl of Albemarle and lord of Holderness, who commanded one of the divisions of the English army at the Battle of the Standard in 1138. This William was the grandson of Odo de Campania, a follower of Duke William, whose daughter Adeliza he married, receiving also from the Conqueror the lands of Holderness by the Humber, with other gifts. His son was Stephen, who married the granddaughter of Malcolm, King of Scotland ; thus William le Gros was of royal blood on both father and mother's side. He, says the Chronicler, "viewing well, and seeing it to be a convenient plot to build a castle upon, helping nature forward with a very costly worke, closed the whole plaine of the rocke with a wall, and built a toure within the very streight of the passage." And from this fortress he ruled over the country N. of Humber with king-like power, until Henry II., bent on putting a stop to the lawless excesses of the nobles, decreed the demolition of a vast number of their castles, Scarborough among the rest. This mandate being resisted by Le Gros, Henry came in person to see his orders carried out, but being struck with the useful situation of the castle, he not only preserved it, but built a new keep and greatly improved its strength and magnificence. But he annexed it to the Crown, and Le Gros in dudgeon retired to Thornton Abbey in Lincolnshire, and died there, 1179. Thenceforth the custodians of this stronghold were appointed by the king, sometimes from among the highest of the nobility. In 1312, when Edward II., desirous of reinstating his minion, Piers Gaveston, who had been banished, recalled him to York, the confederated barons, fearful of Gaveston's power, raised an army, headed by the Earl of Lancaster, and advanced against the king and his favourite, who together fled to Newcastle, and then taking ship at Tynemouth, sailed to Scarborough, where Edward left Gaveston. Thither came the Earl of Pembroke with a strong force to besiege the place. Gaveston repulsed several assaults

with much bravery, but want of provisions compelled him to surrender himself
on terms which were at once set aside; he was taken as a prisoner towards
Warwick, where the Earls of Warwick and Lancaster met him, and struck off
his head at Blacklow Hill; at which place a stone monument has been erected,
marking the spot where he suffered (see *Deddington, Oxon*).

King Robert Bruce after Bannockburn, and later the Earl Douglas, wasted
the northern counties and burned Scarborough, but the castle seems to have

SCARBOROUGH

been too strong for them to master. It was placed in thorough repair by
Edward III. in 1343. The castle, town, and port were granted in 1473 to
the Duke of Gloucester, afterwards Richard III., and Anne his wife, in
exchange for the manor of Bushey.

In 27 Henry VIII. (1536) the fanatics who led the insurrection known
as "The Pilgrimage of Grace" assaulted this castle, but it was bravely defended by Sir Ralph Eure, the governor, and the assailants were beaten off.
Again, at the time of Wyatt's rebellion against Queen Mary in 1553, Thomas,
second son of Lord Stafford, led a daring attack by stratagem on the castle.
Dressing up some thirty followers as countrymen, he strolled with them, on a

market-day, into the castle without exciting suspicion, and suddenly took possession of the entrance and secured the sentries; then admitting the rest of his adherents, he held the castle for three whole days, when the Earl of Westmorland, coming with a considerable force, recovered it without loss. Stafford and four others of the leaders were sent to the Tower of London, where the former was beheaded, and three of his associates were hanged and quartered.

Nothing memorable occurred here afterwards until during the Civil War, when the castle was besieged by a Parliamentary army under Sir John Meldrum, who opened batteries against it in February 1644; besides these, he brought guns into the adjacent Church of St. Mary, firing from the E. window of that church; but these guns were silenced by the fire from the castle, that also brought down the chancel, which indeed is still in ruins. Sir J. Meldrum was wounded and died in June, and the siege was continued by Sir Matthew Boynton. The clever defender of the fortress was Sir Hugh Cholmley, who, being at first Parliamentary governor, had gone over to the Royalist side. He was assisted by his heroic wife, who remained during the whole siege and tended the sick. At last the garrison, reduced by sickness and want of provisions, became disheartened, and Sir Hugh surrendered upon very honourable terms in July 1645.

In 1648 Boynton, who had replaced Cholmley as governor, in his turn declared for the king, but fearing a mutiny of his garrison, he surrendered to Lord Fairfax, and was allowed to march out with all the honours of war in December 1648.

In 1665 George Fox, the founder of the sect of Quakers, was imprisoned here, in one of the rooms facing the sea, now in ruins, remaining there a twelvemonth. We read that in 1745, when the country was in a state of panic on account of the Pretender's invasion of England, the castle received repairs, and next year barracks were built there, but, injured as the fabric was by the siege in 1645, it fell into hopeless decay and ruin, which its exposed position has served to increase.

In spite, however, of the wreckage caused by time and gunpowder, we still see at Scarborough sufficient remains of the "great and goodly castle" to afford an interesting example of what these ancient fortresses were. Approaching from near the E. end of S. Mary's Church, we enter by the barbican, repaired after the great siege, along the narrow causeway and across the ditch, originally defended by a double drawbridge, whence the approach entered the inner ward on the N. side of the keep. The whole enclosure included nearly 20 acres, of which the greater portion is in the outer court or castle green, where were the chapel and the principal offices and barracks for the garrison. The keep or hold is that built by Henry II., but of it only the E. side remains perfect, and also part of the

N. and S. faces; the W. side was destroyed, probably after the siege. It
has been a grand tower, nearly 100 feet in height, of the same character
as that of Rochester, though smaller, having a vaulted crypt, and three
vaulted storeys of rooms, divided by a central wall. The walls are 12 feet
through, built of excellent rubble with ashlar facing, and with round-headed

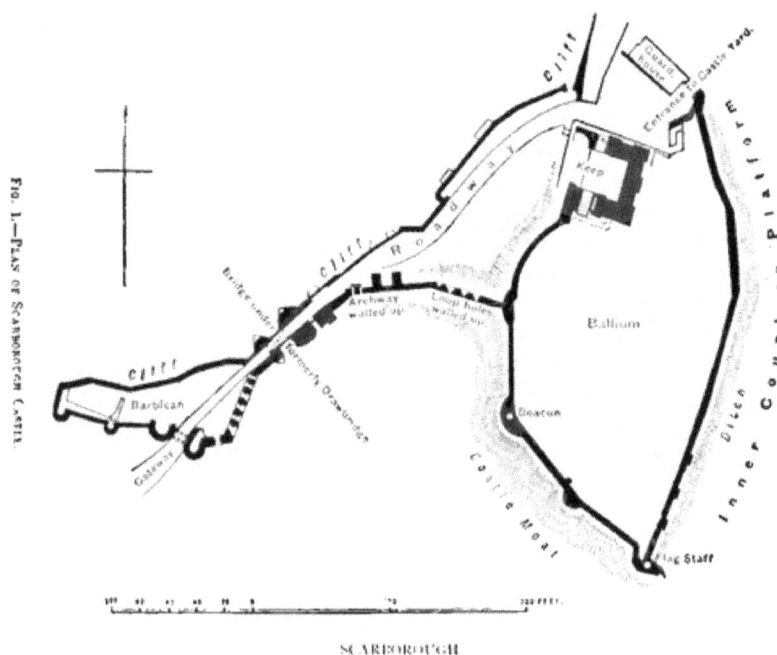

FIG. I.—PLAN OF SCARBOROUGH CASTLE.

SCARBOROUGH

Norman windows. The curtain wall, which was strongly embattled, and
provided with a defencible and machicolated gatehouse and many flanking
towers, was carried across the isthmus between the precipices of cliff on
either side. The remains of a deep well were discovered within the inner
court in 1783, this portion being divided off with the keep by its own moat
and wall; in it were the habitable buildings of the castle, and the towers
mentioned by Leland, containing the queen's lodging.

SHEFFIELD (*non-existent*)

EXCEPT the words "Site of Sheffield Castle" upon the Ordnance maps, there is nothing to show of the existence of this once splendid and important fortress, the home of the great Earls of Shrewsbury, and interesting in history as the scene of the captivity of the hapless Queen of Scots for nearly twelve years. Some vaulted cellars may still exist below the factories and streets that now cover its site, but not a vestige remains aboveground, though the name of Castle Hill preserves its memory.

The castle stood on gently rising ground at the confluence of the rivers Sheaf and Dun, and covered more than four acres. It was one of the strongest places in the north: the broad river Dun on the N. side, and on the E. the Sheaf or Sheath, from which the town is named, flowing beneath the walls, formed its defence, whilst on the S. and W. a wide ditch had been cut connecting the two streams, and thus encircling the walls with water. The entrance was on the S., or the castle-folds side, by a drawbridge across the moat under a gatehouse admitting to the outer bailey, around which were the stables and dwellings. Over the rivers lay the castle orchard, and beyond, the great park, eight miles in circuit, stocked with deer, and full of the finest timber in the country, some trees, says Harrison, being from 12 to 15 feet in girth. A great avenue of walnut trees led from the park gates towards the lodge or manor-house near the centre of the park, built by the fourth earl in the beginning of the fifteenth century.

This strong castle, remote on the moors, and its manor-house, which has disappeared almost as totally as the fortress, were chosen by Elizabeth as a safe prison for her cousin and victim.

The family of De Lovetot held all the lands here temp. Stephen, and in the reign of Richard Cœur de Lion, Maude de Lovetot, lady of Hallamshire, married Gerard de Furnival, of a Norman family, and brought him the lordship. In 50 Henry III., Thomas de Furnival had a licence to crenellate a stone castle on his manor of Shefeld, Ebor. (*Patent Rolls*), perhaps on the site of a former one; and he dying soon after its erection, was succeeded by his son. Other families are mentioned by Hunter ("History of Hallamshire") as possessing the castle, which, however, was acquired early in the fifteenth century by John Talbot, 1st Earl of Shrewsbury, on his marriage with Maud, daughter and heiress of Thomas Nevile, Lord Furnival. He was the celebrated commander of the English in France, when they were making the last struggle to retain their possessions in that country—"the great Alcides of the field." He was, however, routed by Joan of Arc in 1429, and was at last slain by a cannon-ball when eighty years old, at the battle of Chatillon on the Dordon, near Bordeaux, in 1453, where the English made their final stand. His

sword, manufactured at his forges at Sheffield, was found in the river
long after, with the inscription :—

> "Sum Talboti M.III.C.XL.III.
> Pro vincere inimico meo."
> —*Hunter.*

His many titles are thus summed up by Shakespeare (*Henry VI.*, Part I.
Act iv. Sc. 7).

> "Valiant Lord Talbot, Earl of Shrewsbury,
> Created for his rare success in arms,
> Great Earl of Washford, Waterford, and Valence,
> Lord Talbot of Goodrig and Urchinfield,
> Lord Strange of Blackfelde, Lord Verdun of Alton,
> Lord Cromwell of Wingfield, Lord Furnival of Sheffield :
> The thrice victorious Lord of Falconbridge,
> Knight of the noble order of St. George,
> Worthy St. Michael, and the Golden Fleece ;
> Great Marshall to Henry the Sixth,
> Of all his wars within the realm of France."

There is no mention of this castle during the Wars of the Roses, but
John, the second earl, together with his brother Sir Christopher Talbot, was
killed at the battle of Northampton in 1460, on the side of Lancaster ; this
second earl was Lord Treasurer of England. Francis, the fifth earl, was born
here in 1500, and seven Earls of Shrewsbury resided in the castle of Sheffield.
George, the sixth earl, married in February 1567 Lady Cavendish, known as
"Bess of Hardwick," being her fourth husband, and within a year was chosen
by Elizabeth to be the custodian of the captive Queen of Scotland ; she said
"she dyd so trust him as she dyd few." Mary had been removed from Bolton
castle (*q.v.*) and the care of Lord Scrope in January 1569, on account of the
plot for her proposed marriage to the Duke of Norfolk, whose sister was Lady
Scrope, and on Shrewsbury and his grim wife accepting the charge (which they
were possibly obliged to do), the queen was taken to Tutbury Castle (*q.v.*) in
Staffordshire, a place which Shrewsbury held of the Crown. There she
remained, on and off, till December 1570, when the castle of Sheffield, being
the earl's own home, was adopted as her prison, and in it twelve of her
nineteen years (nearly) of captivity were passed in severe durance. Shrewsbury
wrote to Elizabeth : "I have hur sure inoughe, and shall keep hur for the
comyng at your Majesty's commandment, either quyke or ded, . . . so if any
forsabull attempts be gyven for hur, the gretest perell is sure to be hurs." The
standing orders being that in case of any rising or attempt to release her, Mary
should be at once killed, the strictest rules were enforced in regard to the
thirty-nine persons composing her suite. Shrewsbury writes to Burleigh in

1571 that he does not allow the queen "libertie out of the gates, her principall drift," but that he lets her "walk upon the leads in open ayre, and in my large dining chamber and also in this courtyard, so as both myself or my wife be alwaies in her company, for avoiding all others talk either to herself or any of hers." It came out, however, that at Easter 1571 Sir Henry Percy nearly succeeded in a scheme to release her, only failing through an unexpected change of the queen's apartments. The Duke of Norfolk was now imprisoned again, after he had managed to keep up a frequent correspondence with Mary; early in the next year, 1572, Shrewsbury had to preside at his trial, and pronounced sentence of death upon him, Norfolk being beheaded on June 2nd.

During the earl's absence at this time, Sir Ralph Sadler was sent to watch in his place at Sheffield, and during the whole of the queen's captivity Elizabeth constantly kept spies about her, who sent word immediately to London of everything that passed. Five uneventful years were passed at Sheffield after Norfolk's death, during which Mary's sole occupation was her needlework. How she must have groaned for liberty over that "nyddyll." Between 1570 and 1584, when on September 3rd she finally left Sheffield Castle, Mary was on three occasions taken for a short visit to Buxton for her health's sake, and twice to Chatsworth; for imprisonment, and the damp, cold air of her jail, had seriously affected her; in 1581 she is described as weak and bed-ridden, with her hair turned grey, and weak in body, though only thirty-eight years old. Mary Stuart having been defeated at Langside on May 13th, took refuge in Cumberland on May 16th, and wrote to her cousin craving her promised good services and shelter; but Elizabeth, congratulating her upon her escape from Loch Leven, proceeded to close the gates of Carlisle upon her at once, and then fearing the proximity of Scotland, caged her far inland at Bolton Castle. From the date of the queen's landing at Workington on May 13, 1568, to her execution on February 8, 1587, is a period of eighteen years eight months and twenty-two days, and the proportions of her time spent in the various jails she occupied are given by Hunter as follows :—

1 part in Cumberland.
2 parts in Coventry, Worksop, and on journeys.
3 parts at Chartley.
4   „   Bolton.
4   „   Wingfield.
4   „   Buxton.
7   „   Chatsworth.
12 „   Tutbury.
63 „   Sheffield.

During the next fifty years little or nothing is recorded of Sheffield Castle; the later lords seem to have preferred the better, purer air at the manor-house,

and so the old castle was deserted by the family, and fell into disrepair. In
the Civil War, however, it was made strong enough to hold a garrison for the
king. The Earl of Newcastle marched thither, and taking possession in Charles'
name, placed there as governor Sir William Savile, who appointed Major
Beaumont his lieutenant-governor. On August 4, 1644, Major-General Crawford
was sent with a force to summon the castle, "having three of their biggest
peices of ordnance" to take it with, if necessary. Within was "a troop of
horse and 200 foot ; it was strongly fortified with a broad and deep trench of
18 foot deep, and water in it ; a strong breastwork pallizadoed, a wall round
of 2 yards thick, 8 peices of ordnance, and 2 morter-peices." Fire was opened
on the castle, but with the small guns of the Parliamentarians little execution
was done, so word was sent to Lord Fairfax for "the Queen's pocket-pistoll
and a whole culverin," which being obtained and brought to bear on the walls,
speedily shot down a portion of the outer wall into the ditch, doing also very
great execution on one side of the castle buildings. Arrangements were at
once made for storming, but, on a summons being again sent in, the garrison
surrendered. The victors found 400 stand of arms, 12 barrels of powder,
and £400 worth of provisions. An order was then sent from London that
the castle should be made untenable, but this was followed by one directing
that it should be slighted and demolished, which was carried out in
1648, when the walls and most of the buildings were pulled down, and
the lead and materials sold. A part, however, of the fabric survived these
operations, but this, for want of repair, also went to ruin, whilst the growth
of the busy town gradually encroached on the Castle Hill, until all vestiges of
the castle disappeared, so that now a few vaults or undercrofts are all that is
left of it.

From the Talbots the Hallamshire lands passed by the marriage of the
seventh earl's daughter to the family of Howard, and by the middle of the
seventeenth century the property had been restored to the Dukes of Norfolk,
in whose possession the lands remain.

SHERIFF-HUTTON (chief)

THIS fine and interesting ruin stands on a hill, in the middle of the village
of the same name, about ten miles from York, S.W. of Malton. The
castle was built temp. Stephen, by Bertram de Bulmer, the Sheriff of Yorkshire
(whence the name is in part derived), and, together with the manor, belonged to
the demesnes of the bishopric of Durham. During the Civil War that ensued
between Stephen and the Empress Maud the castle was seized for the former
by Alan, Earl of Brittany, but being recaptured, was delivered to the Earl of
Chester. Afterwards it was purchased by Bertram, a descendant of the founder,

who gave it in marriage with his only daughter Emma to Geoffry de Nevill, whose descendant, Ralph de Nevill, 1st Earl of Westmorland, repaired and greatly enlarged the structure, and at his death left it to his grandson, Ralph. This first earl deserted Richard II. when the star of Bolingbroke rose, and was one of the first to attach himself to this claimant of the throne on his landing at Ravenspur. It is he who in Shakespeare's play is called by King Henry "my cousin Westmoreland," his second wife Joan being a daughter of John of Gaunt. The next earl bequeathed this and other lands to his son Richard Nevill, who was created Earl of Salisbury, and during the Wars of York and Lancaster, being taken prisoner at the battle of Wakefield, was beheaded at Pontefract, and his immense estates, attainted by the Parliament at Coventry (1460), were seized by the Crown. Of course, in the see-saw of events during these wars, his son Richard, the great Earl of Warwick, shortly after regained the property, including Sheriff-Hutton, but at the King-maker's death on Barnet Field, King Edward IV. laid hold of the lands and castles, and bestowed them on his own brother, Richard, Duke of Gloucester. When Richard of Gloucester became king he imprisoned at Sheriff-Hutton Sir Anthony Woodville, Lord Rivers, and the Princess Elizabeth, his niece, and future Queen of England; he also incarcerated here his young nephew Edward, Earl of Warwick, son of the unfortunate Duke of Clarence, who continued a prisoner until the death of Richard at Bosworth. But the change of dynasty brought small alleviation of his fate to the poor lad, who, having been a captive from his earliest youth, continued so to his death, and thus grew up ignorant of the ordinary affairs of life and in an almost imbecile condition of mind. After the coronation of Henry VII., Sir Richard Willoughby was despatched to Sheriff-Hutton to fetch the Earl of Warwick to London, where he was closely confined in the Tower for another fourteen years, until the conspiracy of Perkin Warbeck furnished the unscrupulous king with a pretext for attainting his wretched victim, who was beheaded on Tower Hill in 1499.

It was from the gateway of this castle that in 1486 Elizabeth, the White Rose of York, set out for London, to be married to Henry VII.—a destiny little to be envied.

There is a licence to crenellate at "Shirefhoton," obtained 5 Richard II. by Sir John Nevill of Raby, whose buildings, together with those of his successor, above mentioned, constitute the principal remains now existing. It is a venerable and striking ruin, with its stately towers and connecting walls; the S.W. tower being 100 feet high, rising from a vaulted basement or dungeon 40 feet long by 20 wide. There are in it two spacious rooms, the uppermost nearly entire, in which, at the end of the last century, might still be seen the remains of a painting on the wall (*Hinderwell*). The castle stood on a high mound and had a square trace, with a large square tower at each of the four angles. The arched gateway of the chief entrance remains on the E. side,

showing still four shields carved on it, and there are remains of outworks on the
W., and some vestiges of the outer wall. The castle is moated in front, but
only partly so on the N., while there is a double moat on the S. 200 yards
in length and full of water; these meet on the W. with the moat coming from
the N. side.

This castle and manor were retained by the Crown until granted to Charles I.
when Prince of Wales, but it was in so ruinous a condition that it was deemed
best to employ workmen to destroy it still further. Then Charles I. bestowed
the castle and honour on Sir Thomas Ingram and his heirs, whence the ruins
came into the possession of Mr. Meynell Ingram of Temple Newsam, whose
widow now owns them.

The great park was sold in the reign of Charles II. to Edward Thompson,
whose descendant possesses the lands still.

SIGSTON (non-existent)

ON the W. side of Cleveland, three miles from Northallerton, was a castle
of early foundation, called Siggeston and Beresend, variously. It was
allied to another neighbouring castle of West Harlsey (q.v.) by marriage between
the families owning these fortified houses.

No vestige of masonry remains above-ground, but the earthworks and
foundations are well defined, and a considerable area was enclosed by a wide
moat, still to be seen.

Hugh Pudsey, Bishop of Durham (1158–1195) granted to his seneschal Philip
Colville certain townships, including Siggeston, and the estate of Winton, on
which the castle stood. Colville's daughter Joan brought part of these estates
in marriage to John Fitz Michael de Ryhill, between 1260 and 1270, and in
1313 their descendant John Fitz Michael de Siggiston held the lands. In
1323 John de Wauxand and Joan his wife granted to Sir John de Siggeston,
knight, certain lands in Winton; he perhaps having married their daughter.
And this is the probable date of the building of this castle, as about that
time "John de Siggeston, miles, habuit castellum de Bertord in Siggiston"
(Dodsworth, xci. 177), and in 1336 licence was granted at Knaresborough to
the same knight to crenellate his manor-house of Beresende. His daughter
Joan married Thomas Ploys, and their granddaughter, an heiress, carried the
property to Sywardby, from whom it came to the Pygots (middle of fifteenth
century). Thomas Pygot left three daughters, coheiresses, between whom a
division of the property was made, but eventually the estate of Winton,
and this castle, came to Elizabeth, daughter of one of these heiresses, whose
daughter brought it to the Latons. From them it passed to the Frewens, in
which family it continues.

The castle perhaps ceased to be lived in after the partition of the property between the Pygot heiresses, and would in that case fall into decay, as did their Chantry Chapel at Sigston Church, where are some memorials of the families. The last mention of " Bereshend Castle " occurs in 1555.

SKELTON, near Saltburn-by-the-Sea (*non-existent*)

AT Domesday most of the lands here belonged to Robert, Earl of Mortain, whose son William, rebelling against Henry I., lost them (see *Trematon* and others, in *Cornwall*), the king bestowing them on Robert de Brus, whose origin is still in doubt, but it is certain that he founded Guisborough Priory in 1120, near this place.   From the Bruces, Skelton descended with Agnes, daughter of Peter de Brus (55 Henry III.), to her husband Walter de Fauconberg, and their family flourished here through many generations, till early in the reign of Henry VI., when Joan, daughter of Sir Thomas Fauconberg, brought the place in marriage to Sir William Nevill, knight, who was created Earl of Kent by Edward IV.   He left three daughters, coheiresses, of whom Alice, the youngest, married Lord Conyers, and had the manor and castle of Skelton, which remained with their descendants till the 4th year of Queen Mary, when, at the death of Lord Conyers, his property was divided between his daughters.   One of these portions was bought by one Robert Trotter, whose descendants succeeded in acquiring all the Conyers' lands here, and in keeping them till 1727, when they were sold to Mr. Joseph Hall, whose representatives still possess the property—the present owner being Mr. John T. Wharton.

Mr. Atkinson (" History of Cleveland," 1874) quotes from an old Cottonian M.S. an early notice of this castle : " On the righte Haude an antyent castle all rente and torne, and yt seemed rather by the wit and wyolence of men, than by the envye of Tyme, shewed itself on the syde of a broken banke." Of what it was like we have no account, but it is said to have been "a beautiful specimen of antiquity," and Graves says that late in John's reign Peter de Brus "delighted soe much in the beauty of the chapelle, that he gave certain landes unto Henry Percye, upon condition that every Christmasse daye he should come to that castell, and leade his wife by the arme from her chamber to the chapell."   The destruction of the old castle was effected in 1788 by the grandson of John Hall, who assumed the name of Wharton, and " pulled down every remnant of Norman antiquity, including a magnificent tower " (*Ord*).   The present house was erected in 1794.

SKIPTON CASTLE

SKIPSEA (*non-existent*)

ABOUT six miles N. of Hornsea, within Bridlington Bay, is this site of an ancient fortress, said to have belonged to Drugo or Drogo de Beurére, the first Norman lord of Holderness, of which no remains exist. It is, however, supposed to have been placed on the immense circular mound which stands in the low marsh on the W. of the village of Skipsea, and has the usual name of Castle Hill. It is the largest hill-fort in this part of England, being 50 feet high, and 30 yards in diameter at the summit; its circumference at the base is 300 yards, and at the foot is a ditch. The marsh is so low as to be flooded occasionally, and accordingly we find a raised causeway connecting it with its outwork, which is an enormous rampart of crescent shape called the Welts, half a mile long, and with an elevation above the marsh of 20 and 25 feet, protected in front by a ditch. Between this and the great tumulus are remains of an inner or second rampart. The whole is probably an ancient British fortification or camp of refuge, which the Normans fortified. There are fragments on the S. side of the mound of a strong concrete wall of defence.

No history otherwise is attached to the place; but on the W. of the mound are four prints of feet on the turf, which are carefully scoured or cleaned yearly at Martinmas, being by tradition the marks made three centuries ago by two heroes who fought together for the possession of a lady, like farmyard cocks, and killed each other.

Leland writes that the Earl of Albemarle and Holderness, Lord of Skipton in Craven, had "a castle and great manor place at Skipsey in Holderness, not far from the shore."

SKIPTON (*chief*)

THE whole of Craven was shared between the two great families of Percy and Clifford, and the head of the latter lordship was Skipton. It formed part of the extensive patrimony of Earl Edwin, at whose death and forfeiture the Conqueror gave these lands to one of his followers, Robert de Romillé, who is said to have built a castle at Skipton towards the end of William's reign. His daughter, Cecilia, brought Skipton and the barony to her husband, William de Meschines, lord of Coupland, and by her granddaughter's marriage (second) with William le Gros, Earl of Albemarle, the lands and honour went for several generations to this family of De Fortibus, till an heiress, Aveline, by marriage with Edmund Plantagenet, called Crouchback, in 1269, carried them to the Crown.

Among other profuse gifts to his unworthy favourite, Edward II. bestowed Skipton on Piers Gaveston, and after his sudden end, the king gave the manor and castle, in 1310, to Robert de Clifford, in whose race and their descendants Skipton has continued ever since, save in one case of attainder.

The Cliffords, who originated at Clifford Castle, Herefordshire (temp. Henry II.), were a fighting family, and, having done good service for Henry III. and his son, received both endowments and, honours. The Robert who obtained Skipton was summoned to Parliament as Baron Clifford in 1299. He was slain at Bannockburn, 25th June 1314. His eldest son, Roger, rebelling in the unquiet reign of Edward II., and being taken at Boroughbridge, was attainted, and his lands were given to the Le Scropes, but soon after were restored to his brother, whose son, fourth lord of Skipton, fought at Crecy (1340). John, the seventh

GATEHOUSE

lord, was killed in France, his wife being the daughter of Harry Hotspur. The eighth lord was a Lancastrian, and was slain at the first battle of St. Albans, and then came his son John, the "butcher" lord of Clifford and Westmorland, who at Wakefield stabbed the young Earl of Rutland, falling himself next day at Ferrybridge (1461). The next was the "Shepherd Lord," Henry, who, for fear of the reigning Yorks, was hidden for twenty-four years among the fells of Cumberland and moors of Yorkshire, living the life of a shepherd, and residing chiefly in Barden. When Bosworth Field had given him safety, he came back to his own, but from habit he preferred Barden Tower and retirement to a life at Skipton, and therefore resided there chiefly. He led the men of Craven at Flodden in 1513 (when he was sixty years of age), and held a command in the centre of the first line or van. His son, the eleventh lord, was a favourite of Henry VIII., and was made by him Earl of Cumberland and K.G., honours which he repaid by holding out at Skipton for the Crown when besieged in Aske's rebellion of 1536, called the Pilgrimage of Grace. His wife, the daughter of the fifth Earl of Northumberland, added to Skipton the Percy lands of Craven. This earl built the great gallery at the castle, in honour of his son's bride, the Duke of Suffolk's daughter, and niece to the king.

The thirteenth lord left a daughter, Anne Clifford, married first to the Earl

Court Yard, Skipton Castle.

of Dorset, and secondly to the Earl of Pembroke. She repaired the then dilapidated castle in 1657, placing over the gate the still existing inscription regarding this her work, which is also seen in other castles of hers (see *Cumberland*, &c.).

Skipton Castle had been besieged from the end of 1642 until December 1645 by the Parliament, being held for the king by Sir John Mallory, who had at last to surrender it; it was then the property of Henry, 5th Earl of Cumberland, in whom that title was extinguished. Skipton, at the death of the Countess Anne in 1675, went by will to her grandson John Tufton, fourth Earl of Thanet, her daughter, Margaret Sackville, having married the third earl, and with their descendant and representative, Sir Henry Jaques Tufton, the property continued till lately.

Skipton Castle stands on high ground at the end of the town, having on its N. front a ravine which it overhangs. If Robert de Romillé ever built a keep here, there is no part of it remaining, and the only Norman work is perhaps the western door of the inner ward. Robert de Clifford, the grantee, must have built the chief part of the castle on the W., the curtain walls, 9 feet thick, and the seven round towers at the angles of the square enceinte and between them. All this, we are told, had been in a ruinous state from the time of the Albemarles. The range of buildings on the E. having a length of 60 yards, and terminated by an octagon tower, was the work of the first Earl of Cumberland for the reception of his daughter-in-law in 1535, and this part not being destroyed after the Civil War, was the residence of Countess Anne, the great restorer of castles.

The great gatehouse, with its twin round turrets, and the open-work motto of the Cliffords, DES OR MAIS, carved in the parapet, is very fine. Below is a dungeon, and perhaps some of the foundations of the earlier work.

SLINGSBY (*minor*)

ABOUT nine miles from Malton, was anciently a stronghold of the Mowbrays, given, as to the manor, among other rich possessions, to Roger de Mowbray by the Conqueror. Camden affirms that the family had a castle here for many generations, "the ruins of which are still visible." It came from the Mowbrays to the family of Wyvell, possibly on the confiscation of the Mowbray estates by Edward II. after the battle of Boroughbridge in 1322. Leland wrote: "Wyvel of the Northe, that was the ancientest of that name, had his principal house at Slingesby yn Yorkshire. And this Wyvelle was a man of fair landes. The House of Slyngesby and the landes of this Wyvelle be devolvid to the Lord Hastinges by heires general."

In 1338 Ralph de Hastings received a licence to crenellate his house at

Slingsby and to impark his woods, and this was probably the origin of the old castle, which has now quite passed away, since in the first year of James I. Sir C. Cavendish began to build a mansion on the foundations and vaults of the old structure, which he must have pulled down completely.

This Jacobean house was never completed. The plan is a rectangle, measur-

SLINGSBY

ing about 40 yards by 30, with a turret at each angle, and the design and the masonry are excellent, the particular features being the large square Tudor windows, now draped in ivy. Slingsby is the property of the Earl of Carlisle.

SNAPE (manor)

THIS castle, lying one mile from Well, though not mentioned in Domesday, is among the earliest subsequent grants to Richard, lord of Middleham. The word is the same as Knepp or Knapp in Sussex, from Cnœp, the brow of a hill.

The castle is supposed to have been built by the Nevills before they took the name of Latimer, or, may be, the work of John, first Lord Latimer. Leland describes it as "a goodly castel, in a valley longing to the Lord Latimer, and two or three parkes welle wodid about it. It is his chiefe howse, and standith about 2 miles from Great Tanfield." Here lived Katherine Parr, afterwards Queen of England, being then the wife of Lord Latimer.

The Nevills gave way to the Cecils about 1587, and they at once converted a mediaeval castle into an abode better suited to the tastes of the age, transforming Snape into a commodious and well-lighted house with a courtyard. The whole is enclosed in a rectangular form, and is partly Perpendicular and partly Elizabethan, the old foundations having been generally preserved. The interior likewise is changed, but the chapel was not altered; and here in the S.E. corner is an entire survival of the old castle, the walls of which are massive and have the old windows.

The Exeter family inherited this beautiful place until the death of Charles Cecil in 1725, after which time it was wholly neglected and greatly fell to ruin, much of it having been rootless since about 1745. At the beginning of the nineteenth century the then Marquess of Exeter sold the castle and the estate; then the deer were killed off and the park was cultivated. The S. side of the court has, however, been kept in repair, and affords a farm-house to the tenant.

A good drawing of Snape is given by Whitaker, but the fine tower on the N. side is now draped in ivy. It is handed down that the great oaken tables in the hall had, by way of trenchers, holes scooped out to receive the food, while a knife and fork were chained on each side of the hollows. Snape is now the property of Sir Frederick A. Milbank, Bart.

SPOFFORTH (minor)

THREE miles from Wetherby, was a seat of the Percy family before they obtained Alnwick, these lands having formed part of the territory conceded to William de Percy. But it was not until 1309 (2 Edward II.) that Henry de Percy received a licence to fortify his house here. In 1407 Henry, the first Earl of Northumberland, was slain at Bramham Moor, within a few miles of his home, in his revolt against Henry IV. Next, when, at the fatal battle of Towton, in 1462, another Earl of Northumberland and his brother, Sir Richard Percy, were killed, these estates were laid waste, and the buildings injured by the Yorkists under Warwick. They lay in ruins for a long time, until the middle of the sixteenth century, when we had Henry, Lord Percy, obtaining a licence to fortify both Spofforth and Leconfield Castles. Finally, Spofforth was dismantled after the Parliamentary War.

The shape of the building, which was never probably a very strong place, was a parallelogram, with a square tower at the N., and an octagonal tower on the N.W., with a circular stair. The former contains a dungeon-like room lighted by loops. The N. front is about 70 feet long, and contains two storeys.

The great hall has been a magnificent room, 75 feet long and 35 broad, built in the fourteenth century, but after destruction it was rebuilt in the fifteenth. The apartment below is of late Norman style, and attached to it are the kitchen, with a vaulted room, and the withdrawing-room, or solar,—all Edwardian.

The place is the property of Lord Leconfield, inherited, like Wressel, from the Seymours in 1750, with the rest of the Percy property in Yorkshire.

This castle never possessed a moat or other outer defences, but its situation was strong, on an elevation over a brook, and the walls were thick, and loopholed below; therefore it seems to have been erected in troubled times, but when more comfort and better accommodation were designed for the inmates.

TANFIELD (minor)

THE church and castle of this name stand on the N. bank of the river Ure, a few miles N.W. of Ripon, in the beautiful scenery of this rapid stream.

Robert Marmion was here early in the thirteenth century, and in 1215 his grandson, John Marmion, who died in 1323, had a licence to castellate and embattle his house in Tanfield Wood, called the Hermitage. His son was John, married to Maud, daughter of Lord Furnival, who perhaps rebuilt the church where sleep so many generations of Marmions in their sculptured tombs. The Marmions were a devout family, and Maud founded here a chantry also. The architecture of both church and castle is Perpendicular of Edward III., and the windows of the steeple and of the castle gatehouse are identical.

The son of these good people, Robert, the last Marmion, died s.p., and Tanfield went to their daughter Avice, who married Sir John Grey of Rotherfield (died 1359), the children of the marriage taking the mother's name. These Grey-Marmions ended, in the second generation, in a daughter, Elizabeth, who brought the property to her husband, Sir Henry Fitzhugh (died 1424), and the Fitzhughs lasted here till 1513, when, in default of male heirs, Tanfield came to the Parrs by the marriage of Sir William Parr with Elizabeth, sister of the last Fitzhugh, their son, Sir Thomas, being the father of William Parr, Marquess of Northampton, who was attainted, and of Queen Katherine Parr.

After the attainder of the Marquess, Tanfield fell to the Crown, and was granted to the great Lord Burleigh, from whose family it seems to have come to Lord Bruce (temp. James I.), ancestor of the Earls of Aylesbury, with whom it remains.

Leland wrote: "The castelle of Tanfield, or rather, as it is now, a meane manor place, stondeth hard on a ripe of We [Ure], wher I saw no notable building, but a faire toured gatehouse, and a hall of squarid stone." This was in the time of the Parrs, who lived elsewhere.

It was a place of no great extent, and its outline can barely be traced, little of the building remaining now except the gatehouse, which is entire, and is Perpendicular with an oriel window, and shrouded in ivy. Grose informs us that: "Tradition says, when Tanfield Castle was destroyed, the materials were purchased by several of the neighbouring gentry, and the Earl of Exeter's house at Snape, and the seat of the Wandisfords, at Kirklington, were built with them."

THIRSK (*non-existent*)

THIS was one of the fortresses belonging to Roger de Mowbray, as did Kirkby-Malzeard, which, on the suppression of his revolt against Henry II. in 1173, was destroyed by that king. It is supposed to have been a large building, but nothing whatever is to be seen of it now, except the moats, which may still be traced. The materials of it are said to have been taken for the erection of Thirsk Church.

The powerful house of Mowbray possessed four seats, castles attached to their different baronies in this part of Yorkshire—the first at Thirsk, which dominated the Vale of Mowbray, still so called; the second at Kirkby-Malessart or Malzeard, in Craven; the third, controlling the country from the N.W. of Craven to Westmorland; and the fourth was the Isle of Axeholme, with Eppleworth, or Epworth, Castle.

TICKHILL (*chief*)

THIS is the most southern of the Yorkshire fortresses, being seven miles S. of Doncaster, in the West Riding. The manor was held after the Conquest by Roger de Busli, who either erected or rebuilt this castle, and at his death in 1098 the Red King gave it to Robert de Belême, who claimed it as being a kinsman of the founder. After his submission Henry I. took possession of the castle, for it was of importance, standing in the narrow part of the level country between the hills of Derbyshire and Trent, upon the high road to the north, and near the Roman way from Lincoln to York; a position which had been seized on in very early times, and fortified by a mound piled upon a scarped rock. Stephen granted the place to the

Count d'En of Normandy, who also had Hastings, and Ralph, Earl of Chester, held it for him 1151-1153. Then it reverted to the Crown, and Queen Eleanor of Acquitaine, wife of Henry II., held it in dower. John fortified and held this castle against his brother Cœur de Lion, but on King Richard's sudden return from captivity it was given up, and its defenders were hanged by Roger de Leir, the king's custodian. John when king came here six times, although there was no park or chase belonging to the manor. His son

Henry III. restored it to the Count d'En, but Tickhill afterwards returned to the Crown and was settled upon Prince Edward, and in 1254 it formed part of the dower of Eleanor of Castile, his wife. In 1263 Edward granted the place to his cousin Henry, son of Richard, King of the Romans. In 1322 the castle was besieged for three weeks by Thomas, Earl of Lancaster, against Piers Gaveston, and was gallantly defended till relieved by the king in person. Edward III. settled it on his queen, and at her death it was given by Richard II. to his uncle John of Gaunt, who rebuilt or added to it, and it remained an appanage of the duchy thereafter.

At the commencement of the Civil War in the seventeenth century Tickhill was considered a very strong fortress, and it received a garrison for King Charles of eighty men and thirty horses.

TICKHILL.

It sustained a siege in 1646, and after two days was surrendered to a force under Colonel Lilburn, when by order of the Parliament it was slighted and rendered untenable.

Mr. Clark affirms that Tickhill is a fine example of a pre-Norman or English earthwork, consisting of a mound, fosse, and lower ward, converted into a Norman fortress, and demonstrates how such existing forts were treated in the erection of either the square or the shell keep thereon. Here the mound has been placed on the top of a sandstone rock which was scarped around, the material, with the excavations from the ditch around it, being thrown up. This mound is 60 feet in diameter, and is 60 feet above the level of the lands. The keep was ten-sided, and was entered from a flight of seventy-five steps on the W. face; its foundations are visible, and the ditch, with part of the outer walls, is in a tolerably perfect state. The original Early Norman gatehouse remains in a dilapidated state at the S. of the lower ward, between the keep and the castle buildings; it has a round-headed gateway, and in front were added a Decorated gateway with pointed arch and portcullis groove, and four gates in the passage, also walls supporting the drawbridge. The rampart was carried across this gateway in front. The hall and the chapel mentioned by Leland exist no more. The outer ditch, partly a moat, is broad and deep, and was supplied by a stream, the Thorne, which covers the S. front. Outside of all was a bank of earth. The N. part has been converted into a modern residence, and the grounds have been formed into gardens and shrubberies. The area of the whole is about seven acres. Tickhill is now the property of the Earl of Scarborough.

TOPCLIFFE (*non-existent*)

ON the banks of the Swale, N.W. of Ripon, is known to have stood one of the strongholds and residences of the Percy family, who received the manor among their other lands from the Conqueror. The position of the place had been marked in earlier times as a desirable one to hold, as we see from the mound, now called Maiden Bower, about a mile S. from Topcliffe village, where the Danish or Saxon lords had their burh, and which now, thick with fir trees, alone marks the site of the Percys' castle.

Topcliffe enters on more than one occasion into the fatalities which befell the Percy family. It was at Topcliffe that Henry, the fourth earl, was murdered by a mob in 1489, and it was at this castle that the insurrection in Elizabeth's reign, to restore the ancient forms of religion, and called the Rising of the North, was planned, the first meetings of the conspirators being held here. It is said that it was here that, when the Rising had been precipitated by the action of the queen's officers, the Earl of Northumberland was aroused from bed, and caused to ride in haste to Brancepeth to concert with the Earl of Westmorland on the immediate necessity of taking arms (see *Brancepeth* and *Barnard Castle, Durham*).

King Charles I. was a prisoner in the castle of Topcliffe, while the treaty was in progress by the Scots Commissioners for his sale to the Parliamentary authorities. This alone should have caused the preservation of the remains.

UPSALL (*minor*)

THE word seems to be of Scandinavian origin, since Upsala in Sweden is
the name of one of the most important sacrificial places in the North.
At Domesday the lands belonged to Earl Mortain, and next they are found
in the hands of the Mowbrays; then in 1277 one Hugh de Upsall was here,
taking his name from the place, and from this family Upsall must have been
purchased by the successful lawyer Geoffry de Scrope. This founder of the
Scropes of Masham is said to have been a younger son of Scrope of Bolton,
or, at all events, of the family, who, rising under the patronage of the Nevills,
first appears in Coverdale, 5 Edward II. Six years later, adding to his
possessions through extensive practice of the law in Lincolnshire, Kent, and
Northumberland, he grew in wealth, and being in favour with Edward II.,
was by him, in his seventeenth year, made Chief Justice of King's Bench, and
he soon after, on the attainder of Roger de Clifford, received a grant of the
castle and honour of Skipton. As early as 1309 he had a charter of free
warren for his lands (including Upsall), and is said to have obtained a licence
to fortify this manor-house of Upsall, but it does not appear in the Patent
Rolls, and we therefore are not certain of the date or founder of this castle.
Geoffry died, a knight banneret, in 13 Edward III.

His son Henry l'Escrope was a military man, and died 15 Richard II., seised
of Upsall and Clifton. He was succeeded by his son Stephen, who as a soldier
served in his father's train, and in the first year of Richard II. was summoned
to Parliament, in the lifetime of his father, as first Lord Scrope of Masham.
He died 7 Henry IV., leaving issue, his son Sir Henry l'Escrope, 2nd Lord
Scrope, who obtained a grant of Thirsk and Hovingham from Henry IV.,—
a valuable gift to the Lord of Upsall, whose castle overlooked the Vale of
Mowbray.

The third lord was married to Joan, Duchess of York, the sister of Holland,
Earl of Kent; he was made Treasurer of the Exchequer, but joining in the
conspiracy of Richard, Earl of Cambridge, cousin to Henry V., to place on
the throne young Mortimer, brother-in-law to Cambridge, he, together with
the earl and Sir Thomas Grey, lost his head at Southampton (1415), when
his estates were forfeited. His brother, Sir John Scrope, recovered part of
the lands, and signs himself of Masham and Upsall. Whitaker is of opinion
that at this date no castle existed here. Leland has (vol. viii. fol. 56a): "Dominus
Johannes de Scrope de Upsaule obiit 1455." He left a son, Thomas, who,
dying 38 Henry VI., was followed by his son, another Lord Thomas, and other
issue of three sons and three daughters. All the sons died *s.p.*, and their sisters
inherited the property on the death of Thomas, the last lord of Masham, in
1515. In 1520 a division of the estates took place, when Elizabeth, the third

daughter of Lord Thomas, obtained Upsall, and brought it in marriage to Sir Ralph Fitz Randolph, knight, of Spennithorn, by whom she had one son, who died in his father's lifetime, and five daughters, to one of whom, Agnes, Lady Randolph devised Upsall. She was mother to Sir Marmaduke Wyvill, whose son Christopher succeeded to this property. But in the Northern troubles of 1569 this Christopher Wyvill must have fallen a victim, since we find Upsall in the hands of the Crown, and in 1577 Elizabeth granted it to one John Farnham.

Next, early in the reign of James I., Upsall is owned by Joseph Constable of Burton Constable, in Holderness, and it was retained by this family for nearly 200 years, until 1768, when Dr. William Constable, an eminent physician at the court of George III., dying *s.p.*, bequeathed Upsall to Edmund, third son of the Rev. W. Peters, chaplain to the King; Mr. Peters assumed the name of Turton, and his son, Edmund H. Turton, is the present owner.

The old castle was a quadrangular building, measuring about 64 yards by 58 yards, with a courtyard in the centre, and turrets at each angle. The towers at the N.E. and S.W. have been square—as can be made out from their foundations the most perfect fragment being the N.W. tower, which was octagonal, and contained the chief rooms. A piece of the N. wall remains, about 15 feet high, having an arched gateway, which admitted into the outer ward. The site of the N.E. tower and of the interior buildings is occupied by a farm-house, built from the ruins, which have long been used as a quarry. The largest tower, that on the S.W., had a bold projection from the walls. There was a large park of 600 acres attached to Upsall, which was disparked in 1599.

WHORLTON (minor)

A PLACE romantically situated on the E. side of Cleveland, in the North Riding, beneath a lofty range of hills; from one of which, cone-peaked, called Whorl-hill, it obtains its name. Leland wrote: "Whorlton in Cliveland was the principal house of the Lord Meinell, which came since to Master Strangwayes in particion." It was called "old and ruinous" by Camden.

The castle is supposed to have been built by one of the Meinell or Meynell family, who, deriving from a Norman, Robert de Maisnell, had lands in these parts temp. Henry I. Sir Nicholas de Meinell was summoned to Parliament 22 Edward I. According to an inquisition taken 30 Edward III. (1346), on the death of John, Lord Darcy, it was found that the manor and castle of Whorlton, which came to him by marriage with Elizabeth, heiress of Nicholas de Meinell, had been granted in trust to Sir Thomas Swinford, knight; therefore this castle must have an earlier origin than that usually given it, of

Richard II.'s reign. The Dareys continued here till the last lord, Philip, died in 1419, leaving an only daughter, Elizabeth, who brought Whorlton in marriage to Sir James Strangwayes of Harlsey Castle, whose descendants possessed both estates until the last Sir James Strangwayes died in 1541, when in some way not shown Whorlton fell to the Crown, and was given to Matthew, Earl of Lennox. Early in the reign of Charles I. the manor was granted to Edward Bruce, 2nd Lord Bruce, whose brother became the first Earl of Elgin, and it was held by that family until quite lately, when it was purchased by Mr. James Emerson of Easby Hall, Yorks.

The trace of this castle was circular, enclosing an area of about 2 acres, and surrounding the whole was a ditch with drawbridge. But little remains now of all the structure except the gatehouse, which is nearly perfect. The gateway is in a low-pointed arch, whence a once vaulted passage, defended by a double portcullis, leads into the courtyard ; on each side of the entrance are rooms, and a staircase to the guardroom over. There is a second storey above this. Over the gateway are three shields charged with the arms of Meinell, Darcy, and Grey, while another one above has those of Darcy impaling Meinell. The foundations only exist of the kitchens and the lodgings, and there are some huge vaults underground. The remains of ancient earthworks are to be seen also in the vicinity.

There is a tradition that in one of the rooms in this castle was signed the contract betrothing Mary Stuart to Henry, Lord Darnley ; and this is possible, since Whorlton Castle was granted by Henry VIII. to his niece, Margaret, the wife of the Earl of Lennox, and the mother of Darnley.

WILTON (*non-existent*)

ON the northern confines of Cleveland, not far from Redcar, is the modern castle which occupies the site of the Bulmers' ancient abode. The Bulmers were a family who had large possessions in this county and in Durham in very early times ; as to when they became seated at Wilton we have no clue. Emma, the daughter of Bertram Bulmer, married Geoffrey Nevill of Raby, and brought to that family both Brancepeth and Sheriff-Hutton in Yorkshire. John Bulmer was Lord of Wilton 53 Henry III. In 4 Edward II. Ralph de Bulmer obtained a charter of his lands here, and in 1 Edward III. received a summons to Parliament amongst the barons. Three years after he had a licence to fortify his manor-house of Wilton, being at the time Governor of York, and we may therefore take this date of 1330 as that of the late castle.

The lands and castle continued in the hands of the Bulmers for a long series of generations, until Sir John Bulmer in 28 Henry VIII. was attainted for his participation in the rebellion called the Pilgrimage of Grace, and was hanged at

Tyburn, while Lady Bulmer, his unfortunate wife, was, under the infamous law regarding treason in females, drawn on a hurdle from Newgate to Smithfield, and there burnt to death (1537). Generally, after the punishments that followed on this attempt to vindicate the ancient faith of the country, the property of the sufferers was not forfeited, but the lands of the Bulmers were confiscated by the Crown, and were in the reign of Queen Mary granted to Sir Thomas Cornwallis, whose descendant, Lord Cornwallis, sold the estate to Lord Holland (Fox), from whom it was purchased by the Lowther family, and it is now the seat of Sir Charles Lowther, Bart.

Until some time after the beginning of this century there existed a tower of the old castle, and some other buildings, but being very ruinous they were removed, and a new mansion was built upon the site by the Lowthers.

WRESSEL (minor)

THIS fine castle of the Percys is in the flat country S.E. of York, on a site slightly elevated above the bank of the river Derwent, the navigation of which it was evidently intended to command at a short distance from its junction with the Ouse. It was of the usual quadrangular type, of four towers connected by curtains—two of these towers, which are very large, surviving, together with the S. curtain. The moat encompasses three sides, the fourth, wherein is the entrance, being dry. The front contains a basement, and on the first floor is the hall, with the chapel on one side, and the state lodgings on the other. There was a gatehouse once, where the causeway enters, and it was doubtless a strong fortress; but the towers gave no flanking fire, and the main protection was in the broad and deep moat, defended by a high and strong wall. Beyond this there was the power of the Percy name.

Wressel is said to have been founded by Sir Thomas Percy, the brother of the first Earl of Northumberland, who is introduced by Shakespeare in the first part of *Henry IV.* as plotting with Hotspur, his nephew, the overthrow of the unpopular king. He had been made Earl of Worcester and Lord High Admiral of England by Richard II., and joined his nephew in the insurrection that was quelled by the battle of Shrewsbury (1403). Worcester was taken prisoner, and beheaded two days after at the High Cross in Shrewsbury. Since the manor is named in an inquisition of 9 Edward II. as a lordship of William de Percy, it probably came to Worcester by inheritance, and not as Leland says by purchase. Wressel falling to the Crown on his attainder, Henry IV., after keeping it for some time, gave the place to his son John, Duke of Bedford, who died possessed of it 12 Henry VI. (1434), leaving Wressel to the king, who in his thirty-sixth year (1457) granted it to Sir Thomas Percy, son of Henry, 2nd Earl of Northumberland. During the vicissitudes of the Wars of the Roses it seems that this place was at one time held by Nevill, Lord Montague (brother of the King-maker, Warwick), together with all other estates of the Percys, but in 1460 King Edward revoked the grants, and restored Henry, the fourth earl, to the Percy property. The Earls of Northumberland frequently inhabited this castle, and kept up their state therein with royal magnificence, with a household established on the same plan as that of a royal court ; and in September 1541 Henry VIII. was entertained at Wressel for several days, on his excursion into the North ; but at that date the owner was under a cloud, and was not present to receive his sovereign.

At the death of Joceline, the eleventh earl, the barony of Percy went with his daughter and heir, Lady Elizabeth Percy, in 1682 to her husband Charles Seymour, Duke of Somerset. But only the wreck of Wressel was then left. In 1642 it had been garrisoned by the Parliament, when much injury was done to the place, and again in 1648 this was repeated ; but in the latter year the capture of Pontefract Castle by the king determined the London Council to take measures to prevent any similar surprises elsewhere, and sudden orders were sent to the York Committee on April 17 to make Wressel untenable, by throwing down three sides of the quadrangle, and leaving the S. front only, in which face large windows were to be broken out. All this was to be done in four weeks, and without any reference to the owner. In pursuance of this order three sides of the great castle were entirely demolished, but the work was only begun in December 1648, and the destruction was not completed till May 1650.

The Seymours continued lords of Wressel until 1750, when the Duke of Somerset dying *s.p.* male, his estates were divided among the heirs ; those which had come by Lady Elizabeth Percy went with his daughter to her husband, Sir Hugh Smithson, who became Earl of Northumberland, and the rest of the Percy lands in Yorkshire were inherited by his nephew, Sir Charles Wyndham, now represented by Lord Leconfield.

Leland, visiting Wressel about 1538, saw it in its untouched state, and describes it at unusual length. Modernising his spelling, the account runs thus : "Most part of the base court of the castle is all of timber. The castle itself is moated about on three parts, the fourth part is dry where the entry is into the castle. The castle is all of very fair and great squared stone, both within and without, whereof (as some hold opinion) much was brought out of France. In the castle be only 5 Towers, one at each corner, almost of like bigness. The gatehouse is the 5th, having 5 lodgings [storeys] in height, 3 of the other Towers have 4 [storeys]. The 4th containeth the buttery, pantry, pastry, larder, and kitchen.

"The Hall and the great chambers be fair, and so is the chapel and the closets. To conclude, the house is one of the most proper beyond Trent, and seemeth as newly made. . . . The base court is of a newer building, and the last Earl of Northumberland saving one made the brewhouse of stone without the castle walls, but hard joining to the kitchen of it. One thing I liked exceedingly in one of the towers, that was a study called Paradise, where was a closet in the middle of 8 squares latticed about: and on the top of every square was a desk lodged to set books on." . . . "There is a park hard by the castle." He speaks also of the gardens and the orchards.

The remaining S. side is a fine object, with its large, square towers; each of these had a circular newel stair to the roof, ending in an octagonal turret; the turret on the S.W. having borne at top a fire-beacon. The W. tower contained a dining-room ornamented with carved wood, and the chapel was in that on the E.; as the Roundheads ruined the parish church, this chapel was long used in its place. Above the chapel was the library. The S. front contained the state drawing-room and an ante-chamber, with two curious staircases in octagonal cases or screens, the flights of stairs winding round each other, as some are seen in France. These rooms must have been magnificent, having a carved frieze running round the walls, and the windows filled with painted glass, chiefly heraldic. This part was used as a farm-house till the year 1796, when a fire destroyed everything except the walls, which seem imperishable.

Parker calls Wressel a fine specimen of the castellated mansions of the period of Richard II., of early Perpendicular character.

YORK (minor)

SINCE York was in the earliest times the chief town of the land, when London was only a mart for traders, a high antiquity must attach to the great burh or mound upon which subsequently was erected the keep of a Norman castle, and which still bears the curious structure called Clifford's Tower.

The river Ouse flows past what was the W. side of the town, and at the southern point of this it receives the waters of a strong stream called the Foss, coming down from Cleveland. Here, in the very usual manner, on the intervening tongue of land, sheltered thus on both sides, some early settlers had fixed their camp, and at some time or other, two huge mounds of earth, formed by the *déblai* of surrounding moats, were thrown up, one on the fork of land, and the other on the opposite side of the Ouse, between them commanding that river. These mounds would receive the usual Saxon fortification of water ditches defended by wooden stockades, with a dwelling and barracks of timber on the summit of each.

And thus probably they remained on the occasion of the Conqueror's first visit to York in the summer of 1068, when "as usual he ordered a castle

to be built, and equally as usual the place selected was the mound of the
existing stronghold" (*Clark*). The position between the rivers was hurriedly
strengthened, and occupied with a garrison of 500 selected men under Sir
William Malet. Next year, however, the citizens revolted and besieged Malet
in his fortalice, which was strong enough to hold out until the king came to
his assistance and relieved the garrison. A second fort was then ordered to be
built upon the other mound, across Ouse, now called the Bail Hill; and as
this was done in eight days, its construction must have been also of wood.
Next year came an expedition of Danes up the Humber, to their old hunting
grounds, when they were met as friends by the Saxons, and an alliance was
formed to make common cause against the usurping Normans and to thrust
them out. An attack on the castle ensued, and the garrison sallying out were
cut off and overcome, some 3000 being said to have fallen, and the forts taken
and destroyed. When these tidings were brought to William, who was hunting
in the Forest of Dean, he swore "by the splendour of God" that he would
avenge his men, and collecting his forces came northward to Pontefract,
where he bought off the Danes, and then to York, which the enemy, now
scared, had evacuated. Then began the cruel and fiendish harrying of the
North, in which the Norman king destroyed the life of the country, and made
of the land between York and Durham a burnt and desolated desert: the
crowning infamy of his violent life.

The York castles were of course at once renewed, but, in all likelihood, with
such materials as were at hand. It is not probable that, in such pressing
times, architects and masons and workmen could have been procured from
Normandy to build what we call Norman keeps, but they had to content
themselves with lines of palisades along the crest of earthworks, and deep
ditches, with perhaps gatehouses alone of masonry (*Clark*). The more serious
constructions could only have come later, when time had been given for their
preparation. There is but little of Norman work in York, and that is of a later
style. The wall "upon the Foss may, in parts, be early twelfth century, but
the round mural towers cannot be earlier than the reign of Henry III." Little
is known about the different portions of the main fortress, or its builder.
In its best days it must have been a very strong place, encircled by the waters
of the Foss and only approachable by two drawbridges. The approach was on
the E. side, near the castle mills, and there was a gatehouse on the side of the
town, which was rebuilt many years ago, having a drawbridge. The works on
the E. have been entirely swept away, but until the end of the last century the
sallyport and some towers remained, and the moat connected with the fosse,
which latter defence was then filled in.

The chief object of interest now is the great building which clusters on the
Castle Mound, called Clifford's Tower, from the name of its custodian. This is
of singular form, being built as a quatrefoil, or four circular bastions conjoined,

measuring 60 feet and 80 feet in its diameters, with walls 3 yards thick and 40 feet high. Outside, above the first stage, are three circular turrets corbelled out, with a square one in the fourth angle, which latter contains an oratory. The ground floor is defended by loops, and commanded the moat surrounding this tower, and the only entrance from the inner ward was by a drawbridge. Mr. Clark is of opinion that this tower may be of the reign of Richard I. or John.

It could scarcely, however, have been built at the date of the terrible massacre of the Jews which took place in the castle in the reign of Richard (1190); when 500 Jews with their families and goods took refuge in the castle from the fury of the people of York, who had risen against them and their usury.

THE WALLS OF YORK

They managed to get the castellan out of the fortress and shut themselves in, being then besieged by an armed crowd. Soon they were in a starving condition, and in despair a large number of them killed themselves, after slaughtering their wives and children, and having set fire to the tower. When the citizens got in all the surviving Jews were put to the sword.

Clifford's Tower, together with other quarters, was strengthened at the outbreak of the Civil War of the seventeenth century, and carried three guns on the top. Sir Thomas Cobb was governor during the siege of York in 1644, and after the surrender to the Parliament chiefs the castle was dismantled. In 1684 a fire, supposed to be the work of an incendiary, broke out in Clifford's Tower and consumed all within it, greatly injuring the structure. The castle was bought, about 1825, for the formation of a county gaol, and though the main fortress has much disappeared, the keep tower was reserved intact.

SISERGH

Westmorland

APPLEBY (*chief*)

APPLEBY is built on the crest of the hill along the slope of which
stands the county town of Westmorland. It is believed to have
been founded by Randolph de Meschines while in possession of
the earldom of Caerleolium (see *Carlisle*), since from his charter of
1088 he evidently had a castle here. Whitaker ascribes to him the castles of
Appleby, Brough, Brougham, and Pendragon, which must have consisted of the
usual Norman square keep towers only, with their three storeys of chambers.

Appleby had changed ownership three times by heiresses before it came to
Simon de Morville; then from Robert de Veteripont it passed, like Brougham
(*q.v.*), to the Cliffords, by Isabella his daughter. It was much exposed to the
inroads of the Scots, and in the time of Richard II. and Henry IV. great injuries
were done to the fabric. In or before 1454 (temp. Henry VI.), Thomas, Lord
Clifford, built the greater part of what we now recognise as the older portion.

The chief feature still remaining is the great keep, 80 feet in height, and
called, as are many other similar towers, by the inappropriate name of Cæsar's
Tower. The gatehouse is supposed to have been built by John, Lord Clifford,
in 1418, as his arms and those of his wife are upon its walls, and it was his
son Lord Thomas (who fell at St. Albans in 1455) who erected the eastern
portions, that is, the hall, the chapel, and the great chamber. The castle is
said to have been ruined during the insurrection of the Earls of Northumberland and Westmorland in 1569, and it remained in this state and uncovered

APPLEBY CASTLE

for nearly 100 years, until in 1651 Anne, Countess of Pembroke, the famous castle-builder who defied the orders of the Protector himself—repaired and restored the castle, when, as one of many Clifford strongholds belonging to that lady (see *Brough* and others), she made it her residence. She had in 1641 garrisoned Appleby for King Charles, and committed the charge of it to Sir Philip Musgrave; but in 1648 he was forced to surrender the fortress to the Parliament forces, who took prisoner there 121 officers and 1200 horse.

The keep is an interesting structure; it has newel staircases in the S.E. and S.W. corners leading to the several floors, and in the other angles are similar ones to the roof only; there are also mural passages and small chambers with stone seats. About the middle of the wall on the E., towards the river, is the sallyport, which has portcullis grooves. Outside the walls are seen the outer and inner moats, defending all sides of the fortress except the face towards the river. It is the property and the residence of Lord Hothfield.

ARNSIDE TOWER (*minor*)

ARNSIDE TOWER stands in a very exposed situation on the border of Morecambe Bay. It is a fine peel tower of the fifteenth century, which belonged in former times to the Harrington family, and afterwards to the Stanleys, lords Mounteagle; perhaps it may have served as a resting-place for them in breaking their journey from the south to the Isle of Man. It was once a Border stronghold of some importance, and was formerly given to Lancashire, but now under the Parliamentary census is included in Westmorland. It is a quadrangular building,

ARNSIDE TOWER

with walls of amazing thickness, having projecting square turrets, on one of which the battlements and machicoulis remain. The windows are small and square-headed. The interior is a mere shell, with the remains of a narrow staircase; the best defined part is the kitchen, which has a large chimney-corner with seats for the cook and turnspit, and there is an oven, above which are bed-closets cleverly contrived to be warmed by the oven. In the Parish Register is an entry of November 1602, with these words : " M^d that y^t 16 day of October, att nyght, being a myghtie wynde, was Arnchead Tower burned, as it pleased ye Lord to p'mitte."

BROUGH (chief)

THE castle of Brough is in the N.E. part of the county, and occupies a commanding position on a height above the W. bank of the river Eden. The remains consist of the magnificent square keep, with its corner towers of the usual Norman type, similar to those of Rochester, Dover, and the Tower of London ; the walls are of immense strength, and the masonry is admirable ; there are also remains of the castle habitations. It possibly occupies the site of a Roman fort, which may account for the name of "Cæsar's Tower" given to the keep. Camden suggests that it was built before the time of an English conspiracy that was raised against the Conqueror. William the Lion, King of Scotland, invading England in 1174 at the head of an army of Flemings, captured this castle. An inscription plate, formerly placed over the principal gateway, but now removed, declares that the castle was put into proper repair in 1659 by Anne Clifford, Dowager-Countess of Pembroke, and that she had since inhabited it in 1661. It had been burnt in 1521, soon after Henry, Lord Clifford, known as the "Shepherd Lord," had held high Christmas festivity under its roof two years before his death, and had lain ruinous ever since. This Anne was daughter of George Clifford, Earl of Cumberland ; she married, first, Lord Buckhurst, afterwards Earl of Dorset, and secondly, Philip, Earl of Pembroke and Montgomery, and inherited the vast property of the Clifford family, which had been derived from the grants by King John to Robert de Veteripont, and his successors, Barons of Westmorland. She spent the end of her life in the North, repairing her castles, especially those injured by the Parliamentary forces, and her memory was long cherished in the Northern counties. Her death occurred in 1676, when her property was inherited by her daughter and sole heiress, who married the Earl of Thanet, and the Clifford estates passed to the Tufton family (see the castles of *Brougham, Appleby, Pendragon, Barden* (Yorks), and others).

The Tower of Brough, once an important Border fortress, was demolished to the bare walls by Thomas, Earl of Thanet, about 1695, when he was repairing Appleby Castle. Nicolson in 1777 says the ruins then presented "a scene of venerable magnificence."

BROUGHAM (chief)

THIS large, strong, and magnificent edifice—now in utter ruin—stands at the confluence of the Lowther with the river Eamont, about 1½ miles from Penrith, having been in its day one of the most important of the Border fortresses. The entrance to it is along a series of arches by the river-side. One part of the ruin consists of three square towers, with the remains of their connecting wall stretching for a considerable distance towards the S.W., and terminating in a tower.

In the centre of the main group rises the keep, "a lofty square tower, frowning in Gothic strength and gloomy pomp." The turrets on its summit have disappeared, together with the parapet and galleries. The lowest storey has a vaulted stone roof with eight arches, supported by one centre shaft. It is of Norman origin, but the date of its building is uncertain. On the S. are traces of the Roman camp which stood here on the road from

BROUGHAM

York to Carlisle. The Conqueror William granted it and the manor to his nephew, Hugh d'Albini, in whose family, and that of the Meschines, it remained until 1170, when it passed to the De Morvilles, but being forfeited under them to the Crown, King John gave it to a Norman knight of high repute and power, Robert de Veteripont (or Vipont), Baron of Westmorland, together with other lands of great extent in that county. His son and grandson held these possessions in the reign of Henry III., when Robert de Veteripont fought on the side of Simon de Montfort, and died of his wounds after either the battle of Lewes or that of Evesham, the estates being forfeited to the king, but they were soon after restored to the two infant daughters of Earl Robert. These two heiresses, Isabella and Idonea (or Ivetta), being committed by the king to the care of two knights, Roger de Clifford, of Hereford, and Roger de Leybourne, of Kent, were in time married by these guardians to their own eldest sons, when a division of the Veteripont property was made between them; the elder daughter, Isabella, who had married young De Clifford, holding Brougham as a residence. When, however, her sister died without issue, Isabella de Clifford succeeded to the entire estate, and in the possession of her descendants, the Earls of Clifford, it continued for about four centuries.

The castle was rebuilt and added to by the first Roger de Clifford, who indeed reared the greater part of the fortress, and he caused an inscription to be placed over the inner door, with the words "Thys made Roger." He died in the reign of Edward I. Standing as it did on the old Roman "Maiden-way" on the borders of Cumberland, it was subjected to much ill-treatment, being attacked in some of the inroads made by the Scots in Henry IV.'s reign, about 1412, and nearly destroyed. In 1617 James I. was here on a hunting expedition, and was entertained with masquerades. In 1652, the old Countess of Pembroke, Anne, who inherited the vast estates of the Clifford family, thoroughly repaired Brougham Castle and made it one of her principal residences; but after her death it was allowed to go to ruin. In 1691 her grandson, Lord Thomas Tufton, pulled down a great portion of the castle, and in 1708 it was further demolished, and some of the materials were sold.

On the N. of the Norman keep are two distinct gateway towers, connected, and abutting on the keep. On the opposite side of the river is the old castle mill, and this, viewed together with the castle and the river, forms a highly

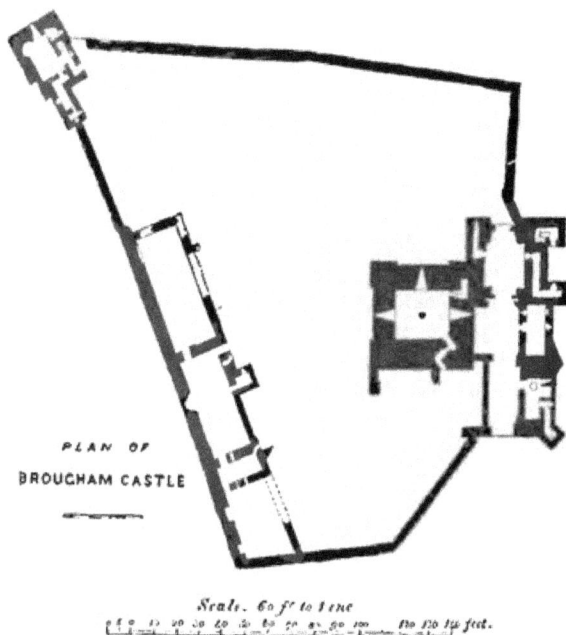

PLAN OF
BROUGHAM CASTLE

Scale. 60 ft to 1 ine

picturesque scene. Licence to crenellate his house was granted (1 Edward II.) to Ricardus de Brun of Dunmaloch (a neighbouring hill), but this refers probably to Brougham Hall, since the castle at that period belonged to the Clifford family. The ruin is owned by Lord Brougham and Vaux.

BROUGHAM HALL (minor)

BROUGHAM HALL is situated about half a mile from the castle, on the brow of a hill, and commands one of the finest views in England. It has been generally rebuilt, but still retains some very ancient portions of the fourteenth and even of the twelfth centuries. The entrance gate is temp. Edward I. The manor, apart from Brougham Castle, is shown to have been in the possession of Gilbert de Broham in the second of King John, and it is still the property of his descendants, having been repurchased in 1727 by the grandfather of Lord Chancellor Brougham. A portion of the estate is held by the curious Border tenure of "cornage," which service has been said to consist in blowing a horn to give notice of the arrival of maranding Scots, or others, in the vicinity. This was a signal for lighting up Penrith beacon, and for communicating by similar signals with Appleby, and so into Yorkshire on one side, and into Lancashire on the other, whereby all the barons of the Marches were put on the alert. The original horn by which this service was performed is still preserved at Brougham Hall, the residence of Lord Brougham and Vaux.

BULEY (non-existent)

BULEY was an ancient residence of the Bishops of Carlisle, on the S. side of the Eden, opposite to Crackenthorpe. Nicolson in 1777 describes it as a mean and ruinous building, and even this has now perished. It was probably built by a John de Bailly, whose daughter Idonea married a Norman knight, Robert de Veteripont, a noble of high repute in the reign of John, to whom that king granted the lands and castles of Appleby and Brough in Westmorland, and other large possessions (see *Brougham*).

BYTHAM or BETHAM HALL (minor)

ON the river Byth, there was anciently a large handsome building, called a castle by Leland, and described by Gough (1762) as then in ruins. The manor was held, temp. 17 King John, by the heir of Thomas de Betham, and in 20 Edward III. Ralph de Betham is directed to send prisoners from his castle to the Tower of London. In 3 Henry VI. Thomas de Betham is the represen-

tative in Parliament of Westmorland, and he is the last found of the name
The tradition is that after Bosworth the manor was forfeited and given to the
Stanleys, but from the absence of records, it was more probably purchased
by that family.

Ascending from the Byth you come to the gateway and grand entrance
into the castle-yard, which measures 70 yards by 44, and has a wall of the
enceinte, with the marks of soldiers' barracks along the side. On the left
is the loopholed castle with a hall of the fourteenth century, now used as
a barn. The windows are small, and are raised high from the ground for
purposes of defence. The greater portion is of the fifteenth and sixteenth
centuries. The fortress stands near the bay at Milthorp, the only seaport in
the county.

CASTLE EDEN (non-existent)

CASTLE EDEN is a place near the coast, a few miles N. of Hartlepool.
It was of some importance in Saxon times, and suffered much from
Danish invaders.

It is said that a castle existed here, but its site cannot be traced, and all
records refer to the manor.

HARTLEY (minor)

THIS was once a noble structure, standing on an eminence over the village
of Hartley and town of Kirkby Stephen. As long as the Musgraves
resided here, the castle was kept in good repair, but nothing now remains
except the venerable ruins of part of the walls. The ancient name of this
manor was Hardclay, indicating the nature of its soil, and its possessors, who
held from the Veteriponts, from earliest times (Henry I.) were called De
Hardclay or Harcla through many succeeding reigns.   In 8 Edward II.
Andrew de Harcla held the manor, and seven years later was created Earl
of Carlisle for his great services to Edward II. in having vanquished the Earl
of Lancaster, together with John de Mowbray and Roger de Clifford, in the
fight at Boroughbridge, Yorkshire.   But the very next year, King Robert
Bruce having raided that part of the Border without hindrance from the king,
the earl repaired privately to the Bruce at Lochmaben, and there made
a treaty for mutual support and defence with him.   This being told to
Edward II., he resented the action of the Earl of Carlisle, proclaimed him
a traitor, and sent Anthony, Lord Lucy, to apprehend him at Carlisle Castle,
which was ably done by Lucy with an armed force.   The Chief Justiciar
was then sent to try the earl, who was next day sentenced to be degraded,
hanged, and quartered, and the sentence was at once carried out with all the

brutality of the law of high treason (see *Carlisle, Cumberland*). The estate was then confiscated by the Crown, and granted to Nevill, Baron of Raby, who sold it to Sir Thomas Musgrave of Musgrave, knight, the representative of an ancient family dwelling in these parts since the days of Stephen. His lineal descendant was created a baronet by James I., and the son of this man, Philip, distinguishing himself on the king's side during the Civil War in the next reign, was given at the Restoration a warrant as Baron Musgrave of Hartley Castle, but never took out the patent. This grand castle was destroyed by Sir Christopher Musgrave in order to build his new house of Edenhall.

The sentence executed on Andrew, Earl of Carlisle, the lord of Hartley, in 1322, was to this effect: "He and his heirs are to lose the dignity of the earldom for ever; he is to be ungirt of his sword, and his golden spurs are to be hacked from his heels. He is further adjudged to be drawn, hanged, and beheaded; one of his quarters to be hanged at the top of the Tower of Carlisle; another at the top of the Tower of Newcastle; the third on the bridge at York; the fourth at Shrewsbury, and his head to be spiked on London Bridge." His remains were collected in to Edward III., fifteen years after, by the king's order, and given for burial to Sir Andrew's sister Sarah, the widow of Robert de Leybourne.

HAZLESLACK TOWER (*minor*)

THIS tower, which is of similar character to Arnside, and probably of the same date, is now a ruined farm-house. These buildings may have been erected for the defence of the lands round Morecambe Bay, as on the opposite side are vestiges of "Broughton Tower" and of "Bazin Tower;" and in the centre of the Bay is "Peel" Castle. Again at Haverbrack Park, near the estuary of the Kent River, is a small hill on the top of which was formerly a circular castle, whence it is still called Castle Hill. There is no history attached to Hazleslack. It possesses garderobes of better construction than are usually found, and may therefore be of comparatively late date.

HOWGILL (*minor*)

THIS was originally a stronghold of the De Stutevilles, who held the manor of Milburn under De Meschines in the reign of Henry I. It lies up in the hills where are the head waters of Tees, about five miles from Appleby. The family of Lancaster, descended from the Barons of Kendal (*q.v.*), succeeded the De Stutevilles, and the last of them, William de Lancaster, dying *s.p.*, his inheritance was divided between his two sisters, Hawise and Alice, an illegitimate son named Roger coming in for certain lands, including this manor and Howgill. This was towards the end of Henry III.'s reign, and Roger Lancaster died 19 Edward I., leaving three sons, John, William, and Christopher. John, who succeeded to Howgill, died 8 Edward II. *s.p.*, when his brother William's son, John, obtained the property, and it descended in the family until, in the time of the Roses (1438), the succession ended in four daughters, one of whom, Elizabeth, brought this Lancaster property to her husband, Robert de Crackenthorpe, the brother of her neighbour at Newbiggin. It went again by an heiress, her great-granddaughter, to Sir Thomas Sandford of Askham, and the Sandfords continued here till the beginning of the eighteenth century, when the property again went, by default of heirs male, to the Essex family of Honeywood. Howgill is now the property of Lord Hothfield.

The site is a strong position, on the brow of a ravine through which runs a hill stream, and seems to have been considered sufficiently defensible without earthworks or ditches. We know nothing as to the nature of the original dwelling of the De Stutevilles, if they had one here ; but it is probable that when Roger de Lancaster succeeded, in the thirteenth century when much castle-building was going on, he erected what was perhaps a North-country tower or peel for his safe abode, to be extended in later times in the form in which we see the place.

Howgill Castle consists of a central block between two immensely strong rectangular towers, each measuring 64 feet long by 33 wide, with walls 9 feet and 10 feet thick ; the basements have barrel-vaulted roofs, with two stages above, and formerly a battlemented roof. Wide-splayed loops gave light to the ground floor of each side tower, and small staircases, in the thickness of the walls, lead to the first floor, from whence each has a newel stair to reach the upper stages. The central block originally contained the hall, which has been destroyed at some time or other, and rebuilt with thin walls, and subdivided, perhaps at the end of the seventeenth century. Access is obtained to the side towers by pointed-arch doorways, and Tudor, with later inserted, windows, give light to the apartments (*Dr. M. W. Taylor*).

KENDAL. (*minor*)

THE original stronghold which occupied this commanding site over the Kent valley was brought in marriage, together with the lands, by Lucy, the heiress of Turold, lord of Spalding, to Ivo de Taillebois of Anjou, a Norman companion of the Conqueror, from whom he obtained the barony of Kendal. His descendants were called De Lancaster, and the male line failing at William de Lancaster, seventh in descent, the Honour of Kendal and its estates passed to his sisters Hawise and Alice. Then Margaret, the

eldest coheir of Hawise by Robert le Brus, married the younger son of
Robert, Lord Roos of Hamlake and Werks, by Isabel, daughter of Alexander II.
of Scotland. Their grandson Sir Thomas de Roos married Katherine, daughter
of Sir Thomas Strickland of Sizergh, Westmorland, and had an only daughter
Elizabeth, who brought Kendal Castle and a rich inheritance to the Parrs,

KENDAL.

by her marriage with Sir William de Parr, knight. Their grandson Sir
William Parr, K.G., married Elizabeth, one of the coheirs of Lord Fitzhugh
by Alice, daughter of Ralph Nevill, Earl of Westmorland, and Joanna
Beaufort, the child of John of Gaunt. Alice's sister was Cicely Nevill, "The
Rose of Raby," mother of Edward IV. and Richard III., and the great-grand-
mother of Henry VIII., who thus married his fourth cousin in Katherine Parr,
the first Protestant Queen of England, born at this old castle in 1513. After
the Crown had granted it to various favourites, it was sold and resold many
times.

The ruin is finely situated on a circular mound about half a mile E. of the town, on the opposite side of the river, having a wide prospect from its walls. There is a good fifteenth-century gatehouse, and parts of the keep and two of the round towers exist. The remains of the chief apartments and of a dungeon or cellar may be traced, the whole being surrounded by a moat.

The place was decayed even in Camden's time, and it has never been repaired. "This crumbling relic rises like a grey crown over the green hills of Kendal, situate on a lofty eminence, with panoramic views over the town and picturesque vale of the clear and rapid Kent. A circular tower is the most considerable portion of the ruins, but there is a large enclosure of ivy-mantled walls remaining, with a few broken arches" (*Agnes Strickland*).

The strength of the walls is very great, but they have been built in rude early Norman fashion. The earliest portion is the tower on the N.W., which may have been erected about the time of Ivo de Taillebois; the tower opposite, on the S.W., is likewise ancient and strong, that on the S.E. being of later construction.

It is probable that during its long possession by the Parrs this fortress of the Barons of Kendal was altered many times and adapted to more modern requirements, and it is difficult now to trace the old Norman arrangements.

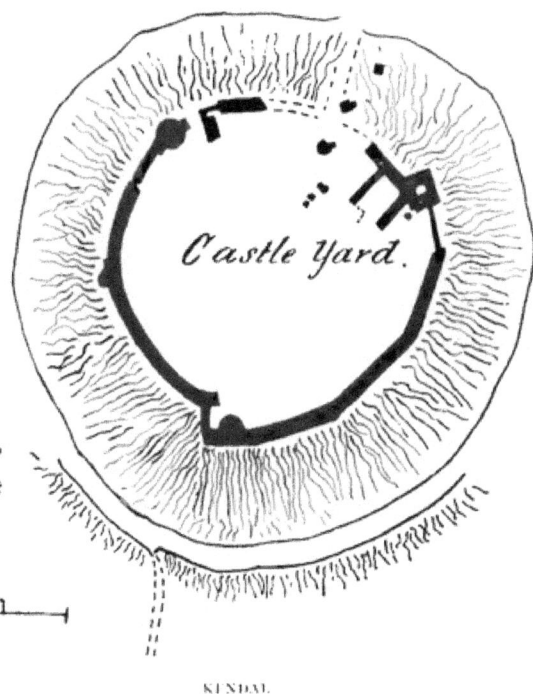

KENDAL.

LAMMERSIDE (*non-existent*)

THIS is an ancient ruin near Wharton, in a fine situation, but only a few remains appear, in fragments of walls and a part of a tower, with its dungeon.

NEWBIGGIN (*minor*)

ALTHOUGH the present hall does not pretend to be a castle, yet it is on the site of an early Norman fortress which gave shelter to the owners of the lands here for many generations. There exist charters of grants to one Laurence de Newbigginge, whose race continued in the male line for seven generations, when Robert de Newbiggin married Emma, daughter of Threlkeld, and left one daughter and heiress, who brought Newbiggin to her husband, Robert de Crackenthorpe. This was early in the reign of Edward III. Then followed fifteen generations of Crackenthorpes of Newbiggin, an ancient family of Danish origin, as the name implies, which held a strong position in the county, and intermarried with most of the leading families of Westmorland and Cumberland. They were Lancastrians, and two brothers of the family shed their blood at Towton Field in 1461.

An inscription over the door shows that the existing manor-house was built by Christopher Crackenthorpe in 1533 (25 Henry VIII.), and this owner added to the estate by the purchase from the Crown of some of the Church lands at the Dissolution.

According to tradition, the original castle was built temp. Edward I., and it was in all likelihood a rectangular peel tower of strength; but there are no vestiges of it left. The situation was in a low ground capable of being flooded, and hence perhaps its chief defence.

The existing building is of the same design, having, like Howgill, a central block supported at either end by strong rectangular battlemented towers.

PENDRAGON (*minor*)

PENDRAGON is said by Camden to have been called anciently the "Castle of Mallerstang," from the neighbouring forest of that name. It takes its name of Pendragon from a Welsh tradition about its founder, and is believed to date from Saxon times. The ruin is finely situated on a mound above the Eden, and a deep moat afforded protection on the other side. One of the flanking towers is still tolerably perfect.

Owned temp. Edward I. by Roger de Clifford, it was burned to the ground by the Scots in 1341 (temp. Edward III.), but was afterwards rebuilt and possessed continually by the Cliffords. This was one of the castles of Anne Clifford, Countess of Pembroke, repaired by her in 1661, and stated on the usual inscription stone set up by her to have lain ruinous without timber or any covering since 1541. This lady also built the bridge over Eden, near the castle. The building was demolished in 1685 by Thomas, Earl of Thanet, its owner.

SIZERGH (minor)

SIZERGH is a venerable fortified mansion belonging to the ancient family of Strickland (orig. *Stirkland*), who have owned estates in that district since the first year of King John. There exists one lofty tower, or peel, of the time of Henry VII., a square building 60 feet in height, defended by two square turrets; it has good battlements and a fine chimney. A few of the original windows are left; but the house has been much altered in the time of Elizabeth and at later periods, being still inhabited (*Parker*). It is three miles from Kendal. To Sizergh came Katherine Parr, about the year 1530, when a young widow of about eighteen, at the death of her first husband, Lord Borough, to live with her kinswoman, Lady Strickland; and here she occupied herself much in embroidery, specimens of which are shown at the castle. The apartment she occupied is still called the Queen's Room,— a fine state chamber in the ancient portion of the building called the D'Eyncourt Tower, opening from the drawing-room, and panelled with richly carved black oak, which is covered with tapestry of great beauty (*Agnes Strickland*).

WHARTON HALL (minor)

WHARTON HALL is the seat of an old Westmorland family, near Kirkby Stephen, dating from the time of Edward I. A considerable portion of the house still remains, partly converted into a farm-house. There is a quadrangle with an entrance gatehouse, showing the date of 1559, possibly erected by Sir Thomas Wharton, ennobled by Henry VIII. The principal tower exists with its staircase, the great hall, and many of the domestic offices. The family of Wharton came to an end at the death of the last heir male, the eccentric Duke of Wharton, born 1698, who was raised to that dignity by George I. in 1718, and whose character is well given by Pope. This place was then purchased by the Lowthers, and is now the property of Earl Lonsdale. The first Baron Wharton won his elevation by his surprising conduct and success in the signal defeat of the Scots at Solway Moss, in November 1542, in which a force of 500 under the Duke of Norfolk routed

King James V.'s army of 10,000; "perhaps," Gough says, "the most considerable victory the English ever gained over the forces of the neighbouring kingdom." He died in 1568, being succeeded by his son Thomas, who died in 1572, and had as successor his son Philip, a distinguished Whig temp. Queen Anne, created Viscount Winchendon and Earl of Wharton, and afterwards Marquis of Wharton in 1715, in which year he died. His only son was the profligate character mentioned above as the last of the family; he is said to have replied in the House of Lords with such vigour to the first Earl of Stanhope, the minister of George I., on the matter of the South-Sea Bubble (1721), as to have caused the death of Stanhope, who succumbed to a fit of apoplexy the next day.

YANWATH HALL (manor)

THE Manor of Yanwath Hall lies nearly three miles S. of Penrith, on the Westmorland side of the Eamont River, a few miles after it leaves the lake of Ullswater, and was placed there to guard an important ford in the river, on one of the main Border roads. A wooded bank slopes precipitously down to the river at the back of the house, and the tower, as is generally the case, commands a wide view over the adjacent country. In one of the papers published by the Archaeological Society of the county, it is said that no part of these counties is so rich in examples of old manorial houses as the district around Penrith. They are generally tenanted now by farmers. Yanwath was a peel, and a good specimen of a fourteenth-century fortress, being built, like all Border towers of the same epoch, for defence and also as a refuge for men and cattle from the incursions of Scottish marauders. It occupies a commanding position on the S. bank of the stream, like all these English peels, in order to impose the river between the castle and the enemy. Parker (vol. ii. p. 216) says that this castle is of two very distinct periods; the original structure is believed to have been built by John de Sutton, who married Margaret, the heiress of the family of De Somerie, in 1322. The heirs of this union became Barons Dudley, and in the reign of Henry VIII., Thomas, the eldest son by the second wife of Edmund, Lord Dudley, settled at Yanwath, and married Sarah, the daughter and coheiress of Sir Lancelot Threlkeld of Yanwath, a member of an ancient county family. It was sold in 1654 to the Lowthers, and is still owned by the Earl of Lonsdale.

The building is in the form of a quadrangle, three sides of which now are standing, enclosing an inner bailey or "barmkin," as it used to be called. The fourth side was possibly closed by a wall, or by wooden buildings. On the S. side are the chief tower, the hall, and the kitchen. The present gateway is modern, the old entrance having existed at the arch of the N.E. angle, where are the guardrooms, and a thick wall, with crenellated parapet. At the W. end stands the great peel tower of three storeys, with its battlements and watch-turrets at each angle. There is a vaulted basement to the tower quite untouched. The hall, which was probably rebuilt in the fifteenth century, was originally a fine apartment, 42 feet by 24 feet, but it was altered then, and later additions have quite spoilt it. The oldest portions of Yanwath are early fourteenth century, but the tower received many alterations in Elizabeth's time. At the N.E. angle is more of the early work, with an interesting look-out and platform for the warder. In Nicolson and Burns's History, it is said that there existed a chapel over the gate, but the buildings here are now used as stables, and it is difficult to say if it was so. The present gateway is entirely modern.

DACRE

Cumberland

ARMATHWAITE (minor)

THIS was the fortified manor-house belonging to the Skeltons of
Skelton, and was their chief seat. John Skelton, the poet laureate of
Henry VIII., was one of this family and was born here. They retained
it till 1712, when it was sold by Richard Skelton to William Sanderson,
from whose family it passed to the Milburns, and in 1846 became the property
of the Earl of Lonsdale, the present proprietor. Jefferson says that the Skeltons
frequently represented this county and Carlisle in Parliament, between the
reigns of Edward II. and Henry VIII., and distinguished themselves in the
Scottish and French wars. Before coming here, they were a considerable
family (temp. Edward II.) in the W. of Cumberland. Richard, a son of Sir
Clement, was at Agincourt in the suite of the Duke of Gloster, and his
nephew, John Skelton, who was also a warrior, and much esteemed by the
duke, was the first to seat himself at Armathwaite, where, in 1445, he built
a house of defence against the Scots.

The castle stands on the site of an ancient fortress, upon a rock washed
by the river Eden. It has a modern front of ashlar stone, and has received the
addition of a new wing of offices.

ASKERTON (*minor*)

THIS is a lonely fortified house, built by Thomas, Lord Dacre, when Warden of the Marches, to guard against inroads from Liddesdale by Bewcastle and the Maiden Way, as an advanced post above Naworth Castle, and for the protection of the barony. It stands on the banks of the Cambock, and was the usual residence of an officer called the Land Serjeant, whose duty it was to take the command of the inhabitants in repelling the inroads of the borderers (*Whellan*).

In a MS. in the British Museum, published in the *Scottish Archæologia*, dated 1590, Askerton is thus mentioned: "Upon the E. side of Eden lyeth the barony of Gilsland, under the government of a Steward who ought to be at Askerton Castle. In his charge is all the safety of that Barony, without either help of warden or other. . . . This Castle since the Rebellion is sore spoyled, and ever since worse governed."

It was a Border watch-tower, whose uses ceased after the union of England and Scotland. Mr. Ferguson calls it a building of great interest, occupying three sides of a quadrangle, the fourth or E. side being completed by a curtain wall. There are towers on the S.W. and S.E. The W. wall is thin and modern, but on that side stood the hall, of which a part remains at the N.W. angle, with a three-light window in its N. end, and part of a staircase to the battlements above it. The fine massive original roof is still in its place. This hall was once embattled. The interiors of the towers have been dismantled, having had formerly two small rooms with fireplaces and windows, and garderobes. On the N. side is a stable with hayloft over. The design of the whole was a quadrangle in which the entire garrison, horses and all, could be contained, the gates shut, and a short siege stood, until rescue from Naworth or Carlisle was forthcoming.

There is nothing to show that any previous building ever existed at this point. The fabric, which was in great decay, as we have seen, in the reign of Elizabeth, has since been repaired and converted into a farm-house. There was once a park attached to it.

BEWCASTLE, OR THE CASTLE OF BUETH (*minor*)

ITS Celtic predecessor (see *Triermain* and *Irthington*) was a remote Cumbrian fortress on the Maiden Way, "rugged and solitary," and not easy of access. There are the remains of a Roman camp. The lands were granted by Henry II., by charter, to Hubert de Vallibus or Vaux, the lord of Gilsland, after the death of Gilles Bueth, but it was rather regarded as a part of the barony of Burg. The De Multons, or Moultons, however, took possession of it after they had obtained Gilsland by marriage. In the reign of Edward III. Bewcastle was held by the Swinburnes, after which time it got into the hands of the Crown, and then was held by the Musgrave family, from the time of Henry VIII. till the seventeenth century, Jack Musgrave being captain of it at the period of the Commonwealth.

Rushworth says Bewcastle had a garrison of a hundred men in 1639, which was afterwards withdrawn to Carlisle, when this castle was dismantled; though Hutchinson states that it was destroyed by the Parliament forces in 1641. Its latter proprietors have been Grahams.

All that remains of the castle is a large enclosure of 87 feet square, with four huge walls, much broken down on the N. and E. The date of its erection is not known, and there are no details whereby this can be traced. As the windows are insertions of late Tudor work, the castle may have been rebuilt when the Tudors came to the throne. A gateway has been added on the W. The lodgings and offices appear to have been built round the walls of the enceinte, as at Askerton, and had two storeys and a basement. The doorways remain, and are furnished with the long holes for the wooden bars to fasten the doors.

Many are the stories of the lawlessness of the Bewcastle folks, in the times of disorder; they were all moss-troopers, "and many of them appear in the lists kept by Lord William Howard of those whom he had either hanged upon the fatal trees at Naworth, or sent to Carlisle, where the officer 'does his work by daylight.'"

CARLISLE (chief)

THE city of Carlisle (Caerluel), placed on the western approach to Scotland from London, is the successor of British, Roman, Saxon, and Danish settlements, whose occupants in earliest ages chose this well-protected, elevated rock of new red sandstone for their stronghold against the Scots. Three rivers—on the N. the Eden, W. the Caldew, and E. the Petterill cover its three sides.

When the Red King settled the boundaries of England and Scotland at this point, he drove out the owner of the lands and commenced the building of a Norman castle upon the N. and most elevated spot of this piece of high ground, rising 60 feet above the Eden. The slopes of the hill on the N., E., and W. are very steep towards the meadows intervening between the three rivers below. Rufus retained the district in his own hands, but Henry I. granted it as the earldom of Caerleolium to Ranulph le Meschines, who soon after (through his mother Maud, sister of Hugh d'Avranches, surnamed Lupus, Earl of Chester) inherited the earldom of Chester, on the drowning of Earl Richard, together with Prince William and many other young nobles, on board the *White Ship* at Barfleur. He thereon surrendered Caerleolium to the king, and the earldom was divided into two parts, the eastern portion going to form the county of Westmorland, and the rest being divided into baronies.

During Stephen's reign, Cumberland was given over to the Scots, and it is probable that Carlisle and its walls were finished by King David of Scotland, who sometimes resided here. Fordun fixes his occupation in 1138, and Carlisle remained in the hands of the Scots till 1157, when King Malcolm surrendered the city and castle to Henry II. In 1174, William the Lion besieged the place with a force of 80,000, as is said; but on his capture at Alnwick the siege was raised. Here in 1186 King Henry attended with a large army to meet this same Scottish king and his brother David, then on friendly terms. But in 1216 King Alexander II. laid siege again to Carlisle, when the castle held out, but from the injuries it received became so dilapidated that in 1256 a survey was ordered for its repair. In 1296 an incursion of the Scots under the Earl of Buchan was beaten off, and a system of fire-beacons was instituted in the surrounding country to give notice of an enemy's approach. Soon after Edward I. arrived here with his army, this being the first of four visits which he paid. The last occasion was in 1307, when he kept his last birthday here, and shortly after died at Burgh-upon-Sands, in the neighbourhood. Most of the Edwardian additions to the castle are of this reign (*Clark*). It was in 1305 that the heroic Sir William Wallace was confined in irons here on his way to his cruel death at Smithfield.

The Bruce laid siege to Carlisle in 1315, directing the attack chiefly against the city walls; but Sir Andrew de Harcla, the governor, drove him off after a hard-fought siege of eleven days, for which service in 1322 Harcla was made Earl of Carlisle and Lord Warden of the Marches; he had also that year earned the gratitude of Edward II. by vanquishing at Boroughbridge the Earl of Lancaster, John de Mowbray, and others, and quelling their insurrection. But the next year, wearied with the weakness of the king, whom perhaps he thought likely to lose his kingdom, Harcla sought Robert Bruce at Lochmaben and entered into traitorous terms with him for mutual support. This was brought to the notice of Edward, who sent at once Sir Anthony de Lucy with three knights to apprehend Earl Harcla. On February 23rd, Lucy with a few followers entered Carlisle Castle, concealing their arms under their cloaks, and passed without challenge into the inner ward, and thence to the great hall, whence they proceeded to the private apartments of the governor, whom they found there unarmed and engaged in writing. He was at once arrested; but the sound of voices alarmed the retainers, who came to the rescue, and the keeper of the inner ward was killed by Sir Richard Denton in his attempt to close the gate. Lucy's warrant, however, prevailed ; the castle was surrendered to him, and the governor made close prisoner. On March 2nd the Chief Justiciary, Sir Jeffrey le Scrope, arrived, and on the following day the earl was arraigned and tried, found guilty, degraded, and sentenced to be hung, drawn, and quartered. The sentence was at once carried out with all its barbarous cruelty, his quarters being distributed over the country, one of them disfiguring the castle keep.

Edward III. in 1334, being in Scotland, sent Edward Baliol to Carlisle to defend Cumberland ; and in 1337 and 1345 the Scots made incursions against the fortress, which must have needed repairs, as a survey was ordered at that period. During the weak reign of Richard II., the Scots made several attempts against the place, in 1380, 1385, and 1387 ; and in the Civil Wars of the fifteenth century Carlisle suffered greatly, though we hear little regarding its castle. Edward IV. made his brother Richard of Gloster governor of it, and he resided here, one of the towers being called after him.

Henry VIII., in order to adapt the castle for artillery, caused many alterations to be made, building a blockhouse or citadel

CARLISLE

on the S. side, of similar form to those which he provided along the S. coast. Pennant describes it as oblong in shape, with three circular bastions, and a strong machicolated gateway, defended in front by a moat and drawbridge.

Elizabeth built the chapel and barracks, her arms being placed thereon ; but the survey of 1563 shows that large repairs were then necessary, 70 feet of the wall of the outer ward, 9 feet thick and 18 feet high, having fallen, and both the keep and the captain's tower needed repair, the parapets also being ruinous and deficient.

In 1568 Mary Queen of Scots was brought here with some state, after her landing at Workington on Sunday, May 16th, by the sheriff, Sir Richard Lowther, and she remained here until her removal to Bolton Castle on July 13th, thus spending six weeks at this castle, where she must have received the insulting and pitiless rejoinders of Elizabeth, and realised the loss of her liberty. She occupied a tower in the S.E. corner of the inner ward, which was of finer architecture than the other parts, and contained the state apartments for distinguished visitors; the lower part was Norman, with a circular-headed gateway, holding a portcullis, and having a postern on the right. The upper part was Early English. A sketch of this tower and its description are given in the "History and Antiquities of Carlisle," published by Jefferson in 1838; three years after, the tower was pulled down on account of its insecure state—a fate shared also by the chapel.

In 1644 General Leslie brought a Parliamentary force to Carlisle, which was occupied for the king by a large garrison under Sir Thomas Glenham and Sir Henry Stradling. After a siege prolonged for ten months, the garrison was starved out and surrendered, when the castle was occupied in force by the Roundheads.

Prince Charles Edward arrived before Carlisle at Stannix Bank on November 9, 1754, with a force of about 7000 men and six six-pounder guns, retreating to Brampton on being fired upon; but on the 13th they returned and opened trenches against the city, and when on the 15th scaling-ladders were brought and an assault ordered, the garrison, which consisted of 300 militia only, hung out a white flag and offered to surrender. The prince required that the castle should be given up as well as the town, and this being agreed to, the Highland army entered, and obtained a large booty of arms and stores and 100 barrels of powder. The people of the neighbourhood had sent their plate and valuable effects into the castle for safety, but these were ordered to be restored to their owners. A garrison was left in the castle of 100 men, and the prince's army then proceeded on their incursion into England, from which they returned on the 20th December, passing one night at Carlisle to change the garrison, and retreating next day into Scotland. The same day the king's army under the Duke of Cumberland marched from Penrith to Carlisle, and being received with artillery fire, raised batteries against the place and summoned it, whereupon the town and castle were delivered up to the royal troops. Nearly 400 prisoners were sent to London with Mr. John Hamilton of Aberdeenshire, the governor, who, with another officer, was hung, drawn, and quartered. There are traces of two field-works in the meadows N. of the castle, evidently prepared for the reception of the Scots army as they approached over the brow at Stannix in November 1745 (Clark).

The plan of the castle is a right-angled triangle, of which its right angle is on the S.W., and the longest side, somewhat curved, from N. to E.; the area contained being about 3 acres. A strong buttressed wall with bastions crowns the edge of the slope, and is carried on the E. and W. sides past the castle to unite with the city walls. The S. front is separated from the town by a deep ditch 30 yards broad and 10 yards deep, and a glacis.

The walls of the inner court converge on a flat salient, in the middle of the outer court at the gatehouse, called the Captain's Tower. This is rectangular, with a low-arched Decorated gateway and vaulted passage furnished with gates and portcullis; in front was once a ditch and a drawbridge. Old plans show a small lunette battery placed near in front, and communicating with the outer gatehouse by a covered-way; but all this outside work has been

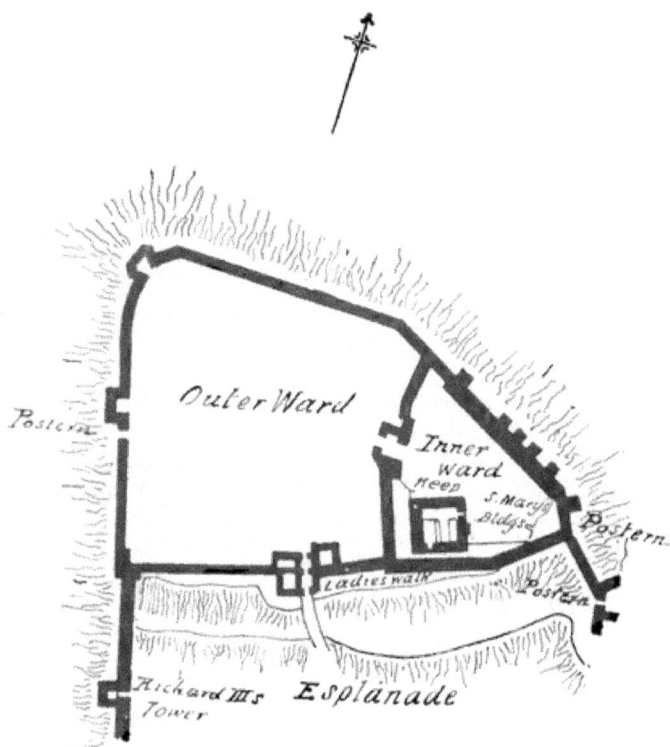

CARLISLE

removed. The wall is backed by a rampart and masonry, probably of the time of Henry VIII.

The keep measures 66 feet N. and S., and 61 feet E. and W., and is now 68 feet high. It has been so much altered that the old plan cannot be well seen. The entrance, which had an Edwardian portcullis, is on the ground level on the E. face. The basement is vaulted in four compartments, and had a stair in the N.W. angle to the first floor, which has been vaulted in brick and is used as a mess-room; it has a large Norman fireplace now walled up.

The second floor, reached from the exterior, has a wooden ceiling, and its E. wall has a mural chamber once used as a prison, and bearing inscriptions by prisoners. The third floor is vaulted in modern brick to carry a gun platform on the roof. An external stair (Edwardian), built against the N. face, leads up to the ramparts.

The hall and the domestic buildings, with Queen Mary's Tower, were at the S.E. angle, but all is now gone save a fragment of panelled work, part of a grand staircase of early Edwardian work which led to the chief apartments (Clark).

The N. wall of the inner ward is protected by a rampart 27 feet thick, and on the outside are six enormous buttresses (Decorated or Perpendicular), to support it. Formerly in the centre a spur curtain wall extended down the slope, ending in a round tower, for flanking this N. wall : it is now removed. The N. face of the curtain and its N.W. corner have been restored in Decorated style, but most of the W. wall is original (Clark). In the centre of this W. wall is a small projecting Norman tower, open at the gorge, with a postern close to it ; it is continued to join the city wall across the outer ditch, and some way along this is the tower called after Richard III., or "Tile Tower," which may be Norman work altered. There was, it is said, an underground passage below this tower and the enceinte. The S. wall is original, with Norman pilasters. Here is another postern in the wall from the S.E. angle to the city wall, now banked up ; this led to what is called the Lady's Walk, at the foot of the S. wall as far as the S. gatehouse, which is alleged to have furnished the usual promenade of the captive Mary Stuart.

CASTLE CRAG (non-existent)

ON the sides of Lake Derwentwater, overlooking the Vale of Keswick, is an eminence of this name which was once occupied by a Roman fort, and afterwards by a fortress of the Norman lords of Der. The materials of this structure are said to have been employed in building a house on one of the three wooded islands of the lake, called Lord's Island, upon which the Radcliffe family had a stately mansion. The island was originally a peninsula, but was cut off from the mainland by a ditch with a drawbridge, remains of which are still visible. This residence was given to a younger branch of the family : Sir John, the brother of Sir Cuthbert Radcliffe, lived and died here. It then fell to decay, and nothing now remains of it, nor of the Roman castrum and the Norman tower ; for it is alleged that the stones of all were carried away to build the town-hall of Keswick. The Derwentwater estate extended for two miles along the shore and for half a mile in depth, between the present road to Ambleside and the Falls of Lodore.

The Derwentwaters appear to have been settled in Cumberland as early as
the time of King John, and continued there till 48 Edward III., when Sir John
de Derwentwater was sheriff of the county, a post he also filled in the reign
of Richard II. He was the last of his race, and his property was inherited by
his daughter Margaret, who, temp. Henry V., married Sir Nicholas de Radcliffe,
of a family coming from the village of that name in Lancashire, near Bury
(see *Dilston*), whose pedigree assumes a De Radcliffe prior to the time of
Henry II. (*Gibson*). Many of these Cumberland Radcliffes were buried at
Crossthwaite.

CASTLESTEADS (*non-existent*)

HUTCHINSON says (vol. i. p. 102) that the ancient mansion-house of
Gilsland was at a place in the parish of Walton called Castle Steed, and
that Gilbert Bueth dwelt here (see *Irthington*); also that the lords of Gilsland
used its ruins for building Naworth Castle. But the fact is, that there is no
evidence for the existence of any castle or tower here at any time: there
seems to have been nothing but a Roman camp, the ramparts and ditches
of which are still very apparent, and from this site many altars and Roman
remains have been dug.

CATTERLEN HALL (*minor*)

THREE miles N.W. of Penrith, situated on a hill at the base of which
flows the Petterill, is a good specimen of a Border peel tower, with later
additions, which increased civilisation required and improved security allowed.
It is not known by whom the ancient tower was erected; it probably dates
from the Wars of the Roses, and is similar to others in the district. It was
added to in the fifteenth century, and, in the middle of the seventeenth, it
received the more imposing buildings, approached by a flight of stairs.

The peel is a small one, 30½ feet long by 19½ broad, and consists of a
single barrel-vaulted basement lighted by narrow slits and old loops enlarged,
the walls being 4 feet thick. In the S.W. angle a low-pointed doorway leads
to the newel stair by which the other floors are reached. The first story is
the solar, in a single apartment, with a small closet having a window on
the E., over which is a shield with the arms of Vaux of Catterlen. The
flooring of both storeys is gone, but the joist corbels remain. The second
floor was the ladies' chamber, with windows on the N. and E. sides. The
parapet round the roof was crenellated.

The ranges of building added at the end of the tower consist of a two-
storeyed erection 22 yards long, with a hall and kitchen and sleeping rooms

overhead. Over the doorway is an inscription by the builder, Rowland Vaux (1577). The hall, with a wooden roof, is a good Tudor building, where the lord and his guests dined in common with his retainers.

The second addition was made by the Richmond family, about 1657, at right angles to the last range ; this contains a courthouse and a retiring-room reached by stairs from the court, with inferior rooms below, all built in the style of the Elizabethan and Jacobean ages.

After the Conquest, Hubert de Vallibus (Vaux) wrested the lands from Wilfrid, son of the Saxon thane, and Henry I. granted them to him, together with Gilsland, despoiled from the Saxon Beuth. The family of Vaux continued to hold the property till the last John Vaux died, *s.p.*, in 1642, when the manor went with his daughter Mabel to a neighbouring squire, Christopher Richmond of Highhead Castle, from whose family it came in 1775 by an heiress to the Duke of Norfolk, and it is now the property of the Howards.

COCKERMOUTH (*chief*)

THIS castle stands on a steep and rocky knoll on the point of land formed by the confluence of the Cocker with the river Derwent. Such a position was in earliest times a favourite one for the placing of a stronghold ; and upon this triangular space of scarped rock, defended on all sides but one by water, and perhaps following Roman foundations, the Norman baron built a keep, with a bastioned curtain wall around the highest ground enclosing his bailey or ward, and protected on the open side by a ditch with a barbican. This early castle must have been that destroyed by Henry III. in his vengeance on William de Fortibus, Earl of Albemarle, in 1221 (see *Bytham, Lincoln*); for the remains of these buildings are traceable, and the greater part of what now exists was erected in Decorated and Perpendicular styles between 1360 and 1400.

When Ranulph de Meschines succeeded to his cousin's great earldom of Chester (see *Carlisle*), he ceded to Henry I. the rights and fief of Caerleol, whereon that king created five new baronies, Copeland or Allerdale above Derwent, Allerdale below Derwent, Wigton, Greystock, and Levington, reserving to the Crown Inglewood Forest and Carlisle ; the rest of the fief went to Westmorland. Ranulph's brother, who had obtained the barony of Gilsland, resigned it in exchange for that of Copeland, between Dudden and Derwent ; while Waldeof, son of Gospatric, Earl of Northumberland, obtained Allerdale below Derwent, which passed, four generations later, to William Fitz-Duncan, Earl of Moray, the nephew of Malcolm, King of Scots. Meanwhile, Copeland had come to Cicely de Meschines, the granddaughter of William, and then to her daughter Alice (by Robert de Romilly, lord of Skipton), who was married to this same William, Earl of Moray; and their only son, who is known in poetry as "the Boy of Egremont," became heir to all these large possessions in England, as well as to his father's vast territory in Scotland. But an even greater future seemed possible for this son—the victim of the Wharfe—for when David, King of Scotland, died, Malcolm his successor was not favoured by the Highland clans, because he had acted as a vassal or feudatory to his cousin King Henry II. of England at the siege of Toulouse, and they desired to see this cousin, this Boy of Egremont, on the throne in his place (Skene's "Celtic Scotland," vol. i. p. 456).

But the catastrophe of Wharfe,

> "When Lady Adaliza mourned
> Her son, and felt in her despair
> The pang of unavailing prayer,"

ended all these bright visions, and the English lands fell to the three sisters of the Boy—Cicely, Annabel, and Alice—who all, in themselves or their descendants, possessed Cockermouth.

Cicely, the eldest daughter of William Fitz-Duncan and his wife Alice de Romilly, carried Skipton to her husband, William le Gros, Earl of Albemarle (see *Scarborough*). And their only daughter Hawise married successively William de Mandeville, William de Fortibus, and Baldwin de Bethune, by the second of whom she left an only son, William, who through her became the second Earl of Albemarle, and was the rebel in the early part of Henry III.'s reign.

Alice was the wife of Robert de Courtenai, as her second husband (1196), and paid to King John a fine of £500, ten palfreys, and ten oxen, to have the liberty of her inheritance, and not to be compelled to marry again. She died *s.p.*, when her property of Allerdale went to the descendants of her sister Cicely, and to those of her other sister Annabel, who had married Reginald de Lucy and had obtained the barony of Copeland.

There is a command of the young King Henry III. in 1221 to the sheriff of Westmorland, following on Albemarle's rebellion, that he should cause the castle of Cockermouth to be besieged and destroyed to its very foundations. This order seems to have been carried out, though, perhaps, only in part, for we see in the W. tower evidence that it was built early in the thirteenth century, and was destroyed very soon after, a fourteenth-century building being afterwards erected on the old foundations. William de Fortibus, however, managed to make his peace, and perhaps rebuilt the castle. He married Aveline, the heiress of Robert de Montfichet, and died in 1241, leaving an only son, William, whose second wife was Isabel de Ripariis (1247), sister and heiress of Baldwin de Redvers, Earl of Devon. William died in 1260, and his widow had Cockermouth as her dower; but the immense possessions of the Earls of Devon and of De Fortibus fell to Aveline, sole heiress of this last William and Isabella de Redvers, so that she became a suitable match for Prince Edmond "Crouchback," Earl of Lancaster, whom she married in 1269. She died six years afterwards, and her vast property was escheated to the Crown, though descendants of the two sisters Cicely and Amabel were still living.

Edward I. retained Cockermouth Castle in his own hands, and Edward II. handed it over first to Piers Gaveston, and afterwards to Sir Andrew Harcla, whose rebellion and destruction are related under Carlisle Castle.

Then Anthony de Lucy, who had claimed the property, being a descendant of Amabel, the second sister of the Boy of Egremont, was, in return for his capture of Harcla, presented with Cockermouth. He died in 1343, and his son Thomas married Margaret, one of the three coheiress sisters of John de Multon; the other two being married, Elizabeth to Robert de Harrington, and Joan to Robert de Fitzwalter; and each of the three became entitled to a third of the Egremont barony. This Thomas de Lucy is given by Froissart as one of the companions of Edward III. in Normandy in 1346, and he probably fought at Crecy. He repaired the bastion at the W. salient of this castle and built the great hall. His son Anthony succeeded him in 1365, but died in the Holy Land, whereupon his sister Maud, the wife of Gilbert de Umfraville, Earl of Angus, became heiress of the Lucy line. This Anthony de Lucy was lord of Cockermouth from 2 Edward II. to 17 Edward III., and being a high military chief on the marches, probably kept his castle in proper order. It may have been he who remodelled the Norman work, and built the new front of the inner ward and the great kitchen, in the Decorated period (*Clark*). The Lady Maud had by the Earl of Angus a daughter, who after the earl's death (8 Richard II.) married Henry Percy, 1st Earl of Northumberland. Failing her own heirs, the honour of Cockermouth was settled on the heirs male of her husband, who were to wear the arms of Percy (a blue lion), and of Lucy (3 lucies), quarterly; and the remainder taking effect, Cockermouth passed to the Percy descendants of Earl Henry's first wife Margaret, daughter of Ralph, Lord Nevill of Raby. The arms of all these families appear on the shields over the castle gatehouse built by this earl, by whom the area of the fortress was trebled by the extension of the outer ward, eastward. Maud died in 1398, and Earl Henry, like many other nobles, after helping to place Bolingbroke on the throne, turned against him and joined Owen Glendower and Roger Mortimer; he was beheaded after the fight on Bramham Moor in 1408, his eldest son, Henry, "Hotspur," having been slain at the battle of Shrewsbury five years before. His grandson, the second earl, fell at St. Albans, and the third earl at Towton (1461), when the estates became forfeited to the Crown by attainder, and this castle and honour were then granted to Richard, Earl of Warwick, and, after his death, to Henry, 4th Earl of Northumberland, who was murdered at his seat of Cock Lodge, Yorkshire. The fifth earl, who did not live here, died in 1527, being the first of these lords who died a natural death during 150 years, and the sixth died s.p., leaving his property to the Crown.

The Percys were thus dispossessed for twenty years, but in 1557 Thomas Percy was restored, and when Queen Mary Stuart landed at Workington, at the mouth of the Derwent, in 1568, and was by the sheriff, Sir Richard Lowther, conducted to Cockermouth Castle, Earl Thomas hastened to receive her there, and desired to bring her to his grander home of Alnwick, which, from the proximity of that castle to the coast, was not permitted by Elizabeth.

In 1577 a survey of the castle was made, which stated that the fabric was then in a great state of decay "as well in the stone work as timber work thereof." This was in the time of Henry, eighth earl, who, being confined in the Tower for complicity in Throgmorton's plot for liberating the Queen of Scots, was in 1585 found dead in his bed in the Bloody Tower, with three bullets in his side. His son Henry, ninth earl, called "The Wizard," was also committed to the Tower on the charge of being concerned in the Gunpowder Plot, and remained there for fifteen years; he died in 1632, and was followed by Earl Algernon, whose son Earl Jocelyn (eleventh) ended the male line of his race, and Cockermouth came by his daughter and sole heiress to Charles Seymour, Duke of Somerset. Their son, Duke Algernon, created Earl Egremont and Baron Cockermouth, died in 1750, leaving a daughter, but Cockermouth Castle and the earldom were settled on Sir Charles Wyndham, the grandson of Duke Algernon, and thus descended to George, the last earl, who died s.p. legitimate, leaving this castle to his natural son.

The entrance is at the N. end of the E. front, formerly through an open barbican with a drawbridge, and thence through a three-storeyed gatehouse (cir. 1400) which has a fine newel staircase with groined roof. Inside the walls are modern buildings and traces of early ones, and on the left is an ascent to the flagstaff tower at the S.E. angle of the wall, and to the wall allure. In front is the great face of the inner ward (1390), which once had before it a dry ditch across the courtyard. Passing through the inner gateway in the centre we cross the cellars or prisons, formed within what was originally the first moat, and by a steep flight of stairs ascend into the inner ward, where, on the right, is the castle well, and an entrance into the great hall which abuts on the kitchen. This is a huge tower, open to the roof, and having a gallery across its N. side which led into the hall, with recessed pantries below it, and on its opposite side a newel staircase in the wall to the roof. The hall measures 48 feet in length by 30 feet, and beyond it runs a range of solar or state apartments, whose inner wall has disappeared. In the salient circular tower at the W. the archers' seats still remain in the windows. Perhaps the chapel stood over the great entrance.

In August 1648 the castle was held for the Parliament, and being attacked by a Royalist force it held out for a month, until relieved by General Ashton. As there are no battlements remaining, there seems good reason to believe that the fortress was dismantled at this period.

CORBY (*minor*)

ON the E. side of the Eden, four miles E.S.E. of Carlisle, stood this fortress, built on a precipitous cliff impending over the river, on the site of a still earlier work. The square walls of its keep were incorporated in the later mansion built about the middle of the sixteenth century.

The manor of Corby was given by Henry II. to Hubert de Vaux, who gave it to one Odard, whose descendants assumed the name of De Corby. In the reign of Edward I. this De Corby family gave way to the Richmonds, who 16 Edward II. conveyed the property to Andrew de Harcla, afterwards Earl of Carlisle, after whose execution (see *Carlisle*) it was bestowed in 1335 on Richard de Salkeld for his former good service in assisting in the capture of the earl. His descendant in the reign of Henry VII. left two daughters, and the families derived from them owned Corby, and in 1606 and 1624 sold their moieties to Lord William Howard, who gave the place to his second son, Sir Francis, ancestor of the present proprietor. Lord W. Howard, or Belted Will, is written of in the Memoir of Naworth (*q.v.*).

There is little of antiquity apparent in the existing structure, so many and various have been the alterations and additions made thereto. The castle is surrounded by celebrated and very beautiful grounds.

DACRE (*minor*)

THE river Eamont, flowing E. from Ullswater, receives at its N. bank the small stream of the Dacre beck, and about a mile from this place up the beck, at the mouth of a pleasant valley, stands this castle on a spur of high ground, with the village of Dacre close beside it. William of Malmesbury, writing A.D. 1131, mentions a castle at Dacre as being the place where Constantine, King of the Scots, and Eugenius, King of Cumberland, put themselves and their kingdoms under Athelstane, the King of England, about the year 927. But whatever may have been the rude fortress of those days, the present one, from its Early English style, was not built till some time in the thirteenth century. It was perhaps erected by Ranulph de Dacre, who was a firm Royalist during the Barons' War, and was sheriff of the county, as his father was before him, dying 14 Edward I.

His family doubtless took their name from the place, and lived here probably
till by the abduction of Margaret de Multon, the heiress of Gilsland, in 1313
(see *Naworth* and *Kirkoswald*), Ralph de Dacre obtained the fine seat of
Kirkoswald, which formed an abode more befitting the increased importance
of his person and family. These Dacres were bold men of high spirit and
reputation, and were as successful in love as in the State. Sir Thomas at
the end of the fifteenth century followed his ancestor's example in acquiring
the lordship of Greystoke by a marriage of elopement.

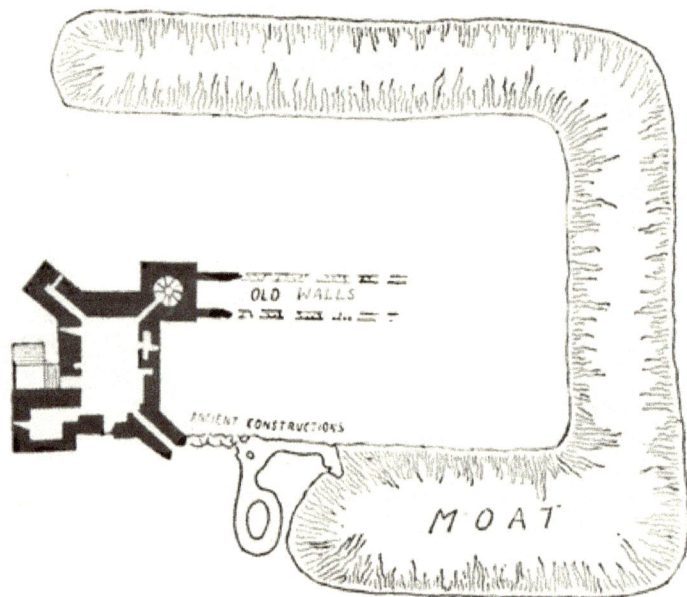

DACRE

In the seventeenth century Thomas, Lord Dacre of the South, created
Earl of Sussex 1674 (see *Hurstmonceaux, Sussex*), made many additions to
the building, inserting also the square-headed windows, and placing his arms
(which quartered Lennard, Fiennes, Dacre, and Multon) over the entrance.
He died in 1715 *s.p.* male, when his earldom ceased, and the barony of
Dacre fell into abeyance between his two daughters, Barbara and Anne, who
sold Dacre to Sir Christopher Musgrave of Edenhall. It was afterwards sold
to Mr. E. W. Hasell of Dalemain.

Dacre Castle consists of a plain massive stone tower, almost square in
form, with large square turrets projecting at the E. and W. corners, square

with the tower, and at the N. and S. angles two other smaller turrets, set diagonally like buttresses. The summit of both tower and turrets has a crenellated parapet, the height of this from the ground being about 66 feet. The large turret on the W. contains a broad newel staircase leading to the upper storeys and the battlements, and the one on the E. side has four small apartments. Against this latter is built, on the outside, a flight of stairs giving access to the pointed doorway of the castle. Of the two smaller turrets, that on the N. contains rooms for sleeping accommodation, and the opposite one was appropriated to garderobes and drains, and is now blocked up.

The outer walls are very strong, being 8½ feet thick. The basement has two barrel-vaulted chambers for cellars or dungeons, dimly lighted. Above these, with its oven and fireplaces, is the original hall or kitchen, formerly a single apartment 36 feet long by 21 feet wide; opposite the fireplace is a curious recess with a shelf and water drain, like a piscina. The chamber of the second floor is called by tradition "The Room of the Three Kings," from the legend of William of Malmesbury; it is 17 feet high to the wooden ceiling, and a minstrels' gallery seems to have formerly occupied its E. wall, reached by a stair from the turret and a mural passage.

A large moat, once 15 to 20 feet deep, and from 30 to 50 feet wide, extends from the N.E. of the castle, and forms a quadrangular enclosure 150 feet square, being still filled with water. The court thus enclosed probably held the stables and offices, and the outer defences were perhaps closed on the tower by palisades.

DALSTON HALL (*minor*)

THE manor-house of Little Dalston, lying four miles to the S.W. of Carlisle, is a building which, like Naworth, has expanded from the original peel, the tower at the E. end of the range of building measuring 31 feet by 25½ feet. Little Dalston was a manor within the barony of Dalston, which was presented by Ranulph de Meschines, Earl of Cumberland, to Robert de Vallibus or Vaux, the brother of Hubert of Gilsland. He took the name of the place, which he enjoyed until Stephen ceded Cumberland to King David; but this manor he gave to a younger brother, whose descendants kept it till 1761.

Sir William Dalston, created baronet in 1640, was a staunch Royalist and suffered considerably in the cause. During the long siege of Carlisle in 1644, he had to retire before General Lesley, who seized on his house and converted it into headquarters. He died in 1657, and the male line failed at the death of Sir George, the fifth baronet, in 1765, who, however, had sold the property five years before to Monkhouse Davison, after whose death it was purchased (1795) by James Sowerby, in whose family it remains.

This old fort is situated on an eminence overlooking the valley of Caldew, and is at present used as a farm-house. It consists of two square embattled towers echeloned 50 feet apart, and connected by inferior buildings. Upon a cornice is seen this old inscription: "𝕵𝖔𝖍𝖓 𝕯𝖆𝖑𝖘𝖙𝖔𝖓 𝕰𝖑𝖎𝖟𝖆𝖇𝖊𝖙𝖍 𝖜𝖎𝖕𝖍𝖊 𝖒𝖆𝖔 𝖞𝖘 𝖇𝖞𝖑𝖔𝖞𝖓𝖌," which is thought to refer to an owner in the middle of the fourteenth century. The fabric itself is ancient, but the square-headed windows are of the date of Henry VIII. The tower is of the same type as all peels, in three storeys, with a staircase in the wall.

DRAWDYKES (non-existent)

THE tower of this name, in the township of Linstock, was built in 1676 by John Aglionby on the site of an old Border fortress, which was removed during that century, but of which there are no remains, nor any history. The vallum of the Roman wall is clearly traceable in front of the castle; the three busts on the top of the tower are said to have come from the wall, but they have nothing Roman about them (*J. C. Bruce*).

DRUMBURGH (manor)

CLOSE to the Roman wall, at the head of the Solway Firth, 4½ miles from Burgh, are considerable remains of a fine specimen of an old fortified manor-house. Leland, writing of it in 1539, says: "At Drumburgh, the Lord Dacres father builded upon old ruines a prety pyle for defence of the country. The stones of the Pict wall were pulled down to build it." It was anciently a seat of the Bruns, lords of Bowness, and afterwards belonged to the barony of Burgh, which passed by heiresses through the several great families of Estriver, Eugaine, De Morville, Dacre, and Howard (see *Naworth*, &c.). It now belongs to the Earl of Lonsdale, since in 1678 Henry, Duke of Norfolk, sold the demesne to John Aglionby, who repaired the castle, then in ruins, and later conveyed it to the earl's ancestor, Sir John Lowther, in exchange for Nunnery, the head of the Armathwaite manor. Thomas, Lord Dacre, rebuilt the structure in the reign of Henry VIII., and in 1680 John Aglionby inserted new square windows; so although built at the end of the fourteenth, or at the beginning of the fifteenth century, its appearance is quite changed, and there is nothing now of a castellated nature remaining.

DUNWALLOGHT (*non-existent*)

THIS castle was in the parish of Cumrew. Here William de Dacre had a manor-house, which in 1 Edward II. (1307) he obtained a licence to fortify. It was then written as Dunmalloght, and there are some existing traces of it.

EGREMONT (*minor*)

THE castle stands on a remarkable hill close to the town, commanding the ford over the Eden and the bridge of later date, a most favourable site for a fortress, but no traces exist of any fortification earlier than the twelfth century, though there may have been a hill-fort in prehistoric times.

When William de Meschines obtained the barony of Copeland from Henry II., he built on this "cop" a fort to protect himself against a hostile population and also from the attacks of the Scots. There is shown under COCKERMOUTH how Allerdale below Derwent came to Alice de Romilly and William Fitz-Duncan, Earl of Moray, and also the disposition of the lands after the death of their son, "The Boy of Egremont,"— so called, perhaps, from having been born here in the castle of his grandmother Cicely de Meschines. His sister Amabel or Annabel married Lambert de Multon, the eldest son of Thomas de Multon of Holbeach, Lincolnshire, and brought to her husband these lands and the castle, to which he is said to have added the great hall. He died in 1247, and the property descended for three generations of the same family to Thomas De Multon in 1293, who, an important man of his day, figures in the Roll of Caerlaverock. He died about the time of the Bruce's raid into England in 1315, leaving a widow Eleanor, who had for her dower the castle of Egremont with its lands.

John de Multon, the last of his race, died *s.p.* in 1335, when the barony passed to his three sisters, the *caput baroniæ*, *i.e.*, the castle and lands, falling through the eldest, Joan, to Robert Fitzwalter.

We next hear of Egremont in 1371, when Walter, the son of this Joan and Robert Fitzwalter, being taken prisoner in the invasion of Gascony, had to mortgage the castle in order to raise £1000 for his ransom. Perhaps this money was furnished by the Percy family and was never redeemed, since in 1449 Thomas Percy, a son of Hotspur, was created Baron Egremont of Egremont Castle; he was slain at the battle of Northampton in 1460, when the title expired, but this property remained with his family.

About the year 1528, Henry Algernon Percy, 6th Earl of Northumberland, the early lover of Anne Boleyn, bought from Robert, Viscount Fitzwalter, one third part of this ancient barony and castle, whereby he seems to have acquired the greater portion of the whole property; but on the death of this earl in 1537 the entire Percy estates fell to the Crown, and were afterwards granted by Philip and Mary in 1557 to his nephew Thomas, at whose execution, in connection with the rising in the North in 1572, his brother Henry inherited.

A survey was then made of the Percy estates, and at Egremont it was found, in 1578, that "the Castle of Egremont is now almost ruinated and decay'd, save that some part of the old stonework & walls thereof are yet standing, & one chamber therein now used for the Court house in like ruin & decay. About which castle is a pleasant dry dich, & without the said dich hath been the base court now called the Castle-garth, the site of which said Castle together with the said Castle-garth contain by est. 2 acres & worth to be lett p. ann. 14s. 6d." Such condition of the old fortress at that date is sufficient to account for its present state, without ascribing its further ruin to the Parliamentary forces of the seventeenth century.

The castle occupies an oval-shaped eminence, the sides of which have been scarped on all sides, its highest point being at the N., where perhaps stood the original tower of the Meschines, and where Buck's drawing of 1739 shows a high raised

EGREMONT

tower fronting the road from St. Bees Abbey (also founded by William de Meschines) to Egremont. Round the crest of this hill ran the enceinte wall, which once had bastion towers at various points.

The square entrance tower remains at the S.W. corner, the lower part of which, with a considerable length of the curtain wall adjoining on the left of it, is of the first half of the twelfth century, according to Mr. Jackson (*Transactions of the Cumberland and Westmorland Antiquarian Society*, vol. iv.), and contains herring-bone work, as appears on the drawing given. There was a steep approach up to the drawbridge, and a circular Norman gateway opened into a groined archway, defended by strong doors.

The outer ward is 120 feet in length and ends in front of the great hall, built cir. 1260, which formed a defensible dwelling of the nature of a keep (as at Knaresborough), with an entrance defended by a portcullis. Traces of screens and window seats remain, but little of this building now exists; the lights were double, and raised far above the court. No chapel is to be found, but as the walls of the inner bailey have nearly perished, this and other buildings which we now seek in vain may have been situated here.

The salient on the S. was formed by a thirteenth-century circular bastion, which has vanished.

Below the upper ground there runs round the castle a broad lower terrace, also scarped: on the inner side of this was the ditch, of which a portion remains near the S.W. entrance. The barbican at the main entrance has gone entirely, as likewise have defences which perhaps stood at two other points of approach up the scarp of the terrace, round which probably ran a strong palisade. Below the S. end of the hill were the pleasaunce and gardens, and perhaps the tilt-yard. This is the castle to which, as told by Wordsworth, is attached the legend of the Horn of Egremont, relating to its possession by the Lucys, which could not, however, have lasted many years after 1335.

GREYSTOKE, or GREYSTOCK (chief)

THIS beautiful mansion of the Howards, occupying the site of the ancient castle, was built in the seventeenth century by the Hon. Charles Howard; but subsequent owners, Dukes of Norfolk, have added to and greatly embellished the work of those days. It stands on an eminence protected on the E. and S. by a rocky bank, below which a small stream flowed on its way to join the Petterill. There are but few remains of the ancient fortress, which was demolished by the Parliament after its capture in the Civil War. "Some broken towers are seen to the E., and in the back part of the present mansion some other old edifice appears" (*Hutchinson*).

The Conqueror gave Cumberland to Ranulph de Meschines, who granted this barony to one Lyulph, to whom it was confirmed by Henry I., and whose posterity assumed the name of Greystock. The Greystocks continued here in unbroken succession, generally from father to son, with much honour and wealth, intermarrying with the best families in the land, until the reign of Henry VII., when Robert, the son of Ralph, Lord Greystock, concluded the line, leaving an only daughter. She, being lady of Greystock and Wem, eloped from Brougham Castle one night and married Thomas, Lord Dacre of Gilsland, whereupon her estates went to the Dacres, whose race ended in the male line at the death of George, an infant, from the effects of a fall in the nursery, in 11 Elizabeth. His sisters then succeeded. The eldest, Anne, became the wife of Philip, Earl of Arundel, eldest son of the Duke of Norfolk, and brought Greystock to that family (see *Naworth*). The old castle must have been built

GREYSTOKE

captured by a Parliamentary force of General Lambert's division, and was then burnt and destroyed. It stood in a park of 500 acres.

HARBY BROW (minor)

NEAR the village of Allhallows and not far from Aspatria, on the N. bank of the Eden, is an old peel tower, 30 feet square and 60 feet high, now used as a farm-house.

HAY, OR HAYES (non-existent)

IN the Whitehaven district, half a mile from Distington, was once the residence of the Moresby family, and the manor-house of the lords of Distington. Little remains of the place except a portion of the N. wall, but its foundations may be traced over a considerable area.

HIGHHEAD (minor)

THIS place lies about eight miles S. of Carlisle, in the township of Ivegill. The tower belonged to the barony of Dalston, and is called in old records "Pela de Hivehead,"—showing that originally it was a peel tower only. The manor belonged to Sir Andrew Harcla (see *Carlisle*), and after his execution to the Crown. In 1326 Ralph Dacre obtained a grant of it and of the tower for ten years, after the expiry of which William L'Angleys, or L'Englise, was made custodian for life. In 1342 (16 Edward III.) Willielmus Lengleys, "dilectus vallettus noster," had a licence to crenellate his house of Heyheved, and this is probably the date of the new buildings then added to the old peel. His son in 1358 built the chapel, which was but a mean edifice. From the Langleys the property passed in 1550 by sale to John Richmond, in whose time the building was altered and enlarged, and all that remains of the old castle was then incorporated. His descendant Christopher Richmond left two daughters, the elder of whom became the wife of S. Gledhill, and the younger, Elizabeth, married Peter Brougham of Skelton, whose son, Henry Richmond Brougham, the High Sheriff of Cumberland, spent £10,000 upon new buildings here, procuring workmen from Italy to carry out the plaster-work. He died in 1749, before the place was finished, and the house passing into the hands of two families, half of it to each, was neglected by both, and fell partially into ruin. In the present century, the famous lawyer, Lord Chancellor Henry Brougham, a descendant of one of the owners, became purchaser of the castle, which has since been placed in better repair, and is now used as a farm-house. There was once a good deal of carved woodwork about the building, which has been removed to Brougham Hall.

Mr. Ferguson says that the remains of the ancient peel have to be sought behind the panels of upper bedrooms. Buck gives a drawing of Highhead as it appeared in 1739.

This grand structure stands on the brink of a rocky ravine, overhanging the Ive rivulet which flows below. Upon three sides the position is strong by nature, and upon the fourth the defences were assured by a massive wall and iron gates. In Buck's view there is shown the ruined gatehouse with a staircase turret in the inner corner, ending in a look-out, and on each side a high embattled wall; on the brink of the rocks stand the shattered remains of a large tower. H. R. Brougham's work must have commenced immediately after the taking of this sketch, and the building as erected by him is in a singularly inappropriate Italian style, with a balustrade parapet at top supporting a grand pediment decorated with figures in high relief. A double flight of stairs leads to the entrance, which conducts to a great hall with rows of Ionic columns, and corridors branching off right and left to the various apartments; in the midst rises a fine staircase, in two flights, to the upper storeys.

The only remaining portion of the ancient building is at the S.W. side, incorporated in the present house, and made to match the new work by a new stone facing.

HUTTON JOHN (*minor*)

THIS is a peel belonging to the chain of Border towers extending through the Eamont and Eden valleys, among which are Yanwath and Dacre, and perhaps Blencowe, which is, however, a Hall of the fourteenth century.

It is a square embattled tower, with added wings of later date, the work of Andrew Hudleston in 1662, when, after being driven away from his other possessions, he retired here with his family. The building was altered again at the end of the last century, but still retains its ancient appearance.

The old peel seems to date from about 1362, when it was the property of William de Hoton, being held under Greystoke. The Hotons were here in the thirteenth century, and possibly began to build at that period.

The structure is in two storeys, and measures 38 feet long by 30 feet wide; it has some interesting masonry and arms upon it. A branch of the Hotons or Huttons held it till 1564, when an heiress, Margaret, sister of the last male heir, brought the property to her husband, Andrew Hudleston, whose family afterwards parted with the greater part of the lands to Charles, 11th Duke of Norfolk. It was a member of this family, Father John Hudleston, who assisted in the escape of Charles II. after the battle of Worcester (September 1651), and followed him in his exile and wanderings, attending him on his deathbed. A portrait of this priest is preserved here.

IRTHINGTON (*non-existent*)

THE Chronicle of Lanercost shows the *caput baroniæ* of the barony of Gilsland to have been at Irthington, a village on the N. side of the river Irthing, 2½ miles from Brampton. Here was once a Roman camp, where now stands the Nook farm-house, alongside of which is an ancient mound, on which the English owners, the Irthingas, built their wooden homestead, and which was perhaps included in the Norman castle afterwards erected upon the site of the Roman camp.

Ranulph de Meschines, after the Conquest, had granted the barony of Gilsland to his kinsman or follower Hubert de Vaux or Vallibus, and with the consent of Henry II. his family continued to possess it. The lands had belonged to a Celtic family called Bueth, one of whom, Gille Mor, was driven out by the Conqueror; but when King David obtained Cumberland from Stephen, he supported Gille Mor Bueth against the Norman possessor, Robert de Vaux. On Henry II. regaining Cumberland from the Scots, this Robert re-entered on his property, and the legend runs that he invited his rival Bueth to a friendly tryst at Castle Steads, and there treacherously murdered him. It was by way of expiating this deed that, about 1169, Robert de Vaux is said to have founded the priory of Lanercost.

There is no evidence as to when Irthington Castle was destroyed; the foundations of it are well ascertained. Maclauchlan ("Memoir of the Roman Wall") says that the centre of the present farm-house occupies what was once the site of the ancient castle: its dimensions were about 96 feet by 75 feet, with a tower at the S. angle, and perhaps at the others. The middle of the castle was about 50 yards from the mound, and the walls were some 10 yards clear of the ditch surrounding that elevation. The mound has been lowered in order to form a garden on its summit. Many Roman remains, coins, &c., have been found here.

IRTON (minor)

THIS is an early Border tower, square and embattled, on the W. side of the county, which has been incorporated in the modern dwelling-house with other portions of the old building—the home of an ancient family who took their name from the place and the river Irt. The manor was held as far back as the reign of Henry I. by their ancestor Bertram de Irton, whose successor Adam became a Knight Hospitaller and went to the Crusades. The family has continued here in high standing and honour through all the vicissitudes of the country. One member, Sir Thomas Irton, was knighted for his conduct at Flodden (1513), and others have filled the office of High Sheriff for Cumberland until late in the last century; the present owner is Mr. Samuel Irton.

KIRKOSWALD (minor)

THE remains of this once magnificent abode of the Dacres are situated on rising ground about 200 yards S.E. of the town, in a fine valley, eight miles from Penrith. The town was called after St. Oswald, King of Northumbria.

This favourite residence of the lords of Gilsland is said to have been built originally by Ranulph or Randolph de Engain, Baron of Burgh, who married the heiress of the Trivers family not long after the Conquest. His grand-daughter Ada brought the inheritance to Simon de Morville, and, in the

second year of John, Sir Hugh de Morville obtained a licence to fortify the
castle and enclose a park. This Hugh, Baron of Burgh and Kirkoswald, has
in error been confounded with his notorious namesake who was one of the
murderers of Becket. The assassin of St. Thomas, however, was Hugh, lord
of Westmorland and Knaresborough at the time when Kirkoswald was held
by Simon de Morville, the grandfather of Sir Hugh, who fortified the castle.

After three generations of this family the lands went with an heiress to the
Multons of Holbeach, who as owners greatly enlarged the fortress (temp.
Edward II.). In the seventh year of this king, the castle and manor passed
by the runaway marriage of Margaret de Multon to Ranulph de Dacre of
Dacre (see *Naworth*), and the new owners made this place their favourite
residence; so that in the fifteenth and sixteenth centuries, Kirkoswald rose
to its full splendour, and in or about 1500 the castle received its last
additions from Thomas, Lord Dacre, who "encompassed it with a large
ditch for better security, and beautified it at great expense." This Sir Thomas
held the property from 1485 till 1525, and by carrying off at night from
Brougham Castle the young heiress Elizabeth, daughter of the last Lord
Greystoke, he united her barony of Greystoke to Kirkoswald. During his
wardenship of the Marches he lived chiefly here, and some of his despatches
are dated from this place.

Upon the division of the vast possessions of the Dacres into the two
branches of Dacres of the North and Dacres of the South, this castle fell
to the latter, that is, to the Fiennes and Lennard families; the last of whom
marrying a natural daughter of Charles II. by the Duchess of Cleveland,
was created Earl of Sussex, and died in 1715, leaving two daughters. The
property was then exposed for sale, and was purchased by Sir Christopher
Musgrave, Bart., of Edenhall, in whose family it continues.

These South Dacres, however, did not live here, and under their rule the
place was little cared for and fell into ruin; at last it was dismantled by
order of Lord Dacre, and was also subjected to spoliation to a vast extent,
a quantity of the carved wood and of painted glass finding its way to Lowther
and Corby. Lord William Howard enriched his castle of Naworth with
curious genealogical glass windows and the panelled ceiling of the hall
all miserably burnt there in the fire of 1844 (see *Naworth*). In 1622 the
beautiful chapel roof of Kirkoswald was removed, and put up over the
library of Belted Will; so that in 1688 Thomas Denton wrote of this castle
as "a bare shell or heap of stones." Buck's drawing of 1739 shows it almost
as ruinous as it is at present; some walls, however, were then standing which
have since been removed for use in other buildings.

The castle stands in the centre of a space of about 1¾ acres, enclosed
by a rectangular moat, 30 to 40 feet wide, and from 12 to 18 feet deep,
which is supplied by a brook in the park above. In the W. angle of the

moat is a separate outwork, an outlying mound which once was fortified, surrounded by water, and flanking the drawbridge on the W. side. There are no traces of the gatehouse which, with this bridge over the moat, gave admittance to the outer ward. The buildings of the castle formed a square of about 150 feet, and two towers partly remain on the S. face of it, having a vaulted basement and two floors. On the N. side stands a tall slender tower, tolerably entire, 65 feet in height, built diagonally to the castle wall; it contains a spiral staircase, admitting to the three floors of the castle by mural galleries, the doorways to the several entrances still remaining. There is a fourth doorway leading to the battlements, which have all disappeared. On this N. face were situated the chapel and chief apartments, the great hall lying probably on the E. side.

Sandford, visiting Kirkoswald in 1610, declares this castle to have been "the fairest fabrick that ever eyes looked upon. The hall I have seen 100 feet long, & the great portraiture of King Brute lying at the end of the roof of this hall and of all his succeeding Kings of England. In this grand Castle I was some 60 years agoe, when there was many fair towres and chambers & chapels."

On the W. face, among grassy mounds and heaps of rubbish, can be traced the site of the inner gatehouse, and in the outer ward that of the stables and offices. It seems possible that before the moat was added by Sir Thomas Dacre, in 1500, there was an outer wall of defence. Nothing remains now of the Norman castle, all that we see being chiefly the buildings of the time of Edward II.

LIDDELL, or LYDDAL (non-existent)

AT Liddell there is a strong earthwork entrenchment, about two miles from Netherby, called the Mote, situated on a lofty cliff overlooking a vast expanse of country. At one end of the enclosure is a high mound, and in the middle lie the foundations of a square building. The work is further strengthened on its weaker side by a curved lunette in front.

Leland appears to be the authority for this work having contained a castle. He says: "This was the noted place of a gentilman cawled Syr Walter Seleby, the which was killed there, & the place destroyed yn King Edward the Thyrde time, when the Scottes went to Dyrham." It is said to have been taken by storm by David II., who caused the two sons of Sir Walter to be strangled before their father's face, and then commanded their parent to be beheaded.

This is all disallowed, however, in a paper on the work by Mr. R. S. Ferguson, published in the *Transactions of the Cumberland Archæological Society*, vol. ix. He affirms it to have been purely a Roman post, and denies that any castle existed here, though perhaps there may have been an early sixteenth-century abode of the Graham family.

The barony of Liddell was held by the Crown from 1343 till the seventeenth century, when James I. granted it to Francis, Earl of Cumberland, who sold Liddell in 1629 to the ancestors of the Grahams of Netherby, of whose estates it still forms a part.

LINSTOCK (minor)

LINSTOCK is a square peel on the Borderland N.W. of Carlisle. It was granted by Henry I. to his chaplain Walter, and given by him to the prior and convent of Carlisle; afterwards, from the foundation of the bishopric in 1133, it was for nearly 200 years the residence of the bishops. Bishop Irton, a prelate employed by the king in negotiations with the Scots, died here in March 1292, after a tedious journey in the snow to attend the Parliament in London. The next year Bishop Halton entertained here John Romaine, Archbishop of York, and a suite of 300 persons, on his way to Hexham. In 1307 Edward I. came with his queen, and was sumptuously lodged for six days by the Bishop. Linstock was, however, an insecure retreat, lying exposed to the incursions of the Scots, who were small respecters of persons, and during the time of the soldier bishop, who was governor of Carlisle, the annoyances and the difficulties of defence were so great that about this time it was abandoned and deserted; and so it remained till about a century ago, when the castle was rebuilt and modernised by one James Nicolson, lessee of the estate.

The ancient square tower or keep, built of red sandstone, still exists. Its walls, which are very massive, contain four chambers; the ground floor is vaulted, and is lighted by a single loop. From the large room on the first floor a stair contrived in the wall leads to the second floor, which is in two rooms. It was repaired and modern windows were inserted in 1768, and it is now used as a farm-house. Part of the moat which once surrounded the building still exists. There is no way of fixing the date of erection, but originally the castle must have been of much larger extent to have accommodated the bishops with their retinue and their visitors.

MILLOM (minor)

MILLOM is on the extreme S.W. point of the county, between the sea and the Duddon sands, in the barony of Egremont, and was granted by William de Meschines to one Godart de Boyville or Boisville, temp. Henry I. His family retained the property till the reign of Henry III., taking the name of De Millom, and ending, after five generations, in an heiress, Joan, who brought the lordship to her husband, Sir John Hudleston, knight, with whose descendants it continued for nearly 500 years. These Hudlestons were a very ancient stock, whose origin is traced back long anterior to the Conquest; Sir John served at the siege of Caerlaverock, and in 1301 signed the celebrated letter of the barons to the Pope, under the title of Lord of Anneys in Millom. Another, Sir Richard, fought as a banneret at Agincourt (1415). Sir William Hudleston was a distinguished and devoted Royalist in the Civil War, being made a knight banneret on the field by Charles I., for his great personal bravery at the battle of Edgehill, where he recovered the royal standard. Millom is said to have been beset by the Parliamentary forces in 1648. The Hudlestons were still living there in 1688, but the castle was then in a ruinous state. William Hudleston left a daughter Elizabeth, who in 1774 sold the estate, for about £20,000, to Sir James Lowther, Bart., and it now belongs to his successor, the Earl of Lonsdale.

There are considerable remains of the castle, which was fortified by Sir John Hudleston by licence obtained 9 Edward III. (1335), on the plea of defending himself against the raids of the Scots. In early time there were the surroundings of a fine park, but most of the timber was cut down in 1690 for fuel to work iron furnaces; as late as 1774 the park was well stocked with deer, but in 1802 it was disparked by the Lonsdales.

Canon Knowles states (1872) that the house of the thirteenth century consisted probably of a hall, a solar chamber and cellars, a palisaded court and offices. It had on the E. a stone gatehouse flanked by two semicircular turrets, of which there are traces. Sir John Hudleston added a kitchen on the site of the old hall, with dormitories above; as well as the present entrance tower and the new hall and solar, with the corridor buildings. In the fifteenth century some rooms occupied the site of the old hall, and late in the sixteenth the great tower, 50 feet square, was built. It is a quadrangular building. The entrance tower on the E., now a ruin, leads into the courtyard, in which can be seen traces of the original gatehouse; on the N. is the kitchen, and S. the solar. On the W. corner is the ancient hall, dismantled perhaps in 1322, and next to it is the great tower, the battlements of which have disappeared.

Of late the fabric has been used as a farm-house.

MUNCASTER (*minor*)

THE manor of Mealcastre or Mulcaster was, like Millom, held of the barony of Egremont, and lay between the rivers Esk and Mite, about a mile from the railway at Ravenglass, where these two streams unite with the Irt in the estuary of Esk, and flow thence into the Irish Sea.

There was an ancient castle here upon an eminence N. of the Esk, belonging to the Penningtons, a family whose domicile, prior to the Conquest, had been at a place of that name in Furness, where they resided till 1242. The fee of Ravenglass had been given to Alan Pennington temp. John, and his descendant Sir John Pennington, a steady Lancastrian, residing at the time at Muncaster, gave shelter there to King Henry VI. after the disaster at Hexham in 1464, on his flight from Bywell Castle in Northumberland to find an asylum in the Lake Country. On leaving the friendly castle, he is said to have presented his entertainer with "an ancient glass vessel of the basin kind, about 7 inches in diameter, ornamented with some white enamelled mouldings," which has been preserved here with pious care ever since, and is called the "Luck of Muncaster." Like a similar relic at Edenhall, it was given with a prayer that as long as it should be preserved the family should prosper, and never want a male heir. There is an old painting representing this incident in what is called King Henry's Bedroom here.

Sir John was a distinguished soldier, and led the left wing of the English army in an expedition into Scotland. His grandson fought at Flodden, and one of his descendants was a trusted admiral of Charles I. In 1783 Sir John Pennington was created Baron Muncaster, and the property continues with his descendants.

The present castle is chiefly modern, but the principal tower of the ancient castle has been preserved, though it has no longer its original outward appearance. The place is surrounded with fine grounds and woods, and has a magnificent prospect over Eskdale.

Near Ravenglass is a very curious relic of a building called Walls Castle, said by Canon Knowles to be decidedly of late Roman construction. It consists of some low walls forming a series of rooms, with doorways and traces of windows.

NAWORTH (chief)

NAWORTH was probably erected about 1385, "in magno periculo propter Scotos," and is a truly beautiful castle, formed by the enlargement of an original peel, which was placed here in very early days. It is an irregular quadrangular building, defended on three sides by a deep ravine, and formerly on the fourth by a moat with gatehouse and drawbridge, and lies about twelve miles N.E. of Carlisle, in the parish of Brampton. Ranulph de Dacre, Sheriff of Cumberland 20 Henry III., was its first possessor, and had a licence to crenellate in 9 Edward III. (1336); he was governor likewise of Scarborough and Pickering, and of Carlisle at his death, 52 Henry III.

Mr. Ferguson says that he found the lower part of the Carlisle or old tower at Naworth and the S. curtain wall of a date not later than the tenth century, and that this was the original peel from which the famous castle grew.

When Henry II. recovered Cumberland from the Scots, he granted the barony of Gilsland to Hubert de Vallibus or Vaux, whose family had come from Normandy some years after the Conquest, and this property descended from ancestor to heir in unbroken series, through the successive noble families of De Vaux, Multon, Dacre, and Howard, to its present possessor, the Earl of Carlisle; it has never been sold or alienated for a period of over 700 years. Robert de Vaux, the second baron, founded the neighbouring abbey of Lanercost, and defended Carlisle in 1174 against William the Lion. In 6 Henry III. we find Robert de Vaux, a crusader, at Gilsland. His son, the fifth baron, who succeeded him 1234, left an only daughter, Maud, who brought Gilsland to her husband, Thomas de Multon, who was of a Lincolnshire family, and thus obtained the De Vaux estates in Cumberland, Yorkshire, Norfolk, Suffolk, Somerset, and Devon. Thomas de Multon, his great-grandson, was summoned to Parliament among the greater barons, and died in 1313, leaving an only daughter and heiress, Margaret, married to Ranulph de Dacre, who came from a place of that name in the same county, in the barony of Greystoke. This Ranulph had eloped in 1313 with Margaret, a girl of seventeen, from Warwick Castle, where she and the Gilsland lands were placed under the tutelage of the Earl of Warwick. He was a man of much importance on the Borders, and suffering from an inroad of Scots under Lord Archibald Douglas in 1333, obtained licence to fortify his house at Naworth in 1336; he died in 1340. His great-great-grandson Ralph, Lord Dacre of Gilsland, was killed at the battle of Towton, and his possessions were forfeited, a great part going to his niece Lady Joan, married to Sir Richard Fiennes, (through her) Lord Dacre of the South. His brother Humphrey, however, made his peace with Edward IV., and was summoned to Parliament as Lord Dacre of the North; he was Lord Warden of the Marches, and died in 1485. To him succeeded Thomas, Lord Dacre, who in 1487, following the example of his ancestor, carried off by night from Brougham Castle Elizabeth, the heiress of Greystoke, a ward of the king, and in the custody of Henry Clifford, Earl of Cumberland, who perhaps intended her for one of his own family. Thus was Greystoke added to the Dacre inheritance, and the united estates were possessed by this lord's descendants till 1569. This Thomas was a notable figure in history; he accompanied, in 9 Henry VII., the Earl of Surrey in his relief of Norham Castle. At Flodden he commanded the cavalry:

> "The right-hand wing with all his rout.
> The lusty Lord Dacres did lead;
> With him the bows of Kendal stout,
> With milk-white coats and crosses red."

He filled the office of Warden of the East and Middle Marches, and later of the West also, and carried out many negotiations with the court of Scotland. In 1523 he led the cavalry in Surrey's attack upon Jedburgh, and after an obstinate conflict, took the castle of Fernhurst. He died a Knight of the Garter in 1525.

William, Lord Dacre, who was governor of Carlisle temp. Edward VI., Mary, and Elizabeth, died in 1563, and was followed by his eldest son, Thomas. He died two years after, leaving an infant son George, who died 1569 from falling off a wooden rocking-horse, when the barony of Dacre of Gilsland (of the North) fell into abeyance between three coheiresses. Their uncle Leonard tried to wrest the lands from them, but failing in this he embarked in the Northern Rebellion. Laying hold of Naworth, he fortified and held it, but being defeated by Lord Hunsden, the governor of Berwick, at the Gelt Bridge, he betook himself to the Low Countries, and died in exile there (1573), as did his next brother Edward.

The mother of the infant Lord George had married, as her second husband, Thomas, Duke of Norfolk, who

NAWORTH

was beheaded by Elizabeth, and who had apportioned the three heiresses, then minors, to his three sons. Ann accordingly married the Earl of Arundel, Mary was given to Thomas, Lord Howard de Walden, and Elizabeth to Lord William Howard, his third son. Mary, however, died before her marriage; Arundel was imprisoned by Queen Elizabeth, and died in the Tower, and Lord William had to purchase Naworth and the estates for £10,000. He and Elizabeth Dacre were married in 1577, and they lived together for sixty years. The persecution of his family ended at the death of the queen, and on the accession of James, Lord William was restored in the blood, and in 1605 made Warden of the Marches. He at once occupied Naworth and commenced repairing and altering the old stronghold, whose chief interest perhaps is gained from him. He was not only a bold soldier and the terror of marauders in the Borderland, but was also a man of culture, the friend of Camden and Cotton, and one of the original members of the Society of Antiquaries. Legend and poetry have thrown a charm over the name of him whom Scott calls "Noble Howard—Belted Will." Another Border name for him was "Bauld (or bold) Willie."

> "Howard, than whom knight
> Was never dubb'd, more bold in fight ;
> Nor when from war and armour free,
> More famed for stately courtesy."

He is said by a strong hand to have given peace to the Borders, and substituted obedience for anarchy. He died at Naworth in 1640, aged seventy-seven. His eldest son Philip died during his lifetime, leaving a son, Sir William Howard, who was by Charles II. created Lord Dacre of Gilsland and Earl of Carlisle, and whose family have since then possessed the lands and Naworth.

The castle stands on a triangular tongue of land formed by the castle stream on the N., and a little rivulet on the S., which unite and flow into the Irthing ; from their banks, which on either side are rocky and precipitous, rise the castle walls. It has been said to be "one of England's choicest architectural monuments."

In the S. front, close to the old tower, is the entrance, admitting under the main building into the courtyard or quadrangle, around which the castle is built. The outer defence in front consisted of a deep ditch extending from one stream to the other, but stopped at each end and crossed by a drawbridge. The E. front contains the chief rooms, the N. side being occupied mostly by the great hall, which is entered by a flight of stairs from the court ; it has sixteenth-century windows on the inner side (enlarged afterwards), and is 70 feet long by 24 feet wide. At the end is the dining-room, and the kitchens are at the W. end of this front. The W. front contained the chapel and the lodgings, the S. side being chiefly a curtain wall.

The hall and gatehouse into the small outer ward, as well as other buildings taken down after the great fire, were erected by Lord Thomas Dacre, the great builder of the family. But the Dacres, who created Naworth, resided principally at Kirkoswald, and the successors of Lord Thomas did little for Naworth, which after 1569 was unoccupied for thirty years ; so that in the

Survey of 31 Elizabeth it is stated to be "in very great decay in all parts." Then succeeded Lord William Howard, who repaired Lord Thomas' work and rebuilt a great part, including the upper portion of the tower bearing his name, and the long gallery in the E. front; some of his work bears the mark 1602, about which time he came to reside here. The first Earl of Carlisle repaired the castle, and the third earl, who built Castle Howard, did more in that way, his architect Vanbrugh adding the music-gallery and the hall-screen. The old or Carlisle Tower is like the Strickland Tower at Rose Castle. The E. front is shown by Buck with its two great flanking towers; that on the S.E. being the old tower, which is 29 feet square, and that on the N.E. Lord William Howard's or Belted Will's Tower.

On the 10th May 1844 a fire broke out, during the absence of the family, which destroyed the greater part of the castle, but was fortunately stopped before it reached the N.E. tower of Belted Will, where the apartments remain much in their original state. These are closed with iron doors, and contain his furniture, and his scholarly library of books is still in the room in which he used to sit. Near this room is an oratory, and the fire revealed below this tower three priests' holes lighted by slits. Beneath the great S.E. tower are three dungeons on the ground floor, and one above, quite unlighted, with iron doors and a ring in the wall to which prisoners might be chained. In the "Legend of Montrose" is mentioned a private stair and passage from Lord William's room to these prisons, and the fire revealed others. Here he used to immure the daring moss-troopers, and there are two magnificent oaks near the entrance on which he is said to have hanged his victims. He kept a garrison of 140 men at Naworth.

PENRITH (*minor*)

SINCE the men of Penrith obtained a licence to fortify their town in 1347 (20 Edward III.), it is evident that no castle of any sort was then in existence here. In 1397 Richard II. granted the manor of Penrith to Ralph Nevill, Earl of Westmorland, and to his heirs, his son Richard succeeding; and it is likely that Penrith Castle was built at this time. When the Earl of Salisbury had been beheaded after the battle of Wakefield, Henry VI. gave Penrith to John, Lord Clifford of Brougham Castle; and when he fell at the battle of St. Albans in 1461, this manor and castle were given by Edward IV. to the Earl of Warwick, the king-maker, on whose death at Barnet, in 1471, they reverted to the Crown. Edward then granted them to his brother Richard, who is said to have lived here when engaged in the defence of Cumberland against the Scots; for five years he is described as sheriff, and of Penrith Castle, which fabric he greatly enlarged, but after this the castle seems to have been neglected. The Crown held it till 1616, when it was devised in trust for

Charles, Prince of Wales, and in 1672 it formed part of the jointure of Queen Catherine of Braganza, who possessed it on the death of Charles II. In 1696 William III. granted the honour and castle of Penrith to his friend William Bentinck, Earl of Portland, and in 1787 the Duke of Portland sold the property to William, 5th Duke of Devon.

In the Survey of Elizabeth's reign in 1572, two towers are mentioned : one the Red Tower, and the other the White, or Bishop Strickland's Tower, with one great chamber adjoining the latter, a bakehouse, brewhouse, &c., all in good repair. The outer gatehouse, with the gates, was in utter ruin, as were also the chapel, the great hall and solar, and the kitchens ; these could not be

PENRITH

repaired, for already much stone material had been abstracted from the ruin and carted away for building purposes since 1547.

Penrith was captured in 1648 by General Lambert, who made it his head-quarters for a month, and the castle seems to have been demolished at this time, the lead and timber being sold for the use of the Commonwealth.

The castle stands on rising ground near the railway station. It was built in the form of a parallelogram, and was fortified with a very deep ditch outside, and a walled rampart. There was one entrance on the side of the town, where an opening still exists, and where the approach lay over a drawbridge.

Buck's view in 1730 shows two large detached fragments of the main building with windows of the hall, and a long range of the outer walls with supporting turrets, having the corbels for carrying a wooden allure outside. There are still many cellars and dungeons remaining.

ROSE (chief)

ROSE, the episcopal palace of the see of Carlisle, is situated by the Caldew river, seven miles S. of the city. The origin or nucleus of the fine group of towers and hanging gardens which we see now, was the baronial manor peel of Dalston, granted to the see by Henry III. in 1228, the remains of this building forming the present Strickland Tower on the N.E. corner of

ROSE

the N. front of the fabric. The name of The Rose was borne by the tower at that time.

The first historical notice we get of the place is in 1300, when Edward I. was residing here, after the siege of Caerlaverock, probably as a guest of Bishop Halton. Whilst here he summoned a parliament to meet him at Lincoln, the writs for which are dated "Apud la Rose, Sep. 25, 1300." In 1322, during an inroad by King Robert Bruce, the buildings were burnt, and the same thing happening a few years later, Bishop John Kirby in 1336 obtained a licence to crenellate his house called La Roos. This bishop then built himself a spacious mansion within the walls, and the works were continued by his successor, Bishop Welton. The castle then formed a quadrangle, the hall being on the E. side, to the S. of the old tower; on the W. side was a council chamber, and at the end of this was the chapel, with the Constable's tower beyond. All this stood within an inner court surrounded by its own moat: outside of this was the outer bailey, around which a second wall was drawn, with towers at intervals, and a strong gatehouse at the point of the present entrance. The whole was encircled by a moat supplied by a spring from the bank above.

In the fifteenth century Bishop Strickland restored the old peel or keep, which has since borne his name, and by the provision of larger windows and better sleeping accommodation, the fortress was rendered more habitable and convenient. Bishop Bell afterwards built another tower on the N. front, which bears his monogram of a bell; and Bishop Kite in the sixteenth century added a third tower on the W. side, and more private apartments; the total number of rooms being sixty. Later in that century Bishop Meye complained, in the reign of Elizabeth, that he was turned out of the Rose by the Warden of the Marches, who occupied it as a stronghold against the Scots. No historical interest attaches to it till 1645, when the castle, being held for the king by Mr. Lowther, the Constable, with only twenty or thirty men, was attacked and taken by a detachment of Colonel Heveringham's regiment, and was used as a prison for Royalists. In 1648 it seems to have changed hands again, and was once more beset and summoned. After suffering a storm of two hours' duration it was taken and burnt, so that in the Survey of 1680 the castle was reported to be in a state of great decay, its materials being valued at only £425; and when Bishop Rainbow came here after the Restoration, no part of the fabric was habitable.

Succeeding bishops repaired the building and added to it, but its present state is due to Bishop Percy, who in 1827 restored the place to a condition worthy of its ancient name, and in the style which prevailed at the date when the older portions were erected, that is, in the fourteenth century. Beyond Kite's Tower at the S.W. angle was another, called Pettenger's Tower, where once some one of that name had hanged himself, but this was removed. The gatehouse contains a room for the warder, above the archway, which may be of as early a date as Bishop Halton: a rose is sculptured on it.

The original retreat of the bishops of Carlisle was at Linstock (q.v.).

SCALEBY (manor)

SCALEBY lies about six miles N.E. of Carlisle. The manor was given by Edward I. to Richard de Tilliol, surnamed the Rider, and in 1307 (1 Edward II.) a licence was granted to Robert de Tylliol to crenellate his house. The last of the family, Robert, died s.p. in 1435, leaving two sisters, the eldest of whom, Isabel, brought this estate to John Colville, whose son

SCALEBY

William left only two daughters; they both married into the Musgrave family, the youngest, Margaret, conferring Scaleby on her husband, Nicholas Musgrave, whose descendant, Sir Edward Musgrave, largely rebuilt the castle in 1596. His grandson, Sir Edward, created a baronet in 1638, was a zealous Royalist, and garrisoned Scaleby Castle for the king in 1644, but during the siege of Carlisle in 1645 it was taken from him. Recovering it, however, he held it again for King Charles in 1648; but the place had suffered so much in the first siege that it was now too weak to hold out, and after firing a single shot, Sir Edward had to surrender to General Lambert, whose soldiers are said to have set fire to the castle.

Then, to relieve himself from his heavy losses in the Civil War, Sir Edward was obliged to sell his property, which was conveyed to Dr. Richard Gilpin, who repaired the castle and fitted it up for his own residence. Here in 1724 was born the Rev. William Gilpin, the voluminous author. Afterwards the place was acquired by the family of Stephenson, or Standish, and is now the property of their descendant, Captain W. P. Standish. After the Gilpins the castle was long deserted, and fell into a state of decay; but it was again put into good repair by a Mr. Rowland Fawcett, whose family inhabited it for many years.

Although the castle stands on a flat site it is a place of considerable strength, having two broad and deep moats for an outer defence, one of which, partly filled with water, still remains: the circumference of the outer one measured nearly a mile. With the *débris* of these moats a mound was formed, upon which part of the castle was built. The entrance was across two drawbridges defended by a strong tower with a portcullis, and a very lofty battlemented wall. A considerable portion of the old work remains in a tolerably perfect state, the walls being immensely thick. The vaulted hall is a fine apartment, and beneath it are large cellars.

Perhaps the large area contained within the moats was intended for the protection and the support of cattle, which would be driven in at a time of alarm on the Border.

SEATON (*non-existent*)

NEAR Workington, on the W. coast and close to the sea, there was a castle, once the seat of the Curwen family, who left it as early as the twelfth century, and removed to Workington Hall, on the other side of the Derwent River. A few remains exist, and are known as the Barrow Walls, being used for shooting-butts by the local volunteer force. The Curwens trace their descent from John de Tailbois, a brother of the Count of Anjou, before the Conquest.

TRIERMAIN (*minor*)

TRIERMAIN, an ancient fief of the barony of Gilsland, is situated at some distance from the left front of Birdoswald, the Roman station of Amboglanna, and the largest one, upon the line of the great wall of Hadrian. The Celtic possessors of Triermain before the Normans were named Bueth, of which family one Gille-mor, or "the big gillie," or servant (hence Gillesland, or Gilsland), was deprived of his lands by Henry I. in favour of one Hubert de Vaux or Vallibus (see *Irthington*). Robert de Vaux had the place in 1169, and

it was held by a succession of male De Vauxes until the reign of Edward IV.,
when Jane, daughter and heiress of the last of them, brought it to Sir Richard
Salkeld of Corby, whose daughter inherited Triermain, and from her it passed
in several changes to the family of Dacre, and finally to that of Howard in the
beginning of the seventeenth century.

This tower may have been erected by an early De Vaux of Triermain, it
being built of stones taken from the convenient neighbouring quarry of the
Roman wall. It was a total ruin temp. Elizabeth, and is thus described in
an inquisition taken in the thirty-first year of her reign : "The scite of the
said manner of Tradermayne, was sometime a fair Castle called Tradermayne
Castle, a house of great strength & of good receipt ; it stood and was built
opposite to the coasts of Scotland and Tyndell, and about vi miles distant
from Lydderesdeli, and was a very convenient place for both annoying of the
enemy and defending the country thereabouts, but now the said Castle is
utterly decayed."

In 1832 great portions of the ruin fell, but before its collapse it was described
as an oblong quadrangle, turreted at the eastern and western extremities and
moated round. The principal entrance was underneath a massive archway in
the western turret. This is the castle celebrated by Scott in his romantic
poem of "The Bridal of Triermain."

WOLSTY (non-existent)

THIS castle, which was two miles from Silloth, must in early times have been
a position of strength and importance, since Roman pottery has been
found in the earthworks. The place became Church property, and a licence
to crenellate a castle was granted to the abbots of Holme by Edward III. in
1349. It was afterwards used by the abbots of Holme Cultram as a stronghold wherein to preserve their treasure. It belonged to nine generations of
the family of Chamber of Holderness, afterwards of Hanworth, Middlesex.
The only existing remains are those of the site of a part of the ditch, which
was large and deep.

DURHAM

Durham

AUCKLAND, or BISHOP AUCKLAND (chief)

AUCKLAND CASTLE stands on a hill ten miles S.W. of Durham. Of the fourteen castles and manor-houses once held by the ancient bishops palatine, this is the only remaining episcopal residence. It stands in a well-timbered park—the remains of the chase which originally perhaps attracted the early bishops, who were mighty hunters, to the manor-house; and it is stated that Bishop Anthony Bec (1283 to 1311) "did sumptuously build and incastellate the ancient manor place of Auckland." He is said to have built "the great hall with its divers pillars of black marble speckled with white"—though this is now thought to be of earlier date—but he certainly added a hall, of which portions are to be seen in the present kitchen, as well as the chapel, the great chamber, and many rooms adjoining. The succeeding three bishops made large additions to the buildings, until their palace became a very grand edifice. It was not a highly defensible place, and was called a manor-house, and not a castle, till the sixteenth century, but it was certainly strong enough to afford protection to the bishops in troublous times. Bishop Ruthal (1509-1522) built a dining-hall, the great window of which was completed in the reign of Henry VIII. by Bishop Tunstall (1529-1558), who also added that part of the castle stretching westward, called "Scotland," from the fact that it was set apart for the lodgings of Scottish hostages. All this has been modernised. Beneath are the cellars, and on the first floor the servants' dwellings, with a long line of bedrooms above, built by Bishop Tunstall.

Thus Auckland remained in the seventeenth century, a stately and luxurious seat, of considerable strength, compassed with a thick stone wall on the side of its hill, below which runs the river. In the park were wild cattle, such as are still seen at Chillingham—"all white, which will not endure your approach, very violent and furious."

In 1611 it was determined to send to Auckland, to the custody of Bishop James, the Lady Arabella Stuart, who had married contrary to the intent of her tyrant cousin, King James. On the road thither she managed to escape from her conductors at Highgate, but being retaken, was afterwards confined in the Tower of London, where she lost her reason and died a prisoner. Six years after this, Bishop James was so roughly upbraided by the king, in his own castle of Durham, that he retired to Auckland and died there three days after of "a violent fit of strangury," brought on by vexation—"scolded to death," as was stated in the Mortality Rolls.

In May 1633, Charles I. spent three days here, on his journey to Scotland, and was magnificently entertained. He was here again in 1647, a prisoner with the Scottish army, at which time the castle was in the hands of his enemies. In this year the castle palace was confiscated and was conveyed by the Parliamentary Commissioners to Sir Arthur Hastlerigg of Noseley, Northants, for the sum of £6102, 8s. 11½d., when the purchaser began to construct for himself a magnificent mansion within the castle yard, using the materials of the chapel, which he destroyed with powder ; but he meddled very little with the castle itself, in spite of the assertions to the contrary of Bishop John Costin, who, coming in at the Restoration, made as an excuse for his own alterations, that Hastlerigg had "ruined and almost utterly destroyed" the castle. This prelate removed the new mansion of Hastlerigg, and built the courtyard walls shown in Buck's drawing of 1728. Succeeding bishops added rooms on the S. front and carried out various "improvements," spoiling thereby much good old work.

All that remains of Bishop Bee's work is the chapel in the N.E. corner, called after its founder, and perhaps a small tower in the S.W. corner of the outbuildings.

BARNARD (minor)

ON the summit of a high rocky cliff, W. of the town of the same name, are the ruins of this once magnificent fortress. The position is an ideal one for security, defence, and picturesqueness, overhanging the Tees at a considerable elevation, with far-reaching prospects up and down the valley, and over the spreading country below. William the Red King gave to

Guy Baliol one of his father's followers from Normandy the forests of Teesdale and Marwood, with the lordships of Middleham and Gainforth, and Guy's eldest son Bernard built this castle about the year 1130. He was one of the barons who defeated the army of the Scots at the Battle of the Standard, and he was taken prisoner with Stephen at Lincoln in 1142, when that restless and valiant king was struck down, fighting against overpowering odds, in the

BARNARD

decisive battle there. In 1174 (20 Henry II.), when the Scots under their king William the Lion laid siege to Alnwick Castle, Bernard de Baliol, Robert de Stuteville, lord of Knaresborough, and others, collected their forces and marched to its relief. A thick fog coming on, a halt was advised, when Baliol exclaimed that he would push on alone if the rest waited, and so they all moved forward, and with such despatch that they surprised the enemy, and in a short skirmish took the Scottish king prisoner, and sent him to Richmond Castle. During the time of the next lord, Hugh Baliol, Alexander, King of Scotland, came before Barnard Castle with an army, and reconnoitred it to ascertain if it were assailable. While the enemy was thus occupied, some one from the walls with a crossbow-shot killed the king's brother-in-law, Eustace de Vesey, lord of Alnwick, whereon the northern force decamped. This Hugh was in great favour with King John. On the forfeiture of the estates of John Baliol, King of Scotland, in 1294, Edward I. gave Barnard Castle to Guy Beauchamp, Earl of Warwick, in whose family it remained through five descents. After them, Anne Nevill, daughter of the King-maker, brought the property in marriage to King Richard III. (at that time Duke of Gloucester), who resided at the castle as one of his favourite seats. The sculpture of his cognizance, the white boar, is still visible on the ruins, and there is a fine oriel window in the W. front which is said to have belonged to his state chamber.

The castle and manor were restored by Henry VII. to Warwick's widow, but that greedy king afterwards obliged her to reconvey them to him. Then they passed, through several other possessors' hands, to Charles, Earl of Westmorland, who with the Earl of Northumberland headed the Catholic insurrection in 1569, known in history as the "Rising of the North." The deep attachment of the northern provinces to the old faith seems to have been stirred by the zealous proceedings of Pilkington, the first Protestant Bishop of Durham, while at the same time the misfortunes of Mary Queen of Scots had evoked general interest, which was quickened by the imprisonment, on her account, of the Duke of Norfolk, head of the ancient nobility of England, and brother-in-law to Westmorland. At the first alarm of a disturbance in the North, Elizabeth summoned both Westmorland and Northumberland to London, as the chief men of those parts both in dignity and property. Being neither of them strong men, they were worked upon to believe that their lives and estates were to be forfeited, and that the royal troops were on their way to seize them. The Earl of Northumberland therefore left his house by night, and sought the Earl of Westmorland at Brancepeth, where he found him similarly alarmed, and arming his followers, the bells ringing backwards, and beacon-fires blazing. The two earls had no difficulty in raising 1500 men, a force which was doubled as they proceeded to Durham. Here they made a Catholic demonstration, celebrated mass in the cathedral, and then proceeded southwards, their forces numbering 4000 foot and 600 horse. Meantime the queen's forces under Radcliffe, Earl of Sussex, and the Earl of Warwick with 3000 men in support, were coming to meet the insurgents, while the bulk of the Catholic nobility and gentry abstained from giving any assistance. At this critical moment the two earls showed neither talent nor decision, but retreated to Raby, and then turned off to besiege Sir George Bowes, who had taken possession of Westmorland's castle of Barnard. The rebels gained the outer bailey and the outer circuit of the castle walls without difficulty, but the strong keep defied them, obstinately defended as it was. Sir George Bowes held out for ten days, and then surrendered upon good terms from want of provisions; but this delay enabled the queen's forces to come up to Northallerton, when the insurgents disbanded and fled. The earls made their way into Scotland, and there Northumberland was betrayed by a faithless Borderer named Graham, to the Regent Moray, who sent him to Berwick, where he was beheaded. The Earl of Westmorland escaped to Flanders, where he survived to old age (see *Raby* and *Brancepeth*). On the forfeiture which followed this foolish rebellion,

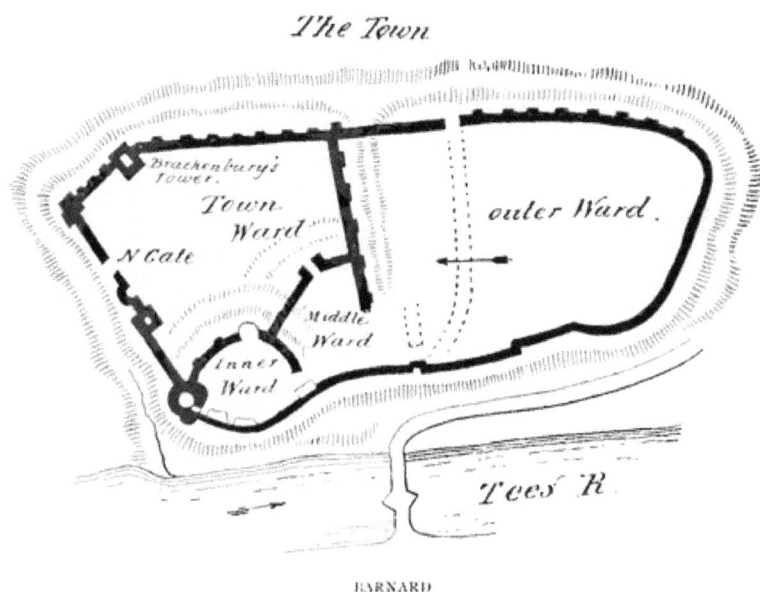

BARNARD

under the Act of Henry VIII., the castles of Barnard, Raby, and Brancepeth, with all the manors, ought to have vested in the see of Durham, but Elizabeth obtained an Act enabling the Crown to retain the whole properties (*Surtees*).

Barnard Castle was then leased to Sir George Bowes, whose own castle of Streatlam had been entirely wrecked by the rebels. James I. gave it to his minion, Robert Carr, Earl of Somerset, on whose attainder it reverted to the Crown, and became part of the provision of the Prince of Wales. Afterwards the castle, honour, and privileges were purchased by an ancestor of the present Duke of Cleveland, and in 1640 Sir H. Vane obtained a grant of these, which were afterwards made into a barony by William III. During the Civil War the castle was held for the king, when it was besieged by

Cromwell, who opened batteries upon it from the other side of the Tees, on Towler Hill, with such effect that the garrison were soon obliged to capitulate.

The circuit of the walls of this grand fortress covers an area of nearly seven acres, but the remains are now nothing more than a shell. The strongest part of the castle, whose situation is so charmingly described in "Rokeby," stands on the brink of the cliff, 80 feet above the Tees at its N.W. corner. The whole is enclosed by the ancient walls, the portion on the N. being the oldest, and the W. front overlooking the river containing the chief apartments. At the N.W. corner is Balol's Tower, a circular structure of great size and antiquity, and of excellent masonry; it was in such good preservation that at one time it was let for a shot factory, an employ-ment which caused some serious damage to the fabric, especially to the vaulting of its curious floor and staircase. The wall on the S. is very thick, and was strengthened by balks of oak, laid in tiers in the centre of the wall, for resisting the blows of battering-rams. The outer court is separated from the inner by a deep ditch which surrounds the rest of the fortress. There is one entrance from the market-place into the outer bailey, where perhaps was the chapel spoken of by Leland as having sculptured figures of the Baliols, but all this has vanished. Another gatehouse, with a circular arch, having a semicircular flanking tower, led from the flats adjacent and the old Roman road communicating with the ford. In the interior is the building known by tradition as Brackenbury's Tower, which was anciently used as the castle keep. It is supposed to be named after Richard's officer, the notorious Constable of the Tower of London, who was entrusted with the murder of the princes.

BRANCEPETH (chief)

OF Brancepeth Sir Bernard Burke writes: "Of all the feudal fortresses of England, whether we regard their venerable antiquity, the rank and authority of their early possessors, or the wealth and taste which have been, in modern times, expended upon them, there are few which can claim precedence over this home of the Nevills." Still, so much of this castle has been rebuilt and so much modernised, that as a building, and standing as it does on a low site, its effect is disappointing.

Brancepeth is five miles S.W. from Durham, on the road by Nevill's Cross. It was originally erected by the family of Bulmer, seated here for many generations, till the death of their last male representative Bertram, whose only daughter Emma married Geoffrey Nevill, a grandson of that Gilbert Nevill who was admiral in the fleet of Duke William of Normandy. Their daughter and heiress, Isabel, married Robert Fitz Meldred, lord of Raby, whose son Geoffrey assumed the name of Nevill, and from whom sprang the noble line of warriors and statesmen of that name, whose principal seat for so long was at Raby (*q.v.*). Ralph, Lord Nevill, in 1398 was created Earl of Westmorland by Richard II., and the lordship and castle of Brancepeth continued with this family till the time of Elizabeth, when Charles, the sixth earl, joining in the Rising of the North (1569), the object of which partly was to effect the marriage of his brother-in-law, the Duke of Norfolk, with Mary Queen of Scots, his lands were forfeited to the Crown (13 Elizabeth), with

BRANCEPETH

the castles of Raby and Brancepeth (see *Barnard Castle*). Under the Act of Henry VIII., all this large property ought to have vested in the see of Durham, but Elizabeth obtained a special Act to retain it in the Crown. James I. granted it to his favourite Robert Carr, who lived here as Baron Brancepeth from 1613 until his trial and condemnation (see *Grey's Court, Oxon*). Thus Brancepeth remained until the eighth year of Charles I., when the castle and lordship were sold to Lady Middleton and others; then to the Cole family; and in 1701 a new sale was made to Sir Henry Bellasys, whose grandson devised the property to the Earl of Fauconberg, and he sold it in 1776 to John Tempest. Twenty years after it was purchased by Mr. William Russell, and his son Matthew, considered the richest commoner in England, at enormous cost reared the present structure in 1818. In 1828 the marriage of Emma

Marie Russell with the eldest son of Viscount Boyne brought Brancepeth into that family.

Leland says that " Ralph, Earl of Westmoreland, builded much of this house A.D. 1398," and as Brancepeth was nearer to Durham and to the Marches than Raby, it was oftener used by the Nevills as their residence ; the fourth, fifth, and sixth earls seem from their correspondence to have spent much time there.

At the present day there is little of the original fortress visible. It consisted of four square towers with their connecting curtain walls built as a quadrangle, each corner tower having four turrets. The entrance gatehouse was on the N., flanked by two square towers, with a portcullis. E. of this was the battlemented wall connecting another large square tower, and so round the enceinte. There may originally have been eight of these towers. On the N. and E. the castle was defended by a moat, but on the W. it stands on a rock with a small stream running below, and this side alone gives a picturesque view of the fortress. An old ruin, roofless and decayed, is a venerable object of interest ; every one of its stones seems imbued with historic associations ; but when the old work gives place to new, and ancient walls are rebuilt or covered up to meet modern requirements and modern taste, with nineteenth-century windows and sham battlements, then, alas, good-bye to all interest in the fabric.

The word Brancepeth is said to have been derived from " Brawn's path," or the track of a great wild boar which tradition says had its lair there and was accustomed to pass through the manor in search of its prey.

In the barons' hall is the original sword of Richard Nevill, with which he fought at Nevill's Cross, bearing his name, with the date 1345.

DURHAM (chief)

EXCEPT at Edinburgh, we have in this kingdom no combination of architecture and scenery so fine as the view of Durham Castle and Cathedral standing over the woods and gorge of Wear. The original church, which was reared over St. Cuthbert's grave in 999, was standing when the Conqueror ordered the rebuilding, in 1072, of the palace of the Saxon bishops of Durham, which had been burnt down two or three years before. This edifice did not perhaps suit the taste or requirements of the proud and wealthy prelates who came after, and in 1174 Bishop Pudsey rebuilt the whole, with great additions, in the best late Norman style of military architecture. Freeman says : " The bishop of the days at once following the Norman Conquest, turned by Norman polity into a military tenant of the Crown, dwelling commonly as a stranger among a strange and often hostile people—often raised to his see as the reward of temporal services to the Crown—as soon as he found himself on his rural estates began to feel like any other baron. He raised for himself, not

a house, not a palace, but a castle in the strictest sense ; a fortress not merely
capable of defence in case of any sudden attack, but capable of being made a
centre of military operations in case the bishop should take a fancy, in times
of civil strife, to make war upon some other baron, or upon the king himself."
William placed Bishop Walcher as a ruler both spiritual and temporal over
the turbulent and wild natives of the district, and him they besieged and
murdered. Then Rufus had to lay siege to Durham, and afterwards Henry II.
took possession of both castle and town. In Clark's work is given a curious
poem by Lawrence, the prior in 1149, describing the castle as it was during
the strife between Stephen and Maud, which raged with great severity in
that part of the kingdom, on account of the claim of King David, Maud's
uncle, to the old inheritance of Northumberland and Cumberland. The castle
still retains many features there depicted.

It is built on a high rocky hill of horse-shoe shape, round which the river
Wear flows, under steep cliffs, 80 or 100 feet below, serving as a moat to the
fortress. The line of walls, with their five gates, extended round that side of the
hill not occupied by the cathedral, enclosing the courtyard or bailey. The
great N. gate, which flanked the keep to the E., and the space leading down to
the town commanded the most important approach, and was rebuilt and much
strengthened by Bishop Langley in 1417 ; it had double gates towards the
bailey, and one towards the city, with portcullis and battlements. The old
gate had a postern and a round tower at the end of the ditch, still existing.
The second gate, called the King's Gate, commanded a ford on the river, but
has disappeared. Two others stood where are now Queen Street and Duncow
Lane ; and the fifth, or water gate, being that of the outer court, stood in its
ancient form until of late years.

The mount on which the keep stands is 44 feet high, and was vaulted beneath.
The tower was an irregular octagon 63½ feet across, and four storeys high, with
an entrance on the W. ; the eight angles were supported by buttresses, and a
battlemented parapet ran round the summit. Nothing, however, remains of
this edifice but the mount, the vaults, and the outer shell ; it was probably the
work of Bishop Hatfield in the middle of the fourteenth century, who also built
the great hall. Bishop Morton entertained Charles I. here and all his retinue,
with a magnificence that cost £1500 a day. The bishops palatine of Durham
seem to have vied with each other in enlarging and beautifying their dwelling,
which continued to be their residence till 1833, when the Durham University
was founded, and the castle given up to accommodate the members.

Many royal visitors have stayed in this grand fortress since William I. Most
of our Angevin and Plantagenet sovereigns came there, and also James I. of
Scotland and his English queen ; the saintly Henry VI. ; the Princess Margaret
on her way to join her husband, James IV. of Scotland ; James I. of England,
and Charles I. his son.

HOUGHTON-LE-SPRING (minor)

THIS tower, like the one of Corbridge in Northumberland, is an instance of a rectory house which the state of the country made it necessary to fortify. In 1483 the then incumbent, John Kelyng, began to crenellate and embattle a peel tower without first obtaining a licence, for which he was called to account by the prince bishop, and only pardoned on payment of a fine. To this was afterwards attached a large dwelling, in which the famous divine, Bernard Gilpin, known as the "Apostle of the North," lived and ministered with profuse hospitality for the many years in which he was rector of Houghton, and where he died in 1583. This building was destroyed in 1664 by a succeeding rector named Davenport, who built it anew and added another tower and a chapel. The whole of Davenport's work, however, was demolished by the last rector.

The appellation added to Houghton is derived from a family named Le Spring, who possessed the manor in the thirteenth century. One of them, Sir John le Spring, was murdered in his house at Houghton in the sixth year of Edward III., as is related in a pathetic ballad given by Surtees. His effigy is in the church at the side of Gilpin's tomb.

HYLTON (chief)

THIS castle, or what is left of the ancient structure, stands on the N. bank of the Wear, about 2½ miles on the W. of Sunderland, in a low situation, surrounded by trees, and well sheltered from the N. by a hill on which formerly stood the vill of Hilton. In the days of its baronial grandeur the castle must have been of great extent and strength, to judge from its gatehouse, the only part of it remaining, which is a massive, imposing edifice, five storeys in height, resembling in form a superior peel tower, 66 feet long by 36 feet deep, having on its W. or principal front angle turrets formed by the junction of broad projecting pilasters on either side, with two equidistant pilasters, one on each side of the gateway; all these turrets are continued above the roof, and are terminated in octagonal super-turrets boldly projected beyond the face on corbels, and machicolated on all sides. The E. front has a circular turret at each angle, and in the centre a single broad projecting tower, the whole of the roofs being screened by a heavy crenellated parapet. The walls are from 8 feet to 12 feet thick. During the restorations in 1869 a square courtyard was disclosed on the W. side, which seems to prove that the main buildings of the castle were on that quarter.

The origin of the Hilton family is hidden in its antiquity. The first member recorded is one Romanus, in the reign of Henry II., who then appears in 1166 in an application for a chaplain to officiate in his chapel of Hylton, and therefore the tradition of the Hiltons being here long before the Conquest is possibly true. The Prince Bishops of Durham were sovereigns in their own domain ; they had a mint, and sustained a court of barons, in which the Hiltons, as powerful lords holding a very extensive territory both in this county and in Northumberland and Cumberland, and in Yorkshire, always had a seat, the name of the Baron of Hylton always standing first on the list.

The names of the successors of Romanus are proved by charters, licences, and other documents as far as the middle of the fifteenth century, with a steady succession throughout from father to son as barons of the bishopric, and nothing is recorded of them of a stirring nature almost throughout their story. Baron Alexander was summoned to Parliament by Edward III., having served in his Scottish wars, where he held a command in 1333, under Lord Nevill. He died in 1361, seised of many manors. William, who was born in 1356, was probably the builder of the existing structure.

Baron William in 1513 is said to have fought at Flodden, and his son Sir Thomas Hilton joined Aske in the Pilgrimage of Grace in 1536 with Lord D'Arcy and others, but does not appear to have suffered for his participation in that rebellion.

HYLTON

Henry Hilton, who died in 1640, "by a will such as a madman only could make," alienated the property and ruined his family. He left his entire estate to the Lord Mayor and Corporation of London, and so reduced the Hilton possessions to little more than a name. His brother Henry was a stout Royalist, and served King Charles under the Marquess of Newcastle. He was included among the malignants, and though his son obtained a re-grant of the lands after the Restoration, the property was little more than a name, when saddled with the encumbrances raised by Baron Henry.

The last baron was John, who died in 1730, having devised the estates to his nephew, Sir Richard Musgrave of Hayton Castle. This owner took the name of Hilton, but obtaining an Act of Parliament to enable him to dispose of the estate, sold the manor of Hilton in 1750 to Mrs. Bowes, widow of Sir George Bowes of Streatlam, from whom it was inherited by the Earl of

Strathmore. Then it passed through several hands, until in 1863 the castle and lands were purchased by Mr. W. Briggs of Sunderland, whose son, Colonel Charles J. Briggs, is the present owner.

Sir Richard Hilton's grandson was Mr. Hylton Joliffe, M.P., created Lord Hylton in 1866. Sir Richard soon after obtaining the property, spent a large sum in Italianising the fabric, adding two huge wings to it, which were found in 1869 to be in so decayed a state that they were removed, and the building was then restored and greatly improved; the windows being remodelled from an ancient one which the S. wing had hidden. On the W. front are a number of heraldic shields exhibiting the arms of various families allied to the Hiltons, the Percys, Viponts, Lumleys, Feltons, Bowes', and others. In the centre is the banner of France and England quartered; that of France bearing only three fleurs-de-lys instead of five, a change made late in the reign of Henry V., and therefore fixing the date of the sculpture and perhaps of the building. The ruins of the castle chapel, dedicated to St. Katherine, lie to the N.E. of the castle. In it most of the Hilton barons were buried. They had also a chantry within the castle.

Many legends hang over this ancient family: amongst others there is that of "The Cauld Lad of Hilton," a brownie, or familiar sprite, whose gambols for many years disturbed the household of Hylton. Sleepers used to be awakened by violent noises in the kitchen; plates and dishes were broken, and pewter thrown about in confusion, when things had been left in good order there. But if, as did happen often, the servants left things in disorder downstairs, then the brownie arranged everything carefully in its proper place; so he was looked on as a benefactor by them. "One night," as the English Fairy Tales so daintily tell, "they heard a noise, and peeping in, saw the brownie swinging to and fro on the jack-chain, and saying:

> 'Woe's me! woe's me!
> The acorn's not yet
> Fallen from the tree
> That's to grow the wood
> That's to make the cradle
> That's to rock the bairn
> That's to grow to the man
> That's to lay me.
> Woe's me! woe's me!'

Then they took pity on the poor brownie, and asked the nearest henwife what they should do to send it away. 'That's easy enough,' said the henwife, and told them that a brownie that's paid for its service, *in aught that's not perishable*, goes away at once. So they made a cloak of Lincoln green, with a hood to it, and put it by the hearth and watched. They saw the brownie come up, and, observing the hood and cloak, put them on, and frisk about, dancing on one leg and saying—

'I've taken your cloak, I've taken your hood :
The Cauld Lad of Hilton will do nae mair good.'

And with that it vanished, and was never seen or heard of afterwards."

This of course is a folk-lore tale, common to other languages, and otherwise told in Grimm's " Elves and the Shoemaker ; " but at Hylton they connect the sprite with the story of an unfortunate stable-boy, whom one of the lairds killed, accidentally as some say, with a pitchfork, and then threw into a pond, where his bones were found in the time of the last Hilton. Surtees tells of the inquest in 1609 on one Roger Skelton, who was killed by Robert Hilton of Hylton accidentally with a scythe, when Hilton got off with a free pardon.

LUMLEY (chief)

A MILE to the S. of Chester-le-Street, near the old Roman road to the north, stands this seat of the Earls of Scarborough, on elevated ground sloping down to the river Wear.

The Lumleys descend from a Saxon thane named Liulph, of high repute in the time of the Confessor ; his son, or grandson, assumed the surname of De Lumley from this place, and from him the property has come down with the name, generally from father to son, in direct succession to the present time.

The original manor-house or castle was built (temp. Edward I.) by Sir Robert Lumley, knight, and was enlarged by his son Sir Marmaduke ; but in 16 Richard II. (1392) a royal licence was obtained by "Ralph de Lomley, chivaler, quoddam castrum apud Lomlay de novo facere et construere," and he had also one from Bishop Skirlaw, to repair and crenellate his castle. He was summoned to Parliament in this reign, but joining in the insurrection of Thomas Holland, Earl of Kent, was slain in a skirmish at Cirencester, and his estates were forfeited. His son Sir John, however, succeeded in obtaining livery of all his lands, castles, and manors, and was restored in blood by the Parliament in 1411, as Baron Lumley. He served in the French wars of Henry IV. and Henry V., and lost his life, with the Duke of Clarence, at Beaugé in 1421.

His descendant John, Lord Lumley, in 28 Henry VIII. joined in the popular religious movement called the Pilgrimage of Grace, but afterwards shared in the king's clemency. His only son, George, who succeeded him, being tried also for treason with Lord Darcy and Sir Thomas Percy, was committed to the Tower, and was convicted and executed.

The son of this man, John, was restored in the blood, and created Lord Lumley in 36 Henry VIII.; he fought at Flodden, and was chosen as one of the peers to sit in judgment on the unhappy Queen of Scots. He is styled by Camden "a person of entire virtue, integrity, and innocence, and in his old age, a complete pattern of true nobility." Dying in 1609, he bequeathed Lumley and all his lands to a distant cousin, Richard Lumley, elevated to the peerage of Ireland as Viscount Lumley in 1628. He was a faithful supporter of Charles I., and held this castle as a garrison for the king, for whom he commanded a force under Prince Rupert, in the W. of England, and at the siege of Bristol. His grandson Richard came next into the estates, being created in 1681 Baron Lumley, and by William

LUMLEY

and Mary, Viscount, and further by them, in 1690, Earl of Scarborough.

The castle forms a quadrangle with a large courtyard, 80 feet square ; in the centre of the building and at each corner rises a projecting massive square tower, the whole of the parapets being battlemented with turrets, octangular in shape and machicolated, at each angle of the towers. The entrance is on the W. side by a broad staircase and large platform, which admits to the great Hall. This is 60 feet long by 30 feet, with a minstrels' gallery at one end.

The S. front is modern, and that on the N. is occupied by the offices. The E. front retains its ancient character, with a noble projecting gatehouse, carrying turrets and a machicoulis gallery. On its face are six stone shields of arms, corresponding to the time of Richard II., bearing the devices of Lumley, Grey, Nevill, and others.

The original house of the family before the present castle was erected seems to have been at a site about a mile distant, where are some traces of it. The whole interior of Lumley Castle was subjected about 200 years ago to a complete remodelling and renovation in an Italian style, whereby its antique character has quite disappeared.

RABY (chief)

THE superb fortress of the Nevills, Earls of Westmorland, "can boast," remarks the Duchess of Cleveland in her interesting Memoir, "of having had a hearth-fire always alight since the days of Edward the Confessor." The name is of course Danish, and tradition assigns to the site of it a palace of King Canute, standing upon a rocky eminence about a mile from the village of Stain-drop. The Saxon Earl Uchtred was one of the very few lords of the soil whom the Confessor permitted to continue in possession, and his family remained here for five centuries. In the fourth generation from Uchtred, Robert Fitz-Maldred married Isabel de Nevill, from whose mother Emma, the daughter and heiress of Bertram de Bulmer, lord of Brancepeth, she inherited that territory as well as Sheriff Hutton in Yorkshire. Emma de Bulmer had married Geoffrey de Nevill, the descendant of Gilbert, admiral of Duke William's fleet, who came from Neuville in Normandy. Geoffrey, the son of Isabel and Robert, lord of Raby, adopted his mother's name of Nevill, and thus commenced the male line of a mighty and princely family, second to none in the kingdom. His son Robert was made by Henry III. captain-general of the royal forces north of Tweed, but he afterwards joined the popular side in the Barons' War. He had a son of the same name, who marrying Mary, daughter of Ralph FitzRandolph, added through his wife the manor and castle of Middleham to the other large estates of the Nevills. His son Ralph de Nevill was summoned to Parliament as a baron in 1294, and served in the Scots and French wars of Edward I. Ralph died in 1331, and his son Ralph, the second baron, held high employment under Edward III. in Scotland and France, and was one of the leaders at the battle of Nevill's Cross; he died in 1367. His son Sir John, whom, when a child of five years, he had taken to witness the great fight near Durham, became an illustrious warrior, and is said to have won during his military service no less than eighty-three walled towns and fortresses. He also filled the post of admiral of the royal fleet from the Thames northward, and he attended Richard II. to Scotland with his own forces of 300 archers and 200 men-at-arms.

In 1378 he obtained from the Prince Bishop of the Palatinate, Hatfield, a licence to crenellate his castle of Raby, and built the Nevill gateway, whereon we see three shields bearing St. George's Cross between the arms of Nevill and Latimer—his second wife being the heiress of the latter family; each shield is encircled by the garter, of which order Lord Nevill was made a knight in 1369. Dying in 1388, he was buried like his father in Durham Cathedral; his brother, Sir Ralph, being slain at the battle of Otterburn (q.v.) or Chevy Chase in the same year. With his son, also Ralph, the fourth baron, the fortunes of the Nevills reached their zenith. Holding high office under Richard II., he was created Earl of Westmorland, but he nevertheless became a strong supporter of Henry IV., whom he assisted in placing on the throne, receiving from that king for his services a grant of the county and honour of Richmond for his life, and the high

RABY

office of Earl Marshal of England. He supported Henry IV. against the Percy rebellion, and did great service for him at the battle of Shrewsbury; and in 1405, by artful treachery towards Archbishop Scrope and the Earl Marshal, he brought their formidable insurrection to an end (see *Pontefract, Yorks*) in a bloodless campaign (*Henry IV.*, Part ii. Act iv. Scene 2). In the next reign we find him at Agincourt, being at that time Earl Marshal, with a following of his own of five knights, thirty men-at-arms, and eighty archers. By his second marriage with Joan de Beaufort he was uncle to King Henry V., though Shakespeare makes the king to call Westmorland his "cousin." By his two wives this earl had twenty-three children; nine by his first wife, Lady Margaret Stafford, and the rest inherited the blood royal through their mother, the daughter of John of Gaunt by Katharine Swynford. The youngest daughter of this large family was Cicely, the fair "Rose of Raby," who married in early youth Richard Plantagenet, Duke of York, by whom she became the mother of the two kings Edward IV. and Richard III. (see *Berkhamstead, Herts*).

This great noble died in 1426, and was followed at Raby by his eldest son Ralph. The elder son of the second marriage was Richard Nevill, created Earl of Salisbury, who, with the rest of his kith, became a strenuous supporter of the White Rose of York, through his youngest sister's marriage, though so closely allied through his father to the house of Lancaster. He fought at the first battle of St. Albans, and afterwards defeated Lord Audley at Blore-heath, and was a leader at Northampton fight in 1460; he was slain, however, at Wakefield with his brother-in-law the Duke of York, as was also his second son, and his head, like that of the duke, was mounted over one of the gates of York. Salisbury's eldest son was Richard Nevill, the stout Earl of Warwick, the King-maker, than whom few better known figures exist in history.

Ralph, fifth lord of Raby and second earl, managed to live through the Wars of the Roses, in spite of, perhaps because of, his close relationship to the chiefs of both the contending factions, and died at Raby the year of the last battle, which placed the crown on the brow of Henry, Earl of Richmond. There is little to remark in the history of the succeeding three earls, who lived out their days at Raby and Brancepeth.

Then came the end of the Nevills, in Charles, the sixth Earl of Westmor-land, who joined with the Earl of Northumberland in the insurrection of 1569 (13 Elizabeth), called the Rising of the North—a movement which resembled the rebellion called the Pilgrimage of Grace during the reign of Henry VIII.

the object of both being the restoration of the ancient faith of the country. The account of the rising of 1569 is given in the Memoir of Barnard Castle, where the two earls were unwise enough to delay until the queen's forces arrived in the neighbourhood; then the rebel party broke up, and the earls sought safety over the Scottish border. The Earl of Westmorland was long concealed by the Kerr family at Fernhurst Castle, Roxburgh, and, more fortu-nate than the Earl of Northumberland, contrived to escape to Flanders. His vast property had, however, been confiscated; his wealth had fled, and his title was gone; so that in poverty he ended his days in 1584, after subsisting mean-while on a "miserable pittance" bestowed on him by the King of Spain. He left four daughters only, from whom Queen Elizabeth, while appropriating their father's estate, withheld even a bare subsistence, leaving them literally without bread.

The possessions of the Nevills under Earl Charles' attainder should have devolved upon the see of Durham, but the queen, by an Act which she obtained, caused them to vest in herself, and the whole, inclusive of Raby, continued Crown property till James I. in 1613 granted them to his worthless favourite Carr, Earl of Somerset; on whose degradation on account of the Overbury murder they were first made over to the citizens of London, and afterwards were devised for the support of the Prince of Wales, under trustees who sold the lands ultimately, with Raby and Barnard Castle, to Sir Henry Vane, a distinguished statesman in the reign of James I., and Treasurer of the Household.

There is a story that Vane, wishing to underrate the value of his purchase to the king, called Raby "a hillock of stones"; and that on a subsequent visit to the place James, remembering what Vane had said, exclaimed : "Gude sakes —ca' ye that a hullock o' stanes ? By me faith, I hae nae sic anither hullock in my realm." The story is ascribed also to Charles I.

Sir Henry's son, likewise so named, was a violent republican and Puritan, and was in the time of the Parliament the principal mover of the Solemn League and Covenant, and of the Self-denying Ordinance. By his evidence he procured the condemnation of Stafford, and after the Restoration he was tried as a regicide and was beheaded (1662) on Tower Hill. In 1645, a Royalist force from Bolton Castle scaled the wall and surprised and took possession of Raby ; but after about six weeks it was invested by a body of 300 men raised by Sir George Vane, Sir Henry's second son (ancestor of the Londonderry family), and the garrison forced to surrender. Again in 1648 the castle was besieged by the Royalists, but no record exists of the fighting, except an entry which appears in the parish register of Staindrop. "Aug. 27, 1648. A souldier slaine at the seidge of Raby Castle was buried in the church. Memo. Many souldiers slaine before Raby castle, which were buried in the Parke, and not registered." Charles I. was here twice.

Sir Henry was followed by his son Sir Christopher, created in 1698 Baron Barnard. It was this owner who in 1714, in order to injure his eldest son, who had displeased him and his virago wife (Lady Elizabeth Holles) by his marriage, endeavoured to ruin Raby Castle. He caused the lead to be stripped off the roofs, and the ironwork and glass and the flooring taken away and sold, employing 200 workmen for the purpose. The old timber was cut down, the deer killed and the park ploughed, and he was beginning to throw down the walls when the heir obtained an injunction against his parents, who were forced by the court to make good all they had injured, under the eye of a Master who was sent down to carry out the order. This unworthy lord died in 1723 ; and Henry Vane, grandson of the last (married to the Lady Grace, daughter of Charles Fitzroy, Duke of Cleveland, the son of Charles II. by Barbara Villiers), succeeding in 1753, was created Viscount Barnard and Earl of Darlington the next year. In 1827 his grandson was made Marquess of Cleveland, and Duke in 1833.

Leland, who visited the place before its forfeiture, says : " Raby is the largest Castel of Logginges in al the North Countery, and is of a strong Building, but not set other on Hil or very strong Ground. . . . The Haul and al the Houses of Offices be large & stately, and the Great Chamber was exceeding large, but now it is fals rofid and divided into 2 or 3 Partes. I saw ther a litle Chaumber

wherin was in Windowes of colerid Glasse al the Pedigree of Neville : but it
is now taken down."

   The position thus spoken of by Leland was rendered a strong one by the
water defences ; a moat, now filled in on all but the S. side, surrounded the
castle, and was supplied by a small burn which, being dammed, formed an
artificial lake around it.   The entrance is on the W. front in the Nevill Tower,

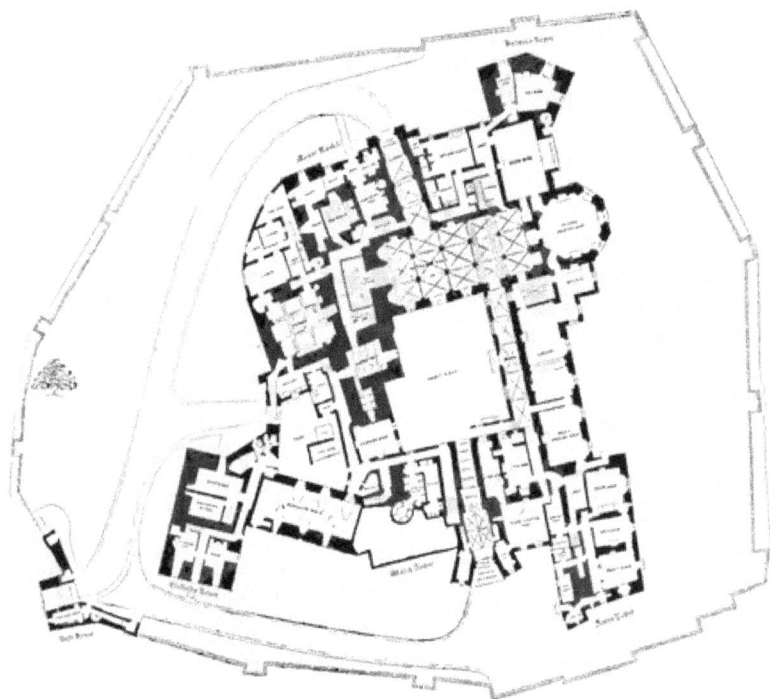

RABY

or inner gatehouse, built by Sir John Nevill in 1378, and bearing the three
stone shields of arms, the passage guarded by an outer and an inner portcullis.
Adjoining this is Joan's Tower, at the S.W. angle of the fortress, called after
Lady Joan of Beaufort, the mother of the King-maker ; in this are the family
apartments, and beyond it the S. front consists of the modern buildings of Inigo
Jones, and later fanciful additions of an octagon tower and a dining-room ;
to fit them in the old vaulted fourteenth-century rooms were sacrificed,
and a huge gap was made in the Bulmer Tower at the S.E. angle, the

Danish arrow-pointed structure of the original castle, which may be considered as the Keep.

Next to this, on the E. front, is the great Chapel Tower, containing the chapel and priest's room, with a guardroom above, and between it and the next tower, called Mount Raskelf (from one of the Nevill manors), is the chapel gateway with its two picturesque turrets, in front of which stood the barbican, destroyed by Lord Darlington in the last century, whereon was sculptured the huge Nevill bull with the saltire banner, now removed to a modern entrance to the home farm.

From Mount Raskelf at the N.E. corner a modern circular curtain leads round to the remarkable Kitchen Tower on the N. front, built about 1370, with its three immense fireplaces, vaulted roof, and mural passages. At its S. wall remain the stairs leading up to the Barons' Hall. Below is a great cellar with vaulted roof supported by a massive central column, and from it descends a long staircase leading to a subterranean passage to Staindrop Priory, but now walled up.

From hence an ancient curtain wall—pierced with a postern into the inner court—conducts the N. front to Clifford's Tower, at the N.W. angle, the largest in the castle, having walls 10 feet thick, in which are mural passages between the loopholes for the bowmen; and thence by the two-storeyed vaulted guardrooms (now the servants' hall) we pass by the W. watch-tower once more to the great entrance with its two splayed turrets. Passing through, we arrive at the central courtyard and at the entrance hall built by Lord Darlington, who opened up a broad avenue through the building to the chapel gateway. This hall, supported on lofty columns, contains the state staircase to the new apartments, and to the ancient Barons' Hall above—"the great historical room, where the 700 knights that held of the Nevills assembled once a year, and where the council that decided upon the fatal Rising of the North was held in 1569"—built by Sir John Nevill in the fourteenth century, but much injured and altered by modern architects.

The park is now reduced in size, but still contains 400 fallow and 100 red deer.

Since the death of the fourth Duke of Cleveland, Raby Castle has become the property of Lord Barnard.

RAVENSWORTH (chief)

RAVENSWORTH, a seat of the Liddells since the fifth year of James I., stands about four miles S. from Gateshead, on gently rising ground a mile from the river Team. The present mansion was built in 1808 on the site of an ancient castle, two towers of which remain. The name is sometimes written Raffensweath, and hence is thought to relate to a defeat of the Danes here, in allusion to the Danish Standard of the Raven; and there is no record of any licence to crenellate, as in other residences of the bishops, which would seem to show the antiquity of the settlement.

The manor was granted by Bishop Flambard to his nephew Richard, for half a knight's fee, and in the twelfth year of Bishop Hatfield (1345-1377), we read of a lady of Ravensworth. In 1370 the family of Lumley is mentioned in connection with the place, and in 1384 Robert de Lumley is seised of the manor of Ravensholm. This Lumley family became extinct in Isabel, wife of Sir Henry Boynton, at the end of the fifteenth century, and their only daughter Elizabeth married Sir Henry Gascoygn, whose descendant, Sir William Gascoygn, 5 James I. (1607), sold Ravensworth to Thomas Liddell, a Newcastle merchant. His son, also Thomas Liddell, defended Newcastle against the Scots, and was made baronet in 1642. Sir Henry, the fourth baronet, was created Baron Ravensworth in 1747, but at his death in 1784 this title became extinct, the baronetcy devolving on his nephew, Sir Henry George, whose son was raised to the peerage as Baron Ravensworth in 1821, and in 1874 the second baron was advanced to an earldom.

The ancient castle was built in the usual form of a quadrangle with a tower at each corner, connected by curtain walls, and before the existing mansion was erected in 1808, two of these old turrets remained, forming a part of the offices, the other two, as now, projecting in front.

STOCKTON-ON-TEES (*non-existent*)

THE bishops palatine had a castle at Stockton, with which the borough was closely connected, erected in early times of the see. In 1214, King John visited Bishop Philip de Poictou here; and in the fourteenth century the castle was rebuilt by Bishop Kellew, and again renovated in 1578 by Bishop Barnes. Several of the bishops between 1241 and 1640 made use of this fortress as a retreat or a refuge in times of danger. It was besieged and captured by the Parliamentary troops in 1644, and in 1652 was dismantled and destroyed. Nothing now remains of the castle except the names of Castle Street and Moat Street, but until lately there was still a fragment of a low massive tower at the end of the High Street.

STREATLAM (*minor*)

STREATLAM lies in the S. of the county, two miles N.E. of Barnard Castle, and between that place and Raby, in a low situation surrounded by a fine timbered park. The present mansion was built early in the eighteenth century, and encases whatever remains of the ancient castle, erected here, as supposed, by the Baliol family, to whom the lands belonged. Bernard Baliol gave Streatlam and other lands in dowry with Agnes his niece, daughter and sole heiress of Ralph de la Haye (Lord Percy), on her marriage with Sir John Trayne, who may have built this castle. The sole issue of the union was a daughter, Alice, who married Sir Adam Bowes in the beginning of the fourteenth century.

The Bowes family were a martial race; Sir Adam's grandson, Sir William Bowes, was created a banneret at the battle of Poictiers in 1346, and his son, Sir Robert, was slain at the battle of Beaugé with the Duke of Clarence in 1419. The son of this man, knighted during the French wars at the battle of Verneuil in 1424, was chamberlain to the Duke of Bedford in France. He sent home a model for the reconstruction of Streatlam Castle, and the plan was carried out on his return from the wars.

Another Bowes, Sir Ralph, received the honour of knighthood after Flodden Field, and his brother Sir Robert was a Privy Councillor to Henry VIII. The direct line ended in Sir George Bowes, the grandson of Ralph, who left three daughters only, and the line was carried on by his cousin, Sir Robert, who acted as ambassador to Scotland. It was this Sir Robert's son, Sir George Bowes, who withstood so strenuously, and unsupported, the insurrection of the Earls of Northumberland and Westmorland, called the Rising of the North, in 1569, in his defence of Barnard Castle (q.v.), in recognition of which service Queen Elizabeth made him Knight Marshal. The last of this valiant race was George Bowes, whose daughter and heiress Mary-Eleanor married in 1767 John, 9th Earl of Strathmore, who took the name of Bowes on the strength of his wife's property.

The story of this Lady Strathmore is a sad one. After the earl's death, when she was but twenty-nine years old, and a "pretty, lively, and accomplished lady," she bestowed her great wealth, her property, and herself, on a worthless scoundrel from King's County, named Andrew Robinson Stoney. This fellow, who had been a lieutenant in the army, and already by cruelty had done one wife to death and dissipated a large fortune, contrived to inveigle the unfortunate countess to marry him, and adopting her name, proceeded to run riot over her property. He spent her money, cut down her splendid old trees, sold her horses, confiscated her plate, and outraged her feelings by leading openly the wildest of lives. At last the broken-hearted woman managed to escape from him, and commenced proceedings at law against him; but, waylaying her, Stoney effected her capture, and shutting her up in Streatlam Castle, recommenced his cruel treatment. Here, however, the people of her estates interfered, and Stoney took to flight, carrying off the countess from the back of the castle, lying across the horse's neck in front of him, and in this way he brought her through deep snow to Darlington. Here, however, they were tracked and overtaken, and the country people, knocking the villain off his horse and nearly killing him, rescued the wife. She obtained a divorce, and Stoney Bowes was shut up for some years in prison.

No traces remain of the two former castles, the earlier of which was cleared away by Sir William Bowes in the fifteenth century when he reconstructed the building, and this castle too, in its turn, was removed when the present one was built at the beginning of this century. The shape of the original castle cannot be known; the existing one was built by Sir George Bowes on the old foundations, and it retains many of the old apartments. The situation is in a low vale, surrounded by high hills, and enshrouded in forests. The moat which encircled the original fortress can still be traced.

Leland's account says that "the Castle had 2 or 3 Towers and a faire Stable."

WITTON-LE-WEAR (minor)

THIS castle stands on the S. bank of the Wear, near Bishop Auckland. The Crown held the lands until Henry II. granted them to Henry Pudsey, nephew of Bishop Pudsey (1153-1196), who was a kinsman of King Stephen. It is not known at what date the Eure or Ever family first came here; they were anciently derived from the old lords of Warkworth and Clavering (temp. Henry II.), and Ralph Eure is found seised of the manor of Witton in the time of Bishop de Bury (1333-1348), it being held of the bishop *in capite*. In 1410 Bishop Langley granted a licence to Sir Ralph Eure to fortify and crenellate his castle of Witton, and "to entower the same"; and this may be taken therefore as the date of the main building. The family of Eure ended in a female representative early in the reign of Henry VII., but before that time the manor and castle of the Eures, Barons of Witton, were sold, we are told, to the Darcys, which family sold them in 1743 to William Cuthbert for about £15,000.

The old castle, so long the home of the Eure family, was burnt down late in the last century, while undergoing repairs, and the present house was built upon its site, preserving what remained of the former structure, including the keep.

These Eures seem to have been a martial family of consequence, and were connected by marriage with many noble houses. One of them, Sir Ralph, was killed at Towton Field, and another of the same name in a fight in Northumberland. Sir William Eure was created Lord Eure in 1584; he was a famous man during the Border warfare, and died in 1592. His descendant was the Colonel William Eure who was slain at Marston Moor on King Charles' side, and his son Thomas also fell in the Civil War. The last Lord Eure, George, who was living in 1674, dying *s.p.* male, the family became extinct.

DURHAM

Sir William Darcy held Witton Castle for the king, and was besieged in it by Sir Arthur Hazlerigg of Auckland Castle (q.v.). The place was taken and its contents were sequestered, but no injury was done to the building by the Parliament. A subsequent owner, however—James, Lord Darcy—in 1681 destroyed the place; he took away the lead, timber, and chimney-pieces to help in building a house at Sudbury, near Richmond, but this plan was never carried out, and the spoil of the old castle of Witton was afterwards sold at a lower price than the demolition had cost him.

It was originally a place of great strength; rectangular in shape, it had strong embattled curtain walls enclosing a large area, with projecting turrets or bartizans, three circular and one square, at the four angles. At one end and on the line of wall stands by itself a lofty square keep with a crenellated parapet throughout; it is two storeys only in height, with a staircase turret in one corner giving access to the roof, and its windows are square and modern. The entrance was in the centre of the N. wall through a gateway which is defended by a projecting gallery.

This important and interesting castle is now the property and residence of Henry Chaytor, Esq.

WARKWORTH

Northumberland

ALNWICK *(chief)*

AFTER the Conquest, the lands and the existing castle at Alnwick, of whatever sort it was, were bestowed upon Ivo de Vesey, a Norman noble, who, dying without male issue, left them to his daughter Beatrice. She married Eustace FitzJohn (temp. Henry I.), one of the Justices Itinerant with Walter Espec, the leader of the English at the Battle of the Standard (see *Helmsley, Yorks*).

In the reign of Rufus, in 1093, Malcolm Ceanmor, King of Scotland, in one of his incursions into Northumberland, was met on the banks of the Aln by a strong force under Morel, the sheriff of the county, the nephew of Robert de Mowbray, and was defeated and slain, together with his son Edward.

The need of a strong fortress at this point, to restrain these murderous Border raids, was naturally felt, and in 1140, or thereabout, Eustace FitzJohn set himself to erect the castle of which the splendid Norman arches of the innermost gateway, and some fragments of the outer curtain wall, still remain. His son William took the name of his mother's family, de Vesey; he sup-

ported the cause of the Empress Maud against Stephen, and he delivered his
castle of Alnwick into the keeping of Maud's uncle, King David of Scotland.
He was afterwards killed in an expedition against the Welsh, when his son
Eustace de Vesey succeeded him. In his day in 1174 King William the Lion
invaded England, on one of his attempts to compel the restoration of the
earldom of Northumberland that had belonged to his ancestors, and his
savage and undisciplined soldiery spread through the country, burning and
destroying as they went. This aroused the indignation of the neighbouring barons in the north of England, and Ralph de Glanville, Bernard
Baliol (see *Barnard Castle, Durham*), Odinel de Umfraville of Prudhoe (*q.v.*),
and others raised a force of 400 heavy armed horsemen, and hastened by a
fatiguing march to Newcastle to check the career of the Scots. Resting here
for the night (11th July), they pressed on early next morning towards Alnwick,
where the Scottish king was lying in fancied security; but on their way they
were overtaken by a mist so dense, that fearing the proximity of the enemy,
and having lost their way, they thought of retreating, and would have done so
but for the intrepidity of Baliol, who urged on the march, and soon the sun,
lifting the mist, showed them the towers of Alnwick. They then came by
surprise on the king, who was attended by sixty horsemen only, all his force
having dispersed in pursuit of plunder. William boldly charged them, but
being unsupported, was speedily overpowered, unhorsed, and made prisoner.
The gallant band then, to secure their prize, wisely galloped off the field and
returned to Newcastle, whence the king was taken prisoner to Richmond, from
whence he was despatched to Falaise Castle in Normandy. The Scottish army,
blind with rage at the loss of their king, at once broke up from Alnwick and
tumultuously dispersed.

King John visited Alnwick on four different occasions. Eustace de Vesey
married a daughter of the King of Scotland, and in 1216 accompanied
Alexander II., his brother-in-law, in an expedition against Barnard Castle
in Durham, and while riding round the fortress reconnoitring it, was slain by
a bolt from the walls, to the grief of the Scottish army, which at once left the
place. His son William succeeded, who was married to Agnes, daughter of
William Ferrers, Earl of Derby, by whom he had two sons, John, who sided
against Henry III., and was made prisoner at Evesham, and who died 1288,
and William, who died 1297, both without issue. Thus the family of de Vesey
came to an end, and the castle and manor of Alnwick became by royal licence
the possession of Anthony Bek, Bishop of Durham, from whom the lands and
castle were purchased in 1309 by Sir Henry de Percy, 1st lord of Alnwick, a
name so intimately connected with the history of this country, and with all
that is chivalrous and martial in it for so many centuries, that a short account
should be here given of the family which at this time acquired Alnwick.

Their ancestor, William de Percy, coming from the quiet little village of

Perci in Calvados, Normandy, had accompanied Duke William to England, and his son and grandson succeeded to the lands bestowed upon him by the Conqueror; but the family of his grandson ended in a daughter and heiress, Agnes de Percy, married to Joscelin, the brother of Adeliza de Louvaine, Queen of England. Their son and successor, Henry, assumed the name of his mother's family, and thus recommenced the family of Percy. He married Isabel de Brus, obtaining with her the lordship of Skelton and its castle in Yorkshire. His son William succeeded, and died 1245, when his son Henry de Percy came into the estates, which included also the lordship of Petworth in Sussex. This Percy marrying Eleanor, daughter of John, the great Earl de Warenne, was led by him to espouse the side of Henry III. in the Barons' War, and he was taken prisoner at Lewes. In the Chronicle of Dover he is spoken of as "unus de melioribus in regno." He died 1272, leaving a son, Sir Henry de Percy, a warrior of distinction, who was knighted by Edward I., and accompanied that king in his wars; he was, together with his grandsire John de Warenne, at the siege of Caerlaverock, and at Berwick 22 Edward I., and, like his father, he took a wife in Sussex, namely, Eleanor, daughter of the powerful noble Richard FitzAlan, Earl of Arundel. He it was who in 1309 purchased Alnwick of Bishop Anthony Bek, but he only enjoyed it for six years, dying in 1315. Up to this date little perhaps had been done on the old fabric in the way of additions, but we are told that his son and successor most excellently repaired the castle. At this period were added or remodelled the barbican and the magnificent gatehouse with its two octagonal towers, and also those called the Abbot's, the postern, the Constable's, and the Friar's Towers, and the gatehouse between the outer and middle bailey; also one on the foundations of the present Record Tower, and all the intermediate ones westward to the barbican. He also added the great hall and the vaults below it, as the latter still exist. This Percy married a daughter of Robert, Lord Clifford, and so we find the Clifford escutcheon carved on the wall of the inner gatehouse. He served throughout the wars of Edward III. in France and in Scotland, and with the Black Prince, fighting at Halidon Hill and at Nevill's Cross, and is described as being a personage only second to the king in importance. He died in 1352, when he was succeeded by the oldest of his four sons, whose marriage with Mary Plantagenet, daughter of Henry, Earl of Lancaster, shows that the Percys were esteemed worthy of alliance with the blood-royal; he fought at Crecy, and died in 1368, after completing the remodelling of Alnwick Castle. His eldest son, the father of "Hotspur," was in great favour at first with Richard II., but transferred his allegiance to Henry IV. on his claiming the crown. He was created Earl of Northumberland, and married as his second wife Maud, the sister of Anthony, Lord Lucy, and widow of Gilbert Umfraville, by whom he obtained the manors and castles of Cockermouth and Langley, and whom he succeeded in those of Prudhoe. Both he and his son Henry "Hotspur" revolted against King Henry, the latter

Alnwick Castle.

being killed at the battle of Shrewsbury in 1403, and the earl at a skirmish on Bramham Moor in 1407.

In 1405 Alnwick sustained a short siege, and was yielded to Henry IV. It was defended by Sir Henry Percy of Athol, as he was called, the grandson of the Earl of Northumberland, but on the fall of Berwick he surrendered. Hotspur's son Henry, the heir, who through his mother inherited the blood of the royal stock of the Mortimers, was an exile in Scotland till 1416, when Henry V. restored him to his family possessions, creating him Earl of Northumberland. He repaired the castles of Alnwick and Warkworth, possibly adding the keep of the latter. He was an active Lancastrian, and was killed at the first battle of St. Albans in 1455. His son Henry, the third earl, had a licence to crenellate the town of Alnwick from Henry VI., and built the Bondgate Tower at Alnwick. He was slain on the bloody field of Towton in 1461, fighting like his father for the Red Rose. The fourth earl was massacred by the mob at Thirsk in 1489, when he was striving to collect Henry VII.'s taxes. In his time Alnwick was the centre of much fighting. In 1462, being held by the Lancastrian William Tailbois, it was besieged by Lord Hastings and Sir Ralph Grey and taken, but on Queen Margaret's landing shortly after at Bamburgh, siege was again laid to Alnwick Castle, which from lack of provisions was forced to surrender. The next year the Earl of Warwick retook it, but a few months after it was treacherously yielded by its governor, Sir R. Grey, to Lord Hungerford and a French force, and again, after the battle of the Linnels at Hexham, it was given up to Warwick.

The Percys, as leaders of the northern barons, resided at Alnwick, and entertained here King Edward II. in 1311 and 1322, and also Edward III. in 1335; but the later earls lived much in Yorkshire and at Petworth, and on the death of the seventh earl and the imprisonment of his brother the family ceased to live at Alnwick, and the castle came to be neglected.

We have recounted seven lords of Alnwick who died violent deaths, and the list increases: Thomas, 7th Earl of Northumberland, was beheaded at York in 1572 for the Rising in the North, and the eighth earl died mysteriously in the Tower of London: with the eleventh earl, Jocelyn, the male line of the Percys the most historic perhaps of all our English families—comes to an end in 1670. The last earl's daughter, Lady Elizabeth Percy, who was twice a wife and twice a widow before she was sixteen, became (1682) the wife of Charles Seymour, Duke of Somerset, to whom she brought her great wealth. Their daughter Catherine married Sir William Wyndham, and conveyed to his family the estates of Petworth, Egremont, and Leconfield. In the next century, Algernon Seymour, Duke of Somerset, left one child, Lady Elizabeth, who inherited Alnwick and married Sir Hugh Smithson, created Earl Percy and Duke of Northumberland in 1766,— the ancestor of the present noble owner of Alnwick Castle.

This magnificent fortress stands on high ground on the S. bank of the Aln

River. The view is comparatively confined. The enclosure of the walls is of irregular shape, in the form of two loops or links, with the great keep and its approaches forming the junction between them. This keep consists of a cluster of towers and walls set round a central court, having a superb gateway with two highly ornate Norman arches, the work probably of Eustace FitzJohn, cir. 1140. There is also a great deal of Norman masonry remaining in the walls of the enceinte. Originally there was a deep dry ditch surrounding the keep, which is spoken of in the Survey of 1587. The Norman gateway was built into the later work of the middle of the fourteenth century, when also the two lofty flanking towers were added.

The central "Prudhoe" Tower is modern, but adds much to the elevation of the castle. There is a curious garrison well in this part, which may have been built by the second Percy lord (1315), who did so much to the structure. The great gatehouse and barbican are fine examples of the military architecture of the fourteenth century. The latter gave access over a drawbridge across a moat which originally encircled the building, besides the bridge operated on from the gatehouse; these were not in existence in 1556. This entrance is the work of the second Lord Percy of Alnwick, who also built most of the towers of the outer wall. After his time little mention is made of the fabric till 1538, when the first survey was made (given by Hartshorne *in extenso*), and there was another in 1586, wherein the chapel is mentioned, removed in 1755. In 1764 repairs were imperative, and Hugh, 1st Duke of Northumberland, was advised to remove the chapel, and the Exchequer Tower, and to "restore" the fabric after the lamentable Strawberry-Hill Gothic taste which then prevailed. The original arrangements of the interior were entirely destroyed at that time, and in 1854, when a new building was carried out in the keep, it was found necessary to pull down the old Hall, which was in a dangerous state: the marks of the dais across the hall were then discovered, and over it a buffet or side-board for the display of cups and plate; also water drains, and the hooks for suspending tapestries upon the walls were found in the old plaster (*Hartshorne*). The hall was rebuilt in 1863, but the vaults below are original.

AYDON (*minor*)

THIS fortress stands on the N. side of Tyne, one and a half miles from Corbridge, in a secluded wood; on two sides the building is protected by a deep ravine and on the others by a ditch. It was built in 1305 by Robert de Reymes or Raymes, who then obtained a licence from Edward I. to crenellate his house ("mansum suum de Eydon"). At the same date this Robert also built under royal licence a similar tower at SHORTFLAT, but Aydon exceeded it greatly in extent.

Robert de Raymes owned the manor, castle, and half the village of Aydon, and his descendants retained some interest in it till the reign of James I., though the family of Carnaby became possessed of the castle in 1542, their arms being cut on a stone mantelpiece in the castle. It was afterwards the property of the Collinsons, "but the last of that family was ruined by being bond for a friend." Then Aydon was purchased by one John Douglas, from whom it descended to the Blacketts of Matfen, and it is now the property of Sir E. W. Blackett, Bart.

In the "Domestic Architecture" of Hudson Turner are admirable drawings and details of Aydon, which in the thirteenth and fourteenth centuries was called Aydon Hall, as being a Border house, in reality, carefully fortified. In plan it was a many-sided enclosure of high walls, forming three courts attached to a strong house of three storeys, gabled at the ends and battlemented throughout, standing on the edge of the ravine. Some good rooms are on the upper floor, one measuring about 30 feet by 20 feet; there are four original fireplaces with good chimneys, and some of the windows are square-headed, with double lights.

BAMBOROUGH, FORMERLY CALLED BAMBURGH (chief)

NO spot in England, remote though this one be, is more intimately bound up with the early memories of the country than Bamborough. A bold plutonic rock of black basalt, a natural fortress overhanging the North Sea was chosen by Ida, at the head of a powerful force of Angles, in 547, as his camp, "which he surrounded with palisades and afterwards with a wall" (*Flores Hist.*). It is not possible to prove the tradition that Agricola had been there before him. Ida became king of that country called Bernicia, extending from the Tyne to the Forth, which joined in the next century to Deira, and reaching to the Humber, long formed, under the name of Northumbria (or lands north of the Humber), the most powerful of the Anglo-Saxon states, whose king was then Ethelfrith, and their capital Bamburgh or Bebbanburgh, so called from Bebba, Ethelfrith's queen. It covered no more ground than the existing castle, but formed in those wild times a camp of refuge, where the Bernician kings and their Thegns might be secure from the inroads of Scots and Danes. It was spoken of in 774 as "a most strongly fortified city;" yet in 993 the Danes broke in and injured its defences, and again in 1015 they took it by assault.

In the spring of 1095, Robert de Mowbray, the third Norman Earl of Northumberland, who had two years before killed Malcolm Ceannmore, the Scottish king, and his son before Alnwick, took on himself to wantonly plunder four Norwegian ships lying in some northern harbour. The merchants preferred a complaint to the king, William Rufus, who, glad perhaps of a cause against this turbulent earl, sent positive orders to de Mowbray to restore what he had taken; but of this the earl took no notice, and on being summoned to court to give an account of himself, stoutly refused to go. This defiance was more than the Red King would endure, so, gathering a strong force together, he put himself at its head and marched to the north to chastise the earl, and put a stop to the conspiracy which he knew existed there. Arrived at Newcastle, the fortress, which his brother Robert had built to defend the Roman road to the north, soon fell into his hands, and he then laid siege to the castle of Tynemouth, which was held by the earl's brother, and which, after a delay of two months, he took, and at once pressed on to attack de Mowbray in his citadel of Bamburgh, where the earl lay, accompanied by his newly married wife, Matilda de l'Aigle. The old fort, described as "a city small but strong, and its steep height approached only by steps," had then been replaced by a Norman castle fortified by all the military science of the age. Rufus found it impregnable, and contented himself with forming close to its walls a strong earthwork, which he called *Malvoisin*, or the Bad Neighbour, as cover for a force placed there, to harass and watch his foe, and then left the place for the south. De Mowbray, deceived by false news that Newcastle wished to open its gates to him, escaped by sea to go there, leaving in charge of Bamburgh his countess and his nephew Morel, the knight who had slain King Malcolm in 1093; but arrived at Newcastle, he found himself mistaken and the enemy in possession, and just managed to throw himself into Tynemouth, where he was besieged, and, after a defence of six days, overcome, wounded, and taken prisoner, awaiting the king's disposal. The lady of Bamburgh continued the defence there, and resolutely refused to yield; whereupon Rufus sent orders to parade her husband before the walls of Bamburgh, with the threat that unless the castle was given up his eyes should be torn out. Then the countess gave in, and the castle was surrendered to the king, but the earl was sent prisoner to Windsor, and condemned to perpetual captivity, which some say he endured for thirty years, another account being that he became a monk at St. Albans and died there. The poor bride, who had seen little of pleasure or quiet in her short married life, after some time received a Papal dispensation to marry again, and she became the wife of Nigel de Albini. Henry I. entrusted this castle to the keeping of Eustace FitzJohn, Lord of Alnwick.

Bamburgh resisted the attack of David, King of Scotland, when he invaded the Marches in the interest of the Empress Maud, and the value of this fortress to the English Crown is shown by the reservation of it in the grant of the earldom of Northumberland to Earl Henry, David's son.

Henry II. was a great castle-builder, and in his time the keep was erected, cir. 1164. King John, in his endless journeys, came here four or five times, and Henry III. in 1221. The Constables of Bamburgh seem to have always

Bamborough Castle.

held royal appointments. It was here that Edward I. vainly summoned John
Baliol to attend and do him homage for Scotland. Edward II. granted the
castle to Isabel de Beaumont, widow of John de Vesey of Alnwick, a favour
which she repaid by giving shelter there to Piers Gaveston. To Bamburgh
they took the young King of Scotland, David, son of the Bruce, when captured
at the battle of Nevill's Cross in October 1346, before sending him to London.
He was only twenty-one years old, and had shown great courage at the battle,
being with difficulty taken prisoner, wounded as he was in face and leg; and he
was now in a pitiable state, since two barber-surgeons were sent for from York
to extract an arrow with which he had been wounded, and to heal him "with
despatch,"—services which they appear to have performed satisfactorily, since

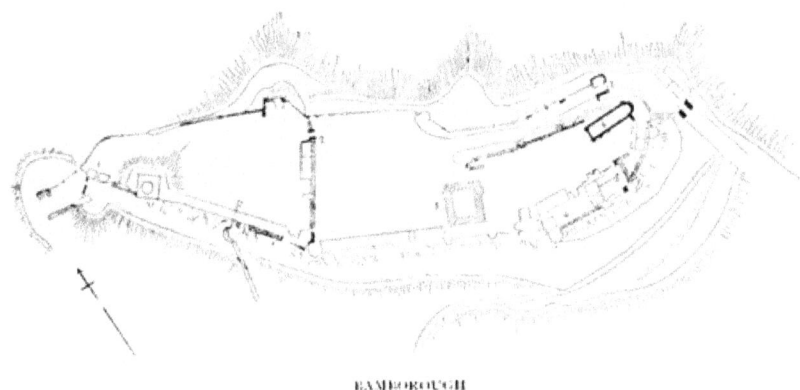

BAMBOROUGH

1. ST. OSWALD'S GATE.   3. KEEP.   5. KITCHEN.
2. SMITH'S GATE   4. THE KING'S HALL 6. CHAPEL

they received the sum of £6 for them, a sum equal to perhaps £120 of our
money, but it was five months before David could be moved to London. In
1336 Edward, proceeding to attack Berwick Castle, left his queen, Philippa, at
Bamburgh, when the Scots, under Archibald Douglas the Regent, attempted
to draw him off by besieging that fortress, but, stimulated by the presence
of their queen, the garrison made so strenuous a defence that they beat off
their assailants, and then Berwick fell. Edward spent ten days here in 1356,
when he was in treaty with Edward Baliol for the surrender of the Scottish
crown. Henry IV. gave the constableship of Bamburgh to Henry Hotspur,
for his assistance in effecting the dethronement of Richard II., but after the
battle of Shrewsbury this post was given to Hotspur's great enemy, the Earl
of Westmorland. In the wars of the Roses Bamburgh played an important
part. Being surrendered to Edward IV. after Towton, it was soon after

recovered by Queen Margaret, who (2 Edward IV.) gave it into the keeping of the Duke of Somerset and Lord Roos, with a garrison of 300 men. Edward coming north with an army of 10,000 men, then laid siege to the three castles of Alnwick, Bamburgh, and Dunstanburgh, the conduct of the operations being superintended by the Earl of Warwick, who, taking up his lodging at Warkworth, rode thence daily to look after the conduct of these three sieges. He commenced the attack on Bamburgh on the 10th December, and the garrison bravely defended the castle till Christmas Eve, when, in the face of the great odds against them, they were forced to surrender. Meantime, the queen had managed to escape in a small ship, intending to go to France, but her ever-pursuing evil fortune prevailing, a violent storm drove her to Berwick, where she was glad to land, with the loss of the treasure she had on board the vessel. After its fall Sir Ralph Grey was left in charge of the castle, but in Lent, 1463, he betrayed it to the Lancastrian troops, with Queen Margaret, who entered Bamburgh with her ill-fated husband, Henry, only to quit it again in April, when she sailed for Flanders. The king, thus left alone in the castle, remained there for a whole year. The next year, after the disastrous battle of Hexham, or the Linnels (May 1464), King Henry fled from Bywell Castle, where he was staying, leaving behind his "bycocket," or coronetted cap, and other effects, and returned to Bamburgh, which, however, he soon quitted for the loyal district of the Lakes. Then Sir Ralph Grey, who had fled at Hexham before the battle, threw himself into Bamburgh, with many other Lancastrian fugitives, and was followed shortly after by Warwick and his brother Northumberland, who laid siege to the castle. Grey, on being summoned, defied them, when he was warned that it was intended to take the fortress, even if the siege lasted seven years, and that for every shot fired from their guns a head should fall from a member of the garrison. The siege was then commenced, and heavy ordnance was opened on the castle, doing great injury to it, and sometimes sending their shot through Sir Ralph Grey's quarters. At last, one of the towers being ruined, in falling injured the captain, Grey, so severely that he was taken up for dead, when the defenders lost heart and at once yielded. Sir Ralph, however, recovered, and being carried to Edward at Doncaster, was executed.

In the sixteenth century, Bamburgh, like all the Border castles, was suffered to fall into decay, and the survey (temp. Elizabeth) shows that it was ruinous. Sir John Foster succeeded as captain, and was charged, 1584, with having by his cupidity laid parts of it waste; yet in 1610 James I. bestowed it and the lordship upon Claudius Foster, the son of one of Sir John's illegitimate children. The estates of the Fosters were sold in 1704 to meet their debts, and were purchased by Lord Crewe, Bishop of Durham, who had married the beautiful Dorothy Foster. The bishop dying without heirs in 1720, left the greater part of this property to trustees for charitable purposes, and in 1757 the restoration of Bamburgh Castle began under the auspices of Dr. Sharp, Archdeacon of Northumberland, who carried out his own plans very zealously, and partly at his own cost. He repaired the Norman keep, and lived in it with his family, managing the various charitable designs of the founder, dispensing corn to the poor and housing shipwrecked seamen.

The enceinte of the castle follows the bends of the cliff, enclosing nearly five acres of ground, and from the entrance to the brink of the cliff, where the wall stands 150 feet above the sea, is nearly ¼ mile. There were three wards or courts ; the W. or lower ward, and the E. or middle ward, have been at one time covered with the buildings of the ancient town, and at the extreme W. end was situated the Church of St. Peter. The original entrance was by a flight of steps at the N.W. or lowest corner, where now are modern stairs. The great quadrangular Norman keep was built (temp. Henry II.) after the foreign pattern adopted at London, Dover, Newcastle, and other places ; it had originally only two storeys, with galleries and staircases in the wall. A deep draw-well exists in the keep ; it is 145 feet deep, cut through the hard rock, and the water, "sweet and very pure," is said in the Chronicle to have existed in 774. There has been much fanciful restoration, but happily some old work has escaped, and on the W. is the wall of the Captain's Lodgings, where probably the shot from the brazen gun penetrated Sir Ralph Grey's quarters. The gatehouse is all changed. Dr. Sharp kept exact drawings of the old work as he found it, and he gave these to an antiquary, one Edward King, but they cannot now be traced. Under the Captain's Hall is a very fine vaulted chamber of the best masonry in the castle ; it is now divided and used as a coal-cellar. Above this were the kitchens. It is deplored by Mr. Bates in his "Border Holds of Northumberland" that a grand old fortress of such historic interest as this, which was successfully defended by Margaret l'Aigle, by Queen Philippa, and by Queen Margaret of Anjou, "sanctified for more than a year by the solitary agony of Henry VI.," should now be "degraded into a £5 a year boarding-school for thirty girls, with its keep let as a lodging-house during the summer months," and he urges that the fabric should be made use of in ways consonant with the wishes of Lord Crewe. This is right, and one is therefore glad to read (April 30, 1894) that "the historic Castle of Bamburgh has just been purchased from the trustees of Lord Crewe's Charity by Lord Armstrong, who has undertaken not to alter the historic character of the building, but to restore all the parts that have fallen into decay in accordance with the original design. A considerable portion of the castle will be devoted to an endowed Home for the reception of impoverished persons of cultivated habits and acquirements." The good work was at once set in hand, and ranges of buildings, commensurate with the scheme and of a dignified character, are now rising upon the ancient foundations.

BELLISTER (*minor*)

WITHIN a short distance to the E. of this castle, and opposite to it on the S. bank of the South Tyne, in a beautiful situation near Haltwhistle, stands Bellister Castle, the seat of a younger branch of the Blenkinsops. It is a rude irregular structure, and a gloomy-looking one, built upon an artificial mound, and surrounded by a broad moat. It belonged to a Thomas Blenkinsop in the reign of Edward VI., and to George Blenkinsop temp. Elizabeth. The manor came during this century into the possession of the Ellisons of Hebburn, and this castle and estate to the Bacon family.

BELSAY (*minor*)

THIS ancient seat of the Middleton family dates from the reign of Edward II., cir. 1317, the modern mansion of Belsay Hall being the residence of a descendant of the founder, Sir Arthur E. Middleton, Bart. It lies about nine miles S.W. from Morpeth, and in the park is the old castle, or rather peel tower, one of the largest in the country. The Middleton family continued here through all the vicissitudes of the country, till at the Restoration the proprietor was, in 1662, created a baronet, and was high sheriff in 1666, from which time the succession to the present holder has been unbroken.

The tower is described as a highly picturesque structure, built of a rich yellow sandstone, and environed with fine timber. It is four storeys in height, and measures at its base an area of 56 feet by 47 feet. The ground-floor is vaulted, and the second floor contains a state apartment, 41 feet long and 21 feet wide, with a height of 17 feet. A newel stair in a square turret leads to the roof, which is masked by a fine embattled parapet, projected on corbels over the face of the wall, and having overhanging circular bartizans at the angles. Additions were made to it temp. James I., one of which remains in a steward's house, with the date 1614.

BLENKINSOP (*minor*)

IS a peel castle or Border fortress, 2½ miles from Haltwhistle, on the S. side of the Tippalt, in a cold bare country. The number of these fortified houses is very great, because every chief residence in these lawless regions had to be protected against, not only the enemies of England across the Border, but also from the raids and injuries of thieves and moss-troopers. This one is a strong square tower with a vaulted basement, surrounded by a high wall at the distance of four yards, and again by a deep ditch on the N. and W. sides, a brook on the S. and a steep bank E. It appears to have been built out of the Roman wall, from which it is not far removed, being, next to Thirlwall, the most westerly of the Northumbrian castles. It is in a ruinous state, but partly inhabited, having a farm-house added to it. The family of Blenkinsop held it in Henry III.'s reign: it was perhaps built about 1340 by a Ralph Blenkinsope de Boltby, Baron of Tynedale, and continued for centuries in that family, going by marriage at last to the Coulsons of Jesmond, Jane, the heiress of the Blenkinsops, who in the seventeenth century lived at Dryburnhaugh, marrying in 1727 William Coulson. In Murray is given the tradition that exists in this family of a black dog which appears as a warning before the death of any member of it, and reappears in the house again at the moment of dissolution.

BOTHAL (minor)

THE site no doubt of a very early fortress or "Bottle." This ancient seat of the Ogle family stands on an eminence above the Wansbeck River, on its N. bank, in a romantic situation, enveloped in woods, between Morpeth and the sea. The lands here belonged to the Bertrams, one of whom, Robert Bertram, served in the Welsh War of 1277, and his son was sheriff of the county. Robert, fifth of his name, built the castle of Bothal 1343, under licence to crenellate 17 Edward III., when twenty-one years of age. He was knighted and received the thanks of Edward III. for his bravery at Nevill's Cross; dying in 1362, his only child Helen married Robert Ogle, and as she had four husbands, it was not until 1405 that her son Sir Robert Ogle came into possession of Bothal. This estate he entailed on his second son John, who took his mother's name of Bertram, with remainder to his elder brother Sir Robert Ogle, who the next day after their father's death in October 1409, came with a force and besieged Bothal Castle, and took it after four days' fighting. Sir John Bertram died in 1449, and his male line failing with his grandson, Bothal passed to the Ogles. Sir Robert Ogle had been created Lord Ogle by Edward IV., 1461. The seventh Lord Ogle died 1601, s.p. male, when the barony fell into abeyance between his two daughters, the younger of whom, Catherine, marrying Charles Cavendish of Welbeck, Notts, was mother of William Cavendish, the famous Marquis of Newcastle, King Charles I.'s general. Again, on the death of the second Duke of Newcastle in 1691, the title of Ogle again fell between his three daughters, the eldest of whom, Margaret, married Edward Harley, Earl of Oxford, and acquired the property of Bothal, which has descended to her representative, the present Duke of Portland.

A Decorated gatehouse, which is still inhabited, is the principal feature of this fortress, having two semi-octagon towers covering the entrance, with portcullis groove under the archway. Above are sculptured a curious series of shields giving the arms of Edward III. and the Black Prince, with those of the warrior families of Wake, Aton, Greystock, Percy, Bertram, Conyers, Darcy, and Felton. Around the courtyard were placed the great hall, parlour, seven bed-chambers, chapel, kitchens, stables, and all the domestic offices. Bates gives a drawing of the castle dated 1724, and Grose another of 1773, since which time it has been kept in good order, and a great deal remains. The outer wall runs round the edge of the cliff, and encloses half an acre.

BYWELL. (*minor*)

STANDS on the N. side of the Tyne, about seven miles E. of the town of Hexham, in the most picturesque part of the Tyne Valley. It was an ancient barony of the Baliols and the Nevills, having attached to it a large park, which in the middle of the sixteenth century was full of "redd deare." The castle seems to have been the stronghold of a large barmkin, or walled enclosure, built at the E. end of the town for the protection of the people and their cattle from the raids of Tynedale robbers. Formerly it was a seat of the Baliols held *in capite* by five knights' fees, from the time of the Red King; then in the reign of Richard II. it came to the Nevills, lords of Raby, and afterwards Earls of Westmorland, who lost the property in 1571, when it was purchased by the Fenwicks. This family held it till 1713, when an heiress brought Bywell to another family of Fenwicks, of Stanton and Brink-burn; in 1802, the proprietor dying *s.p.*, bequeathed it to his widow, and the estate was sold to Thomas Wentworth Beaumont for £145,000. It was to the shelter of this castle that Henry VI. fled after the battle of the Linnels, or Hexham (1464), but not feeling safe here, he escaped to Bamburgh, leaving behind him at this castle his helmet and sword, with the war trappings of his horse, and also a cap of state adorned with a double crown.

The building is actually a grand fifteenth-century gatehouse, with turrets, battlements, and machicolis (*Parker*), whose walls are almost intact. It is an oblong structure, measuring about 61 feet by 38 feet, standing close over the steep bank of the river. There was a portcullis in the gateway, and the old oak gate is still in its place. In the gateway passage are two doors facing each other; one leads to the vaults below, and the other, which is an ancient one with an iron grating, opens to a staircase leading to a good chamber above, having a garderobe in the corner, and good windows. A newel stair leads to the upper room, nearly 50 feet long, with two fireplaces and Perpendicular windows. Above is the heavily battlemented roof, with four fine turrets. A portion of the enceinte wall remains.

CALLALY (*minor*)

THIS place is two miles W. from Whittingham, and was the residence of the ancient family of the Claverings. The building includes at the W. end an original Border tower of great antiquity, that on the E. and the centre being of a later date.

Callaly was the vill of William de Callaly, early in the reign of Henry III., and his son Gilbert granted it to Robert Fitz-Roger, Lord of Warkworth and of Clavering in Essex. The family of Fitz-Roger descended from the Norman De Burghs, ancestors of many noble families in England, and this Robert was called to Parliament in 23 Edward I., and died 4 Edward II. At this time the want of surnames was found to be of great inconvenience, and in the general adoption of territorial names, King Edward gave to John the son of this Robert that of Clavering, from the name of the chief part of his estates. He inherited the vast property left by his father, but left only a daughter, Eva, who had four husbands, the second being Ralph, Lord Nevill of Raby. At his death he left his lands in this county to the Crown, by whom they were passed on to the Percys. The youngest brother of this John Clavering was the ancestor of the Claverings of Callaly, which place remained their home until of late years. It is now the property of Major Alexander H. Brown.

CARTINGTON (*minor*)

THE castle is two miles N.W. of Rothbury, on the hillside. It was a detached portion of the barony of Ditchburn, and was in early times held by the owner of Embleton, whose lands after the death of Simon de Montfort were added to the possessions of the Earls of Lancaster. Although the Cartington family became tenants originally of the place about the year 1316, yet the tower is first mentioned only in 1415. The last John Cartington (they were almost all named John) died about 1494, when the place came to the Radcliffes, his daughter and heiress Anne having become the wife of Edward, son of Sir Thomas Radcliffe of Derwentwater. In November 1518, Queen Margaret, the widow of James IV. of Scotland, who had married Archibald Douglas, Earl of Angus, soon enough after Flodden, came to Cartington from Harbottle with her newly-born daughter, Margaret Douglas, born at Harbottle a month before, and remained here a week. This little child afterwards married the Earl of Lennox, and was the mother of Darnley, and so grandmother to James VI. and I. of England. In 1601 Cartington was settled on an elder daughter, Elizabeth Radcliffe, married to Roger Widdrington, and their son was in 1642 made a baronet by Charles I.,—Sir Edward Widdrington of Cartington. The Scottish army when it moved south entered and plundered this castle, and after Marston Moor the owner, who had fought there on Charles's side, was sequestrated, the castle being valued at £8000, and ordered to be slighted. But in 1648 it was strong enough to make front against the Parliamentary troops and sustain a siege for a short while ; this was on the occasion when the Royal troops, 1200 strong, under the command of Sir Richard Tempest, commander of the forces of Durham, and Colonel Edward Grey, in command of the forces in Northumberland, being encamped carelessly along the Coquet, allowed themselves to be surprised in their beds by the Roundheads, when the greater part were made prisoners. From the Widdringtons, Cartington passed by marriage to the Charltons, and again to one or two other families, till at last, when in a woeful state of neglect, it was sold in 1883 to Sir William G. Armstrong of Cragside, now Lord Armstrong ; he rescued the old stronghold from ruin, and rebuilt and restored the castle. There are two good towers at the E. and W. extremities of the other buildings, remains of the ancient structure ; the tower on the E. was originally four storeys in height, having bartizans at the angles, and rising one storey above the W. tower. The paved courtyard has been restored and some seventeenth-century work removed.

CASTLE STONE-NICK (minor)

THIS is the name given to a fortified building surrounded by a ditch which stands about a quarter of a mile from the great bridge over Tweed opposite to Coldstream. It is the only remaining portion of the stronghold besieged and captured in the incursion of the French auxiliaries from Scotland into England, which took place in 1549. It is described as a house of considerable strength, and much booty was found in it. This happened during the Protectorate of Somerset.

CHILLINGHAM (chief)

THE castle stands on rising ground in the midst of a wild and picturesque park. Licence was granted 18 Edward III. (1344) to Thomas de Heton to crenellate "mansum suum ac castrum sive fortalitium inde facere" at Chevelyngham. The Hetons possessed it till the death of William de Heton s.p. male, when the property passed to married female heirs. It is not known how and when the Greys of Wark first obtained this castle. There is a splendid altar tomb to Sir Ralph Grey, who died 1443, in the parish church, in a side chapel. His son, the Lancastrian leader of the same name, who defended Bamburgh Castle against the Earl of Warwick, and was beheaded after the final surrender of that fortress in 1464, wisely had this property and castle conveyed to trustees, and thus his widow Jacquetta was able to enjoy them after his death. After the insurrection in defence of the old faith in 1536, called the Pilgrimage of Grace, some of the king's supporters took refuge here, whereupon Sir Ingram Percy sent for heavy guns from Berwick to besiege the castle. In 1541 it was owned by Ralph Grey, a minor, and in the custody of his stepfather, and was then in fair repair. The Greys remained lords of Chillingham until the death of Ford Grey, Earl of Tankerville, in 1701, when the whole went to his only daughter and heiress, Lady Ossulton, whose husband was created Earl of Tankerville, and his family are still the possessors. On the N. side of the estuary of the River Seine, not far from the town of Havre, is the county of Tanquerville, which was granted by Henry V. to Sir John de Grey, a brother of the ancestor of these Greys of Chillingham, for services rendered in the French war in 1419; it was lost by his son Henry de Grey in 1449, when the armies of France overran Normandy, in the weaker days of Henry VI.

The chief remains of the mediæval castle are the corner towers, two of which, those on the S.E. and S.W. angles, belong to the middle of the fourteenth century, together with a dungeon in the N.W. tower, and are probably the work of Thomas de Heton; but the structures connecting these towers, that is, the N. and S. fronts, are of much later construction. Inside is an arcade by Inigo Jones, with a stone staircase leading to the dining-room. In the beautiful and extensive park attached to the castle exists a famous breed of wild cattle, all white, very shy and fierce, but of unknown origin.

CHIPCHASE (minor)

AN ancient and beautiful structure, nine miles N.W. from Hexham, situated on a declivity on the E. bank of the North Tyne amid the finest scenery of that river: it is in a state of good preservation. The original tower is a rectangular building, about 52 feet long and 38 wide, by 50 feet in height. Adjoining it on the S.E. is the old manor-house built in 1621 by Cuthbert Heron; it is said to be the finest specimen of Jacobean architecture in the county. The entrance to the tower is through an archway next to the manor-house, and over this entrance is a small room for working the portcullis, the groove of which remains, and the framework of which is still in place, being made of oaken bars (*Hartshorne*). On the first floor there is a single dark, gloomy apartment, but the second floor has a good pointed window with two lights; a small oratory is contrived in the wall, adjoining the large room. There were good rooms on the third floor, which is provided with mural passages and a garderobe; a wheel stair leads to a square turret. The old stone roof is very perfect. At each corner there is an embattled turret,

corbelled out over the face of each wall, and between them was a heavy
parapet with bold machicoulis projecting 2 feet from face of walls.

Chipchase was a portion of the manor of Prudhoe, belonging to Odinel
de Umfraville in 18 Henry II.; and he had a small fort here. In the reign of
Edward I. it was possessed by Peter de Insula (De Lisle), and next by a branch
of the Herons of Ford. In Elizabeth's reign Chipchase belonged to Sir George
Heron, High Sheriff 13 Elizabeth, who was killed in a Border fray. He was
succeeded by his cousin Cuthbert Heron, whom Charles II. made a baronet
in 1662, perhaps because his brother was killed at Marston Moor. He built
the manor-house. His grandson sold the castle, which in 1732 became the
property of the Reeds. In the first quarter of the present century, owing to
losses by banking failures, the estate came to the hammer, and is now the
property of Mr. Hugh Taylor. There is a chapel in the park S. of the castle.

COCKLAW TOWER (minor)

THIS small peel tower stands near the conflux of the Erring burn—coming
from the N.E.—with the North Tyne River, N. of Hexham, and within sight
of the Roman wall. It also has the name of West Errington Tower, and is
supposed to have been built by the Errington family in the fifteenth century.
Mr. Bates remarks, in regard to the rude and ancient appearance which some of
these fortalices bear, that " it is necessary to remember that towers of this class
were the work of the country people themselves, and consequently look considerably earlier than they really are."

There are two floors above the basement or ground floor, which is entered
by a low-pointed doorway on the S. front, the door of which was fastened in
the usual way by a wooden bar in sockets. At its right hand is a circular stair,
in the S.E. angle, leading to the upper stages and roof, and opposite to this in
the vaulted passage is a small dungeon, the sole admission to which is by a hole
in the vaulting of it. At the end of the entrance passage of 10 feet is a fine
pointed doorway leading into the basement vault, the usual feature of Border
peels, measuring about 32 feet by 20½ feet, into which the stock was accustomed to be driven for security; a narrow loop or slit being given for light and
air. It has a masonry barrel roof.

The first floor has a fireplace, and two lights, and a loop, and on the E. wall
is a passage which led to an outside building, perhaps a chapel, now vanished.
The top floor has only two small windows and a fireplace. On the S.W. of
each floor is a small chamber apart, and on the first there is a mural passage
leading to a garderobe.

COCKLE or COCKLEY PARK TOWER (*minor*)

ON the road northward, four miles from Morpeth, is the ruin of a fine
fifteenth-century peel of the Ogles, Lords of Bothal, whose scutcheon is
borne on a large panel on the E. wall. A farm-house has been formed in the
centre with the N. end wall which remains, since it was the property of Lord
Oxford in 1724. The tradition is that the S. end was destroyed by fire several
centuries ago.

It is probable that the tower, which stands in a bleak position, with a very
extended prospect, was reared by Robert, 1st Lord Ogle, who came into actual
possession of Bothal in 1465 ; it does not appear in the list of these fortalices in
the survey made in 1415. Hodgson shows that in 1543 Sir Robert, 5th Lord
Ogle, settled the building and lands upon his wife Jeyne, prior to which they
had been in the occupancy of his mother, Anne Ogle. Lord Robert was killed
at the battle of Ancrum Moor a few days after he had made the above disposition "in case of being slain by the chance of war." Since then the place
has descended in the same way as Bothal to its present possessor, the Duke
of Portland.

The length of the W. front is 54 feet, and that of the N. 30 feet, including
its projection at the E. end, which carries the staircase,—this N. end being
the only original part left. The entrance doorway is near the staircase, which
leads up to the first and second floors, and terminates in a small gable giving
to the battlements. These are carried on boldly projecting brackets, the
corners being rounded at the four angles, which seem to have thus formed
angle turrets. In the centre of the N. wall is a fine pointed fifteenth-century
window, the others being of later date.

COLDMARTIN TOWER (*non-existent*)

WAS a small peel situated on an eminence on the E. marches, opposite
to the Cheviots—about 27 feet square. In the inquest of 1584 it is thus
spoken of : "Cadmertowne, one tower of stone and lime, of Roger Fowberry's
of Fowberry, gent.,—utterly decayed, notwithstanding it hath land belonging
to it able to keep two men and horse fit for service."

The remains consist of a fragment 9 feet high of the S.W. wall, 6 feet thick,
standing above Wooler Water.

CORBRIDGE (*minor*)

IN a corner of the market-place of this town is a massive peel tower of Edward II., 33 feet in height, which has been used sometimes for a rectory house and sometimes as a prison. The parapet is embattled, and forms square projecting bartizans at the four corners. The walls are four feet thick, and there is a garderobe outside carried on corbels. The interior is in perfect condition, and exhibits completely the domestic arrangements peculiar to the period.

COUPLAND (*minor*)

THIS Border tower stands on the N. bank of the Glen stream, on the N.W. of Wooler, to which barony the manor belonged, and which was held, together with Akeld Manor, under the Muschamps, the grantees of Wooler from Henry I., by the family of de Akeld. These de Akelds were here until late in the reign of Edward II., when they are lost sight of. Previous to this, about the middle of the thirteenth century, there appears in the district a family of the name of Coupland, though not apparently holding any land in the manor of Coupland. One of them, John de Copeland, was chosen as one of the twelve English knights appointed in 1245 to settle disputes on the Border marches; and it is possible that his namesake, who at the battle of Nevill's Cross in 1346 took prisoner David, King of Scotland, was also of this family; for this deed Sir John Copeland was made a knight banneret, and had £500 a year settled upon himself and his heirs.

The Prenderguests next appear as owners of the Akeld estates, perhaps by an heiress, and after them, in the reign of Henry IV., the Greys are lords of Akeld and Coupland, a family which continued to exercise signorial rights here, and to own Coupland until the middle of the last century. Then, in 1734, the Earl of Tankerville, representing the old Greys of Chillingham, sold Coupland to Robert Paul of Tower Hill, London.

Other families also held lands in this lordship, amongst them the Forsters of Bamburgh and the Halls of Otterburn. The first of these introduced the family of Wallis as landowners here, and this family, originally written Whaleys or Wallace, became later the chief proprietors after the Greys.

Leland speaks of no castle here, and in the survey of Border castles and towers made in 1552 it is said "the towneshippe of Coupland hath yn it neither fortresse or barmekyne;" therefore this tower must be of late date. On a chimney-piece in the oldest part of the tower there is the date 1619, with the initials G. W. and M. W., which probably represent George Wallis and his wife, who are said to have erected or rebuilt the stronghold, at a time when these Border lands were in a very disturbed state, and protection for life and property was necessitated. The oldest portion consists of a strong tower and side turret containing eleven rooms, with a curious newel stair; the walls being 6 and 7 feet thick (*Paper by the Rev. Matthew Culley*).

The Coupland Castle estate had come to the Ogles from the Wallises in 1713, and in 1806 passed to the family of Bates of Brunton, and in 1830 Matthew Culley of Akeld (who had obtained those lands in 1765) succeeded to the whole of this property in right of his mother, the sister and heir of Thomas Bates. His son, the Rev. Matthew Culley of Akeld and Coupland, is the present owner.

DALLEY, OR DALA (*non-existent*)

THE site of this old fortress is about a mile S. of Tarset, on the opposite side of Tyne, on the N. bank of Chirdon burn, and is said by the tradition of the country to have a subterranean communication with Tarset (*q.v.*).

It is thought that this is the tower in Tynedale alluded to in a letter (still extant) written in 1237 to Henry III. by Hugh de Bolebec, his "custos" of Northumberland, complaining that a certain Scottish knight, David de Lyndesey, was building a house in Tynedale (which was then held by the King of Scotland); that it was already built up to the walks of the battlements (allures), and was intended to be crenellated. This Lindsay, as Justiciary of Lothian, was at the head of the Scottish Commission for determining the marches at Carham; and in 1255 Henry III. confirmed to him and his heirs the property in Chirdon given him by Margery, the sister of Alexander II. Henry, therefore, did not take the same view as Bolebec.

There are vestiges of the walls of this fortalice, in some places standing 7 feet above the ground.

DILSTON (*minor*)

SOUTH of the Tyne, and E. of Hexham, stand, on the brink of a deep ravine, through which runs the stream of the Devil's-water, the shattered remains of the old castle which was once the home of the Radcliffe family. One John d'Eivill is said by Dugdale to have been a powerful personage at the time of the Barons' War, in Henry III.'s reign. His family, seated here from the days of Henry I., probably gave their name in a corrupted form to the river and the locality. Robert de Dyvilston was assessed for scutage 18 and 23 Henry III., and his grandson, Sir Thomas de Dyvilston, was sheriff of the county in the ninth year of Edward I. His barony was inherited by his cousin, William de Tynedale, Lord of Langley, a barony about ten miles distant westward. Thomas de Tynedale left a son, William, who succeeded to Dyvilston at his mother's death in 1317, and whose grandson, Walter de Tynedale, dying during the reign of Richard II., left two daughters. Both these ladies died without issue in 1416, whereon Sir William Claxton, a grandson of Thomas de Tynedale's wife, succeeded to Dyvilston and to all the estates of the Barons of Tynedale. In the second year of Richard III., Johanna, second daughter of Sir Robert Claxton, became Lady of Dyvilston, being married to John Cartington of Cartington Tower, whom she survived. By her will (A.D. 1521), Dyvilston was devised to her grandson, Sir Cuthbert Radcliffe, knight, and his heirs male by reason that her daughter and heiress, Anne Cartington, had (before 1494) married Sir Edward Radcliffe, knight-banneret, who was High Sheriff of Northumberland in 17 Henry VII. Anne Cartington inherited the Cartington, Whittonstell, and Hawthorn estates; and her husband's father, Sir Nicholas Radcliffe, had succeeded to the possessions of the old lords of Derwentwater, Cumberland, by his marriage with Margaret, daughter of the last of the Derwentwater family (see *Castle Crag, Cumberland*). This Margaret had issue Sir Thomas, who married Margaret, daughter of Sir William Parr of Kendal Castle (*q.v.*), the ancestor of the last queen of Henry VIII., and Sir Edward Radcliffe was their third son; he finally inherited all the property. He had two sons by his marriage with Anne Cartington, Sir Cuthbert and Sir John—both knights—the eldest succeeding him as Sir Cuthbert Radcliffe of Dilston, Sheriff of Cumberland, 19 Henry VIII. Sir Cuthbert married in 1514 Margaret, daughter of Henry, Lord Clifford, and, dying in 1545, was succeeded by his son, Sir George Radcliffe of Dilston and Derwentwater.

Sir George's son and heir was Sir Francis, created baronet in 1619, who was succeeded in 1622 by his son, Sir Edward. Being a distinguished Royalist, and also a Catholic, Sir Edward suffered sequestration at the hands of the Parliamentarians. He had married, clandestinely it is supposed, Elizabeth Barton, heiress of Whenby, Yorkshire, and lived at Dilston, dying in 1663 at the age of seventy-five. To his already large property he had added the estates of Alston, and of Langley with its castle, his heir being his only surviving son, Sir Francis Radcliffe.[*]

Sir Edward built an addition to the ancient tower and mansion of Dilston, where he lived and died, and the whole was incorporated with the large additions made by his son, the second Sir Francis, which for a century and a half formed the abode of the family. These new buildings were on the N. of the existing tower, and being chiefly of brick, fell into such decay that in 1768 they were removed, leaving once more standing alone the older stone tower, whose ruins we still see. An avenue of chestnuts led up to the large

---

[*] The rent-roll of Sir Francis at this time (1672) was £6263.

gateway (now removed), and the approach road passed round the side of the hill nearest the river, and to the W. of the mansion. The chapel still remains, and is on the N. side, adjacent to the old gateway, built about 1616 by the first Sir Francis.

In the third year of James II., Sir Francis married his son Edward to the Lady Charlotte, the youngest natural daughter of Charles II. by the Duchess of Cleveland, then aged fourteen. This Edward was created in 1688 Earl of Derwentwater, Baron Tynedale, and Viscount Radcliffe and Langley. He died in 1696, aged seventy-two, and was succeeded by Edward, his son, the second earl. He also left three daughters. Earl Edward, who died 1705, had issue James, his elder son and heir, born 1689, and Charles, who was beheaded in 1745; also a daughter, Lady Mary. He and his countess separated in 1700. James Radcliffe, the third earl, was brought up at St. Germains at the court of James II., in company with his young cousin, the royal prince, afterwards called the "Pretender," whom he served with attachment and devotion to the end. He first visited his estates in 1710, when twenty-one years old, going first to Dilston and then to his Derwentwater property. He is described as a gentle and lovable youth, of rather short stature, slender of person, and of a handsome countenance, with light hair and grey eyes, being also of active habits. He wrote his name Darwentwater, which is the old and correct pronunciation. At Dilston Earl James kept up a generous hospitality, and was much beloved by rich and poor. In 1712 he married Anne Maria, eldest daughter of Sir James Webb, Bart., of Canford, Dorset, like himself a Catholic, educated in France, where, at the court of St. Germains, he first made her acquaintance. Some additions were at this time made to Dilston Castle while the earl and his wife lived with the Webbs at Hatherhope, near Fairford, Gloucestershire.

King James II. dying on September 16, 1701, the English at St. Germains saluted his son as James III., but it was not until August 1715 that the Earl of Mar raised the standard proclaiming this prince as James VIII. of Scotland. It is not known if the Earl of Derwentwater was in the secret of this rising, but, in their precautions against a rebellion, the Government issued warrants for the apprehension of him and his brother Charles, so as to prevent their joining. Being warned of this, the earl and his brother withdrew from Dilston and hid themselves in the country during the whole of September. The earl seems to have hesitated long before risking his life and large possessions in the cause of the Pretender, and it is said to have been his lady who at length goaded him on to action, reproaching him "for continuing to hide his head in hovels from the light of day when the gentry were in arms for the cause of their rightful sovereign, and, throwing down her fan before her lord, bade him take it and give his sword to her." At all events he soon did espouse the cause, heart and soul, and having arranged a meeting with his friends, ordered every retainer in his castle to be ready to follow him in the early morn of October 6, 1715, when from his ancient halls

> " Lord Derwentwater rode away
> Well mounted on his dapple-grey,"

accompanied by his brother and "some friends and all his servants, mounted, some on his coach-horses and others upon very good useful horses, and all well armed." They crossed the Devil's-water at Nunsborough Ford, and rode on to meet the main party at the Waterfalls Hill, crossing the Tyne close to Hexham, where their force was increased to almost sixty horse. After halting near Errington's at Beaufront, they proceeded to the Coquet and the small town of Rothbury. Continuing their ride through the night, they came on the morning of the 7th to Warkworth Castle, where Lord Widdrington, another Catholic peer, joined the party with others. By Lord Mar's arrangement, Mr. Forster of Bamburgh Castle was elected leader, who, though a civilian and a Protestant, forthwith with sound of trumpet proclaimed James III. The party then moved to Alnwick, described as being at that time "an old dilapidated house of the Duke of Somerset," and thence to Morpeth, which place had through the accession of Border volunteers grown to the strength of 300 fighting men. From thence they intended to proceed to and enter Newcastle, but the loyal folk of that town had closed their gates and manned the walls, which still existed at that time, being reinforced by some Government troops under Lieutenant-General Carpenter. So Earl Derwentwater and his party returned to Hexham, and from thence, being joined by Lord Kenmure and his followers, they retreated to Rothbury. Their next move was northwards to Kelso, where Lord Mar's contingent was to unite. At this place serious deliberation took place whether to continue the march north to attack the force under Argyll, and so to secure Scotland, or whether to invade England. The latter counsel prevailed, and the Pretender's forces marched to Hawick and thence to Penrith, which place they entered, 1700 strong, on November 2nd. The militia forces had disbanded before their advance, and General Forster at once proclaimed the prince as James III., levying £500 in his interest from the town. Next day the force marched to Appleby, where they rested till the 5th, and from thence went to Kendal, Lord Derwentwater taking up his lodging in the "White Lion" in Strickland Gate.

On November 7th the force entered Lancaster in parade order, with colours flying, and to the music of drums and pipes. First came 200 English noblemen and their followers, all mounted; next came the Highlanders; then 200 Lowlanders, followed by the Scottish horse. Here in Lancaster Lord Derwentwater and his colleagues were the guests of Mr. Dalton at Thurnham Hall, where they spent a day. On the 9th the whole party marched by way of Garstang to Preston, preceded by an advance-guard of Northumbrian horse, the infantry arriving on the morning of the 10th. At Preston they were joined by 1200 half-armed followers of the Roman Catholic gentry of the district, but it was evident that the county itself stood aloof from the rising, and that the support calculated upon was not forthcoming. Meantime the Government troops were advancing on the invaders, and ultimately took them by surprise, for General Willes, with five regiments of foot and one of cavalry, marched to Wigan, and thence, early on the 12th, set out for Preston. The unexpected news of this advance seems to have paralysed the prince's amateur general ; a council was held, and, brought to bay as the invaders were, they proceeded to defend themselves in the centre of the town by barricading the streets in three places, each barricade being defended by two pieces of ordnance. But they omitted to secure the bridge over the Ribble, and the hollow pass from it to the town, by doing which they might have greatly checked the enemy. As it was, the town was left open on all sides to Willes, who, arriving at one o'clock, at once attacked the barricades in two places. These were, however, gallantly defended, and after a fight which continued until midnight, King George's troops withdrew, having lost about 260 men ; a result which is said to have been greatly due to the bravery and the example of Lord Derwentwater and his brother.

Next day the fortunes of war changed, for, Carpenter's troops having come up, the town was invested on all sides, and it was evident that the Jacobite cause was lost. The prevailing thought among the Northern forces was to cut their way out through the ranks of the enemy. Forster, however, of his own accord sent overtures for a truce to General Willes, and a capitulation ensued, the besieged laying down their arms. Then the six insurgent lords, Derwentwater, Nithsdale, Kenmure, Widdrington, Carnwath, and Nairn, were arrested at the Mitre Tavern, and being sent with many other prisoners to London, were lodged in the Tower. Altogether, some 1700 of the insurgent force were captured at Preston, and were imprisoned at Chester and Lancaster and in other jails, the rest making good their escape.

The utmost efforts were made to obtain remission of the capital punishment passed on the young Lord Derwentwater, but George II. was incapable of generosity to a fallen foe, and his reply to a petition of the House of Lords was an order, issued on the 23rd February, for the immediate execution of Lords Derwentwater, Nithsdale, and Kenmure. Lady Derwentwater, supported by many other ladies of high rank, made repeated touching appeals for mercy personally, but without any effect. When the news of Lord Nithsdale's escape on the eve of his intended execution, by means of his brave and clever wife, reached the king, he gave way to an excess of passion at having his vengeance thus thwarted. Lord Derwentwater saw his wife for the last time twenty-four hours before his death, which took place on the morning of February 24th.

At ten o'clock he was taken from the Tower to the scaffold on Tower Hill, and there beheaded. The body was brought back to the Tower, but the earl's friends contrived to get possession of it, and it was taken to Dagenham Park, near Romford, to a house which the countess had rented. Finally it was removed to Dilston after being embalmed. The countess survived her husband seven years; aged but thirty years, she died in 1723 at Louvain, where she was buried. Her eldest son died from an accident, and was buried there also in 1731, before he reached his twenty-first year. Thereby the estates devolved on Charles Radcliffe, the brother of Lord Derwentwater, who, being also condemned to death in 1716, managed to escape from Newgate, and lived for many years abroad. In November 1745 Charles and his son were by accident captured on board a French privateer, being at first supposed to be the Pretender and his son; when their true identity was recognised, Charles Radcliffe was arraigned on the old conviction for high treason, recorded in 1716, and being sentenced to death, was executed on this charge, now thirty years in abeyance, on the 8th December 1746, aged fifty-three.

The vast estates of the Derwentwater family, inherited at the death of Earl James's son in 1731 by Charles Radcliffe, should, at the death of the latter, have passed to his son James Bartholomew Radcliffe, but they had become vested in the Crown after 1749, when the Government caused an Act to be passed, vesting them absolutely in the hands of trustees for the benefit of Greenwich Hospital, which institution enjoyed their possession until quite recently. The confiscated lands included, besides the manor and demesne of Derwentwater, the estates of Langley, Meldon, Wark, and many others in Northumberland and Hexhamshire, as well as the Cumberland property; in all about 41,000 acres. The rental returned in 1816 was £43,487, besides what was brought in by the mines, whose produce in 1823 was estimated at £23,000. Of late years these princely inheritances of the Derwentwater family have been claimed by a crazy person calling herself the heiress of the Radcliffes. She attempted to take forcible possession of Dilston, encamping in gipsy fashion near the castle, from whence she was with difficulty ejected by the agents of Greenwich Hospital.

Dilston Hall, as it stood in the days of Earl James, is stated, in the exhaustive narrative of Mr. Gibson, to have been "a plain, extensive building, two storeys in height, which occupied three sides of an oblong, rectangular figure, enclosing a courtyard paved with dark-veined limestone in diamond-shaped slabs, and entered by the great gateway, which was built in the reign of James I. This gateway is still standing in another site. The longest range of building occupied the northern side; in the centre was a large entrance hall, approached from the paved court by a few raised steps. The courtyard was bounded on the western side by the old tower or castle, which still remains, and against the W. front of which a range of building was added by Lord Derwentwater, but never finished in the interior." There is a vault said to exist below the old tower, and some subterranean passages with a chamber attached. As soon as the Royal Commissioners obtained possession, the materials of Dilston were valued. The house was dismantled and its contents sold and dispersed, while the walls were demolished piecemeal for building purposes, only the more ancient castle being left. This, the "old original" tower of the Dyvilstons, was probably at first a strong Border peel, to which the newer mansion was eventually attached.

The last request of the ill-fated young earl, that he might be buried with his ancestors, was refused, in view of the excitement prevailing in the North, and it was supposed that the body had been interred in the churchyard of St. Giles, Holborn. But, in fact, the coffin was removed, and carried secretly by friends, resting by day, and travelling by night only, into Northumberland, and was deposited with the remains of his father in the chapel vault of Dilston.

In 1805 an unworthy curiosity to ascertain if the earl's head had been buried with his body moved the Commissioners of Greenwich Hospital to open the interment, when the body was found well embalmed, and but little decayed, the head lying beside it, with the mark of the axe clearly visible. The coffin had been placed in a row with five others of his line, and below was found a leaden box, in which the heart had been deposited.

It is noteworthy, in connection with Lord Derwentwater's memory as retained in his own country, that the aurora borealis, which appeared very vividly on the night of his execution, is still known there by the name of Lord Derwentwater's lights.

Dilston was purchased in 1874 from Greenwich Hospital by Mr. W. B. Beaumont, when the remains in the crypt were removed. The old gateway, once the entrance to Dilston Hall, now stands near the chapel, bearing its date of 1616, with the initials F. R. and J. R.

DUDDO (minor)

THIS was another Border tower in Norhamshire, two miles on the N. side of the Till, standing on a precipitous crag of rock, 300 feet above sea-level. Only the S. side of the tower remains, but it appears to have been a square in form, measuring about 36 feet square, with a staircase turret. The wall is rent from bottom to top. Over the entrance is a round bartizan, well corbelled out, but there is little to remark as to the architecture (*Bates*).

The manor was anciently held by the Stryvelings or Stirlings, and it descended in 1391 to the Claverings. When James IV. invaded England in support of Perkin Warbeck in 1496, he caused this fortress to be partly thrown down; but between 1541 and 1561 the remaining half of it was repaired, and an enclosure or barmkin was built round it for the safe-guarding of cattle. There is nothing remaining of the fifteenth-century tower of William Clavering of Duddo, who was third son of Robert Clavering of Callaly, killed in a skirmish with the Scots in 1586.

DUNSTANBURGH (chief)

THE castle is six miles N.E. of Alnwick, and two from Embleton; it stands on the brow of a great basaltic headland of the same range as that of Bamburgh, which here is displayed in black perpendicular columns, above which the fortress frowns over the wild North Sea like Scarborough and Bamburgh. Its name shows that it was originally a "burh" of the Angles, but nothing is known about its early history. The manor named Dunstan was granted by Henry I. to a family whose founder, Liulf of Bamburgh, and his son Odard, having been Sheriffs (vicecomites) of Northumberland, retained in later times the title of "Viscount" as a family name. John de Viscount, the last of his race, dying in 1244, left a daughter, Rametta, his sole heiress, whose husband, Hereward de Marisco, sold the barony in 1256 to Simon de Montfort, Earl of Leicester. John de Vesci, lord of Alnwick, fleeing from the slaughter at Evesham (1265), carried home one of the feet from the earl's mutilated body, and deposited it, encased in a silver shoe, as a relic in Alnwick Abbey. Henry III. seized this barony and granted it to his younger son, Edmund Crouchback, Earl of Lancaster, whose son, Thomas Plantagenet, succeeding (1296) to the earldom, proceeded to build at Dunstanburgh. He erected the gatehouse with towers 80 feet high, and formed the moat, and we hear of coal being brought from Newcastle for burning the lime. In 9 Edward II. Thomas, Earl of Lancaster, has a licence to crenellate. He was a great builder, as his castles of Kenilworth and Pontefract testify, and, as the king's cousin, was the greatest and most powerful and opulent nobleman in the kingdom; he headed the movement against Piers Gaveston which ended in the beheading of the favourite near Warwick, for which the king vowed vengeance on him. Lancaster was also suspected of taking bribes from the Scots, because he abstained from assisting the king in his expedition to Scotland in 1314, and is said to have jeered at his army and himself as they passed Pontefract Castle on the return from Bannockburn. Certain it is that in the subsequent invasion of England by a Scottish army, his castle of Dunstanburgh was respected by them, and his property was not molested. In 1322 it was to Dunstanburgh that the confederate Earls of Lancaster and Hereford were retreating, in order to unite with their Scottish contingent, when the fight of Boroughbridge took place, ending in the capture and execution of Lancaster. Two years after, Edward restored Dunstanburgh and the earldom to the late earl's younger brother, Henry, whose son, Henry "Tort-col" or Wryneck, created Duke of Lancaster 1351, left three daughters, the youngest of whom, Blanche, married John of Gaunt (his first wife), and brought him Dunstanburgh among other places, and the dukedom. Coming to the castle, he made many additions to it, building a new gatehouse, with a barbican and drawbridge, and a postern. When his son Henry ascended the throne, Dunstanburgh became Crown property, and continued a Lancastrian stronghold throughout the Wars of the Roses. After Towton this castle, as well as others in Northumberland, was provisioned and manned with an English, French, and Scottish garrison.

In October 1462 Queen Margaret landed from the Continent, and divided her forces between Alnwick, Bamburgh, and Dunstanburgh, whereupon the king, Edward IV., marched north with a large army to attack them, the sieges of all three being superintended by the Earl of Warwick (see *Bamburgh*). The siege of Dunstanburgh was committed to the Earl of Worcester and Sir Ralph Grey, while in

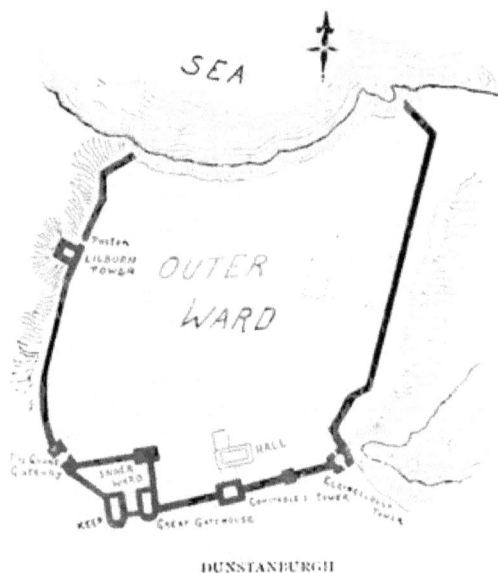

DUNSTANBURGH

its garrison were Sir Richard Tunstall, Sir Philip Wentworth, Dr. Morton, and 700 men. The place was forced to capitulate, honourably, at Christmas, and was, together with Bamburgh, placed under the custody of Sir Ralph Percy, on his swearing allegiance to King Edward; this, however, did not prevent him from yielding both places to the Lancastrians the ensuing spring. After the rout at the Linnels (Hexham) in May 1464, Dunstanburgh was taken by storm, and its captain, John Gosse, was carried to York and beheaded, when the great Earl of Warwick entered the fortress as a victor.

In 1538 the Royal Commission, consisting of Bellasis, Collingwood, and Horsley, reported to Henry VIII. regarding this castle as "a very reuynus house, and of smalle strengthe," but little could have been done to the fabric, since a report in Elizabeth's time is equally condemnatory. James I. gave it to Sir William Grey of Wark, and it continued the property of his descendants until the Earl of Tankerville sold it in 1869 to the trustees of Mr. Samuel Eyres of Leeds.

The original walls and towers built by Thomas, Earl of Lancaster, must have been of better materials and workmanship than the buildings of John of Gaunt, for while they have withstood the climate and storms in their so exposed situation, the latter have almost disappeared under the same conditions. The outer walls, ranging on three sides of an oblong enclosure of about nine acres extent, stand on the bank of a deep chasm or indentation of the rock on the E. side, and along the edge of the cliff on the W., the S. or landward face having the great gatehouse and three mural towers, while the N. front faces the ocean. The principal feature remaining is the gatehouse, which consists of two huge semicircular towers, 80 feet in height, flanking a circular archway under a building of two storeys ; the room over the passage having an opening along the back wall for containing the portcullis, and side chambers in the front wall for firing from cross-loops. The passage was at one time walled up to convert the structure into a keep, when the entrance to the castle was through a postern added by John of Gaunt, about 20 yards along the W. wall. The inner ward, now a mass of ruin, perhaps contained the chapel. The Lilburn Tower on the W. was built by a Constable of that name in 1325, and E. of the gatehouse is the Constable's Tower, of two storeys, having in rear of it the ruins of the hall, which we read was glazed in 1444. Farther on, at the S.E. angle, stands the Egginclough Tower, on the very brink of the rocky chasm, now called the Rumble Churn ; its S. wall has collapsed, and one side of it is given up to a series of latrines or garderobes having an outside shaft, lately fallen down.

EDLINGHAM (minor)

THE village lies six miles to the S.W. of Alnwick, and near it, at the head of a narrow valley, are the ruins of a twelfth-century castle, of which the tower remains, and contains carved stone in fireplaces and doorways of some interest ; there is also a spiral staircase in the tower.

In the reign of Henry II., John, son of Walden, held it under Earl Patrick ; and in the fourteenth century it belonged to Sir John Felton. In the end of Henry VII., the manor and castle were owned by Sir Roger Hastings, knight, and temp. Henry VIII., by Thomas Swinburn of Nafferton Hall. By the failure of heirs male to his descendant, John Swinburne, in the reign of Charles I., his daughter and heir, Margaret, brought Edlingham in marriage to William Swinburne of Capheaton, thus uniting the two properties as well as the families, and the present owner is Sir John Swinburne of Capheaton, Bart.

E T A L (manor)

THE remains of this fortress stand on the E. side of the river Till, opposite to the Field of Flodden, near the borders of Norhamshire, on gently rising ground. This was the principal seat of the Manners family, who were persons of distinction even in the reign of Henry II. At that time Robert de Manners held Ethale for a half knight's fee under the barony of Muschamp, and his descendants were there in the time of Henry III. In 1341, the date of the fortress, Sir Robert Manners obtained a licence to crenellate his house of Etal. He was Constable of the important castle of Norham, and must therefore have been a personage of note ; he died in 1354, and was succeeded by his son, whose posterity continued at Etal, from father to son, till towards the end of the fifteenth century.

In 1487 Sir George Manners succeeded to his mother's inheritance of the barony of Ros, and of the baronies of Vaux, Trusbut, and Belvoir, and became twelfth Lord de Roos, or Ros. His father had possibly deserted the small castle of Etal for the larger halls of Belvoir, on his marriage with the heiress, Eleanor, sister and coheir of Edmund, 11th Lord Ros (see *Belvoir, Leicestershire*).

Thomas, 13th Lord Ros, was chosen for many honourable posts by Henry VIII., and was made a Knight of the Garter by him in the seventeenth year of his reign ; and in the same year he was created Earl of Rutland. The tenth Earl of Rutland was raised in 1703 to the dignity of Marquess of Granby and Duke of Rutland.

In 1522, when the Borders were set in a state of defence, Etal, then the property of Lord de Ros, was given a garrison of twenty men under John Collingwood.

Then, in 1542, the Survey of Sir Robert Bowes says of Etal, that it was "for lack of reparacons in very great decaye, and many necessary houses within the same becom ruynous and fallen to the ground ;" but that it might be fit for a garrison of 100 men or more in war time. The bridge of Etal had at that time fallen down. And in the survey made in 1584 this castle is described as lying in the same neglected state.

The fortress is square in form, enclosing a quarter of an acre ; at the S.E. corner is a strong gatehouse, with the shield and crest of the Manners family carved on it. Portcullis grooves exist at the outer doorway, but there was no door at the side next the courtyard. The keep stands in the S.W. corner of the quadrangle, measuring 30 feet by 17 feet ; it is four storeys in height, its lower basement having been vaulted. A spiral staircase to the different stages was contained in the N. wall, and there are many mural recesses. Its mullioned windows, with transoms, betray the date of the castle. The wall on the S. side is massive and strong, and is 30 feet high, and a small tower is found in the S.E. corner.

Etal Castle is now the property of Mr. James Laing of Etal Manor.

FEATHERSTONE (*minor*)

ABOUT 2½ miles S. of Haltwhistle, on a grassy spot (haugh) on the S. side of Tyne, in an open and fertile country, is this picturesque old castle, originally a strong square peel tower with two watch-turrets, and surrounded by a ditch; the lower floor is vaulted in a chamber provided for the protection of the cattle and flock. To this has been attached a modern castellated house with a fine gallery.

It was the seat of the ancient family of Featherstonehaugh, who possessed it in the reigns of Edward I., II., and III. Sir Albany Featherstonehaugh was High Sheriff, 2 Elizabeth, as his eldest son was thirty years after; his second son being appointed by James I. receiver of the king's revenues in Cumberland and Westmorland. The son of this man, Timothy Featherstonehaugh, espoused the side of King Charles and raised a troop of horse for him; he was knighted under Charles's banner, and fought bravely at the fatal field of Worcester (September 3, 1651), where he was taken prisoner, and was afterwards beheaded at Bolton in Lancashire. His lineal descendant, Matthew Featherstonehaugh of Newcastle, afterwards obtained a re-grant of the castle and the estate, but was unable to keep them, and the manor was sold to the Earl of Carlisle. His descendant, Sir Matthew Featherstonehaugh, Bart., sold the rest and the castle to the father of the Right Hon. Thomas Wallace, in whose family the place remains.

FORD (*chief*)

THE river Till meanders in the low lands below and E. of Branxton Hill, which originally gave its name, in English mouths, to the battle of 1513, afterwards known only by its Scottish title of Flodden Field, the Gilboa of Scotland; and the road beneath Branxton crosses the Till to the village of Ford, above which, on the hill, stands the castle of the same name, on the E. side of the river. In 1338 (12 Edward III.), William Heron had licence to crenellate "the mansion of his manor," and this was in all probability the date of the erection of Ford Castle by Sir William Heron, since in 1385, when the Scots, under the Earls of Douglas, Fife, and March, broke into England at the same time as the English host was wasting the Lowlands, they took by assault Ford Castle and dismantled it, as they did also to Wark and Cornhill. When, on 22nd August 1513, King James IV., previous to the battle of Flodden, broke through the English Border at Coldstream and other points, he was unable to leave these hostile fortresses in his rear, while proceeding into the heart of Northumberland, and therefore directed part of his host upon the castles of Norham and Wark, Etal and Ford, and took them.

This must have occupied some time, and meanwhile his army lay encamped principally on the high ground about Flodden, the king himself taking up his quarters in the Castle of Ford, a short distance in front. This place was partly burnt by his soldiers, who, it is said, "threw down that stronghold, by falling of the timbers thereof, whereby several of his men were injured." The owner of Ford, Sir William Heron, was at the time a prisoner in Scotland, but in the castle were his wife Elizabeth and her daughter ; and although tradition has taken great liberties with the reputation of the former lady, nothing is recorded in history but that Lady Heron prayed the king to spare her house, and that he agreed on condition that certain friends of his, prisoners in England, the Laird of Johnstoun and Alexander Hume, should be given up to him by September 5th ; that she went to Alnwick and met the Earl of Surrey with his army advancing against the Scots, when the king's request was agreed to, provided he guaranteed under his royal seal protection to the castle ; then came challenges of battle and defiances between heralds and the king, who replied by burning Ford Castle (*Ridpath*).

This is all that is known in history as to the proceedings before the battle at Ford, the burning of which is confirmed by the report of the Border Survey of 1541. The treatment of Lady Heron and her property is certainly much at variance with the story of "an affair of gallantry." which is probably an entire fiction.

Sir William Heron died 1535, leaving a grandchild six years old, his heiress general, to inherit Ford. In 1549 Scottish invaders again entered England under a French General D'Essé, with four field-guns ; they attacked Ford, and again burnt the greater part of the place, but had to retire, leaving one of the towers unreduced, which was defended by Thomas Carr, a younger son of the governor of Wark, and his brave conduct led the heiress of Ford to bestow her hand on him. Soon afterwards the heirs male of the Heron family made a serious disturbance, claiming the property, and blood was shed in the quarrel, but in the end Carr regained the castle, which in 1584 was in possession of a William Carr, "decayed by want of reparation of a long continuance." These Carrs of Ford came to an end in 1685, and Ford went by successive heiresses to the families of Blake and Delaval, and finally to the Marquess of Waterford in 1822. Sir John H. Delaval in 1761 destroyed the architectural beauty of Ford by sham Gothic additions of evil taste, but the late owner, Louisa, Marchioness of Waterford, repaired the mischief and made this castle "one of the most beautiful houses in the N. of England " (*Bates*).

The situation commands a fine view up the Till Valley to Wooler, bounded by high hills. There are two ancient towers, one on the E., and one on the W. flank, and these are nearly the only remains of the old castle. The top room in the tower which goes by the name of King James, who is said to have slept there before Flodden, has a narrow staircase contrived in the thickness of the wall, which was lately brought to light, and is now said to be connected with the king's intrigue with Dame Heron. Hodgson (vol. ii. part 3, p. 191) gives at length Sir Robert Bowes' Report of 1550 upon the state of the frontiers (thirty-seven years after Flodden). He says it "was brounte by the laste Kinge of Scots a lytle before he was slayne at Flodden Fielde some parte thereof hath bene rep'elled again sythence that tyme, but the great buyldinges and most necessarye houses resteth ever sythens waste and in decaye."

HALTON (*minor*)

ABOUT four miles to the N. of Hexham the Roman Wall is crossed at right angles by the Watling Street, or the continuation of this great southern road from Yorkshire, made by Agricola through Durham county to Corbridge-on-Tyne, and thence direct round the N. of lofty Carter Fell in the Cheviots into Scotland to Jedburgh. Though in some places grass-grown and lost, the road is here, as in many places, still the highway, retaining for miles together the features of its original construction (*Bruce*). Within half a mile E. of this crossing is the Wall Station of Hunnum, a sort of English Pompeii, like many other places along this most interesting track; and close under the Roman camp, on the side of a ravine, and a stream which protected the situation on the W., stand the remains of Halton Castle. Bates describes it as "set in a quaint garden of old-fashioned flowers;" and at a short distance to the E. of it is a curious little chapel with an early round chancel arch; this perhaps marks the spot where Alfwold, King of Northumbria, was assassinated in 788.

In the middle of the twelfth century the place appears in the possession of Waldief de Haulton, and it was held by his descendants till the death of Sir John de Haulton in 1345, when Halton passed, through the marriage of his daughter, to the Lowthers; but in 1383 William de Carnaby (Yorkshire) took possession of Halton, and his son William was alive and died there in 1453. After the Pilgrimage of Grace, Sir Thomas Percy sent his priest to take possession of the dwelling of Sir Reynold Carnaby's grandfather at Halton, "as Sir Reynold was fled and was against the Commons." Sir William Carnaby fought against the Parliament at Marston Moor in the Northumbrian regiment, commanded by the Marquess of Newcastle; his lands were seized and he fled the country. The last Carnaby buried in Halton Chapel was William Carnaby, who died 1698, the last perhaps of his race. Halton was bought in 1706 by John Douglas, a Newcastle lawyer, and in 1713 it went with a daughter and heiress to Sir Edward Blackett, Bart., whose descendants hold it still. Attached together are the original tower of 1415 (if not older), and a seventeenth-century house. The tower has one room on the first floor, and two above, which until recently were unroofed. In the N.E. angle is a small stair leading to the roof. Here the low circular corner turrets have been boldly corbelled out, and the battlements are very good.

HARBOTTLE (minor)

THIS old fortress formed an outlying post to the N. of the wild and dangerous country of Redesdale, on the verge of the Cheviot Hills. It must have been of considerable utility to England from early times for protection on the W. of the county among the dreary wastes which stretch along the Marches of Scotland. The castle of Harbottle was built by King Henry II. cir. 1159, on a high eminence standing over the Coquet. It lay within about ten miles of the Border, and in the direct road of a Scottish army breaking into Northumberland from Jedburgh. The land belonged to the Umfraville family, who had settled in those parts so early as nine years after the Conquest, when Robert de Umfraville, surnamed "cum barba," obtained a grant of the Redesdale country and other large estates. In 1174 Odinel de Umfraville's men had to defend it against an attack by King William the Lion, on which occasion it was taken and partly destroyed. His grandson Richard, taking up arms against King John, lost his estates, but recovered them again from Henry III. in 1221. He probably added greatly to the strength of the place, since in 1296 it withstood a desperate attack made by the whole Scots army for two days. After Bannockburn the Scots again besieged Harbottle and took and destroyed it a second time. It belonged to Robert de Umfraville, 18 Edward II., and to Gilbert de Umfraville at the close of the reign of Edward III., and after the extinction of the male line of this family in 1436 it still continued the property of their representatives.

In 1515, two years after the battle of Flodden, Queen Margaret, widow of King James IV. and daughter of Henry VII., having married Douglas, Earl of Angus, retired to this fortress for the birth of her daughter, who afterwards became the mother of Darnley, and consequently the grandmother of James I. of England. In the reign of Henry VIII. a complete survey was made of this place, with an estimate of the cost of repairing the work. Again in 1546, when it was still in bad repair, Sir Robert Bowes in his report recommended that the king should take this fortress into his own hands, it being the key and chief defence to one half of the Middle Marches, and the Crown obtained it in exchange for the manor of Brailes in Warwickshire. It was evidently at one time a place of very great strength, but has now a sadly ruinous appearance, as most of the massive building has slipped, and huge portions lie half-way down the hill-side, embedded in the ground. There was formerly an outer bailey, with a deep ditch crossed by a drawbridge. The keep stood on an insulated mound, and the masonry generally partakes of the character of that of Prudhoe, and also of Northampton Castle, which was built about the same time by Simon de Liz. The termination "bottle" shows the importance of Harbottle before the Norman Conquest.

HARNHUM (*minor*)

THIS was a small fortress, but situated in a position of great strength, on an eminence protected on the N. and W. by a high range of rocks, and a morass on the S. A lofty wall crossed the neck of ground uniting the position with the heights, and there was an iron gate of great strength at the entrance, said by Wallis to have been standing within the recollection of people living at the end of the last century.

The place was held in 1272 by Bernard de Babington, of an ancient family in England, which appears to have continued at Harnhum till the end of the seventeenth century. In the reign of Charles II., either the old tower or the later mansion was inhabited by Colonel Philip Babington, the governor of Berwick, who was married to Katherine, the widow of Colonel George Fenwick of Brinkburn, and daughter of Sir Arthur Haselrigg, both famous characters in the Puritan Commonwealth. This lady was a celebrated beauty, who having strong Covenanting tendencies, felt herself privileged to oppose the re-entry, after the Restoration, of the regular clergy into their pulpits. She caused the new vicar at Shortflat to be pulled out of his, and thereby incurred episcopal excommunication, so that when she died in 1670 (aged thirty-five only), burial in the church being refused, her husband had to excavate a cave in the rock under the garden, where the body of the lovely Kate lay until quite lately. A window-pane in the house had her name written on it with a diamond, " K. Babington, June 9, 1670. How vain is the help of man. Omnia Vanitas." This date was only two months before her death.

The remains of the old fortalice are considerable in rear of the present house. One of the ceilings is painted with a pedigree and arms of the Babingtons, with the motto " Foy est tous," acquired by Sir John Babington when serving in France under Henry V. The king sent him on some special service with five other young knights, and on quitting the presence, young Babington brandished his sword, using this expression, which was adopted by the family.

HAUGHTON (minor)

THIS ancient stronghold, first mentioned in 1373, stands about 3 miles E. from Simonburn, in a most picturesque situation on the sloping S. bank of Tyne, a little below Chipchase and Wark. From original charters in the possession of Sir J. E. Swinburne, it is shown that William the Lion, King of Scotland, granted in 1177 to Reginald Prath of Tynedale the one-third part of Haluton, and that he re-granted the same lands between 1236 and 1245 to William de Swyneburn : a grant which was confirmed in 1267 by Alexander III., coupled with further gifts at the instance of Queen Margaret, whose treasurer he was.

Haughton Castle was in 1415 the property of Sir John Widdrington, in whose family it remained till its purchase by Robert Smith of Tecket in 1642. It now belongs to Mr. W. Donaldson Cruddas.

It has been a place of immense strength, and the fabric has still that character ; the figure of the tower is an oblong rectangle, measuring 100 feet by 44 feet, built on two parallel vaults, and crowned with five square turrets ; that at the S.W. is 63 feet in height, and contains a staircase from the ground to the top. Its S. front has the most ornamental work, and on the N. side are projecting garderobes and work on corbels.

There was an outer wall of defence, surrounding the castle at a distance of about 60 yards, which was taken down early in this century by the owner to build a farm-house. The ruins of a chapel are in the field in front. There is a large room left in its original state in the upper storey, and on a lower floor is seen in one of the walls a fine Early English ornamental doorway. The external walls have been built with relieving arches, which improve the effect outwardly, and add to the strength of the building, the walls being generally 8 feet thick.

HEBBURN TOWER (minor)

THIS, a fine peel tower in the S.E. corner of Chillingham Park, is the ruin of the home of the ancient family of Hebburn, which can be traced back to one Nicholas de Hebburn in 1271 ; and owners of the same name held it temp. Elizabeth, when, in 1588, there occurred here the settlement by arbitration of a blood-feud between the Hebburns and a family named Story for the slaughter of one John Story. The family possessed the place till the end of the last century, when their heiress married a clerical adventurer named Brudenell, and it was soon after sold to the Earl of Tankerville (cir. 1770).

The tower is a large oblong block, a "bastle" or bastille house, with a vaulted basement and a dungeon. It is two storeys high above the entrance, with gables at the E. and W. ends, and the windows are good.

HEPPLE TOWER, or HEPPEDALE (minor)

THE lands here were united in a barony by King John in favour of the heiress of the Heppedale family, who had married a favourite, Ivo de Tailbois, but later the barony was divided between these two families, and in 1331 Jane de Hepple brought her portion in marriage to the all-pervading Ogle family. Hepple continued with the Ogles and their successors until the third Duke of Portland sold it in 1803 to the father of its present possessor, Sir Walter B. Riddell, Bart.

It lies on the N. side of the Coquet, about 5 miles W. of Rothbury, and is a small peel tower, probably of the fourteenth century, of oblong shape, 26 feet long by 17 feet wide. It belonged to Sir Robert Ogle, who fought at Nevill's Cross, 1346, and in Leland's time was, like so many other towers and castles, in bad repair.

A high stone vault runs through the basement, the entrance being by a pointed doorway on the S. side, closed by a door with wooden bar, the sockets of which remain. The entrance passage is defended from its roof by a meurtrière opening. A circular staircase in a mural shaft on the W. side leads to the upper stages. Late buildings have been erected against the old tower, as at Whitton.

HETON (minor)

HETON, or Heaton Castle, stands upon high ground, 100 yards from the Till on its W. bank, and about two miles from where that river falls into the Tweed. The manor belonged temp. Edward I. to William de Heton, but soon afterwards became the chief property of the Grey family. In 1415 its owner was Sir Thomas Grey, who was executed at Southampton for plotting against Henry V. When James IV. of Scotland was invading England in 1496 in favour of Perkin Warbeck, this fortress stood in his way and was "casten down," and at the time of his next invasion in 1513, before Flodden, it was still in ruins. Sir Robert Bowes, in his Survey of the Marches, reports regarding Heton that "a great part of the vaults and walls are yet standing w'out any rouffes or flores, a great pyte." At this time it was the property of the Greys of Chillingham, who, living at that castle, allowed Heton to be neglected. In a survey temp. Elizabeth it is said to have been formerly "a pleasant and beautifull beuilding, with goodlie towers and turretts, as yet remaininge," but the report says that the large room, which in the preceding reign was considered fit to receive a hundred horses, was "now ruinsome & all in decaie." Heton was a large and very strong rectangular enclosure with four heavy battlemented towers at each corner, and buildings on the wall and detached ones within the enclosure. It was considered fit to receive a garrison of 300 horsemen. It had on the W. a large tower called the Lion's Tower. Now it is almost entirely demolished, and its site occupied by farm buildings, the chief remains of the ancient castle being a large stable 70 feet long, with vaulted roof.

HOLY ISLAND (minor)

THIS stronghold was anciently called Landisfarne, and consisted of two separate castles, both built since the Reformation. The older building stands, facing the south, on a high rocky eminence of trap, which rises some 60 feet above the beach and is called Beblowe, which name it gave to the fort itself. Raine places the date of this castle at 1539, at which period the coasts of England were placed in a state of defence by Henry VIII. It is mentioned in Sir Robert Bowes' Survey of 1550, with the recommendation that an outer wall with flanking bastions should be added, together with a wet ditch towards the land. Another survey of the year 1560 reports on its efficiency. The outer fort, supporting it on the W., was built in 1675. This is of irregular form, following the shape of the rock on which it was built. The ruined walls still remain of a small tower, 24 feet by 21 feet, with parts of an outer surrounding wall and terrace, the whole only occupying a rood of ground. Architecturally there is nothing worthy of remark concerning these buildings, to which access is given by a winding path on the south side of the rock on which they stand.

In 1584, when certain Scottish nobles fled across the Tweed for protection, an asylum was offered them in Holy Island; but in later days that castle was considered too important for strangers to be allowed in it, and a captain was appointed with a garrison under him. Occupied at first for King Charles, the fort fell during the Civil Wars into the hands of the Parliament, and in the beginning of 1646 the Commons sent a force thither, as it was considered "of such consequence to the northern parts of the kingdom."

In the month of October 1715, at the time of Lord Mar's rising, the castle was the subject of a daring capture perpetrated by one Launcelot Errington, master of a ship then lying in the harbour. This man, with the aid of his brother, succeeded in seizing the fortress for the Pretender, obtaining entrance at a moment when but two out of the garrison of fourteen were present. Errington, by merely presenting a pistol at them, managed to secure and eject these two men, and then signalled for help from his ship. The castle was, however, soon retaken, and the Erringtons were sent to Berwick jail, from whence they eventually escaped. Launcelot Errington, who was a zealous Jacobite, afterwards kept an inn in Newcastle, and is said to have died of grief after the battle of Culloden.

The castle is still used as a station for the Royal Artillery Coast Brigade.

HORTON-NEXT-THE-SEA (*non-existent*)

HERE was once a strong castle of high antiquity, standing near the road from Newcastle to Blyth, cir. three miles from the coast. Temp. Henry III. the lands belonged to a family who took their name from the place, but in 1293 one Guischard de Charron had a licence to crenellate his house of Horton. His successors were the Monbouchers, and after them the Delaval family, through a conveyance to them by Sir Edward Fitton, the lineal descendant of the Monbouchers, temp. Elizabeth, to Sir Robert Delaval, who died seised of Horton in 1606. In that family it passed regularly to its possessor when Hodgson wrote (1832), Sir Jacob Astley of Seaton Delaval. He became in 1841 Baron Hastings, and his grandson, the present peer, now owns the estates.

The whole was razed to the ground, and even the foundations were taken up in 1809 to build a farm-house close to the old site. The castle was defended by a double moat and earthen rampart, which latter was levelled and the moat filled up with it. Some thick walls of the building remain in the farm-house.

HOWTELL TOWER (*minor*)

STANDS in the open valley between the hill of Flodden and the Beaumont. The lands were granted with many others to Robert de Ross, the Lord of Wark, who married Isabella, daughter of William the Lion, King of Scotland, and held the office of Chief Justice of the northern forests in England from 21 to 28 Henry III. The tower was one of those thrown down by King James IV. when he invaded England in the interests of Perkin Warbeck in 1496. In 1541 it belonged to John Burrell, when the greater part of it was standing. Now there is but little to be seen.

A part of the S. front, three storeys high, remains, in excellent masonry, but the quoins have been abstracted. It was a small building, the interior of the basement measuring but 17½ feet by 16½ feet. There seem to have been two doorways on the S. side, and in the N. wall are traces of a first-floor window ; the floors were of timber (*Bates*).

The ruin is the property of Mr. Watson Askew-Robertson of Pallinsburn.

LANGLEY (*minor*)

THIS castle stands on sloping ground at the junction of two small streams about 1½ miles S. of the Tyne, near Haydon Bridge, and is called "a noble and tolerably perfect remain of feudal grandeur." The ancient barony of Langley, 13,000 acres in extent, was the property of Adam de Tindal, who died in 1191, and in 1195 his son Adam paid a half-year's rent (£12, 4s. 4d.), on the barony towards the ransom of King Cœur de Lion.

In 1235 Langley was possessed by Nicholas de Boltby of Ravensthorp, near Thirsk, who had married Philippa, the daughter of the younger Adam de Tindal, and succeeded to the entire barony of Langley; he formed a park there, and received from Henry III. a grant of free warren. Dying in 1273, he was followed by his son Adam de Boltby, who left Langley to his daughter Isabel, the wife of Alan de Malton (from Moulton near Spalding), who had adopted his mother's name of Lucy. Their son Sir Thomas de Lucy succeeded, and after him his brother Anthony de Lucy, the latter being best known as a baron of Parliament, and lord of Egremont and Cockermouth in Cumberland; the fee of which latter fortress he obtained 17 Edward II., with its honour, having previously for his services to the Crown been made governor of Carlisle and Appleby. These appointments were in return for his clever capture in 1323 of Sir Andrew de Harcla, the traitor Earl of Carlisle (see *Carlisle*).

Anthony's son, Sir Thomas Lucy, was a valiant knight who in 1339 had so distinguished himself as to receive from Edward III. a grant of forty sacks of wool for his better support in Flanders. He it was who brought relief so ably to the English garrison of Lochmaben in Dumfries in 1343 (in which year he succeeded to Langley), and in 1346 he sailed with King Edward in his expedition to raise the siege of Aguillon, which led to the glorious victory of Creçy. After Creçy, when Edward sat down to reduce Calais, fearing an invasion of the Scots at home, he sent Sir Thomas de Lucy with two other knights to conclude a treaty with King David, or, on failure, to assist in the defence of the country. But when they arrived in the North the war had already begun, and de Lucy took part in the great battle of Nevill's Cross (17th October), where he held a command in the fourth division, or the reserve. In their advance from the peel of Liddel and Lanercost to Beaurepaire near Durham, the Scots army had passed Langley, and there is a petition from Sir Thomas for compensation for damages caused to his property by the invaders. It is probable that the unprotected state of the place occasioned the founding of Langley Castle, in about 1350, with funds acquired in the French war, and with what Lucy received for the Scottish depredations.

Sir Thomas died in 1365, and three years after his son Anthony died, leaving an infant daughter Joan, when Langley passed to Maud, the daughter of Sir Thomas, the wife of Gilbert de Umfraville, Earl of Angus. At his death she married Henry Percy, 1st Earl of Northumberland, to whom she brought the honour of Cockermouth, with Langley, in 1383. Maud de Lucy died in 1398, and the earl and his son, the Hotspur of history and of Shakespeare, having acquired so great wealth, commenced to intrigue against King Henry IV., with a view to their own aggrandisement in the North.

After Hotspur had fallen at the battle of Shrewsbury, his father was called on to give up his castles to the king, who, proceeding in force to Berwick, took the castle there at once with his artillery, and then Alnwick, and Warkworth, and other castles belonging to the Percy family.

In July 1405 Langley was surrendered to Henry IV. without showing any fight, being taken over with its arms, artillery, and victuals by Sir Robert Umfraville in the king's name. Nor did its garrison show greater courage when summoned to surrender to the victorious Lord Montagu after the battle of Hexham in May 1464.

Under the will of the ruined sixth Earl of Northumberland, Langley became the property of King Henry VIII. It was, however, leased for a long term to a branch of the ancient family of Carnaby. Edward VI. restored the estate to the heir of the unfortunate Percys, but when, on the accession of Queen Mary, Thomas Percy became seventh Earl of Northumberland, and obtained possession of all the other lands of his house, it was forgotten to insert Langley, which he owned already in the general entail.

Then, on this earl's attainder and execution, after the Rising in the North in 1569, instead of passing with the estates in tail to his brother the eighth earl, the ancient barony of Langley was escheated by the Crown.

In Sir Robert Bowes' Survey of 1542, Langley is described as : "The walles of an olde Castell, . . . late thinherytance of therle of Northumberland. All the roofes and flores thereof be decayed, wasted, and gone, and nothyng remayning but only the walls, . . . and it standes in a very convenyant place for the defence of the Incourses of the Scottes of Lyddesdale and of the theves of Tyndale, Gyllesland, and Boweastell when they ryde to steall or spoyle in the byshoprycke of Durham."

Again in 1608 a Survey describes this "auncient stone Castell" as "utterly ruined and decayed, and soe hath been tyme out of mynde."

The Carnabys parted with their leasehold interest in 1619 to the fortunate adventurer John Murray, 1st Earl of Annandale, who seems to have acquired the whole barony in 1625. Sir Edward Radcliffe of Dilston purchased it in 1632, and his son Sir Francis was created by James II. Baron Tindal, Viscount Langley, and Earl of Derwentwater. His son James, the second earl, was beheaded on Tower Hill after the Jacobite rising, connected with Lord Mar's rebellion, of 1715 (see *Dilston*); and on the death of his son, Langley was confiscated. In 1749 the Radcliffe estates were settled on the Governors of Greenwich Hospital, and Langley has been sold by the Lord of the Admiralty to Mr. Cadwallader J. Bates.

The castle is a structure oblong in shape, with massive rectangular towers at the four corners; the walls are 4 feet thick, and had ashlar facing on both sides. The interior space measures 82 feet by 25 feet. There was no original vaulting, and the upper floors were carried on timber beams.

For a building in so good a state of preservation, the absence of any clue to the ancient destination of the various rooms is most remarkable. In this respect Langley is quite the antithesis of Warkworth. The entrance was in a block attached to the E. tower, on the N. side at the ground level, where the sole defence was a portcullis, whence a large circular staircase gave access to the different storeys, of which there were three, the corner turrets having four successive rooms, each 14 feet square. The S.W. tower was given up to a series of garderobes, four on each floor, of singular construction : as Viollet-le-Duc says : "d'une manière tout-a-fait monumentale." There were two fireplaces on each floor of the main block, and the upper rooms of the corner towers had each one, the chimneys being carried up in the thickness of the wall.

The elaborate tracings of the pointed windows is typical of the last half of the fourteenth century, passing stage by stage from pure Decorated, through traces of flamboyancy, up to forecasts of Perpendicular (*Bates*). Parker gives a sketch and plan of the building. Hodgson remarks that " Langley Castle seems to bid a stern defiance to the attacks of time, as if determined once again to resume its roof and hang out over its battlements its blue flag and pillared canopy of morning smoke, as emblems that joy and high-minded hospitality have returned to reside in it."

LONG HORSLEY TOWER (*minor*)

THE number of these strong houses, or peel towers, is very great in this part of the country, and is accounted for by the fact that in early and lawless times every possession of importance had to be defended against not only the enemies of the country—such as the Scots—but also against the attacks of robbers and moss-troopers coming from the uplands. Among a selected number of these peels, Long Horsley is one of the larger, lying about six miles to the N.W. of Morpeth, and long the residence of an ancient family of the name, the last of them being Sir Thomas Horsley, who received General Monk here, with his force, in January 1660, and entertained him with much hospitality.

The peel is a rectangular building, about 42 feet by 30 feet, containing a vaulted basement and two upper stages, a circular staircase leading from the ground at the S.E. corner up to the battlements, and ending in a small turret, with a bell. A gabled building seems to have been added on the E. face, towards the end of the seventeenth century, and originally there were two entrances on the E. and S. sides at the ground level.

The knightly family of Horsley early acquired an estate here, which descended by marriage to the Widdringtons and Riddells. The tower was probably built by the Horsleys about the reign of Henry VII. Long Horsley was a manor of the De Merlays, Barons of Morpeth (*q.v.*), and of their descendants the lords Greystock, and the Dacres and Howards. The castle now belongs to Mr. John Gifford Riddell of Felton Park, but is under long lease to the Catholic Bishop of Hexham and Newcastle, as the residence of the clergy of the village; the present priest and occupier being the Rev. Matthew Culley of Coupland Castle (q.v.).

MITFORD (*minor*)

TWO miles above Morpeth, situated amid the beautiful scenery of the Wansbeck, where that river is joined by the Font, is the ancient village of Mitford. Here the river makes a sharp bend, enclosing on its right bank a small tract of land, upon which we see three successive generations of house-building. First there is the original mediæval fortress, built probably temp. Henry II., cir. 1150–1170; second, the seventeenth-century Tudor hall of the Mitfords, built partly from the ruins of the first, and itself a wreck; and third, the modern mansion of the present family; and with these there is the Church of St. Andrew. Mitford appears to have been erected into a barony by Henry I., for William Bertram, a brother of Bernard Baliol, the founder of Barnard Castle. Roger Bertram, his great-grandson, having espoused the cause of the confederate barons in John's time, that king sent an army of Flemings to seize the castle and burned the town; he visited it in 1216, staying three days there. It had its share, too, of the incursions of the Scots, for in 1217 it was besieged for seven days by Alexander II., who despoiled and dismantled it. The Bertrams retained the property for eight generations, until Agnes, the heiress of the family, in 1275 sold the estate to Alexander de Baliol, from whom it passed to Adomer de Valence, Earl

MITFORD

of Pembroke. This noble was one of the favourites of Edward II., and sat at the trial of Thomas, Earl of Lancaster, at Pontefract; he was killed at a tournament on his third wedding day, and of his property Mitford was assigned to his widow for her life. His heirs were John de Hastings, and John Cumyn of Badenoch, whose sister Johanna married David de Strathbolgi, Earl of Athol, and with her other sister Elizabeth Cumyn shared their father's property in Mitford. This David, Earl of Athol, was slain s.p. male, leaving only two daughters, Elizabeth, who was married to Sir Thomas Percy, and the other to his brother Ralph, but the entire property of Mitford and Athol came to the son of Sir Thomas Percy, namely, Sir Henry Percy, lord of Athol. He again left only daughters, by one of whom the half of Mitford came to the family of Borough, and the other half to Sir Henry Grey, knight. Lord Borough possessed this castle and manor temp. Henry VIII., but they were granted by Charles II. to Robert Mitford, a descendant of Sir John de Mitford of Molesden, a knight of considerable note in the fourteenth century. Three moles still figure in the arms of the Mitfords, to whom the castle now belongs.

The ancient castle, built probably by Roger Bertram in the early part of the reign of Henry II., stands on an eminence of freestone rock, 70 feet above the river, and is protected on the N.E. and W. by the Wansbeck, which flows around, and S. by the small stream Font. The walls of the enceinte, enclosing about an acre, are built along the edge of the cliff, being about 20 feet high, and much broken; that on the N. is tolerably perfect. A cross wall with a strong doorway parts off the inner ward, in which stands the square Norman keep, built upon a raised portion of rock. Its N. front projects in a salient angle, the basement only remaining, divided into two vaulted cellars. The entrance into the inner ward is commanded by the keep; the gatehouse is ruined. On the marshy ground also at the foot of the Castle Hill there appears to have been a wet ditch, and in its prime this castle must have been an important and strong fortress.

MORPETH (minor)

MORPETH CASTLE is well situated on a lofty ridge of land, with the ground sloping away on all sides except on the W., where a deep ditch formed its defence. The site measures 82 yards N. and S., and 33 from E. to W.

As early as 1095 there seems to have been a small fortalice (munitiuncula) at Morpeth (Bates), and a castle is mentioned as existing in 1138, which King John demolished in 1215. In early Norman times William de Merlay, called "the good lord," had the barony and honour of Morpeth, and he probably built the first castle; his property was held in succession by his descendants till the last owner, Roger de Merlay, died, in 1265, and Morpeth went to his daughters, one of whom, Mary, was married to William, Lord Greystock. The issue of all the other sisters dying out, Morpeth came to the family of Lord Greystock, who died 17 Edward I. His son John died *s.p.*, having settled the estate upon Ralph Fitz William, a near relative, who assumed the title of Lord Greystock, and the third in descent from him, William, was summoned to Parliament 26 Edward III. (1352). This lord built the castle of Morpeth and that of Greystock in Cumberland, and died in 1358, his family continuing here till the death in 2 Henry VII. (1486) of Lord Ralph, whose granddaughter succeeded him as Baroness Greystock. This heiress was carried off and married by Thomas, Lord Dacre of Gilsland, from Brougham Castle (see *Kirkoswald* and *Greystoke, Cumberland*), and through her the Dacres obtained Morpeth and continued in possession till the death of George, Lord Dacre, *s.p.* and under age, when his property came to his two sisters; Ann, married to Philip, Earl of Arundel, and Elizabeth to Lord William Howard, second son of Thomas, Duke of Norfolk, the "Belted Will" of Border story (see *Naworth*). As the family preferred to live at Naworth, it is possible that Morpeth thenceforth became neglected. The great-grandson of Elizabeth and Lord William, Charles Howard, was in 1661 created Baron Dacre of Gilsland, Viscount Howard of Morpeth, and Earl of Carlisle.

Leland, writing after visiting this place about 1540, says : "Morpeth Castle stondythe by Morpethe Towne. It is set on a highe Hill, and about the Hill is moche Wood. The Towne & Castle belongeth to the Lord Dacors. It is well mayntayned."

William, Lord Greystock, built the tower between 1342 and 1359. It is said to be the only instance of one built with a peaked roof, and is a square massive structure, defended by machicoulis and angle turrets or bartizans. The original Norman walls are now but broken fragments. The only circumstance connected with the history of the county regarding this fortress is its being occupied in 1646 by the Scottish army for twenty days, at the end of which they were turned out of it by the great Montrose. It still belongs to the Earls of Carlisle.

Wallis wrote in 1769 : "Only an old tower of this castle is standing, with part of two speculating turrets."

NAFFERTON (minor)

THIS castle stands in the open country N. of the road from Heddon on the Wall to Corbridge, midway between Ovington and the Roman wall. It was built by Philip de Ulecote, a man of no great origin, who was forester of Northumberland in the reign of John. He managed to get into the favour of that king, and is said by Roger of Wendover to have been his "iniquitous councillor," obtaining from him the baronies of Matfen, Natterton, and Lorbottle. In 14 John he became sheriff of the county, when, presuming on his influence with the Crown, he began to erect a castle, taking the materials from the Roman wall in the vicinity. But Richard de Umfraville made complaint of the injury this castle would be to his fortress of Prudhoe, and got the Crown to issue a writ to Philip commanding him to desist. Hartshorne says that the building remains much in the same state as it was left by the workmen when they were stopped, 6 Henry III., at which date the sheriff had orders to cast down the *bretesches*, or outside defences of wood; which, however, seems to show that the castle had been nearly completed. There are the remains of a keep, 20 feet square, and of two outer baileys, placed on sloping ground.

NEW BEWICK (*non-existent*)

THIS was a tower or stronghold, built in 1509, about three miles S. of Chillingham near the Till River, which was owned by the Priory of Tynemouth. The Itinerary of Leland (1538) says: "At Bewyke ys a good Tower of the Kinge's majestie inheritance, late belonging to the suppressed monastery of Tynmouthe. A parte thereof ys newly covered with leade and thother parte ys not well covered nor in good reparacions. It is able in tyme of warre to conteyne fyftye men in garryson, and yt is much requysyte that the said tower were kept in convenyent repare for yt standeth in a fytte place for the defence of the countrye thereaboutes."

In 1608 it was still standing, "a faire stronge tower," but much decayed. Nothing remains at this time but the foundations, across which is carried the high road, to form which this once royal stronghold was probably destroyed.

NEWCASTLE-UPON-TYNE (*chief*)

THE important Roman station of Pons Ælii stood here on an eminence fortified by Agricola. It commanded the bridge built by the Emperor Hadrian (whose family name was Ælius) in A.D. 118 across the Tyne, protecting also at this point the Roman wall which passed here towards its termination at Wall's End. The Chronicles state that Robert Courthose, having been sent by his father, the Conqueror, in 1080 against King Malcolm of Scotland, built on his return a castellum or small fortress upon the Tyne, in the vill now called Novum Castrum, but then Monke Chestre. Perhaps it was merely a wooden and palisaded structure on a mound, of the usual Danish or Saxon character; but it was Robert's brother, the Red King, who placed here a strong masonry fortress, utilising, perhaps, stone from an ancient work. Ere this the old

Roman bridge had disappeared, and the place was called, according to Huntingdon, Novum Castellum. Hardyng's account runs thus:

> " He buylded then the Newcastell upon Tyne,
>   The Scottes for to gaynstande and to defende,
>   And duelte therein."

And the townspeople he made to build the town also, and "to wall it all aboute." Stow places the date of this at A.D. 1090. Five years afterwards the Earl of Northumberland, Robert Mowbray, being in possession of this castle, formed a conspiracy with others to rid the land of the Red King (see *Bamborough*). Rufus came north with an all-England army, besieged and took the earl's castle at Tynemouth, and then, turning to Newcastle, captured that fortress also, and with it the best followers of the earl. After the imprisonment of Mowbray his earldom was held by Rufus, and next by Henry I., but on the accession of Stephen in 1135 King David of Scotland, who pretended to Northumbria *jure uxoris*, espoused the cause of Maud and took possession of the castle upon the Tyne, by craft. Thither in 1137 King Stephen came with an army, and a temporary truce was made between them. After the second invasion of England in the following year, when he had been defeated at the Battle of the Standard, David made a more lasting treaty with Stephen, by which Northumbria was ceded to Scotland, and, according to Wynton, after this event " in New Castell then Kyng Dawy of Scotland dwelt than comownaly." After the death of Stephen Henry II. in 1157 repudiated this treaty and seized Northumberland, setting aside the claim of William the Lion.

The next record of the Newcastle fortress dates in 1168, when the present keep was commenced by Conan, Earl of Brittany. It was finished in 1171, and after that time the castle was so strong under the command of the valiant chevalier Robert Fitz Richard, that William the Lion on coming before it, "with armed people and naked," during his invasion of 1174, was fain to leave it alone, and to turn and besiege Carlisle instead. In the July of that same year, however, the Scottish king was captured by Odinel de Umfraville and other knights at Alnwick (see *Alnwick*), and brought prisoner to Newcastle for a night on his way to Richmond and the South. Large sums continued to be spent on the keep, according to the Pipe Rolls, until 1176, when a sum equal to about £80,000 of our money had been expended on it. In the reign of John further expenditure was incurred on a tower and ditches, and on outworks between the castle and the river.

In 1237 King Alexander of Scotland met Henry III. at this castle, on which occasion the English king had his chamber in the Old Tower, and also used the "old hall and old kitchen," a new hall and chamber being in course of construction for him. It was at this meeting that Alexander renounced his rights in Northumberland, Cumberland, and Westmorland. In 1292 John Baliol did homage for his crown to Edward I. in the king's hall of the castle, and in the succeeding reign this fortress was used for stores during Edward's expedition into Scotland. Early, however, in the year 1334 the castle is described as being in so very dilapidated a condition that not one gate of it could be closed. Repairs were executed, and we find in 1341 Lord John Nevill of Hornby captain of the castle, and holding the Earl Murray in custody therein. Five years later John de Coupland, the sheriff, kept the Scotch king David Bruce here in ward, he having been taken prisoner, grievously wounded, at the battle of Nevill's Cross in 1346. In 1388 Percy Hotspur threw himself into the castle to defend it from the attack of Earl Douglas, who found the place too strong for him, and retired to Otterburn, where followed Chevy Chase, or the battle of Otterburn.

In 1400 Henry IV., preparing to invade Scotland to enforce his absurd claim of over-lordship, lay at Newcastle from July 25th to August 7th, and came thither again on his return from his futile expedition.

NEWCASTLE-UPON-TYNE

Later in this same reign, however, the building fell again into neglect, and remained thus during the reign of Edward IV., so that at the end of the fifteenth century the keep was used as the county gaol, and the king's hall as the courthouse of assize; and to these ends the building was appropriated until our own times.

In Elizabeth's day this Northern fortress was described as "an old and ruinous castle," and its buildings were rented out to various persons. In

1619 one Alexander Stevenson, a page of King James I., obtained a lease for fifty years, having begged the castle of the king; and under him and those that followed him, the structure went further to neglect and disrepair. The castle, nevertheless, bore a part in the siege of Newcastle in 1644, being the last resort of the gallant defenders of the town, after the surrender of which it also was ceded to the Parliament army. At the expiration of Stevenson's lease in 1664, Lord Gerard obtained a grant of the castle for ninety-nine years, but litigation ensued between him and the Corporation, who obtained from James II. certain rights, which on the earl's death were confirmed, possession of the castle being retained by the civic authorities in 1701.

In the year 1811 the original mound to the S.W. of the keep was levelled and removed, and Castle Street was laid out. Eleven baronies, holding fifty-six knights' fees for their lands by service at the castle of Newcastle, possessed houses in the castle ward, distinct from the towers on the walls. Until 1790 much remained of the outer walls, particularly in the south and west, as well as an ancient south postern to the Old Half-Moon Battery. The site was well planned for defence, being protected on two sides by a precipitous and scarped hill, and by a moat or ditch at the junction of the neck with the main ground. The whole enclosure of walls was of the shape of a quadrant, the arc portion lying towards the river, and the entrance by the Black Gate being at the apex on the north. This same Black Gate, all Early English work, was built in 1247, and, though it had become ruinous in Tudor times, still remains the sole relic of Henry III.'s extensive works. It is a huge oval structure, protected in part by a barbican built in 1358, the vaulted passage through which is defended by two portcullises, the outer groove being still visible. From this gate a drawbridge over the moat gave access to the second gate, which stood in Black Gate Street, having had on its east side a square tower called the Great Pit, which was used as a prison, the basement having no lights, and being entered only by a trap-door. Three sides of this tower have vanished, but that on the east remains.

On the opposite side, and behind the second gate, stood another prison, called the Heron Pit (Heron having been a sheriff from 1247 to 1257), and both these structures were ruinous in the year 1334, when they received repairs. The prison of Heron Pit was likewise in the dreadful lower storey of the tower, and was entered by a trap-door. Part of its lower walls are in the cellars of the "Two Bulls' Heads Inn."

Passing the second gate, the way led into the castle garth, a large triangular space, with the ancient mound in its S.W. corner, and its S.E. angle formed by a huge semicircular tower, called the Half-Moon, which was reinforced on its face by several large projecting square turrets or buttresses, with similar smaller ones between them. The whole structure rose high above the rest of the walls, dominating the ground below and the bridge, and was called the Tower. From the Roman remains found on this site, it would seem to be the original position chosen and fortified by Agricola, and afterwards occupied by the old castle of Monkchester. This tower was destroyed in 1787, and its site utilised for the building of the new Moot Hall and County Courts, while the front of it was encased with a row of houses.

Immediately at the northern abutment of the Half-Moon, Henry III. built in 1237 his "New Hall and New Chamber." The former became the Great or Moot Hall, being the same that witnessed the homage of Baliol in 1292, and which was used centuries after for assizes, and at its S. end was the King's Chamber, converted in later days into the Grand Jury Room. These interesting structures were all pulled down in 1809, and the site occupied by the New County Court.

The original entrance to the castle ward or bailey was in the centre of the W. wall, through a circular arched gateway between two square towers. It had in front low wooden palisades, called "The Barriers," and was built in 1178; but after the erection of the Black Gate it became a postern merely, and was finally destroyed in 1811.* Here it was that in 1388 took place the encounters between the Scottish force under James, Earl Douglas, and the English who held the fortress under the Percys. During one of the many feats of arms performed here, the following incident is said to have occurred. Hotspur and his brother Ralph were, as ever, foremost at the barriers, when the Douglas, tilting against Sir Henry Percy, not only had the fortune to drive him out of his saddle, but also to snatch from him his lance with its silken pennon. Waving this aloft, the Douglas vowed he would plant it on his castle at Dalkeith. "That shalt thou never accomplish," cried Percy, grieved at his loss. "Then you must come," replied the Douglas, "and seek it to-night, for I shall plant it in the ground before my tent, and we will see if you will venture to take it away." That night the Scots drew off and marched to Otterburn, followed next day by the English, and two nights after (August 19th) was fought the fierce fight of Otterburn, or Chevy Chase, at which Percy was captured, and the Douglas slain (see *Otterburn*).

From the W. or old gate of the castle, ran E. and W. the wall of the inner ward, called the Cross Wall, which terminated at the Half-Moon. The W. face of the curtain contained two other square towers, one being at the S.W. corner, from whence extended the S. front round to the Half-Moon. On this S. wall was another square tower, and the S. postern, over which was the county gaoler's house. There was another postern on the E. face near the second gate. The whole face to the N. and W. was defended by a ditch, 22 yards broad, which also extended on the eastern and partly on the southern sides. Beyond this moat was an outer wall of defence.

* Jefferson's drawing of it, with the keep, is given in vol. iv. N. S. Arch. Æliana.

After the castle and its buildings were leased out, which had already taken place, as we have seen, in the sixteenth century, houses began to be erected round about it. An old description in 1790 states that "the castle yard is now crowded on all sides with shops," most of these being for the sale of old clothes, and that the inhabitants were numbered by "many hundreds."

There remains to describe the old "Donjon" keep, which is still standing. It is of late Norman style, and was built by Henry II. between the years 1172 and 1177, at a cost of £892, 18s. 9d. It stands at about 30 feet from the centre of the W. wall of the castle enclosure, and is a building of four stages and a basement. It is nearly square, three of its angles being carried up by pilasters in square projecting turrets, ending in machicolations and battlements, with other strong pilasters in the intervals. The N. angle is a half polygon of six faces. The keep is entered by a forebuilding on the E. side, where is a stair giving access to the great hall on the third floor. Below is the chapel, which had a separate entrance on the E. The chancel has at its further end an oriole, and in the stage above is a highly ornate room, formerly an oratory, to which access is given by a staircase passing half-way up a small gateway tower. The lowest stage was the prison, and still holds the rings to which prisoners were attached when the place was converted into a gaol.

The roof vaultings spring from a centre column, which perhaps served as a drain for the upper storeys. The second stage is now divided, and used as a library; it appears to have formed, with the third stage, the dwelling, and is provided with fireplaces and garderobes. The third stage, till the building of the new hall, formed the king's chamber, a newel stair communicating with the floor below. A "well-room" was at the end of the hall, and mural passages and closets extend around. The fourth stage was for the defence of the castle, and has a mural gallery, with loops in the outer wall.

It was customary to display on the walls of the keep the heads and quarters of traitors, as was certainly done at Carlisle Castle in the case of Andrew Harcla, Earl of Carlisle, temp. Edward II.

In 1644, when the town of Newcastle was taken, its defenders sought refuge in this keep, but they had to surrender it after three days.

NORHAM (*minor*)

IN Northumberland, the land of castles, there is no more interesting fortress than "Norham's castled steep," wrapped as it is in the chivalrous story of the Border, and the halo of Scott's undying song. No stouter stronghold than this existed between Berwick and Carlisle. For twelve miles along the Border from

Berwick to Coldstream, the lands belonged to the mighty and wealthy bishops of Durham, Counts Palatine, and here early in the twelfth century, upon a rocky elevation on the S. side of Tweed, which at this place forms a large bend, Ralph Flambard, Prince Bishop from 1099 to 1128, reared Norham Castle; and Hugh Pudsey, the reputed nephew of Stephen, his successor in St. Cuthbert's chair from 1153 to 1195, with his immense wealth rebuilt the

NORHAM

work and added to it. In 1136, King David, invading England in the cause of his niece, the Empress Maud, took the castle and held it until its restoration under treaty to Stephen; but two years after he took it again and dismantled it. Henry II. laid his hands on both castles of Durham and Norham, but afterwards restored them to the see of Durham for a fee of 2000 marks (or £1333, 13s. 4d., equal to about £35,000 of our time), but on terms that allowed it to fall again to the Crown at the death of Bishop Pudsey in 1195. King John came to Norham four times, one of these being at the time he was preparing to invade Scotland, and again when he was negotiating a treaty with William the Lion.

In 1215 he came and besieged the castle in revenge for the homage paid by
the Northumbrian barons to King Alexander, but after forty days was forced
to raise the siege and depart. The place was Crown property in the reigns of
Henry III. and Edward I., and the latter came here in 1291 to decide regarding
the claimants to the Scottish throne, and to advance his own claims. He
resided in Norham Castle, while the Scots' camp lay at Ladykirk, on the
opposite side of Tweed. This was the time of the warlike Bishop of Durham,
Anthony Bek, who attended Edward at the head of 140 knights, 1000 foot, and
500 horse himself clad in complete armour—and with them proceeded as far
as Aberdeen. In 1318 the Scots attacked the castle again and raised two forts
against it, but without any effect; however, four years after, they succeeded in
taking the fortress, but Edward II. coming in person, retook it after ten days'
fighting. At this time extensive repairs were carried out, and afterwards the
bishop recovered his property. It was in this reign that the gallant feat of
arms occurred at Norham related by Leland, and woven into Bishop Percy's
ballad of "The Hermit of Warkworth"; when Sir William Marmion of
Scrivelsby came to this "dangerest place in England" to "fame" his golden-
crested helmet among the Scots of Berwick (see Note 9 of "Marmion"). Again
in 1327 there was a fire and sword raid, when the Scots laid siege to Norham,
and succeeded in taking it the next year; but it was retaken at last in 1355.
The castle had its share in all the military occurrences going on at the
Border during the reigns of Henry IV., Henry V., and Henry VI., being
within sight of the battlements of Berwick when the former of these kings
was battering that castle with his guns in 1405. In 1435 the bishops began
the practice of letting the castle to some nobleman or knight of approved
merit, which saved them much cost in upkeep. Bishop Richard Fox, a
great prelate, and the strenuous supporter of Henry VII., held the see of
Durham from 1494 till 1501, and as, in the words of Richard III. to the
Pope, the first duty of a Bishop of Durham was to protect the realm
against the Scots, he came to Norham at an early date to superintend, as
an engineer, various improvements there; he deepened the outer ditch, and
uniting it with the stream on the E. side, dammed up the water and thus
formed a moat. Lord Bacon says that Fox "caused his castle of Norham
to be strongly fortified and furnished with all kinds of munitions, and
had manned it likewise with a very great number of tall soldiers;" and
that "he had caused the people to withdraw their cattle and goods into
fast places that were not of easy approach," when in 1497 King James IV.
coined his golden chain to provide funds for his raid into Northumberland
in favour of Perkin Warbeck. But the bishop, according to Polydore Vergil,
held the castle of Norham against his attack for fifteen days, and the Earl
of Surrey, summoned by him in haste, coming to the rescue with a strong
force, James raised the siege and retired to his own country (Chisholm

Batten's "Life of Fox"). In 1513, King James on his way to Flodden Field again laid siege to Norham, and for five days assaulted it in front with his artillery in vain. Then, according to the Ballad of Flodden, the weak point in the fortifications was pointed out to him by a traitor from the garrison: the wall soon yielded, and the castle fell. King James hanged the traitor, and passed on to Ford Castle. After the battle of Flodden, Bishop Ruthall repaired and strengthened the castle, and when in 1530 another hostile visit was paid by the Scots, they were driven off by the valour of Archdeacon Franklin, to whom Henry VIII. assigned a special coat of arms for his services. In Elizabeth's reign Norham, like all other northern fortresses, was in bad repair, and Sir George Bowes made a report on the place: then various works were set in hand there—a storey was taken off the keep, and the outworks were strengthened. At the death in 1559 of Bishop Tunstall, who had laid out large sums on this castle, Norham was finally and by law detached from the see of Durham and held thereafter by the Crown. Elizabeth gave a lease of it to Lord Hunsdon, which his representatives, the Careys, were induced to part with to

NORHAM

Home, Earl of Dunbar, in favour of whom Norham was converted into a freehold. It was kept in a state of defence as late as 1583, but of course, with the accession of James VI. to the English throne, all use for Border castles was at an end.

The Tweed forming the front defence of the castle, a deep ravine with a small stream in it divides the platform on which it is placed from the rest of the high ground on the E., and a broad ditch is continued from it round the S. and S.W. of the fortress. There are on the S. the remains of earlier entrenchments. The area of the castle works is 2680 square yards, and the inner ward with the keep stands on the E. over the ravine and river, protected by an immense wall N.E. and S.E. The keep, built by Hugh Pudsey (Bishop of Durham

1153 1197), is a mere ruin, rectangular in shape and originally 90 feet in height : this is all Norman work, in which Decorated windows have been inserted : in the W. wall is a spiral stair leading to the roof, and terminating in a square turret. A large part of the N. front has disappeared. The second floor was originally the topmost and state floor, having two apartments entered from the well stair ; then a third floor was added with timber joists, containing two chambers. In the Decadent period there were many alterations made in the western half of the keep—doors and windows were opened, and the well stair formed — perhaps by Bishop Bek —the whole building being heightened at the same time. The broad outer wall from the keep to the N. side seems to have been made by filling up the hall and chapel. This was done some time after the introduction of artillery, and nearly all the face of this wall is now gone. From the S.W. angle of the keep the wall, here 30 feet high, extends to a large rectangular

NORHAM

bastion which projects from it so as to look down the S. ditch on both sides ; and further W. was the gatehouse of the inner ward. The outer ward stretched in a bold curve round the S. and S.W. sides of the keep to the N., and was enclosed by a wall 30 feet high, still partly remaining at E. and S. On the N. the scarped rock constituted the chief defence, the wall there being only a breastwork, while at its junction with the W. wall is the lower entrance, the gatehouse of which is 40 feet long, and of Norman work. From thence southwards was a wall with mural towers and the great gateway of the castle, all of which have vanished.

OGLE (non-existent)

ABOUT twelve miles N.W. of Newcastle, on a rounded hill or ridge from which the ground slopes away northward towards Blyth, is this castle, probably built about 15 Edward III., when Sir Robert Ogle obtained, in reward for his good services on the marches, a licence to crenellate his "mansum" of Ogle.

To this castle at the hour of vespers on October 17, 1346, came John Copeland and his eight companions with their captive, King David Bruce of Scotland, riding from the field of battle at Nevill's Cross, where Copeland had with difficulty effected his capture: the brave young king fought desperately, though wounded by one arrow in his leg and another in the face, and could scarcely be taken alive. Before yielding himself he had struck out several of Copeland's teeth with his gauntlet. The battle joined at nine in the morning, and was not decided until noon, when the party, to make sure of their capture, started for Ogle; a distance which Froissart gives as fifteen miles, but which is more like twenty-five miles, and hither they managed to convey the king, wounded as he was, before nightfall. It is somewhat difficult to see why Copeland should have come northward instead of to the south, and Froissart says that Queen Philippa complained of his carrying off the king without her leave, but he was made a knight-banneret, and afterwards Constable of Berwick. From Ogle King David was brought to Bamburgh, where he remained until sufficiently recovered to be taken to the Tower of London (q.v.). During his long captivity he experienced durance in many castles.

There exists an account of this castle, drawn up in 1664, which describes it as "not large, yet it hath been a strong and handsome structure. Several towers were upon the wall, built in a half round outwardly, and in a square within, surrounded with a double moat and drawbridge before the gate, seated in as pleasant a soil as the country doth afford."

Hutchinson says that in 1776 very little remained of the old castle; part of a circular tower then existed, adjoining the E. end of the farm-house, which stands on the castle site, the windows of it being small pointed Early English. Between the two moats stood originally a stone wall, which was levelled when the moats were filled in. Hodgson states that not a vestige of the castle was remaining in 1827, except the W. end of the moat, and some 60 yards of the dividing wall. The present farm-house seems to have been built towards the end of the seventeenth century.

The Ogles' pedigree begins in the middle of the twelfth century, and a Sir Thomas de Oggell, knight, held Oggil about 1240. Robert Ogle, his descendant, performed good services under Edward III., perhaps in France, and built the castle. He fought at Nevill's Cross, and received letters of thanks for his services there. He died in 1368, holding an extensive property. Sir Robert, the first Lord Ogle, espoused the Yorkist side, and was in favour with Edward IV., from whom he obtained many grants of land, including the lordship of Redesdale, and also the castle of Harbottle, after the battle of Towton. He fought at Hexham, and was at the siege of Bamburgh Castle, dying in 1469. Cuthbert, the seventh and last Lord Ogle, died in 1597, seised of Ogle and Bothal, and of the large property of his forefathers. In the insurrection called the Rising of the North, in 1569, he was a strenuous opponent of the Earls of Northumberland and Westmorland. His eldest daughter, Jane, was married to Edward Talbot, 8th Earl of Shrewsbury, but left no issue, and her sister Catherine, the wife of Sir Thomas Cavendish, youngest brother of the first Earl of Devonshire (of that family), carried on the Ogle line. Their son was Sir William Cavendish, "the loyal Duke of Newcastle," who was created successively Baron Ogle of Bothal, Viscount Mansfield, Baron Cavendish of Bolsover, and Earl and Marquis of Newcastle in 1643, and finally Earl of Ogle and Duke of Newcastle in 1664. He was the great Royalist general in the Civil War, and was the soul of that cause in the North.

OTTERBURN (minor)

THE present tower is a modern building, but it encloses the relics of the ancient structure which saw the great fight between the Scots and the English, 508 years ago, famous in poetry and history as Chevy Chase, or the battle of Otterburn. It stands in Redesdale, on the Otter stream, about twenty-eight miles from Newcastle, along the road which passes into Scotland over the Cheviots by Carter Fell; the position is a strong one, and the tower was a fortress suited to the desolate and unsupported situation in which it was built.

It was long the stronghold of the Halls, a doughty family in Redesdale in the reign of Henry VIII., and there is an inscription on the front with the initials of one of them. From some acts of treachery they earned in Tynedale the sobriquet of "the faus' hearted Ha's." John Hall, the head of the family in 1715, joined in Lord Mar's rebellion, with Forster of Bamburgh and Lord Derwentwater (see *Dilston*). He was taken at Preston, brought to London, and hung at Tyburn for high treason, by George II., in July 1716. His estates were forfeited and sold, and, after many changes of masters, this tower is now the property of Mr. Thomas James.

Froissart has given a close account of all the circumstances leading to the battle of Otterburn and of the fight itself, which, indeed, is the only one we have. He tells how after the loss by Sir Henry Percy of his pennon

at the barriers in Newcastle, as is related in the account of that fortress (q.v.),
the Scots next morning, under Earl Douglas, broke up and took the road
homewards, and coming at the dawn of day to the tower of Ponteland,
belonging to Sir Aymer de Athol, they assaulted and captured it and its
lord, and then burnt it : proceeding during the day to Otterburn, where they
encamped for the night. Their force consisted of 300 lances and 2000 foot
soldiers, and next day an assault was made against the tower of Otterburn,
which Froissart says was "a strong one and situated among marshes,"—too
strong for them in fact, for they were beaten off, and retired to their quarters,
having formed a sort of camp with huts made of trees and branches within
a strong entrenchment, placing their baggage with the camp followers in
their rear across the road to Newcastle, and driving their cattle into the
marsh lands.

To return to Newcastle. When Percy found that Douglas had started for
Scotland, and that his force was under 3000 strong, he at once determined
to follow, having a superior force of 600 spears, of knights and squires, and
upwards of 8000 infantry. So they left Newcastle after dinner, and took the
road leisurely for Otterburn, arriving at the Scottish camp just as that host,
tired out with its siege of the tower, were turning in to repose. By good
generalship the Scots were not, however, taken at a disadvantage, having
during the day learnt the ground, and every man his post, in the expectation
of this attack. Fortunately for them, the English arriving at the quarters
of the camp followers, mistook them for those of the soldiers, and made a
fierce onslaught on them, which gave the knights time to arm, and for the
men to form under their respective leaders, the Earls of Douglas, Moray,
and March, who each had arranged their special posts, that were evidently
far removed from where the English now were.

Night had by this time well advanced, but a bright August moon in a
clear sky gave ample light for the fight, which now began in earnest. The
main body of the Scots, instead of moving direct against Percy, skirted the
hillside, according to a preconcerted plan, and fell on the English flank while
engaged with the troops drawn up to defend the camp. Then commenced
a close struggle, in which the English archers were of no avail. One side
shouted "Percy" and the other "Douglas," and a general mêlée took place,
in which the chiefs of either side fought hand to hand, the two rival
banners meeting in the crush. Earl Douglas dashed into the midst of his
enemies, laying about him with his battle-axe, but was borne to the ground
by three spears driven into his shoulder, his middle, and his thigh, and as
he fell he was struck on the head with an axe, and the fight passed over
him. In the dusky light his fall was not noticed by his men, who pressed
on with the Douglas banner to a slight eminence, where the whole Scots
force collected, and then attacked the English, already wearied with their

forced march, so vigorously, that they repulsed and drove them from the field in spite of their superior numbers.

In the fight Sir Henry Percy, unhorsed, was made prisoner by Lord Montgomery, and his brother Sir Ralph was desperately and mortally wounded. Froissart, a contemporary, whose account is carefully written, says that the English were pursued for five miles, losing, as prisoners and left dead on the field, 1840 men, and more than 1000 being wounded; while of the Scots about 100 were slain, and 200 taken prisoners.

The ground where the engagement took place is called the Battle Riggs, and a cross was set up where Douglas fell, which is erroneously called Percy's Cross.

The appellation of Chevy Chase must have attached from the traditional boast of Earl Douglas, that the reason of his foray was to chase the deer on the English Cheviots, and it is curious that it should remain still the everyday schoolboy term for a running hunt.

Roger Widdrington, the head of the house, seems to have been slain at this fight, from the following verse in the ballad of Chevy Chase—

> " For Wetharryngton my harte is wo,
>   That ever he slayne shuld be ;
>   For when both hys leggis wear hewyne in to,
>   Yet he knyled and fought on hys kne."

PRESTON TOWER (minor)

ABOUT a mile S.E. from Ellingham, near the E. coast, is a relic of a good specimen of the old Border keep; it is spoken of in 1415 as in the possession of Robert Harbottle, who perhaps built it. He was much in favour with Henry IV., and in 1408 was made sheriff of Northumberland, and afterwards captain of Dunstanburgh. He managed to obtain rights over pieces of land about Preston by leases, and married Isabel de Monboucher, the widow of the lord of Chillingham. He died in 1419, and his son Robert, 1424, married Margerie, daughter of Sir Robert Ogle, whose lands of Newstead were conveyed to him. The marriage contract contains an odd bargain, that Sir Robert should maintain his daughter for two years, keeping her still at home, and also support her husband and his servant (un vadlet) and horses whenever he came there; and the bride was to find her own attire. He is Sir Robert in 1439, and sheriff of the county. In 1499 Sir Ralph grants a lease of the tower, manor, and town of Preston to John Harbottle of Falloden at an annual rent of £8, 13s. 4d., and the place has a new timber roof found between them, thatched with "flaggs or strawe." Sir Ralph married Margaret, daughter of Sir Ralph Percy, who fell at Hedgeley Moor, and their granddaughter, Eleanor Harbottle, became the wife of Sir Thomas Percy, beheaded after the insurrection of the Pilgrimage of Grace. She obtained Preston as coheir of her brother, and was the mother of Thomas, seventh Earl of Northumberland, on whose attainder Preston fell to the Crown. In the Survey of 1570 it is said to be let to Margaret Harbottle for £4, 13s. 4d., and afterwards it passed into the family of Armourer, and then to that of Craster: at present it belongs to Miss Baker Cresswell.

It is a narrow oblong building with square towers at the four corners. The S. front alone remains, with the S.E. and S.W. corner turrets and parts of their side walls. It is entered by a doorway cut through the S. front in the seventeenth century; the turret rooms are vaulted and have fireplaces (*Bates*).

PRUDHOE (*chief*)

PRUDHOE was erected by Odinel de Umfraville during the first twenty years of the reign of Henry II. The situation is well chosen, being at a considerable height above the river Tyne, flowing on its N. face, while it is defended on the other sides by ditches. It lies about seven miles W. of Newcastle. The founder of this family was called Robert cum barba, who received after the Conquest a grant of the lordship of Redesdale on the service "of defending it from enemies and wolves with that sword which King William had by his side when he entered Northumberland," and in that district he possessed also the castle of Harbottle. Prudhoe Castle must have been built before 1174, since in that year it was attacked by King William the Lion, whom it beat off after a three days' siege, to be noticed later.

Robert's son was Odinel de Umfraville, who was succeeded by another Odinel, who died in 1182; then, after three generations, came Gilbert (1226–1244), called by Matthew Paris "the defender of the North and flower of chivalry." His son Gilbert succeeded, and bore his maternal grandfather's title of Earl of Angus; he served Edward I. in all his wars, dying in 1303, and was followed by his brother Robert, who died 18 Edward II., 1325, leaving an only son, Gilbert, as third Earl of Angus; he married as second wife, Maud, heiress of Thomas, Lord Lacy. On their deaths without issue, Prudhoe passed under an entail to Henry Percy, 1st Earl of Northumberland, who had married Angus's widow, and after his rebellion against Henry IV., it was not recovered by the Percys till 1441. To return to Umfraville, the chronicler relates that Odinel, in building his castle, laid the people of the neighbourhood under sad exactions in order to complete it, which gives us an insight into the way in which the Norman barons obtained the requisite labour for their castle-building. In his incursion of 1174, the Scottish king first took Harbottle, and then Warkworth fell before him, when he next invested Prudhoe. This castle was strong and was well defended, but Hoveden and three other chroniclers relate that Odinel, fearing for the fate of Prudhoe, as the garrison was weak, determined to seek assistance, and for that end managed to leave the castle by night "mounted on a good brown bay horse." Spurring night and day, he beat up his friends till he had gathered together 400 knights and their followers with their shining helmets; among them Ralph de Glanvile, Barnard Balliol of Barnard Castle, and several Yorkshire barons. The laborious ride of this heavy armed cavalcade, and their march to Alnwick and their return to Newcastle, is told in the account of Alnwick. They found that the Scottish Lion had been repulsed at Prudhoe, and had gone back to attack Alnwick, where they captured him. This expedition, occasioned by Umfraville on behalf of Prudhoe, and leading to so important a result, was a great feat of arms; to perform a ride of 71 miles in heavy armour after the fatigue of a long previous march, to charge the enemy, and to wrest their king from the midst of so powerful a force, and carry him off a prisoner with them, shows the stuff of which men, and also horses, of that day were composed. No harm was done by the Scots to Prudhoe Castle, but before leaving the place they are said to have "destroyed the corn-fields, ravaged the gardens, and even barked the apple-trees."

The castle walls, covering an area of about three acres, follow on the N. the line of the slope 60 feet above the river, and are flanked towards the west by two semicircular towers of fourteenth-century work. The entrance and gatehouse on the S. side with its barrel vault are Norman; the barbican in front was probably built by Gilbert, 3rd Earl of Angus, in the middle of the fourteenth century. On the first floor of the gatehouse was a chapel, and as it was not large enough to contain the altar, a portion of its E. end was built out on corbels to afford additional space, lighted by three small lancet windows.

Within the walls are the outer and inner courts, divided by a dwelling-house, rebuilt in the present century, the inner bailey containing a fine lofty Norman keep, of oblong shape, buttressed by corner turrets of flat relief, with the usual Norman apartments and divisions, a straight staircase in the thickness of the W. wall, and another spiral one in the N.E. corner. It was in a ruinous state (temp. Elizabeth).

SEATON DELAVAL (*non-existent*)

A SHORT distance to the S.W. of the fire-eaten wreck of the modern mansion of the Delaval family lies the site of their ancient fortress, of which nothing whatever remains except the beautiful little Norman chapel that belonged to it, and even this has been partly destroyed

The now extinct family of Delaval was one of the most ancient in England; Hamon, second son of Guy de Laval of Maine, where their old castle still exists, came over with Duke William, whose niece, Dionysia or Denise, his son Guy married. Father and son shared largely in the spoils of the Saxons, and their descendants kept the lands and manors granted to them, as well as their estates in France, until the reign of John, when they lost them by rebellion. It is evident that they were established in Northumberland shortly after the Conquest in the barony of Delaval, constituted by William himself, and held by two knights' fees *in capite*, connected with the defence of the new castle; the first baron of whom there is record being Hubert de Laval or De la Val, temp. Rufus. The generations of the Delavals run on with tolerable regularity to sons or brothers till the death of Sir Henry (12 Richard II.), when the succession was taken up by his sister Alice, the wife of John de Whitchester, and their son and grandson, which latter was in possession of Seaton cir. 1416. At his death *s.p.*, his sister Elizabeth succeeded, being the wife of Sir John Burchester, knight, and she dying (9 Edward IV.), settled the estate on a kinsman, James Horsley. His mother was a Delaval of Newsham, and he came in for all the estates, assuming the Delaval name. His grandson is thus written of in a Survey of the Borders: "Sir John Delaval of Seaton, may serve the king with fifty men; he keepeth a good house, and is a true gentleman." He died in 1562, and his posterity continued at Seaton in regular succession, one being knighted by James I. in 1617, and at the Restoration the further honour of a baronetcy was conferred on Sir Ralph, who was member for the county during the entire reign of Charles II. Sir John, third and last baronet, died in 1720, aged seventy-four, when his cousin, Admiral Delaval, became proprietor of Seaton, and being a wealthy man, proceeded to build here a stately palace from the designs of Sir John Vanbrugh. This sumptuous edifice was destroyed by a fire in 1822, and being partially repaired, gives still some idea of the grandeur which excited so much admiration in past years.

The Chapel of Our Lady was attached to the old feudal fortress of Seaton, and is a very interesting relic of perfect Norman style, with its short columns and the zigzag mouldings of its semicircular arches; it is still used for service.

The Delaval baronetcy was revived in Sir John Hussey Delaval, who was raised to the peerage in 1786 as Lord Delaval. He obtained Ford

Castle from his brother, and almost entirely rebuilt the fabric, and at his death in 1888, at the age of eighty, he left Ford to a lady whom he had espoused three years before, and after her to his granddaughter, Lady Susan Carpenter, the wife of Henry, second Marquess of Waterford, in whose family it remains.

The entailed estates passed to his brother Edward, who died in 1814, the last of his name, when they went to his nephew, Sir Jacob Astley, Bart., whose son claimed and obtained the ancient barony of Hastings, and holds Seaton Delaval.

SEWINGSHIELDS (*non-existent*)

ON the N. side of Tyne, near the wall at Housesteads, is a place which represents the Roman station of Borcovicus, and is full of interesting remains. In the reign of Edward I. the lands belonged to William de Haulton, and in 1362 Robert de Ogle died seised of Sewin-sheles. Again, in 1407, Sir Robert Ogle, knight, gave this manor to William Thimilby, clerk, but is returned as the owner still in 1434; after him no mention is made of an owner until 1568 and again in 1663, when the property is reckoned among the estates of the Herons of Chipchase. In later years it was included in the possessions of the Erringtons of High Wardon.

The Survey of 1542 speaks of this place as "an old castle or fortress of Sewynge-sheales of James Heron of Chipchase, in great decay both in roof and floors, and hath great bounds of good ground either for corn or pasture; both the same house and ground lie waste and unplenished at this present." Perhaps the reason of this neglect is to be found in the fact of the castle standing in the track of the Liddisdale and Tynedale thieves and moss-troopers, so that its inmates, like the pastoral folk dwelling hereabout, were never safe from molestation and violence.

Hodgson says that a square, low mass of ruins, overgrown with nettles, is all that remains of the building, which was possibly never more than a tower or peel. Its site is at the end of a long ridge, overlooked from the S. by the basaltic cliffs along which the Roman wall is built. There are traces of ditches about it, but as these are on the N. side of the wall, they were probably made in later times as security against marauding parties from the dales.

There is an ancient legend that beneath this tower is an enchanted cave in which lie King Arthur and Queen Guinevere and their court, all fast bound in sleep until some deliverer shall blow the horn at the entrance to the cave, and shall cut with a sword of stone the garter lying beside it. And the tradition runs that a shepherd who once found his way in, saw the king and all of them lying asleep. The garter he managed to cut, but neglecting to blow the horn, the king awoke and cried out :

> " O woe betide that evil day
>> On which this hapless wight was born,
>> Who drew the sword, the garter cut,
>> But never blew the bugle-horn."

Whereupon the intruder was so dazed with fright that he fled away, nor could he ever again find the entrance to the magic cave. There are other legends regarding Arthur and Guinevere associated with this locality, the reason of which connection it would be interesting to trace.

SHORTFLAT TOWER (minor)

THIS edifice was built by Robert de Raymes of Bolan by licence from Edward I., dated 1305, and resembles in many of its features the tower built by the same owner at Aydon. It is embattled, and the walls at the ground level are seven feet thick. It belonged to a branch of the Fenwicks, after the Raymes, but its subsequent possessors are unrecorded. The tower is still inhabited, and is the property of Mr. E. J. Dent.

SIMONBURN (minor)

ABOUT half a mile N. from the church of this old town is the picturesque ruin of a stronghold of the Herons of Chipchase Castle, in the neighbourhood. It stands on a hill, below which flows a stream, called from it Castle Burn, in a well-wooded locality. The account of this place as given in the MS. quoted by Hodgson (vol. ii. part 3, p. 235, note) shows that it was an important post for controlling the Tynedale district, its garrison acting with others in the district and at Chipchase, and it was here that the "kepar" or warden of Tynedale resided, with a force of fifty horsemen "allwaies a this commandement." It says, "Symondburne ys a greatt and strongly buylded toure standinge very defencyble upon the corner of an hyll, envyrowned upon thre q'ters thereof wth a depe staye hyll almost inaccessyble, so that a barmekyn wall of a meane height sett upon the toppe of that hyll were defencyble enough." Another sixteenth-century Survey reports : ".At Symondburne ys a stronge toure of fonre house height of thinherytaunce of John Heron."

Sir Charles Heron, Bart., sold the manor and demesnes to Robert Allgood, whose heirs possessed Simonburn at the beginning of this century. Walls, who was curate of the parish and wrote his Antiquities here, declares the fabric to have been pulled down by the country people in searching vainly, "like King John at Corbridge," for reported hidden treasure. Part of the W. end was rebuilt in 1766 in Wallis's time, "with two small turrets (i.e., bartizans) at the angles."

TARSET (minor)

THIS strong fortalice is situated on Tyne, four miles W. of Bellingham. One of the Scottish barons called to give service to the king in the Barons' War was John Comyn of Badenoch, Earl of Buchan, who received in 52 Henry III. a licence to fortify and crenellate his building of "Tyrsete" in Tynedale (1267). It was his son, the Red Comyn, who was a competitor for the crown of Scotland, and who was stabbed by Robert Bruce in the Grey Friars' Church of Dumfries. The Comyn property went in the female line in 19 Edward II., when this lordship came to the Strathbolgys, Earls of Athol, and Earl David, cir. 1375, left it and his other property to his daughters Elizabeth and Philippa, who being committed to the wardship of Henry, Lord Percy, he prudently married them to his two younger sons, when Tarset came by the elder girl to Sir Thomas Percy, and became afterwards attached to the dukedom of Northumberland.

The castle was burnt in 1525 by Tynedale marauders "at a tyme when Sir Rauffe Fenwyke lay with a certain garrison in the tower at Tarsett hall for the reformaçon of certayne mysorders within the said countrye of Tyndall."

The old tower, standing in a commanding situation, was built of the finest masonry, with walls 4 feet thick, and turrets at the corners, covering an acre of ground with its buildings, and surrounded by a ditch ten yards broad and an outer wall. It was destroyed at the beginning of this century for the sake of its stones.

The country story runs that there exists an underground passage cut between this place and Dalley Castle—a mile asunder—below the bed of the river, and that the noise is heard at midnight of carriages driving through this passage, which may be seen to emerge at Dalley, drawn by headless horses.

THIRLWALL (minor)

THIS ruin stands on the N. side of the Roman wall (which in the Middle Ages was itself called the Thirlwall), in that short space of flat land near Haltwhistle where the two rivers South Tyne and Tithing approach each other. Opposite to it, across the wall, is the interesting station of Magna, now called Caercoran. The castle is a large, sombre-looking place, called by Hutchinson "a horrid, gloomy dungeon;" the whole of it was built with stones taken from the wall, and in its turn the ruin has been robbed of its stone for other buildings.

The castle, which until 1297 was practically in Scotland, was for many centuries the residence of an ancient Northumbrian family of the same name, and was built probably early in the fourteenth century, after a visit there of Edward I. in 1306. The first mention of it occurs in 1309, and in 1386 John de Thirlwall had it, his family having been established here already for a century at least. This John had served with Edward III. in his expedition to Paris in 1360, in Gascony with the Black Prince, and in Brittany with the Duke of Lancaster in 1378. In 1415 it belonged to Roland de Thirlwall, and in the Survey of the marches in 1542 its owner was Robert Thyrewall. The castle was garrisoned by a Scottish force for the Parliament in 1645, but after the Restoration, John Thirlwall, the head of the family, left it to live at Newbiggin near Hexham. His granddaughter, the heiress of the family, married in 1738 Matthew Swinburne of Capheaton, who sold the castle and manor of Thirlwall to the 4th Earl of Carlisle, with whose descendants the property has remained.

Not much is left of this the most westerly of Northumbrian fortresses; part of a rectangular oblong keep remains, with a tower on the E. in line with the S. wall, the E. wall of the building having fallen down in 1831. In this wall was the entrance, near its N. corner, where, in 1767, were still the remains of an iron gate, and inside this is a staircase, contrived in the thickness of the wall, leading into the first floor in the N.W. angle. In the basement is a small dungeon, and the walls seem to be 9 feet thick. A hill stream, called the Tipalt, flows past the castle on its way S. to the Tyne.

TOSSON TOWER (minor)

ON the S. of the Coquet, about a mile from the town of Rothbury, are the remains of this building. In the middle of the fifteenth century it is spoken of as belonging to the Lords Ogle, and at that time "not in good reparacions." Mr. Bates says that the Ogles obtained lands here cir. 1330 by marriage with a daughter of Sir Robert Hepple, but that the tower is of later construction. It has been a small peel measuring only 25 feet by 18 feet, having probably two stages above the basement. A stair was in the N.E. corner, but little remains now of the fabric except part of the N. and E. fronts, from which most of the ashlar facing has been abstracted.

TWIZEL (*non-existent*)

THIS old Border stronghold, standing on a rocky cliff on the E. of the Till, is thus described by Leland : " At Twysle, nere unto the said ryver of Twede, there ys standinge the walls of an old fortresse or castell rased and caste downe by the King of Scotts in a warre xl^{ti} yeres and more since." This destruction was done by James IV. of Scotland when he started to harry Northumberland in support of Perkin Warbeck against Henry VII., and the occasion of its razing is the first notice we find of the castle. The lands were held of the Mitford barons in 1272, and in 1329 they belonged to Sir William Riddell ; on the failure of whose family they came to the Herons. Afterwards the manor belonged to the ancient family of the Selbys (temp. Edward VI. and Elizabeth), and at the beginning of the present century was owned by the Blakes, also an old family of British extraction.

The early fortress was never rebuilt, and the ruins now seen are those of a castle commenced to be built in 1770 and never finished.

TYNEMOUTH (*minor*)

THE situation of the Priory of Tynemouth, whose origin dates from the seventh century, was a very exposed one, on a promontory on the north bank of the Tyne, and its oft-repeated destruction by the Danes necessitated the fortification of its precincts for protection both landward and from the sea. Earl Tostig had a stronghold here shortly before the Norman Conquest, probably a stockaded one of timber ; but between then and 1095 a strong castle must have been erected, perhaps by the great Robert de Mowbray, since in that latter year it sustained a violent siege for two months by the Red King.

No grant of the castle is found after this event, and it is probable that being built on church ground, it vested in the prior and convent after falling to the Crown by capture ; indeed, what was called a castle could have been little more than the defences of the priory—that is, a wall and ditch, with ramparts and a strong gatehouse. There never probably was a keep.

The next heard of the castle is in 1346, after the battle of Nevill's Cross, when Sir Ralph Nevill of Raby, keeper of the marches, and no friend to the Church, proposed to send all the Scottish prisoners for keeping to Tynemouth, a suggestion which was strenuously opposed by the churchmen, and petitioned against to the king. Again, in 1379, Richard II. made a grant to enable the prior and monks to repair their fortifications, these being treated as a part of the priory ; after which time there is scarcely any notice of the fortress till the reign of Henry VIII., after the suppression of the convent, when it is stated that the defences had been strengthened by the Crown; and in 1550 Tynemouth is mentioned as one of the king's castles in the middle marches. In Elizabeth's reign a garrison of six gunners and a master-gunner were kept in the castle, a governor being always appointed. In 1584, Sir Henry Percy, 8th Earl of Northumberland, and his sons held this appointment, with the castle, for life; but Elizabeth, mistrusting them, and believing that they were in collusion with the Throgmorton plot concerning Mary Queen of Scots, sent and apprehended Percy, removing him to the Tower, where he was kept till his supposed murder in June 1585 (see *Tower of London*). While this earl was castellan he received the Earl of Bothwell as a prisoner in 1563-64. Camden wrote: "Tynemouth glories in a noble and strong castle, which, in the language of an old writer, is made inaccessible on the E. and N. side by a rock over the ocean; but on the other sides, on account of its lofty situation, is easily defended."

In 1633 Charles I. rested at Tynemouth Castle on his way to visit Scotland, accompanied by a gallant train of nobles and courtiers; but when civil war had become imminent in 1642, the Earl of Newcastle placed the castle in a state of defence for the king, sending to it from Newcastle guns and stores, and placing a new fort at the river's mouth.

Then, after the victory of Marston Moor, the Parliamentary forces came (1644), and besieged and captured the fortress, where they obtained a great store of arms and ammunition.

Two years after, Sir Arthur Haslerigg being governor, his deputy, Colonel Lilburne, with a Scottish garrison, declared for the king, whereupon Haslerigg sent a force to capture the place, and to put to the sword all they found under arms. The castle was accordingly stormed and taken, and Lilburne's head was struck off and placed on a pole.

In 1660 Haslerigg gave way to General Monk, and about this time various repairs and works were undertaken on account of the war with Holland, when, to lessen expenses, the lead and roofing and the buildings of the priory were laid hands on and adapted.

Thenceforward, however, the castle was neglected, and it was not till 1783 that the buildings were again made serviceable for holding stores and a garrison, and some of the present disfiguring constructions were put up.

The old castle gatehouse is the entry to the priory ruins; it was a strong one, provided with three gates, the second having a portcullis; in front was a ditch, with a drawbridge of entry. Little is left of the old works, the whole place having been modernised into an ordinary barrack; but beneath, in the rock, are known to exist many chambers and passages, which afforded secret access to the convent from the river and haven.

WARK (*minor*)

THE parish of Carham occupies the extreme N.W. corner of the border of
Northumberland, and at a point two miles from this corner, where the
Tweed begins to form the march between England and Scotland, on a high
bank 60 feet above the river, stood the castle of Werk or Wark. Here, in the
time of Stephen, Walter Lespec of Helmsley (*q.v.*, *Yorkshire*), the great leader
at the Battle of the Standard, founded the original fabric. This underwent a
siege by the Scots temp. David I., who invaded Northumberland in 1136, in
support of the Empress Maud, his niece, when this castle, defended by Lespec's
nephew, Jordan de Bussei, withstood him. David was supplied with all the
machines necessary for battering the fortress, and remained three weeks
before it : then he broke up, and leaving a sufficient force to mask it, marched
to the Tyne, devastating the country with great barbarity. Stephen brought an
army against him and crossed the Tweed, ravaging in his turn, whereupon the
Scots returned to their own side, and Stephen also retired south. Finding
the country again unprotected, David advanced into the counties of Durham
and Yorkshire, which having devastated, he laid siege to the castle of Norham
and took it. Then he returned again to Wark, but was compelled again to
retire with great loss, revenging himself by destroying the English grain crops.
The Battle of the Standard, however (22nd August 1138), drove him back to
his own dominions, but he returned soon to Wark, to conduct the siege in
person. All his attacks again failing, David sat down to reduce the place by
famine, and the garrison in their extremity received an order from Lespec
to yield up the fortress, which they gladly did, upon good terms. It was
found that they had no more provisions left than one live horse and one
salted. Then David caused the castle to be demolished ("*funditus,*" *i.e.*, to
the ground).

Stephen purchased the Scottish king's neutrality by ceding to him the border
counties of Northumberland and Cumberland, but when Henry II. succeeded
he resumed the royal demesnes thus alienated, and took possession of both
counties in 1157, rebuilding Wark. This loss of territory rankled in the heart
of the succeeding king, William the Lion, who preferred claims which Henry
refused to recognise ; whereon he invaded England in 1173, and appearing
before Wark, demanded its surrender. The captain, who was Robert de
Stuteville, sheriff of the county, begged and obtained a respite of forty days,
in order to consult his king, Henry II., who was in Normandy ; but he spent
the time in strengthening his defences and preparing for a siege, and when
William, who had been carrying a campaign into Cumberland, once more
appeared, at Easter 1174, he found himself defied, and the castle so strong
that all his efforts to break in failed ; and in a frenzy of wrath he was at

last obliged to leave the place. He was taken prisoner soon after at Alnwick (*q.v.*).

After this Wark seems to have come, like Helmsley, to Robert de Roos or Ross (*i.e.*, "Furstan," who married a daughter of William the Lion), by disposition of Henry III. Edward I. came here for three days, after receiving at Norham the homage of Edward Baliol (1292), and that same winter the owner of the castle, Robert de Roos, left Wark for Scotland, in order to follow a Scottish lady, Christiana de Mowbray, with whom he had fallen in love, and for whose sake he joined the Scots army; whereon the English king took possession of Wark, though afterwards he restored it to the brother of De Roos.

In 1342 David II. led a raid into England as far as Newcastle, where, being repulsed, he came to Durham, which place he took and treated barbarously; then, returning across the Border, his followers, with their train of rich spoils, passed in view of Wark Castle, and this was more than the garrison could endure passively. Edward III. had given the fortress in 1333 to William Montagu, afterwards Earl of Salisbury (see *Nottingham*), whose nephew was at this time in charge of the castle, with the countess, Katherine de Grandison, who was esteemed one of the most beautiful women in England. Young Montagu, with his men, fell on the rear of the Scots force as it passed the Tweed, and killing 200 of them, carried off into the castle 160 horses laden with their English spoils. This so exasperated King David that he at once laid close siege to the castle; whereon the garrison, doubting their strength, managed to send word to the King of England at Alnwick of their condition, begging his assistance. Edward at once started in person to their relief, and at his approach the Scots retired over the Border. Great was the joy of the garrison, and on Edward's coming into Wark Castle, their gratitude, as expressed by the beautiful countess, awoke in him an attachment which, as related by Froissart, was the commencement of the romance to which a few years after the famous Order of the Garter owed its origin.

The Earl of Salisbury's heir exchanged Wark for other lands, and in 2 Henry IV. it was in the possession of the Greys of Heaton, a family now represented by Earl Tankerville of Chillingham, who is its present owner.

In 1419 the Scots took Wark, then in the custody of Robert Ogle, and put its garrison to the sword; but soon after an English force came there, and some of them managed to creep up a large drain leading from the river to the kitchen of the castle, and made an entrance for their comrades, who in turn massacred the Scots.

At the death of James II. before Roxburgh Castle, a party of Scots again seized Wark, and so injured it that in 1519, when Henry VIII. caused the defences of the Border to be put into repair, its condition was found

ruinous, and considerable sums were devoted to its rebuilding, as a post
of importance; since in conjunction with Norham and Berwick, which
fortresses could both be seen from the ramparts of Wark, it formed an
efficient guard for the North Border.   At this time it was possessed by
Sir Edward Grey, from whom it came to his son Sir Ralph, whose son
Sir William was created Lord Grey of Wark by James I. in 1624.   Lady
Mary Grey, daughter and heir of Forde, Lord Grey and Earl of Tankerville,
in 1695 married Charles, 2nd Baron Ossulton, in whom the Tankerville title
was renewed.

From a drawing of Wark Castle temp. Elizabeth, it appears that the
enceinte was rectangular and oblong, surrounded by a high wall, the N. end
abutting on the river bank, with a strong tower at the N.E. corner, close to
which on the E. face was the great gatehouse, which has now entirely
disappeared. The enclosure was divided into the outer, or nether, and middle
wards by a wall, the line of which is now shown by a hedge. The middle
ward contained the Constable's lodgings and domestic offices, and there was
a postern in the W. face. The keep, which was octangular with a turret of
the same form, stood in the S.W. corner of an inner ward, protected by
another wall or palisade.   The structure is said to have been destroyed at
the time of the Union, and little remains but the ramparts. Some foundations
of the corner tower may be traced in a garden over the river bank.

WARKWORTH (chief)

THE Coquet River, about a mile from where it loses its bright stream in
the dark waters of the North Sea, forms a bend round a peninsula of
somewhat elevated land, at the neck of which, overhanging the river on the
west, stands the castle of Warkworth. The walls are built in the trace of a
triangle, the keep at the N. end overlooking the town being the apex, while the
entrance and its towers and curtains form the base at the S., from each end of
which the two straight side walls, with their flanking towers, run up to the keep.
The whole area enclosed is an acre and a half.

The lands of Warkworth, as far back as the eighth century, were the property of the Church of Lindisfarne, or the Holy Island of St. Cuthbert, and it
is possible that owing to the visits of the ruthless Northmen to this coast, or
perhaps far anterior to these, the position on the peninsula was early selected
for a defensible post, since we find the existing keep built upon an artificial
mound which probably existed before the Norman Conquest. No mention
occurs of this castle till the reign of Henry II., when one Roger Fitz-Richard, a
valiant knight and Constable of Newcastle-upon-Tyne, became master of Warkworth, holding *in capite* from the Crown : this was in 1158, when the oldest por-

Markworth Castle.

tions of the castle may have been erected. Fitz-Richard was grandson of
Eustace Fitz-John, Lord of Alnwick, and his grandson Robert obtained confirmation of the grant from King John, but had to pay 300 marks for it; and the king
received as much more for giving him permission to marry. The castle and lands
were held for five generations, from father to son, without the possession of any
surname by this family, until 1299 (28 Edward I.); but when John Fitz-Robert
was summoned to Parliament he assumed the name of his estate in Essex,
namely, Clavering, the king, it is said, objecting to the iteration of "Fitz." He
died in 1332 without male issue, and his northern estates passed to the Percys
under an existing settlement.

Warkworth remained with this family until the forfeiture of Henry, 4th lord
and 1st Earl of Northumberland, in 1403. This great noble was the most
remarkable man of his age; inheriting a mighty name from his father and grandfather, he was one of the chief men of Richard II.'s court, being Marshal and
Constable of England, Guardian of the Welsh Marches, Governor of Calais, and
Lord of the Isle of Man; but he deserted that king when Bolingbroke aspired
to the throne, and was the first to support him on his landing at Ravenspur.
The attachment, however, was brief, and both the earl and his son Hotspur,
estranged by Henry's meanness and impecuniosity, before the lapse of two
years were in rebellion against him. The earl kept away from Shrewsbury,
where his son was slain, but afterwards made cause with Archbishop Scrope and
Mowbray, Earl of Nottingham, in their plot against Henry. When the king
came northwards with an army (1405) Northumberland fled to Berwick, and
thence into Scotland, and in 1407 was killed in an engagement at Bramham
Moor in Yorkshire. The king took Berwick after a siege, and then proceeded
to make himself master of the Percy castles. Prudhoe fell at once, and Henry
proceeded to Warkworth, where its captain declared he would hold the castle
for the earl, but on cannon being brought to bear on the walls, the same effect
was produced as had moved the garrison of Berwick, and after the seventh
shot the castle was yielded up. Henry gave Warkworth to his third son John,
afterwards Duke of Bedford, together with Prudhoe, Alnwick, and Langley;
they were restored to the grandson of the first earl, Henry, son of Hotspur,
together with the dignities of the house, by Henry V., in 1416. Warkworth
was well garrisoned for Lancaster after the battle of Towton in 1461; then
Edward IV. granted it to his brother George, Duke of Clarence, but on his
rebellion resumed possession in 1470. Shakespeare places three of the scenes
in *Henry IV.* at this castle, and with all propriety, since Warkworth was
the favourite abode of those who possessed it, and two of the Percy lords
died there.

Henry, 9th Earl of Northumberland, was confined in the Tower of London
for complicity in the Gunpowder Plot, and died therein; and during these
troubles Warkworth was dismantled, both lead and timber from it being sold.

The ruin was completed by the widow of Jocelyn, the eleventh earl, who gave away the materials of the castle.

A large part of the outer walls is of the twelfth century, but the keep was built at the end of the fourteenth or the beginning of the fifteenth century upon the ancient mound. This is a structure of unusual form— a square central block, with large projecting towers on each face, which give a sort of cruciform shape to it (good details of it are given by Parker). It is of the Perpendicular period (1435–1440), and is described in the minute survey of 1538 as "a marvellous proper dongeon of viiij towyres all joined in one house together." The masonry is admirable throughout, and the fact that it is possible to assign on internal evidence the exact original use of nearly every apartment in this complicated pile, enables us to realise the exigencies and the discomforts of mediaeval life. Surmounting the top is a lofty watchtower, commanding wide prospects over sea and land. The Lion Tower was built or remodelled by Henry, 4th Earl of Northumberland (1471–1489), as shown by the badges over the door. On the W. or river side were the principal apartments of the older castle, the hall, the kitchen, and the chapel ; and on the E. side are two mural towers in their original state, as also are the postern, and some other portions. The gatehouse is grand and severe ; the entrance deeply recessed between two half-octagon buttressed towers, with deep machicolations over. There are no original windows, and no traces now exist of the drawbridge across the ditch which remained in 1567. The S.W. tower is called Crayfargus in the Survey, built probably in 1200 ; its W. side has fallen. Much interest must attach to this part of the castle, since it was probably here that the two first Percy lords lived and died. Of late years repairs have been effected ; a portion has been re-roofed, and renovations have been carried out, but without much impairing the features of the old fabric.

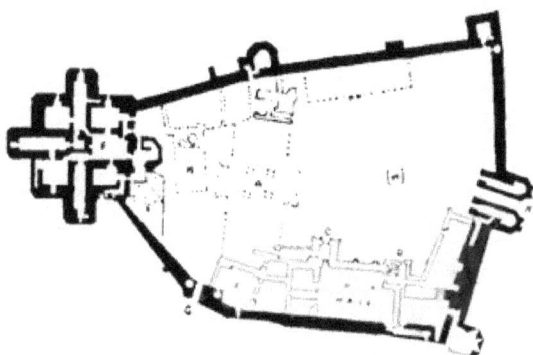

WARKWORTH

A. FOUNDATIONS OF CHURCH.
C. HALF TOWER.
D. GRREAT TURRET.
E. LION TURRET.
F. KEEP.

G. POSTERN.
H. OVENS.
I. KITCHEN.
K. CHIEF ENTRANCE.
W. WELL.

WHITTON TOWER (*minor*)

THIS ancient hold stands on the S. side of the Coquet, opposite to Rothbury, and is built on the slope of the hill, so that its N. wall is founded some 20 feet below the level of the S. wall. It seems to have been the parsonage of Rothbury, built by some warlike priest of that parish in the fourteenth century, being entered in the list of county strongholds in 1415 as the possession of the rector of the town. Additions made by rectors in the last century were since extended into "a modern Tudor mansion," the ancient tower forming the corner of the double range.

The basement chamber, with its vaulted roof, is entered by two pointed doors and a passage between, the roof being a barrel vault of stone; and in the floor of it is the well. A newel stair in the S.E. angle leads to the upper floor from the first stage, the only means of communication between this and the basement having been by a man-hole in the vaulted floor. The dwelling-room of this first stage is now lighted by a large S. window.

The second stage has been divided into bedrooms, and there is a large window recess which held formerly a small oratory, and has a piscina. Here was the dwelling of the mediæval rectors. Above is found little to remark; there is a plain modern parapet, with raised crenellations at the three outer angles.

WHITTON TOWER

WIDDRINGTON (*non-existent*)

THE original castle was the seat of one of the most ancient and worthy families in the North, and stood on an eminence near the sea, about nine miles N.E. of Morpeth.

The Widdringtons are believed to have existed here since the time of Henry II., and they held the manor in the first year of Edward III., in whose reign one of them, Sir Roger, was High Sheriff of the county, as were his son and others of his descendants in successive reigns. The bravery of one

of the family, temp. Richard II., is recorded in the ballads on the battle of
Otterburn (see *Otterburn*).

Gerard de Widdrington obtained a licence from King Edward I. to
crenellate his house, which is doubtless the date of the building that has
passed away. Sir John Widdrington was sheriff in the reigns of Henry VIII.,
Edward VI., and Elizabeth; and the widow of Sir Henry married Sir Robert
Carey, Lord Warden of the Middle Marches, afterwards created Earl of
Monmouth, who lived here, and carried the news of Queen Elizabeth's death
to James VI. at Edinburgh. This castle was thereafter chosen by James as
a resting-place on his progress south to assume the English crown. He
spent part of the day at a deer hunt, which his soul loved, and stayed the
night here. Sir William represented the county in Parliament in Charles I.'s
time, and was among the first to raise troops at his own expense to defend
the king, who created him Baron Widdrington of Blankney in 1643. After
Marston Moor he retired abroad with his friend and general, the Marquis of
Newcastle and others, and his estate was sequestrated by Parliament. He
was slain by a Parliamentary troop, which surprised a force which he had
joined on its way to Worcester Field. Lord Clarendon bears witness to
his worth and services, and says he was "one of the goodliest persons of
that age, being near the head higher than most tall men, and a gentleman
of the best and most ancient extraction of the county."

As a good family supporter of the Stuarts, his grandson William, fourth lord,
joined the Earl of Mar's rising in 1715 against King George, with Lord Derwentwater, his brother being aide-de-camp to "General" Forster. Lord Widdrington
being taken at Preston, was pardoned, but his estates were confiscated and
sold first to a building company, and then to Sir George Revel, whose daughter
brought the estate in marriage to Sir George Warren. This castle meantime
fell into decay, and towards the end of the last century was destroyed by
Sir George Warren, who built a grand pseudo-Gothic edifice, which was
speedily consumed by fire, and a second building raised in its place was
also burned in 1862; a single octagon tower being all that was left of it. The
ancient building of the Widdringtons was a massive pile, and, as shown in the
drawing of 1728 by S. and N. Buck, consisted of the original square tower,
like that of Belsay, with doubly machicolated bartizans overhanging each of
its angles, supported by a smaller tower at the side, and connected with this
by the entrance portion of the house; there being outer wings on each flank
for the offices, and a stone wall defending a square area in front.

WILLIMOTESWICK (minor)

THIS ancient seat of the Ridley family is in a fine position on the right bank of the Tyne, midway between Haltwhistle and Bardon Mill. Bruce (*Roman Wall*) gives it as the birthplace of Nicholas Ridley, the Oxford Martyr. That prelate, however, was first-cousin of the owner of this stronghold, to whom his last letter was written, his father being Christopher, third son of Nicholas Ridley of Willimoteswick, and he was born at the neighbouring house of Unthank, which still retains the "Bishop's Room." There was a family of this name temp. Henry II., and in 1279 the place is held by Nicholas de Rydeley. In 1484 Nicholas Ridley was one of the commissioners for completing the truce with Scotland, and was probably grandfather of the bishop. In 1620 the heir had run through the property; he was married to a daughter of Sir Richard Musgrave of Norton, and before the Civil War this place had been sold to the Nevills of Chevet, Yorkshire, who sold it to the Blacketts, and it is now the property of Sir Edward Blackett of Matfen. Dr. Nicholas Ridley, Bishop of London, the prelate and martyr of Mary's reign, was born at the beginning of the sixteenth century. In 1545 he was joined by Cranmer in rejecting the doctrine of transubstantiation, and he made an enemy of the Princess Mary during her brother's reign; he then espoused the Protestant cause of Lady Jane Grey, and was at once committed to the Tower, whence he was conveyed to Oxford, and there condemned to death for heresy. On October 15, 1555, he "suffered the cruellest death with the greatest courage," in company with Bishop Latimer.

At Willimoteswick there is a courtyard entered through a late gatehouse in the N.E. angle; on the left the yard is formed by a range of old stables and byres, with the manor-house on the S. front, and at the E. end is a very early building standing between two narrow towers. The entrance in the gatehouse has two doorways, one to the basement chamber, and the other to the battlements. The first floor is low, and there are two rooms on the second floor. The old manor-house has been much altered and injured; it has still a great fireplace and a Gothic doorway. Bates says that the two towers taper upwards, and are relics of the defensive architecture of Northumberland.

WOOLER (minor)

ON a round hill are the remains of a tower belonging, with the manor, to the very ancient family of Muschamps, which has long been extinct. The barony was given by Henry I. to Robert de Muschamp, and included a wide tract of country. Belford, Etal, Ford, Brankston, Fenton, Elswick, and others were members of it, and were held *in capite* by the service of four knights' fees. The Robert de Muschamp temp. Henry III. was counted the mightiest baron in the north of England, but the fortress of Wooler must even then have been an old one, as in 1254 it is returned as of no value. The son of this baron, also Robert, left three daughters, coheirs, whereby the great estate was divided up, and Wooler must have come in some way later to the Percys, since in 41 Edward III. Joan, the widow of Earl Henry, has it in dower. Afterwards it passed through the families of Hevell, Scrope, Darcy, and Percy again, from the last of whom it came to the Greys of Chillingham : it is now the property of Lord Tankerville.

The fortalice must have been rebuilt after the time of Henry III. and again fallen to decay, since the Survey of 1541 speaks of it as a little tower of which one half had fallen down for want of repairs, that very year, and recommends its immediate repair, as being "a mervelous convenyent place for the defence of the countrye thereaboute," as it lay in the usual track of the Scots raiders when invading the realm. It was still decayed in 1584. There is but little left now of the walls, which were very thick and strong, and apparently as old as the Muschamps' time.

BERWICK-ON-TWEED (non-existent)

THIS town of ancient Bernicia, of importance since the time of Agricola, stands on the north of the Tweed, on a high promontory of land. The river flowed originally on two sides of the town, around which a broad water-defence was formed, surrounding it completely, while the castle stood on a lofty hill in the N.W., overlooking the town, about 400 yards from the Border bridge. At the beginning of the twelfth century Berwick belonged to Scotland, and was not a place of consequence, Bamborough being so near. It possessed, however, some sort of fortress from the time of the Saxons, who fortified the hill with a ditch and ramparts, these being added to by the Danes, and doubtless also by the Normans, although no record exists on the subject. When William the Lion was taken prisoner at Alnwick, in order to regain his freedom he gave up Berwick to Henry II., to whom the Norman castle is due. For, although Henry was a destroyer of the smaller castles of his barons, he built several of our finest fortresses, such as the keeps of Newcastle and Dover, this one at Berwick being intended to command the bridge between England and Scotland. The importance of Berwick was seen as soon as Henry had recovered the northern provinces from Malcolm, the young

King of Scots, for then the Tweed became the boundary between the two peoples. In 1177 Geoffrey de Nevill of Raby was made keeper of the castle of Berwick; and in 1204 we find King John, who coveted Berwick Castle, throwing up, as a step towards its acquisition, a fortification opposite to it at Tweedmouth, but this work was twice hindered by William the Lion, who finally razed it to the ground. In 1214 the barons of Northumberland and Yorkshire had recourse, for protection against their furious king, to Alexander, the young King of Scotland, who had recently succeeded his mighty father,

BORDER WALL, BERWICK-ON-TWEED

and to create a diversion, the castle of Norham was besieged. This attempt, though a failure, had the effect of drawing the English king northward at once, *ira accensus*, destroying and burning the barons' houses and towns, amongst which were Morpeth, Alnwick, Metford, Wark, and Roxburgh, after which he retired before the forces of Alexander II. The town and castle of Berwick were, however, taken, and great cruelties perpetrated on the unhappy towns-people. This town, too, was burnt, the king himself setting fire with his own hand to the house in which he had lodged.

In 1291, and again in the following year, Edward I., after his royal progress into Scotland, held a great council of the English and Scottish laity and clerics in the chapel of Berwick Castle, in order to settle the rival claims of Bruce and

Baliol to the Scottish throne. The disputed succession was settled at the last meeting on November 20, 1292, when, in presence of a vast assemblage in the hall of the castle, John Baliol was declared "the illustrious King of Scotland." In 1296, while marching against the Scots who had thrown off their allegiance to him, King Edward came again to Berwick and encamped by Halidon Hill (a mile to the N.W.), whence he proceeded to assault and take the town, which was almost undefended, slaughtering the inhabitants and fighting men to the number of 8000. The castle was surrendered, and the king slept in it the same night. He remained here fifteen days, meantime improving the defences by causing a ditch to be cut across from the sea to the Tweed, 80 feet broad and 40 feet deep, the traces of which can still be made out. Edward received the submission of John Baliol at Brechin, and after invading the country as far north as Elgin in Moray, returned to Berwick, where he held an English parliament. He then retired south, leaving John de Warenne, Earl of Surrey, Guardian of Scotland. In 1297 the army under Sir William Wallace retook the town of Berwick, but the castle was too strong to be reduced, being further relieved by Earl Warenne in the following year. The next year Edward came again to Berwick on his way to carry war into Scotland, and spent Christmas in the castle. Of this king's unfeeling cruelty in his testy old age, we have instances when he sought to wreak vengeance on women as well as on men, for the queen of Robert Bruce was imprisoned by him, and the Countess of Buchan, who in the absence of her brother, the Earl of Fife, had performed his hereditary office and placed the crown of Scotland on the head of Bruce, was condemned by Edward to be shut up in a wooden cage in one of the towers of Berwick Castle, there to be exhibited as a reproach to all passers-by,—a sentence which was actually carried out.

King Edward II. entered Scotland in 1310 with a large army, and coming to Berwick, stayed there with Queen Isabella through the winter, and during the greater part of the year 1311. Here also he collected together his army in 1314 on the march to Bannockburn, when his force mustered 40,000 horse and 52,000 archers, and to Berwick he again returned after that crushing defeat. Berwick was betrayed in 1318 to the Scots army, which after a siege of six days took the castle : King Robert Bruce then came and took up his residence therein, holding his court also in the castle. On quitting Berwick, the Bruce left it in the keeping of his son-in-law, young Sir Walter Stewart, who the next year defended the town in the severest siege it had ever experienced. For the English army under King Edward himself besieged both town and castle with all the warlike appliances of the age, and only retreated at last when, on the Earl of Lancaster leaving the camp and retiring with all his men, Edward raised the siege and concluded a truce with the Scottish king. In 1332, the truce which had been made in 1328 between England and Scotland on the marriage of "Makepeace" Joan, youngest

daughter of the murdered Edward II., with David, son and heir of Robert
Bruce, was broken by the English nobles, who prevailed on their young king,
Edward III., to take up arms against his brother-in-law, for the Scottish king
had refused either to pay homage or to deliver up Berwick. A great expedition
was undertaken, and in April 1333 Edward III. appeared with a vast host at
Tweedmouth, overlooking Berwick. The strength of this latter place seemed
so great, that a formal investment of both castle and town was entered upon,
in order to reduce the place by famine. Edward remained a month before
Berwick, when he left the siege and proceeded to Edinburgh, and as far
as Scone and Dundee, ravaging the country, and finally returning to
Berwick. The following episode connected with this siege of Berwick is
related by the historians Boece and Buchanan, on the Scottish side. Two
sons of Sir Alexander Seton, commanding in the town, had been taken
prisoners by the English in a skirmish, and were retained as hostages on
the strength of a truce entered into by the opposing forces, which stipulated
that, if not relieved by the Scots army during the truce, both town and
castle should be surrendered to the English. The Scots army, however,
under Douglas, passed by to besiege Bamborough, where Queen Philippa
was dwelling for safety, and the prescribed time expired without Berwick
being either relieved or given up. Thereupon Edward, it is related, caused
the two sons of Seton, as hostages, to be hung on a gallows erected on the
opposite side of the river Tweed, in sight of the garrison and of the "agonised
father." The place of execution is still called "Hang-a-dyke Nook," and two
skulls are there shown as testimony of the deed. But in favour of King
Edward it is affirmed that Seton was not governor of Berwick at that time,
nor were his sons hostages; nevertheless it is possible that Edward did hang
two prisoners to enforce the surrender of the place. The capitulation, in
fact, was signed on the 15th or 16th of July, Sir William Keith, and Dunbar,
Earl of March, being governors of the town and castle respectively. Two
days after this event (July 18th) Lord Douglas and his large army crossed the
Tweed and gave battle to Edward, who took up a position on Halidon Hill,
which lies a mile to the N.W of Berwick. The Scottish army was utterly
defeated, and numbers of their nobles were slain; the town and castle of
Berwick were ceded to Edward, who rested his army there for twelve days,
returning thence to England. The English king now assisted Edward Baliol
to recover the throne of his father, on condition of his remaining a vassal of
the British crown, receiving Baliol's homage and fealty as such in Henry III.'s
hall of the fortress of Newcastle. Baliol was then granted the castle, town,
and county of Berwick, together with Edinburgh, Dumfries, and other territory, to the great resentment of the Scots. In 1335 King Edward came with
an army to assist his vassal Baliol at Berwick, whither he had retired, and
he next year further granted him a subsidy of five marks per day towards

his expenses. Edward was again at Berwick for a few days in 1337, and in 1341 passed through on his way to invade Scotland with an army of 40,000 foot and 6000 lances, to assist at the siege of Stirling. After the truce which then followed he returned to Berwick to spend Easter, and held a magnificent tournament in the castle courtyard, at which two Scottish knights and one Englishman, Sir James Twyford, were killed. Again, in February 1343, Edward III., returning from France, summoned all his forces to meet him at Berwick in order to take vengeance on the Scots for their infringements of the truce. In 1346 occurred the battle of Nevill's Cross, resulting in the captivity of the Scottish king, and followed by another truce which lasted until 1355.

At the termination of this period, which had been more than once disturbed by attempts at recapture, and by reprisals, in which many men were slain, the Scots formed a plan for the recovery of Berwick. That year (1355), the Earls of Angus and March, collecting a number of ships, well manned and armed, came to the mouth of the Tweed on a dark night, and disembarked a strong force on the N. side of the river; then approaching the town they scaled the walls and overpowered the English garrison in it, killing the governor, Sir Alexander Ogle, and two other knights. The defenders then took refuge in the castle, which the Scots in vain attempted to capture. It is a proof of the vast importance attached at this time to the possession of Berwick that King Edward, who was in France, on learning its loss, returned to England with all speed, and resting only three days in London, came on to Newcastle, where he had summoned the whole force of the county to meet him, and arrived before Berwick on January 14, 1356, his navy, according to his invariable tactics, meeting him in the Tweed. Edward at once threw himself into the castle, which still held out, whereon, the Scottish story says, the garrison abandoned the town, and returned into their own country, after destroying the walls. English history, however, relates that the king prepared to undermine the town walls with the aid of skilful Forest-of-Dean miners, under Sir Walter Manny, while his army was to assault it on the far side, and that seeing resistance hopeless, the townsfolk yielded the place.

In 1378, when both Edward III. and King David were dead, and during the continuance of a truce, seven filibustering Scottish Borderers, under one Alexander Ramsay, surprised and actually captured Berwick Castle; coming at night, they managed to cross the ditch, which was dry, and to scale the wall with a ladder, thus entering the castle without opposition. Then they went to the quarters of the governor, Sir Robert Boynton, and began to batter the door of his room with axes. Boynton awaking, thought this an attack by his own men, with whom he had lately quarrelled, and opening a window looking on the ditch, made a fatal leap out, breaking his neck. The sleeping guard, few in number, were then overpowered by the Scots, but not before their cries had warned the townspeople of what had occurred, and they at once cut off the communication between the town and castle, and sent a messenger to Alnwick to apprise Earl Percy of what had happened. He, as Warden of the Marches, without delay called up a large force from Newcastle, with the Lords Nevill, Lucy, Bellasis, Stafford, and others to meet him at Berwick, whither he marched at once with his own men. Meanwhile the crew within, now increased to forty-eight in number, defended the fortress, and returned a defiant answer to the summons of Percy, who at the head of a force of 7000 archers and 3000 men-at-arms attacked the castle both by mining and by assault. This siege was prolonged for eight days without any result, but on the ninth the English troops, with ladders at different points, entered and took the place, putting to the sword all whom they found. At this siege we hear of the gallant behaviour of the earl's son Henry, known afterwards as Harry Hotspur, then a mere lad (*Froissart*, i. 529).

BERWICK-ON-TWEED

Again, in 1384, this bone of contention between the two kingdoms changed hands, being betrayed to the Scots for a bribe by the deputy of Earl Percy, who was himself charged with treason; but, being at the time on the Northern Marches, he at once proceeded to retake Berwick for the king, and, partly aided by a bribe of 2000 marks, succeeded in recovering possession of the castle, and was reinstated by Richard.

Then followed the change of kings, the revolt of Northumberland and his son, and the death of Hotspur at the battle of Shrewsbury (1403), after which defeat Percy with his friends took shelter within Berwick Castle, and there awaited the rising in Yorkshire of Scrope and the Earl Marshal with the Archbishop of York. When this had been cleverly, if treacherously, quelled by Nevill, Earl of Westmorland (see *Brancepeth* and *Raby, Durham*), King Henry, gathering a large army of 37,000 men, at Newcastle, marched forthwith against Earl Percy, who, unable to resist such a force, fled into

Scotland, taking with him the son of Hotspur (afterwards the second earl), and leaving the defence of Berwick to Sir William Greystock.

When Henry IV. appeared before Berwick town on July 9, 1405, at the head of this army, the walls of the place were in a very bad state, crumbling to pieces at some points for a length of 200 to 300 yards, and at other places being in actual ruin. We learn that the castle had so fallen into the power of the town that, if opposed to each other, the castle could not hurt the town, though the town might greatly injure the castle. The town wall was at this time nearly two miles (3105 yards) in circumference, being 3 feet 4 inches in thickness. On the S.W. side it was connected with Tweedmouth by a timber bridge, the river forming a defence on this side. There were no towers on this division of the walls, but on the N. and E. rose at intervals of 120 yards small towers, the outer walls of which were 4 feet 8 inches thick, strengthened with timber and counter-forts. The towers of the wall, 14 feet to 60 feet in height, were known as the Percy, the Broadstair Head, the Murderer, the Middle Tower, the Red Tower, the Conduit, Windmill, Blackwatch House, Plommer's Towers, and others. To the E., on the sea side and the Ness, there were other bulwarks and earthworks among the pools and moats on the low-lying lands. On the W., about 50 yards from the Percy Tower, stood the keep or dungeon of the castle, which had been strengthened by Edward I. a hundred years previously. It was approached from the town by a drawbridge, and was surrounded by a wall with towers like those of the town. From the S.W. angle, a wall 94 yards long—called the White Wall—ran down to the Tweed, ending in a tower at the river's brink. At the N.W. corner was a moat with a postern strengthened by a barmkin, or apron of stone.

Henry IV. had no great difficulty in entering the town, and he at once passed through it to attack the castle. Then, as stated by some writers (including Speed), heavy guns or cannon were for the first time used in England, and the effect of this trial of artillery against the Castle of Berwick was the belief in men's minds that no wall could withstand the fire of such guns.

This fire was directed against the S. front of the castle wall, until a breach was effected 40 yards in width near an iron gate known as "the postern entry behind the court." At last a stone shot was sent through an iron grating into the Constable Tower, killing a man who was mounting the stair. Then the garrison, demoralised no doubt by the novel force employed, lost heart and surrendered the fortress, whereupon the royal troops took possession, and many of the defenders were hung by them at their entry.[*]

The next record of Berwick is when, after their terrible defeat at Towton

* Henry IV., at the siege of Berwick Castle, "caused a peece of Artillerie to be planted against one of the Towers, and at the first shot overthrowing part thereof, they within were put in such feare that they simplie yeelded themselves" (*Holinshed*, i, 530).

in April 1461, Henry VI. and his queen and son, with several nobles, fled thither on their way to take refuge in Scotland; and then it was that, with a view to attaching that kingdom to the interest of the Red Rose, King Henry surrendered Berwick to the King of Scots, after it had been held by England, with a few interruptions, for 128 years.

King James III. executed many repairs in the castle, and furnished it with artillery, appointing a garrison of 500 men between it and the town.

In July 1482 Edward IV. sent Richard, Duke of Glo'ster, with the Earl of Northumberland and the Duke of Albany, into Scotland with an army 22,500 strong. The force was marshalled at Alnwick, and marched to Edinburgh, where, in the absence of King James, a truce was concluded with England, of which the chief article was the restitution of Berwick Castle and town to the English Crown, and on August 24th Lord Hales, the governor, who had hitherto bravely defended the place, finally surrendered it to the English.

In 1502 the Princess Margaret, daughter of Henry VII., came to Berwick, on the way to her nuptials with James IV., and was received in the castle during two days, her escort, according to Leland, being formed of from 1800 to 2000 knights; in a truce between the two kings at this time Berwick is recognised as a neutral point between the two realms.

A new fort built in 1552 was for the defence of the town, but the work seems to have been cleared away in 1559, when alterations were made, the defences in this part of the country set in order, and the fortifications strengthened.

In 1603 King James, who had passed through Berwick on his way to take possession of the English throne, and had visited the castle, reduced the garrisons of Berwick and Carlisle, no need existing for a state of war to be kept up thenceforward on the borders of the two united kingdoms.

Strype tells us that the castle of Berwick was in complete repair in the reign of Elizabeth, that it had "mounts, rapiers, flankers, well replenished with great ordnance, and fair houses therein; the walls and gates made beautiful with pictures of stone, the work curious and delicate." But during the reign of Charles I. it seems to have been sold to the Earl of Suffolk, and from him to have been afterwards purchased by the Town Corporation for £320, at which time the place is reported as "much dilapidated"; and naturally so, for the Parliament in Cromwell's time had, in the usual way, stripped and sold the lead and the timber, and had built the church of Berwick with materials from the castle. In the time of Charles II. the remains were sold for £100.

Dr. Fuller's history (1799) says, as to the place in his time, that few of its buildings then remained: "Scattered fragments of them, and confused heaps of stone are everywhere to be seen." At the northern extremity of the town, some 400 yards from the castle, he speaks of the ancient Bell Tower, a pentagonal work, four storeys high, in which a bell was rung to give notice of an enemy's approach, giving as many strokes as there appeared ships or horsemen. Being placed on high ground, it commanded a wide range of sea and land, and there was a covered way from it to the castle by the town ditch. This old relic fortunately still remains on its hill.

The final destruction was wrought in 1845, when the works of the railway from Berwick to Edinburgh, and of Stephenson's Border Bridge, were carried out. The ground for the station and the termination of this great bridge was chosen on the summit of the Castle Hill; and then all the ancient buildings which interfered with the levelling and the formation of the castle courtyard into a railway station were destroyed, the walls being thrown into the ditch. The little that was left we still see near the station, and on the slope to the river and by the river bank.

An early map, which Sheldon gives, shows the castle standing on its hill at the W. of the town, separated from it by King Edward's great ditch which carried the river water into the broad moat surrounding the W., N., and E. sides of the town; a deep central moat also divided this area and formed the outer defence on the W. of the line of irregular fortifications which environed Berwick, between which and the castle lay a flat piece of land called Castle Gate.

The castle is represented with a long curtain wall on its W. side, a very solid and bulky work, the other defences being formed by many semicircular mural flanking towers and bastions connected by short curtains. No keep is shown, and though we know that the ground inside was occupied by "fayre houses," it is singular that we possess so few particulars regarding the construction and details of one of the most important castles in the kingdom.

Index

INDEX

INDEX

Printed by Ballantyne, Hanson & Co.
London & Edinburgh

www.ingramcontent.com/pod-product-compliance
Lightning Source LLC
Chambersburg PA
CBHW031810270326
41932CB00008B/367